AN EXEGETICAL SUMMARY OF
ACTS 1–14

AN EXEGETICAL SUMMARY OF
ACTS 1–14

Belinda Cheng

Robert Stutzman

SIL International®
Dallas, Texas

©2017 by SIL International®

ISBN: 978-1-55671-412-2

Library of Congress Control Number: 2017934199
Printed in the United States of America

All Rights Reserved
No part of this publication may be reproduced, stored in a retrieval system, or transmitted in any form or by any means—electronic, mechanical, photocopy, recording, or otherwise—without the express permission of SIL International®, with the exception of brief excerpts in journal articles or reviews.

Copies of this and other publications of SIL International® may be obtained through distributors such as Amazon, Barnes & Noble, other worldwide distributors and, for select volumes, www.sil.org/resources/publications:

SIL International Publications
7500 West Camp Wisdom Road
Dallas, TX 75236-5629, USA

General inquiry: publications_intl@sil.org
Pending order inquiry: sales_intl@sil.org
www.sil.org/resources/publications

PREFACE

Exegesis is concerned with the interpretation of a text. Thus, exegesis of the New Testament involves determining the meaning of the Greek text. Translators must be especially careful and thorough in their exegesis of the New Testament in order to accurately communicate its message in the vocabulary, grammar, and literary restraints of another language. Questions occurring to translators as they study the Greek text are answered by summarizing how scholars have interpreted the text. This is information that should be considered by translators as they make their own exegetical decisions regarding the message they will communicate in their translations.

The Semi-Literal Translation

As a basis for discussion, a semi-literal translation of the Greek text is given so that the reasons for different interpretations can best be seen. When one Greek word is translated into English by several words, these words are joined by hyphens. There are a few times when clarity requires that a string of words joined by hyphens have a separate word, such as "not" (μή), inserted in their midst. In this case, the separate word is surrounded by spaces between the hyphens. When alternate translations of a Greek word are given, these are separated by slashes.

The Text

Variations in the Greek text are noted under the heading TEXT. The base text for the summary is the text of the fourth revised edition of *The Greek New Testament,* published by the United Bible Societies, which has the same text as the twenty-sixth edition of the *Novum Testamentum Graece* (Nestle-Aland). The versions that follow different variations are listed without evaluating their choices.

The Lexicon

The meaning of a key word in context is the first question to be answered. Words marked with a raised letter in the semi-literal translation are treated separately under the heading LEXICON. First, the lexicon form of the Greek word is given. Within the parentheses following the Greek word is the location number where, in the author's judgment, this word is defined in the *Greek-English Lexicon of the New Testament Based on Semantic Domains* (Louw and Nida 1988). If the specific reference for the verse is listed in *A Greek-English Lexicon of the New Testament and Other Early Christian Literature* (Danker and Bauer 2000), the outline location and page number is given. Then English equivalents of the Greek word are given to show how it is translated by those commentaries which have translations of the whole Greek text and, after a semicolon, by twelve major versions. "All versions" refers only to those versions used in the lexicon. "All translations" refers to both the versions and the commentaries used in the lexicon. Sometimes further comments are made about the meaning of the word or the significance of a verb's tense, voice, or mood.

The Questions

Under the heading QUESTION, a question is asked that comes from examining the Greek text under consideration. Typical questions concern the identity of an implied actor or object of an event word, the antecedent of a pronominal reference, the connection indicated by a relational word, the meaning of a genitive construction, the meaning of figurative language, the function of a rhetorical question, the identification of an ambiguity, and the presence of implied information that is needed to understand the passage correctly. Background information is also considered for a proper understanding of a passage. Although not all implied information and background information is made explicit in a translation, it is important to consider it so that the translation will not be stated in such a way that prevents a reader from arriving at the proper interpretation. The question is answered with a summary of what commentators have said. If there are contrasting differences of opinion, the different interpretations are numbered and the commentaries that support each are listed. Differences that are not treated by many of the commentaries often are not numbered, but are introduced with a contrastive 'Or' at the beginning of the sentence. No attempt has been made to select which interpretation is best.

The Use of this Book

This book does not replace the commentaries that it summarizes. Commentaries contain much more information about the meaning of words and passages. They often contain arguments for the interpretations that are taken and they may have important discussions about the discourse features of the text. In addition, they often have information about the historical, geographical, and cultural setting. Translators will want to refer to at least four commentaries as they exegete a passage. However, since no one commentary contains all the answers translators need, this book will be a valuable supplement. It makes more sources of exegetical help available than those to which most translators have access. Even if they had all the books available, few would have the time to search through all of them for the answers.

When many commentaries are studied, it soon becomes apparent that they frequently disagree in their interpretations. That is the reason why so many answers in this book are divided into two or more interpretations. The reader's initial reaction may be that all of these different interpretations complicate exegesis rather than help it. However, before translating a passage, a translator needs to know exactly where there is a problem of interpretation and what the exegetical options are.

Before Belinda Cheng and Robert Stutzman were available to begin their work on the Exegetical Summary of Acts, Charlie Law volunteered to use his spare time to provide a preliminary presentation of how the twelve translations treated the Greek text. Then over a period of several years he did this for chapters 1–8.

ABBREVIATIONS

COMMENTARIES AND REFERENCE BOOKS

AB	Munck, Johannes. The Acts of the Apostles. The Anchor Bible. Revised by William F. Albright and C. S. Mann. Garden City, NY: Doubleday, 1967.
Bar	Barrett, C. K. The Acts of the Apostles, A Shorter Commentary. London & New York: T & T Clark, 2002.
BDAG	Danker, Frederick William (Editor), Walter Bauer (Author). A Greek-English Lexicon of the New Testament and Other Early Christian Literature, 3rd Edition. Chicago: University of Chicago Press, 2000.
BECNT	Bock, Darrell L. Acts. Baker Exegetical Commentary on the New Testament. Grand Rapids: Baker Academic, 2007.
CBC	Packer, J. W. The Acts of the Apostles. Cambridge Bible Commentary. Cambridge: Cambridge University Press, 1973.
EBC	Longenecker, Richard N. "The Acts of the Apostles." The Expositor's Bible Commentary, Vol. 9. Grand Rapids: Zondervan, 1981.
LN	Louw, Johannes P., and Eugene A. Nida. Greek–English Lexicon of the New Testament Based on Semantic Domains. New York: United Bible Societies, 1988.
NAC	Polhill, John B. Acts. The New American Commentary. Nashville: Broadman and Holman, 2001.
NICNT	Bruce, F. F. The Book of the Acts, Revised Edition. The New International Commentary on the New Testament. Grand Rapids: Eerdmans, 1988.
PNTC	Peterson, David G. The Acts of the Apostles. The Pillar New Testament Commentary. Grand Rapids: Eerdmans, 2009.
TH	Newman, Barclay M., and Eugene A. Nida. A Translator's Handbook on the Acts of the Apostles. London: United Bible Societies, 1972.
TNTC	Marshall, I. Howard. Acts. The Tyndale New Testament Commentaries. Grand Rapids: Eerdmans, 1980.
TRT	Carlton, Matthew E. Acts of the Apostles. Translator's Reference Translation. Dallas: SIL International, 2001.

GREEK TEXT AND TRANSLATIONS

GNT	The Greek New Testament. Edited by B. Aland, K. Aland, J. Karavidopoulos, C. Martini, and B. Metzger. Fourth ed. London, New York: United Bible Societies, 1993.
LXX	The Septuagint. The Greek translation of the Jewish Scriptures, translated between 300–200 BC in Alexandria, Egypt.
CEV	The Holy Bible, Contemporary English Version. New York: American Bible Society, 1995.
ESV	The Holy Bible, English Standard Version. Wheaton: Crossway Bibles Div, Good News Publishers, 2001.
GW	God's Word. Grand Rapids: World Publishing, 1995.
KJV	The Holy Bible. Authorized (or King James) Version. 1611.
NASB	New American Standard Bible. La Habra, CA: Lockman Foundation, 1995.
NCV	New Century Version. Dallas: Word Publishing, 1991.
NET	The NET Bible, New English Translation. Version 6r,715, Biblical Studies Press, 2006.
NIV	The Holy Bible, New International Version. Grand Rapids: Zondervan, 1995.
NLT	The Holy Bible, New Living Translation. Wheaton: Tyndale House, 1996.
NRSV	The Holy Bible: New Revised Standard Version. New York: Oxford University Press, 1989.
REB	The Revised English Bible. Oxford: Oxford University Press and Cambridge University Press, 1989.
TEV	Good News Bible, Today's English Version. Second edition. New York: American Bible Society, 1992.

GRAMMATICAL TERMS

act.	active		mid.	middle
fut.	future		opt.	optative
impera.	imperative		pass.	passive
imperf.	imperfect		perf.	perfect
indic.	indicative		pres.	present
infin.	infinitive		subj.	subjunctive

EXEGETICAL SUMMARY OF ACTS 1–14

DISCOURSE UNIT—1:1–5:42 [CBC, NICNT]. The topic is the beginnings of the Church [CBC], the birth of the Church [NICNT].

DISCOURSE UNIT—1:1–2:47 [NAC]. The topic is the Spirit empowers the Church for witness.

DISCOURSE UNIT—1:1–2:41 [EBC]. The topic is the introduction: the constitutive events of the Christian mission.

DISCOURSE UNIT—1:1–26 [NICNT]. The topic is the forty days and after.

DISCOURSE UNIT—1:1–14 [Bar]. The topic is the introduction and recapitulation.

DISCOURSE UNIT—1:1–11 [BECNT; NET, NIV, REB]. The topic is the prologue to the book of Acts [REB], the introduction: Jesus ascends to the Father and gives a mission [BECNT], Jesus ascends to heaven [NET], Jesus taken up into heaven [NIV].

DISCOURSE UNIT—1:1–8 [NASB]. The topic is the introduction.

DISCOURSE UNIT—1:1–5 [AB, BECNT, CBC, EBC, PNTC, TNTC; CEV, ESV, NCV, NLT, NRSV, TEV]. The topic is Luke writes another book [NCV], the prologue [TNTC], the prologue to the book of Acts [CEV, TEV], the author's preface [CBC], a presumptive preface [EBC], the preface to Acts [AB], a review of book 1 to the ascension [BECNT], the promise of the Spirit [PNTC], the promise of the Holy Spirit [ESV, NLT, NRSV].

DISCOURSE UNIT—1:1–3 [NICNT]. The topic is the prologue.

DISCOURSE UNIT—1:1–2 [NAC; GW]. The topic is the introduction [GW], the literary prologue [NAC].

1:1 O Theophilus, in my first book I-wrote[a] about all Jesus began both to-do and to-teach **1:2** until (the)-day when he-was-taken-up[b] after having-given-instructions[c] through[d] (the)-Holy Spirit[e] to-the apostles whom he-had-chosen.

LEXICON—a. aorist mid. indic. of ποιέω (LN 90.45) (BDAG 7a. p. 841): 'to make, to do' [BDAG, LN]. The clause 'in my/the first book I wrote about' [AB, LN; GW, NRSV, TEV] is also translated 'the first book I wrote was about' [NCV], 'in the first book I have dealt with' [ESV], 'in my first book I told you about' [NLT], 'in the first part of my work I wrote of' [CBC], 'in the first part of my work I gave an account of' [REB], 'in the first account I treated' [BECNT], 'I wrote my first book about' [Bar], 'I wrote the former account' [NET], 'I first wrote to you about' [CEV], 'the first account I composed about' [NASB], 'in the former book I wrote about' [NIV], 'the former treatise have I made of' [KJV]. This verb is a marker of an agent relation with a numerable event [LN].

b. aorist pass. indic. of ἀναλαμβάνω (LN 15.203) (BDAG 1. p. 66): 'to be taken up' [AB, BDAG, BECNT, CBC, LN; ESV, KJV], 'to be taken up to heaven' [CEV, NASB, NET, NIV, NLT, NRSV, REB, TEV], 'to be taken up into heaven' [NCV], 'to be taken to heaven' [GW], 'to be received up' [Bar]. This verb means to lift up and carry (away) [LN, BDAG].

c. aorist mid. (deponent = act.) participle of ἐντέλλομαι (LN 33.329) (BDAG p. 339): 'to give instructions' [AB, BDAG, CBC; GW, NIV, NLT, NRSV, REB, TEV], 'to give orders' [BDAG; CEV, NASB, NET], 'to give commands' [BDAG, LN; ESV], 'to give commandments' [KJV], 'to give a command' [BECNT], 'to give a charge' [Bar]. The phrase 'having given instructions to the apostles' is also translated 'told the apostles what they should do' [NCV]. This verb means to give definite orders, and it implies that it is given by someone in authority or who has official sanction [LN]. It means to give instructions [BDAG].

d. διά (LN 90.4): 'through' [AB, Bar, BECNT, CBC, LN; ESV, GW, KJV, NIV, NLT, NRSV, REB], 'by' [LN; NASB, NET], 'with the help of' [CEV, NCV], 'by the power of' [TEV]. This preposition marks an intermediate agent [LN]. Jesus is the primary agent and the Holy Spirit is the secondary agent [TH].

e. πνεῦμα (LN 12.18) (BDAG 5.c.β. p. 834): 'Spirit' [AB, Bar, BDAG, BECNT, CBC, LN; all versions except KJV], 'Ghost' [KJV]. This noun denotes the third person of the Trinity whose titles are 'Spirit, Spirit of God, and Holy Spirit'. In many religious systems the significant difference between the gods and the spirits is that the gods are regarded as supernatural beings which control certain aspects of natural phenomena, while the spirits are supernatural beings, often impersonal, which indwell or inhabit certain places, including rivers, streams, mountains, caves, animals, and people. Spirits are often regarded as being primarily evil, though it may be possible to induce them to be favorable to people. It is extremely difficult to find in some languages a fully satisfactory term to speak of the Spirit of God. If one uses a term which normally identifies local supernatural beings, there is a tendency to read into the term the meaning of an evil or mischievous character. If, however, one uses a term which may identify the spirit of a person, the problems may even be greater, since according to many systems of religious belief, the spirit of an individual does not become active until the individual dies. Therefore, the activity of the Spirit of God would presumably suggest that God himself had died. However, if one uses a term which means 'heart' or 'soul' (and thus the Spirit of God would be literally equivalent to 'the heart of God'), there may be complications since this aspect of human personality is often regarded as not being able to act on its own. The solutions to the problem of 'Spirit' have been varied. In some languages the term for Spirit is essentially equivalent to 'the unseen one,' and therefore the Spirit of God is essentially equivalent to 'the invisibleness of God.' In a number of languages the closest equivalent for Spirit is 'breath,' and in a number of indigenous religious systems, the 'breath' is regarded as having a kind of independent existence. In other languages the term for Spirit is equivalent to what is often translated as 'the soul,' that is to say, the immaterial part of a person. There is, of course, always the difficulty of employing a term meaning 'soul' or 'life,' since it often proves to be impersonal and thus provides no basis for speaking of the Spirit of God as being a person or a personal manifestation of God. In quite a few languages the equivalent of Spirit is literally 'shadow,' since the 'shadow' of a person is regarded as the immaterial part of the individual. Moreover, in many systems of religious thought the shadow is regarded as having some significant measure of independent existence. In a few cases the term for Spirit is literally 'wind,' but there are frequently difficulties involved in this type of terminology since a term for wind often suggests calamity or evil intent. One meaning of Spirit which must be clearly avoided is that of 'apparition' or 'ghost.' Frequently it is not possible to find a fully satisfactory term for 'Spirit,' and therefore in all contexts some characterizing feature is added, for example, either 'of God' or 'holy,' in the sense of 'divine.' [LN]. It denotes God's being as controlling influence, with focus on association with humans [BDAG].

QUESTION—Who was Theophilus?

The etymology of 'Friend of God' or 'Loved by God' and this name could have been used to suggest an ideal or representative man of the Christian faith or a Christian inquirer. He might have been a patron or simply the most important intended reader of this book [BECNT]. Probably he was a representative member of the intelligent middle-class public at Rome [NICNT]. The name occurred as a proper name at least three centuries before Luke and the practice of dedicating books was common at that time [EBC]. The Greek text inserts the name 'Theophilus' in the middle of the first sentence after the word πάντων 'everything'. It would probably be more natural in many languages to begin this book with the vocative, 'Oh/Dear Theophilus. I wrote the first book…' [TRT]. This is done in several translations which start out, 'Theophilus, I first wrote to you' [CEV], 'To Theophilus, The first book I wrote' [NCV], 'Dear Theophilus: In my first book' [TEV]. Other translations move his name closer to the beginning of the sentence [ESV, GW, NASB, NET, NIV, NLT, NRSV, REB].

QUESTION—What does the 'first book' refer to?

The first book refers to the Gospel of Luke. Luke was a physician who wrote the two books known as Luke and Acts [EBC].

QUESTION—What is meant by the verb ἤρξατο 'began' in the statement 'Jesus *began* both to do and teach'?

1. Luke had written in the 'Gospel of Luke' about what Jesus had done and taught until the day he was taken up to heaven. Now Luke intends to show what Jesus continued to do and teach through his church [EBC]. This is

also translated 'began to do and teach' [AB, Bar, BECNT, EBC, NAC, NICNT, TNTC; ESV, GW, KJV, NASB, NCV, NET, NIV, NLT].
2. Although some think that the word 'began' is emphatic and should be included in the translation, others take the phrase 'began both to do and teach' as simply an equivalent of 'to do and to teach' [TH] 'Began' is probably not emphatic: 'from the very first' [CEV], 'from the beginning' [CBC; NRSV, REB], from the time he began his work' [TEV].

QUESTION—Who were the apostles that Jesus had chosen?
The word 'apostles' occurs twenty-eight times in Acts and it always refers to 'the Twelve' (or the eleven in this verse before Judas was replaced) except in 14:4, 14 where it refers to Barnabas and Paul [TH].

QUESTION—What is meant by Jesus giving orders διὰ *'through* the Holy Spirit' to the apostles before he was taken up?
It means that Jesus instructed the apostles by means of the Holy Spirit, that is, Jesus had the Holy Spirit instruct them [TH]. Another interpretation is that the Holy Spirit was the source of guidance for Jesus in choosing the apostles [TNTC]. In the account of the commission that Jesus laid on his disciples in John 20:22, Jesus indicated that the power by which the disciples would carry out their commission when he breathed on them and said 'Receive the Holy Spirit' [NICNT]. The instructions Jesus had in mind were those already given in Luke 24:48–49 where at the climax of his earthly teaching he told them: 'You are witnesses of these things. I am going to send you what my Father has promised, but stay in the city until you have been clothed with power from on high.' Now, in a slightly revised form, Luke gives those instructions again. Jesus' mandate to witness was given to the apostles who would act through the power of the Holy Spirit whose coming would be a direct result of Jesus' ascension [EBC].

DISCOURSE UNIT—1:3–11 [GW]. The topic is Jesus ascends to heaven.

DISCOURSE UNIT—1:3–5 [NAC]. The topic is the instruction preparatory to Pentecost.

1:3 He- also -presented[a] himself alive[b] to-them after suffering-death[c] by many proofs,[d] appearing[e] to-them during forty days and speaking[f] about the kingdom of-God.

LEXICON—a. aorist act. indic. of παρίστημι (LN 85.14) (BDAG 1.b.α. p. 778): 'to present' [BDAG, BECNT, LN; ESV, NASB, NET, NRSV], 'to show' [AB, Bar, CBC; GW, KJV, NCV, NIV, REB], 'to appear' [CEV, NLT, TEV]. This verb means to cause to be in a place [LN]. It means to cause to be present in any way [BDAG].

b. pres. act. participle of ζάω (LN 23.93) (BDAG 1.a. β. p. 425): 'alive' [AB, Bar, CBC; all versions except CEV], 'to-live/to-live-again' [BECNT, LN], 'to become alive again' [BDAG], 'to be raised from death' [CEV]. This verb means to come back to life after having once died [LN].

It means to be alive physically in regard to dead persons who return to life [BDAG].
c. aorist act. infin. of πάσχω (LN 24.78) (BDAG 3.a.α. p. 785): 'to suffer death' [BDAG], 'to suffer and die' [CEV], 'to suffer' [Bar, BDAG]. The phrase 'after suffering death' is also translated 'after his death' [CBC; GW, NCV, REB, TEV], 'after his suffering' [BECNT; ESV, NASB, NET, NIV, NRSV], 'after his passion' [AB; KJV], 'after his crucifixion' [NLT]. This verb means to suffer pain [LN].
d. τεκμήριον (LN 28.45) (BDAG p. 994): 'proof, evidence' [LN], 'convincing proof' [BDAG, LN]. The phrase 'by many proofs' [BECNT; ESV] is also translated 'by many certain proofs' [Bar], 'by many infallible proofs' [KJV], 'by many convincing proofs' [NASB, NRSV], 'with many convincing proofs' [NET], 'with many clear proofs' [AB], 'a lot of convincing evidence' [GW], 'proved in many ways' [CEV, NCV, NLT], 'gave many convincing proofs' [NIV], 'gave ample proof' [CBC; REB], 'many times in ways that proved' [TEV]. This noun denotes that which causes something to be known as verified or confirmed [LN]. It denotes that which causes something to be known in a convincing and decisive manner [BDAG].
e. pres. mid./pass. (deponent = act.) participle of ὀπτάνομαι (LN 24.17) (BDAG p. 717): 'to appear' [AB, Bar, BDAG, BECNT, CBC; CEV, ESV, GW, NASB, NIV, NLT, NRSV], 'to be seen' [LN; KJV, NET, REB]. The phrase 'appearing to them' is also translated 'They saw him' [TEV], 'The apostles saw Jesus' [NCV]. This verb means to become visible to someone [BDAG, LN].
f. pres. act. participle of λέγω (LN 33.69) (BDAG 3. p. 590): 'to speak' [AB, BDAG, Bar, BECNT, LN; all versions except GW, NLT, TEV], 'to talk' [GW, NLT, TEV], 'to teach' [CBC]. This verb means to speak or talk, with apparent focus upon the content of what is said [LN].

QUESTION—What were the many proofs?

The 'many proofs' were the events that Luke recorded in Luke 24:13–52 [EBC]. These are some of the appearances of Jesus: on the Emmaus road (24:13–32), to Peter (24:34), and to the disciples (24:36–43). The appearances of Jesus to the apostles were absolutely essential for their role as witnesses of Jesus' resurrection in Acts [NAC].

QUESTION—What is meant by Jesus appearing 'over a period of forty days'?

This wording could be taken to mean either that he did not leave the presence of his disciples throughout the entire period of forty days or that he appeared to them at intervals during that time [LN]. Most understand it to mean that during the forty days the risen Jesus showed himself to the disciples at intervals [BECNT, EBC, NAC, NICNT, TNTC, TRT]. The Gospels tell about His appearances to the women at the tomb, Mary Magdalene, the disciples on the road to Emmaus, Peter in Jerusalem, ten disciples, eleven disciples, seven disciples, and James, the Lord's brother [BECNT].

QUESTION—What does 'the kingdom of God' refer to?
The kingdom of God refers to the sovereign authority and rule of God in the lives of his people rather than to the territory or the people over which God rules [TH]. In the Gospels the kingdom is presented as having been inaugurated in time and space by Jesus' presence and ministry. In Acts, 'the kingdom of God' usually appears as a convenient way of summarizing the content of the earliest Christian preaching. And in this proclamation by the early Christians Jesus is explicitly identified as the king [EBC]. God's kingdom is a central concern of Acts, and the book begins (1:3) and ends (28:31) on this theme [NAC].

DISCOURSE UNIT—1:4–8 [NICNT]. The topic is the apostles' commission.

1:4 And (while)-eating/staying-with[a] (them) he-commanded[b] them not to-depart[c] from Jerusalem, but to-wait-for[d] the promise of-the Father which, (he said) "you-heard[e] from-me;

LEXICON—a. pres. mid/pass. (deponent = act.) participle of συναλίζομαι (LN 23.13, 41.37) (BDAG 1. p. 964): 'to eat with' [Bar, BDAG (1), LN (23.13); NCV, NIV, NLT]. Others think it means 'to be in fellowship with' [LN (41.37)], 'to stay with' [ESV, NRSV], 'to meet with' [GW], 'to gather together' [NASB], 'to come together' [TEV], 'to be assembled together' [KJV]. The verb συναλιζόμενος 'while staying with them' is also translated 'while he was in their company' [AB, CBC; REB], 'while he was still with them' [CEV], 'while he was with them' [NET], 'while [sharing table] with them' [BECNT]. This verb means 'eating together' and the emphasis is upon the fellowship during the meal [LN (23.13)] or it means 'while they were still together in fellowship, he commanded them', but this meaning would seem to be somewhat alien to general Greek usage, and therefore it is more frequently understood in the context of Acts 1:4 as meaning 'to be eating with' [LN (41.37)].

b. aorist act. indic. of παραγγέλλω (LN 33.327) (BDAG p. 760): 'to command' [Bar, BDAG, BECNT, LN; KJV, NASB, NLT], 'to give this command' [NIV], 'to order' [LN; ESV, GW, NRSV], 'to give this order' [TEV], 'to enjoin' [AB], 'to tell' [CBC; NCV], 'to say' [CEV], 'to declare' [NET], 'to direct' [BDAG; REB]. This verb means to announce what must be done [LN]. It means to make an announcement about something that must be done [BDAG].

c. pres. pass. infin. of χωρίζω (LN 15.49) (BDAG 2.b. p. 1095): 'to depart' [AB, LN; ESV, KJV], 'to leave' [Bar, BECNT, BDAG, CBC, LN; all versions except ESV, KJV], 'to be taken away' [BDAG]. This verb means to separate from, as the result of motion away from [LN]. It means to separate by departing from someone [BDAG].

d. pres. act. infin. of περιμένω (LN 85.60) (BDAG p. 802): 'to wait for' [BDAG, CBC, LN; all versions except NCV, NLT], 'to await' [AB, Bar, BECNT, LN], 'to wait' [NCV]. The phrase 'not to depart from Jerusalem but to wait for' is also translated 'do not leave until' [NLT]. This verb

means to remain in a place and/or state with expectancy concerning a future event [LN].
e. aorist act. indic. of ἀκούω (LN 24.52) (BDAG 1.b.β. p. 37): 'to hear' [BDAG, LN]. The phrase ἣν ἠκούσατέ μου 'which, (he said) "you heard from me;..."' [BECNT; ESV] makes a change to a direct quotation that goes on through the next verse. It is also translated '"Which," he said, "you heard of from me;..."' [NASB], '"This," he said, "is what you have heard from me;..."' [NRSV], 'which, (saith he), ye have heard of me' [KJV], 'about which you have heard me speak' [CBC], 'that which', he said, 'you heard from me...' [Bar], 'which "you have heard about from me;..."' [AB], '"You must wait", he said. "for the gift promised by the Father, of which I told you;..."' [REB], 'he gave them this order: "Do not leave Jerusalem, but wait for the gift I told you about, the gift my Father promised..."' [TEV], 'Jesus said to them, "I've told you what the Father promises..."' [GW]. Others have included all of the preceding instructions in the direct quote: 'he declared, "Do not leave Jerusalem, but wait there for what my Father promised, which you heard about from me..."' [NET], 'he commanded them, "Do not leave Jerusalem until...as I told you before..."' [NLT], 'he gave them this command: "Do not leave Jerusalem, but wait for the gift my Father promised, which you have heard me speak about..."' [NIV], 'he said: Don't leave Jerusalem yet. Wait here for the Father to give you the Holy Spirit, just as I told you he has promised to do' [CEV], 'He said, "Wait here to receive the promise from the Father which I told you about..."' [NCV]. This verb means to hear [BDAG, LN].

QUESTION—What was the promise of the Father?

God had already made a promise to send them the Holy Spirit, and this is about waiting for God to fulfill that promise [TRT]. In Luke 24:49 Jesus had spoken about sending 'the promise of the Father' upon his disciples, and then they would be 'clothed with power from on high'. In the following verse we learn that the gift promised by God is being baptized with the Holy Spirit' [AB, BECNT, EBC, NAC, NICNT, TH, TNTC].

1:5 for John on-the-one-(hand)[a] baptized[b] with-water, but-on-the-other-(hand) you will-be-baptized with (the)-Holy Spirit not many[c] days from now."

LEXICON—a. μέν...δέ (LN 89.136): This combination of conjunctions means 'on the one hand..., but on the other hand' [LN]. The words ὅτι Ἰωάννης μέν..., δέ 'for John on the one hand..., but on the other (hand)...' [BECNT] is also translated 'for/For John..., but...' [AB, Bar; ESV, KJV, NASB, NET, NIV, NRSV], 'John..., but...' [CBC; CEV, GW, NCV, NLT, REB, TEV]. The combination of conjunctions μέν..., δέ 'for..., but...' marks one set of items in contrast with another set [LN].

    b. aorist act. indic. of βαπτίζω (LN 53.41): 'to baptize' [LN; all versions]. This verb means to employ water in a religious ceremony designed to symbolize purification and initiation on the basis of repentance [LN].

    c. πολύς (LN 59.1) (BDAG 1.a.α. p. 848): 'many' [BDAG, LN]. The phrase οὐ μετὰ πολλὰς ταύτας ἡμέρας 'not many days from now' [Bar; ESV, NASB, NET, NRSV] is also translated 'in a few days' [CEV, GW, NCV, NIV, NLT, TEV], 'within the next few days' [CBC; REB], 'within a short time' [AB], 'not many days hence' [KJV], 'before many days' [BECNT]. This adjective indicates a relatively large quantity of objects or events [LN].

QUESTION—Who was the man named John?

    This John is never referred to as 'John the Baptist' in Acts. However, to make it clear that he is not the apostle John, a footnote could explain that this was the John who had baptized people [TRT].

QUESTION—What is going to be explained by the beginning conjunction ὅτι 'for'?

    This verse explains why the disciples have to remain in Jerusalem. It reminds them that the promise of the Father is going to be fulfilled in a few days. When the gift of the Holy Spirit comes, they will be baptized by the Holy Spirit in contrast with the baptism with water by John. This contrast is clearly brought out in the original Greek by μέν ... δέ 'on the one hand ... but on the other hand' [LN 89.136]. On the one hand, there was John the Baptist with his preparatory washing; on the other hand, there is the Spirit's coming which is the sign that the Messiah has come and a new era had begun [BECNT]. Except for TW and BECNT, none of the commentaries and versions literally translate μέν ... δέ. Most common translations of this verse are 'for John baptized with water, but you will be baptized with the Holy Spirit...'.

QUESTION—How do the baptism with water and the baptism with the Holy Spirit differ?

    To baptize literally means to immerse a person in water or to deluge him with it, usually done as a means of cleansing. When the term is applied to the Holy Spirit, it refers to the 'pouring out' of the Spirit from on high by God, but the metaphor of pouring out a liquid is inadequate to do justice to the gift of the Spirit who brings power, wisdom, and joy [TNTC]. The baptism of John the Baptist was an eschatological, preparatory washing. When someone was baptized by John it meant that he or she was ready for God to come. The baptism with the Holy Spirit is the fulfillment of the promise of the gift of the Holy Spirit and it was the sign that the Messiah had come and the new era had begun [BECNT]. Whoever received the baptism of the Holy Spirit was one who was saved and protected from judgment. That baptism portrayed not only the cleansing from sin but also the indwelling of God as a result of the cleansing. The bridge from the old era to the new era is crossed when Jesus brings the Spirit [BECNT].

QUESTION—What is meant by 'not many days from now'?

The Greek negative-positive expression 'not many' is often rendered as 'a few' [TH]. According to the chronology of Acts, the time frame was about ten days, since Pentecost was fifty days after Passover and Jesus appeared for forty days [BECNT].

DISCOURSE UNIT—1:6–14 [AB]. The topic is the mission to the world and the ascension.

DISCOURSE UNIT—1:6–11 [BECNT, CBC, TNTC; CEV, ESV, NCV, NLT, NRSV, TEV]. The topic is the ascension [ESV, TNTC], the ascension of Jesus [NLT, NRSV], Jesus is taken to heaven [CEV], Jesus is taken up into/to heaven [NCV, TEV], the ascension and final testament: a promise for the disciples now and a promise to return [BECNT], Jesus' farewell [CBC].

DISCOURSE UNIT—1:6–8 [EBC, NAC, PNTC]. The topic is Christ's legacy: the call to witness [NAC], the mandate to witness [EBC], the commissioning of the apostles [PNTC].

1:6 So when they-had-come-together,[a] they-asking him, saying, "Lord[b], is-it at this time you-are-restoring[c] the kingdom to-Israel?"

LEXICON—a. aorist act. participle of συνέρχομαι (LN 15.123) (BDAG 1. p. 969): 'to come together' [BDAG, BECNT, LN; ESV, GW, KJV, NASB, NRSV], 'to gather together' [BDAG; NET], 'to meet together' [NIV, TEV], 'to assemble' [Bar, BDAG], 'to be all together' [AB, CBC; NCV, REB], 'to be with Jesus' [CEV, NLT]. This verb refers to the movement of two or more objects to the same location [LN]. It means to come together with others as a group [BDAG].

b. κύριος (LN 12.9): 'Lord' [AB, Bar, BECNT, CBC, LN; all versions]. This noun denotes one who exercises supernatural authority over mankind, a title for God and for Christ [LN]. In some other Scriptures, this word may mean 'Sir' when it is addressed to a man. It is used to address someone in a very respectful way such as the Master/Owner, one who has full control [TRT].

c. pres. act. indic. of ἀποκαθιστάνω (LN 13.65) (BDAG 1 p. 111): 'to restore' [AB, Bar, BDAG, BECNT, LN; ESV, GW, KJV, NASB, NET, NIV, NLT, NRSV, REB], 'to give back' [NCV, TEV], 'to give again' [CEV], 'to establish once again' [CBC]. This verb means to change to a previous good state [BDAG, LN].

QUESTION—What is meant by 'restoring' the kingdom to Israel?

Like all Jews, the apostles thought that the coming of the King would bring about the restoration of sovereignty to Israel [AB, Bar, BECNT, NICNT, PNTC]. The Israelites not only would be freed from the rule of Rome but Israel would then rule over all other nations [EBC, TH, TNTC, TRT]. They saw the promise of the coming gift of the Holy Spirit from the Father as a mark of the final great messianic Day of the Lord when Israel would be restored to the former glory of the days of David and Solomon [NAC, TH, TRT].

QUESTION—Why did the apostles ask if the restoration of the kingdom would be 'at this time'?

They wanted to know how soon the nation of Israel would be restored [TNTC]. They wanted to know if this restoration would happen in the immediate future. The question reflects a nationalist's concern for Israel's vindication and the completion of the OT promises of Israel being restored to a place of great blessing [Bar, BECNT]. In Jewish expectations, the restoration of Israel's fortunes would be marked by the renewed activity of God's Spirit, which had been withheld since the last of the prophets. The promise of the coming gift of the Holy Spirit had rekindled their old nationalistic hopes [EBC, NICNT].

1:7 But he-said to them, "It-is not for-you to-know times[a] or seasons[b] which the Father has-set[c] by his-own authority.[d]

LEXICON—a. χρόνος (LN 67.1) (BDAG 1. p. 1092): 'time' [BDAG, LN]. 'period of time' [BDAG]. The plural form χρόνους 'times' [Bar, BECNT; ESV, GW, KJV, NASB, NET, NIV, NRSV, TEV] is also translated 'the time of those events' [CEV], 'dates' [AB, CBC; NCV, NLT, REB]. This noun denotes a point of time that consists of an occasion for a particular event [LN]. It denotes an indefinite period of time during which some activity or event takes place [BDAG].

b. καιρός (LN 67.1) (BDAG 3.b. p. 498): 'season' [BDAG], 'time' [BDAG, LN], 'occasion' [LN]. The plural form καιρούς 'seasons' [Bar, BECNT; ESV, KJV] is also translated 'periods' [GW, NET, NRSV], 'epochs' [NASB], 'dates' [NIV], 'occasions' [TEV], 'events' [CEV], 'times' [AB, CBC; NCV, NLT, REB]. This noun denotes points of time consisting of occasions for particular events [LN]. It denotes a period of time characterized by some aspect of special crisis. It is one of the chief terms relating to the end time [BDAG].

c. aorist mid. indic. of τίθημι (LN 13.9) (BDAG 4.b. p. 1004): 'to set' [BECNT, CBC; NET, NIV, NLT, NRSV, REB, TEV], 'to fix' [BDAG; ESV, NASB], 'to establish' [BDAG, LN], 'to cause to be' [LN], 'to determine' [GW], 'to decide' [NCV], 'to reserve' [AB], 'to place' [Bar], 'to put' [KJV], 'to control' [CEV]. This verb means to cause a state to exist [LN]. It means to bring about an arrangement [BDAG].

d. ἐξουσία (LN 37.35): 'authority' [Bar, BECNT, LN; ESV, GW, NASB, NET, NIV, NLT, NRSV, TEV], 'power' [KJV], 'sovereignty' [AB]. The phrase ἐν τῇ ἰδίᾳ ἐξουσίᾳ 'by his own authority' is also translated 'within his own control' [CBC; REB], 'that only the Father controls' [CEV]. 'is the only one who has the authority (to decide)' [NCV]. This noun denotes the right to control or govern over others [LN].

QUESTION—What is the difference between χρόνους 'times' and καιρούς 'seasons'?
Most commentaries think that χρόνους 'times' refers to a span/duration of time and καιρούς 'seasons' refers to specific events/times. However, some think the two terms are synonyms [TRT]. It is quite likely that in a set phrase such as this no basic distinction is to be made between the two terms [BECNT, NICNT, TH].

1:8 **But you-will-receive power[a] (when) the Holy Spirit has-come upon[b] you, and you-will-be my witnesses[c] in Jerusalem and in all Judea and Samaria, and to (the)-end[d] of-the earth."**

LEXICON—a. δύναμις (LN 76.1) (BDAG 1.a. p. 262): 'power' [Bar, BDAG, BECNT, CBC, LN; all versions]. The clause λήμψεσθε δύναμιν 'you will receive power' is also translated 'you will be filled with power' [TEV], 'you will be empowered' [AB], '(the Holy Spirit) will give you power' [CEV]. This noun denotes the potentiality to exert force in performing some function [BDAG, LN].
  b. ἐπί (LN 90.57): 'on, to' [LN]. The phrase ἐπελθόντος…ὑμᾶς 'has come upon you' [Bar; ESV, NASB, NET, NRSV] is also translated 'comes on/upon you' [AB, BECNT, CBC; NIV, NLT, REB, TEV], 'is come upon you' [KJV], 'will come upon you' [CEV], 'comes to you' [GW, NCV]. This preposition refers to the one who experiences the action of the verb, and often it is about the action of a superior force or agency [LN]. This is another way of talking about being 'baptized with the Holy Spirit' (verse 5) [TRT].
  c. μάρτυς (LN 33.270) (BDAG 2.c. p. 620): 'witness' [Bar, BDAG, BECNT, LN; all versions except CEV, REB]. The clause ἔσεσθέ μου μάρτυρες 'you will be my witnesses' is also translated 'you will bear witness for me' [AB, CBC; REB], 'you will tell everyone about me' [CEV]. This noun denotes a person who witnesses [LN]. It refers to the disciples of Jesus who are witnesses of his life, death, and resurrection [BDAG].
  d. ἔσχατος (LN 61.13) (BDAG 1. p. 397): 'end' [BDAG, LN]. The phrase ἕως ἐσχάτου τῆς γῆς 'to the end of the earth' [Bar, BDAG; ESV] is also translated 'to the ends of the earth' [AB, CBC; GW, NIV, NLT, NRSV, TEV], 'as far as the end of the earth' [BECNT; LN], 'even to the remotest part of the earth' [NASB], 'unto the uttermost part of the earth' [KJV], 'to the farthest parts of the earth' [NET], 'even in the farthest corners of the earth' [REB], 'in every part of the world' [NCV], 'everywhere in the world' [CEV]. This adjective indicates being the last in a series of objects [LN]. It pertains to being at the farthest boundary of an area [BDAG].

QUESTION—How is the conjunction ἀλλά 'but' used in this verse?
It is not contradicting what has just been said. It is a transitional expression that shifts the focus of attention from the previous statement to something

else that has other, and perhaps even more, significance [TH]. However, it is important for you to know that you will receive power...' [TRT].

QUESTION—What is meant by the disciples 'receiving power'?

The apostles would receive power when the Holy Spirit comes upon them. This will happen in Acts 2 and be the fulfillment of v. 5 where it says that the apostles would be baptized with the Holy Spirit. [EBC, NAC, PNTC]. They would receive the power to work miracles [TH], speak boldly about Jesus [BECNT], and accomplish their mission [EBC]. The Spirit's power will enable them to speak boldly when testifying to the message of God's work through Jesus. Their direct and real experience of Jesus and his resurrection qualifies them as witnesses, but the Spirit will give them the capability to articulate their experience with boldness [BECNT, PNTC].

QUESTION—Where were the apostles to be witnesses for Jesus?

The apostles were commissioned to witness for Jesus, first beginning in Jerusalem, and then moving out to all Judea and Samaria, and then extend out to the end of the earth [TRT]. Samaria was of non-Jewish constituency [NAC]. The 'end of the earth' is often taken to refer to all the world [AB, Bar, BECNT, CBC, NAC, TNTC]. The phrase 'the end of the earth is geographic and ethnic in scope, including all people and locales [BECNT]. The final verse in Acts (28:31), with Paul preaching without hindrance in Rome, suggests that the story has not reached its final destination and the witness continues [NAC]. Readers are left with an implied challenge to continue the work of worldwide testimony to Jesus [PNTC]. It has often been pointed out that the geographical scope of this verse provides a rough outline for Acts: Jerusalem (1–7), Judea and Samaria (8–12), the end of the earth (13–28). Jesus' last words before his ascension, his direct commission to the apostles, 'you will be my witnesses' becomes the theme of Acts [BECNT, EBC, NAC, NICNT, TNTC].

DISCOURSE UNIT—1:9–14 [PNTC]. The topic is the ascension of Christ and its aftermath.

DISCOURSE UNIT—1:9–11 [EBC, NAC, NICNT; NASB]. The topic is the ascension [NASB, EBC, NICNT], the ascension of Christ [NAC].

1:9 And when-he-had-said these-things, as-they were-watching,[a] he-was-taken-up,[b] and (a)-cloud took him out-of their sight[c].

LEXICON—a. pres. act. participle of βλέπω (LN 24.7) (BDAG 1.b. p. 179): 'to watch' [AB, BDAG, CBC; CEV, NCV, NET, NLT, NRSV, TEV], 'to look on' [BDAG; ESV, NASB], 'to look' [Bar, BECNT, LN], 'to behold' [KJV], not explicit [GW, NIV, REB]. This verb means to see, frequently in the sense of becoming aware of or taking notice of something [LN]. It means to perceive with the eye [BDAG].

b. aorist pass. indic. of ἐπαίρω (LN 15.105) (BDAG 1. p. 357): 'to be taken up' [BDAG, LN; CEV, KJV, NIV, NLT, TEV], 'to be lifted up' [Bar, BECNT, CBC; ESV, NASB, NCV, NET, NRSV, REB], 'to be taken to

heaven' [GW], 'to ascend' [AB]. This verb means to cause something to move up [LN]. In the passive it means to be taken up [BDAG].
- c. ὀφθαλμός (LN 24.16) (BDAG 1. p. 744): 'sight' [BDAG, LN]. The clause νεφέλη ὑπέλαβεν αὐτὸν ἀπὸ τῶν ὀφθαλμῶν αὐτῶν 'a cloud took him out of their sight' [ESV, NRSV] is also translated 'a cloud took him from their sight' [REB], ' a cloud took him up from their sight' [Bar], 'a cloud hid him from their sight' [LN; NCV, NET, NIV, TEV], 'a cloud removed him from their sight' [AB, CBC], 'a cloud received him from their sight' [BECNT], 'a cloud received him out of their sight' [KJV, NASB], 'a cloud hid him so that they could no longer see him' [GW], 'he was taken up into a cloud, and they could not/no longer see him' [CEV, NLT]. This noun denotes the capacity to see [LN].

QUESTION—What happened when Jesus finished speaking with his disciples?

After Jesus had commissioned his apostles to witness, he was lifted up and a cloud took him out of the sight of the apostles. The passive verb ἐπήρθη 'he was taken up' indicates that Jesus was lifted up by someone, and that one was God the Father [BECNT, TH]. It doesn't mean that God grabbed Jesus by the head and hauled him to heaven, and it could be translated God caused him to go to heaven' [TH]. The cloud represents God's presence and glory [BECNT, EBC, NAC, PNTC, TNTC, TRT]. The cloud is meant to symbolize the *shekinah*, the visible manifestation of God's presence and glory. Such a cloud hovered above the tabernacle in the wilderness as a visible token of the glory of God that dwelt within the tabernacle (Ex. 40:34) [EBC, NICNT]. Such a cloud had also enveloped Jesus and three of his disciples on the Mount of Transfiguration as a visible sign of God's presence and approval of his Son (Luke 9:28–36) [EBC, NAC, NICNT]. Jesus was enveloped in the cloud of the divine presence [BECNT, NICNT, PNTC].

1:10 And as they-were looking-intently[a] into the sky[b] (while) he was-going[c], behold, two men in white clothing stood-by[d] them.

LEXICON—a. pres. act. participle of ἀτενίζω (LN 24.49) (BDAG 1. p. 148): 'to look intently' [BDAG, LN; NIV], 'to look stedfastly' [KJV], 'to look' [NCV], 'to gaze intently' [CBC; NASB, REB], 'to gaze up' [AB; NRSV], 'to gaze' [Bar, BECNT; ESV], 'to stare' [BDAG; GW, NET], 'to keep looking up' [CEV], 'to strain to see' [NLT], 'to fix their eyes' [TEV]. This verb means to fix one's eyes on some object continually and intensely [LN].
- b. οὐρανός (LN 1.5, 1.11) (BDAG 2.b. p. 739): 'sky' [AB, CBC, LN (1.5); CEV, ESV, GW, NASB, NCV, NET, NIV, REB, TEV], 'heaven' [Bar, BDAG, BECNT, LN (1.11); KJV, NRSV]. The clause 'they were looking intently into the sky while he was going' is also translated 'they strained to see him rising into heaven' [NLT]. This noun denotes the space above the earth, including the vault arching high over the earth from one horizon to another, and the sun, moon, and stars [LN (1.5)] or it denotes the supernatural dwelling place of God and other heavenly beings. In a

number of languages precisely the same term is used to designate both 'sky' and 'heaven' (as the abode of God). But in many instances a completely separate term must be employed in speaking of the dwelling place of God, for example, 'where God lives', 'where God is' or 'from where God governs' [LN 1.11].
  c. pres. mid./pass. (deponent = act.) participle of πορεύομαι (LN 15.34) 'to go' [Bar, BDAG, CBC, LN; ESV, NASB, NCV, NET, NIV, NRSV, REB], 'to go up' [CEV, KJV], 'to go away' [LN; TEV], 'to depart' [AB, BECNT; GW], 'to rise' [NLT]. This verb means to move away from a reference point [LN].
  d. pluperfect act. indic. of παρίστημι (LN 17.3) (BDAG 2.b.α. p. 778): 'to stand by' [AB, BDAG, BECNT; ESV, KJV, NRSV], 'to stand near' [LN; GW, NET], 'to stand beside' [Bar, CBC; CEV, NASB, NCV, NIV, REB, TEV], 'to stand among' [NLT]. This verb means to stand near or alongside of someone [LN].

QUESTION—What is indicated by the use of the verb ἀτενίζω 'to look intently'?

This underscores the intensity of the way that the apostles were staring at the sky for the departing Jesus [BECNT, EBC, TH]. Some of the apostles, remembering the Mount of Transfiguration experience, might have expected that the cloud would dissolve and Jesus would be left with them [EBC, NICNT, PNTC, TNTC].

QUESTION—How is the word ἰδού 'behold' used in this verse?

The word ἰδού 'behold' is a particle which generally is used to call attention to what follows, but in certain contexts like this it may be translated in other ways, and the meaning 'suddenly' seems best suited to this context [BECNT, NAC, PNTC, TH].

QUESTION—Who were the two men in white clothing?

The two men dressed in white were angels, the heavenly messengers [AB, Bar, BECNT, CBC, EBC, NAC, NICNT, TH, TNTC, TRT]. 'White' is the traditional dress of angels in Jewish and Christian tradition. Even though the two men were angels, it is better to preserve the wording of the original text and say 'two men.' A footnote could be used to indicate that angels are often spoken of in Scripture in this manner [TH]. It might be important to specify 'God's angels', since there are also evil angels [TRT]. The appearance of these two men resembled that of the two men who met the women at the tomb of Jesus (Luke 24:4–7). Supernatural beings attended both the resurrection and the ascension events [Bar, BECNT, NAC, NICNT, PNTC, TNTC]. The fact that there were two suggests that they are viewed as witnesses, two being the minimum number for credible witness-bearing (Deut. 19:15) [BECNT, NICNT].

1:11 And they-said, "Men of-Galilee, why do-you-stand looking[a] into the sky? This Jesus, who has-been-taken-up[b] from you into heaven, will-come[c] in-(the-same)-way[d] as you-saw him going into heaven."
LEXICON—a. pres. act. participle of ἐμβλέπω (LN 24.9) (BDAG 3. p. 179): 'to look' [Bar, BDAG, BECNT, LN; ESV, GW, NASB, NCV, NIV], 'to look up' [AB, CBC; CEV, NET, NRSV, REB, TEV], 'to gaze up' [KJV], 'to stare' [NLT]. This verb means to direct one's vision and attention to a particular object [LN]. It means to look at something directly and therefore intently [BDAG].
  b. aorist pass. participle of ἀναλαμβάνω (LN 15.203) (BDAG 1. p. 66): 'to be taken up' [BDAG, CBC, LN; ESV, KJV, NASB, NCV, NET, NRSV, REB], 'to be taken' [AB, BECNT; CEV, GW, NIV, NLT, TEV], 'to be received up' [Bar]. This verb means to lift up and carry (away) [BDAG, LN].
  c. fut. mid. (deponent = act.) indic. of ἔρχομαι (LN 15.81) (BDAG 1.b.α. p. 394): 'to come' [AB, Bar, BDAG, BECNT, CBC, LN; ESV, KJV, NASB, NRSV, REB], 'to come back' [CEV, GW, NCV, NET, NIV, TEV], 'to return' [NLT]. This verb means to move toward or up to the reference point of the viewpoint character or event [LN].
  d. τρόπος (LN 89.83) (BDAG 1. p. 1017): 'way' [AB, Bar, BDAG, CBC, LN; all versions except KJV], 'manner' [BDAG, BECNT, LN; KJV]. This noun denotes the manner in which something is done [LN].
QUESTION—What does the phrase Ἄνδρες Γαλιλαῖοι 'Men of Galilee' mean?
  The phrase 'Men of Galilee' is equivalent to 'you men who come from Galilee' or 'you men whose homes are in Galilee'. All languages have a means by which people may be identified as coming from a particular locality [TH].
QUESTION—Is the meaning of οὐρανόν 'heaven/sky' different in verses 10 and 11?
  Greek uses the same word οὐρανόν in either the singular or plural form to refer to both 'heaven' and the 'sky', which seems to imply that the place where God lives and rules from (that is, heaven) is the same place that the sun, moon and stars are (that is, the sky). Some commentaries and versions take all four occurrences (one in verse 10 and three in verse 11) to refer to heaven [AB, Bar, BECNT, NICNT, TNTC; ESV, KJV, NLT, NRSV]. Many other commentaries and versions distinguish between the two. 'Heaven' is used in contexts where God or God's dwelling place is in focus while 'sky' is used in other contexts. So the first two occurrences (the one in verse 10 and the first one in verse 11) refer to 'the sky' into which the men were looking and the last two in verse 11 refer to 'heaven' where Jesus had gone [CBC, EBC, NAC, PNTC. TH, TRT; CEV, GW, NASB, NCV, NET, NIV, REB, TEV].

QUESTION—What is indicated by the use of the demonstrative pronoun 'this' in the phrase οὗτος ὁ Ἰησοῦς 'this Jesus'?

This speaks of the identity between the ascended Jesus and the Jesus yet to come [EBC]. This same person named Jesus will return in the same manner as he went [EBC, NAC, NICNT, TH, TRT]. At his future coming Jesus will be enveloped in the *shekinah* cloud of divine presence and power [Bar, EBC, NICNT, PNTC, TNTC].

QUESTION—Why did the two men (angels) ask why the disciples were standing there looking into the sky?

This was a rhetorical question that did not expect an answer. It was a mild rebuke, letting them know that they should not be surprised that the risen Jesus is lifted up into God's presence. His departure means that they now have work to do before his return [BECNT].

QUESTION—How will Jesus come back in the same way as they saw him going into heaven?

This probably means that Jesus will be enveloped in the cloud of the divine presence and glory as he returns [EBC]. It does not answer the apostles' question of when the restoration occurs, but it assures them that Jesus' return will complete the messianic task. At that time, they were to believe Jesus' promise and obey his command, returning to the city to wait for empowerment by the Spirit and witness to what they had seen [BECNT, NAC, PNTC, TNTC].

DISCOURSE UNIT—1:12–26 [BECNT, CBC, EBC, TRT; CEV, ESV, GW, NASB, NCV, NET, NIV, NLT, NRSV, REB, TEV]. The topic is a new apostle is chosen [NCV], a new apostle takes Judas' place [GW], a replacement for Judas is chosen [NET], someone to take the place of Judas [CEV], Matthias chosen to replace Judas [ESV, NIV, NRSV], Matthias is chosen to replace Judas [TRT], Matthias replaces Judas [NLT], Judas' successor [TEV], community life: replacing Judas by depending on God and reconstituting the Twelve [BECNT], the full complement of apostles [EBC], the upper room [NASB], the company in Jerusalem [CBC], the church in Jerusalem [REB].

DISCOURSE UNIT—1:12–14 [EBC, NAC, NICNT, TNTC]. The topic is the return of the disciples to Jerusalem [TNTC], the preparation in the upper room [NAC], in the upper room [EBC, NICNT].

1:12 Then they-returned to Jerusalem from (the)-mount[a] called Olivet[b], which is near Jerusalem, a Sabbath day's journey[c] away.

LEXICON—a. ὄρος (LN 1.46) (BDAG p. 725): 'mount' [BDAG, BECNT, LN; CEV, ESV, KJV, NASB, NCV, NLT, NRSV, TEV], 'mountain' [AB, Bar, BDAG; GW, NET], 'hill' [BDAG, CBC; NIV, REB]. This noun denotes a relatively high elevation of land, in contrast with βουνός hill [LN]. It refers to the Hill or Mount of Olives about 17 meters higher than Jerusalem [BDAG].

b. ἐλαιών (LN 3.12) (BDAG p. 313): 'olive grove, olive orchard' [BDAG, LN]. The phrase ὄρους τοῦ καλουμένου Ἐλαιῶνος 'the mount called Olivet' [BDAG, LN; ESV, KJV, NASB, NRSV] is also translated 'the Mount of Olives' [BECNT; CEV, NCV, NLT, TEV], 'the mountain called the Mount of Olives' [AB; GW, NET], 'the mountain called Olive Grove' [Bar], 'the hill called Olivet' [CBC; REB], 'the hill called the Mount of Olives' [NIV]. This noun denotes a number of olive trees planted in a garden or grove. Instead of calling it 'the hill called The Olive Grove' it may be well to employ the more common designation for the hill in question, 'Hill of Olives' or 'Mount of Olives' [LN].
c. ὁδός (LN 81.28) (BDAG 2. p. 691): 'way, journey' [BDAG, LN]. The phrase σαββάτου ἔχον ὁδόν 'a Sabbath day's journey away' [AB, BDAG, LN; ESV, NET, NASB, NRSV] is also translated 'a Sabbath day's journey off' [Bar], 'a Sabbath day's trip away' [BECNT], 'from Jerusalem a Sabbath day's journey' [KJV], 'a Sabbath day's walk from the city' [NIV], 'no farther than a Sabbath day's journey' [CBC; REB], 'about half a mile away' [GW], 'about half a mile from Jerusalem' [CEV, NCV], 'about half a mile away from the city' [TEV], 'a distance of half a mile' [NLT]. This noun denotes the action of traveling [BDAG].

QUESTION—How far is 'a Sabbath day's journey'?

'A Sabbath day's journey' is an idiom which is used here as a measure of distance, not to indicate that it was a Sabbath day. The Sabbath day was the day of the week when Jewish Law did not permit them to do any work, in obedience to God's command in Exodus 20:8–11. Jewish Law allowed a person to walk no more than 2,000 cubits/steps on a Sabbath day. That was about three-fourths of a mile or 1.2 kilometers [Bar, BECNT, EBC, NAC, NICNT, PNTC, TNTC, TRT].

1:13 And when they-had-entered (the city), they-went-up to the upper-room[a] where they-were-staying,[b] Peter and John and James and Andrew, Philip and Thomas, Bartholomew and Matthew, James (the-son)-of-Alphaeus and Simon the Zealot and Judas (the-son)-of-James.

LEXICON—a. ὑπερῷον (LN 7.27) (BDAG p. 1034): 'upper room' [AB, BDAG, BECNT; ESV, KJV, NASB], 'upstairs room' [Bar, LN; CEV, NCV, NET, NIV, REB], 'upstairs room of the house' [NLT], 'upper story' [BDAG], 'second-story room' [GW], 'room upstairs' [BDAG, CBC; NRSV], 'up to the room' [TEV]. This noun denotes a room on the level above the ground floor (second story in American usage and first story in most other languages) [LN].
b. pres. act. participle of καταμένω (LN 85.55) (BDAG p. 522): 'to stay' [AB, Bar, BDAG, BECNT, LN; all versions except KJV, REB], 'to abide' [CBC; KJV], 'to lodge' [REB]. This verb means to remain in the same place over a period of time [LN].

QUESTION—What was the upper room like?
Upper rooms in Palestinian cities were usually the choicest rooms because they were above the tumult of the crowded streets and beyond the prying eyes of passersby. For the wealthy, the upper room was the living room. Sometimes upper rooms were rented out. Often they served as places of assembly, study, and prayer [EBC]. The upper room mentioned here may or may not be the same upstairs room where Jesus and his disciples had celebrated the Passover (Luke 22:12) and where Jesus appeared to some of them on Easter Day (Luke 24:33; John 20:19, 26) [TRT]. The various meetings recorded in Acts 1:13; 2:1–4; 4:23–31; 12:12–17 could all have been in different locations. There is not enough evidence to be certain [PNTC].

QUESTION—Is there any significance in the listing of the apostles' names?
The list of apostles is identical with that of Luke 6:14–16, but in a different order and with the omission of Judas Iscariot [Bar, BECNT, CBC, EBC, NAC, NICNT, PNTC, TNTC, TRT]. The reordering of the names is possibly deliberate. Andrew was moved from second place in the Gospel to fourth place in Acts, and John was moved to second place. This gives prominence to Peter, John and James, the only apostles who have any individual role in the narrative of Acts [NAC, PNTC].

1:14 These all with-one-mind[a] were devoting-(themselves)[b] to-prayer, together-with (the)-women and Mary the mother of-Jesus, and his brothers.
LEXICON—a. ὁμοθυμαδόν (LN 31.23) (BDAG p. 706): 'with one mind' [BDAG, LN; NASB, NET], not explicit [CBC; NCV, NIV, NLT, NRSV]. The phrase 'with one mind' is also translated 'with one accord' [ESV, KJV, REB], 'with one purpose' [BECNT, BDAC], 'with a single purpose in mind' [CEV], 'had a single purpose' [GW], 'in union with one another' [Bar], 'in common' [AB], 'as a group' [TEV]. This adverb pertains to mutual consent or agreement [LN]. It means with one mind, purpose [BDAG]. Ten of the eleven NT occurrences of this term appear in Acts 1:14; 2:46; 4:24; 5:12; 15:25 [BECNT].
b. pres. act. participle of προσκαρτερέω (LN 68.68) (BDAG 2.a. p. 881): 'to devote oneself' [BECNT, LN; ESV, GW, NASB], 'to keep on, to persist in' [LN], 'to be busily engaged in, to be devoted to' [BDAG]. The phrase 'were devoting themselves to prayer' is also translated 'were continuing in prayer' [Bar], 'continued together in prayer' [NET], 'continued praying together' [NCV], 'joined together constantly in prayer' [NIV], 'were constantly at prayer' [REB], 'were constantly united in prayer' [NLT], 'engaged in common prayer continuously' [AB], 'were constantly devoting themselves to prayer' [NRSV], 'were constantly at prayer together' [CBC], 'often met together and prayed' [CEV], 'gathered frequently to pray' [TEV], 'continued...in prayer (and supplication)' [KJV]. This verb means to continue to do something with intense effort,

with the possible implication of doing so despite difficulty [LN]. It means to persist in something [BDAG].

QUESTION—Who were with the apostles in the upper room?
There were Jesus' mother Mary, his brothers and some women. Jesus had four half-brothers James, Joseph, Judas and Simon according to Mark 6:3. They were the natural offspring of Mary and Joseph after the birth of Jesus. The women would be those who accompanied Jesus from Galilee and witnessed his crucifixion and resurrection and might include the wives of the apostles [BECNT, EBC, NAC, NICNT, PNTC]. Mary the mother of Jesus is referred to only here in Acts. This is the point of reference to Mary and of that to his brothers. These are never again mentioned in Acts [Bar]. Here indicates that the earthly family of Jesus was taken up into his spiritual family [Bar, EBC, PNTC, TNTC].

QUESTION—What did they do in the upper room?
Having obeyed Jesus' command to return to Jerusalem and wait for the promised gift of the Spirit, they stayed together in the upper room and devoted themselves to prayer while waiting. It is striking that at most every important turning point in the narrative of God's redemptive action in Acts, there is a mention of prayer like here (e.g. 1:24; 8:14–17; 9:11–12; 10:4, 9, 30; 13:2–3) [CBC, NAC, PNTC].

DISCOURSE UNIT—1:15–26 [AB, Bar, EBC, NAC, NICNT, PNTC, TNTC]. The topic is the twelfth apostle [TNTC], the twelfth apostle is chosen after the death of Judas [AB], a replacement for Judas Iscariot [NICNT], Judas and Matthias [Bar], Matthias chosen to replace Judas Iscariot [EBC], restoration of the apostolic circle [NAC], completion of the apostolic circle [PNCT].

1:15 **And in those days Peter stood-up among the brothers[a] (a)-crowd[b] of-(people)[c] that-was about (a)-hundred (and)-twenty in all, and he-said,**

LEXICON—a. ἀδελφός (LN 11.23): '(Christian) brother, fellow believer' [LN]. The phrase τῶν ἀδελφῶν 'the brothers' [Bar, BECNT; ESV] is also translated 'his brothers' [Bar], 'the brethren' [AB; NASB], 'the assembled brotherhood' [CBC; REB], 'the believers' [NCV, NET, NIV, NLT, NRSV, TEV], 'the disciples' [GW, KJV], 'the Lord's followers' [CEV]. This noun denotes a close associate of a group of persons having a well-defined membership, and in the NT the word 'brothers' refers specifically to fellow believers in Christ [LN].
b. ὄχλος (LN 11.1) (BDAG 1.b.β. p. 745): 'crowd' [BDAG, BECNT, LN; NRSV], 'company' [ESV], 'gathering' [AB; NASB, NET], 'meeting' [NCV, TEV], 'group' [NIV], 'number' [Bar; KJV], 'large number' [BDAG], 'assembled [CBC; REB], not explicit [CEV, GW, NLT]. This noun denotes a casual non-membership group of people, fairly large in size and assembled for whatever purpose [LN]. It denotes a group or company of people with common interests or of distinctive status gathered together [BDAG].

c. ὄνομα (LN 9.19, 33.126) (BDAG 2. p. 714): 'people' [LN (9.19); NET], 'person' [AB, Bar, BDAG, BECNT, LN (9.19); ESV, NASB, NRSV], 'name' [LN (33.126); KJV]. The phrase ὄχλος ὀνομάτων 'a crowd of people' is also translated 'a group numbering' [NIV], 'assembled brotherhood' [CBC; REB], not explicit [CEV, GW, NCV, NLT, TEV]. This noun denotes a person, with the possible implication of existence or relevance as individuals [LN (9.19)], or it denotes the proper name of a person or object [LN (33.126)].

QUESTION—What is meant by ἐν ταῖς ἡμέραις 'in those days'?

'In those days' indicates either a transition to a new section [EBC, NAC, PNTC, TH], or the beginning of a new story [TH]. In this context, it refers to the period of time between the Ascension and Pentecost [Bar, PNTC].

QUESTION—Who were these ἀδελφῶν 'brothers'?

In this context, 'brothers' refers to 'followers of Jesus Christ', including both men and women [TRT]. They were 'fellow believers' [PNTC], 'members of God's reconstituted family' [Bar].

QUESTION—Why did Luke make a point of telling how many people were there?

Luke might have intended to show that they were a legally formed community. Based on the Jewish Law, it was required to be at least 120 members for a community to be established and have its own council [TNTC, TRT]. In rabbinic tradition 120 was the minimum requirement for constituting a local Sanhedrin [NAC].

1:16 "Men[a], brothers, the Scripture had to-be-fulfilled,[b] which the Holy Spirit foretold[c] through (the)-mouth of-David concerning Judas, who became[d] (a)-guide to-those who-arrested[e] Jesus.

LEXICON—a. ἀνήρ (LN 9.24): 'man' [LN]. The beginning phrase Ἄνδρες ἀδελφοί 'Men, brothers' is also translated 'Men and brethren' [KJV], 'Brothers' [AB, Bar; ESV, GW, NET, NIV, NLT], 'Brethren' [BECNT; NASB], 'Brothers and sisters' [NCV], 'Friends' [NRSV], 'My friends' [CBC; CEV, REB, TEV]. This noun denotes an adult male person of marriageable age [LN].

b. aorist pass. infin. of πληρόω (LN 13.106) (BDAG 4.a. p. 829): 'to be fulfilled' [LN], 'to be caused to happen' [LN]. The phrase ἔδει πληρωθῆναι 'had to be fulfilled' [AB, Bar; ESV, NASB, NET, NIV, NLT, NRSV] is also translated 'had to come true' [GW, TEV], 'was bound to come true' [CBC; REB], 'must needs have been fulfilled' [KJV], 'that must happen' [NCV], 'it was necessary (that Scripture) be fulfilled' BECNT], 'has now happened' [CEV]. This verb means to cause to happen, with the implication of fulfilling some purpose [LN]. It means to bring to a designed end, here referring to the fulfillment of a divine prediction [BDAG].

c. aorist act. indic. of προεῖπον (LN 33.281) (BDAG 1. p. 868): 'to foretell' [AB, BDAG, LN; NASB, NET, NRSV], 'to speak beforehand' [BECNT;

ESV], 'to speak in advance' [Bar], 'to speak long ago' [NIV], 'to predict' [GW, NLT], 'to make a prediction' [TEV], 'to speak before' [KJV], 'to say' [CEV, NCV], 'to utter' [CBC; REB]. This verb means to say in advance what is going to happen [LN]. It means to tell beforehand [BDAG].
d. aorist mid. (deponent = act.) participle of γίνομαι (LN 13.48) (BDAG 7. p. 199): 'to become' [BDAG, LN; ESV, NASB, NET]. The phrase γενομένου ὁδηγοῦ 'who became a guide' [BECNT; NRSV] is also translated 'who served as guide' [NIV], 'who acted as guide' [AB, Bar, CBC], 'Judas acted as guide' [REB], 'who guided those' [NLT], ' was the guide' [TEV], 'which was guide' [KJV], 'he brought the mob' [CEV], 'He led those' [NCV], 'Judas led the men' [GW]. This verb means to come to acquire or experience a state [LN]. It means to come into a certain state [BDAG].
e. aorist act. participle of συλλαμβάνω (LN 37.109) (BDAG 1.a. p. 955): 'to arrest' [AB, Bar, BDAG, BECNT, CBC, LN; all versions except KJV], 'to take' [KJV]. This verb means to seize and to take along with [LN]. It means to take into custody [BDAG].

QUESTION—What does Ἄνδρες ἀδελφοί 'Men, brothers' refer to?

This phrase represents a type of formal address found in first-century synagogues [EBC]. The expression 'men, brothers' is using the word 'men' in a general sense that does not exclude women, so it is usually best left untranslated. The term 'brothers' can also cause difficulties in languages in which the term for 'brother' is not generalized. Often the terms 'relatives, kinsmen' or 'companions' must be used for a term that can include women [TH]. Similar to verse 15, the 'brothers' here refers to 'followers of Jesus Christ', 'fellow believers', including men and women, and it may have to be translated 'brothers and sisters'. The term 'Christians' should not be used until after Acts 11.26 [TRT].

QUESTION—What does ἔδει 'it was necessary' imply?

'It was necessary' indicates that what follows has to be fulfilled and it concerns Judas, the betrayer of Jesus [NAC, TH, TNTC, TRT]. Such betrayal was a necessary part of the divine plan for Christ, the Messiah [EBC, PNTC].

QUESTION—What was foretold through the mouth of David?

This points to Psalm 69:25 and Psalm 109:8 that Peter is going to quote in verse 20. Both Psalms were written by King David [BECNT, NAC, TNTC]. Peter meant that what had been prophesied in these Scriptures would come to fulfillment [Bar, BECNT, NAC, TNTC]. The real author of these Scriptures was the Holy Spirit, who spoke through the prophet David. In other words, David was a mouthpiece of the Spirit [NICNT].

1:17 For he-was counted[a] among us and received (his) share of-this ministry[b]."

LEXICON—a. perf. pass. participle of καταριθμέω (LN 34.33) (BDAG 2. p. 526): 'to belong to' [BDAG, LN], 'to be counted as a member, to be counted as a part' [LN]. The clause κατηριθμημένος ἦν ἐν ἡμῖν 'he was/had-been counted among us' [Bar; NASB] is also translated 'he was counted as one of us' [LN; NET], 'he was numbered among us' [BECNT; ESV, NRSV], 'he was numbered with us' [KJV], 'he was one of our number' [CBC; NIV, REB], 'he belonged to our number' [BDAG], 'he was one of our group' [NCV], 'he had been one of us' [GW], 'Judas/He was one of us' [AB; CEV, NLT], 'Judas was a member of our group' [TEV]. This verb means to be counted as a member of a group [LN]. It means to include as an entity in a group [BDAG].

b. διακονία (LN 35.21) (BDAG 3. p. 230): 'ministry' [BDAG, LN], 'service, office' [BDAG]. The clause ἔλαχεν τὸν κλῆρον τῆς διακονίας ταύτης 'he received his/a share in/of this ministry' [NASB, NET] is also translated 'he was allotted his/a share in this ministry' [BECNT; ESV, NRSV], 'he had obtained part of this ministry' [KJV], 'he had been given an active role in this ministry' [GW], 'he has his place in this ministry' [AB, CBC; REB], 'he shared in the ministry with us' [NLT], 'he shared in this ministry' [NIV], 'he had been chosen to have a part in our work' [TEV], 'he had worked with us' [CEV], 'he served together with us' [NCV], 'he obtained the lot of this ministry' [Bar]. This noun denotes the role or position of serving [LN]. It denotes a service functioning in the interest of a larger public [BDAG].

QUESTION—What is the function of this verse?

The mention of Judas as one of the twelve apostles sets the stage for talking about the replacement of Judas for his ministry work among the Twelve in verse 20 [NAC, TNTC].

1:18 (Now this-man acquired[a] (a)-field with (the)-reward[b] of-his wickedness,[c] and falling headlong[d] he-burst-open (in-the)-middle and all his intestines[e] gushed-out.[f] **1:19** And it-became known to-all who were-living-in Jerusalem, so-that in (their)-own language that field was-called Akeldama, that is, Field-of-Blood.)

LEXICON—a. aorist mid. (deponent = act.) indic. of κτάομαι (LN 57.58) (BDAG 1. p. 572): 'to acquire' [BDAG, LN; ESV, NASB, NET, NRSV], 'to buy' [AB, BECNT, CBC; CEV, GW, NCV, NIV, NLT, REB, TEV], 'to purchase' [Bar; KJV], 'to get, to gain' [LN]. This verb means to acquire possession of something [LN]. It means to gain possession of [BDAG].

b. μισθός (LN 38.14) (BDAG 1. p. 653): 'reward' [AB, Bar, BECNT, LN; ESV, KJV, NET, NIV, NRSV], 'money' [BDAG; CEV, NCV, GW, NLT, TEV], 'price' [CBC; NASB, REB]. This noun denotes a recompense based upon what a person has earned and thus deserves, and the nature of

the recompense may be either positive or negative [LN]. It denotes the remuneration for work done, and in this case it refers to the money paid for his treachery [BDAG].
c. ἀδικία (LN 88.21) (BDAG 2. p. 20): 'wickedness' [BDAG; ESV, NASB, NIV, NRSV], 'unjust deed' [LN; NET], 'evil deed' [TEV], 'evil act' [NCV], 'evil thing' [CEV], 'unrighteous act' [Bar], 'unrighteousness' [BDAG, BECNT], 'sin' [AB], 'wrong' [GW], 'iniquity' [KJV], 'treachery' [NLT], 'villainy' [CBC; REB]. This noun denotes an activity which is unjust [LN]. Here it means that Judas paid the fee for the field with the fee paid him for his crime [BDAG].
d. πρηνής (LN 17.20) (BDAG p. 863): 'headlong' [AB, BDAG, BECNT, LN; ESV, KJV, NASB, NIV, NRSV, REB], 'headfirst' [CEV, NET, NLT], 'headfirst to death' [GW], 'to death' [NCV, TEV], 'flat on his face' [Bar], 'forward on the ground' [CBC]. This adjective pertains to being stretched out in a position facedown and headfirst [LN].
e. σπλάγχνον (LN 8.58) (BDAG 1. p. 938): 'intestines' [Bar, LN; NCV, NASB, NET, NIV, NLT], 'bowels' [BECNT; ESV, KJV, NRSV], 'insides' [CEV, TEV], 'inward parts' [BDAG], 'internal organs' [GW], 'entrails' [AB, BDAG, CBC; REB]. This noun denotes the inner parts of the body, especially the viscera [LN].
f. aorist pass. indic. of ἐκχέω (LN 14.18) (BDAG 1.b. p. 312): 'to gush out' [BDAG; ESV, KJV, NASB, NET, NRSV], 'to pour out' [AB, Bar BECNT, CBC, LN; NCV], 'to come out' [CEV, GW], 'to spill out' [NIV, NLT, REB, TEV]. This verb means for solid objects to flow out of a container [LN]. Here it refers to all his bowels gushing out [BDAG].

QUESTION—Why are verses 18–19 enclosed by parentheses?
Verses 18–19 are not part of Peter's speech but constitute an aside that Luke provided for his readers. In translation, this is indicated by a parenthesis at the beginning of verse 18 and at the end of verse 19 [NAC, NICNT]. In these two verses, Luke explains what happened to Judas in order to underscore the horrific judgment he experienced and his death [BECNT, EBC, NICNT, PNTC]. According to verse 19, this incident became so well known to everyone in Jerusalem that it was not necessary for Peter to tell his hearers. Luke has included this for his readers [Bar].

QUESTION—Did Judas buy the field himself?
Judas was already dead when the chief priests bought the field with the thirty pieces of silver, the money he got from his wicked act of leading the soldiers to arrest Jesus. However, Judas was still considered the owner of the money and so the one who bought the field [BECNT, EBC, PNTC, TNTC, TRT]. In fact, the chief priest might have bought the field in Judas' name [TRT].

QUESTION—How did Judas die?
Luke says that Judas fell headlong, burst open and his insides poured out. Matthew 27:5 says that Judas hanged himself. What Luke describes here suggests that Judas jumped/fell down from a great height [Bar, PNTC, TRT]. It is possible that the rope he was using broke and his body hit rocks below,

or his body might have hit something sharp during the fall [TNTC, TRT]. We can picture that his fall was so severe as to open his body cavity and cause his inner organs to spill out [NAC]. Packer's comment is that the dead body hanging from a tree was torn down and ripped open by wild dogs [CBC].

QUESTION—What was the language mentioned in this verse?

The language mentioned here was Aramaic [Bar, BECNT, CBC, EBC, NAC, PNTC, TRT]. During that time, most Jews probably spoke Aramaic as their first language [TRT]. It is probably that Luke wrote for the benefit of his Greek-speaking readers, now Peter spoke for his Aramaic-speaking hearers [Bar].

QUESTION—Why was the field called Ἀκελδαμάχ 'Akeldama'?

Akeldama or Hakeldama is a transliteration of the Aramaic word *haqeldama, Field of Blood* [Bar, TNTC]. Field of Blood does not mean a field consisting of blood, or a 'bloody field', but rather a field with which blood was associated [TH]. In Matthew 27:6, the chief priests considered the money returned from Judas as blood money. The field was purchased with 'blood money' [AB, EBC, PNTC, TNTC]. Barrett states that the last two syllables should be derived from *damka*, sleep (in death), i.e. cemetery [NAC]. Note that Matthew 27:7 records that the potter's field bought by the chief priests was a burial place for strangers, i.e., a cemetery.

1:20 "**For it-is-written in (the)-book of-Psalms, 'Let his homestead[a] become deserted,[b]' and let there be no one living in it.' and 'Let another receive[c] his position.'**

LEXICON—a. ἔπαυλις (LN 7.4) (BDAG p. 360): 'homestead' [AB, BDAG, CBC, LN; NASB, NRSV, REB], 'residence' [BDAG, LN], 'house' [LN; CEV, NET, TEV], 'home' [GW, NLT], 'habitation' [BECNT; KJV], 'place' [NCV, NIV], 'farm' [BDAG, LN], 'camp' [ESV], 'steading' [Bar]. This noun denotes property in which a person was expected to reside, either as the result of ownership or legal contract [LN]. It denotes property that serves as a dwelling place whether personally owned or by contract [BDAG].

b. ἔρημος (LN 85.84) (BDAG 1.a. p. 391): 'deserted' [BDAG, LN; GW, NET, NIV], 'uninhabited/empty' [CEV, NCV, TEV], 'desolate' [AB, Bar, BDAG, BECNT, CBC; ESV, KJV, NASB, NLT, NRSV, REB]. This adjective pertains to an absence of residents or inhabitants in a place [LN]. It pertains to being in a state of isolation [BDAG].

c. aorist act. impera. of λαμβάνω (LN 57.125) (BDAG 10.b. p. 584): 'to receive' [BDAG, LN]. The clause 'let another receive his position' is also translated 'let another take his position of responsibility' [NET], 'let another take his position of overseer' [NRSV], 'let another take his office' [ESV], 'let another take over his charge' [CBC], 'let another man take his office' [NASB], 'let another man replace him as leader' [NCV], 'let someone else take his position' [GW, NLT], 'let someone else take his office' [Bar], 'let someone else have his job' [CEV], 'let his charge be given to another' [REB], 'his office let another take' [BECNT], 'his bishopric let another take' [KJV], 'may another take his place of leadership' [NIV], 'may someone else take his place of service' [TEV], 'another shall have his work of overseeing' [AB]. This verb means to receive or accept an object or benefit for which the initiative rests with the giver, but the focus of attention in the transfer is upon the receiver [LN].

QUESTION—How is the conjunction γάρ 'for' used at the beginning of this verse?

The account of Peter's speech has been interrupted by verses 18 and 19 and now it is resumed with γάρ 'for', which refers back to verse 16 to give Peter's explanation of the reason why it was necessary that Judas should have been the guide of those who arrested Jesus. In some languages, it is best to omit the conjunction entirely in a construction such as this since 'because' serves only to show that the argument is proceeding after the interruption of verses 18 and 19 [TH].

QUESTION—How did Peter apply the passages in the book of Psalms?

Peter quoted Psalm 69:25 and Psalm 109:8. In each case the quotation uses the Greek Septuagint translation (LXX) with some modification [Bar, TH]. Peter modified the subject in Psalm 69:25 from plural to singular to apply the meaning of it solely to Judas [PNTC, TH]. He altered the verb in Psalm 109:8 from optative to imperative to apply more emphatic meaning in Acts [BECNT]. Psalm 69 discusses the enemies of God. The Psalmist cries to God to be delivered from the enemies and calls for God's judgment so that their camp is left desolate and no one is able to live in their tents. Peter applied it to indicate that God's judgment had been fulfilled on Judas and his property, as Luke described in verses 18–19 [PNTC]. Psalm 109:8 is a lament. The Psalmist requests that the enemy's days may be few and another may seize his position. Peter applied it to refer to Judas' replacement. Another should replace his position as one of the twelve apostles [BECNT, NICNT, PNTC, TNTC].

QUESTION—What is the significance of the use of the imperative verb form?

These three Greek verbs are in imperative form: Γενηθήτω 'let become', ἔστω 'let be', and λαβέτω 'let receive'. The imperative form adds an emphatic obligatory mood to an action [TH]. These verbs are not expressing doubts or asking someone for permission [TRT]. In other words, Judas' homestead must become desolate, no one must live in it and someone else must do what Judas was supposed to do [TH].

1:21 Therefore it-is-necessary for one of-the-men (who) have-accompanied[a] us during all (the)-time[b] that the Lord Jesus went-in and out among us, **1:22** beginning from the baptism of-John until the day on-which he-was-taken-up[c] from us—one of-these-men must become (a)-witness[d] of-his resurrection (together) with us."

LEXICON—a. aorist act. participle of συνέρχομαι (LN 15.148) (BDAG 2. p. 970): 'to accompany' [Bar, LN; ESV, GW, NASB, NET, NRSV], 'to company' [KJV], 'to come/go with, travel together' [BDAG], 'to bear (us) company' [CBC; REB], 'to be with (us)' [AB; CEV, NIV, NLT], 'to come with (us)' [BECNT], 'to be part of (our group)' [NCV], 'to be in (our group)' [TEV]. This verb means to come/go together with one or more other persons [BDAG, LN].

b. χρόνος (LN 67.78) (BDAG 1. p. 1092): 'time, period of time' [BDAG, LN].The clause 'all-the/the-whole time that the Lord Jesus went in and out among us' [Bar; ESV, KJV, NASB, NIV, NRSV] is also translated 'all the time in which the Lord Jesus came in and went out among us' [BECNT], 'throughout the time when the Lord Jesus came and went among us' [AB], 'all the while we had the Lord Jesus with us, coming and going' [CBC], 'all the time the Lord Jesus associated with us' [GW, NET], 'the-entire/all-the time the Lord Jesus was among us' [NCV], 'the entire time we were traveling with the Lord Jesus' [NLT], 'the whole time that the Lord Jesus traveled about with us' [TEV], 'all the while the Lord Jesus was going about among us' [REB], not explicit [CEV]. This noun denotes an indefinite unit of time (the actual extent of time being determined by the context) [LN]. It denotes an indefinite period of time during which some activity takes place [BDAG].

c. aorist pass. indic. of ἀναλαμβάνω (LN 15.203) (BDAG 1. p. 66): 'to be taken up' [BDAG, CBC; ESV, KJV, NASB, NET, NIV, NRSV, REB], 'to be lifted up and carried away' [LN], 'to be received up' [Bar], 'to be taken to heaven' [CEV], 'to be taken up to heaven' [NCV, TEV], 'to be taken (from us)' [AB, BECNT; GW, NLT]. This verb means to carry something away from some location [LN]. It means to lift up and carry away [BDAG].

d. μάρτυς (LN 33.270) (BDAG 2.c. p. 620): 'witness' [Bar, BDAG, BECNT, CBC, LN: ESV, KJV, NASB, NCV, NET, NIV, NLT, NRSV, REB, TEV], 'one who testifies' [LN], not explicit [GW]. This noun is also translated as a verb: 'to bear witness' [AB]. The phrase 'must become a witness of his resurrection with us' is also translated 'we need someone else to help us tell others that Jesus has been raised from death' [CEV]. This noun denotes a person who witnesses [LN].

QUESTION—What does 'went in and out among us' mean?

'To go in and out among' is a Semitic idiom meaning 'to live or be with someone' [TH]. This idiom refers to having a familiar and unhindered association with someone [EBC].

QUESTION—What was 'the baptism of John'?
1. The baptism of John refers to Jesus' baptism by John [CBC, NAC, TH, TRT]. This interpretation seems to fit this context best.
2. The baptism of John' refers to John's baptizing ministry, similar to the account in Acts 10.37 [AB, Bar, BECNT, EBC, NICNT, TH, TNTC, TRT].

1:23 **And they-proposed[a] two-(men), Joseph the-one called Barsabbas, who was-also-called Justus and Matthias.**
LEXICON—a. aorist act. indic. of ἵστημι (LN 30.87 or 33.343) (BDAG A.2. p. 482): 'to propose' [AB, BDAG, LN (33.343); NET, NIV, NRSV, TEV], 'to recommend' [LN (33.343)], 'to nominate' [Bar; NLT], 'to put forward' [BDAG, CBC, LN; ESV, NASB, REB], 'to send forward' [BECNT], 'to select, to choose' [LN (30.87)], 'to appoint' [KJV]. The phrase 'they proposed two men' is also translated 'they put the names of two men before the group' [NCV], 'two men were suggested' [CEV], 'the disciples determined that two men were qualified' [GW]. This verb means to speak of someone or something as being well qualified or suited for a particular purpose [LN (33.343)] or to propose or put forward a particular selection [LN (30.87)]. It means to propose someone for an obligation [BDAG].
QUESTION—Who is this Joseph?
Luke tells that this Joseph is the one who has two other names, Barsabbas and Justus [TH]. 'Barsabbas' can mean 'Son of Saba' [Bar, BECNT, PNTC, TRT] or 'Son of the Sabbath', that is, one born on the Sabbath [Bar, BECNT, EBC, NAC, NICNT, PNTC, TNTC, TRT]. 'Justus' suggests a connection with the Roman world, a Roman name, possibly like Paul that he was a Roman citizen [Bar, EBC, PNTC]. He is not mentioned again in the New Testament [BECNT, TH].
QUESTION—Who is this Matthias?
'Matthias' means 'gift of God' [BECNT, NAC]. It is a shortened form of Mattathias [EBC, PNTC], of Mattithiah [TNTC]. Matthias is not mentioned again in the New Testament [BECNT, TH]. He might be one of the 70 disciples who Jesus sent out as messengers in Luke 10.1, and later became a missionary to the country of Ethiopia [BECNT, NAC, NICNT, TRT].

1:24 **And they prayed and said, "Lord, you who-know-(the)-hearts[a] of-all (men), show[b] (us) which one of these two you-have-chosen 1:25 to-take the place of-this ministry and apostleship from which Judas turned-aside[c] to-go to his-own place."**
LEXICON—a. καρδιογνώστης (LN 28.12) (BDAG p. 509): 'one who knows the hearts' [BDAG, LN], 'knower of hearts' BDAG], 'one who knows what people think' [LN]. The phrase 'you who know the hearts of all-(men)/everyone' [ESV, NASB, similarly BECNT, CBC, LN; NET, REB], is also translated 'you know everyone's heart' [NIV, NRSV, similarly AB, Bar; KJV], 'you know every heart' [NLT], 'you know the thoughts of

everyone' [NCV, TEV], 'you know everyone's thoughts' [GW], 'you know what everyone is like' [CEV]. This noun denotes one who knows what someone else thinks (literally 'to know what is in the heart') [LN].
b. aorist act. impera. of ἀναδείκνυμι (LN 28.54) (BDAG 1. p. 62): 'to show' [Bar, LN; all versions except REB], 'to show clearly' [BDAG], 'to point out' [BECNT], 'to declare' [CBC; REB], 'to let (us) know' [AB]. This verb means to make known that which has presumably been hidden or unknown [LN]. It means to make something known by clear indication [BDAG].
c. aorist act. indic. of παραβαίνω (LN 68.39) (BDAG 1. p. 758): 'to turn aside' [BDAG, BECNT, LN]. The phrase 'turned aside to go to his own place' [ESV, NASB, NET, NRSV] is also translated 'turned away and went where he belongs' [NCV], 'fell away to go to his own place' [Bar], 'left to go to his own place' [AB], 'abandoned to go where he belonged' [CBC; REB], 'abandoned his position to go to the place where he belongs' [GW], 'left to go to the place where he belongs' [TEV], 'left to go where he belongs [NIV], 'has deserted and gone where he belongs' [NLT], 'might go to his own place' [KJV], 'got what he deserved' [CEV]. This verb means to cease by removing oneself from some activity or position [LN]. It means to go aside [BDAG].

QUESTION—Why did they pray to the Lord and ask him which men he had chosen?

It is because apostleship is not a humanly ordained office [TNTC]. The Lord Jesus had chosen the original Twelve and so they now asked the Lord to choose this replacement for Judas; the choice was left to Jesus [AB, Bar, BECNT, EBC, NAC, NICNT, PNTC]. Jesus also prayed before he chose the original Twelve, so this demonstrated that they followed the example set by Jesus [NAC].

QUESTION—What is meant by 'Judas has gone to his own place'?

Saying that Judas has gone to his own place means that he ended up in a place different from the Eleven, a euphemism for eternal judgment among the lost [BECNT, NAC, NICNT, PNTC]. This is probably a nice way of saying that he has gone to hell for punishment [TRT], his destination would presumably be hell as a consequence of his act [Bar, EBC, TNTC].

1:26 And they-cast lots[a] for-them, and the lot fell to Matthias, and he-was-added[b] to the eleven apostles.

LEXICON—a. κλῆρος (LN 6.219) (BDAG 1. p. 548): 'lot' [AB, Bar, BDAG, BECNT, CBC, LN; all versions except CEV, GW]. The phrase 'they cast lots' is also translated 'they drew names' [CEV, GW], This noun denotes a specially marked pebble, piece of pottery, or stick employed in making decisions based upon chance [LN]. It denotes a specially marked object such as a pebble, a piece of pottery, or a stick that was used to decide something [BDAG].

b. aorist pass. indic. of συγκαταψηφίζομαι (LN 60.5) (BDAG p. 951): 'to be added' [BDAG; NASB, NIV, NRSV, TEV], 'to be counted' [BECNT, LN; NET], 'to be numbered' [AB; ESV, KJV], 'to be assigned' [CBC], 'to be elected' [REB], 'to be chosen and joined' [GW, CEV], 'to be voted in' [Bar], 'to be selected to become' [NLT], 'to become' [NCV]. This verb means to be counted as belonging to a particular group [LN]. It means to be chosen by a vote, or to be added to the eleven disciples [BDAG].

QUESTION—What method was used as a means for finding the Lord's choice of the twelfth apostle?

The apostles used the cast lots method to decide who would replace Judas. They believed that God guided the decision (Proverbs 16.33) [BECNT, EBC, NAC, NICNT, PNTC, TNTC, TRT]. This method of choice was frequently used in the Old Testament for both religious and social purposes [Bar]. The way Jews cast lots was to put names or marks on stones (or wood, animal bones), put the stones into a cup (or jar, vessel) and then shake the cup until one of the stones came out. The one whose name/mark was on the stone that came out was the one chosen. [BECNT, NAC, TRT]. After this instance, this practice is not reported again in the New Testament because after Pentecost, the Holy Spirit becomes their guide [NAC, PNTC, TNTC, TRT].

QUESTION—Was there any significance in restoring the number of apostles to twelve?

Matthias was added to the eleven apostles; the number of apostles was restored to twelve. It is significant to restore the number to twelve since then their number corresponds to the twelve tribes of Israel, and in a real sense they represent the restored Israel, the people of God. The continuity with Israel necessitates the restoration of the full number of twelve. Luke 22:28–30 tells us the apostles' unique role of judging the twelve tribes of Israel with God in His kingdom [NAC, TRT]. Note that James was not replaced after his martyrdom (Acts 12.2). It was necessary to replace Judas because he had abandoned his position. His betrayal, not his death, forfeited his place in the circle of Twelve. Even after death James continued to be considered an apostle [NAC].

DISCOURSE UNIT—2:1–47 [NICNT]. The topic is the day of Pentecost.

DISCOURSE UNIT—2:1–41 [BECNT, EBC]. The topic is Pentecost [BECNT], the coming of the Holy Spirit [EBC].

DISCOURSE UNIT—2:1–40 [PNTC]. The topic is the restoration of Israel begins.

DISCOURSE UNIT—2:1–13 [AB, Bar, BECNT, CBC, EBC, NAC, PNTC, TNTC; CEV, ESV, GW, NASB, NCV, NET, NIV, NLT, NRSV, TEV]. The topic is the event: the coming of the Spirit [BECNT], the Pentecost event [Bar], the Pentecostal miracle [AB], the miracle of Pentecost [EBC, NAC], the Holy

Spirit at Pentecost [CBC], the Holy Spirit comes at Pentecost [NIV], the Holy Spirit and the day of Pentecost [NET], the day of Pentecost [NASB], the Holy Spirit comes [NLT], the coming of the Holy Spirit [CEV, ESV, NCV, NRSV, TEV], the coming of the Spirit [BECNT, PNTC], the pouring out of the Spirit [TNTC], the believers are filled with the Holy Spirit [GW].

DISCOURSE UNIT—2:1–4 [NICNT]. The topic is the descent of the Spirit.

2:1 And when the day of-Pentecost had-come,[a] they-were all together[b] in one place.

LEXICON—a. pres. pass. infin. of συμπληρόω (LN 67.70) (BDAG 2. p. 959): 'to come' [Bar, BDAG; GW, NASB, NCV, NET, NIV, NRSV, REB, TEV], 'to arrive' [BECNT; ESV], 'to begin' [AB]. The phrase 'when the day of Pentecost had come' is also translated 'when the day of Pentecost was fully come' [KJV], 'on the day of Pentecost' [CEV, NLT], 'while the day of Pentecost was running its course' [CBC]. This verb refers to the culmination of a particular period of time, with emphasis on the completion of an implied purpose or plan [LN]. This verb means to arrive at the timely moment for an event to take place [BDAG].

    b. ὁμοῦ (LN 89.116) (BDAG 1. p. 709): 'together' [Bar, BDAG, BECNT, CBC, LN; CEV, ESV, GW, NASB, NCV, NET, NIV, NRSV, REB]. The phrase 'were all together in one place' is also translated 'were all with one accord in one place' [KJV], 'all...were meeting together in one place' [NLT], 'all...were gathered together in one place' [TEV], 'were all assembled in one place' [AB]. This adverb is a marker of association based on similarity of activity or state [LN]. It pertains to being together in the same place [BDAG].

QUESTION—What was the day of Pentecost?

In the Old Testament, Pentecost was known as the Festival of Weeks (Exodus 34:22a), or of the Firstfruits (Numbers 28:26) and the Feast of Harvest (Exodus 23:16a). Thousands of Jews would go to Jerusalem to celebrate this festival. Before 70 A.D., it was the day when the Jews celebrated the wheat harvest (Leviticus 23:15–21). After 70 A.D., it was the day they celebrated that God had given Moses the Laws to give to their ancestors [BECNT, CBC, EBC, NAC, NICNT, PNTC, TNTC, TRT]. The gift of Torah (the Laws) was a divine revelation in which the nature and will of God were made known on the basis of his gracious act of deliverance and with the result of a covenant between himself and his people [Bar]. Pentecost which means 'fiftieth' came fifty days after the Passover and Jesus' death [BECNT, CBC, PNTC, TRT]. The Christian Pentecost is the new revelation through the Holy Spirit that is based on the new act of redemption and deliverance and issuing in the formation of a new, or renewed, people of God, based upon a new covenant [Bar, PNTC]. The coming of the Spirit at Pentecost is not only a parallel to the Spirit's coming upon Jesus at his baptism; it is also both in continuity with and in contrast to the Law [EBC].

QUESTION—Who does 'they' refer to?
1. It refers to the 120 mentioned in Acts 1:15, which includes the apostles [AB, Bar, BECNT, NAC, NICNT, PNTC, TH, TNTC, TRT], and the believers [EBC].
2. It only refers to the 12 apostles, because they are the last ones mentioned in Acts 1:26 and they are the ones in focus in 2:7, 14, 37 [Bar, TH, TRT].

QUESTION—What does 'in one place' refer to?
The expression 'in one place' means 'at the same place' and the place refers to the house referred to in verse 2 [AB, BECNT, EBC, NAC, NICNT, PNTC, TH, TNTC].

2:2 **And suddenly there came from heaven (a)-sound[a] like (the)-rushing[b] of-(a)-violent[c] wind, and it-filled (the)-entire house where they-were sitting.**
LEXICON—a. ἦχος (LN 14.75) (BDAG 1. p. 441): 'sound' [AB, Bar, BDAG, BECNT, LN; ESV, GW, KJV, NET, NIV, NLT, NRSV], 'noise' [BDAG, CBC, LN; CEV, NASB, NCV, REB, TEV]. This noun can denote any type of sound other than human speech [LN]. It is an auditory impression of varying degrees of loudness [BDAG].
  b. pres. pass. participle of φέρομαι (LN 15.11) (BDAG 3.c. p. 1051): 'to rush' [AB, BDAG, BECNT; ESV, KJV, NASB, NRSV], 'to blow' [LN; GW, NCV, NET, NIV, TEV], 'to come, to move' [LN]. The phrase 'like the rushing of a violent wind' is also translated 'like the roaring of a mighty windstorm' [NLT], 'like a strong, driving wind' [REB], 'like the sound of a mighty wind' [CEV], 'of a powerful rushing wind' [Bar], 'of a strong driving wind' [CBC]. This verb means to move from one place to another, with the possible implication of causing the movement of some other object or objects. In this verse it is possible that it should be understood in the idiomatic sense of a 'blowing' wind. In any event, one must often translate it as 'blowing' since this is frequently the appropriate type of term to use in speaking of the movement of wind. [LN]. It means to cause to follow a certain course in direction or conduct and it is used to refer to the rushing of the wind itself [BDAG].
  c. βίαιος (LN 20.8) (BDAG b. p. 176), 'violent' [BDAG, LN; GW, NASB, NET, NIV, NRSV], 'strong' [BDAG, CBC; NCV, REB, TEV], 'mighty' [BECNT; CEV, ESV, KJV, NLT], 'forcible' [LN], 'powerful' [Bar], 'great' [AB]. This adjective pertains to the use of a violent or strong force [LN]. It pertains to being violent or strong in the use of force, and here it refers to the natural force of a wind [BDAG].

QUESTION—What does the word οἶκον 'house' refer to?
It refers to a house that may have been near the temple complex, possibly the house mentioned in Acts 1:13 [EBC, NAC, NICNT, PNTC, TRT]. It is not likely to be the temple but a public place since a crowd is quickly drawn to the event. That houses could hold a group of 120 or so has been shown by an unearthed mansion in the Jewish Quarter of Jerusalem, with its meeting hall of 11 by 6.5 meters [BECNT]. However there are some who think it might

refer to the temple complex where Jesus' followers spent much of their time [EBC, TRT].

QUESTION—What is the function of this verse?

This verse describes the audible manifestation of the coming of the Holy Spirit [AB, NAC, PNTC]. It is described as coming suddenly from heaven like the blowing of a violent wind. The word 'suddenly' gives a hint of a wondrous and awesome coming [Bar]. Wind phenomena often accompany an appearance by God in the Old Testament. In Greek the word πνοή 'wind' has the double connotation of 'wind' and 'Spirit', and that connection is to be seen here [BECNT, EBC, NAC, NICNT, PNTC, TNTC].

2:3 And there appeared to-them divided[a] tongues just-like fire and it-remained on each one of-them,

LEXICON—a. pres. mid./pass. participle of διαμερίζω (LN 63.23, 15.140) (BDAG 1 or 2. p. 233): 'to be divided [BDAG (1), LN (63.23)] 'to be disunited' [LN (63.23)], 'to be separated' [BDAG (1)], 'to be spread out, to be dispersed' [LN (15.140)]. Taken in the passive sense, the divided tongues appeared to them: 'divided tongues as of fire appeared to them' [ESV], 'tongues that looked like fire appeared to them' [GW], 'what looked like flames or tongues of fire appeared' [NLT], 'there appeared to them flames like tongues of fire' [REB], 'there appeared to them tongues, like tongues of flame' [AB], 'there appeared to them tongues as of fire' [NASB], 'there appeared to them tongues like flames of fire' [CBC], 'there appeared to them tongues as if of fire' [Bar], 'there appeared unto them cloven tongues like as of fire' [KJV], 'divided tongues as of fire appeared to them' [ESV], 'divided tongues, as of fire, appeared among them' [NRSV], 'they saw something like flames of fire' [NCV], 'they saw what seemed to be tongues of fire' [NIV], 'they saw what looked like fiery tongues moving in all directions' [CEV], 'they saw what looked like tongues of fire' [TEV]. Taken in the middle sense, the tongues were being divided among them: 'there appeared to them tongues like fire being distributed to them' [BECNT], 'tongues spreading out like a fire appeared to them' [NET], 'there appeared to them tongues as if of fire, dividing up among them' [Bar]. In the passive sense this verb means to be divided into separate parts [LN 63.23)], and in the middle sense it means to disperse, on the basis of having been divided up [LN (15.140)]. It probably means to be divided into separate parts and in this verse it refers to the imagery of the jagged effect produced by a flame [BDAG (1)], but some think it means to distribute objects to a series of people and in this verse it would then refer to tongues of fire being distributed among the people [BDAG (2)].

QUESTION—What is the function of this verse?

This verse describes the visible manifestation of the coming of the Holy Spirit [AB, NAC, PNTC]. Throughout the Old Testament, fire phenomena are used to depict the presence of God (Exodus 3:2; 19:18; 1 Kings 18:38–39;

Ezek. 1:27) [BECNT, EBC, NAC, NICNT, PNTC, TNTC, TRT]. The fire is described as being divided, which gives a picture of one great flame separating into many tongues of flame so that a flame rested on each individual. Here Luke was dealing with something beyond ordinary human experience and it could only be expressed in an earthly analogy [NAC]. What appeared to them were not actual tongues of fire, but what looked like tongues of fire. The tongues were not cloven tongues or divided tongues, rather they were many tongue-like objects looking like fire that darted out separately to touch or rest on someone, with the result being that there was one on each person [TH]. These tongues would allow the disciples to speak about God's activity in the foreign languages of their audience [BECNT].

2:4 and they-were- all -filled[a] with-(the)-Holy Spirit, and they-began to-speak in-other languages[b] as the Spirit gave- them -(the ability) to-speak.[c]

LEXICON—a. aorist pass. indic. of πίμπλημι (LN 59.38) (BDAG 1.a.β. p. 813): 'to be filled' [AB, Bar, BDAG, BECNT, CBC; all versions except CEV], 'to be filled completely, to be filled up' [LN]. The phrase 'they were all filled with the Holy Spirit' is also translated 'the Holy Spirit took control of everyone' [CEV]. This verb means to cause something to be completely full [LN]. It means to cause to be completely full, and in the case of a person it refers to the inner life [BDAG].

b. γλῶσσα (LN 33.2) (BDAG 2.a. p. 201): 'language' [AB, Bar, BDAG, LN; CEV, GW, NCV, NET, NLT, NRSV], 'tongue' [BDAG, BECNT, CBC; ESV, KJV, NASB, NIV, REB, TEV], 'dialect, speech' [LN]. This noun refers to a language, perhaps implying a distinctive form. The miracle described in Acts 2:4 may have been a miracle of speaking or a miracle of hearing, but at any rate people understood fully, and therefore it seems appropriate in this context to speak of 'languages' [LN]. It refers to a body of words and systems that makes up a distinctive language [BDAG]. In this verse the 'tongues' are best understood as 'languages' [EBC]. They spoke in languages different from the one they normally spoke, the languages of other peoples, of foreigners [TH]. It denotes a body of words and systems that make up a distinctive language [BDAG].

c. pres. mid./pass. (deponent = act.) infin. of ἀποφθέγγομαι (LN 33.76) (BDAG p. 125): 'to speak' [LN], 'to speak out, to declare to someone with urgency' [BDAG]. The phrase καθὼς τὸ πνεῦμα ἐδίδου ἀποφθέγγεσθαι αὐτοῖς 'as the Spirit gave them the ability to speak' [GW] is also translated 'as the Holy Spirit gave them this ability' [NLT], 'as the Spirit gave them ability' [AB; NRSV], 'as the Spirit enabled them' [NET, NIV], 'as the Spirit enabled them to speak' [TEV], 'the Spirit let them speak' [CEV], 'as the Spirit gave them utterance' [ESV, KJV], 'as the Spirit gave utterance to them' [BECNT], 'as the Spirit was giving them utterance' [NASB], 'as the Spirit gave them power of utterance' [CBC; REB], 'as the Spirit granted them to give utterance' [Bar], 'by the power the Holy Spirit was giving them' [NCV]. This verb means to speak with the focus upon verbal sound rather than upon content [LN]. It means to express oneself orally [BDAG].

QUESTION—What is meant by the phrase 'filled with the Holy Spirit'?

It means to be guided or empowered by the Holy Spirit [TRT]. The Holy Spirit was the object which filled them, not the agent of the filling. He possessed them completely, he came into them entirely [TH]. This was the fulfillment of the spiritual baptism foretold by John and promised afresh by the Lord [Bar, CBC, NICNT, PNTC]. The gift of the Holy Spirit at Pentecost was permanent and eschatological [PNTC]. This experience was an event which took place once for all [NICNT].

QUESTION—What is the function of this verse?

Here the presence of the Holy Spirit was manifested by the effects wrought upon the disciples who were inspired to speak in languages of which they had no command in normal circumstances [BECNT, EBC NAC, NICNT, PNTC, TNTC]. The verse describes the manifestation of the Holy Spirit himself in his coming on those gathered in the upper room. From this point on in Acts, the gift of the Spirit became a normative concomitant of becoming a Christian believer (2:38) [NAC]. The work of the Spirit also involves more than mission. It includes salvation (2:38–39) and transformed lives (2:42–47) [BECNT].

DISCOURSE UNIT—2:5–13 [NICNT]. The topic is the crowd's amazement.

2:5 Now there-were Jews dwelling in Jerusalem, devout[a] men from every nation[b] under heaven.

LEXICON—a. εὐλαβής (LN 53.8) (BDAG p. 407): 'devout' [AB, BDAG, CBC; ESV, GW, KJV, NASB, NLT, NRSV, REB], 'religious' [CEV, NCV, NET, TEV], 'God-fearing' [NIV], 'reverent' [LN], 'pious' [Bar, BECNT, LN]. This adjective pertains to being reverent toward God [LN]. It refers to the religious attitude of being devout or God-fearing [BDAG].

b. ἔθνος (LN 11.55): 'nation' [AB, Bar, BECNT, CBC, LN; ESV, GW, KJV, NASB, NET, NIV, NLT, NRSV, REB], 'country' [CEV, NCV, TEV], 'people' [LN]. This noun denotes the largest unit into which the people of the world are divided on the basis of their constituting a sociopolitical community [LN].

QUESTION—Who were these 'devout men' who were dwelling in Jerusalem?

These devout men were Jews who faithfully and regularly worshipped and obeyed God. They were not believers in Christ at that time [TRT]. 'Pious' here need not equal "saved," since these people will later be told that they must repent to be delivered [BECNT]. They were all currently living in Jerusalem, but many were visitors who had come to celebrate Pentecost [TRT]; Jews from all over gathered in Jerusalem for the feast or for permanent residence [Bar, EBC, NICNT, PNTC, TNTC]. The phrase 'from every nation under heaven' tells us that the Jews present for Pentecost have come from every direction of the globe, as verses 9–11 will specify [BECNT].

2:6 And (when) this sound[a] occurred, the crowd came-together,[b] and they-were-bewildered[c] because each one was-hearing them speak in-his-own language.

LEXICON—a. φωνή (LN 14.74) (BDAG 1. p. 1071): 'sound' [AB, Bar, BDAG, BECNT, CBC, LN; ESV, NASB, NET, NIV, NRSV, REB, TEV], 'noise' [BDAG; CEV, NCV], 'loud noise' [NLT]. The phrase 'when this sound occurred' is also translated 'when they heard the wind' [GW], 'when this was noised abroad' [KJV]. This noun denotes any type of sound, including human speech, but normally a distinctive type of sound as opposed to confused noise [LN]. It as an auditory effect [BDAG].
   b. aorist act. indic. of συνέρχομαι (LN 15.123) (BDAG 1. p. 969): 'to come together' [LN; ESV, KJV, NASB, NCV, NIV], 'to gather' [BDAG, CBC; CEV, GW, NET, NRSV, REB, TEV], 'to gather together' [BECNT, LN], 'to assemble' [Bar, BDAG, LN], 'to come flocking' [AB]. The phrase 'the crowd came together' is also translated 'everyone came running' [NLT]. This verb refers to the movement of two or more objects to the same location [LN]. It means to come together with others as a group [BDAG].
   c. aorist pass. indic. of συγχέω (LN 25.221) (BDAG p. 953): 'to be bewildered' [CBC; ESV, NASB, NIV, NLT, NRSV, REB], 'to be surprised' [BDAG; CEV, NCV], 'be amazed' [BDAG], 'to be confounded' [Bar, LN; KJV], 'to be perplexed' [BECNT], 'to be excited [BDAG; TEV], 'to be startled' [GW], 'to be troubled, to be stirred up' [BDAG], 'to be struck with awe' [AB], 'to be in confusion' [BDAG; NET], 'to experience consternation' [LN]. This noun means to cause such astonishment as to bewilder and dismay [LN]. It means to cause dismay [BDAG].

QUESTION—What kind of sound was this?
   1. It was the sound like wind mentioned in v. 2 [Bar, EBC, NAC, TH, TRT].
   2. It was the sound of the apostles speaking in the foreign languages referred to in vv. 4 and 8 [Bar, PNTC, TH, TRT]. The sound, probably a reference to the tongues which in light of the next few verses draw a crowd to an unspecified location [BECNT, NAC, NICNT, TNTC].
   3 It could be referring to both [TRT].

QUESTION—What is meant by 'his own language'?
   Speaking 'in his own language' refers to the languages of the people in the crowd that gathered, not the languages of Jesus' followers. It may be clearer to say, 'heard his own language being spoken by the apostles' [EBC, NAC, NICNT, PNTC, TH, TRT]. The crowd heard the message 'in their own language' as the disciples spoke to them in tongues. They were bewildered that supposedly uneducated Galileans were exhibiting this surprising array of linguistic expertise [BECNT].

2:7 And they-were-amazed[a] and astonished,[b] saying, "Look! Are not all these (who) are speaking Galileans?
LEXICON—a. imperf. mid. indic. of ἐξίστημι (LN 25.220) (BDAG 2.b. p. 350): 'to be amazed' [BDAG, CBC; ESV, KJV, NASB, NCV, NIV, NLT, NRSV, REB], 'to be astonished' [BDAG, BECNT], 'to be astounded' [Bar], 'to be astonished greatly, to be greatly astounded, to be astounded completely' [LN], 'to be excited' [CEV], 'to be stunned' [GW], 'to be in amazement' [TEV], not explicit [AB]. The phrase 'they were amazed and astonished' is also translated 'completely baffled' [NET]. This verb means to cause someone to be so astounded as to be practically overwhelmed [LN]. It means to be out of one's normal state of mind [BDAG].
  2. imperf. act. indic. of θαυμάζω (LN 25.213) (BDAG 1.a.α. p. 444): 'to be astonished' [BDAG; ESV, NASB, NRSV], 'to marvel' [Bar, BDAG, LN; KJV], 'to be amazed' [BDAG, LN; CEV, GW], 'to be in astonishment' [CBC; REB], 'to wonder' [BECNT], 'to be in wonder' [BDAG, LN; TEV], not explicit [NCV, NIV, NLT]. The phrase 'they were...astonished' is also translated 'They were filled with astonishment' [AB]. The phrase 'they were amazed and astonished' is also translated 'completely baffled' [NET]. This verb means to wonder or marvel at some event or object [LN]. It means to be extraordinarily impressed or disturbed by something [BDAG].
QUESTION—What did the people of Jerusalem think of the people of Galilee?
  Jews from Jerusalem considered the people from Galilee Province to be culturally backward and uneducated [BECNT, TRT]. Galileans had difficulty pronouncing the Hebrew gutturals and they were in the habit of swallowing syllables when they spoke, so they were looked down upon by the residents of Jerusalem [EBC]. The expression 'Are not all...'? suggests that a contrast with pious men in v. 5 is intended, but here Luke is interested in language, not piety, possibly in the degree of education that might be expected of Galileans [Bar]; the expected answer to the question is 'Yes' [TH].
QUESTION—Why are two synonyms ἐξίσταντο 'amazed' and ἐθαύμαζον 'astonished' used here?
  1. The synonyms are used to increase the prominence/importance of what is being said [TH, TRT]: 'utterly amazed' [NAC]. Reinforcing the reference to perplexity in v. 6, the combination stresses how surprised they are at what is taking place and that they are unable to explain it [BECNT]. God did something that defied rational explanation [PNTC].
  2. The words are related but have a different focus: 'amazed' is the initial reaction, whereas 'astonished' is the reaction that continues after the initial surprise and often includes a verbal response [TRT].

2:8 **And how-is-it-that we-each-hear (them) in-our-own language in which we-were-born[a]?**

LEXICON—a. aorist pass. indic. of γεννάω (LN 23.52) (BDAG 2. p. 194): 'to be born' [BDAG, LN]. The phrase 'in our own language in which we were born' [NASB] is also translated 'in our own tongue, wherein we were born' [KJV], 'in our own native language' [BECNT; NET, NRSV], 'in his own native language' [CBC; ESV, NIV, REB], 'in our own native languages' [Bar; NLT, TEV], 'in our native dialects' [GW], 'in our very own languages' [CEV], 'in our own languages' [NCV], 'his own language which he has heard from early childhood' [AB]. This verb means to give birth to a child [BDAGLN].

QUESTION—What is the function of this verse?

This prepares for verses 9–11 which list the various areas of the diaspora represented [NAC]. This verse basically repeats v. 6b with the added note that it was in their 'native' tongue, the language into which they were born [NAC]. God is using for each group the most familiar linguistic means possible to make sure the message reaches the audience in a form they can appreciate. Thus the miracle underscores the divine initiative in making possible the mission God has commissioned. In a real sense, God is bringing the message of the gospel home to those who hear it [BECNT]. The Jews could not by themselves have learned so many different languages [EBC, PNTC].

2:9 **Parthians and Medes and Elamites, and the-ones living-in Mesopotamia, together-with Judea and Cappadocia, Pontus and Asia, 2:10 Phrygia and Pamphylia, Egypt and the parts of-Libya near Cyrene, and the visiting Romans, 2:11 both Jews and proselytes,[a] Cretans and Arabs—we hear them in-our-(own) languages[b] speaking about the mighty-acts[c] of God."**

LEXICON—a. προσήλυτος (LN 11.54) (BDAG p. 880): 'proselyte' [AB, Bar, BECNT, CBC, LN; ESV, KJV, NASB, NET, NRSV, REB], 'convert' [BDAG, LN; GW], 'one who has chosen to be a Jew' [CEV], 'one who had become a Jew' [NCV], 'convert to Judaism' [NIV, NLT], 'Gentile converted to Judaism' [TEV]. This noun denotes a person who has converted to Judaism [LN]. It denotes one who has come over from polytheism to Judean religion and practice [BDAG].

b. γλῶσσα (LN 33.2) (BDAG 2.a. p. 201): 'language' [AB, BDAG, LN; CEV, GW, NCV, NET, NLT, NRSV, TEV], 'tongue' [Bar, BDAG, BECNT, CBC; ESV, KJV, NASB, NIV, REB], 'dialect, speech' [LN]. This noun denotes a language, with the possible implication of its distinctive form. The miracle described in Acts 2:4 may have been a miracle of speaking or a miracle of hearing, but at any rate people understood fully, and therefore it seems appropriate in this context to speak of 'languages' [LN]. It denotes a body of words and systems that makes up a distinctive language [BDAG].

c. μεγαλεῖος (LN 76.8) (BDAG p. 622): 'mighty act' [LN], 'great deed' [Bar, LN; NET], 'mighty deed' [BDAG, BECNT; NASB], 'great thing' [CBC, LN; NCV, REB, TEV], 'wonderful thing/work' [CEV, KJV, NLT], 'great/mighty work' [AB; ESV], 'wonder' [NIV], 'miracle' [GW], 'deed of power' [NRSV]. The substantive form of this adjective denotes a deed of importance or power [LN].

QUESTION—Where were the people and places mentioned in verses 9–11?

After the Babylonian captivity of 605–538 B.C., not all of the Jews returned to Palestine. Many stayed in some of the places mentioned here or were later deported to other places by other rulers. They learned the languages of the people they were living among [TRT]. The list in verses 9–11 mixes peoples (Parthians, Medes, Elamites, Romans, Cretans, and Arabians) with lands (Mesopotamia, Judea, Cappadocia, Pontus, Asia, Phrygia, Pamphylia, Egypt, and Libya) [BECNT]. The list of places from which the Jews had come is probably intended to indicate every country in the world (v. 5) [EBC, NAC, PNTC, TNTC, TH]. The list moves from east to west and also from northwest to southwest [BECNT, EBC]. They can be grouped into 6 groups: (1) Parthians, Medes, Elamites and those who dwell in Mesopotamia, (2) Judea and Cappadocia, (3) Pontus and Asia, (4) Phrygia and Pamphylia, (5) Egypt and parts of Libya belonging to Cyrene, (6) visitors from Rome, both Jews and proselytes, Cretans and Arabians. The first group lists the communities located to the east in Mesopotamia and beyond. Parthia is the farthest east. Mesopotamia covers the Tigris and Euphrates Valley and is where the Parthian and Roman empires met. The second group covers larger Judea and Cappadocia to the north. The third group is farther north, to Pontus on the edge of modern Asia Minor (Turkey) and beyond to Asia, which here is probably western Asia Minor. The fourth group moves west to Cappadocia to the central and southern edge of Asia Minor, to Phrygia and Pamphylia. The third and fourth groups cover what is today modern Turkey. The fifth group goes further west and south across the Great Sea (Mediterranean) to Egypt. Next to Libya as far west as Cyrene. The last group comes back north to Rome, mentioning that both Jews and Gentile proselytes have come to Jerusalem from there and referring to Crete and the Arabians, probably meaning Nabataea, making almost a full circle as the list is completed. Rome is in the last grouping and is important, for it is where Acts will end [BECNT].

QUESTION—Who were the 'visiting Romans'?

It refers to people from the city of Rome who are visiting Jerusalem; they may or may not be Roman citizens [BECNT, EBC, NICNT, TH, TRT]. A few think it refers to Roman citizens who are not necessarily from the city of Rome and have moved to live in Jerusalem [Bar, TRT].

QUESTION—What does the comment 'both Jews and proselytes' refer to?

1. It refers back only to the visiting Romans [BECNT, EBC, NAC, NICNT, PNTC. TH]. If this refers back to only the visiting Romans, this phrase could be put within parentheses or dashes [TRT].

2. It refers to the entire list of people in verses 9–10 who are staying in Jerusalem [AB, Bar, TNTC].

QUESTION—Who were the proselytes?

They were Gentiles who had changed their religion to Judaism. In order for a person to convert to the Jews' religion, he/she had to receive a purifying baptism in front of some witnesses, offer a sacrifice at the temple, and if the person was a man, be circumcised [BECNT, NICNT, TH, TRT].

QUESTION—What is the function of these verses 9–11?

These verses praise God's mighty acts through the descent of the Holy Spirit on the Day of Pentecost. The national list of Jews is a hint of where the gospel message is going—from Jerusalem out into the entire world [BECNT].

2:12 And (they) all were-amazed[a] and perplexed,[b] saying to one another, "What can this mean?"

LEXICON—a. imperf. mid. indic. of ἐξίστημι (LN 25.220) (BDAG 2.b. p. 350): 'to be amazed' [BDAG, CBC; ESV, KJV, NCV, NIV, NLT, NRSV, REB, TEV], 'to be excited' [CEV], 'to be stunned' [GW], 'to be astounded' [Bar; NET], 'to be astonished' [AB, BDAG, BECNT], 'to be astonished greatly, to be greatly astounded, to be astounded completely' [LN]. The phrase 'they all were amazed' is also translated 'they all continued in amazement' [NASB]. This verb means to cause someone to be so astounded as to be practically overwhelmed [LN]. It is a feeling of astonishment mingled with fear that is caused by events which are miraculous, extraordinary, or difficult to understand [BDAG].

b. imperf. act. indic. of διαπορέω (LN 32.10) (BDAG p. 235): 'to be perplexed' [Bar, BECNT, CBC; ESV, NIV, NLT, NRSV, REB], 'to be very perplexed' [LN], 'to be greatly perplexed' [BDAG], 'to be in great perplexity' [NASB], 'to be confused' [CEV, NCV, TEV], 'to be very confused' [LN], 'to be greatly confused' [NET], 'to be puzzled' [KJV], 'to be bewildered' [AB], 'to be in doubt' [KJV], 'to not know what to do' [LN], 'to be at a loss' [BDAG]. This verb means to be thoroughly perplexed [LN].

QUESTION—What is the function of this verse?

This verse picks up the theme introduced at the beginning of verse 7, that while the people did understand what the apostles were saying [TH], they did not understand the reason for what was happening [Bar, TH, TRT]. It reinforces verses 7–8 and shows the people's inability to discern what was taking place, thus setting up Peter's speech [BECNT, EBC, PNTC, TNTC].

2:13 But others mocking,[a] said, "They-have-been filled-with-sweet-wine.[b]"

LEXICON—a. pres. act. participle of διαχλευάζω (LN 33.408) (BDAG p. 240): 'to mock' [Bar, BECNT; ESV, KJV, NASB], 'to make fun of' [CEV, NCV, NIV, TEV], 'to joke' [GW], 'to jeer at' [BDAG, LN; NET], 'to ridicule' [NLT], 'to sneer' [NRSV], 'to taunt' [AB], 'to show contempt' [CBC; REB]. This verb means to make fun of someone by joking or jesting [LN]. It means to laugh at someone in scorn [BDAG].

b. γλεῦκος (LN 6.199) (BDAG p. 201): 'sweet wine' [AB, Bar, BECNT, LN; GW, NASB], 'new wine' [LN; ESV, KJV, NET, NRSV], 'sweet new wine' [BDAG]. The phrase 'they have been filled with sweet wine' is also translated 'they are drunk' [CEV], 'these people are drunk' [TEV], 'they have had too much wine' [NCV, NIV], 'they're just drunk, that's all' [NLT], 'they have been drinking' [CBC; REB]. This noun denotes a new, sweet wine in the process of fermentation [LN].

QUESTION—What did they mean by saying that the apostles have been filled with sweet wine?

The focus is not on what type of wine they had drunk [TRT]. Although the 'sweet wine' was only a partially fermented wine, their intent was to insist that the apostles were drunk [Bar, TH]. These mockers thought that what they were hearing in unrecognized languages was just drunken gibberish [BECNT, TNTC]. Being spiritually insensitive, they attributed it to drunkenness [EBC, NAC, NICNT, PNTC].

DISCOURSE UNIT—2:14–42 [TNTC; CEV, NCV, TEV]. The topic is Peter preaches the gospel [TNTC], Peter speaks to the people [NCV], Peter speaks to the crowd [CEV], Peter talks to the crowd [GW].

DISCOURSE UNIT—2:14–41 [EBC, NAC; ESV, GW, NIV, NLT]. The topic is Peter's sermon at Pentecost [EBC, NAC; ESV], Peter's message [TEV], Peter addresses the crowd [NIV], Peter preaches to the crowd [NLT].

DISCOURSE UNIT—2:14–40 [Bar, PNTC]. The topic is Peter's Pentecost Sermon [Bar], Peter's interpretation of the event [PNTC].

DISCOURSE UNIT—2:14–36 [AB, BECNT, CBC, NICNT; NASB, NET, NRSV]. The topic is Peter's Pentecostal address [AB], Peter's address on the day of Pentecost [NET], Peter's proclamation [NICNT], Peter's sermon [NASB], Peter addresses the crowd [NRSV], Peter speaks to the crowd [CBC], the explanation: the Spirit's coming shows Jesus is Lord-Messiah [BECNT].

2:14 **But Peter, standing with the eleven, raised**[a] **his voice and declared to-them, "Men**[b] **of Judea, and all who dwell in-Jerusalem, let-this-be known to-you and give-ear**[c] **to my words.**[d] **2:15** **For these-men are- not -drunk, as you suppose, for it-is (only) (the)-third hour of-the day.**

LEXICON—a. aorist act. indic. of ἐπαίρω (LN 33.78) (BDAG 2. p. 357): 'to raise [AB, CBC, LN (15.105); NET, NIV, NRSV], 'to lift up' [Bar, BECNT; ESV, KJV]. The phrase 'raised his voice and declared' is also translated 'in a loud voice began to speak' [TEV], 'in a loud voice he said/spoke' [GW, NCV], 'in a loud voice addressed' [NCV, REB]. 'spoke in a loud clear voice' [CEV], 'shouted' [NLT]. The idiom 'to raise the voice' means to increase the volume with which one speaks, so as to

overcome existing noise or the speech of someone else [LN]. It means to cause to move upward and here it means 'to raise' one's voice [BDAG].
b. ἀνήρ (LN 9.24, 9.1): 'man' [LN (9:24)], 'human being' [LN (9.1)]. Peter addressed the people as Ἄνδρες Ἰουδαῖοι 'Men of Judea' [BECNT; ESV, GW, NASB, NRSV], 'You men of Judea' [NET], 'Ye men of Judea' [KJV], 'Fellow Jews' [Bar, CBC; NIV, NLT, NRSV, REB, TEV], 'My fellow Jews' [NCV], 'Jews' [AB], 'Friends' [CEV]. The noun ἀνήρ 'man' denotes an adult male person of marriageable age in both the singular and plural forms [LN (9.24)], or the noun denotes a human being. Then in the singular form it means 'person, human being, individual' and in the plural form it means 'people, persons, mankind' [LN (9.1)].
c. aorist mid. (deponent = act.) impera. of ἐνωτίζομαι (LN 24.62) (BDAG p. 343): 'to give ear' [Bar, BDAG; ESV], 'to let one's ears hear' [BECNT], 'to listen carefully to' [LN; CEV, NET, NIV, NLT], 'to listen to' [NRSV, TEV], 'to mark someone's words' [LN], 'to pay attention to' [BDAG, LN; GW, NCV], 'to hearken to' [KJV], 'to give heed to' [NASB]. The phrase 'let this be known to you and give ear' is also translated 'listen and take note' [REB], 'mark this' [CBC], 'understand this' [AB]. This verb means to listen carefully to (someone) and pay attention [LN]. It means to listen carefully to what is said [BDAG].
d. ῥῆμα (LN 33.98) (BDAG 1. p. 905): 'word' [Bar, BDAG, BECNT, LN; ESV, KJV, NASB], 'saying' [BDAG, LN], 'statement' [BDAG, LN], not explicit [NLT, TEV]. The phrase 'my words' is also translated 'what I have to say' [CEV, GW, NCV], 'what I say' [NET, NIV, NRSV, REB]. The phrase 'give ears to my words' is also translated 'give me a hearing' [CBC], 'give me your attention' [AB], 'pay attention to what I am proclaiming' [BDAG]. This noun denotes that which is stated or said, with the primary focus being upon the content of the communication [LN]. It denotes that which is said [BDAG].

QUESTION—Who were 'the eleven'?
The apostle Peter was the one who stood up and gave a speech [TH] The eleven present with him were the rest of the twelve apostles. Matthias had replaced Judas by this time [NAC, NICNT, TRT].

QUESTION—Who were the 'men of Judea and all those who lived in Jerusalem'?
Some think 'men of Judea' means the Jews from the Judea Province [TRT]. Many others think it means 'fellow Jews', both men and women [BECNT, EBC, NAC, PNTC, TRT]. 'All those inhabiting Jerusalem' refers to both Jews and non-Jews who lived in Jerusalem [Bar, BECNT, EBC, NAC, PNTC].

QUESTION—What does 'give ear to my words' mean?
'Give ear to my words' means 'pay close attention/listen carefully to what I am going to say' [BECNT, NAC, PNTC]. Peter wished to correct a misunderstanding, so he started his speech with two imperatives: 'let this be known to you' and 'give ear to my words' [BECNT].

QUESTION—What is important about it being 'the third hour of the day'?

The third hour of the day is nine o'clock in the morning [Bar, BECNT, CBC, EBC, NAC, PNTC, TNTC, TH]. This hour was the hour of prayer for the Jews. They normally ate their first meal of a day at ten o'clock in the morning after the hour of Morning Prayer [NAC, TH]. Thus, Peter wanted to make the point here that the apostles had not yet eaten, they could not possibly be drunk [BECNT, CBC, NAC, TH]; it was too early in the day for men to be drunk [Bar, EBC, NICNT, PNTC, TNTC].

2:16 But this is what was-spoken through the prophet Joel, **2:17** 'And it-will-be in the last[a] days,' says God, '(that) I-will-pour-out[b] my Spirit on all people,[c] and your sons and your daughters will-prophesy,[d] and your young-men will-see visions, and your old-men will-dream dreams.

LEXICON—a. ἔσχατος (LN 61.13) (BDAG 2.b. p. 397): 'last' [AB, Bar, BDAG, BECNT, CBC, LN; all versions], 'final' [LN]. This adjective refers to the last in a series of events or objects [LN]. It refers to the last days before the second coming of Christ [BDAG].
   b. fut. act. indic. of ἐκχέω (LN 47.4) (BDAG 2. p. 312): 'to pour out' [AB, Bar, BDAG, BECNT, CBC, LN; all versions except GW, CEV, NASB], 'to pour' [GW], 'to pour forth' [NASB], 'to give' [CEV]. This verb means to cause something to pour out [LN]. It means to cause to fully experience something, and is a figurative extension of 'pour out' in which according to Joel's prophecy the Holy Spirit is poured down on people like rain from heaven [BDAG].
   c. σάρξ (LN 9.11) (BDAG 3.a. p. 915): 'person' [BDAG. LN; NET, NIV, NLT], 'everyone' [BDAG, CBC; CEV, GW, TEV], 'mankind' [NASB, REB], 'flesh' [AB, Bar, BECNT; ESV, KJV, NRSV], 'human being' [BDAG, LN], 'a man of flesh and blood' [BDAG]. The phrase 'all people' is also translated 'all kinds of people' [NCV]. This is a figurative usage of 'flesh' that refers to humans as physical beings [LN]. It denotes one who is a physical being [BDAG].
   d. fut. act. indic. of προφητεύω (LN 33.459) (BDAG 1. p. 890): 'to prophesy' [AB, Bar, BDAG, BECNT, CBC, LN; all versions except GW, TEV], 'to make inspired utterances' [LN], 'to speak what God has revealed' [GW], 'to proclaim my message' [TEV]. This verb refers to the act of speaking by divine inspiration, with or without reference to future events [LN]. It means to proclaim an inspired revelation [BDAG]. In the Biblical setting 'to prophesy' primarily means to 'proclaim God's message to people' [TH].

QUESTION—What was it that the prophets had spoken about?

The pronoun 'this' in v. 16 refers to the speaking in tongues event. The apostles spoke about the mighty acts of God in languages which were not their first or second language [NAC, TH, TRT].

ACTS 2:16–17

QUESTION—From where did Peter quote the sayings of the prophet Joel?
Peter's speech in verses 17–21 is a quotation from the Old Testament book, Joel 2:28–32 [AB, BECNT, CBC, EBC, NAC, NICNT, PNTC, TH, TNTC]. The quotation is largely from the Greek Septuagint version of the Old Testament [BECNT, CBC, NAC, TNTC]. Peter pointed out that the ecstasy was not the result of drunkenness. It was the outpouring of God's spirit on all people as prophesied by the prophet Joel [CBC, NAC, PNTC].

QUESTION—What does 'in the last days' refer to?
'In the last days' is a typical Jewish expression used to describe the time of the Messianic age in which God would fully accomplish those promises that he had made to his people [TH]. It refers to the period that began when Jesus Christ came into the world, and especially from the time of his resurrection onward. It will end when he returns to earth [NAC, NICNT, TH, TRT]. The coming of the Spirit upon all people is the fulfillment of Joel's prophesy [BECNT, EBC, PNTC, TNTC].

QUESTION—What is a prophet?
A prophet is someone who speaks for God. In this case here, Joel spoke for God and said what God wanted him to say [TRT]. The focus is on his function as a revealer of God's will and word, rather than his role as a foreteller of the future [TH].

QUESTION—What are visions?
Visions are usually spiritual experiences that people have while they are awake, possibly in a trance [PNTC, TRT]. People have dreams when they are asleep. Some languages do not distinguish between 'visions' and 'dreams' [TRT]. In this context, both visions and dreams are spoken of as vehicles for the communication of divine truth from God [TH].

2:18 And even on my male-slaves[a] and on my female-slaves[b] in those days I-will-pour-out[c] of my Spirit, and they-will-prophesy.[d]

LEXICON—a. δοῦλος (LN 87.76) (BDAG 1.a., 2.b.β. p. 260): 'male slave' [NCV], 'male servant' [ESV], 'man slave' [AB, Bar], 'slave' [BDAG, CBC, LN; NRSV], 'bondservant' [LN; NASB], 'servant' [BECNT; CEV, GW, KJV, NET, NIV, NLT, REB, TEV]. This noun denotes a man who is considered the property of another [LN]. It especially refers to the relationship of humans to God. They are recipients of gifts from God's Spirit. It can refer to Christian prophets and in this verse it refers to the apostles [BDAG].

b. δούλη (LN 87.83) (BDAG p. 259): 'female slave' [BDAG; NCV], 'female servant' [ESV], 'woman slave' [AB, Bar], 'maidservant' [BECNT], 'handmaiden' [KJV], 'handmaid' [REB], 'slave woman' [LN], 'slave girl' [LN], 'bondwoman' [BDAG]. The phrase 'on my male slaves and on my female slaves' is also translated 'on my servants, both men and women' [CEV, NET, NIV, TEV], 'on my servants, on both men and women' [GW], 'on my bond slaves, both men and women' [NASB], 'upon my slaves, both men and women' [NRSV], 'on my servants—men

and women alike' [NLT] 'endure even my slaves, both men and women' [CBC]. This noun denotes a female slave [LN]. It denotes a female slave, a bondwoman claimed by God [BDAG].
- c. fut. act. indic. of ἐκχέω (LN 47.4) (BDAG 2. p. 312): 'to pour out' [AB, Bar, BDAG, BECNT, CBC, LN; all versions except GW, CEV, NASB], 'to pour' [GW], 'to pour forth' [NASB], 'to give' [CEV]. This verb means to cause to pour out [LN]. It means to fully experience something, and is a figurative extension of 'pour out' in which according to Joel's prophecy the Holy Spirit is poured down on people like rain from heaven [BDAG].
- d. fut. act. indic. of προφητεύω (LN 33.459) (BDAG 1. p. 890): 'to prophesy' [AB, Bar, BDAG, BECNT, CBC, LN; all versions except GW, TEV], 'to make inspired utterances' [LN], 'to speak what God has revealed' [GW], 'to proclaim my (i.e., God's) message' [TEV]. This verb means to speak under the influence of divine inspiration, with or without reference to future events [LN]. It means to proclaim an inspired revelation [BDAG].

QUESTION—Who does 'my male slaves and female slaves' refer to?
1. Some think that 'my male slaves and female slaves' refers literally to slaves or servants who are God's people, a different group of people from those mentioned in v. 17 [BECNT, TRT]. Even the lowest of classes will be blessed [BECNT].
2, Others think it is a further definition to the same people mentioned in v. 17 and it emphasizes the fact that God owns his people, [NAC, PNTC, TRT].

QUESTION—What does 'in those days' refer to?
It refers to 'in the last days' of the preceding verse [PNTC, TH, TNTC].

2:19 And I-will-show[a] wonders[b] in the sky above and signs[c] on the earth below, blood and fire, and vapor[d] of-smoke.

LEXICON—a. fut. act. indic. of δίδωμι (LN 13.128) (BDAG 4. p. 242): 'to show' [CBC; ESV, KJV, NCV, NIV, NRSV, REB], 'to perform' [LN; NET, TEV], 'to cause' [AB, BDAG, LN; NLT], 'to produce, to make, to cause to happen' [BDAG, LN], 'to work' [CEV, GW], 'to grant' [NASB], 'to give' [Bar, BECNT]. This verb means to cause something to happen and it is used particularly in relationship to physical events [BDAG, LN].
- b. τέρας (LN 33.480) (BDAG p. 999): 'wonder' [AB, BDAG, BECNT; ESV, KJV, NASB, NET, NIV, NLV], 'miracle' [BDAG; CEV, GW, NCV, TEV], 'portent' [Bar, BDAG, CBC, LN; NRSV, REB], 'sign' [LN], 'omen' [BDAG]. This noun denotes an unusual sign, especially one in the heavens, that serves to foretell impending events [LN]. It denotes something that astounds because of its transcendent association [BDAG].
- c. σημεῖον (LN 33.477) (BDAG 2.b. p. 921): 'sign' [AB, Bar, BECNT, CBC, LN; ESV, GW, KJV, NASB, NET, NIV, NLT, NRSV, REB], 'portent' [BDAG], 'wonder' [CEV, TEV], not explicit [NCV]. This noun denotes an event that has some special meaning [LN]. It refers to

terrifying appearances in the heavens that had never before been seen [BDAG].
d. ἀτμίς (LN 1.36) (BDAG p. 149): 'vapor' [Bar, BDAG, BECNT; ESV, KJV, NASB], 'steam' [LN], 'mist' [NRSV], 'cloud' [CEV, GW, NET, NLT]. The phrase 'vapor of smoke' is also translated 'thick smoke' [NCV, TEV], 'drifting smoke' [CBC], 'billows of smoke' [NIV], 'billowing of smoke' [AB], 'a pall of smoke' [REB]. This noun denotes a hot steamy vapor [LN]. It is a smoky vapor like that of a volcanic eruption [BDAG].

QUESTION—What is the difference between miracles, wonders and signs?
Each word has a slightly different focus that should be preserved in a translation. 'Miracle' (δυναμις) focuses on the supernatural power of a miracle. Here 'sign' (σημεῖον) focuses on the significance of a miracle that draws attention to God. 'Wonder' (τέρας) focuses on the effect the miracle has on the audience. It causes fear, awe, amazement and surprise all at the same time [TRT].

QUESTION—What is the 'vapor of smoke'?
The equivalent of 'vapor of smoke' is in many languages 'a cloud of dark smoke', 'heavy smoke', or 'big smoke'. The closest normal equivalent is the smoke and vapor which comes from a volcano [TH].

QUESTION—What will be signified by the signs on the earth?
Blood, fire, and vapor of smoke and the imagery of the darkened sun and bloody moon in the next verse (v. 20) are all connected with the day of the Lord and judgment [BECNT, NAC, NICNT, PNTC, TNTC].

2:20 **The sun will-be-changed**[a] **into darkness and the moon into blood, before the-coming (of) the great and glorious**[b] **day of-(the)-Lord. 2:21 And it-will-be-(that) every one-who calls-upon the name of-(the)-Lord will-be-saved.**[c]

LEXICON—a. fut. pass. indic. of μεταστρέφω (LN 13.64) (BDAG p. 641): 'to be changed' [BDAG, LN; NET], 'to be turned to' [AB, CBC; ESV, NIV, NRSV, REB], 'to be turned into' [Bar, BECNT, LN; KJV, NASB], 'to be caused to be different from, to be transformed' [LN], 'to be altered' [BDAG]. The phrase 'the sun will be changed into darkness' is also translated 'the sun will turn dark' [CEV], 'the sun will become dark' [GW, NCV, NLT], 'the sun will be darkened' [TEV]. This verb means to undergo a change of state [LN]. It means to cause a change in state or condition. The resulting state is often the opposite of the initial state [BDAG].
b. ἐπιφανής (LN 79.22) (BDAG p. 386): 'glorious' [AB, BDAG, BECNT, LN; NASB, NCV, NET, NIV, NLT, NRSV, TEV], 'wonderful' [LN; CEV], 'marvelous' [LN], 'magnificent' [ESV], 'splendid, remarkable' [BDAG], 'notable' [KJV], 'resplendent' [CBC; REB], 'manifest' [Bar]. The phrase 'the great and glorious day of the Lord' is also translated 'the terrifying day of the Lord' [GW]. This adjective describes something as

being glorious or wonderful [LN]. It pertains to being resplendent [BDAG].
c. fut. pass. indic. of σῴζω (LN 21.27) (BDAG 2.b. p. 983): 'to be saved' [AB, Bar, BDAG, BECNT, CBC, LN; all versions], 'to attain salvation' [BDAG]. This verb means to experience divine salvation [LN].

QUESTION—What is meant by the moon being changed to blood?
Some Bible scholars think this means that the moon will become red like blood, not that it will actually become blood. Be sure to choose the color that refers to the color of blood in the receptor language [TRT].

QUESTION—What is 'the great and glorious day of the Lord'?
The great and glorious day of the Lord is the last day, the day on which the Lord Jesus Christ returns to earth [Bar, NAC, PNTC]. It is the day of judgment [TNTC]. He will descend from heaven to judge the nations and consummate the story of the people of God [Bar, PNTC]. It is a day of judgment, but that means the day of God's salvation to all who invoked his name [NICNT]. The reference to the Lord in Joel means calling out to Yahweh, Israel's God, for salvation. Here in Peter's speech, he showed that Jesus is Lord [BECNT, TNTC].

2:22 Men of Israel, listen to these words: Jesus the Nazarene, (a)-man attested[a] to you by God with miracles[b] and wonders[c] and signs[d] which God did through him in your midst, as you yourselves know,

LEXICON—a. perf. pass. participle of ἀποδείκνυμι (LN 28.50) (BDAG 2. p. 108): 'to be attested' [BDAG, BECNT; ESV, NASB, NET, NRSV], 'to be clearly shown' [LN], 'to be demonstrated, to be shown, to be made clearly known' [LN], 'to be shown forth, to be displayed' [BDAG], 'to be approved' [KJV], 'to be accredited' [AB; NIV], 'to be proven' [CEV], 'to be clearly proven' [TEV], 'to be publicly endorsed' [NLT], 'to be singled out and made known' [CBC; REB], 'to be marked out' [Bar]. The phrase 'a man attested to you by God' is also translated 'a man whom God brought to your attention' [GW], 'God clearly showed this to you' [NCV]. This verb means to cause something to be known as genuine, possibly focusing upon the source of such knowledge [LN]. It means to show forth the quality of an entity [BDAG].
b. δύναμις (LN 76.7) (BDAG 3. p. 264): 'miracle' [BDAG, BECNT, CBC, LN; CEV, GW, KJV, NASB, NCV, NIV, REB, TEV], 'powerful miracle' [NLT], 'powerful deed' [AB; NET], 'mighty deed' [LN], 'mighty work' [Bar; ESV], 'deed of power' [BDAG; NRSV], 'wonder' [BDAG]. This noun denotes a deed that manifests great power and it is implied that it was accomplished by some supernatural force [LN]. It denotes a deed that exhibits the ability to function powerfully [BDAG].
c. τέρας (LN 33.480) (BDAG p. 999): 'wonder' [AB, BDAG, BECNT; all versions except GW, REB], 'amazing thing' [GW], 'portent' [Bar, BDAG, CBC, LN; REB], 'sign' [LN], 'prodigy, omen' [BDAG]. See entry at v. 2:19.

d. σημεῖον (LN 33.477) (BDAG 2.a.α. p. 920): 'sign' [AB, Bar, BECNT, CBC, LN; all versions except NET, TEV], 'miraculous sign' [NET], 'portent' [BDAG], not explicit [TEV]. See entry at v. 2:19.

QUESTION—Who are the 'Men of Israel' referred to?

These are the same people whom he had addressed in verse 14 as 'Men of Judea and all who dwell in Jerusalem' The expression 'Men of Israel' is a more general term, meaning 'People of the nation of Israel' [NICNT, TH, TNTC]. The use of this term in the New Testament is not a reference to descent from Israel but to the nation as a religious and ethnic entity [TH].

QUESTION—What are the people to listen to?

The command 'listen to these words' refers to what Joel is now going to say about Jesus after having quoted from the prophet Joel in verses 17–21 [TH]. Now Peter was continuing his own speech [TRT].

2:23 this (Jesus), delivered-up according-to the definite[a] plan and foreknowledge of-God, you crucified[b] and killed by (the)-hand(s) of-lawless men.

LEXICON—a. perf. pass. participle of ὁρίζω (LN 30.83) (BDAG 2.a.c. p. 723): 'to be determined' [BDAG, LN], 'to be decided, to be resolved' [LN]. The phrase 'according to the definite plan and foreknowledge of God' [ESV, NRSV] is also translated 'according to the marked-out will and foreknowledge of God' [BECNT], 'according to God's appointed plan and foreknowledge' [AB], 'in accordance with his own plan God had already decided' [TEV], 'by the predetermined plan and foreknowledge of God' [NASB, NET], 'by a plan that God had determined in advance' [GW], 'by the determinate counsel and foreknowledge of God' [KJV], 'by God's determinate counsel and foreknowledge' [Bar], 'by God's set purpose and foreknowledge' [NIV], 'by the deliberate will and plan of God' [CBC; REB], 'God had already planned and decided' [CEV], 'this was God's plan which he made long ago; he knew all this would happen' [NCV], 'God knew what would happen, and his prearranged plan was carried out' [NLT]. This verb means to come to a definite decision or firm resolve [LN].

b. aorist act participle of προσπήγνυμι (LN 20.76) (BDAG p. 884): 'to crucify' [LN], 'to nail (to a cross)' [BDAG]. The phrase 'you crucified and killed by the hand(s) of lawless men' (ESV) is also translated 'you executed by nailing him to a cross at the hand of Gentiles' [NET], 'you killed him, using heathen men to crucify him' [REB], 'this one…you killed having him crucified through the hands of lawless men' [BECNT], 'you took him and had evil men put him to death on a cross' [CEV], 'you crucified and killed by the hands of those outside the law' [NRSV], 'you nailed to a cross by the hands of godless men and put him to death' [NASB], 'you killed him by letting sinful men crucify him' [TEV], 'ye have taken, and by wicked hands have crucified and slain' [KJV], 'you, with the help of wicked men, put him to death by nailing him to the cross'

[NIV], 'you killed when you had him crucified by heathen hands' [AB], 'By using men who don't acknowledge Moses' Teachings, you crucified Jesus, who was given over to death' [GW], 'you used heathen men to crucify and kill him' [CBC], 'with the help of those who don't know the law, you put him to death by nailing him to a cross' [NCV], 'With the help of lawless Gentiles, you nailed him to a cross and killed him' [NLT], 'you, making use of men outside the law, nailed up and killed' [Bar]. The idiom 'to hang on a tree' means: to execute by nailing to a cross. It is rare that one can find in receptor languages a technical term or phrase meaning specifically 'to crucify.' In general, a phrase must be employed, since this type of execution is no longer practiced. One can, for example, use such expressions as 'to nail to a cross bar' or 'to nail up on wood' or even 'to nail up high.' [LN]. It means to fasten to something [BDAG].

QUESTION—What does the expression 'by the predetermined plan and foreknowledge of God' mean?

It means that God was very much in control of events that are tied to Jesus and included a plan for suffering and death as a part of Jesus' calling [BECNT, PNTC].

QUESTION—What does the 'you' refer to in the phrase 'you killed him'?

The 'you' here refers to the Jewish leadership and Jews in Jerusalem [BECNT, CBC, NAC, NICNT, PNTC, TNTC].

QUESTION—Who were the 'lawless men'?

The phrase 'the hands of lawless men' refers to the Romans who did not obey God's Law/laws, men outside the Law [Bar, EBC, NICNT, PNTC, TRT]. Some others think it refers only to the Romans who gave out the penalty of crucifixion and executed Jesus [BECNT, TNTC]. 'Lawless men' is a term used by Jews to designate Gentiles [NAC]; either because of their actual sins or simply because they did not possess the Mosaic Law [EBC].

QUESTION—What does this verse tell us?

This verse tells us that Jesus' death is at one and the same time determined by God and carried out by the Jews with the assistance of the Romans who nailed him to the cross [AB, Bar, BECNT, EBC, NICNT, PNTC, TNTC]. Peter balanced all the participants in the drama of Jesus' death – the guilt of Jew and Gentile alike, and the triumphal sovereignty of God [NAC].

2:24 God raised-him-up,[a] having-destroyed the pains[b] of-death, because it-was not possible-(for) him to-be-held[c] by it.

LEXICON—a. aorist act. indic. of ἀνίστημι (LN 23.94) (BDAG 2. p. 83): 'to raise up' [AB, Bar, BDAG, BECNT; ESV, KJV, NET, NRSV], 'to raise up again' [NASB], 'to raise to life' [LN; CEV, GW], 'to raise to life again' [CBC; REB], 'to raise back to life' [NLT], 'to raise from death' [TEV], 'to make live again' [LN], 'to raise from the dead' [NCV, NIV]. This verb means to cause someone to live again after having once died [LN]. It means to raise up by bringing back to life [BDAG].

b. ὠδίν (LN 24.87) (BDAG b.α. p. 1102): 'pains' [GW, KJV, NET], 'pain' [NCV], 'great suffering, great pain' [LN], 'birth pains' [BDAG], 'pangs' [Bar, BECNT, CBC; ESV, REB], 'agony' [AB; NASB, NIV], 'horrors' [NLT], 'power' [TEV], not explicit [CEV, NRSV]. This noun is a figurative extension of 'to suffer birth pain' and it denotes intense pain or suffering, similar to the pain of childbirth [LN]. It denotes great pain (as the pain in giving birth) [BDAG].

c. pres. pass. infin. of κρατέω (LN 37.16) (BDAG 5. p. 565): 'to be held' [AB, Bar, BECNT; ESV, KJV, NCV], 'to be held in its power' [BDAG; NASB, NET, NRSV], 'to be in the power of' [LN], 'to be controlled' [LN]. The phrase 'it was not possible for him to be held by it' is also translated 'death could not hold him in its power' [CEV], 'death had no power to hold him' [GW], 'death could not keep its hold on him' [NIV], 'death could not keep him in its grip' [NLT], 'it could not be that death should keep him in its grip' [CBC; REB], 'it was impossible that death should hold him prisoner' [TEV], 'it was impossible for him to be held in (death's) power' [BDAG]. This verb in its active form means to exercise power or force over someone or something [LN]. It means to control in such a way that something does not happen [BDAG].

QUESTION—Why was it not possible for Jesus to be held by death?

It means that Jesus would not stay dead [CBC, EBC, NICNT, PNTC, TNTC, TRT]. God, the one with power over life and death, was able to overcome death's grip and bring Jesus to life [BECNT]; God raised Jesus up from the dead [AB, Bar, NAC, NICNT, TNTC].

2:25 For David says of him, 'I-saw^a the Lord always before me, because he-is on my right-(hand),^b so-that I-may- not -be-shaken.^c

LEXICON—a. imperf. mid. indic. of προοράω (LN 24.5) (BDAG 3. p. 873) 'to see beforehand, to have seen previously' [LN], 'to see before one' [BDAG]. The clause 'I saw the Lord always before me' [AB; ESV, NIV, NRSV] is also translated 'I saw the Lord before me always' [BECNT], 'I saw the Lord always in my presence' [NASB], 'I saw the Lord always in front of me' [NET; similarly GW], 'I set the Lord always in my sight before me' [Bar], 'I always see the Lord near me' [CEV], 'I see that the Lord is always with me' [NLT], 'I keep the Lord before me always' [NCV], 'I saw the Lord before me at all times' [TEV]. Others take this to refer to seeing in advance: 'I foresaw the Lord always before my face' [KJV], 'I foresaw that the Lord would be with me forever' [REB], 'I foresaw that the presence of the Lord would be with me always' [CBC]. This verb means to have seen someone beforehand or prior to an event or in a temporal sense, i.e., to foresee [LN]. In the middle voice, instead of seeing something in advance, it means to have before one's eyes [BDAG].

b. δεξιός (LN 82.8) (BDAG 1.a. p. 217): 'right hand' [AB, Bar, BECNT, CBC; ESV, KJV, NASB, NET, NIV, NRSV, REB], 'right side' [BDAG, LN; CEV]. The phrase 'he is on my right hand' is also translated 'he is by

my side' [GW], 'he is close by my side' [NCV], 'he is right beside me' [NLT], 'he is near me' [TEV]. This adjective pertains to being to the right of some point of reference [LN]. It means to stand at someone's side [BDAG].
  c. aorist pass. subj. of σαλεύω (LN 25.242) (BDAG 2. p. 911): 'to be shaken' [BDAG, BECNT, CBC; ESV, NASB, NET, NIV, NLT, NRSV, REB], 'to be deeply distressed, to become unsettled' [LN], 'to be upset' [LN], 'to be afraid' [CEV], 'to be moved' [Bar; GW, KJV], 'to be hurt' [NCV], 'to be troubled' [TEV], 'to be disturbed' [BDAG], 'to be made to stumble' [AB]. This verb is a figurative extension of being physically shaken and it means to be emotionally unsettled and distraught [LN]. It means to be disturbed inwardly [BDAG].

QUESTION—What is the function of this verse?

In verses 25–28 Peter quoted King David's prophecy about Jesus Christ, the Messiah [TRT]. The quotation is from Psalm 16:8–11 where King David is not speaking of himself but of the Messiah [Bar]. This quotation is from the Greek Septuagint version of the Old Testament. Peter used it to support Jesus' resurrection from the dead, a defense to his claim in the last verse, v. 24 [AB, BECNT, CBC, EBC, NAC, NICNT, PNTC, TNTC]. The term 'Lord' here refers to Jesus [TH].

QUESTION—What does the expression 'he is on my right side' mean?

The expression 'he is on my right' is an idiom which means someone is being present to help and defend someone else. Therefore, this expression may be interpreted as 'he (the Lord) is with me' here [TRT].

2:26 **Therefore, my heart was-glad[a] and my tongue rejoiced,[b] and, in-addition, my body[c] also will-live in hope.**

LEXICON—a. aorist pass. indic. of εὐφραίνω (LN 25.122) (BDAG 2. p. 415): 'to be gladdened' [BDAG; all versions except KJV, TEV], 'to be glad' [BECNT, CBC], 'to be cheered up' [LN], 'to rejoice' [AB, Bar, BDAG, LN; KJV]. The phrase ηὐφράνθη καρδία μου 'my heart was glad' is also translated 'I am filled with gladness' [TEV]. This verb means to rejoice as an expression of happiness [LN].
  b. aorist mid. indic. of ἀγαλλιάω (LN 25.133) (BDAG p. 4): 'to rejoice' [BECNT, LN; ESV, GW, NCV, NET, NIV, NRSV, REB], 'to be extremely joyful, to rejoice greatly' [LN], 'to be glad' [BDAG; KJV], 'to exult' [Bar, BDAG; NASB], 'to be overjoyed' [BDAG, LN]. The phrase 'my tongue rejoiced' is also translated 'my words will be joyful' [CEV], 'my words are full of joy' [TEV], 'my tongue shouts his praises' [NLT], 'my tongue speaks my joy' [CBC], 'my tongue was jubilant with happiness' [AB]. This verb means to experience a state of great joy and gladness, and it often involves a verbal expression of that joy along with appropriate body movement [LN].
  c. σάρξ (LN 8.4) (BDAG 2.a. p. 915): 'body' [AB, BDAG, LN; GW, NCV, NET, NIV, NLT]; 'flesh' [Bar, BECNT, CBC; ESV, NASB, KJV, NRSV,

REB], 'I' [CEV], 'I, mortal though I am' [TEV]. This noun denotes a living body [LN]. It denotes the physical body as a functioning entity [BDAG]. The word 'flesh' is used here in parallelism to the heart and the tongue. It is a figure of speech for the person himself [BECNT].

QUESTION—What is meant by the expression 'my heart was glad'?
This means 'I am very glad' [TRT]. 'Glad' is a state of mind; while 'rejoice' is an outward expression of joy [TRT].

QUESTION—What is meant by the expression 'my body will live in hope'?
This concerns a hope in what God will do for the person, a hope in God's promises [TH]. Here the word 'flesh' is a figure of speech for the person himself [BECNT]. The expression 'my body will live in hope' means 'I am completely sure that I am safe' [TRT]. After death his physical body will rest in hope of a resurrection [Bar]. It is a hope that after death he will not descend to Sheol but be taken into the presence of God [TNTC].

2:27 Because you-will- not -abandon^a my soul to Hades,^b nor will-you-allow your Holy-One^c see decay.^d

LEXICON—a. fut. act. indic. of ἐγκαταλείπω (LN 13.92) (BDAG 2. p. 273): 'to abandon' [BECNT, BDAG, CBC; ESV, GW, NASB, NIV, REB, TEV], 'to leave' [AB, Bar, BDAG, LN; CEV, KJV, NCV, NET, NLT, NRSV], 'to allow to remain' [BDAG], 'to cause to remain, to leave to exist' [LN. This verb means to cause someone to continue to exist in a certain location [LN]. It means to separate connection with someone [BDAG]. This means that God will not let Jesus stay in Hades [TW].

b. ᾅδης (LN 1.19) (BDAG 1. p. 19): 'Hades' [Bar, BDAG, BECNT, CBC, LN; ESV, NASB, NET, NRSV], 'hell' [KJV], 'the world of the dead' [LN; TEV], 'the kingdom of the dead' [AB], 'the grave' [CEV, GW, NCV, NIV, NLT], 'death' [REB], 'the nether world' [BDAG]. This noun denotes a place or abode of the dead, including both those who were righteous and unrighteous. In most contexts ᾅδης is equivalent to the Hebrew term Sheol [LN]. It is the place of the dead [BDAG].

c. ὅσιος (LN 53.46) (BDAG 1.b. p. 728): 'Holy One' [AB, BECNT; all versions except REB, TEV], 'godly one' [Bar], 'faithful servant' [REB, TEV], 'loyal servant' [CBC], 'devout, pious' [BDAG, LN]. This pronominal adjective pertains to being dedicated or consecrated to the service of God [LN]. It means to be one who is without fault relative to deity, to be devout, pious, pleasing to God, holy [BDAG]. It is used in the sense of being one who belongs to and serves God [TH].

d. διαφθορά (LN 23.205) (BDAG p. 239): 'decay' [LN; CEV, GW, NASB, NET, NIV], 'corruption' [AB, Bar, BDAG, BECNT, CBC; ESV, KJV, NRSV, REB], 'destruction' [BDAG]. The phrase 'nor will you allow your Holy one see decay' is also translated 'you will not let your Holy One rot' [NCV], 'you will not...allow your Holy One to rot in the grave' [NLT], 'you will not allow your faithful servant to rot in the grave' [TEV]. The noun 'decay' is derived from a verb meaning to rot or to decay [LN]. It is the condition or state of rotting or decaying [BDAG].

QUESTION—Who does the pronoun 'you' refer to?

The pronoun 'you' in this verse refers to God [TH].

QUESTION—What is 'Hades'?

'Hades' is a transliteration of the Greek word which refers to 'the place or world of the dead' [TH, TRT], It is Sheol, the realm of the dead [BECNT, NAC, PNTC, TNTC]. It does not refer to hell, nor does it refer to a cemetery or grave [TRT].

QUESTION—What does 'your Holy One' refer to?

'Your Holy One' points to Jesus Christ, the Messiah [NAC, TNTC]. The Greek word for 'Holy One' especially means Christ is faithful/loyal to God or that He is perfect/sinless and that God loves Him [TRT].

QUESTION—What is the point of this verse?

Peter is pointing out that King David could not have been speaking about himself since he did indeed die, was buried, and suffered decay; nor did he ascend to heaven. Peter asserted here that King David had been prophesying about the resurrection of the Messiah [EBC, NAC, NICNT]. God would not let Jesus stay in the world of the dead and he would not permit the corpse of Jesus to decay [NAC, TH]. Peter is arguing that Scripture predicted Jesus' resurrection, as all can now see [BECNT, NICNT].

2:28 **You-made-known to-me (the)-ways**[a] **of-life, you-will-fill me with-joy with your presence.**[b]'

LEXICON—a. ὁδός (LN 41.16) (BDAG 3.a. p. 691): 'way' [BDAG, LN], 'way to live, way of life' [LN]. The phrase 'the ways of life' [AB, BECNT, CBC; KJV, NASB, NRSV] is also translated 'the way of life' [NLT], 'ways of life' [Bar], 'the paths of life' [ESV, NET, NIV, REB], 'the path of life'[GW], 'the path to life' [CEV], 'the paths that lead to life' [TEV], 'how to live a holy life' [NCV]. This noun is a figurative extension of meaning of ὁδός 'road' and denotes a customary manner of life or behavior, with probably some implication of goal or purpose [LN]. It denotes a course of behavior [BDAG].

b. πρόσωπον (LN 85.26) (BDAG 1.b.ɳ. p. 888): 'presence' [AB, Bar, BECNT, CBC, LN; all versions except CEV, KJV, NCV], 'countenance' [KJV]. The phrase 'you will fill me with joy with your presence' is also translated 'he makes me glad by being near me' [CEV], 'being with you will fill me with joy' [NCV], 'with your presence you will fill me with joy' [LN]. This noun is a figurative extension of the word meaning 'face' and denotes the personal presence of an individual at a particular place [LN]. God's abiding presence gives gladness/joy to David [BECNT, PNTC, TH].

QUESTION—What is meant by knowing 'the ways of life'?

It refers to the way one lives [AB, Bar, BECNT, CB, Bar, NAC, LN. TH, TRT; all versions]. It refers to the ways out of death back into life [Bar] and it might be translated 'you have shown me the paths which I must take in order to truly live' [TH]. It means 'you have shown me the ways of life that I will live again' or 'you will raise me back to life' [TRT]. The one who experiences God's protection has had the ways of life revealed to him [BECNT]. Jesus is the author of life who leads others in the path to new life [NAC]. It affirms his belief that after death he will be taken into the presence of God [TNTC]. Following verse 27 about not abandoning his soul, it now refers to the Messiah of David's line with the meaning that he has been rescued from the grave and raised up to ascend to heaven [EBC, NICNT].

2:29 **Men,[a] brothers, it-is-possible[b] to-speak to you with confidence about (our) ancestor[c] David, that he- both -died and was-buried, and his tomb is with us to this day.**

LEXICON—a. ἀνήρ (LN 9.1): The combination Ἄνδρες ἀδελφοί 'Men, brothers' is also translated 'Men and brethren' [KJV], 'Brethren' [BECNT; NASB], 'Brothers' [AB, BAR; ESV, GW, NET, NIV], 'Dear brothers' [NLT], 'Brothers and sisters' [NCV], 'My friends' [CBC; CEV, REB, TEV], 'Fellow Israelites' [NRSV]. This noun denotes a person, a human being, or an individual, and in its plural form it refers to people or persons. It is not uncommon in languages for a term which is often used to refer to an adult male to also be employed in a generic sense of 'person' [LN].

b. pres. act. part. of ἔξεστι (LN 71.1) (BDAG 2. p. 349): 'to be possible' [BDAG, LN]. The phrase 'it is possible to speak to you with confidence' is also translated 'it is possible to speak confidently to you' [AB], 'I can speak confidently to you' [NET], 'I tell/can-tell you confidently' [GW, NIV], 'I say to you with confidence' [BECNT], 'I may confidently say to you' [NASB], 'I may say to you with confidence/confidently' [ESV, NRSV], 'I may say to you with all freedom' [Bar], 'it is right for me to speak to you' [CEV], 'I can tell you truly' [NCV], 'I must speak to you plainly' [TEV], 'let me freely speak unto you' [KJV], 'let me tell you plainly' [CBC], 'nobody can deny' [REB], 'you can be sure that' [NLT]. This verb marks an event as being possible in a highly generic sense. The possibility of speaking confidently about David evidently is based upon well-known facts [LN]. It means to be within the range of possibility [BDAG].

c. πατριάρχης (LN 10.22) (BDAG p. 788): 'ancestor' [BDAG; CEV, GW, NCV, NRSV], 'our famous ancestor' [TEV], 'patriarch' [AB, Bar, BDAG, BECNT, CBC, LN; ESV, KJV, NASB, NIV, NLT, REB], 'our forefather' [NET]. This noun denotes a particularly noted male ancestor either because of his role in initiating an ethnic group or in the case of David, because of his important exploits and accomplishments [LN]. It denotes a prime ancestor of a national entity, or it refers to David as being their ancestor [BDAG].

QUESTION—Who are the people being addressed?
Here 'men, brothers' refers to both men and women. After quoting from the OT, Peter now continues his speech to all the people who are present [BECNT, TRT]. After applying the citation from the Psalm to Jesus, he now addresses the audience as brothers because they are fellow Jews [EBC, PNTC, TNTC].

QUESTION—What does the term 'patriarch' mean?
This term is usually reserved for Abraham, Isaac, Jacob and his twelve sons [BECNT, NAC]. The term 'patriarch' implies progenitor and 'founder of the nation'. However in this context it is an honorary title applied to David, the king of Israel [TH], the founder of a dynasty [NICNT]. The term 'patriarch' is equivalent in many languages to 'forefather' or 'grandfather' [TH].

QUESTION—What was a tomb like in the apostolic time?
A tomb was either a place inside a cave or a small room cut out of a rock hillside that was used to bury the dead [TRT]. By saying that David's tomb is with us to this day, Peter implies that David's tomb has not been disturbed and his body has not raised. David has not experienced a bodily resurrection [BECNT, PNTC]. Peter was entitled to make his point with confidence since the proof of David's burial was visible for all to see [TNTC]. David's tomb is mentioned in Nehemiah 3:16. It was on the south of Jerusalem, near the pool of Siloam [NAC, NICNT].

2:30 Therefore being (a)-prophet, and knowing that God had-sworn to-him with-an-oath^a to-seat (one) from (the)-fruit of his loins^b on his throne, 2:31 he-foresaw^c and-spoke about the resurrection of the Messiah,^d that he-was-not -abandoned to Hades, nor did his body experience decay.

LEXICON—a. ὅρκος (LN 33.463) (BDAG p. 723): 'oath' [AB, Bar, BDAG, BECNT, LN; ESV, GW, KJV, NASB, NET, NIV, NLT, NRSV]. The phrase 'God had sworn to him with an oath' is also translated 'God had sworn to him' [CBC; REB], 'God had promised him' [NCV], 'God had made a promise he would not break' [CEV], 'God had made a vow that' [TEV]. This noun denotes an affirmation of the truth of a statement by calling on a divine being to execute sanctions against the person if the statement in question is not true. In a number of languages it is necessary to be quite specific in referring to the swearing of an oath, for example, 'to say something by calling upon God to listen' or 'to state that something is true and asking God to punish if it is not true' or 'to make God responsible for what one has said' [LN].

b. ὀσφῦς (LN 8.43, 10.34) (BDAG 2. p. 730): 'loins' [BDAG, LN (8.43)], 'genitals' [LN (8.43)]. The phrase 'one/that from the fruit of his loins' [BECNT; KJV] is also translated, 'one of his descendants' [AB, Bar, LN (10.34); ESV, NASB, NET, NIV, NRSV], 'one of his own direct descendants' [CBC; REB], 'one of David's descendants' [GW, TEV], 'one of David's own descendants' [NLT], 'a person from David's family' [NCV], 'someone from his own family' [CEV]. The idiom 'fruit of the

genitals' refers to a descendant as being the result of the male role in procreation [LN (10.34)]. The word ὀσφῦς refers to the loins as the place of the reproductive organs, so the fruit of someone's loins refers to someone's son or descendants [BDAG].
  c. aorist act. participle of προοράω (LN 28.6) (BDAG 1. p. 873): 'to foresee' [AB, Bar, BDAG, BECNT, LN; ESV, NET, NRSV], 'to know beforehand, to know already, to have foreknowledge' [LN], 'to know what would happen' [CEV], 'to look ahead' [NASB], 'to see what was ahead' [NIV], 'to look into the future' [NLT], 'to know something before it happened' [NCV, similarly KJV], 'to know' [GW]. The phrase 'he-foresaw and spoke about' is also translated 'he spoke with foreknowledge' [CBC; REB], 'David saw what God was going to do in the future' [TEV]. This verb means to know about something prior to some temporal reference point, for example, to know about an event before it happens [LN]. It means to see in advance [BDAG].
  d. Χριστός (LN 53.82) (BDAG 1. p. 1091): 'Messiah' [BDAG, CBC, LN; GW, NLT, NRSV, REB, TEV], 'Christ' [AB, Bar, BDAG, BECNT, LN; CEV, ESV, KJV, NASB, NCV, NIV, NET], 'the Anointed One' [BDAG]. This name is literally 'the one who has been anointed' and in the NT it functions as a title for the Messiah. It is also translated into English as either 'Messiah' or 'the Christ'. In some languages an attempt is made to represent the significance of the term by translating it 'God's appointed one' or 'God's specially chosen one' [LN]. It is the name for the fulfiller of Israelite expectation of a deliverer and it is also translated 'the Messiah, the Anointed One, the Christ' [BDAG]. This title occurs in verses 3:31, 36; 9:22; 17:3; 18:5, 28; 26:23.

QUESTION—What is meant by the expression 'to seat upon his throne'?
This is an idiom which implies that one of David's descendants would be king just as David was [TH]. It looks back to Luke 1:32, where the child Jesus is said to be given the throne of David and a kingdom that will never end [BECNT].

QUESTION—What is meant by 'God had sworn to him with an oath'?
In many other contexts, one can translate 'to make an oath' as 'to promise, calling God to witness'. In this context, it is God who makes the oath. One needs to communicate the essential components of this expression. For example, 'God made a strong promise to David' or 'God promised David with powerful words' [TH]. The combination of oath and swearing emphasizes the certainty of God's commitment [BECNT].

QUESTION—What is the function of this verse?
Psalm 16:10 is cited again in this verse [BECNT, TRT]. Note that the first 'he' in 'he spoke' refers to David and the following 'he' and 'his' refer to Christ. Some texts have 'his soul' instead of 'he' here, i.e., Christ's soul was not abandoned to Hades [TRT]. Also note that a significant change is made in this verse from the citation: the past tense is employed to emphasize fulfillment here [PNTC]. Peter intends to use David's words to support his

witness for the resurrection of Christ [TRT]. Christ was not abandoned to Hades and his body did not experience decay [BECNT]; he would be raised from the dead [TNTC]. Peter's point is that only through resurrection from the dead could a descendant of David rule forever over God's people [PNTC].

2:32 This Jesus God raised-up,^a of-which we are all witnesses.^b **2:33** Then, having-been-exalted^c to-the right-hand^d of-God, and having-received from the Father the promise of-the Holy Spirit, he-has-poured-out this that you both see and hear.

LEXICON—a. aorist act. indic. of ἀνίστημι (LN 23.94) (BDAG 2. p. 83): 'to raise up' [AB, Bar, BDAG; ESV, KJV, NET, NRSV], 'to raise up again' [NASB], 'to raise to life' [LN; CEV, NIV], 'to make live again' [LN], 'to bring to life' [BDAG], 'to bring back to life' [GW], 'to raise from the dead' [BECNT; NCV, NLT], 'to raise from death' [TEV], 'to be raised' [CBC; REB]. This verb means to cause someone to live again after having once died [LN]. It means to raise up by bringing back to life [BDAG].
  b. μάρτυς (LN 33.270): 'witness' [AB, Bar, BECNT, CBC, LN; all versions except CEV], 'one who testifies' [LN]. The clause 'This Jesus God raised up, of which we are all witnesses' is also translated 'All of us can tell you that God has raised Jesus to life' [CEV]. This noun denotes a person who witnesses [LN].
  c. aorist pass. participle of ὑψόω (LN 87.20) (BDAG 1. p. 1046): 'to be exalted' [AB, Bar, BDAG, CBC, LN; ESV, KJV, NASB, NET, NIV, NLT, NRSV, REB, TEV], 'to be lifted up' [BDAG, BECNT], 'to be raised high' [BDAG], 'to be given a high position' [LN]. The phrase 'having been exalted to the right hand of God' is also translated 'Jesus was taken up to sit at the right side of God' [CEV], 'God used his power to give Jesus the highest position' [GW], 'Jesus was lifted up to heaven and is now at God's right side' [NCV]. This verb means to cause someone to have high status [LN]. It means to lift up spatially [BDAG].
  d. δεξιός (LN 76.4) (BDAG 1.b. p. 218): 'right hand' [AB, Bar, BDAG, BECNT, CBC; ESV; KJV, NASB, NET, NIV, NLT, NRSV, REB], 'right side' [CEV, NCV, TEV], 'right' [BDAG], 'power' [BDAG, LN; GW]. This noun is a figurative extension of meaning of δεξιά 'right hand' power, with the added implication of authority [LN]. It denotes the power of God [BDAG].

QUESTION—Who are those who are witnesses to the fact that Jesus had been raised up?

It is not clear from the Greek text who 'we all' refers to [TRT]. Since Jesus appeared only to his disciples and followers, 'we' included Peter and the believers, but not the crowd [TH]. They were the apostles [PNTC].

QUESTION—What is the significance of being at the right hand of God?
The place to the right of God is the place of highest honor, power, and authority [TH, TNTC, TRT]. In the ancient world, 'the right hand' was often identified with greatness, strength, goodness and divinity [PNTC].
QUESTION—What is it that they had both seen and heard?
The pronoun 'this' refers to the gift of the Spirit [TRT] when they were filled with the Holy Spirit [BECNT, NAC]. Jesus' resurrection and ascension has led to all of this activity involving the Spirit [BECNT].
QUESTION—What is indicated by the conjunction ουν 'then'?
Peter brings out the sequel of events following Jesus' resurrection. Jesus was then exalted to the right hand of God, and received from the Father the promise of the Holy Spirit and in turn he has poured out the Spirit to the disciples that they now see and hear [Bar, BECNT, NICNT, PNTC].

2:34 For (it-was) not David who-ascended into the heavens, but he-himself says, 'The Lord said to my Lord, "Sit at (the)-right[a] of-me **2:35** until I-make your enemies[b] (a)-footstool[c] for your feet."'
LEXICON—a. δεξιός (LN 87.34) (BDAG 1.b. p. 218): 'right' [LN], 'right side' [LN; CEV, NCV, TEV], 'right hand' [AB, Bar, BDAG, BECNT, CBC; ESV, KJV, NASB, NET, NIV, NLT, NRSV, REB]. The phrase 'sit at the right of me' is also translated 'sit in the place of honor at my right hand' [NLT], 'take my highest position of power' [GW]. This noun denotes a high status or position [LN]. To sit at someone's right hand means to be at the place of honor [BDAG].
b. ἐχθρός (LN 39.11) (BDAG 2.b.β. p. 419): 'enemy' [AB, BDAG, Bar, BECNT, CBC; LN; all versions except KJV], 'foe' [KJV]. This noun derives from an adjective meaning to be in opposition to someone or something [LN]. It refers to the enmity between humans and God [BDAG].
c. ὑποπόδιον (LN 6.117, 37.8) (BDAG p. 1040): 'footstool' [AB, Bar, BDAG, BECNT, CBC, LN (6.117); all versions except GW, NCV]. The phrase 'make your enemies a footstool for your feet' is also translated 'put your enemies under your control' [GW, NCV]. This noun denotes a piece of furniture on which one may rest one's feet [LN (6.117)]. The idiom 'to make someone a footstool for one's feet' means to put someone under the complete control of another person [LN (37.8)]. Making someone a footstool for someone means to subject one person to another so that the other can put a foot on the subject's neck [BDAG].
QUESTION—How is the conjunction 'until' to be properly translated?
In many languages the conjunction 'until' specifies the end of a period, after which some other arrangement is presumed. However, here the Lord Messiah will not cease to sit at the right of God and it will be more proper to translate 'until' as 'in the meantime' or 'during that time'. For example, 'sit at my right side and during that time I will make your enemies…' [TH].

QUESTION—To whom do the two references to the Lord in the clause 'the Lord said to my Lord' refer?

The quotation in vv. 34–35 is a citation from Psalm 110:1 [Bar, BECNT, EBC, NAC, NICNT, PNTC, TNTC]. The first 'Lord' refers to God the Father and the second 'Lord' refers to Jesus, David's descendant who is to be the Messiah [TH]. David's authorship of Psalm 110:1 is critical for its messianic application [PNTC].

QUESTION—What is meant by making someone's enemies a footstool for his feet?

The clause 'I make your enemies a footstool for your feet' is a figure of speech that means 'I make your enemies subject to you, I will put them under your rule' [TH, TRT]. The concept of being subjected to one's authority might have to be translated with a non-metaphorical equivalent such as, 'until I cause you to have victory over your enemies' or 'I cause your enemies to be subjected to your authority' [TH].

2:36 Therefore, let all (the)-house^a of-Israel know with-certainty^b that God made him both Lord and Messiah,^c this Jesus whom you crucified."

LEXICON—a. οἶκος (LN 11.58) (BDAG 3. p. 699): 'house' [AB, Bar, BDAG, BECNT, LN; ESV, KJV, NASB, NRSV], 'nation' [BDAG, LN], 'people' [LN; GW, NCV, NET, TEV], 'descendants' [BDAG]. The phrase 'all the house of Israel' is also translated 'everyone in Israel' [CEV, NLT], 'all Israel' [CBC; NIV, REB]. This noun refers to the people of Israel as an ethnic entity [LN]. 'House' refers to a whole clan or tribe of people descended from a common ancestor [BDAG].

b. ἀσφαλῶς (LN 31.42) (BDAG 2. p. 147): 'with certainty' [LN; NRSV], 'for a certainty' [AB], 'with assurance' [BECNT], 'beyond a doubt' [BDAG; GW, NET], 'certainly true, worthy of being believed, completely believable' [LN], 'for certain' [Bar; CEV, ESV, NASB, NLT], 'as certain' [CBC; REB], 'assuredly' [BDAG; KJV], 'for sure' [TEV], 'truly' [NCV]. The phrase 'let all the house of Israel know with certainty' is also translated 'let all Israel be assured of this' [NIV]. This adverb pertains to being certain and thus completely believable [LN]. It pertains to being certain [BDAG].

c. Χριστός (LN 53.82) (BDAG 1. p. 1091): 'Messiah' [AB, BDAG, CBC, LN; NLT, NRSV, REB, TEV], 'Christ' [Bar, BDAG, BECNT, LN; CEV, ESV, GW, KJV, NASB, NCV, NET, NIV]. This name is literally 'the one who has been anointed' and in the NT it functions as a title for the Messiah. It is also translated into English as either 'Messiah' or 'the Christ'. In some languages an attempt is made to represent the significance of the term by translating it 'God's appointed one' or 'God's specially chosen one' [LN]. It is the name for the fulfiller of Israelite expectation of a deliverer and it is also translated 'the Messiah, the Anointed One, the Christ' [BDAG]. This title occurs in verses 3:31, 36; 9:22; 17:3; 18:5, 28; 26:23.

QUESTION—What is the function of this verse?
Peter now concludes his speech to those Jewish people who had been responsible for the crucifixion of Jesus. 'The Lord' refers to Jesus, the Messiah. Peter makes an emphatic statement to the people of Israel (house of Israel) that they are now to be assured about who Jesus is. The Jesus whom people crucified, but God has exalted and chosen him as Lord and Messiah to them [Bar, PNTC, TH]. The two titles, 'Lord' and 'Messiah' given to Jesus relate back to the Psalm citation in vv. 25–28 and the prior claim of Joel 2:32 that whoever calls on the name of 'the Lord' will be saved (v. 21) [NAC, NICNT, PNTC]. The term 'Lord' in this context shows in particular Jesus' lordship over salvation and the distribution of the benefits of salvation [BECNT]. In Jewish thought, no one had the right to the title Messiah until he accomplished the work of the Messiah. Now that Jesus had accomplished his messianic mission, was raised by God, and has been exalted 'at the right hand', the titles Lord and Messiah (Christ) are legitimately his [BECNT, EBC, TNTC].

DISCOURSE UNIT—2:37–47 [CBC; NASB]. The topic concerns what happened afterwards [CBC], the ingathering [NASB].

DISCOURSE UNIT—2:37–42 [NRSV]. The topic is the first converts.

DISCOURSE UNIT—2:37–41 [BECNT; NET]. The topic is the reaction: repent and receive the promised gift [BECNT], the response to Peter's address [NET].

DISCOURSE UNIT—2:37–40 [AB, NICNT]. The topic is a call to repentance [NICNT], the great baptismal act on the day of Pentecost [AB].

2:37 And having-heard-(this), they-were-pierced[a] to-the heart and they-said to Peter and the rest of the apostles, "Men, brothers,[b] what shall-we-do?"

LEXICON—a. aorist pass. (deponent = act.) indic. of κατανύσσομαι (LN 25.281) (BDAG p. 523): 'to be pierced, to be stabbed' [BDAG]. The idiom 'they were pierced to the heart' [NASB] is also translated '(Peter's words) pierced their hearts' [NLT], 'they were cut to the heart' [BECNT, BDAG, CBC; ESV, NIV, NRSV, REB], 'they were pricked in their fear' [KJV], 'they were acutely distressed' [NET], 'they were deeply troubled' [LN; TEV], 'they were deeply upset' [GW], 'they were very upset' [CEV], 'they felt guilty' [NCV], 'they were pricked in their consciences' [Bar], 'they felt a deep grief' [AB]. The idiom κατανύσσομαι τὴν καρδίαν 'to pierce the heart' means to experience acute emotional distress, implying both concern and regret [LN]. This verb means to be pierced or stabbed and it is used figuratively of the feeling of the sharp pain connected with anxiety, remorse, etc. [BDAG].
  b. ἀδελφός (LN 11.25): 'brother' [LN], 'fellow countryman, fellow Jew [LN]. The phrase 'men, brothers' is also translated 'men and brethren'

[KJV], 'brothers' [AB, Bar, BECNT; ESV, GW, NET, NIV, NLT, NRSV, TEV], 'brethren' [NASB], 'friends' [CBC; CEV, REB], not explicit [NCV]. This noun denotes a person belonging to the same socio-religious entity and being of the same age group as the so-called reference person [LN].

QUESTION—What is meant by them being 'pierced to the heart'?

They were conscience-stricken, remorseful, brokenhearted [PNTC, TNTC]. They felt a sharp pain associated with anxiety and remorse [EBC]. Being convinced, they wanted to know what to do [BECNT, NICNT]. They realized their need and were open to God's working [EBC]. Luke's remark about the heart shows the sincerity and depth of the people's response [BECNT].

2:38 And Peter-(said) to them, "Repent,[a] and each of-you be-baptized in the name[b] of-Jesus Christ for (the)-forgiveness of your sins, and you-will-receive the gift[c] of-the Holy Spirit.

LEXICON—a. aorist act. impera. of μετανοέω (LN 41.52) (BDAG 2. p. 640): 'to repent' [AB, Bar, BDAG, BECNT, CBC, LN; ESV, KJV, NASB, NET, NIV, NRSV, REB], 'to change one's way' [LN], 'to be converted' [BDAG]. The command 'repent' is also translated 'turn back to God' [CEV], 'turn to God and change the way you think and act' [GW], 'change your hearts and lives' [NCV], 'repent of your sins and turn to God' [NLT], 'turn away from your sins' [TEV]. This verb means to change one's way of life as the result of a complete change of thought and attitude with regard to sin and righteousness [LN]. It means to feel remorse [BDAG].

b. ὄνομα (LN 33.126) (BDAG 1.d.γ.ⵧ. p. 713): 'name' [BDAG, LN]. The phrase 'in the name of Jesus Christ' [Bar, BECNT; all versions except REB] is also translated 'in the name of Jesus the Messiah' [CBC; REB], 'calling on the name of Jesus the Messiah' [AB]. This noun denotes the proper name of a person [LN]. 'In the name of God or Jesus usually means 'with mention of the name' or 'calling on the name'. At a baptism it usually refers to being baptized 'while naming the name of Jesus Christ' [BDAG].

c. δωρεά (LN 57.84) (BDAG p. 266): 'gift' [BDAG, LN]. The phrase 'you will receive the gift of the Holy Spirit' [AB, Bar, CBC; ESV, NASB, NCV, NET, NIV, NLT, NRSV, REB] is also translated 'you will receive the Holy Spirit as a gift' [GW], 'you will be given the Holy Spirit [CEV], 'you will receive God's gift, the Holy Spirit' [TEV], 'you will receive the gift of the Holy Ghost' [KJV], 'you shall receive the gift, the Holy Spirit' [BECNT]. This noun denotes that which is given or granted [LN]. It denotes that which is given or transferred freely by one person to another [BDAG].

ACTS 2:38

QUESTION—What is meant by 'repent'?

'Repent' means 'to stop sinning and serve/obey God', that is, 'turn to God from one's evil/sinful thoughts/heart and ways' [TRT], 'turn away from sin and turn to God' [Bar, NICNT, PNTC, TH]; 'turn away from a sinful and godless way of life' [TNTC], 'turn away from the rejection of the Messiah and call upon his name' [NAC], 'make a conscious turn toward God and God's actions through Jesus' [BECNT]. It implies that there will be a complete change of heart and that a confession of sin will be made [EBC]. Repentance is the key response from Peter. Repentance leads to public participation in the rite of baptism, to the forgiveness that the rite signifies, and to the receiving of the Spirit [BECNT, NAC, NICNT].

QUESTION—What is meant by being baptized 'in the name of Jesus Christ'?

In the Greek text the phrase 'in the name of Jesus Christ' can either mean 'in the name of' or 'into the name of' and the two meanings complement each other. 'In the name of' focuses on the authority or power of the one who creates the new relationship [BECNT, NICNT, PNTC, TRT]. 'Into the name of' was commonly used in commerce to show transfer of ownership, the focus being on the new relationship/union that was being formed [CBC, TNTC, TRT]. The latter is more commonly used with baptism [TH]. The expression reflects what Peter has proclaimed in v. 21, 'calling on the name of the Lord in order to be saved' [BECNT, NAC]. Baptism is a self-evident expression of conversion, and calling upon Jesus to be one's Lord is a way of confessing one's faith in him [BECNT, PNTC, TNTC]. It is a way of committing oneself to Jesus and identifying with him [EBC]. The washing signifies the forgiveness of sins that Jesus brings and then comes the emergence into a new, clean life [BECNT].

QUESTION—What is meant by 'the forgiveness of your sins'?

'The forgiveness of your sins' means 'not to punish you for your sins even though you deserve it', and 'to erase your guilt' or 'not be angry with you for sinning'. After God forgives someone, he no longer holds anything against the person; things are completely settled so that their relationship is restored. Since God is aware of all sins and does not ignore or hide sins, avoid translations using words such as 'overlook', 'ignore', or 'hide' [TRT]. God cleanses an unclean person by granting forgiveness so that the indwelling and presence of the Spirit can become possible [BECNT].

QUESTION—What is meant by 'the gift of the Holy Spirit'?

The Holy Spirit is the gift that you will receive from God. It should not sound like the gift is something from the Holy Spirit [EBC, NAC, NICNT, PNTC, TH, TRT]. The gift of the Holy Spirit is what God has promised for the last days [Bar]. The offer of the gift of the Spirit and what the Spirit provides to the one who believes is the core of the gospel [BECNT].

2:39 For the promise is for you and for your children and for-all those (who-are) far-off,[a] everyone (the)-Lord our God calls-to-himself.[b]"

LEXICON—a. μακράν (LN 83.30) (BDAG 1.a.α or 2. p. 612): 'far off' [BECNT; ESV, KJV, NASB, NIV], 'far away' [AB, Bar, BDAG (1.a.α), CBC, LN; GW, NCV, NET, NRSV, REB, TEV], 'at a distance' [LN]. The phrase 'for all those who are far off, everyone the Lord our God calls to Himself' is also translated 'for everyone our Lord God will choose, no matter where they live' [CEV], 'even to the Gentiles—all who have been called by the Lord our God' [NLT]. This adjective pertains to a position at a relatively great distance from another position [LN]. It pertains to either being at a relatively great distance from some position [BDAG 1.a.α.] or to a position in time relatively far removed from the present time [BDAG 2. p. 612].

    b. aorist mid. subj. of προσκαλέω (LN 33.308) (BDAG 1.b. p. 881): 'to call' [AB, Bar, BDAG, BECNT, CBC, LN; all versions except CEV, GW]. 'to choose' [CEV]. The phrase 'everyone the Lord our God calls to himself' is also translated '(The promise) belongs to everyone who worships the Lord our God' [GW]. This verb means to call to someone [LN]. It means to call to or notify in order to secure someone's presence, and here it is about God's invitation to share in the benefits of salvation [BDAG]. It refers to all those whom God invites to come to him [TH].

QUESTION—What is meant by the people being μακράν 'far off'?

It refers to a location that is far away [AB, Bar, BECNT, EBC, LN, NAC, NICNT, TH, TNTC]. The promise includes the Jews living far away in other lands [AB]. It probably refers to the Diaspora Jews and also the God-fearers [BECNT]. There is no need to restrict this to just the Diaspora Jews [Bar, NICNT, TH, TNTC]. Here it refers to the Gentiles, those 'who are far off' [NAC]. Although 'far away' could be taken in a temporal sense to refer to those who were not yet born, it is more natural to take it to mean 'persons in far-off distant lands [TH]. Others have taken the Greek word μακράν to refer to future Jewish generations, but that Greek word is not used temporally in the Greek version of the Old Testament nor anywhere else in the Greek NT [EBC].

QUESTION—What does the clause 'all whom the Lord our God will call to himself' mean?

People everywhere must call on the name of the Lord for deliverance, but God must first call them and enable them to respond to his gracious initiative [NICNT, PNTC, TNTC]. God is the main acting agent of the deliverance [BECNT].

2:40 And with many-more other words he-insisted[a] and kept-on-exhorting[b] them, saying, "Be-saved from this crooked[c] generation."

LEXICON—a. aorist mid. (deponent = act.) indic. of διαμαρτύρομαι (LN 33.319) (BDAG 2 p. 233): 'to insist' [LN], 'to solemnly urge, to exhort' [BDAG], 'to press a case' [CBC; REB], 'to make an appeal' [LN; TEV],

'to testify' [Bar, BECNT; KJV, NET, NIV, NRSV], 'to solemnly testify' [NASB], 'to bear witness' [ESV], 'to set forth his case' [AB], 'to warn' [BDAG; GW, NCV], not explicit [CEV, NLT]. This verb means to be emphatic in stating an opinion or desire [LN]. It means to exhort with authority in matters of extraordinary importance [BDAG].
  b. imperf. act. indic. of παρακαλέω (LN 33.168) (BDAG 2. p. 765): 'to exhort' [AB, Bar, BDAG; ESV, KJV, NASB, NET, NRSV], 'to keep exhorting' [BECNT], 'to encourage' [BDAG], 'to urge' [BDAG; GW, NLT, TEV], 'to appeal to' [BDAG, LN], 'to ask for earnestly, to request' [LN], 'to beg' [CEV, NCV], 'to plead' [CBC; LN; NIV, REB]. This verb means to ask for something earnestly and with propriety [LN]. It means to urge strongly [BDAG].
  c. σκολιός (LN 88.268) (BDAG 2. p. 930): 'crooked, unscrupulous, dishonest' [BDAG, LN]. The command 'Be saved from this crooked generation' is also translated 'Be saved from this twisted generation' [BECNT], 'Be saved from this perverse generation' [NASB], 'Save yourselves from this corrupt/crooked/perverse generation' [GW, ESV, NET, NIV, NLT, NRSV], 'Save yourselves from this crooked age' [CBC; REB], 'Save yourselves from this untoward generation' [KJV], 'Save yourselves from the evil of today's people' [NCV], 'Save yourselves from the punishment coming on this wicked people' [TEV], 'I beg you to save yourselves from what will happen to all these evil people' [CEV], Accept your salvation from this crooked generation' [Bar], 'Let yourselves be saved from this vicious generation' [AB]. In its figurative sense, the adjective means to be unscrupulous or dishonest [LN]. It pertains to being morally bent or twisted [BDAG].

QUESTION—What is mean by 'be saved'?
  Here the verb 'to save' is expressed in the passive imperative [Bar]. 'Be saved' means 'let God save you' [TRT]. God is the main acting agent of the deliverance [BECNT].

QUESTION—What is meant by 'this crooked generation'?
  It refers to everyone who rejects Jesus. Peter may have been thinking especially of the leaders of the Jews [TRT]. Peter gave a warning about the fate of this generation that is ethically crooked, spiritually off the path to God, rebellious and not faithful to God, and thus subject to judgment, so be saved/rescued from it [BECNT, NAC, NICNT, PNTC, TNTC]. It was a big step for people to break away from the control of their religious leaders and become Jesus' followers as those did in the following verse 41 [TRT].

DISCOURSE UNIT—2:41–47 [AB, Bar, NICNT, PNTC]. The topic is the Pentecost community [Bar], the community created by the Spirit [PNTC], the first Christian church [NICNT], life in the growing church [AB].

2:41 So those who-had-received[a] his word were-baptized, and there-were-added that day about three-thousand souls.[b]

LEXICON—a. aorist mid. (deponent = act.) participle of ἀποδέχομαι (LN 31.52) (BDAG 2. p. 109): 'to receive' [BECNT, LN; ESV, NASB], 'to receive gladly' [KJV], 'to accept' [AB, Bar, BDAG, CBC, LN; GW, NCV, NET, NIV, REB], 'to believe' [CEV, NLT, TEV], 'to welcome' [NRSV]. This verb means to come to believe something to be true and to respond accordingly, with some emphasis upon the source [LN]. It means to show approval by accepting [BDAG].

b. ψυχή (LN 9.20) (BDAG 3. p. 1099): 'soul' [AB, Bar, BECNT; ESV, KJV, NASB], 'person' [BDAG, LN; NRSV], 'people' [LN; GW, NCV, NET, TEV], not explicit [CBC; CEV, NIV, NLT, REB]. This noun refers to a person as a living being [LN]. It is an extension of the word 'soul' by metonymy to denote an entity with personhood [BDAG].

QUESTION—What does 'in that day' refer to?

The phrase 'in that day' is ambiguous in the Greek text. Most Bible scholars think it refers to that very day, that is, a 24-hour period [TRT]; a period of time beginning at sunset and ending at the following sunset [LN]. However, a few think it is more general and means 'at that time' which can refer to several days [TRT].

QUESTION—What does the clause 'there were added that day about three thousand souls' imply?

The population of Jerusalem was immensely swollen at this time of the pilgrim festivals and it was possible for a crowd of three thousand to hear Peter in the open air [TNTC]. The clause 'there were added that day about three thousand souls' implies that after having listened to what Peter said, about three thousand more people believed, repented and got baptized on that day to join the existing group of believers [EBC, NICNT, TH]. The group grew from about 120 waiting for the Spirit to about 3000 more [BECNT, EBC, NAC, PNTC, TNTC].

DISCOURSE UNIT—2:42–12:24 [EBC]. The topic is the Christian mission to the Jewish world.

DISCOURSE UNIT—2:42–6:7 [EBC]. The topic is the earliest days of the Church at Jerusalem.

DISCOURSE UNIT—2:42–47 [BECNT, EBC, NAC; ESV, GW, NET, NIV, NLT]. The topic is the common life of the community [NAC], the summary: community life [BECNT], a thesis paragraph on the state of the early church [EBC], the believers form a community [NLT], the fellowship of the believers [ESV, NIV], the fellowship of the early believers [NET], life as a Christian [GW].

2:42 And they-were devoting-(themselves)ᵃ to-the teaching of-the apostles and the-fellowship,ᵇ to-the breakingᶜ of-bread and the prayers.

LEXICON—a. pres. act. participle of προσκαρτερέω (LN 68.68) (BDAG 2.b. p. 881): 'to devote oneself to' [BECNT, LN; ESV, NASB, NET, NIV, NLT, NRSV], 'to be devoted to' [GW], 'to continue steadfastly in' [KJV], 'to persevere in' [AB, BDAG], 'to persist steadily' [Bar], 'to keep on, to persist in' [LN], 'to continue in, to hold fast to' [BDAG]. The phrase 'they were devoting themselves to' is also translated 'they spent their time' [CEV, NCV, TEV], 'they met constantly to' [CBC; REB]. This verb means to continue to do something with intense effort, with the possible implication of doing so despite difficulty [LN]. It means to persist in doing something [BDAG]. 'They were devoting themselves to' can be translated as 'they spent their time in', 'they gave themselves to', or 'they were eager for', 'they were very desirous of' [TH]

b. κοινωνία (LN 34.5) (BDAG 1. p. 553): 'fellowship' [AB, Bar, BDAG, BECNT, LN; all versions except CEV, NCV, REB], 'the common life' [CBC; REB], 'close association' [BDAG, LN], 'association, communion, close relationship' [BDAG], 'sharing' [NCV]. The phrase 'they were devoting themselves to…fellowship' is also translated 'they were like family to each other' [CEV]. This noun denotes an association involving close mutual relations and involvement [LN]. It denotes a close association involving mutual interests and sharing [BDAG].

c. κλάσις (LN 19.34) (BDAG 2. p. 546): 'breaking' [AB, Bar, BDAG, BECNT, CBC, LN; all versions except NLT, TEV]. The phrase 'breaking of bread' is also translated 'sharing of meals (including the Lord's Supper)' [NLT], 'sharing in the fellowship meals' [TEV]. This noun is used in the New Testament exclusively of the breaking of bread [LN]. It denotes the cultic action of breaking the bread [BDAG].

QUESTION—How were they devoting themselves to the teaching of the apostles?

The believers regularly listened to the apostles' teaching and lived according to what the apostles taught [Bar, TRT]. Apostolic instruction is an important part of the new community and it continued to be at the center of church life later in Gentile contexts [BECNT, NAC, PNTC].

QUESTION—What does 'fellowship' refer to?

This fellowship refers to a spiritual fellowship/unity in Christ [EBC, TH, TRT]. There was a real sense of connection to, between, and for each other [BECNT]. The root word κοινων normally means 'to give someone a share in something'. The sharing in this case could simply refer to material blessings, as described in vv. 44–45 [NAC, PNTC, TNTC]. A few think it refers to communal living [EBC, TH, TRT].

QUESTION—What is meant by 'the breaking of bread'?

This refers to the Lord's Supper or to the Agape/Love Meal which was followed by the Lord's Supper. The Agape/Love Meal was a time when the believers gathered to eat a meal together [Bar, BECNT, EBC, NAC, NICNT,

PNTC, TH, TNTC, TRT]. Perhaps it includes their communal living which included eating regular meals together [BECNT, EBC, PNTC, TRT].

QUESTION—What were 'the prayers'?

'The prayers' refers to the prayers of the Christian community as well as the Jewish prayers at their stated hours [EBC, NAC, NICNT, TH, TNTC]. The plural, with the article, implies that they did not merely pray but used certain specific prayers [Bar, BECNT, EBC, NAC, PNTC]. Some have suggested the Psalter, the Eighteen Benedictions, the Lord's Prayer [Bar]. The prayers may be translated as 'they prayed to God together' [TH]. Community life seeks God's direction and is dependent upon God [BECNT, PNTC].

DISCOURSE UNIT—2:43–47 [TNTC; CEV, NCV, NRSV, TEV]. The topic is a summary of the life of the early church [TNTC], life among the Lord's followers [CEV], life among the believers [NRSV, TEV], the believers share [NCV].

2:43 And awe[a] came-upon every soul,[b] and many wonders[c] and signs[d] were-being-done through the apostles.

LEXICON—a. φόβος (LN 53.59) (BDAG 2.a.α. p. 1062): 'awe' [AB, LN; ESV, NIV, NRSV, TEV], 'a sense of awe' [CBC; NASB, REB], 'a deep sense of awe' [NLT], 'reverence' [LN], 'reverential awe' [NET], 'fear' [Bar, BDAG, BECNT; KJV], 'a feeling of fear' [GW], 'respect' [BDAG], 'great respect' [NCV]. The phrase 'awe came upon every soul' is also translated 'everyone was amazed' [CEV]. This noun denotes a profound respect and awe for deity [LN]. The expression 'awe came upon every soul' means that every person was filled with awe which is equivalent in some languages to 'everyone has great respect for', or 'everyone is deeply impressed by' [TH]. It denotes the product of an intimidating or alarming force [BDAG].

b. ψυχή (LN 9.20) (BDAG 2.c. p. 1098, 3. p. 1099): 'soul' [Bar, BDAG (2.c.), BECNT; ESV, KJV], 'person' [BDAG (3), LN]. The phrase 'every soul' is also translated 'everyone' [BDAG (3); CEV, GW, NASB, NCV, NET, NIV, NRSV, REB, TEV], 'them all' [NLT], 'all' [AB], 'everywhere' [CBC]. This noun refers to a person as a living being [LN]. It denotes an entity with personhood [BDAG (3)].

c. τέρας (LN 33.480) (BDAG p. 999): 'wonder' [AB, BDAG, BECNT; ESV, KJV, NASB, NET, NIV, NRSV], 'miracle' [CEV, NCV, TEV], 'portent' [Bar, BDAG, LN; REB], 'sign' [LN], 'miraculous sign' [NLT], 'prodigy, omen' [BDAG], 'marvel' [CBC], 'amazing thing' [GW]. This noun denotes an unusual sign, especially one in the heavens, serving to foretell impending events [LN]. It denotes something that astounds because of a transcendent association [BDAG].

d. σημεῖον (LN 33.477) (BDAG 2.a.α. p. 920): 'sign' [AB, Bar, BECNT, CBC, LN; ESV, KJV, NASB, NRSV, NCV, REB], 'miraculous sign' [GW, NET, NIV], 'miracle' [BDAG], 'wonder' [CEV, NLT, TEV]. This noun denotes an event that is an indication or confirmation of intervention by transcendent powers [LN]. It denotes an event that is an indication of intervention by transcendent powers [BDAG].

QUESTION—What caused every person to have a feeling of awe?

It may be more natural to reverse the order of this verse so that one can see the cause: 'God was doing many wonders and signs through the apostles, so that fear/awe came on every soul/person' [TRT]. Here 'miracles and signs' is the same expression which was discussed in vv. 19, 22 [BECNT, EBC, PNTC, TH, TNTC].

2:44 And all those who believed were in the same-(place/fellowship)ᵃ and had all-(things) (in)-common.ᵇ

LEXICON—a. αὐτός (LN 58.31): 'same' [LN]. The phrase 'were in the same' is also translated 'were together' [BECNT; ESV, KJV, NASB, NCV, NET, NIV, NRSV], '(whose faith) had drawn them together' [CBC], 'met together in one place' [NLT], '(all the members of the believing) community' [Bar], 'often met together' [CEV], 'came as a group' [AB], 'continued together in close fellowship' [TEV], 'kept meeting together' [GW], 'agreed (to hold everything in common)' [REB]. When occurring together with the article this adjective pertains to that which is identical to something else [LN].

b. κοινός (LN 57.99, 89.118) (BDAG 1.a. p. 551): 'in common' [AB, Bar, BDAG, BECNT, CBC, LN (89.118); ESV, KJV, NASB, NET, NIV, NRSV, REB]. The phrase 'had all things in common' is also translated 'they shared everything they had' [CEV, NLT], 'they shared everything with each other' [GW], '(they) shared everything' [NCV], '(they) shared their belongings with one another' [TEV]. This adjective pertains to being in common between two or more persons [LN (89.118)] and the phrase 'to have in common' means 'to share with one another equitably' [LN (57.99)]. It pertains to being shared collectively [BDAG].

QUESTION—What is meant by the abstract statement that all the believers were in the same (place/fellowship)?

Some think it means they were in the same place, meaning that the believers lived together or regularly met together for fellowship. But some others think it is an idiom that refers to spiritual unity, so that they lived in harmony or fellowship with one another [TRT].

1. It refers to a spiritual unity, that is, they lived in harmony/close fellowship with one another, similar to 'fellowship' in v. 42 [NAC, NICNT, PNTC, TNTC, TRT], They remained near one another and they continued as one group [TH]. It emphasizes the unity of the new community [NICNT].
2. It means that the believers lived together or regularly met for fellowship together [TRT]. They met together in one place [Bar, BECNT; CEV, NLT].

QUESTION—What is meant by the statement 'they had all things in common'?

The expression 'had all things in common' in this verse and the way believers treat their properties in the following verse 45 bear the same point:

when people became believers, those who had money or owned property made some of it (an amount they decided) available to those who were in need. They shared belongings with one another but did not give up all of their wealth [Bar, NAC, NICNT, TH, TNTC, TRT]. They truly demonstrated a community of love and compassion [BECNT].

2:45 **And they-were-selling (their) properties^a and possessions^b and distributing the (proceeds) to-all, as anyone had need.**
LEXICON—a. κτῆμα (LN 57.15) (BDAG 1. p. 572): 'property' [Bar, BDAG, CBC, LN; CEV, GW, NASB, NET, NLT, REB, TEV], 'possession' [BDAG, BECNT, LN; ESV, KJV, NIV, NRSV], 'land' [AB; NCV]. This noun denotes something which is owned or possessed and may specifically refer to land [LN]. It denotes that which is acquired or possessed [BDAG].
  b. ὕπαρξις (LN 57.16) (BDAG 1. p. 1029): 'possession' [Bar, BDAG, CBC, LN; CEV, GW, NASB, NET, NLT, REB, TEV], 'property' [AB, LN], 'belongings' [ESV], 'goods' [BECNT; KJV, NIV, NRSV], 'things owned' [NCV]. This noun denotes that which constitutes someone's possession [LN]. It denotes that which one has [BDAG].
QUESTION—What is the distinction between the two terms 'property' and 'possessions'?
  'Properties' refer to real estate and land, while 'possessions' refer to personal property [AB, EBC, NICNT, PNTC, TH]. The two terms can be collectively translated as 'what they owned' or 'what belonged to them'. The last clause of v. 44 is a general statement and this verse is a more specific description of how they practically shared belongings with people among them who were in need [TH]. There is no evidence that the sharing of property was ever widely practiced in primitive Christianity. The Christians did as they willed, no one compelled them as each acted voluntarily [Bar, NICNT, PNTC, TNTC].

2:46 **And day-by-day continuing^a with-one-mind in the temple, and breaking^b bread from-house-to-house, they-were-taking their meals together with gladness^c and humbleness^d of-heart,**
LEXICON—a. pres. act. participle of προσκαρτερέω (LN 68.68) (BDAG 2.a. p. 881): 'to devote oneself to, to keep on, to persist in' [LN], 'to be engaged in, to be devoted to' [BDAG]. The phrase 'day by day, continuing with one mind in the temple' [NASB] is also translated 'day by day, attending the temple together' [ESV], 'day by day, as they spent much time together in the temple' [NRSV], 'day after day they met together in the temple' [CEV], 'day after day they met as a group in the Temple' [TEV], 'each day, attending the temple together' [BECNT], '(they) had a single purpose and went to the temple every day' [GW], 'continuing daily with one accord in the temple' [KJV], 'daily they continued together in the Temple' [Bar], 'every day they continued to meet together in the temple courts' [NIV], 'every day they continued to

gather together by common consent in the temple courts' [NET], 'the believers met together in the Temple every day' [NCV], 'they worshiped together at the Temple each day' [NLT], 'they continued to meet every day in the temple' [AB], 'one and all they kept up their daily attendance at the temple' [REB], 'with one mind they kept up their daily attendance at the temple' [CBC]. This verb means to continue to do something with intense effort, with the possible implication of doing so despite difficulty [LN]. It means to persist in something [BDAG].

b. κλάω (LN 23.20) (BDAG p. 546): 'to break' [BDAG, LN]. The phrase κλῶντές κατ' οἶκον ἄρτον 'breaking bread from house to house' [KJV, NET] is also translated 'breaking bread in their homes' [ESV, REB], 'broke bread in their homes' [NIV], 'broke bread together in different homes' [CEV], 'broke bread at home' [NRSV], 'had their meals together in their homes' [TEV], 'taking their meals together' [NASB], 'ate at each other's homes' [GW], 'ate together in their homes' [NCV], 'breaking bread at home (they took food with rejoicing…)' [Bar], 'breaking bread at home (they ate their meals with joy…)' [AB], 'breaking bread in private houses, (shared their meals with unaffected joy)' [CBC], 'breaking bread in their homes, (they were partaking of food with…)' [BECNT], 'met in homes for the Lord's Supper' [NLT]. The idiom 'to break bread' means to eat a meal without reference to any particular time of the day or to the type of food involved [LN]. This verb as used in the New Testament refers exclusively to breaking bread [BDAG].

c. ἀγαλλίασις (LN 25.132) (BDAG p. 4): 'extreme gladness, extreme joy,' [LN], 'exultation' [BDAG]. The phrase 'with gladness' [KJV, NASB] is also translated 'with glad (hearts)' [BECNT; ESV, NET, NIV, NRSV, TEV], 'with rejoicing' [Bar], 'with joy' [AB, CBC; REB], 'with great joy' [NLT], 'happily' [CEV], 'happy (to share)' [NCV], 'were joyful' [GW]. This noun denotes a state of intensive joy and gladness [LN].

d. ἀφελότης (LN 88.55) (BDAG p. 155): 'simplicity' [BDAG, LN], 'humbleness, humility' [LN]. The phrase 'humbleness of heart' is also translated 'simplicity of heart' [Bar, BDAG], 'simplicity' [AB], 'sincere hearts' [NIV], 'sincerity of heart' [NASB], 'humble hearts' [NET, TEV], 'grateful hearts' [BECNT], 'singleness of heart' [KJV], 'generous hearts' [ESV, NRSV], 'with generosity' [NLT], 'with joyful hearts' [NCV], 'with unaffected (joy)' [CBC; REB], 'were humble' [GW], 'freely' [CEV]. This noun denotes a humility that is associated with a simplicity of life [LN].

QUESTION—What did the believers do day by day?

The expression 'day by day' means every day. Being at the beginning of the first sentence (vv. 46–47a), it is in the emphatic position and it is repeated in v. 47b. Day by day, the believers were together in the temple. Regular attendance at the temple reflects Jewish practice for those in Jerusalem. Nothing about this is seen as unusual for Jewish believers in Jesus, and it was there they bore their witness. Their fellowship extends beyond the temple as, they shared meals at each other's home with joy and sincerity [BECNT, EBC, NAC].

QUESTION—What does τῷ ἱερῷ 'the temple' refer to?
In this context 'temple' refers to all the buildings and courts area that made up the entire temple complex [TRT]. 'Temple' in many languages is the 'house of God' or 'holy place' [TH].

QUESTION—What is meant by κλῶντές...ἄρτον 'breaking bread'?
1. This refers to having meals [AB, Bar, BECNT, CBC, EBC, NAC, NICNT, TH; GW, NASB, NCV, TEV, and probably CEV, ESV, KJV, NET, NIV, REB]. Since there is no article to refer to '*the* breaking of bread', it refers to their communal living which included eating regular meals together [TH]. It is only a reference to regular meals with no special meaning to the meals. [BECNT]. The common meal could not conveniently be eaten in the temple precincts so they ate by households [NICNT]. It means they shared a common meal together, but it probably included the Lord's Supper as well [NAC, TNTC].
2. This has the same meaning that τῇ κλάσει τοῦ ἄρτου 'the breaking of the bread' has in v. 42 and refers to the Lord's Supper [PNTC; NLT], or to the Agape/Love Meal that was followed by the Lord's Supper [PNTC].

2:47 praising God and having favor[a] with all the people. And the Lord was-adding to their number day-by-day those who were-being-saved.

LEXICON—a. χάρις (LN 25.89) (BDAG 2.a. p. 1079): 'favor' [Bar, BDAG, BECNT, CBC, LN; ESV, KJV, NASB, NIV, REB], 'good will' [BDAG, LN; GW, NET, NLT, NRSV, TEV], 'grace, gracious care, help' [BDAG]. The phrase 'having favor with all the people' is also translated 'everyone liked them' [CEV], 'were liked by all the people' [NCV], 'were well liked by all the people' [AB]. This noun denotes a favorable attitude toward someone or something [LN]. It denotes a beneficent disposition toward someone [BDAG].

QUESTION—Who does ὁ κύριος 'the Lord' refer to?
1. This refers to the 'Lord God' [AB, Bar, BECNT, NAC]. It is the 'Lord God' who calls people to himself in v. 39, so it is the Lord God who adds to his community [BECNT].
2. This refers to the 'Lord Jesus' [PNTC, TH].
3. Although most people think it refers to the Lord Jesus, God is mentioned in verses 33 and 47, so 'the Lord God' also fits the context. It is best to leave it 'the Lord' if possible [TRT].

QUESTION—What does the expression 'having favor with all the people' imply?
'All the people' indicates people outside the community of believers. The expression 'having favor with all the people' implies that others are appreciative of this new community. The believers enjoyed great popular goodwill from outsiders. Their reputation with outsiders is good and that

brings positive impacts to their witnesses [BECNT, NAC, NICNT, PNTC, TNTC].

QUESTION—What did the Lord do day by day?
Corresponding to what the believers did day by day, the Lord added the number of believers to the group day by day [TRT]. The Lord himself was continuing to draw people/call the saved into the fellowship of the redeemed community [Bar, EBC, NAC, NICNT, PNTC, TNTC]. The Lord was saving people from eternal punishment for their sins [TRT].

DISCOURSE UNIT—3:1–5:42 [NAC, TNTC]. The topic is the apostles' witness to the Jews in Jerusalem [NAC], the church and the Jewish authorities [TNTC].

DISCOURSE UNIT—3:1–4:31 [NICNT]. The topic is an act of healing and its consequences.

DISCOURSE UNIT—3:1–26 [EBC, PNTC; GW]. The topic is a crippled beggar healed [EBC], a lame man is healed [GW], a particular sign of the Messianic restoration [PNTC].

DISCOURSE UNIT—3:1–11 [NAC; NLT]. The topic is Peter heals a crippled beggar [NLT], Peter's healing a lame beggar [NAC].

DISCOURSE UNIT—3:1–10 [AB, Bar, BECNT, CBC, EBC, NICNT, PNTC, TNTC; CEV, ESV, NASB, NCV, NET, NIV, NRSV, TEV]. The topic is Peter and John heal a lame man [CEV], Peter and John heal a lame man at the temple [NET], Peter heals a crippled man [NCV], Peter heals the/a crippled beggar [NIV, NRSV], a cripple cured [NICNT], the healing of the/a lame man [BECNT, TNTC], healing the lame beggar [NASB], 'healing in the name of Jesus [AB, PNTC], a lame beggar is healed [TEV], the lame beggar healed [ESV], the healing [EBC], at the beautiful gate [CBC], temple miracle [Bar].

3:1 Now Peter and John were-going-up to the temple at the hour of-prayer, the ninth[a] hour. **3:2** And a man lame[b] from his mother's womb[c] was-being-carried, whom they-would-put every day at the gate of-the temple that is-called Beautiful (Gate) to-ask-for alms[d] from those entering the temple.

LEXICON—a. ἔνατος (LN 60.56) (BDAG p. 331): 'ninth' [AB, Bar, BDAG, BECNT; ESV, KJV, NASB]. The phrase 'the ninth hour' is also translated 'at three o'clock' [NCV], 'at three o'clock/three in the afternoon' [CBC; CEV, NET, NIV, NRSV, REB, TEV]. The phrase 'at the hour of prayer, the ninth hour' is also translated 'to take part in the three o'clock prayer service' [NLT], 'for the three o'clock prayer' [GW]. The adjective 'ninth' refers to 'the ninth hour' or 'three o'clock in the afternoon [LN]. It denotes the time for prayer [BDAG].

b. χωλός (LN 23.175) (BDAG p. 1093): 'lame' [Bar, BDAG, BECNT, LN; all versions except NCV, NIV, REB], 'crippled' [AB, BDAG; NCV, NIV]. The phrase 'a man lame from his mother's womb' is also translated 'a man who had been a cripple from birth' [CBC; REB]. This adjective describes someone who has a disability in one or more limbs, especially the leg or foot, often as the result of some deformity [LN].

c. κοιλία (LN 8.69) (BDAG 2. p. 550): 'womb' [BDAG, LN]. The phrase 'from his mother's womb' [AB, Bar, BECNT; KJV, NASB] is also translated 'from birth' [CBC; ESV, GW, NET, NIV. NLT, NRSV. REB], '(who) had been born lame' [CEV], 'from earliest youth' [BDAG], 'all his life' [NCV, TEV]. This noun denotes the womb [BDAG, LN].

d. ἐλεημοσύνη (LN 57.112) (BDAG 2. p. 316): 'alms' [BDAG], 'gift, money given to the needy, charity donation' [LN]. The phrase 'to ask for alms' [BECNT; NRSV], is also translated 'to beg alms' [AB; NASB], 'asked for alms' [REB], 'to ask alms' [Bar; KJV], 'asked to receive alms' [ESV], 'beg for money' [NCV, NET, TEV], 'begged for donations' [LN], 'beg for handouts' [GW], 'begged (from the people)' [CEV], 'to beg' [CBC; NIV, NLT]. This noun denotes that which is given to the needy. In some languages the closest equivalent of this word is simply 'money' [LN]. It denotes that which is benevolently given to meet a need [BDAG].

QUESTION—What time is 'the ninth hour' of the day?

The ninth hour was at three o'clock in the afternoon, the time for the second daily hour of prayer [AB, Bar, BECNT, CBC, EBC, NAC, NICNT, PNTC, TH, TNTC, TRT]. There were public sacrifices at the temple twice a day, at nine in the morning and three in the afternoon, each being accompanied by public prayer [BECNT, EBC, NAC, NICNT, TH, TNTC, TRT].

QUESTION—What does 'lame from his mother's womb' mean?

It means that the man was born lame. Never in his entire life had he stood on his own two feet unaided [AB, EBC, NAC, NICNT, PNTC, TH, TNTC]. 'Lame' refers specifically to people who cannot walk or who have difficulty walking [TRT]. It does not refer to a complete paralysis but to damage to feet, ankles, knees, or hips that left the man crippled but not completely paralyzed [BECNT].

QUESTION—Why was this beggar placed at this door of the temple?

This door was a gate that separated the outer court of the Gentiles from the inner courts where only the Jews were allowed. The first of the inner courts was the Women's Court where Jews, both men and women, held public assemblies [Bar, BECNT, CBC, EBC, NAC, NICNT, PNTC, TNTC, TRT].

3:3 Seeing Peter and John about to-go into the temple, he-asked to-receive alms. **3:4** But Peter, looking-intently[a] at him, as did John, said, "Look at us." **3:5** And he-fixed-his-attention[b] on-them, expecting to-receive[c] something from them.

LEXICON—a. aorist act. participle of ἀτενίζω (LN 24.49) (BDAG p. 148): 'to look intently at someone' [BDAG; NLT, NRSV], 'to look straight at' [LN; CEV, NCV, NIV, TEV], 'to gaze at' [BECNT], 'to gaze intently at' [AB], 'to direct one's gaze at' [ESV], 'to fix one's gaze upon/on' [Bar; NASB], 'to fix one's eyes on' [CBC; REB], 'to stare at' [BDAG, LN; GW], 'to keep one's eyes fixed on' [LN], 'to fasten one's eyes upon'

[KJV], 'to look directly at' [NET]. This verb means to fix one's eyes on some object continually and intensely [LN]. It means to look intently at, to stare at someone [BDAG].
b. imperf. act. indic. of ἐπέχω (LN 24.33) (BDAG 2. p. 362): 'to fix one's attention' [BDAG; ESV, NRSV], 'to pay attention' [Bar; NET], 'to give attention' [NASB, NIV], 'to fix one's gaze upon' [BECNT], 'to look straight at' [NCV], 'to look earnestly at' [AB], 'to look at eagerly' [NLT], 'to look at' [TEV], 'to stare at' [CEV], 'to watch closely' [GW], 'to give heed unto' [KJV], 'to notice, to watch' [LN]. The phrase 'he fixed his attention on them' is also translated 'the man was all attention' [CBC; REB]. This verb means to direct one's attention to a particular object or event [LN]. It means to be mindful of or especially observant [BDAG].
c. aorist act. infin. of λαμβάνω (LN 57.125) (BDAG 10.c. p. 584): 'to receive' [AB, Bar, BDAG, BECNT, LN; ESV, GW, KJV, NASB, NET, NRSV], 'to get' [BDAG; CEV, NIV, TEV], 'to obtain' [BDAG], 'to accept' [LN]. The phrase 'expecting to receive something from them' is also translated 'thinking they were going to give him some money' [NCV], 'expecting some money' [NLT], 'expecting a gift from them' [CBC; REB]. This verb means to receive or accept an object or benefit for which the initiative rests with the giver, but the focus of attention in the transfer is upon the receiver [LN].

QUESTION—Was it common to ask for alms at the temple gate?

The giving of alms in Old Testament Israel and in New Testament Christianity was a practice expected by God of his people. Giving alms was a responsibility that Judaism took seriously as an expression of compassion that God honored [BECNT]. It was a meritorious act [EBC, TNTC]. The three pillars for the Jewish faith were the Torah, worship, and the showing of kindness or charity. Almsgiving was one of the main ways to show kindness and was thus considered a major expression of one's devotion to God [NAC].

QUESTION—Why did Peter tell the lame man to look at them?

Peter wanted to have eye contact with the man in order to have his full attention [BECNT, NICNT]. They wanted him to listen carefully to what they would say to him [PNTC].

QUESTION—How did the lame man respond to Peter?

The lame man did listen to Peter and turned his attention to them in the hope of receiving financial help from them [BECNT, NICNT, PNTC].

3:6 And-then Peter said, "Silver and gold is- not -possessed[a] by-me, but what I-do-have, this I-give to-you. In the name of-Jesus Christ the Nazarene, get-up and walk."

LEXICON—a. pres. act. indic. of ὑπάρχω (LN 57.2) (BDAG 1. p. 1029): 'to belong to' [LN], 'to be at one's disposal' [BDAG]. The clause 'Silver and gold is not possessed by me' is also translated 'Silver and gold I do not possess' [Bar], 'Silver and gold I do not have' [BECNT], 'Silver and gold have I none' [KJV], 'Silver or gold I do not have' [NIV] 'I don't have any silver or gold' [CEV, NCV, NLT], 'I don't possess silver and gold' [NASB], 'I have no silver and/or gold' [AB, CBC; ESV, NET, NRSV, REB], 'I don't have any money' [GW], 'I have no money at all' [TEV]. This verb means to belong to someone [LN]. It means to be at one's disposal [BDAG].

QUESTION—What is it that Peter did not have?

'Silver and gold' was a common expression that was especially used for a great deal of money, so Peter meant that he had no money and therefore alms were not possible [Bar, BECNT, TNTC, TH].

QUESTION—What did Peter have and give to the lame man?

Peter did have something he could give to the lame man, the gift of healing, the power to walk, through Jesus Christ the Nazarene. He used his given power and in the name of Jesus Christ, he told the man to get up and walk [BECNT, NAC, NICNT, TNTC]. 'In the name of' is a frequently occurring biblical phrase meaning 'by the authority or power of the person whose name is mentioned' [NAC, TH]. 'In the name of Jesus Christ' represents Jesus' divine authority and continuing power to grant the blessings of salvation [EBC, PNTC, TNTC]; in the authority of Jesus' still active messianic person [BECNT].

3:7 And, having-grasped[a] him by-the right hand, he-raised- him -up.[b] And immediately his feet and ankles were-made-strong.[c]

LEXICON—a. aorist act. participle of πιάζω (LN 18.3) (BDAG 1. p. 812): 'to grasp' [BDAG, CBC; REB], 'to grasp firmly' [LN], 'to take hold of' [BDAG, LN; GW, NET], 'to take firm hold of' [BDAG], 'to seize' [AB, BDAG, LN; NASB], 'to take' [Bar, BECNT; CEV, ESV, KJV, NCV, NIV, NLT, NRSV, TEV]. This verb means 'to take hold of firmly with a considerable measure of force' [LN].

b. aorist act. indic. of ἐγείρω (LN 17.10) (BDAG 3. p. 271): 'to raise up' [AB, Bar, BECNT; ESV, NASB, NET, NRSV], 'to raise, to help to rise' [BDAG], 'to cause to stand up, to get up' [LN], 'to help up' [CEV, GW, NIV, NLT, REB, TEV], 'to lift up' [KJV, NCV], 'to pull up' [CBC]. This verb means 'to cause to stand up, with a possible implication of some previous incapacity' [LN]. It means to cause to stand up from a position lower than that of the person rendering assistance [BDAG].

c. aorist pass. indic. of στερεόω (LN 79.67) (BDAG 1. p. 943): 'to be made strong' [ESV, NET, NRSV], 'to be made sound' [Bar], 'to become strong' [BDAG, LN; CEV, GW, NCV, NIV, TEV], 'to be strengthened' [AB, BDAG, BECNT; NASB], 'to receive strength' [KJV], 'to grow strong' [CBC; REB]. The phrase 'immediately his feet and ankles were made strong' is also translated 'the man's feet and ankles were instantly healed and strengthened' [NLT]. This verb means to be physically strong and vigorous [LN]. It means to make physically firm [BDAG].

QUESTION—What do all the 'he', 'his' and 'him' words in this verse represent?
This verse re-written with all the 'he', 'his' and 'him' words clarified in brackets reads: And, having grasped him (the lame man) by the right hand, he (Peter) raised him (the lame man) up. And immediately his (the lame man's) feet and ankles were made strong. This is made quite clear in English by some translations: 'Then Peter took the lame man by the right hand and helped him up. And as he did, the man's feet and ankles were instantly healed and strengthened' (NLT), 'Then Peter took hold of him by the right hand and raised him up, and at once the man's feet and ankles were made strong'. (NET).

QUESTION—Why did Peter grasp the man's hand?
It was a friendly gesture that Peter grabbed the man's hand to help him stand up from a sitting position [TH, TRT]. He grabbed the man's right hand which perhaps had been extended expecting alms [BECNT].

3:8 **And, leaping-up,ᵃ he-stood and began-to-walk, and he-entered the temple with them, walking and leapingᵇ and praising God.**

LEXICON—a. pres. mid./pass. (deponent = act.) participle of ἐξάλλομαι (LN 15.240) (BDAG 2. p. 345): 'to leap up' [AB, Bar, BDAG, BECNT, LN; ESV, KJV], 'to jump up' [LN; CEV, NCV, NET, NLT, NRSV, TEV]. The phrase 'leaping up, he stood' is also translated 'he leaped/leapt up and stood' [AB, Bar], 'with a leap he stood upright' [NASB], 'he jumped to his feet' [NIV], 'springing to his feet, he stood up' [GW], 'he sprang up, stood on his feet' [CBC], 'he sprang to his feet' [REB]. This verb means to leap up to a standing position [BDAG, LN].
  b. pres. mid./pass. (deponent = act.) participle of ἅλλομαι (LN 15.238) (BDAG 1. p. 46): 'to leap' [AB, Bar, BDAG, BECNT, CBC, LN; ESV, KJV, NASB, NET, NLT, NRSV, REB], 'to jump' [LN; CEV, GW, NCV, NIV, TEV], 'to spring up' [BDAG]. This verb means to leap or to jump into the air [LN]. It means to make a quick leaping movement. He was showing by slow and fast movements that he was really healed [BDAG].

QUESTION—What had happened to the lame man?
A miracle had happened, the lame man had been healed instantly. He was not only able to stand, but also able to walk and leap into the air. He was filled with joy and praising God [AB, EBC, NICNT, PNTC, TNTC]. Not only had he received physical healing, but he has found spiritual acceptance as well. For the first time he was deemed worthy to enter the house of worship [NAC]. 'Praising God' does not mean that the healed man has yet identified Jesus as the one who has healed him, but Peter's words were clearly designed to help him and all those standing by to make that connection and to acknowledge Jesus as Messiah and Lord [PNTC, TNTC]. The now healed man knew that God had been at work through Jesus [BECNT]. In some languages, an expression such as praising God must be

put into direct discourse, for example, 'he said, God is wonderful' or 'he declared, how great God is!' [TH].

3:9 And all the people saw him walking and praising God. **3:10** And they-recognized[a] him as the-one- who-sat at the Beautiful Gate of-the temple, (asking) for alms. And they-were-filled with-wonder[b] and amazement[c] at what had-happened to-him.

LEXICON—a. imperf. act. indic. of ἐπιγινώσκω (LN 27.61) (BDAG 3. p. 369]: 'to recognize' [AB, Bar, BDAG, BECNT, CBC, LN; ESV, NCV, NET, NIV, NRSV, REB, TEV], 'to realize' [NLT], 'to know' [CEV, GW, KJV], 'to take note of' [NASB]. This verb means to identify newly acquired information with what had been previously learned or known [LN]. It means to connect present information or awareness with what was known before [BDAG].
- b. θάμβος (LN 25.208) (BDAG p. 442): 'wonder' [AB, Bar, BECNT, CBC; ESV, KJV, NASB, NIV, NRSV, REB], 'astonishment' [BDAG; NET], 'amazement' [BDAG]. It is also translated as a verb phrase: 'they were amazed' [GW, NCV], 'they were completely surprised' [CEV], 'they were all surprised' [TEV], 'they were absolutely astounded' [NLT]. This noun denotes a state of astonishment at such an unusual event [BDAG, LN].
- c. ἔκστασις (LN 25.217) (BDAG 1. p. 309): 'amazement' [AB, BDAG, BECNT, CBC, LN; ESV, KJV, NASB, NET, NIV, NLT, NRSV, REB], 'astonishment' [Bar, BDAG, LN], 'distraction, confusion, terror' [BDAG]. It is also translated as a verb phrase: 'they were amazed' [TEV], 'they wondered (how his could happen)' [NCV], 'they were stunned to see' [GW], 'they could not imagine' [CEV]. This noun denotes a state of intense amazement, to the point of being beside oneself with astonishment [LN]. It denotes a state of consternation or profound emotional experience to the point of being beside oneself [BDAG].

QUESTION—Who were 'all the people' who saw him walking and praising God?

They were the people in the temple complex who well knew this lame man, who had been daily carried to the temple gate and had asked them for alms [BECNT, NICNT, TH]. 'All the people' indicates a widespread reaction, perhaps including those who were not initially present for the healing [PNTC].

QUESTION—What was the reaction of the people when they saw the former lame man healed and walking?

They were filled with wonder and amazement [AB, Bar, EBC, PNTC]. Such a response is often noted at the end of miracle stories, without suggesting that the observers believed in Jesus [PNTC, TNTC]. 'Filled with wonder and amazement' is a parallelism, that is, it expresses the same idea in two different ways in order to increase its prominence/importance. If it is possible and natural, a translation should keep both parts of the parallelism [TRT].

DISCOURSE UNIT—3:11–26 [AB, Bar, BECNT, CBC, EBC, NICNT, PNTC, TNTC; CEV, ESV, NASB, NCV, NET, NIV, NRSV, TEV]. The topic is Peter's miracle speech [Bar], Peter's second sermon [NASB], Peter's address in Solomon's Colonnade [NICNT], Peter speaks in Solomon's portico [ESV, NRSV], Peter speaks in the temple [CEV], Peter's sermon in Solomon's Colonnade [EBC], Peter's message in the temple [TEV], Peter's interpretation of the sign [PNTC], Peter's explanation of the miracle of healing [AB], Peter speaks to the people [NCV], Peter speaks to the onlookers [NIV], Peter addresses the crowd [NET], Peter preaches Jesus from Torah and promise [BECNT], Peter explains the incident [TNTC], the meaning of the sign [CBC].

3:11 (While)- he -was-holding-onto[a] Peter and John, all the people, utterly-astonished,[b] ran-together[c] to them in the portico,[d] the-one called Solomon's (Portico).

LEXICON—a. pres. act. participle of κρατέω (LN 18.6) (BDAG 2.a. p. 564): 'to hold on to' [Bar, BECNT, LN; CEV, NCV, NIV, TEV], 'to hold' [BDAG; KJV], 'to cling to' [AB; ESV, NASB, NRSV, REB], 'to hang on to' [NET], 'to hold tightly to' [NLT], 'to clutch' [CBC], 'to retain in the hand, to seize' [LN]. The phrase 'while he was holding onto Peter and John' is also translated 'the man wouldn't let go of Peter and John' [GW]. This verb means to hold on to something [LN]. It means to hold someone fast with the hand so that person cannot get away [BDAG].
  b. ἔκθαμβος (LN 25.211) (BDAG p. 303): 'utterly astonished' [BDAG, LN; NRSV], 'astonished' [NIV], 'utterly astounded' [ESV], 'astounded' [LN], 'completely astounded' [NET], 'greatly wondering' [KJV], 'filled with wonder' [AB], 'amazed' [LN; NCV, TEV], 'completely amazed' [BECNT], 'alarmed' [LN], 'excited' [GW], 'in astonishment' [CBC; REB], 'in amazement' [CEV, NLT], 'full of amazement' [Bar; NASB]. This adjective describes someone who is amazed or alarmed [LN]. It means to be greatly astonished [BDAG].
  c. aorist act. indic. of συντρέχω (LN 15.133) (BDAG 1. p. 976): 'to run together' [Bar, BDAG, BECNT, LN; ESV, KJV, NASB, NET, NRSV], 'to rush together, to assemble quickly' [LN], 'to run' [CEV, GW, TEV, NCV], 'to come running' [CBC; NIV, REB], 'to come running and surround' [AB], 'to rush out' [NLT]. This verb means to come together quickly to form a crowd [LN]. It means to run together to a place and gather there [BDAG].
  d. στοά (LN 7.40) (BDAG p. 946): 'portico' [BDAG, LN]. The phrase 'the portico, the one called Solomon's' is also translated 'the portico called Solomon's' [ESV], 'the portico that was called Solomon's' [BECNT], 'the portico called Solomon's Portico' [Bar; NRSV], 'the so-called portico of Solomon' [NASB], 'Solomon's Portico, as it is called' [REB], 'Solomon's Cloister, as it is called' [CBC], 'the porch that is called

Solomon's' [KJV], 'Solomon's Porch, as it was called' [TEV], 'Solomon's Porch' [NCV], 'the place known-as/called Solomon's Porch' [CEV, GW], 'the place called Solomon's Colonnade' [NIV], 'Solomon's Colonnade'[NLT], 'the colonnade called Solomon's' [AB], 'the covered walkway called Solomon's Portico' [NET]. This noun denotes a covered colonnade, open normally on one side, where people could stand, sit, or walk, protected from the weather and the heat of the sun. In many parts of the world the closest equivalent would be a veranda, an extensive type of porch. Such a porch may be described as 'a long outside room' or 'a room made with pillars and open'. In some areas where there is no construction which is parallel to this type of colonnade, one can use a more general term such as 'a long shelter' or 'a roofed-over shelter'. In many areas such a shelter is constructed for special festivities and therefore the name of this type of even temporary construction can probably be employed as the closest natural equivalent [TH]. It is a roofed colonnade that is normally open on one side [BDAG]

QUESTION—Where was Solomon's portico?

Solomon's portico was situated in the eastern part of the temple buildings/area [AB, CBC, NICNT]. It was a covered portico that ran the entire length of the eastern portion of the outer court of the temple known as the court of Gentiles [BECNT, EBC, NAC, PNTC, TNTC].

QUESTION—Why was the healed man holding onto Peter and John?

This man had been healed so he was not holding onto Peter and John because he needed their physical support to stand. After walking, leaping and praising God, he came back to hold onto Peter and John at Solomon's Portico to show the utterly astonished people who healed him [BECNT]. He had attached himself enthusiastically to the men who had brought such a dramatic change into his life [PNTC] and he did not want not to let his two benefactors get away [EBC, NICNT, TNTC].

DISCOURSE UNIT—3:12–26 [NAC; NLT]. The topic is Peter's sermon from Solomon's Colonnade [NAC], Peter preaches in the temple [NLT].

3:12 **And when Peter saw-(this), he addressed[a] the people, "Men, Israelites, why are-you-amazed[b] at this, or why are-you-staring[c] at-us as-(though) by-our-own power[d] or piety[e] we-have-made him walk?**

LEXICON—a. aorist mid. (deponent = act.) indic. of ἀποκρίνομαι (LN 33.28) (BDAG 1. p. 113): 'to address' [Bar; ESV, NLT, NRSV], 'to say' [LN; CEV, GW, NCV, NIV, REB], 'to speak' [AB; LN], 'to declare' [LN; NET], 'to reply' [BDAG; NASB], 'to answer' [BDAG; KJV], 'to respond' [BECNT]. The phrase 'when Peter saw this, he addressed the people' is also translated 'Peter saw them coming and met them with these words' [CBC; REB]. This verb means to introduce or continue a somewhat formal discourse [LN].

b. pres. act. indic. of θαυμάζω (LN 25.213) (BDAG 1.a.β. p. 444): 'to be amazed' [BECNT, LN; GW, NASB, NET], 'to be astonished' [Bar,

BDAG], 'to be surprised' [CBC; CEV, NCV, REB, TEV], 'to marvel' [AB, BDAG, LN; KJV], 'to wonder' [BDAG, LN; ESV, NRSV]. The phrase 'why are you amazed at this' is also translated 'why does this surprise you' [NIV], 'what is so surprising about this' [NLT]. This verb means to wonder or marvel at some event or object [LN]. It means to be extraordinarily impressed by something, and here it means to wonder to oneself [BDAG].

c. pres. act. indic. of ἀτενίζω (LN 24.49) (BDAG p. 148): 'to stare at' [AB, BDAG, CBC, LN; all versions except KJV, NASB, NCV], 'to look straight at, to keep one's eyes fixed on' [LN], 'to look intently at' [BDAG], 'to look earnestly on' [KJV], 'to gaze at' [Bar, BECNT; NASB]. The phrase 'why are you staring at us as if by our own power or piety we have made him walk' is also translated 'you are looking at us as if it were our own power or goodness that made this man walk' [NCV]. This verb means to fix one's eyes on some object continually and intensely [LN].

d. δύναμις (LN 76.1) (BDAG 1.a. p. 262): 'power' [AB, Bar, BDAG, BECNT, CBC, LN; all versions], 'might, strength, force' [BDAG]. This noun denotes the potentiality to exert force in performing some function [LN]. It refers to a power provided by one's own capability [BDAG].

e. εὐσέβεια (LN 53.5) (BDAG p. 412): 'piety' [Bar, BDAG, BECNT, LN; ESV, NASB, NET, NRSV], 'godliness' [CBC, LN; NIV, NLT, REB, TEV], 'godly life' [GW], 'holiness' [AB; KJV], 'goodness' [NCV]. The phrase 'by our own...piety' is also translated 'because we are so religious' [CEV]. This noun denotes behavior reflecting correct religious beliefs and attitudes [LN]. It refers to an awesome respect accorded to God [BDAG].

QUESTION—Who are the people that Peter addressed as 'Men, Israelites'?

This expression is a means of identifying Peter with those to whom he speaks, and it includes both men and women [PNTC, TH]. In some languages this is simply equivalent to 'fellow tribesmen' or even 'my relatives' if this involves the extended ethnic unit [TH].

QUESTION—Why did Peter ask this question?

Peter had raised a question about the power behind the man's healing. He wanted to make it clear that it was not by Peter and John's own power and piety that this miracle had occurred [Bar, BECNT, NAC, NICNT]. Peter wanted to deflect attention from himself and John by identifying the risen Lord as the one responsible for the healing miracle [PNTC, TNTC]. It was not by their own power that the lame man was walking, nor was it due to mere piety that caused God to act [BECNT, NAC].

3:13 The God of-Abraham, the God of-Isaac, and the God of-Jacob, the God of our fathers, glorified[a] his servant[b] Jesus, whom you delivered[c] and disowned[d] in (the)-presence of-Pilate, when he-had-decided to-release[e] that one.

LEXICON—a. aorist act. indic. of δοξάζω (LN 87.24) (BDAG 2. p. 258): 'to glorify' [AB, Bar, BDAG, BECNT, LN; ESV, GW, KJV, NASB, NET, NIV, NRSV], 'to make gloriously great' [LN], 'to give glory to' [NCV], 'to bring glory to' [NLT], 'to give divine glory to' [TEV], 'to bring honor to' [CEV], 'to give the highest honor to' [CBC; REB]. This verb means to cause someone to have glorious greatness [LN]. It means to cause someone to have a splendid greatness, and here it is the glory that comes in the next life [BDAG].

b. παῖς (LN 87.77) (BDAG 3.b.γ. p. 750): 'servant' [AB, BDAG, BECNT, CBC; all versions except CEV, KJV, TEV], 'Servant' [Bar; TEV], 'slave' [BDAG, LN], 'Son' [CEV, KJV]. This noun denotes 'a slave, possibly serving as a personal servant and thus with the implication of kindly regard' [LN]. It denotes one who is committed in total obedience to another, and here it refers to Christ's special relationship to God [BDAG].

c. aorist act. indic. of παραδίδωμι (LN 37.111) (BDAG 1.b. p. 762): 'to deliver over' [ESV], 'to deliver up' [KJV], 'to deliver' [BDAG; NASB], 'to hand over' [AB, Bar, BDAG, BECNT, LN; GW, NCV, NET, NIV, NLT, NRSV, REB, TEV], 'to turn over' [BDAG, LN], 'to betray' [LN; CEV], 'to commit' [CBC], 'to give up a person' [BDAG]. This verb means to deliver a person into the control of someone else, involving either the handing over of a presumably guilty person for punishment by the authorities or the handing over of an individual to an enemy who will presumably take undue advantage of the victim [LN]. It means to hand over, turn over, give up a person to the police and court [BDAG].

d. aorist mid. (deponent = act.) indic. of ἀρνέομαι (LN 33.277) (BDAG 3.b. p. 132): 'to disown' [BDAG; NASB, NIV, REB], 'to deny' [Bar, BDAG, BECNT, LN; ESV, KJV], 'to repudiate' [AB, BDAG, CBC], 'to reject' [GW, NET, NLT, NRSV, TEV], 'to turn against' [CEV], 'to not want' [NCV]. This verb means to say that one does not know about or is in any way related to a person or event [LN]. It refers to repudiating Christ by disclaiming any association with him [BDAG].

e. pres. act. infin. of ἀπολύω (LN 37.127) (BDAG 1. p. 117): 'to release' [AB, Bar, BDAG, BECNT, CBC, LN; ESV, NASB, NET, NLT, NRSV, REB], 'to set free' [BDAG, LN; CEV, TEV], 'to let go' [KJV, NIV], 'to let go free' [GW, NCV], 'to pardon' [BDAG]. This verb means to release from one's control [LN]. It is a legal term that refers to granting an acquittal to a prisoner' [BDAG].

QUESTION—How many Gods are referred to here?

It is important to translate in a way that there is only one God mentioned, not four different ones. Abraham, Isaac, Jacob and the fathers, all the Jewish ancestors worshipped the same God [TRT]. The God of Abraham, Isaac and Jacob is a phrase which goes back to Exodus 3:6, 15 [AB, PNTC, TH]. It is a familiar Old Testament way of addressing God as the God of those men who were the founders of the Jewish nation [TH]. When Peter said the God of our fathers, he identified himself as a member of the nation [BECNT]. To avoid the suggestion that there were four or five gods some translate this as 'The God of Abraham, Isaac, and Jacob, the God of our fathers/forefathers/ancestors' [AB, CBC, similarly Bar; NASB, NCV, NET, NIV, NLT, REB, TEV].

QUESTION—Why did Peter refer to Jesus as God's servant?

Peter directed the people to turn their eyes onto God. He told them that God had glorified his servant Jesus in this miraculous act. Peter has identified Jesus as the promised Messiah whom the prophet Isaiah described as the servant of the Lord in Isaiah 42:1, 49:6, 52:13 and 53:11 [AB, Bar, BECNT, CBC, EBC, PNTC, TNTC, TRT]. In the Greek Septuagint translation of Isaiah 52:13 and other related passages 'the servant of the Lord' was a Jewish Messianic title [TH]. The concept of a suffering servant is prominent throughout the NT and in verses 3:13 and 26 the emphasis is on the election of Christ as servant. God has chosen him, sent him, and exalted him, yet these Jews have rejected God's chosen servant [NAC].

QUESTION—In what way did God glorify his servant?

There is not enough of the specific involvement of Jesus for the reader to understand just how Jesus is glorified. The concept of giving glory to him could be stated 'caused him to be very important' or 'caused people to look at Jesus as being very great' [TH]. Many think that God glorified Jesus by raising him from the dead and taking him to heaven [TRT].

QUESTION—Who was 'that one' whom Pilate had wanted to release?

It refers to Jesus, whom Pilate originally intended to release because he could find no fault in Jesus [NAC, NICNT, PNTC, TH, TNTC, TRT]. Pilate, the Roman governor of Judea was therefore reluctant to condemn and execute Jesus [Bar].

3:14 And you rejected[a] the Holy[b] and Righteous-One, and asked-for (a)-man, (a)-murderer, to-be-granted[c] to-you.

LEXICON—a. aorist mid. (deponent = act.) indic. of ἀρνέομαι (LN 33.277) (BDAG 3.b. p. 132): 'to reject' [CEV, GW, NET, NLT, NRSV, TEV], 'to disown [BDAG; NASB, NIV, REB], 'to not want' [NCV], 'to repudiate' [AB, BDAG, CBC], 'to deny' [BDAG, Bar, BECNT, LN; ESV, KJV]. This verb means to say that one does not know about or is in any way related to a person or event [LN]. It means to disclaim association with a person or event [BDAG].

b. ἅγιος (LN 88.24) (BDAG 2.c.β. p. 11): 'holy, pure, divine' [LN], 'the holy (person) [BDAG]. The phrase 'the holy and righteous one' [AB, Bar; REB] is also translated 'the one who was holy and righteous' [CBC], 'the One who is holy and good' [NCV], 'Jesus, who was holy and good'

[CEV], 'the man who was holy and innocent' [GW], 'this holy, righteous one' [NLT], 'he was holy and good' [TEV]. Some translate this as a title: 'the Holy and Righteous One' [BECNT; ESV, NASB, NET, NIV, NRSV], 'the Holy One and the Just' [KJV]. This adjective describes one who is holy in the sense of superior moral qualities and possessing certain essentially divine qualities in contrast with what is human [LN]. In this verse it is used as a substantive and refers to Christ [BDAG].

c. aorist pass. infin. of χαρίζομαι (LN 37.30) (BDAG 1. p. 1078): 'to be handed over to someone, to be put into the control of someone' [LN], 'to be given freely' [BDAG]. The phrase 'asked for a man, a murderer, to be granted to you' is also translated 'asked for a murderer to be granted to you' [NASB], 'asked for a murderer to be given to you' [BECNT], 'asked to have a murderer given to you' [GW], 'desired a murderer to be granted unto you' [KJV], 'asked that a murderer be released to you' [ESV, NIV], 'asked that a man who was a murderer be released to you' [NET], 'asked that a man who was a murderer should be granted you as a favor' [Bar], 'demanded that a murderer should be released to you' [AB], 'demanded the release of a murderer' [NLT], 'asked for a murderer to be set free' [CEV], 'asked Pilate to give you a murderer' [NCV], 'asked to have a murderer given to you' [NRSV], 'asked for the reprieve of a murderer' [REB], 'asked Pilate to do you the favor of turning loose a murderer' [TEV], 'begged as a favor the release of a murderer' [CBC]. This verb means to hand someone over into the control of another person without some reasonable cause [LN]. It means to give freely as a favor. Here the one who is 'given' escapes death or further imprisonment by being handed over to those who wish to have him freed [BDAG].

QUESTION—What did Peter try to communicate to the people?

Peter further told the people that the servant of the Lord they had disowned and denied was the Holy One and the Righteous One. Peter again identified Jesus with the Old Testament prophecy about the Messiah who would be known as the Holy One of Israel (Psa. 78:41; Isa. 49:7) [BECNT, NAC, NICNT, TNTC].

QUESTION—What is meant by calling Jesus the 'Righteous One'?

'Righteous' refers to more than just good behavior. It means that Jesus obeyed God's Law perfectly. He was sinless. He did what was right in God's eyes [TH, TRT]. Jesus as the Righteous One points to a title that has roots in Isa. 53:11. 'The Righteous One' was a messianic description in Judaism (Isa. 32:1, 53:11; Zech. 9:9) [BECNT, NAC, PNTC, TNTC]. It was a title for Jesus [AB]. In some languages a translation of 'righteous' may be rendered as 'straight', in the sense of 'conforming to a standard'. This standard is naturally that which God expects [TH].

QUESTION—Who is the murderer referred to here?

Barabbas is the murderer referred to here. See Luke 23:18–25 [AB, Bar, BECNT, NAC, NICNT, TRT].

3:15 And you-killed the Author/Prince[a] of-life, whom God raised from (the)-dead, (a fact) to-which we are witnesses.[b]

LEXICON—a. ἀρχηγός (LN 68.2, 36.6) (BDAG 1. p. 138): 'author' [Bar, BECNT; ESV, NIV, NLT, NRSV], 'prince' [AB, BDAG 1; KJV, NASB, REB], 'founder' [LN (68.2)], LN (68.2); NET], 'source' [GW], 'the One who gives life' [NCV], 'ruler, leader' [BDAG], 'founding leader' [LN (36.6)], 'the one who leads people to life' [CEV], 'the one who leads to life' [TEV], 'him who has led the way to life' [CBC]. This noun denotes one who causes something to begin' [LN (68.2)] or a person who as originator or founder of a movement continues as the leader [LN (36.6)]. It refers to one who has a preeminent position [BDAG].
  b. μάρτυς (LN 33.270) (BDAG 2.c. p. 620): 'witness' [AB, Bar, BDAG, BECNT, CBC, LN; all versions except CEV], 'one who testifies' [LN]. The phrase 'a fact to which we are witnesses' is also translated 'all of us can tell you what he has done' [CEV]. This noun denotes a person who witnesses [LN]. It denotes someone who affirms or attests something, and in this case it refers to Jesus' disciples who were the witnesses of his life, death, and resurrection [BDAG].

QUESTION—Who are the 'we' in 'we are witnesses'?
  The witnesses are the apostles Peter and John [TRT]. Their charge was to bear witness to the person of Jesus and to the fact and significance of his resurrection [NAC, NICNT, PNTC, TNTC].

3:16 And his name, by faith in his name, has-made-strong[a] this man whom you-see and know. And the faith that is through (Jesus) has given him this perfect-heath[b] before you all.

LEXICON—a. aorist act. indic. of στερεόω (LN 79.68) (BDAG 1. p. 943): 'to be made strong' [Bar, BDAG, LN; CEV, ESV, KJV, NET, NIV, NRSV], 'to be strengthened' [BDAG, BECNT, CBC, LN; NASB], 'to be given strength' [AB; REB, TEV], 'to make well' [NCV], 'to heal' [NLT], not explicit [GW]. This verb means to make physically strong [LN]. It means to render physically firm [BDAG].
  b. ὁλοκληρία (LN 23.131) (BDAG p. 703): 'perfect health' [Bar, BECNT, LN; ESV, NASB, NRSV], 'complete health' [LN; NET], 'complete healing' [NIV], 'wholeness, completeness' [BDAG], 'perfect soundness' [KJV]. The phrase 'the faith that is through Jesus has given him this perfect health' is also translated 'faith in Jesus made this man completely well' [CEV], 'this faith has made him completely well' [CBC; REB], 'faith in Jesus' name has healed him' [NLT], 'he was made completely well because of trust in Jesus' [NCV], 'through his power alone this man...was healed' [GW], 'it was faith in Jesus that has made him well' [TEV], 'the faith that is called out by him (Jesus) gave this man the full use of his limbs' [AB]. This noun denotes a state of complete health or soundness in all parts of the body [LN]. It is a state of soundness or well-being in all parts [BDAG].

QUESTION—Whose faith is being referred to here?

It is the faith of both the apostles and the man [BECNT, NAC, PNTC, TNTC]. It is the faith of the apostles, since the man was looking only for money. But he did respond to the apostles. Given that faith can refer to the start of faith or its ongoing character, it is not impossible in this case that all three are meant. The lame man's response to his healing shows that he did respond to what God had done and was thankful for it. Thus the apostles had demonstrated faith as a characteristic of their lives and the lame man had demonstrated his initial faith in responding to God's work through his servant Jesus [BECNT]. Faith on the part of the apostles was a necessary factor in this healing and so was the rudimentary faith on the part of the man [PNTC]. It refers to the faith of the man, not to that of the apostles [AB]. Once the response of faith was made, the man was filled with the power of Christ and his body was filled with strength and health [NICNT].

3:17 And now, brothers, I-know that you-acted in ignorance,[a] as (did) also your rulers.[b]

LEXICON—a. ἄγνοια (LN 28.13) (BDAG 2.a. p. 14): 'ignorance' [AB, Bar, BDAG, CBC, LN; ESV, KJV, NASB, NET, NIV, NLT, NRSV, REB, TEV]. The phrase 'I know that you acted in ignorance, as did also your rulers' is also translated 'I know that you acted without understanding, just as also your rulers' [BECNT], 'I am sure that you and your leaders didn't know what you were doing' [CEV], 'I know that like your rulers you didn't know what you were doing' [GW], 'I know you did those things to Jesus because neither you nor your leaders understood what you were doing' [NCV]. This adjective means not to have information about something [LN]. It means they were unaware of what they were doing [BDAG].

b. ἄρχων (LN 37.56) (BDAG 2.a. p. 140): 'ruler' [Bar, BECNT, CBC, LN; ESV, GW, KJV, NASB, NET, NRSV, REB], 'authority' [BDAG], 'official' [BDAG], 'leader' [AB, BDAG; CEV, NCV, NIV, NLT, TEV], 'governor' [LN]. This noun denotes one who rules or governs [LN]. It denotes one who has administrative authority and here it refers to the Jewish leaders [BDAG].

QUESTION—Who are the 'brothers' that Peter addressed?

'Brothers' reflects their shared Jewish identity, not as if they were already Christians [BECNT]. They were fellow Israelites [EBC, PNTC].

QUESTION—Who are the rulers?

The rulers are Caiaphas, the other chief priests, and the scribes who took the leading part in accusing Jesus before Pilate [NICNT, TH]. They are often seen as the driving force behind Jesus' death in Luke 23 [BECNT].

QUESTION—What were they ignorant about?

They did not realize who Jesus was [PNTC]. They did not know that they were wrong in asking that Jesus be crucified. Jesus had cried out to the Father from the cross to forgive the executors and rulers as they did not know what they did (Luke 23:34) [AB, NICNT]. They did not know that Jesus was the Messiah [NICNT, TRT]. They did not realize Jesus was the Holy and Righteous One, the anointed Servant of God, the author of life [NAC]. They did not understand the meaning/significance of what they were doing [TH]. They did not know that they were killing the holy and innocent originator of life [Bar].

3:18 **But what God foretold[a] by (the)-mouth of-all the prophets, (that) his Messiah would-suffer, he-has- thus -fulfilled.[b]**

LEXICON—a. aorist act. indic. of προκαταγγέλλω (LN 33.283) (BDAG p. 871): 'to foretell' [BDAG, BECNT, CBC, LN; ESV, NIV, NLT, NRSV, REB], 'to foretell long ago' [NET], 'to announce beforehand' [Bar; NASB], 'to make known beforehand' [AB], 'to predict' [LN; GW], 'to announce long ago' [TEV], 'to show before' [KJV], 'to tell' [CEV], 'to say' [NCV]. This verb means to announce openly what is to happen in the future' [LN]. It means to announce beforehand by prophetic utterances [BDAG].

    b. aorist act. indic. of πληρόω (LN 13.106) (BDAG 4.a. p. 829): 'to fulfill' [AB, Bar, BDAG, BECNT, CBC, LN; ESV, KJV, NASB, NET, NIV, NLT, NRSV, REB], 'to cause to happen, to make happen' [LN], 'to make come true' [GW, NCV, TEV]. The phrase 'he has thus fulfilled' is also translated 'now he has kept that promise' [CEV]. This verb means to cause to happen, with the implication of fulfilling some purpose [LN]. It means to bring to a designed end, to fulfill a prophecy. It is God who brings divine prophecies to fulfillment [BDAG].

QUESTION—What was Peter explaining in this verse?

Peter explained that what the people and the rulers had done in ignorance had actually fulfilled God's plan as revealed in the prophets. That plan taught that the Christ would suffer [Bar, BECNT, EBC, NICNT, TNTC]. Human responsibility and divine design are side by side. Ignorance does not alleviate the need to repent because the penalty and responsibility for the ignorance are still present, as shown in the following verses 19–23 [BECNT]. 'All the prophets' could be a generalization covering the rest of the Old Testament apart from the Law of Moses. Most prophecies of the suffering servant in Isaiah and passages reflecting the experience of David or some other righteous sufferer in the Psalms were applied to the passion of Jesus (e.g., Psalms 22, 31, 34, 69) [NAC, PNTC, TNTC].

3:19 **Repent[a] therefore, and turn[b] so-that your sins may-be-wiped-out[c]**

LEXICON—a. aorist act. impera. of μετανοέω (LN 41.52) (BDAG 2. p. 640): 'to repent' [AB, Bar, BDAG, BECNT, CBC, LN; ESV, KJV, NASB, NET, NIV, NRSV, REB, TEV], 'to feel remorse, to be converted' [BDAG], 'to change one's way' [LN]. The command 'repent' is also translated 'repent of your sins' [NLT], 'give up your sins' [CEV], 'change the way you think and act' [GW], 'you must change your hearts and lives!' [NCV]. This verb means to change one's way of life as the result of a

complete change of thought and attitude with regard to sin and righteousness [LN]. It means to feel remorse [BDAG].
  b. aorist act. impera. of ἐπιστρέφω (LN 31.60) (BDAG 4.a. p. 382): 'to turn' [BDAG], 'to return' [BDAG]. The command 'turn' [Bar, BECNT] is also translated 'turn again' [ESV], 'turn back' [NET], 'turn to God' [AB, CBC; CEV, GW, NIV, NLT, NRSV, REB, TEV], 'return' [NASB], 'come back to God' [NCV], 'be converted' [KJV]. This verb means to change one's belief, with the focus on that to which one turns [LN]. It means to change one's mind or course of action [BDAG].
  c. aorist pass. infin. of ἐξαλείφω (LN 13.102) (BDAG 2. p. 344): 'to be wiped out' [AB, CBC, LN; NET, NIV, NRSV, REB], 'to be wiped away' [NASB, NLT], 'to be washed away' [BECNT], 'to be blotted out' [Bar; ESV, KJV], 'to be removed' [BDAG; GW], 'to be eliminated, to be done away with' [LN], 'to be destroyed, to be obliterated' [BDAG]. The phrase 'your sins may be wiped out' is also translated 'you will be forgiven' [CEV], 'he will forgive your sins' [NCV, TEV]. This is a figurative extension of the verb 'to wipe away' and it means to cause something to cease by obliterating any evidence of it [LN]. It means to remove so as to leave no trace [BDAG].

QUESTION—What is meant by the command to turn'?
It means to turn from sinful thoughts/ways and turn to God [Bar, EBC, NICNT, TH, TNTC, TRT], to turn from their rejection of Christ and turn to God [NAC], to acknowledge the centrality of Jesus to God's purpose [PNTC], It stresses the need for a change in direction, to change one's mind about where one is and to end up in line with God [BECNT].

QUESTION—What is meant by their sins being 'wiped out'?
It means that their sins will be forgiven by God [NAC, TRT]. This is another way to describe obtaining forgiveness: their sins will be removed completely, leaving no trace [BECNT, PNTC, TNTC].

3:20 in-order-that times of-relief/encouragement[a] may-come from (the)-presence of-the Lord, and (that) he-may-send the Messiah appointed[b] for you, Jesus,

LEXICON—a. ἀνάψυξις (LN 22.35, 25.148) (BDAG p. 75): 'relief' [BDAG, LN (22.35)], 'rest' [NCV], 'relaxation, 'time of rest' [BDAG], 'refreshing' [BECNT, LN (25.148); ESV, KJV, NASB, NET, NIV, NRSV], 'refreshment' [Bar; NLT], 'fresh strength' [CEV], 'spiritual strength' [TEV], 'renewal' [AB], 'recovery' [CBC; REB], 'encouragement, recovery of happiness' [LN (25.148)]. The phrase 'in order that times of relief/encouragement may come from the presence of the Lord' is also translated 'Then times will come when the Lord will refresh you' [GW]. In this verse the phrase translated 'times of relief' is generally regarded as a reference to the Messianic age. The entire expression in this verse may be restructured as 'so that the Lord may cause you to have relief from trouble' or 'so that the Lord may cause you

to no longer be troubled' [LN (22.35)]. Or the phrase 'times of encouragement' denotes a state of cheer and encouragement after a period of having been troubled or upset [LN (25.148)]. It denotes an experience of relief from trouble [BDAG].
  b. perf. pass. participle of προχειρίζομαι (LN 30.89) (BDAG p. 891): 'to be appointed' [Bar, BDAG, BECNT, CBC; ESV, GW, NASB, NET, NIV, NLT, NRSV, REB], 'to be selected' [BDAG], 'to be already chosen' [LN; TEV], 'to be chosen' [AB; CEV, NCV], 'to be preached before' [KJV], 'to be selected beforehand, to be chosen in advance, to be designated in advance' [LN]. This verb means to choose for a particular purpose in advance [LN]. It means to express preference of someone for a task [BDAG].

QUESTION—What is meant by 'times of relief/encouragement'?

It refers to times in every believer's life when God refreshes and strengthens that one. It refers to spiritual refreshment, not physical refreshment [TRT], times of rest and renewing for the spirits, not physical rest [TH], periods of time that include rest and spiritual refreshment [BECNT], moments of relief during the time men spend in waiting for that blessed day, the End [PNTC]. The plural 'times' shows that the phrase is not a synonym for the sending of the Messiah at the time of the End, and it is consistent with this that 'refreshment' suggests temporary relief rather than finality. There are repeated conversions, moments of collective inspiration, and marvelous works of healing [Bar, TNTC]. It is unclear whether it refers to a temporary period of respite during the period of messianic woes preceding the end time or it pictures the final time itself, probably the latter is intended [NAC].

QUESTION—Who does 'the Lord' refer to?

Here 'the Lord' refers to God rather than Jesus. It is the Lord God who might send Jesus [TH, TRT]. Where it is necessary to make a distinction in the use of 'Lord' it is possible to employ the wording 'Lord God' [TH].

3:21 whom heaven must receive[a] until (the)-times of-restoration[b] of-all (the-things) about-which God spoke by (the)-mouth[c] of-his holy prophets long-ago.[d]

LEXICON—a. aorist mid. (deponent = act.) of δέχομαι (LN 57.125) (BDAG 3. p. 221): 'to receive' [AB, BDAG, BECNT, CBC, LN; ESV, GW, KJV, NASB, NET, REB], 'to receive and keep' [Bar], 'to accept' [LN]. The phrase 'whom heaven must receive' is also translated 'but Jesus must stay in heaven' [CEV, NCV], 'who/he must remain in heaven' [NIV, NLT, NRSV, TEV]. This verb means to receive or accept an object or benefit for which the initiative rests with the giver, but the focus of attention in the transfer is upon the receiver [LN]. It means to be receptive of someone [BDAG].
  b. ἀποκατάστασις (LN 13.65) (BDAG p. 112): 'restoration' [BDAG, BECNT, LN; NASB, NRSV, REB], 'restitution' [KJV], 'reestablishment' [AB], 'final restoration' [NLT], 'universal restoration' [CBC], 'making

things new' [LN]. The phrase 'until the times of restoration of all the things' is also translated 'until the times when all things are restored' [Bar], 'until the time for restoring all the things (about which God spoke)' [ESV], 'until the time all things are restored' [NET], 'until the time comes for God to restore everything' [NIV], 'until the time when everything will be restored' [GW], 'until the time comes when all things will be made right again' [NCV], 'until God makes all things new' [CEV], 'until the time comes for all things to be made new' [TEV]. This noun denotes a change to a previous good state [LN]. It is used of states restored by benefactors to normal conditions and stability [BDAG].

c. στόμα (LN 33.101) (BDAG 1.a. p. 947): 'mouth' [Bar, BDAG, BECNT; ESV, KJV, NASB], 'mouths' [AB], 'lips' [BDAG], 'utterance' [LN], 'what is said, talk' [LN]. The phrase 'about which God spoke by the mouth of his holy prophets' is also translated 'as God promised through his holy prophets' [GW], 'as God/he promised...through his holy prophets' [NLT, NIV], 'that God announced...through his holy prophets' [NRSV], 'as God announced through his holy prophets' [TEV], 'of which God has spoken through his holy prophets' [REB], 'God told about this...when he spoke through his holy prophets' [NCV], 'which God declared from times long ago' [NET], 'of which God spoke by his holy prophets' [CBC], 'just as his holy prophets promised long ago' [CEV]. This noun denotes the content of what is spoken by the mouth [LN]. The phrase 'through the mouth' means 'by the lips of someone' [BDAG].

d. αἰών (LN 67.25) (BDAG 1.a. p. 32): 'long ago' [LN; CEV, ESV, GW, NCV, NET, NIV, NLT, NRSV, TEV], 'very long ago' [LN], 'very long time, the past, the earliest times' [BDAG]. The phrase 'long ago' is also translated 'from ancient time' [NASB], 'from the earliest days' [AB], 'from the beginning' [Bar; REB], 'from of old' [BECNT], 'since the world began' [KJV], 'not explicit' [CBC]. The idiom ἀπ' αἰῶνος 'from an age' refers to a point of time preceding another point of time, with a very long interval between [LN]. This idiom refers to a long period of time without referring to the beginning or the end. In respect to time it refers to the time gone by, the past, to earlier times [BDAG].

QUESTION—What is meant by the clause 'whom heaven must receive until the times of restoration of all the things'?

This clause means that Jesus must remain in heaven [TH], Jesus is received in heaven at God's side until the day he is revealed in return [BECNT]. The word 'must' indicates that Jesus' present withdrawal from the earthly scene is an important stage in the divine plan of salvation. His withdrawal will continue until the times of restoration of all things [PNTC]. The phrase 'times of restoration of all things' refers to the times for all things to be made new [TH]; all things will be restored in the return of the Messiah: a final and complete restoration [BECNT]; the time of universal restoration: when God's purpose for the world will be realized and a new life established [CBC]; the restoration of the human race to the state in and for which it was created [Bar]. The whole clause means that Jesus will remain in heaven until the time comes for His return while the restoration of all things has begun and will continue until it is consummated at His return. By the End, all things will be made new to their original creation's pristine character [BECNT, NAC, PNTC, TNTC, TH].

3:22 Moses said, '(The)-Lord God will-raise-up^a for-you (a)-prophet like me from your brothers.^b You(pl)-must-listen^c to-him in everything he-tells you.

LEXICON—a. fut. act. indic. of ἀνίστημι (LN 13.81) (BDAG 4. p. 83): 'to raise up' [Bar, BDAG, BECNT, CBC; ESV, KJV, NASB, NET, NIV, NLT, NRSV, REB], 'to raise' [AB], 'to cause to arise, to bring into existence, to cause to appear' [LN]. The clause 'the Lord your God will raise up for you a prophet like me from your brothers' is also translated 'the Lord your God will choose one of your own people to be a prophet, just as he chose me' [CEV], 'the Lord your God will send you a prophet, an Israelite like me' [GW], 'the Lord your God will give you a prophet like me, who is one of your own people' [NCV], 'the Lord your God will send you a prophet, just as he sent me, and he will be one of your own people' [TEV]. This verb means to cause to come into existence, with the implication of assuming a place or position [LN]. It means to cause someone to appear for some role or function [BDAG].
   b. ἀδελφός (LN 11.57) (BDAG 2.b. p. 19): 'brother' [AB, Bar, BECNT; ESV, KJV, NASB, NET], 'fellow countryman' [LN], 'your own people' [CEV, NCV, NIV, NLT, NRSV, TEV], '(an) Israelite' [GW]. The phrase 'from your brothers' is also translated 'from among yourselves' [CBC; REB]. This noun denotes a person who is a member of the same nation or ethnic group [LN]. It denotes a compatriot [BDAG].
   c. fut. mid. indic. of ἀκούω (LN 31.56) (BDAG 4. p. 38): 'to listen to' [Bar, BDAG, BECNT, CBC; CEV, ESV, GW, NCV, NIV, NRSV, REB], 'to give heed to' [NASB], 'to listen carefully' [NLT], 'to listen and respond, to pay attention and respond, to accept' [LN], 'to obey' [AB, BDAG; NET, TEV], 'to heed' [BDAG, LN], 'to hear' [BDAG; KJV]. This verb means to believe something and to respond to it on the basis of having heard it [LN]. It means to give careful attention to something, to listen to it, to heed it [BDAG].

QUESTION—What scripture is being cited?
   Peter cited a passage from Deut. 18:15 where Moses wrote about the coming of a great deliverer and what is at stake in responding to him [AB, Bar, BECNT, CBC, EBC, NAC, NICNT, PNTC, TNTC].

QUESTION—Who are the 'brothers' referred to in this context?
   Their 'brothers' are those who are from the same tribe or people group, not just those who are from the same father, or only those who are fellow believers [TRT].

QUESTION—What is implied by the command 'you must listen to him'?
Listening to this prophet involves more than merely hearing what he has to say. Here the plural 'you' together with the usage of the plural forms of 'for you' and 'to you' emphasizes the need for all the listeners to respond collectively to Jesus as the prophet like Moses [PNTC]. The implication is 'you must obey him' [AB, BECNT, EBC, TNTC, TH].

3:23 And it-will-be-(that) every person^a who does- not -listen-to that prophet will-be-destroyed^b from the people.'

LEXICON—a. ψυχή (LN 9.20) (BDAG 3. p. 1099): 'person' [BDAG, LN; NET], 'soul' [BECNT; ESV, KJV, NASB], 'man' [AB]. The phrase 'every person who does not listen to that prophet' is also translated 'No one who disobeys that prophet' [CEV], 'anyone who does not obey that prophet' [TEV], 'those who won't listen to that prophet' [GW], 'anyone who does not listen to that prophet' [Bar; NCV], 'anyone who does not listen to him' [NIV], 'anyone who will not listen to that Prophet' [NLT], 'anyone who refuses to listen to that prophet' [CBC; REB], 'everyone who does not listen to that prophet' [NRSV]. This is a figurative extension of meaning of 'inner self, mind' and refers to a person as a living being' [LN]. It is an entity with personhood [BDAG].
b. fut. pass. indic. of ἐξολεθρεύω (LN 20.35) (BDAG p. 351): 'to be destroyed' [AB, BECNT, LN; ESV, KJV], 'to be destroyed and removed' [LN; NET], 'to be destroyed utterly' [BDAG; NASB], 'to be completely cut off' [NIV, NLT], 'to be cut off' [Bar; REB], 'to be rooted out' [BDAG], 'to be rooted out utterly' [NRSV], 'to be excluded' [GW], 'to be extirpated' [CBC]. The phrase 'will be destroyed from the people' is also translated 'will die, cut off from God's people' [NCV], 'will (not) be one of God's people any longer' [CEV], 'shall be separated from God's people and destroyed' [TEV]. This verb means to destroy and thus eliminate someone [LN]. It means to eliminate by destruction [BDAG].

QUESTION—What part of the Bible is Peter citing?
Peter cites Deut. 18:19 and links it with Lev. 23:29. Here the negative consequences for rejection appear as a prophetic warning [AB, Bar, BECNT, CBC, EBC, NAC, PNTC, TH, TNTC]. The concept of listening to the prophet is from Deut. 18:19, and the penalty of destruction and separation from God's people comes from Lev. 23:29 [BECNT].

QUESTION—Who are the people from whom those who do not listen to the prophet will be removed?
The people here refers to God's people. Those who do not listen to and obey the prophet will no longer be a part of God's people [EBC, NAC, PNTC, TH]; those who fail to respond to the person and work of Jesus, who is the prophet like Moses, will have no place among God's people [BECNT], might be called excommunication [Bar].

3:24 And all the prophets who-have-spoken, from Samuel and those who came-after[a] him, also announced[b] these days.

LEXICON—a. καθεξῆς (LN 61.1) (BDAG p. 490): 'in order' [BDAG, LN], 'in sequence, one after another' [LN], 'one after the other' [BDAG]. The phrase 'from Samuel and those who came after him' [ESV] is also translated 'from Samuel and those that follow after' [KJV], 'from Samuel and those who followed afterward' [BECNT], 'from Samuel and those that followed in order' [LN], 'from Samuel and those who followed him' [Bar; NET], 'from Samuel and those after him' [NRSV], 'from Samuel and his successors onward' [NASB], 'Samuel, and all the other prophets who spoke for God after Samuel' [NCV], 'starting with Samuel, every prophet' [NLT], 'including Samuel and those who came after him' [TEV], 'from Samuel onwards, every prophet' [REB], 'all the prophets from Samuel on' [NIV], 'all the prophets, from Samuel onwards' [CBC], 'Samuel and all the prophets who followed him' [GW], 'Samuel and all the other prophets who came later' [CEV], 'all the later prophets too, from Samuel onward' [AB]. This adverb describes a sequence of one after another in time, space, or logic [LN]. It pertains to being in sequence in time. With the article, it means 'the successors' [BDAG].

b. aorist act. indic. of καταγγέλλω (LN 33.204) (BDAG a. p. 515): 'to announce' [Bar, BDAG, LN; NASB, NET, TEV], 'to proclaim' [BDAG, BECNT, LN; ESV], 'to speak out about' [LN], 'to speak about' [LN; CEV, GW, NLT], 'to preach' [AB], 'to foretell' [KJV, NIV], 'to predict' [CBC; NRSV, REB], 'to tell about' [NCV]. This verb means to announce, with the focus upon the extent to which the announcement or proclamation extends [LN]. It means to make known in public, and it implies a broad dissemination [BDAG].

QUESTION—What do 'these days' refer to?

They probably refer to everything that has happened since Christ came to earth and everything that will yet happen, including Christ's return [TRT], the days of divinely promised activity—all aspects of Jesus' career, from death and glorification to return [BECNT], the last days, of which the events of resurrection, ascension, and the gift of the Spirit mark the beginning [Bar], the days of salvation, the coming of Christ [NAC].

3:25 You are the sons of-the prophets and of-the covenant[a] that God made with your ancestors, saying to Abraham, 'And in your offspring[b] all the people[c] of-the earth will-be-blessed.'[d]

LEXICON—a. διαθήκη (LN 34.44) (BDAG 2. p. 228): 'covenant' [AB, Bar, BDAG, BECNT, CBC, LN], 'pact' [LN]. The phrase 'the covenant that/which God made' [Bar, CBC; ESV, KJV, NASB, NET, REB, TEV] is also translated 'the covenant God made' [AB; NIV], 'the covenant God promised' [NLT], 'the covenant that God gave' [BECNT; NRSV], 'the agreement God made' [NCV], 'the promise that God made' [CEV, GW]. This noun denotes the verbal content of an agreement between two persons specifying reciprocal benefits and responsibilities [LN]. This covenant is decreed by God and cannot require the death of the testator to make it operative. It is a declaration of one person's initiative, not the result of an agreement between two parties. In the covenants of God, it was God alone who set the conditions. Here God has issued a declaration of his purpose that goes back to ancestral days. One may speak of it as a decree [BDAG].

b. σπέρμα (LN 10.29) (BDAG 2.a. p. 937): 'offspring' [CBC, LN; ESV, NIV, REB], 'descendant' [BDAG, LN; GW, NCV, NET, NLT, NRSV, TEV], 'seed' [Bar, BECNT; KJV, NASB], 'posterity' [BDAG, LN], 'family' [AB]. The phrase 'in your offspring' is also translated 'because of someone from your family' [CEV], 'through your family' [AB]. This noun is a figurative extension of the word 'seed' and it refers to one's posterity with an emphasis upon the ancestor's role in founding the lineage [LN]. It denotes the product of insemination, and contrary to normal OT usage 'seed' is used here with reference to a single individual descendant. In this verse the promise of Gen. 22:18 refers to a single individual, the Messiah, who is exalted above the mass of Abraham's descendants [BDAG].

c. πατριά (LN 11.56) (BDAG 2. p. 788): 'people' [BDAG, LN; GW, NIV, TEV], 'nations' [BDAG, LN; CEV, NCV, NET], 'families' [AB, Bar, BECNT, CBC; ESV, NASB, NLT, NRSV, REB], 'kindred' [KJV]. This noun denotes a relatively large unit of people who constitute a sociopolitical group, sharing a presumed biological descent [LN]. It denotes a relatively large body of people existing as a totality at a given moment and linked through ancestry and sociopolitical interests [BDAG].

d. fut. pass. indic. of ἐνευλογέω (LN 88.69) (BDAG p. 336): 'to be blessed' [AB, Bar, BDAG, BECNT, LN; all versions except REB], 'to find blessing' [CBC; REB], 'to be acted kindly toward' [BDAG, LN]. This verb means to be provided benefits, often with the implication of certain supernatural factors involved [LN]. It means to confer special benefits [BDAG].

QUESTION—What verse in the Bible is Peter citing?

The basic covenant that Abraham originally received is in Gen. 12:1–3, but part of the wording is closer to its repetition in Gen. 22:18, with the use of the key phrase 'in your seed' or 'offspring' [BECNT, EBC, NAC]. However, the reference to the word 'families' comes neither from Gen. 12:3 nor 22:18 where 'all peoples on earth' and 'nations' are used respectively [BECNT].

QUESTION—What is meant by being 'the sons of the prophets and of the covenant that God made with your ancestors'?

Peter makes the point that his audience consists of descendants of the prophets and of those who possess the covenant that Abraham originally received [AB, BECNT]. Being the sons of the prophets implies that they ought to be the beneficiaries of everything promised by the prophets concerning the messianic era. They are in line to experience the ultimate blessing of the covenant made with Abraham, Isaac, and Jacob realized in Christ [NICNT, PNTC, TNTC]. In this context, the meaning of 'sons' as 'heirs' has to do with inheriting the blessings that God promised to His people, not with being natural sons/descendants of the prophets [TRT]. It implies that the blessings that God promised and the covenant that God made with the ancestors are also for you, apply to you, all the listeners [TH].

QUESTION—What was the covenant God had made with the fathers?

God's covenant with the fathers was a one-sided peace treaty or agreement in that God was the One who made promises and set the conditions of the covenant for mankind and Himself; Abraham had no part in making that covenant. God made the covenant for the benefit of mankind and breaking it has serious consequences [TRT].

QUESTION—Who are 'all the families of the earth'?

It refers to 'all the people groups' on the earth [TRT]. The blessings that God promised and the covenant that God made with the ancestors of Israel are also for all the people on the earth [AB, BECNT, TH], for all nations on earth [PNTC, TNTC]. The word 'nations' might be interpreted to mean the Gentiles [TNTC].

3:26 God, having-raised-up[a] his servant,[b] sent him to-you first, to-bless[c] you by turning[d] each-one of-you from your wickedness.[e]"

LEXICON—a. aorist act. participle of ἀνίστημι (LN 23.94) (BDAG 2. p. 83): 'to raise up' [Bar, BDAG, BECNT, CBC; all versions except CEV, GW, TEV], 'to raise' [BDAG], 'to raise to life, to make live again' [LN], 'to bring back to life' [GW], 'to make appear' [AB], 'to choose' [CEV, TEV]. This verb means to cause someone to live again after having once died [LN]. It means to raise up by bringing back to life [BDAG].

b. παῖς (LN 87.77) (BDAG 3.b.γ. p. 750): 'servant' [AB, BDAG, BECNT; all versions except CEV, KJV, TEV], 'Servant' [Bar, CBC; TEV], 'Son' [CEV, KJV]. This noun denotes a slave, possibly serving as a personal servant and thus with the implication of kindly regard [LN]. It denotes one who is committed in total obedience to another and here it refers to Christ's special relationship to God [BDAG].

c. pres. act. participle of εὐλογέω (LN 88.69) (BDAG 3. p. 408): 'to bless' [AB, Bar, BDAG, BECNT, CBC, LN; all versions], 'to act kindly toward' [BDAG, LN], 'to provide benefits' [BDAG]. This verb means to provide benefits, often with the implication of certain supernatural factors involved [LN]. It means to confer special benefits on someone [BDAG].

d. pres. act. infin. of ἀποστρέφω (LN 31.70) (BDAG 2. p. 123): 'to turn from' [Bar, BECNT, CBC; ESV, GW, NASB, NCV, NET, NIV, NRSV, REB], 'to turn back from' [NLT], 'to turn away' [AB, BDAG; KJV], 'to cause to turn away' [LN], 'to make someone turn away from' [CEV, TEV]. This verb means to cause someone to turn away from a previous belief [LN]. It means to cause a positive change in belief or behavior [BDAG].

e. πονηρία (LN 88.108) (BDAG p. 851): 'wickedness' [BDAG, BECNT, LN; ESV], 'sinfulness, baseness, maliciousness' [BDAG], 'sins' [CEV], 'evil ways' [GW], 'wicked ways' [Bar, CBC; NASB, NIV, NRSV, REB, TEV], 'sinful ways' [NLT], 'wicked deeds' [AB], 'iniquities' [KJV, NET]. The phrase 'turning each one of you from your wickedness' is also translated 'turning each of you away from doing evil' [NCV]. This noun denotes an evil, wicked nature [LN]. It denotes a state or condition of a lack of moral or social values [BDAG].

QUESTION—Who is this servant of God?

God's servant is Jesus. It is the same word used in verse 3:13 where it talks about God glorifying his servant Jesus [TRT].

QUESTION—What is meant by God 'having raised up' his servant?

In some contexts it could refer to the resurrection, but since it precedes the first sending of this servant, 'raise up' is probably used in the same way as in verse 23 and it refers to bringing somebody onto the stage of history [Bar, TNTC]. Jesus was raised up to be their leader and deliverer, just as centuries before God had raised up his servant Moses to be their leader and deliverer [NICNT].

QUESTION—What does the phrase 'to you first' imply?

'To you first' here implies that the servant was raised and sent to those in Israel first of all, and first and foremost he was Israel's Messiah. It is the first sending of the Messiah, initially to and for the benefit of Jews, but it will turn out to be of benefit to the Gentiles also [AB, Bar, BECNT, EBC, NAC, NICNT, PNTC, TNTC].

QUESTION—What is the function of this verse?

This verse serves as a conclusion to Peter's message. God has raised his servant, Jesus the Messiah, the seed of Abraham. Through him all peoples/nations on earth will be blessed. He blesses each person by turning each one from their wicked ways. In other words, he forgives and leads each repented person, Jew and non-Jews, to walk on God's road, to become righteous as he is [BECNT, NAC, TH].

DISCOURSE UNIT—4:1–31 [EBC]. The topic is Peter and John before the Sanhedrin.

DISCOURSE UNIT—4:1–22 [Bar, BECNT, CBC, NAC, PNTC, TNTC; CEV, ESV, GW, NCV, NET, NIV, NLT, NRSV, TEV]. The topic is Peter and John before the Sanhedrin [NAC; NIV], Peter and John before the Council [ESV, NLT, NRSV, TEV], Peter and John at the Council [NCV], Peter and John are brought in front of the Council [CEV], Peter and John's trial in front of the Jewish Council [GW], the arrest of Peter and John [TNTC], the arrest and trial of Peter and John [NET], arrest and examination of Peter and John [Bar], the arrest and the leadership's deliberation [BECNT], the leadership of the new Israel [PNTC], a skirmish with the rulers [CBC].

DISCOURSE UNIT—4:1-12 [NAC, PNTC; NASB]. The topic is Peter and John arrested [NASB], arrested and interrogated [NAC], proclaiming in Jesus the resurrection from the dead [PNTC].

DISCOURSE UNIT—4:1-7 [EBC]. The topic is the arrest of Peter and John.

DISCOURSE UNIT—4:1-4 [AB, NICNT]. The topic is Peter and John arrested [AB], arrest of Peter and John [NICNT].

4:1 And as they were-speaking to the people, the priests and the commander[a] of-the temple (guards) and the Sadducees approached[b] them,

LEXICON—a. στρατηγός (LN 37.91) (BDAG 2. p. 948): 'commander' [BDAG, LN]. The phrase 'the commander of the temple/temple guards/guard' [AB; NET] is also translated 'the captain of the temple/Temple guards/guard' [Bar, BECNT; CEV, NASB, NIV, NLT], 'the captain of the soldiers that guarded the Temple' [NCV], 'the officer in charge of the temple guards' [GW], 'the captain of the temple' [ESV, KJV. NRSV], 'the controller of the temple' [CBC; REB], 'the officer in charge of the Temple guards' [TEV]. The title στρατηγὸς τοῦ ἱεροῦ is literally 'official of the temple' and it refers to the commander of Jewish soldiers responsible for guarding and maintaining order in the Jewish Temple [LN]. It denotes the commander who is responsible for the temple in Jerusalem [BDAG]. This title also occurs in Acts 5:24.

b. aorist act. indic. of ἐφίστημι (LN 85.13) (BDAG 1. p. 418): 'to approach' [BECNT, LN; GW], 'to arrive' [CEV, TEV], 'to come up to' [NASB, NCV, NET, NIV], 'to come to' [NRSV], 'to be near' [LN], 'to stand near' [BDAG], 'to come upon' [AB, Bar, CBC; ESV, KJV], 'to confront' [NLT], 'to break in on' [REB]. This verb means to be near [LN]. It means to stand at or near a specific place [BDAG].

QUESTION—Who were the priests mentioned here?
Some manuscripts have "chief/high priests" rather than "priests" [TH, TRT]. The chief priests are meant here [NICNT]. These priests were the ones who offered prayers and sacrifices to God on behalf of His people. In other words, they were mediators between God and the people. Chief priests were like an executive/ruling committee within the 71-member Jewish Supreme Court, the Sanhedrin [TRT].

QUESTION—What was the role of the commander of the temple guards?
The commander of the temple guards was in charge of the temple police force that maintained order in the temple area, with power to arrest. He was the highest ranking priest after the high priest [AB, BECNT, EBC, CBC, NAC, NICNT, PNTC, TNTC, TRT]. He also assisted the high priest in the performance of his ceremonial duties [NAC, PNTC].

QUESTION—Who were the Sadducees?
The Sadducees were a wealthy well-educated Jewish party. They were very powerful in the Jewish community, both religiously and politically. They controlled the high priesthood and they held the most seats in the Sanhedrin,

the Jewish Supreme Council/Court [TRT]. They had no specific authority in the temple, but many of the priests came from their ranks [PNTC]. They claimed that their roots went back to Zadok, high priest under Solomon (1 Kings 2:35) [BECNT, CBC, NAC, TRT]. They only believed the five books Moses wrote, the Torah of the Pentateuch. They rejected the oral law and the traditions that other sects held [BECNT, CBC, EBC, NAC, TRT]. They were very materialistic in their worldview, and cooperated with Rome in order to maintain their status, but less devoted to detailed questions about the law and piety than the Pharisees [BECNT]. They did not believe in a resurrection from the dead, nor in angels or spirits (Acts 23:6–8) [AB, BECNT, EBC, NAC, NICNT, TNTC, TRT]. They believed that there was no life beyond this life [NAC].

4:2 **being-greatly-annoyed**[a] **because they were-teaching the people and proclaiming**[b] **in**[c] **Jesus the resurrection from (the)-dead.**

LEXICON—a. pres. mid./pass. (deponent = act.) of διαπονέομαι (LN 88.190) (BDAG p. 235): 'to be greatly annoyed' [ESV, GW], 'to be annoyed' [BDAG, BECNT; REB, TEV], 'to be much annoyed' [NRSV], 'to be greatly disturbed' [BDAG; NASB, NIV], 'to be very disturbed' [NLT], 'to be provoked' [LN], 'to be irked' [LN], 'to be angry' [LN; CEV, NET], 'to be grieved' [KJV], 'to be upset' [NCV], 'to be indignant' [AB], 'to be vexed' [Bar], 'to be exasperated' [CBC]. This verb means to be strongly irked or provoked at something or someone [LN]. It means to feel burdened as the result of someone's provocative activity [BDAG].

    b. pres. act. infin. of καταγγέλλω (LN 33.204) (BDAG a. p. 515): 'to proclaim' [Bar, BDAG, BECNT, CBC; ESV, NASB, NIV, NRSV, REB], 'to announce' [BDAG, LN; NET], 'to proclaim throughout, to speak out about' [LN], 'to spread the message' [GW], 'to preach' [AB; KJV, NCV], not explicit [CEV, NLT, TEV]. This verb means to announce, with the focus upon the extent to which the announcement or proclamation extends [LN]. It means to make known in public, and implies a broad dissemination [BDAG].

    c. ἐν (LN 90.6): 'by, from' [LN]. The phrase 'in Jesus' [Bar, BECNT; ESV, NASB, NIV, NET, NRSV], is also translated 'through Jesus' [AB; GW, KJV, NLT], 'though the power of Jesus' [NCV], '(by teaching the people) about Jesus' [REB], 'were teaching the people that Jesus (had risen from death)' [TEV], '(the resurrection) of Jesus' [CBC], 'just as Jesus (had been raised)' [CEV]. This preposition refers to an agent, often with the implication of an agent being used as an instrument, and in some instances relating to general behavior rather than to some specific event [LN].

QUESTION—What does the expression 'proclaiming in Jesus the resurrection from the dead' refer to?

The expression 'proclaiming in Jesus the resurrection from the dead' could refer to the proclamation of the resurrection of Jesus alone or to Jesus' resurrection as proof of a coming general resurrection. The flow of the argument in Acts 3–4 suggests the latter [PNTC], with the latter meaning as well [EBC]. The Sadducees were annoyed because Peter and John were affirming what they denied [Bar, EBC, NICNT] and brought out the idea of Jesus as the messianic-like figure which would undercut their own power and authority [BECNT, NAC]. They feared for their own position if the apostles' preaching brought about Roman interference [CBC].

4:3 **And they-laid- their hands -on[a] them and put-(them) in jail[b] until the next-day, for it-was already evening.**

LEXICON—a. aorist act. indic. of ἐπιβάλλω (LN 37.110) (BDAG 1.b. p. 367): 'to lay on' [BDAG; KJV, NASB], 'to lay upon' [AB, Bar], 'to put on' [BDAG], 'to arrest' [CBC, LN; CEV, ESV, GW, NLT, NRSV, REB, TEV], 'to seize' [BECNT, LN; NET, NIV], 'to grab' [NCV]. The idiom 'to lay hands on' means to take a person unto custody for alleged illegal activity. Here it means that they arrested them [LN]. They put their hands on them violently [BDAG].

b. τήρησις (LN 7.24) (BDAG 2. p. 1002): 'jail' [CEV, GW, NASB, NCV, NET, NIV, NLT, TEV], 'prison' [BDAG, CBC; REB]. The phrase 'put them in jail' is also translated 'put them in/into custody' [BECNT; ESV, NRSV], 'put them in hold' [KJV], 'put them under guard' [Bar], 'placed them under arrest' [AB]. This noun denotes a place of detention [LN]. It denotes a place for custody [BDAG].

QUESTION—What does the expression 'laid their hands on them' mean?

This is an idiom that means 'arrested them' [AB, NAC, TNTC, TRT], 'seized and arrested them' [BECNT, PNTC], 'took them into custody' [Bar, EBC]. It implies that the arrest was done forcefully [TRT]. The pronoun 'them' refers to Peter and John [AB, Bar, BECNT, EBC, NAC, NICNT, PNTC, TNTC] or Peter, John, and the man who had been crippled, see verse 14 [TRT].

4:4 **But many of-those who-had-heard the message[a] believed.[b] And the number of-the men came-to about five thousand.**

LEXICON—a. λόγος (LN 33.98) (BDAG 1.a.β. p. 599): 'message' [BDAG, CBC, LN; CEV, GWNASB, NET, NIV, NLT, REB, TEV], 'word' [AB, Bar, BDAG, BECNT, LN; ESV, KJV, NRSV], 'proclamation, instruction, teaching' [BDAG]. The phrase 'many of those who had heard the message believed' is also translated 'many of those who had heard Peter and John preach believed the things they said' [NCV]. This noun denotes that which has been stated or said, with the primary focus upon the content of the communication [LN]. It denotes a communication whereby the mind finds expression [BDAG].

b. aorist act. indic. of πιστεύω (LN 31.35, 31.102) (BDAG 1.d. or 2.b. p. 817): 'to believe' [AB, Bar, BDAG (1.d.), LN (31.35), BECNT; ESV, KJV, NASB, NET, NIV, NRSV, TEV], 'to think to be true' [BDAG (1.d), LN (31.35)], 'to believe (in)' or 'to trust' [BDAG (2.b), LN (31.102)]. This verb is also translated as a noun: 'became believers' [CBC; GW,

REB]. Some translations supply the object of what they believed: 'believed the things they said' [NCV], 'believed it (the message)' [CEV, NLT], 'believed it (the fact of the Resurrection)' [BDAG (1.d.)]. This verb means to believe something to be true, and hence worthy of being trusted [LN (31.35)] or to believe in the good news about Jesus Christ and become his follower [LN (31.102)]. It means to consider something to be true and therefore worthy of one's trust, and here the belief is in the fact of the Resurrection [BDAG (1.d.)] or it means to entrust oneself to an entity in complete confidence, here referring to those who became believers, that is, the Christians [BDAG (2.b)].

QUESTION—What is meant by the statement 'the number of men came to about five thousand'?

This means that the total number of believers was now five thousand, not that an additional five thousand were added to the group [AB, Bar, BECNT, CBC, EBC, NAC, NICNT, PNTC, TH, TNTC]. It is impossible to say whether the term 'men' includes women as well [TH]. It is hard to be certain who is included in the count, men only or both men and women [BECNT]. The term men refers to men alone [NICNT].

DISCOURSE UNIT—4:5–22 [AB]. The topic is the apostles' defense before the Sanhedrin.

DISCOURSE UNIT—4:5–12 [NICNT]. The topic is Peter and John before the Sanhedrin.

4:5 On the next-day their rulers[a] and elders[b] and scribes[c] were-gathered-together[d] in Jerusalem,

LEXICON—a. ἄρχων (LN 37.56) (BDAG 2.a. p. 140): 'ruler' [AB, Bar, BECNT, CBC, LN; all versions except CEV, TEV], 'leader' [BDAG; CEV, TEV], 'official' [BDAG]. The phrase 'their rulers and elders and scribes were assembled' is also translated 'the council of all the rulers and elders and teachers of religious law met' [NLT]. This noun denotes one who rules or governs [LN]. It denotes one who has administrative authority [BDAG].

b. πρεσβύτερος (LN 53.77) (BDAG 2.a.β. p. 862): 'elder' [AB, Bar, BDAG, BECNT, CBC, LN; all versions except GW, NCV], 'leader' [GW], 'older Jewish leader' [NCV], 'presbyter' [BDAG]. This noun denotes a person of responsibility and authority in matters of socio-religious concerns [LN]. It denotes an official among the Jews who is a member of a group in the Sanhedrin [BDAG].

c. γραμματεύς (LN 53.94): 'scribe' [AB, Bar, BECNT; ESV, GW, KJV, NASB, NRSV, REB], 'expert in the law' [LN; NET], 'teacher of the law' [NCV, NIV, TEV], 'teacher of the Law of Moses' [CEV], 'teacher of religious law' [NLT], 'doctor of the law' [CBC], 'expert in the Law of Moses, one who is learned in the Law, one who is learned in the Law of Moses' [LN]. This noun denotes a recognized expert in Jewish law [LN].

d. aorist pass. infin. of συνάγω (LN 15.125) (BDAG 1.b. p. 962): 'to be gathered together' [Bar, BECNT, LN; KJV, NASB], 'to be called together' [BDAG, LN], 'to be brought together' [BDAG], 'to be assembled' [NRSV], 'to meet' [CBC; CEV, GW, NCV, NIV, NLT, REB], 'to gather' [AB, BDAG; ESV, TEV], 'to come together' [BDAG; NET]. This verb means to cause to come together [LN]. It means to bring or call together. This verb also occurs at 4:31 in regard to the Christians [BDAG].

QUESTION—Who were the three groups of people assembled on the next day? The first group are the rulers: the religious figures or senior priests [BECNT], a general term that certainly includes the chief priest [Bar, PNTC, TNTC], priestly representation on the Sanhedrin [NAC, TNTC]. The second group are the elders, the civic leaders, the chief tribal and family heads, who often were more senior in age, as the term literally means 'old men' [BECNT], a general term applicable to both priests and laymen [Bar, PNTC], the lay leaders from the Jewish aristocratic families [NAC, TNTC]. The third group are the scribes, who studied and interpreted the law [BECNT], the teachers of the law, the lay Pharisaic scholars who were gradually increasing their influence in what had been a predominantly Sadducean assembly [Bar, PNTC, TNTC], students and interpreters of the law [NAC]. Among them would have been a mixture of Sadducees and Pharisees, with most of the power lying with the Sadducees and the scribes being mostly Pharisees [EBCNT, CBC]. These three groups constituted the Jewish council called the Sanhedrin in the Roman period [Bar, CBC, EBC, NICNT, PNTC, TNTC].

4:6 **with Annas the high-priest[a] and Caiaphas and John and Alexander, and all who were of high-priestly[b] descent.**

LEXICON—a. ἀρχιερεύς (LN 53.89) (BDAG 1.b. p. 112): 'high priest' [AB, Bar, BECNT, CBC, LN; all versions except GW], 'chief priest' [GW], 'most important priest' [LN]. This noun denotes the principal member among the chief priests [LN].

b. ἀρχιερατικός (LN 53.90) (BDAG p. 139): 'high-priestly' [Bar, BDAG, BECNT, CBC, LN; ESV, NASB, NRSV, REB], 'of the high priest' [LN; KJV, NLT], 'high priest's' [AB; CEV, NCV, NET, NIV, TEV], 'chief priest's' [GW]. The phrase 'all who were of high-priestly descent' is also translated 'all/many who were of the high-priestly family' [BECNT, CBC; ESV, NRSV, REB], 'those who belonged to the high-priestly clan' [Bar], 'all who were of the high priest's family' [AB], 'others who were members of the high priest's family' [NET], 'other members of the high priest's family' [CEV], 'other men of the high priest's family' [NIV], 'others who belonged to the High Priest's family' [TEV], 'everyone from the high priest's family' [NCV], 'the rest of the chief priest's family' [GW], 'other relatives of the high priest' [NLT]. This adjective refers to what pertains to the high priest [LN].

QUESTION—Who was the high-priest Annas?
Annas was the patriarch of a family that held high-priestly power for several decades, and so he is given the title here. He served from A.D. 6 to 14 [AB, BECNT, TH, TNTC], for nine years from A.D. 6 to 15 [Bar, CBC, EBC, NAC, NICNT, PNTC].

QUESTION—Who was Caiaphas?
Caiaphas was the son-in-law of Annas [Bar, CBC, EBC, NAC, NICNT, PNTC, TH, TNTC]. He was actually the high priest at the time, officiating from A.D. 18 to 36 [AB, Bar, BECNT, CBC, EBC, NAC, NICNT, PNTC, TH, TNTC]. He served during the entire time that Pilate ruled over Judea [BECNT].

QUESTION—Who was John?
Some manuscripts read Jonathan, son of Annas instead of John. If this was Jonathan, then he was the high priest who replaced Caiaphas and served from A.D. 36 to 37. If this was not Jonathan, then he was unknown [AB, Bar, BECNT, CBC, EBC, NAC, NICNT, PNTC, TH, TNTC].

QUESTION—Who was Alexander?
Alexander was the fourth member of the family noted, was otherwise unattested [BECNT]. He was an unknown member of the high priest's family [AB, Bar, CBC, EBC, NAC, NICNT, PNTC, TH, TNTC].

4:7 And having-placed them in the midst,[a] they-inquired,[b] "By what power[c] or by what name[d] did- you -do this?"

LEXICON—a. μέσος (LN 83.10) (BDAG 1.b. p. 635): 'midst' [Bar, BECNT, LN; ESV, KJV, NET, NRSV], 'middle' [BDAG, LN; CEV], 'center' [NASB], 'before (them)' [AB, BDAG]. The phrase 'having placed them in the midst' is also translated 'they brought in Peter and John and made them stand in the middle' [CEV], 'they made Peter and John stand in front of them' [GW], 'they made Peter and John stand before them' [NCV], 'they made the apostles stand before them' [TEV], 'they had Peter and John brought before them' [NIV], 'they brought in the two disciples' [NLT], they brought the apostles before the court' [CBC; REB]. This adjective describes a position in the middle of an area [LN]. It pertains to a middle position [BDAG].
  b. imperf. mid./pass. (deponent = act.) indic. of πυνθάνομαι (LN 33.181) (BDAG 1. p. 898): 'to inquire' [Bar, BDAG, BECNT, LN; ESV, NASB, NET, NRSV], 'to ask' [AB, BDAG, LN; GW, KJV, NCV, TEV], 'to question' [CEV, NIV], 'to interrogate' [REB], 'to demand' [NLT], 'to make an inquiry' [BDAG], 'to begin the examination' [CBC], 'to seek to learn' [BDAG]. This verb means to inquire about something [LN]. It means to seek to learn by inquiry [BDAG].
  c. δύναμις (LN 76.1) (BDAG 1.b. p. 264): 'power' [AB, Bar, BDAG, BECNT, CBC, LN; all versions], 'might, strength' [BDAG]. This noun denotes the potentiality to exert force in performing some function [LN]. It denotes the power that works wonders [BDAG].

d. ὄνομα (LN 33.126) (BDAG d.γ.ℶ. p. 713): 'name' [AB, Bar, BDAG, BECNT, CBC, LN; all versions except NCV], 'authority' [NCV]. This noun denotes the proper name of a person or object [LN]. In many passages it seems to be a formula [BDAG].

QUESTION—What is referred to by 'power' and 'name'?

Power refers to supernatural force, capable of curing disease. Name links the force with a person. The answer to this question is given in v. 10 [Bar].

QUESTION—What was the leadership's concern that triggered their inquiry to Peter and John?

The leadership knew that they had not given Peter and John the authority to do what they had done in the temple area. In their view, it was theirs to give or withhold. In other words, the leadership inquired of Peter and John what power or authority had given this right to them [BECNT]. They already knew the answer, since Peter had proclaimed the resurrection of Jesus in connection with the healing miracle (3:12–21). However, the challenge was presumably made to expose their theology before the court and provide grounds for accusing them of blasphemy [PNTC]. The leadership's concern was about authority, proper accreditation, law and order, and keeping the peace [NAC]. They questioned by what authority men like Peter and John had presumed to act as they had done [NICNT, TNTC]. They asked this with a scornful tone [AB].

DISCOURSE UNIT—4:8–12 [EBC]. The topic is Peter's defense and witness.

4:8 Then Peter, filled[a] with-(the)-Holy Spirit, said to them, "Rulers of-the people and elders, **4:9** if we are-being-examined[b] today because-of (a)-good-deed-(done-to)[c] (a)-sick[d] man, by what-(means) this-one has-been-healed,

LEXICON—a. aorist pass. participle of πίμπλημι (LN 59.38) (BDAG 1.a.β. p. 813): 'to be filled' [AB, Bar, BDAG, BECNT, CBC, LN; all versions except TEV]. The phrase 'filled with the Holy Spirit' is also translated 'full of the Holy Spirit' [TEV], 'because he was filled with the Holy Spirit' [GW]. This verb means to cause something to be completely full [BDAG, LN], and here it refers to a person's inner life in regard to the Holy Spirit [BDAG]. The verb tense indicates that at that very moment Peter was filled with the Holy Spirit, intimating that the gift of the Holy Spirit was granted on specific occasions to carry out a particular task: 'The Holy Spirit filled Peter's heart and therefore he answered them' [TH].

b. pres. pass. indic. of ἀνακρίνω (LN 56.12) (BDAG 2. p. 66): 'to be examined' [ESV, KJV, NET], 'to be interrogated' [LN], 'to be investigated in court' [LN], 'to be questioned' [BDAG, LN; CEV, NCV, NLT, NRSV, REB, TEV], 'to be asked' [AB], 'to be judged' [BECNT], 'to have one's case heard' [LN], 'to be cross-examined' [Bar; GW], 'to be on trial' [NASB], 'to be called to account' [NIV]. The phrase 'if we are being examined' is also translated 'if the question put to us' [CBC]. This verb means to be the subject of a judicial inquiry [LN]. It means to conduct a judicial hearing. Here with Peter in effect challenging his audience to avoid shame [BDAG].

c. εὐεργεσία (LN 88.7) (BDAG 2. p. 405): 'good deed' [Bar, BDAG, LN; ESV, KJV, NET, NLT, NRSV, TEV], 'benefit' [BDAG; NASB], 'a kindness' [AB, BDAG], 'kind deed' [CEV], 'act of kindness' [NIV], 'good' [GW], 'good thing' [NCV], 'good work' [BECNT], 'help' [CBC; REB]. This noun denotes something which is good and beneficial to someone [LN]. It denotes the content of beneficial service [BDAG].

d. ἀσθενής (LN 23.145) (BDAG 1. p. 142): 'sick' [AB, Bar, BDAG, BECNT, CBC, LN; NASB, NET, NRSV, REB], 'ill' [BDAG, LN], 'weak' [LN], 'crippled' [CEV, ESV, GW, NCV, NLT], 'lame' [TEV], 'disabled' [LN], 'impotent' [KJV]. The phrase 'a sick man' is also translated 'a cripple' [NIV]. This adjective describes someone who is ill and, as a result, is in a state weakness and incapacitation [LN]. It pertains to a state of debilitating illness [BDAG].

QUESTION—Who were the rulers of the people and the elders?

This refers to the leaders of the Jews [TH, TNTC, TRT]. Some Greek manuscripts have 'of Israel' after rulers of the people [TH, TRT]. This begins Peter's testimony before the Sanhedrin [NAC] and Peter has addressed these members of the Sanhedrin politely and respectfully [Bar, BECNT, NAC, TRT].

4:10 **let-it-be known[a] to-all (of) you and to-all the people of-Israel that by the name[b] of-Jesus Christ the Nazarene, whom you crucified,[c] whom God has-raised from (the)-dead by this-(name) this-man stands before you well.[d]**

LEXICON—a. γνωστός (LN 28.21) (BDAG 1.a. p. 204): 'known' [AB, Bar, BDAG, BECNT, LN; ESV, KJV, NASB, NET, NRSV]. The phrase 'let it be known to all of you and to all the people of Israel' is also translated 'there is something we must tell you and everyone else in Israel' [CEV], 'you and all the people of Israel must understand' [GW], 'we want you and all the Jewish people to know' [NCV], 'know this, you and all the people of Israel' [NIV], 'you should all know, and all the people of Israel should know' [TEV], 'let me clearly state to all of you and to all the people of Israel' [NLT], 'this is our answer to all of you and to all the people of Israel' [REB], 'here is the answer, for all of you and for all the people of Israel' [CBC]. This adjective pertains to that which is known [LN]. It pertains to things being familiar or known [BDAG].

b. ὄνομα (LN 33.126) (BDAG 1.d.γ.⅃. p. 713): 'name' [AB, Bar, BDAG, BECNT, CBC, LN; ESV, NJV, NASB, NET, NIV, NRSV, REB], 'power' [CEV, GW, NCV], 'powerful name' [NLT], 'power of the name' [TEV]. This noun denotes 'the proper name of a person or object' [LN]. It refers to the name of God or Jesus, meaning 'with the mention of the name' or 'while calling on the name' [BDAG].

c. aorist act. indic. of σταυρόω (LN 20.76) (BDAG 1. p. 941): 'to crucify' [AB, Bar, BDAG, BECNT, CBC, LN; all versions except CEV], 'to nail to the cross' [BDAG], 'to put to death on a cross' [CEV]. This verb means to execute by nailing to a cross [LN]. It means to fasten to a cross [BDAG].

d. ὑγιής (LN 23.129) (BDAG 1.a. p. 1023): 'well' [LN; ESV, NCV], 'completely well' [CEV, TEV], 'healed' [NIV, NLT], 'cured' [AB], 'healthy' [BDAG, BECNT, LN; NET], 'in good health' [NASB, NRSV], 'with a healthy body' [GW], 'whole' [KJV], 'sound' [BDAG], 'fit and well' [Bar, CBC; REB]. This adjective describes the state of being healthy, well (in contrast with sickness) [LN]. It pertains to persons being physically well or sound [BDAG].

QUESTION—What question is Peter answering?

Peter is answering the question raised in v. 7 'By what power or by what name did you do this?' He addressed his answer to the leaders as well as to the people of Israel. He told them that it was by the name of Jesus Christ that the man got healed. This Jesus was the one they had crucified and then God had raised from the dead [AB, Bar, BECNT, CBC, NAC, NICNT, PNTC, TNTC].

QUESTION—What was 'this man' standing before them?

It refers to the lame man who had been healed and could then walk [TRT]. It indicates the presence of the healed man among them [BECNT, TH]. The Greek word ὑγιής 'well' placed at the end of the verse is emphatic in Greek and it refers to physical health, without damage [BECNT].

4:11 This-one is the stone^a which-was-rejected^b by you, the builders, which has-become (the)-head^c of-(the)-corner.

LEXICON—a. λίθος (LN 2.24) (BDAG 2.f. p. 596): 'stone' [AB, Bar, BDAG, BECNT, CBC, LN; all versions]. This noun denotes a piece of rock, whether shaped or natural [LN]. It denotes a stone of a special kind, here of a building stone of the Father's temple [BDAG].

b. aorist pass. participle of ἐξουθενέω (LN 88.195) (BDAG 2. p. 352): 'to be rejected' [AB, CBC; all versions except CEV, KJV, TEV], 'to be despised' [Bar, BECNT, LN; TEV], 'to be rejected disdainfully' [BDAG]. The phrase 'the stone which was rejected by you, the builders' is also translated 'the stone that you builders thought was worthless' [CEV], 'the stone which was set at naught of you builders' [KJV]. This verb means to despise someone or something on the basis that it is worthless or of no value [LN]. It means to have no use for something, as being beneath one's consideration [BDAG].

c. κεφαλὴ γωνίας (LN 8.10, 7.44) (BDAG p. 209): The phrase 'the head of the/a corner' [Bar; KJV], is also translated 'the head cornerstone' [BECNT], 'the cornerstone' [AB; ESV, GW, NCV, NET, NLT, NRSV, REB], 'the chief corner stone' [NASB], 'the capstone' [NIV], 'the keystone' [CBC], 'the most important stone of all' [CEV], 'the stone that...turned out to be the most important of all' [TEV]. The phrase 'the head of the corner' refers to the cornerstone or capstone of a building that is essential to its construction. Some scholars have assumed that the phrase refers to the capstone occurring at the high point of a peaked roof, but in the NT it would probably refer to the type of stone which would have been used in the Temple in Jerusalem, and therefore it is far more likely to understand it as a cornerstone rather than a capstone of a peaked roof. It would not have referred to the keystone of an arch. Since, however, in many societies the use of 'cornerstone' is not known and in others it may have an entirely different function. It may be more satisfactory to use an expression such as 'the most important stone' or 'the very important stone.' This serves to describe the function and significance of the cornerstone without trying to indicate precisely its location or form [LN (7.44)]. It is either a corner-stone or a keystone [BDAG].

QUESTION—What is meant by saying that Jesus is a 'stone'?

It does not literally mean that Jesus is a stone. It figuratively speaks of Jesus being like a stone that builders use for building [TRT].

QUESTION—Who were the builders?

The builders were the leaders and people of Israel who had put Jesus to death [NAC, TRT]. Builders in Judaism were often associated with teaching or leading. Those close to the stone have failed to appreciate it for what it is [BECNT].

QUESTION—What message is Peter conveying?

This verse is a quote from the Old Testament book of Psalms 118:22 [Bar, BECNT, CBC, NAC, NICNT, PNTC, TH, TNTC, TRT]. Originally it applied either to the king of Israel or to the people of Israel who were rejected by the other nations living at that time but chosen by God for the accomplishment of his purpose [NICNT, PNTC, TNTC, TRT]. Here Jesus is compared with a stone rejected by the builders that had become the cornerstone [AB, CBC]. Peter refers to a prophecy that had been fulfilled when God had raised Jesus from the dead to place him at his His right hand [NICNT, TRT]. Peter declared that the builders rejected the stone (figuratively referring to Jesus) that God elevated to be the cornerstone. What they rejected God vindicated [BECNT, PNTC].

4.12 And there-is salvation[a] in no one else, for there-is no other name[b] under heaven given among men, by which we must[c] be-saved."

LEXICON—a. σωτηρία (LN 21.25) (BDAG 2. p. 986): 'salvation' [AB, Bar, BDAG, BECNT, CBC, LN; all versions except CEV, GW, NCV]. The phrase 'there is salvation in no one else' is also translated 'no one else can save us' [GW], 'only Jesus has the power to save' [CEV], 'Jesus is the only One who can save people' [NCV]. This noun denotes a state of having been saved [LN].

b. ὄνομα (LN 33.126): 'name' [AB, Bar, BECNT, CBC, LN; ESV, NASB, NET, NIV, NLT, NRSV]. The phrase 'no other name under heaven' [AB, Bar, BECNT, CBC; ESV, NASB, NET, NIV, NLT, NRSV] is also translated 'none other name under heaven' [KJV], 'his name is the only one in all the world' [CEV], 'his name is the only power in the world' [NCV], 'in all the world no other name' [REB], 'in all the world there is no one else' [TEV], '(we can be saved) only by the power of the one named Jesus' [GW]. This noun denotes the proper name of a person or object [LN].

c. pres. act. indic. of δεῖ (LN 71.34) (BDAG 1.a. p. 214): 'must, to be necessary' [BDAG, LN]. The phrase 'by/through which we must be saved' [AB, BECNT; ESV, NASB, NET, NIV, NLT, NRSV] is also translated 'whereby we must be saved' [KJV], 'by which we can be saved' [REB], 'by which we are to be saved' [Bar], 'by which we may receive salvation' [CBC], 'and not by any other person' [GW], 'who can save us' [TEV], 'that can save anyone' [CEV], 'We must be saved through him' [NCV]. This verb means to be that which must necessarily take place [LN]. It means to be under necessity of happening [BDAG].

QUESTION—What does 'under heaven' mean?

'Under heaven' means in all of God's creation [PNTC], under the sun [Bar].

QUESTION—What does the word δεῖ 'must' in 'must be saved' imply?

The word 'must' implies that God has determined that one must be saved by Jesus only, not by anyone else [TRT]. There is no one else other than Jesus who has the means to provide salvation, even for Jews who have access to God's revelation [AB, Bar, BECNT, NAC, NICNT, PNTC, TNTC]. This concludes Peter's testimony before the examiners [BECNT, NAC].

DISCOURSE UNIT—4:13–31 [NASB]. The topic is threat and release.

DISCOURSE UNIT—4:13–22 [EBC, NAC, PNTC]. The topic is the apostles warned and released [EBC], warned and released [NAC], teaching the people in the name of Jesus [PNTC].

DISCOURSE UNIT—4:13–17 [NICNT]. The topic is the debate in the Sanhedrin.

4:13 And seeing the boldness[a] of-Peter and John and having-realized that they-were uneducated[b] men and untrained,[c] they-were-amazed,[d] and recognized[e] that they had-been with Jesus.

LEXICON—a παρρησία (LN 25.158) (BDAG 3.a. p. 781): 'boldness' [AB, Bar, BDAG, BECNT, CBC, LN; ESV, KJV, NET, NLT, NRSV, REB], 'courage' [BDAG, LN; NIV], 'confidence' [BDAG; NASB], 'fearlessness' [BDAG]. The phrase 'seeing the boldness of Peter and John...they were amazed' is also translated 'the officials were amazed to see how brave Peter and John were' [CEV], 'the members of the Council were amazed to see how bold Peter and John were' [TEV], 'they were surprised to see how boldly they spoke' [GW], 'the Jewish leaders saw

that Peter and John were not afraid to speak...so they were amazed' [NCV]. This noun denotes a state of boldness and confidence, sometimes implying intimidating circumstances [LN]. It denotes a state of boldness and confidence [BDAG].
- b. ἀγράμματος (LN 27.23) (BDAG p. 15): 'uneducated' [BDAG, LN; ESV, NASB, NET, NRSV, REB], 'unlearned' [LN; KJV], 'unlearned in the Law' [AB], 'unschooled' [NIV], 'untaught' [BECNT], 'untrained' [CBC], 'unlettered' [Bar], 'having no education' [LN; GW, NCV], 'of no education' [TEV], 'not well educated' [CEV], 'illiterate, unable to write' [BDAG]. The phrase 'they were uneducated men and untrained' is also translated 'they were ordinary men with no special training in the Scriptures' [NLT]. This adjective describes someone who has not acquired a formal education [LN]. It refers to being uneducated and illiterate [BDAG].
- c. ἰδιώτης (LN 27.26) (BDAG 1. p. 468): 'untrained' [NASB], 'layman' [AB, Bar, BDAG, CBC, LN; REB], 'ordinary person' [LN], 'ordinary man' [CEV, NET, NIV, NLT, NRSV, TEV], 'common man' [BECNT; ESV], 'having no special training' [GW, NCV], 'amateur' [BDAG], 'ignorant' [KJV]. This adjective describes a person who has not acquired systemic information or expertise in some field of knowledge or activity [LN]. It denotes a person who is relatively unskilled or inexperienced in some activity or field of knowledge [BDAG].
- d. imperf. act. indic. of θαυμάζω (LN 25.213) (BDAG 1.a.α. p. 444): 'to be amazed' [LN; CEV, NASB, NCV, NET, NLT, NRSV, TEV], 'to be astonished' [Bar, BDAG; ESV, NIV, REB], 'to marvel' [AB, BDAG, LN; KJV], 'to wonder' [BDAG, BECNT, CBC, LN], 'to be surprised' [GW]. This verb means to wonder or marvel at some event or object [LN]. It means to be extraordinarily impressed or disturbed by someone [BDAG].
- e. imperf. act. indic. of ἐπιγινώσκω (LN 27.61) (BDAG 3. p. 369): 'to recognize' [AB, Bar, BDAG, BECNT, CBC, LN; ESV, NASB, NET, NLT, NRSV], 'to realize' [GW, NCV, TEV], 'to be certain' [CEV], 'to take knowledge of' [KJV], 'to take note' [NIV, REB]. This verb means to identify newly acquired information with what had been previously learned or known [LN]. It means to connect present information or awareness with what was known before [BDAG].

QUESTION—What does the clause 'they had been with Jesus' indicate and imply?

'They had been with Jesus' indicates that the apostles had been companions with Jesus over a period of time [TH]. The examiners recognized that Peter and John had been with Jesus which spells out what was in their mind. They had associated the apostles' power with Jesus. They knew that the unlettered and unskilled apostles had been trained when they were with Jesus and shared something of his wisdom, insight into the Scriptures and prophetic authority [BECNT, PNTC]. This Jesus was himself just a 'commoner' but also with an amazing boldness and knowledge beyond his training [NAC,

ACTS 4:13

NICNT]. In their mind, just as Jesus' teaching was coupled with demonstrations of miraculous powers, which reinforced among the people the impression of authority; the apostles were now beginning to do the same [EBC, NICNT].

4:14 **And seeing the man who had-been-healed standing with them, they-had nothing to-say-in-opposition.**[a]

LEXICON—a. aorist act. infin. of ἀντιλέγω, (aorist ἀντεῖπον) (LN 33.455) (BDAG p. 87): 'to oppose, to speak in opposition to' [LN]. The clause οὐδὲν εἶχον ἀντειπεῖν 'they/the-leaders had nothing to say in opposition' [BECNT; ESV, NRSV] is also translated 'they had nothing to say against this' [NET], 'they could say nothing against them' [NCV], 'they could say nothing against it' [KJV], 'there was nothing the-council/they could say' [NLT, NIV], 'they couldn't say anything against the two apostles' [GW], 'they had nothing to say in reply' [BDAG, CBC; NASB, REB], 'there was nothing that they could say' [TEV], 'they could give no answer' [AB], 'they could find no reply' [Bar], 'But they could not deny what had happened' [CEV]. This verb means to speak against something or someone [LN]. It means to say something in reply, to say in return [BDAG].

QUESTION— Why couldn't they reply?

The examiners had nothing to say in reply as there was nothing they could say in opposition to or against the man's healed condition. He, the well-known beggar in the community, was no longer crippled and stood there with the apostles [AB, BECNT, EBC, NICNT, PNTC]. He was hard to overlook [NAC].

4:15 **And having-ordered**[a] **them to-go-away**[b] **outside the-meeting-room-of-the-Sanhedrin,**[c] **they-were-conferring**[d] **with one-another,**

LEXICON—a. aorist act. participle of κελεύω (LN 33.323) (BDAG p. 538): 'to order' [BDAG, CBC, LN; GW, NASB, NCV, NET, NIV, NLT, NRSV, REB], 'to command' [AB, Bar, BDAG, BECNT, LN; CEV, ESV, KJV], 'to tell' [TEV]. This verb means to state with force and/or authority what others must do [LN]. It means to give a command that ordinarily is of an official nature [BDAG].

b. aorist act. infin. of ἀπέρχομαι (LN 15.37) (BDAG 1.a. p. 102): 'to go away' [BDAG, LN], 'to go' [AB, Bar; BECNT; NET], 'to go aside' [KJV], 'to depart' [BDAG, LN], 'to leave' [CBC, LN; CEV, ESV, GW, NASB, NCV, NRSV, REB, TEV], 'to withdraw' [NIV], not explicit [NLT]. This verb means to move away from a reference point with emphasis upon the departure [LN]. It means to move away from a reference point [BDAG].

c. συνέδριον (LN 11.80) (BDAG 3. p. 967): 'the meeting room of the Sanhedrin' [BDAG], 'the council room' [CEV, GW], 'the Council room' [TEV], 'the council chamber' [NLT], 'the Sanhedrin' [LN; NIV], the Council' [Bar; NASB], 'the council' [BECNT; ESV, KJV, NET, NRSV],

'the council of the Jews' [LN], 'the court' [CBC; REB], 'the meeting' [NCV], not explicit [AB]. This noun denotes the highest Jewish council, which exercises jurisdiction in civil and religious matters, but having no power over life and death or over military actions or taxation [LN]. Here it denotes a council meeting room [BDAG].
    d. imperf. act. indic. of συμβάλλω (LN 33.159) (BDAG 1.a. p. 956): 'to confer' [BDAG, BECNT, LN; ESV, KJV, NASB, NET, NIV, NLT, REB], 'to discuss' [Bar, CBC; GW, NRSV, TEV], 'to consult' [AB], 'to converse' [BDAG], 'to say' [CEV], 'to talk' [NCV]. This verb means to confer, implying a series of proposals [LN].

QUESTION—Who are the 'them' referring to in 'having ordered them to go away'?
    This refers to Peter and John and probably the healed man [TH].
QUESTION—Is this a normal procedure of hearing?
    This is a normal procedure for the Sanhedrin to order the apostles out of the meeting room. The custom after hearing the witnesses was to dismiss them in order to have as clear and open a discussion among themselves as possible [NAC].

4:16 saying, "What should-we-do with-these men? For on-the-one-(hand), (a)-remarkable[a] miracle[b] has-occurred through them (is)-quite-well-known[c] to-all those living in-Jerusalem, and we-are- not -able to-deny-(it).[d]
LEXICON—a. γνωστός (LN 28.32, 58.55) (BDAG 1.a. p. 204): 'remarkable' [LN (28.32), BDAG], 'well known' [LN (28.32)], 'extraordinary' [LN (58.55); TEV], 'unusual' [LN (58.55)], 'known' [BDAG], 'notable' [BECNT, CBC; ESV, KJV, NET, NRSV, REB], 'noteworthy' [NASB], 'great' [NCV], 'outstanding' [NIV], 'clear' [AB], 'manifest' [Bar], not explicit [CEV]. The phrase 'that a remarkable miracle has occurred through them is quite well known to all those living in Jerusalem' is also translated 'clearly, they've performed a miracle that everyone in Jerusalem knows about' [GW], 'they have performed a miraculous sign, and everybody in Jerusalem knows about it' [NLT]. This adjective describes something that is well known or famous because of some outstanding quality [LN (28.32)] or it pertains to that which is unusual in the sense of being extraordinary [LN (58.55)]. It pertains to being familiar or known [BDAG].
    b. σημεῖον (LN 33.477) (BDAG 2.a. p. 920): 'miracle' [BDAG, CBC, LN; CEV, GW, KJV, NASB, NCV, NIV, REB, TEV], 'miraculous sign' [NET], 'sign' [AB, Bar, BECNT, LN; ESV, NLT, NRSV]. This noun denotes an event which is regarded as having some special meaning. As an event with special meaning was inevitably an unusual or even miraculous type of occurrence in a number of contexts, it may be rendered as 'miracle' [LN]. It denotes an event that is an indication or confirmation or intervention by transcendent powers [BDAG].

c. φανερός (LN 28.28) (BDAG 1. p. 1047): 'quite well known' [BDAG], 'well known, widely known' [LN], 'obvious' [BECNT; NRSV], 'evident' [Bar, BDAG; ESV], 'manifest' [KJV], 'apparent' [NASB], 'plain' [AB, BDAG; NET]. The phrase 'quite well known to all those living in Jerusalem' is also translated 'everyone in Jerusalem knows' [CEV, GW, NCV, TEV], 'everybody in Jerusalem knows' [NLT], 'everyone living in Jerusalem knows' [NIV], 'it is common knowledge in Jerusalem' [CBC; REB]. This adjective describes something that is widely and well known [LN]. It pertains to being evident so as to be readily known [BDAG].

d. pres. mid./pass. (deponent = act.) infin. of ἀρνέομαι (LN 33.277) (BDAG 2. p. 132): 'to deny' [AB, Bar, BDAG, BECNT, CBC, LN; all versions except CEV, NCV]. The phrase 'we are not able to deny it' is also translated 'we cannot say it didn't happen' [CEV], 'we cannot say it is not true' [NCV]. This verb means to say that one does not know about or is in any way related to a person or event [LN]. It means to state that something is not true [BDAG].

QUESTION—Who do 'these men' refer to?

'These men' refers to the apostles Peter and John [TH].

4:17 But-on-the-other-(hand), in-order-that it-may-spread[a] no further among the people, we-must-warn[b] them to-speak no-more[c] to-anyone in this name."

LEXICON—a. aorist pass. subj. of διανέμω (LN 28.24, 84.2) (BDAG p. 234): 'to spread' [AB, Bar, BDAG, BECNT, CBC, LN (28.24, 84.2); all versions], 'to be caused to spread' [LN (84.2)], 'to become known' [LN (28.24)]. This verb means to become known as the result of information spreading abroad [LN (28.24)] or to cause the spread or extension of something' [LN (84.2)]. It means to distribute [BDAG].

b. aorist mid. subj. of ἀπειλέω (LN 33.291) (BDAG p. 100): 'to warn' [BDAG, BECNT; all versions except GW, KJV, REB], 'to threaten' [Bar, BDAG, LN; GW, KJV], 'to forbid with threats' [AB], 'to caution' [CBC; REB]. This verb means to declare that one will cause harm to someone, particularly if certain conditions are not met [LN]. It means to warn [BDAG].

c. μηκέτι (LN 67.130) (BDAG d. p. 647): 'no more' [ESV, NET, NRSV], 'no longer' [BDAG, LN; NASB, NIV], 'never again' [CBC; CEV, REB, TEV], 'never' [GW], 'anymore' [AB, BECNT], 'not from now on' [BDAG]. The phrase 'we must warn them to speak no more to anyone in this name' is also translated 'we must warn them not to talk to people anymore using that name' [NCV], 'we must warn them not to speak to anyone in Jesus' name again' [NLT], 'let us straitly threaten them, that they speak henceforth to no man in this name' [KJV], 'let us threaten them not to speak in this name to a single person' [Bar], 'let us forbid them with threats to say any more to anyone about this name' [AB]. This adverb describes 'the extension of time up to a point but not beyond' [LN].

QUESTION—Who does 'this man' refer to?

'This man' refers to Jesus. The examiners were showing disrespect for Jesus by saying 'this name' instead of 'Jesus' name' [TRT].

QUESTION—What is the objective of the examiners?

The beginning of this verse gives the clear objective of the examiners. They determined that the teaching growing out of the miracle about Jesus spread no further among the people [AB, BECNT, EBC, NICNT, PNTC]. The word ἀπειλέω 'to warn' is not a soft term for warning; it often means to threaten someone with something [BECNT]. In their view, the past must be left alone; the future may be secured by threatening the apostles to no longer speak in Jesus' name [AB, Bar, NAC].

DISCOURSE UNIT—4:18–22 [NICNT]. The topic is the apostles dismissed with a caution.

4:18 And, having-summoned[a] them, they-gave-orders[b] not to-speak[c] or teach at-all in the name of-Jesus.

LEXICON—a. aorist act. participle of καλέω (LN 33.307) (BDAG 3.c. p. 503): 'to summon' [Bar, BDAG, LN; NASB], 'to call' [BECNT; ESV, GW, KJV, NRSV], 'to call in' [AB, BDAG, CBC, LN; CEV, NCV, NET, NIV, NLT, REB, TEV]. This verb means to communicate directly or indirectly to someone who is presumably at a distance, in order to tell such a person to come' [LN]. It is a legal term meaning to call in, to summon before a court [BDAG].

b. aorist act. indic. of παραγγέλλω (LN 33.327) (BDAG p. 760): 'to give orders' [BDAG], 'to order' [Bar, BDAG, CBC, LN; GW, NET, NRSV, REB], 'to command' [AB, BDAG, LN; KJV, NASB, NIV, NLT], 'to instruct, to direct' [BDAG], 'to charge' [BECNT; ESV], 'to tell' [CEV, NCV, TEV]. This verb means to announce what must be done [LN]. It means to forbid to do something [BDAG].

c. pres. mid./pass. (deponent = act.) infin. of φθέγγομαι (LN 33.76) (BDAG p. 1054): 'to speak' [Bar, BDAG, BECNT, LN; all versions except CEV, GW, REB], 'to utter' [BDAG, LN], 'to mention' [GW], 'to proclaim' [BDAG], 'to preach' [AB], 'to speak publicly' [CBC; REB], not explicit [CEV]. This verb means to speak, with a focus upon verbal sound rather than upon content [LN].

QUESTION—What were the apostles ordered not to do?

They were ordered not to make any public proclamation and private teaching in the name of Jesus. Any form of testimony about God's work through Jesus had to be completely halted [AB, Bar, BECNT, EBC, NICNT, TNTC]. Such control might set up the apostles for further punishment if they refused what was in effect an initial warning that could lead to contempt-of-court charges later [BECNT, EBC, TNTC].

4:19 But Peter and John answered and said to them, "If it-is right in-the-sight[a] of-God to-listen[b] to-you rather than to-God, you-judge,[c] **4:20** for we are- not -able[d] not to-speak (of) what we-saw and heard."

LEXICON—a. ἐνώπιον (LN 90.20) (BDAG 3. p. 342): 'in the sight of' [LN], 'in the opinion of, in the judgment of' [BDAG, LN]. The phrase 'in the sight of God' [Bar, BECNT; ESV, KJV, NASB] is also translated 'in God's sight' [NIV, NRSV, TEV], 'in God's eyes' [CBC], 'in the eyes of God' [REB], 'before God' [NET], 'in duty to God' [AB]. The phrase 'if it is right in the sight of God' is also translated 'do you think God wants us to' [CEV, NLT], 'whether God wants' [GW], 'what God would want' [NCV]. This preposition marks a participant whose viewpoint is relevant to an event [LN]. It pertains to an exposure to value judgment [BDAG].

b. pres. act. infin. of ἀκούω (LN 36.14) (BDAG 4. p. 38): 'to listen' [Bar, BDAG; ESV, GW, NRSV], 'to hearken' [KJV], 'to pay attention and obey' [LN], 'to obey' [AB, BECNT, CBC; CEV, NCV, NET, NIV, NLT, REB, TEV], 'to give heed to' [NASB], 'to follow' [BDAG]. This verb means to listen or pay attention to a person, with resulting conformity to what is advised or commanded [LN]. It means to give careful attention to someone' [BDAG].

c. aorist act. impera. of κρίνω (LN 30.108) (BDAG 3. p. 568): 'to judge' [AB, BDAG, BECNT, CBC, LN; ESV, KJV, NIV, NRSV, REB, TEV], 'to decide' [BDAG; GW, NCV, NET], 'to think' [BDAG; CEV, NLT], 'to evaluate' [LN], 'to consider, to look upon' [BDAG], 'to make up your own minds' [Bar]. The phrase 'you judge' is also translated 'you be the judge' [NASB]. This verb means to make a judgment based upon the correctness or value of something [LN]. It means to make a judgment based on taking various factors into account [BDAG].

d. pres. mid./pass. (deponent = act.) indic. of δύναμαι (LN 74.5) (BDAG 1.a. p. 207): 'to be able' [BDAG, LN]. The phrase 'we are not able not to speak of/about' [BECNT] is also translated 'we cannot but speak (of)' [Bar; ESV, KJV], 'we cannot stop talking/speaking about/of' [GW, NASB, TEV], 'we cannot possibly give up speaking of/about' [CBC; REB], 'we cannot keep from speaking about' [NRSV], 'we cannot refrain from speaking of' [AB], 'we cannot keep quiet about' [CEV], 'it is impossible for us not to speak about' [NET], 'we cannot stop telling about' [NLT], 'we cannot help speaking about' [NIV], 'We cannot keep quiet. We must speak about' [NCV]. This verb means to be able to do something [LN]. It means to possess the capacity (whether because of personal or external factors) for experiencing or doing something [BDAG].

QUESTION—What is the stand of the apostles in responding to the examiners' warning?

Despite the warning, the apostles held their stand in believing Jesus and witnessing for his teaching, crucifixion, resurrection and ascension. They in turn challenged the examiners to judge for themselves whether their command could actually be obeyed. The apostles could not abandon their obedience to God and their responsibility to witness to the risen Lord no matter what the cost [AB, Bar, BECNT, CBC, EBC, NICNT, PNTC, TNTC]. The clause 'we (the apostles) are not able not to speak' creates a double negative stating the refusal to obey most emphatically [BECNT]. The apostles' response was in direct discourse; it was bold and almost defiant [NAC, NICNT, TNTC].

4:21 And, having-threatened-(them)-further,[a] they-released[b] them, finding no way they-might-punish them, because-of the people; for all were-praising[c] God for what had-happened. **4:22** For the man on whom this miracle of-healing was performed was more-than forty years (old).

LEXICON—a. aorist mid. participle of προσαπειλέω (LN 33.292) (BDAG p. 876): 'to threaten further' [BDAG, LN; ESV, KJV, NASB, NET, NLT], 'to threaten even more' [GW], 'to threaten still more' [AB], 'to threaten again' [NRSV], 'to threaten' [CEV], 'to warn again' [NCV], 'to warn even more strongly' [TEV], 'to repeat the caution' [CBC]. The phrase 'having threatened them further' is also translated 'had further threatened them' [BECNT], 'repeated their threats' [Bar], 'after further threats' [NIV], 'with a repeated caution' [REB]. This verb means to add to or extend one's threats [LN]. It means to threaten further [BDAG].

b. aorist act. indic. of ἀπολύω (LN 37.127): 'to release' [AB, LN; NET], 'to set free' [LN; TEV], 'to let go' [BECNT; CEV, ESV, GW, KJV, NASB, NIV, NLT, NRSV], 'to let go free' [NCV], 'to discharge' [CBC; REB], 'to send away, to dismiss' [Bar]. This verb means to release from control [LN].

c. imperf. act. indic. of δοξάζω (LN 87.24) (BDAG 1. p. 258): 'to praise' [AB, BDAG, BECNT; all versions except KJV, NASB, REB], 'to glorify' [Bar, LN; KJV, NASB], 'to give glory to' [CBC; REB], 'to honor, to extol' [BDAG], 'to make gloriously great' [LN]. This verb means to cause someone to have glorious greatness [LN]. It means to influence one's opinion about another so as to enhance the latter's reputation [BDAG].

QUESTION—What is the authorities' final response to this matter?

The authorities still refused to change their view that they were against God's will even though the sign was so real and that people were all praising God. They gave further threat to the apostles to be silent before letting them go [AB, BECNT, EBC, NICNT, PNTC, TNTC].

QUESTION—What information does Luke try to give by telling that the healed man was more than forty years (old)?

The lame man is healed of a condition he has had from birth for more than forty years; regenerative cures do not occur of themselves at such an age [EBC, NICNT]. The man's mature age makes the cure particularly striking and remarkable, that the crowd would not have been glorifying God had the man been only twenty [Bar, NAC, TNTC]. Luke brings out this final key observation about how anyone could be punished for this miracle, an act of God through the apostles [BECNT, NAC]. The lame man's restoration after forty years establishes a temporal link to Israel in the wilderness, so that the healed man represents an image of restoration for the entire nation. That makes it clear why the authorities found the evidence for miraculous healing so hard to deny [PNTC].

DISCOURSE UNIT—4:23–37 [PNTC]. The topic is the boldness and generosity of the new Israel.

DISCOURSE UNIT—4:23–31 [AB, Bar, BECNT, CBC, EBC, NAC, NICNT, PNTC, TNTC; CEV, ESV, GW, NCV, NET, NIV, NLT, NRSV, TEV]. The topic is the church's praise and petition [EBC], the prayer of the community [NAC], the Christians pray for boldness during their persecution [AB], the believers pray for boldness [ESV, NRSV, TEV], the followers of Jesus pray for boldness [NET], the disciples pray for further boldness [TNTC], their prayer for boldness [PNTC], prayer for boldness [BECNT], Peter and others pray for courage [CEV], the believers pray for courage [NLT], the prayer for strength [CBC], the apostles pray for God's help [GW], the believers pray [NCV], the believers' prayer [NIV], return of Peter and John [Bar], Peter and John rejoin their friends [NICNT].

4:23 And having-been-released,[a] they-went to their own-(friends)[b] and reported what the chief-priests[c] and the elders[d] had-said to them.

LEXICON—a. aorist pass. participle of ἀπολύω (LN 37.127) (BDAG 3. p. 117): 'to be released' [AB, Bar, BECNT, LN; ESV, GW, NASB, NET, NRSV], 'to be set free' [LN; CEV, TEV], 'to be let go' [BDAG; KJV], 'to be freed' [NLT], 'to be discharged' [CBC; REB], 'to be dismissed, to be sent away' [BDAG]. The phrase 'And, having been released, they went to their own friends' is also translated 'After Peter and John left the meeting of Jewish leaders, they went to their own group' [NCV], 'On their release, Peter and John went back to their own people' [NIV]. This verb means to release from control, to set free [LN]. This verb means to permit or cause someone to leave a particular location [BDAG].

b. ἴδιος (LN 57.4) (BDAG 4.a. p. 467): The phrase τοὺς ἰδίους 'their own' [LN] is also translated 'their friends' [BECNT, CBC; ESV, NRSV, REB], 'their own company' [KJV], 'their own companions' [NASB], 'their fellows' [AB], 'their fellow believers' [NET], 'their own people' [Bar; NIV], 'their own group' [NCV], 'their group' [TEV]. The phrase 'they went to their own friends and reported' is also translated 'they went back and told the others' [CEV], 'they went to the other apostles and told them' [GW], 'Peter and John returned to the other believers and told them' [NLT]. This noun denotes someone or something that is considered to belong exclusively to someone [LN]. It denotes associations or relations, here, fellow Christians [BDAG].

c. ἀρχιερεύς (LN 53.88): 'chief priest' [Bar, BECNT, CBC, LN; all versions except NCV, NET, NLT], 'high priest' [AB; NET], 'leading priest' [NCV, NLT]. This noun denotes a principal priest, in view of belonging to one of the high-priestly families [LN]. It denotes a priest of high rank [BDAG].

d. πρεσβύτερος (LN 53.77) (BDAG 2.a.β. p. 862): 'elder' [AB, Bar, BDAG, BECNT, CBC, LN; all versions except CEV, GW, NCV], 'leader' [CEV, GW], 'older Jewish leader' [NCV], 'presbyter' [BDAG]. This noun denotes a person of responsibility and authority in matters of socio-religious concerns, both in Jewish and Christian circles [LN]. It denotes a member of a group in the Sanhedrin [BDAG].

4:24 And when they-heard (this) they-raised[a] (their)-voices to God with-one-mind[b] and said, "Lord,[c] you who-made the heaven[d] and the earth[e] and the sea[f] and everything that is in them,

LEXICON—a. aorist act. indic. of αἴρω (LN 33.78) (BDAG 1.b. p. 28): 'to lift up' [Bar, BDAG, BECNT], 'to raise the voice, to cry out, to speak loudly' [LN]. The phrase 'they raised their voices' [AB, CBC; NET, NIV, NLT, NRSV, REB] is also translated 'they lifted (up) their voices' [Bar; ESV, KJV, NASB], 'those who heard it lifted their voices up' [BECNT], 'they loudly prayed' [GW], 'they prayed' [CEV, NCV], 'they joined (together) in prayer' [TEV]. The idiom literally 'to raise the voice' means to increase the volume with which one speaks, so as to overcome existing noise or the speech of someone else [LN]. This is a figurative use of the verb 'to lift up' and means to raise one's voice, to cry out loudly [BDAG].

b. ὁμοθυμαδόν (LN 31.23) (BDAG p. 706): 'with one mind' [BDAG, LN; NET], 'with one accord' [KJV, NASB, REB], 'as one man' [CBC], 'together' [Bar, BECNT; CEV, ESV, NCV, NIV, NLT, NRSV, TEV], 'all' [AB], 'they were united' [GW], 'by common consent, unanimously' [LN], 'with one purpose, with one impulse' [BDAG]. This adverb pertains to mutual consent or agreement [LN]. It pertains to being one and the same [BDAG].

c. δεσπότης (LN 37.63) (BDAG 1.b. p. 220): 'Lord' [AB, BDAG, LN; KJV, NASB, NCV], 'Sovereign Lord' [BECNT, CBC; ESV, NIV, NLT, NRSV, REB], 'Master' [Bar, BDAG, LN; CEV, GW, TEV], 'Master of all' [NET], 'ruler' [LN]. This noun denotes 'one who holds complete power or authority over another' [LN]. It denotes one who has legal control and authority over persons, and it is used especially in reference to God [BDAG].

d. οὐρανός (LN 1.3) (BDAG 1.a.α. p. 737): 'heaven' [AB, Bar, BDAG, BECNT, CBC, LN; all versions except GW, NCV], 'sky' [GW, NCV]. The Greek phrase ὁ οὐρανὸς καὶ ἡ γῆ 'the heaven and the earth' denotes 'the totality of God's creation', the universe [LN]. It denotes the portion or portions of the universe generally distinguished from planet earth, and here it is mentioned with the earth, thus forming a unity with it as the totality of creation [BDAG].

e. γῆ (LN 1.3): 'earth' [AB, Bar, BECNT, CBC, LN; all versions except GW], 'land' [GW]. The Greek phrase ὁ οὐρανὸς καὶ ἡ γῆ 'the heaven and the earth' denotes 'the totality of God's creation', the universe [LN].
f. θάλασσα (LN 1.69) (BDAG 1.a. p. 442): 'sea' [AB, Bar, BDAG, BECNT, CBC, LN; all versions]. This noun is 'a generic collective term for all bodies of water…contrasted with the sky and the land' [LN]. The combination heaven, earth, and sea denotes the whole universe [BDAG].

QUESTION—What is meant by raising their voices to God with one mind?

It means that all the apostles offered their praises to God and prayed to God in unison [AB, NAC]. It is most likely that one person prayed with the whole community sharing in the spirit and nature of the request, expressing the convictions and concerns of all [AB, BECNT, PNTC].

QUESTION—What did the apostles pray?

The apostles addressed God as their Lord or Master [Bar, EBC, NAC, NICNT, PNTC, TNTC]. This title is a common designation for God in the Old Testament, but comparatively infrequent in the New Testament [Bar, NICNT]. It expresses God's sovereign position and absolute authority [BECNT]. They began their prayer with the words similar to the Old Testament Scripture in Exodus 20:11a where God was addressed as the Creator, Maker of heaven, earth, sea and all that was in them [NAC, TH]; similar words and phrases are found in Psalm 146:6 as well [Bar, PNTC, TNTC, TRT]. Such a claim shows their belief in God, who has control over nature, is also sovereign in human affairs, even in the lives of those who rebel against him [BECNT, PNTC, TNTC].

4:25 who through-(the)-mouth of our ancestor[a] David, your servant, said by[b] (the)-Holy Spirit, 'Why did- (the)-nations[c] -rage[d] and (the)-peoples plot[e] foolish-(things)?

TEXT—The phrase 'our ancestor' is not present in some manuscripts, including those on which the KJV and the REB are based.

LEXICON—a. πατήρ (LN 10.20): 'ancestor' [LN; CEV, GW, NLT, NRSV, TEV], 'forefather' [LN; NET], 'father' [AB, Bar, BECNT; ESV, NASB, NCV, NIV], not explicit [CBC; REB]. The phrase 'our ancestor' is also translated 'thy servant' [KJV]. This noun denotes a person several preceding generations from the reference person [LN].
b. διά (LN 90.4) (BDAG p. 224): 'by' [AB, Bar, BDAG, CBC, LN; CEV, ESV, NASB, NCV, NET, NIV, NLT, NRSV, REB], 'by means of' [TEV], 'through' [BDAG, BECNT, LN; GW], not explicit [KJV]. This genitive indicates an intermediate agent [LN]. It is a marker of instrumentality whereby something is accomplished [BDAG].
c. ἔθνος (LN 11.55): 'nation' [BECNT, LN; GW, NCV, NET, NIV, NLT], 'people' [LN], 'Gentile' [AB, Bar, CBC; CEV, ESV, NASB, NRSV, REB, TEV], 'heathen' [KJV]. This noun denotes the largest unit into which the people of the world are divided on the basis of their constituting a socio-political community [LN].

d. aorist act. indic. of φρυάσσω (LN 88.185) (BDAG p. 1067): 'to rage' [BECNT, CBC; ESV, KJV, NASB, NET, NIV, NRSV, REB], 'to rave' [LN], 'to be incensed' [LN], 'to be furious' [CEV, TEV], 'to be arrogant, to be haughty, to be insolent' [BDAG], 'to behave insolently' [Bar], 'to act arrogantly' [GW], 'to boast' [AB]. The phrase 'Why did the nations rage' is also translated 'Why are/were the nations so angry' [NCV, NLT]. This verb means 'to show insolent anger' and evidently combines not only anger but a considerable measure of opposition, both verbal and nonverbal [LN].

e. aorist act. indic. of μελετάω (LN 30.60) (BDAG 3. p. 627): 'to plot, to plan to act' [LN], 'to think about, to meditate upon' [BDAG]. The phrase 'plot foolish things' [NET] is also translated 'plot in vain' [LN; ESV, NIV], 'make their useless plots' [TEV], 'devise futile things' [NASB], 'devise useless plots' [GW], 'lay their plots in vain' [CBC], 'hatch their futile plots' [REB], 'waste their time with futile plans' [NLT], 'are making useless plans' [NCV], 'imagine vain things' [KJV, NRSV], 'imagine useless things' [BECNT], 'make foolish plans' [CEV], 'make vain plans' [Bar], 'make plans in vain' [AB], 'waste their time with futile plans' [NLT]. This verb means to think seriously about a particular course of action [LN]. It means to fix one's mind on something [BDAG].

QUESTION—In the apostles' prayer, what did God speak through David?

In the prayer, the apostles referred to the prophecy that God made through David under the inspiration of the Holy Spirit. The reference was in the Old Testament Scripture Psalm 2:1–2. Here the verse said the people plot foolish things while the psalter said the people plot in vain. The content of the prophecy is quoted in this verse and completed in the following verse. The prophecy is about Christ the Messiah whom people would be against [Bar, BECNT, CBC, EBC, NAC, NICNT, TH, TNTC]. The opposition to God's plan would be foolish and in vain because the one they plotted against was the Creator and who even knew in advance of their scheming [BECNT, NAC]; it was God's will that would be done [Bar].

QUESTION—What did the raging nations and the people represent?

The raging nations represented the Gentile rulers and their cohorts, the soldiers who executed Jesus. The people were the people of Israel who plotted against God and his Messiah [BECNT, EBC, NAC, NICNT].

4:26 **The kings of-the earth took-their-stand,[a] and the rulers[b] were-gathered[c] together against the Lord[d] and against his Messiah.[e]'**

LEXICON—a. aorist act. indic. of παρίστημι (LN 17.3) (BDAG 2.a.β. p. 778): 'to stand near' [LN], 'to be present' [BDAG]. The phrase 'took their stand' [CBC; NASB, NRSV, REB] is also translated 'take their stand' [GW, NIV], 'were there' [LN], 'stood there' [Bar], 'stood in array' [AB], 'stood together' [NET], 'stood up' [KJV], 'set themselves' [ESV], 'set themselves in array' [BECNT], 'prepare for war/battle' [CEV, NLT], 'prepare to fight' [NCV], 'prepared themselves' [TEV]. This verb means

to stand near or alongside of someone with either friendly or hostile intent. To indicate merely that the kings of the earth were present may not be sufficient to communicate the hostile intent implied by the context of this verse. It may therefore be important to translate 'the kings of earth prepared themselves' or even 'the kings of earth armed themselves' [LN]. It means to be present with a hostile intent [BDAG].
- b. ἄρχων (LN 37.56) (BDAG 1.a. p. 140): 'ruler' [AB, Bar, BDAG, BECNT, CBC, LN; all versions except NCV], 'leader' [NCV], 'governor' [LN]. This noun denotes one who rules or governs [LN]. It denotes one who has eminence in a ruling capacity [BDAG].
- c. aorist pass. indic. of συνάγω (LN 15.125) (BDAG 1.b. p. 962): 'to gather together' [AB, Bar, BECNT, LN; ESV, KJV, NASB, NIV, NLT, NRSV], 'to assemble' [NET], 'to join together' [CEV], 'to meet together' [TEV], 'to call together' [BDAG, LN], 'to gather' [BDAG]. The phrase 'The kings of the earth took their stand and the rulers were gathered together' is also translated 'Kings take their stand. Rulers make plans together' [GW], 'The kings of the earth prepare to fight, and their leaders make plans together' [NCV], 'The kings of the earth took their stand and the rulers made common cause' [CBC; REB]. This verb means to gather together [BDAG, LN].
- d. κύριος (LN 12.9) (BDAG 2.b.α. p. 578): 'Lord' [AB, Bar, BDAG, BECNT, CBC, LN; all versions], 'Ruler, One who commands' [LN], 'master' [BDAG]. This noun is a title for God and for Christ and refers to one who exercises supernatural authority over mankind' [LN]. It denotes one who is in a position of authority, and is used as a designation for God [BDAG].
- e. Χριστός (LN 53.82) (BDAG 1. p. 1091): 'Messiah' [AB, BDAG, CBC, LN; CEV, GW, NLT, NRSV, REB, TEV], 'Christ' [Bar, LN; KJV, NASB, NCV, NET], 'anointed' [BECNT], 'Anointed' [ESV], 'Anointed One' [BDAG; NIV]. Literally 'one who has been anointed' is a title for Jesus as the Messiah [LN]. It denotes the fulfiller of Israelite expectation of a deliverer [BDAG].

QUESTION—Who were together against the Lord and his Messiah in the prophecy?

Together with the raging nations and the people of Israel, kings of the earth and rulers were against the Lord and his Messiah [Bar, EBC, NICNT, PNTC].

4:27 For truly in this city there-were-gathered-together against your holy servant[a] Jesus, whom you-anointed,[b] both Herod and Pontius Pilate along-with (the)-Gentiles and (the)-people of-Israel, **4:28** to-do whatever your hand[c] and your will[d] had-predestined[e] to-occur.

LEXICON—a. παῖς (LN 87.77) (BDAG 3.b.γ. p. 750): 'servant' [BDAG], 'slave' [LN]. The phrase 'your holy servant' [AB, BECNT; all versions except KJV] is also translated 'thy holy servant' [Bar, CBC], 'thy holy

child' [KJV]. This noun denotes a slave, possibly serving as a personal servant and thus with the implication of a kindly regard toward him' [LN]. It denotes one who is committed in total obedience to another. In this case, it is the special relationship of Christ with God and in this connection it has the meaning of 'servant' because of the identification of the 'servant of God' of certain OT passages with the Messiah [BDAG].
  b. aorist act. indic. of χρίω (LN 37.107) (BDAG b. p. 1091): 'to anoint' [Bar, BDAG, BECNT, LN; ESV, GW, KJV, NASB, NET, NIV, NLT, NRSV], 'to assign, to appoint' [LN], 'to anoint as Messiah' [CBC; REB], 'to appoint Messiah' [AB]. The phrase 'Jesus, whom you anointed' is also translated 'Jesus, your chosen Messiah' [CEV], 'Jesus…whom you made Messiah' [TEV], 'Jesus…the one you made to be the Christ' [NCV]. This verb means to assign a person to a task, with the implication of supernatural sanctions, blessing, and endowment [LN]. It has the sense of an anointing by God that sets someone apart for special service under divine direction [BDAG].
  c. χείρ (LN 76.3) (BDAG 2.b.β. p. 1083): 'hand' [AB, Bar, BDAG, BECNT, CBC, LN; ESV, KJV, NASB, NRSV, REB], 'power' [LN; CEV, GW, NCV, NET, NIV, TEV], not explicit [NLT]. This noun is a figurative extension of meaning of the word 'hand' as an expression of the activity of a person or supernatural being [LN]. The hand of deity denotes God's divine power as ruler, helper, worker of wonders, and regulator of the universe [BDAG].
  d. βουλή (LN 30.57) (BDAG 2.b. p. 182): 'will' [AB, BECNT; GW, NCV, NIV, NLT, TEV], 'purpose' [LN; NASB], 'counsel' [Bar; KJV], 'wisdom' [CEV], 'plan' [LN; ESV, NET, NRSV], 'intention' [LN], 'decree' [CBC; REB]. This noun denotes that which has been purposed and planned [LN]. It denotes that which one decides and here it refers to the divine will [BDAG].
  e. aorist act. indic. of προορίζω (LN 30.84) (BDAG p. 873): 'to predestine' [BECNT; ESV, NASB, NRSV], 'to predetermine' [BDAG], 'to foreordain' [Bar, CBC; REB], 'to decide beforehand' [LN; NET, NIV], 'to decide already' [CEV, GW, TEV], 'to determine beforehand' [NLT], 'to determine before' [KJV], 'to determine' [AB], 'to determine ahead of time, to decide upon ahead of time' [LN]. The phrase 'to do whatever your hand and your will had predestined to occur' is also translated 'made your plan happen because of your power and your will' [NCV]. This verb means to come to a decision beforehand [LN]. It means to decide upon beforehand [BDAG].
QUESTION—Who were those who were against Jesus?
  Herod and Pontius Pilate (kings of the earth and the rulers in the prophecy), along with the Gentiles and the people of Israel (the raging nations and people in the prophecy) were against Jesus [Bar, EBC, NICNT, PNTC, TNTC].

QUESTION—Who did Herod, Pilate, and Jesus represent?
Herod represented the 'kings of the earth' and Pilate, represented 'the rulers'. Jesus was God's Messiah as related to the prophecy. The prophecy which was predestined by God had been fulfilled on Jesus Christ [AB, Bar, EBC, NAC, NICNT, PNTC, TNTC].

QUESTION—Had the opponents of Jesus upset God's plans?
The opponents of Jesus were doing just what Scripture predicted. The apostles saw both God's power and will in the events [PNTC]. The opponents were simply carrying out God's appointed counsel and foreknowledge [NICNT]. The opponents were in fact tools in the hand of God who used them to carry out his own purposes [Bar]. The human rejection Jesus experienced fell within God's plan and the activity of God's hand, that is, God's will and power [BECNT]. All that was plotted and done against Jesus was no more than God had foreordained to happen [TNTC]. That gave the apostles conviction that God was able to carry out his purpose even through rebellious human beings who did not accept his revealed will [BECNT, PNTC]. In the paradox of human freedom and divine sovereignty, despite all the raging of humanity, God's purposes prevail [NAC].

4:29 And now, Lord, look[a] upon their threats and grant[b] that your servants may-speak your word with all boldness[c] **4:30** while you stretch-out your hand to heal, and signs[d] and wonders[e] take place through[f] the name of-your holy servant Jesus."

LEXICON—a. aorist act. impera. of ἐπεῖδον (LN 30.45) (BDAG p. 360): 'to look at, to fix one's glance upon' [BDAG] 'to concern oneself with' [BDAG, LN], 'to take notice of, to consider, to pay attention to' [LN]. The imperative form ἔπιδε ἐπὶ 'look upon' [Bar, BECNT; ESV] is also translated 'look at' [NRSV], 'behold' [KJV], 'pay attention to' [GW, NET], 'take note of' [NASB], 'take notice of' [AB; TEV], 'mark' [CBC; REB], 'listen to' [CEV, NCV], 'hear' [NLT], 'consider' [NIV]. The verb means to take special notice of something, with the implication of concerning oneself about it [LN]. It means to fix one's glance upon something and here it is about God's concern with human things [BDAG].
   b. aorist act. impera. of δίδωμι (LN 90.51) (BDAG 13, p. 243]: 'to grant' [AB, Bar, BDAG, BECNT; ESV, KJV, NASB, NET, NRSV], 'to cause, to bring about' [LN], 'to allow' [BDAG; GW, TEV], 'to help' [NCV], 'to enable' [CBC; NIV, REB]. The clause 'grant that your servants may speak your word with all boldness' is also translated 'make us brave enough to speak your message' [CEV], 'give us…great boldness in preaching your word' [NLT]. This verb indicates a causal relation [LN]. It means to grant by formal action the power to speak courageously [BDAG].
   c. παρρησία (LN 25.158) (BDAG 3.a. p. 781): 'boldness' [AB, Bar, BDAG, BECNT, CBC, LN; ESV, KJV, NIV, NLT, NRSV, REB, TEV], 'courage' [BDAG, LN; NET], 'fearlessness' [BDAG], 'confidence'

[BDAG; NASB]. The phrase 'grant that your servants may speak your word with all boldness' is also translated 'make us brave enough to speak your message' [CEV], 'allow us to speak your word boldly' [GW], 'help us, your servants, to speak your word without fear' [NCV]. This noun denotes a state of boldness and confidence, sometimes implying intimidating circumstances [LN]. It denotes a state of boldness and confidence [BDAG].

d. σημεῖον (LN 33.477) (BDAG 2.a.α. p. 920): 'sign' [AB, Bar, BECNT, CBC, LN; ESV, KJV, NASB, NRSV, REB], 'miraculous sign' [NET, NIV, NLT], 'proof' [NCV], 'miracle' [BDAG, LN; CEV, GW], 'wonder' [TEV]. This noun denotes an event which is regarded as having some special meaning [LN]. It refers to an event that is an indication or confirmation of intervention by transcendent powers [BDAG].

e. τέρας (LN 33.480) (BDAG p. 999): 'wonder' [AB, BDAG, BECNT, CBC; all versions except GW, NCV, REB], 'amazing thing' [GW], 'miracle' [NCV], 'portent' [Bar, BDAG, LN; REB], 'omen' [BDAG], 'sign' [LN]. This noun denotes an unusual sign, especially one in the heavens, serving to foretell impending events [LN]. It denotes something that astounds because of transcendent association [BDAG].

f. διά (LN 89.76): 'through, by means of, by' [LN]. The phrase 'through the name of' [AB, Bar, BECNT, CBC; all versions except CEV, KJV, NCV] is also translated 'in the name of' [CEV], 'by the name of' [KJV], 'by the power of' [NCV]. This preposition indicates the means by which one event makes another event possible [LN].

QUESTION—What does the phrase 'And now' indicate?

The phrase 'And now' indicates a shift to the prayer's request now [BECNT], a shift of attention from the historical event to the circumstances faced by the believers [TH].The phrase 'And now' is a bridging formula as also used in Acts 5:38; 20:32; 27:22 [PNTC]. The prayer now passes from the past to the future [Bar].

QUESTION—What were the apostles asking God?

Based on the apostles' understanding about God's sovereignty in nature and human affairs, they did not ask God for further deliverance [NAC], relief from opposition [EBC], nor for crushing the opponents [BECNT]. They asked God to take note of the threats and act on their behalf, and they also asked God to grant them boldness in speaking God's word. They asked for further healing acts, signs and miracles performed by them, but through the name of Jesus Christ [AB, Bar, BECNT, EBC, NAC, NICNT, PNTC, TNTC]. They did not ask this for their own power over the enemies but for God's word to go forth and in Christ's name to be glorified [EBC, NAC].

QUESTION—What is implied by asking God to stretch out his hand to heal?

The apostles acknowledged that it was God's power that healings, signs, and miracles were performed, and they were asking for enablement to match God's visible activity and sovereign ability to heal with their proclamation of God's word [BECNT, PNTC]. The image of God stretching out his 'hand' to perform signs and wonders through Moses is common in the book of Exodus (e.g., 3:20; 6:6; 7:3, 5). And now in the book of Acts, such activity is normally associated with the apostles (e.g., 2:43; 3:6–8; 5:12–16; 6:8; 8:6–7) [PNTC]. A nonfigurative equivalent in some languages is 'show your power', 'make people see your strength', or 'cause people to see that you are strong' [TH].

4:31 **And when- they -had-prayed, the place in which they-were-gathered-together was-shaken,ᵃ and everyone was-filledᵇ with-the Holy Spirit and continued to-speak the wordᶜ of-God with boldness.ᵈ**

LEXICON—a. aorist pass. indic. of σαλεύω (LN 16.7) (BDAG 1. p. 911): 'to be shaken' [AB, Bar, BDAG, BECNT, LN; all versions except GW, NLT, REB], 'to shake' [GW, NLT], 'to be rocked' [CBC; REB]. This verb means to cause something to move back and forth rapidly, often violently [LN]. It means to cause to move to and fro, and in this verse it is a sign of the divine presence [BDAG].

b. aorist pass. indic. of πίμπλημι (LN 59.38) (BDAG 1.a.β. p. 813): 'to be filled' [AB, Bar, BDAG, BECNT, CBC; all versions], 'to be filled up, to be filled completely' [LN]. This verb means to cause something to be completely full [LN]. It means to cause something to be completely full, here of a person's inner life in reference to the Holy Spirit [BDAG].

c. λόγος (LN 33.260) (BDAG 1.a..β. p. 599): 'word' [AB, Bar, BECNT, CBC; all versions except CEV, TEV], 'message' [CEV, TEV]. This noun denotes the content of what is preached about Christ or about the good news [LN]. It denotes a communication whereby the mind finds expression. In this verse the apostles and other preachers were speaking the word, and of their hearers it is said that they were hearing the 'word of God'. In many places 'the word of God' is simply the Christian message, the gospel [BDAG].

d. παρρησία (LN 25.158) (BDAG 3.a. p. 781): 'boldness' [AB, Bar, BDAG, BECNT, CBC, LN; ESV, KJV, NASB, NLT, NRSV, REB, TEV], 'courage' [BDAG, LN], 'confidence, fearlessness' [BDAG]. The phrase 'continued to speak the word of God with boldness' is also translated 'bravely spoke God's message' [CEV], 'continued to speak the word of God boldly' [GW], 'spoke God's word without fear' [NCV], 'to speak the word of God courageously' [NET], 'spoke the word of God boldly' [NIV]. This noun denotes a state of boldness and confidence, sometimes implying intimidating circumstances [LN]. It is a state of boldness and confidence [BDAG].

QUESTION—How did God respond to the prayer of the apostles?

God gave the apostles immediate responses. The shaking of the house gave the apostles a tangible sense of God's presence and his divine response to their prayer. They were then filled with the Holy Spirit and were enabled to speak the word of God with boldness [AB, Bar, BECNT, EBC, NAC, NICNT, PNTC, TNTC].

QUESTION—Was this a second Pentecost?
This was not a 'second Pentecost' [BECNT, CBC, NAC, NICNT, PNTC], it was a fresh renewal [CBC]. The apostles had already received the Holy Spirit. The Spirit had helped Peter and John in a mighty way before the Sanhedrin, the examining leaders. This was a fresh filling, a renewed awareness of the Spirit's power and presence in their life and witness [NAC, NICNT]. Such a fresh filling experience enabled them to continue their work of proclaiming God's word and testifying to the resurrection of the Lord Jesus [BECNT, PNTC, TNTC].

DISCOURSE UNIT—4:32–5:12a [CBC]. The topic is the common life.

DISCOURSE UNIT—4:32–5:11 [EBC, NICNT]. The topic is Christian concern expressed in sharing [EBC], all things in common [NICNT].

DISCOURSE UNIT—4:32–37 [AB, BECNT, NAC, PNTC, TNTC; CEV, ESV, GW, NASB, NCV, NET, NIV, NLT, NRSV, TEV]. The topic is the common life of the community [NAC], the common ownership of property among the Christians [AB], a further summary of the life of the early church [TNTC], the example of Barnabas [BECNT], their impressive generosity [PNTC], sharing possessions [CEV], sharing among believers [NASB], they have everything in common [ESV], the believers share their possessions [NLT, NRSV, TEV], the believers share their property [GW], the believers share [NCV], conditions among the early believers [NET].

DISCOURSE UNIT—4:32–35 [Bar, EBC, NICNT]. The topic is believers share their possessions [EBC, NIV], sharing and witnessing community [Bar], community of goods [NICNT].

4:32 Now the large-number[a] of-the-ones who-believed were (of) one[b] heart[c] and soul,[d] and not one was-saying-(that) any of-the-possessions-(belonging) to-him was his-own, but to-them all-things were (in)-common.[e]

LEXICON—a. πλῆθος (LN 59.9) (BDAG 2.b.δ. p. 826): 'large number' [BDAG, LN], 'full number' [ESV], 'multitude' [BDAG, LN; KJV], 'crowd' [LN], 'company' [BECNT], 'whole company' [Bar; REB], 'whole community' [BDAG], 'whole body' [CBC], 'whole group' [GW, NRSV], 'group' [BDAG; CEV, NCV, NET, TEV], 'congregation' [NASB], 'band' [AB], 'fellowship, community, church' [BDAG]. The phrase 'the large number of the ones who believed' is also translated 'all the believers' [NIV, NLT]. This noun denotes a large number of countable objects or events, with the probable implication of some type of grouping [LN]. This noun denotes a large amount, and in the usage of religious communities it is a title for the whole body of the members [BDAG].

b. εἷς (LN 63.4) (BDAG 2.b. p. 292): 'one' [AB, Bar, BECNT, LN], 'single, only one' [BDAG]. The phrase 'were of one heart and soul' [ESV, NASB, NRSV] is also translated 'was of one heart and soul' [BECNT], 'were of one heart and of one soul' [KJV], 'all felt the same way about everything'

[CEV], 'lived in harmony' [GW], 'were united in their hearts and spirit' [NCV], 'were united in heart and mind' [NLT], 'was united in heart and soul' [CBC; REB], 'was one in mind and soul' [TEV], 'were of one heart and mind' [NET], 'were one in heart and mind' [NIV]. This adjective describes that which is united as one in contrast with being divided or consisting of separate parts [LN]. It refers to a single entity with the focus on uniformity or quality [BDAG].

c. καρδία (LN 26.3) (BDAG 1.b.η. p. 509): 'heart' [AB, Bar, BDAG, BECNT, CBC, LN; all versions except CEV, GW, TEV], 'mind' [LN; TEV], 'inner self' [LN], not explicit [CEV, GW]. This noun is a figurative extension of the 'heart' and denotes the causative source of a person's psychological life in its various aspects, but with special emphasis upon thoughts [LN]. The 'heart' is considered to be the center and source of the whole inner life [BDAG].

d. ψυχή (LN 26.4) (BDAG 2.c. p. 1099): 'soul' [AB, Bar, BDAG, BECNT, CBC; ESV, KJV, NASB, NRSV, REB], 'mind' [LN; NET, NIV, NLT], 'spirit' [NCV], 'heart' [LN; TEV], 'inner self, thoughts, feelings, being' [LN], not explicit [ESV, GW]. This noun denotes the essence of life in terms of thinking, willing, and feeling [LN]. It is the seat and center of the inner human life concerning feelings and emotions [BDAG].

e. κοινός (LN 89.118) (BDAG 1.a. p. 551): 'in common' [AB, Bar, BDAG, CBC, LN; ESV, NET, NRSV, REB], 'common' [BDAG; KJV], 'communal' [BDAG]. The phrase 'to them all things were in common' is also translated 'they shared everything they had with each other' [CEV], 'they shared everything' [BECNT; GW, NCV], 'all things were common property to them' [NASB], 'they shared everything they had' [NIV, NLT], 'they all shared with one another everything they had' [TEV]. This adjective pertains to that which is in common between two or more persons [LN]. It pertains to being shared collectively [BDAG].

QUESTION—What is the relationship of the believers when they were of one heart and soul?

This implies both their friendship and unity of purpose [PNTC]. It points to a real friendship, and these believers were committed to each other in terms of resources [BECNT]. It reflects their unity and oneness in sharing their personal possessions with those in need [EBC, NAC]. It identifies them with the Greek proverb 'Friends have all things in common' [Bar]. It exhibits a remarkable unanimity that expresses itself even in their attitude to private property [NICNT]. They did not regard possessions as being exclusively for their own benefit and were consequently not captivated by the need to hold on to them [PNTC]. They believed that one's property was for the use of the community as a whole [TNTC]. There was no selfishness and no poverty [CBC].

4:33 And with-great power[a] the apostles were-giving (their) testimony[b] to-the resurrection of-the Lord Jesus, and great grace[c] was upon them all.

LEXICON—a. δύναμις (LN 76.1) (BDAG 1.a. p. 262): 'power' [AB, Bar, BDAG, BECNT, CBC, LN; all versions except CEV, NLT], 'might, strength, force, capability' [BDAG]. The phrase 'with great power' is also translated 'in a powerful way' [CEV], '(testified) powerfully' [NLT]. This noun denotes the potentiality to exert force in performing some function [LN]. It denotes the potential for functioning in some way [BDAG].
  b. μαρτύριον (LN 33.264) (BDAG 1.b. p. 619): 'testimony' [Bar, BDAG, BECNT, LN; ESV, NASB, NET, NRSV], 'witness' [CBC, LN; KJV, REB, TEV]. The phrase 'were giving their testimony' is also translated 'continued to testify' [GW, NIV], 'told everyone' [CEV], 'were telling people' [NCV], 'testified' [NLT], 'witnessed' [AB]. This noun denotes the content of what is witnessed or said [LN]. It denotes a statement that is brought out as a testimony [BDAG].
  c. χάρις (LN 25.89) (BDAG 2.b. p. 1079): 'grace' [AB, Bar, BDAG, BECNT; ESV, KJV, NASB, NET, NIV, NRSV], 'favor' [BDAG, LN], 'good will' [BDAG, LN; GW], 'blessing' [NLT, TEV], 'gracious care' [BDAG]. The phrase 'great grace was upon them all' is also translated 'God greatly blessed his followers' [CEV], 'God blessed all the believers very much' [NCV], 'all were held in high esteem' [CBC; REB]. This noun denotes a favorable attitude toward someone [LN]. It denotes the beneficent disposition that one experiences from another [BDAG].

QUESTION—From whom was the great grace and what did it refer to?

The great grace was from God [AB, Bar, BECNT, NAC, NICNT, PNTC, TNTC]. It refers to God's grace that was so powerfully at work in the apostles enabling them to proclaim Jesus with great power and boldness [AB, BECNT, EBC, NICNT, PNTC, TNTC]. Besides that, God's grace was at work moving the believers to share their belongings among the community so that there was no needy person in the community as described in the following two verses [AB, BECNT, EBC, PNTC, TNTC]. It was primarily God's blessing on their lives and witnesses [NAC].

4:34 For (there) was not anyone needy[a] among them, for as-many-as were owners of-lands[b] or houses sold-(them), and brought the proceeds[c] of-what was-sold **4:35** and laid-(it) at the feet of-the apostles, and it-was-distributed to-each-one who had need.

LEXICON—a. ἐνδεής (LN 57.51) (BDAG 1. p. 331): 'needy' [BECNT, CBC, LN; ESV, NASB, NET, NIV, NLT, NRSV, REB], 'in need' [AB, LN; CEV, TEV], 'in want' [Bar], 'poor' [BDAG, LN], 'impoverished' [BDAG]. The phrase 'there was not anyone needy among them' is also translated 'None of them needed anything' [GW], 'Neither was there any among them that lacked' [KJV], 'No one in the group needed anything' [NCV]. This adjective means lacking what is needed or necessary for

existence [LN]. It pertains to being in need of material possessions [BDAG].
  b. χωρίον (LN 1.95) (BDAG 1. p. 1095): 'land' [AB, Bar, BECNT, CBC, LN; all versions except NCV, TEV], 'field' [BDAG, LN; NCV, TEV], 'place, piece of land' [BDAG]. This noun denotes land under cultivation or used for pasture [LN]. It denotes a piece of land other than a populated area [BDAG].
  c. τιμή (LN 57.161) (BDAG 1. p. 1005): 'proceeds' [BECNT, CBC; ESV, NASB, NET, NRSV, REB], 'money' [AB; CEV, GW, NCV, NIV, NLT, TEV], 'price' [Bar, BDAG, LN; KJV], 'amount, cost' [LN], 'value' [BDAG]. This noun denotes 'the amount of money or property regarded as representing the value or price of something' [LN]. It denotes the amount at which something is valued [BDAG].

QUESTION—What does 'laid them (the proceeds) at the feet of the apostles' mean?

It means the proceeds were turned over to the authority of the apostles who oversaw the distribution of the resources to whoever was in need in their community [BECNT, TH, TNTC].

DISCOURSE UNIT—4:36–37 [Bar, EBC, NICNT]. The topic is an example: Barnabas [Bar], the generosity of Barnabas [EBC, NICNT].

4:36 And Joseph, (a)-Levite,[a] of-Cyprus by-nationality,[b] whom the apostles also called Barnabas, (which translated means Son of-Encouragement[c]), 4:37 sold (a)-field[d] belonging to-him, brought the money and laid-(it)[e] at the feet of-the apostles.

LEXICON—a. Λευίτης (LN 53.91) (BDAG p. 593): 'Levite' [AB, Bar, BDAG, BECNT, CBC, LN; all versions except GW, NLT], 'descendent of Levi' [GW], 'from the tribe of Levi' [NLT]. This noun denotes a member of the tribe of Levi and having the responsibility to serve as an assistant to Jewish priests [LN]. It denotes a member of the tribe of Levi, the tribe whose duty was to perform the lowlier services connected with the temple ritual [BDAG].
  b. γένος (LN 10.1) (BDAG 3. p. 194): 'nation' [BDAG, LN], 'country' [KJV], 'race, ethnic group' [LN], 'people' [BDAG]. The phrase 'of Cyprus by nationality' is also translated 'from Cyprus' [CEV, NIV], 'a native of Cyprus' [ESV, NRSV], 'had been born on the island of Cyprus' [GW], 'of the country of Cyprus' [KJV], 'of Cyprian birth' [NASB], 'born in Cyprus' [NCV, TEV], 'who was a native of Cyprus' [NET], 'came from the island of Cyprus' [NLT], 'a Cypriot by birth' [BECNT], 'a Cypriote by birth' [Bar], 'by birth a Cypriot' [CBC; REB], 'whose family was from Cyprus' [AB]. This noun denotes a relatively large group of persons regarded as being biologically related [LN]. It denotes a relatively large people group [BDAG].
  c. παράκλησις (LN 25.150) (BDAG 3. p. 766): 'encouragement' [BECNT, LN], 'consolation' [AB, BDAG; KJV], 'exhortation' [Bar, CBC],

'comfort' [BDAG]. The phrase 'Son of Encouragement' [ESV, NASB, NET, NIV, NLT, NRSV, REB] is also translated 'one who encourages others' [CEV], 'a person who encourages' [GW], 'one who encourages' [NCV, TEV]. This noun denotes encouragement or consolation, either by verbal or non-verbal means [LN]. It refers to the lifting of another's spirits [BDAG].
- d. ἀγρός (LN 1.95) (BDAG 3. p. 16): 'field' [AB, BDAG, BECNT, LN; ESV, NCV, NET, NIV, NLT, NRSV, TEV], 'land' [LN; GW, KJV], 'piece of property' [CEV], 'tract of land' [NASB], 'a piece of land' [Bar], 'estate' [CBC; REB]. This noun denotes 'land under cultivation or used for pasture' [LN]. It denotes land put under cultivation [BDAG].
- e. aorist act. indic. of τίθημι (LN 57.82) (BDAG 1.a.β. p. 1003): 'to lay' [AB, Bar, BDAG, CBC; ESV, KJV, NASB, NRSV, REB], 'to place' [NET], 'to put' [BDAG; NIV], 'to set' [BECNT]. The phrase 'brought the money and laid it at the feet of the apostles' is also translated 'brought the money and set it at the apostles' feet' [BECNT], 'brought the money to the apostles' [CEV], 'turned the money over to the apostles' [GW], 'brought the money, and gave it to the apostles' [NCV], 'brought the money to the apostles' [NLT], 'brought the money, and turned it over to the apostles' [TEV]. The Greek phrase τίθημι τοὺς πόδας 'to put at someone's feet' means 'to turn over to' [LN], 'to put at someone's disposal' [LN]. It means to put or place in a particular location [BDAG].

QUESTION—What is the function of these two last verses of the chapter?

These two verses serve to give a prime example of how one person sold a field that was his own property, and then turned all the money from the sale to the apostles [AB, Bar, BECNT, CBC, EBC, NAC, NICNT, PNTC, TNTC].

DISCOURSE UNIT—5:1–16 [PNTC; NASB]. The topic is the awesome presence of God [PNTC], the fate of Ananias and Sapphira [NASB].

DISCOURSE UNIT—5:1–11 [AB, Bar, BECNT, EBC, NAC, PNTC, TNTC; CEV, ESV, GW, NCV, NET, NIV, NLT, NRSV, TEV]. The topic is a serious threat to the common life [NAC], a negative example: Ananias and Sapphira [Bar], deceiving the spirit and judgment: Ananias and Sapphira [BECNT], the judgment on Ananias and Sapphira [NET], the sin of Ananias and Sapphira [TNTC], the deceit of Ananias and Sapphira [EBC], Peter condemns Ananias and Sapphira [CEV], Ananias and Sapphira die [NCV], Ananias and Sapphira [ESV, GW, NIV, NLT, NRSV, TEV], judgment in the church [PNTC], the first deaths in the church [AB].

DISCOURSE UNIT—5:1–6 [NICNT]. The topic is the deceit and death of Ananias.

5:1 But a man named Ananias, with his wife Sapphira, sold a-piece-of-property[a] **5:2** and with his wife knowing-it,[b] he-kept[c] back some of the

proceeds[d] for himself, and having-brought just a part (of the money), he-laid-(that) at the feet of-the apostles.

LEXICON—a. κτῆμα (LN 57.15) (BDAG 2. p. 572): 'a piece of property' [CEV, ESV, NASB, NET, NIV, NRSV], 'some property' [GW, NLT, TEV], 'a property' [Bar, CBC, LN; REB], 'some land' [NCV], 'landed property, field, piece of ground' [BDAG], 'a field' [AB, BECNT], 'a possession' [LN; KJV]. This noun denotes that which is owned or possessed and it is usually used in reference to land [LN]. It denotes landed property [BDAG].

b. perf. act. participle of σύνοιδα (LN 28.5) (BDAG 1. p. 973): 'to share knowledge with' [BDAG, LN]. The phrase 'with his wife knowing it' is also translated 'with his wife's full knowledge' [NASB, NIV], 'with his wife's knowledge' [BECNT; ESV, NET, NRSV], 'with her knowledge' [AB], 'with the full knowledge of his wife' [CBC], 'with his wife's consent' [NLT], 'with his wife's agreement' [TEV], 'with the connivance of his wife' [REB], 'his wife also being privy to it' [KJV], 'his wife was privy to this' [Bar], 'his wife sharing in knowledge of that too' or 'his wife also knew about it' [LN], 'his wife knew about this and agreed to it' [NCV], 'they agreed to cheat and keep some of the money' [CEV], 'they agreed to hold back some of the money' [GW]. This verb means to know something together with someone else [LN]. It means to share information or knowledge with someone in the sense of being an accomplice [BDAG].

c. aorist mid. indic. of νοσφίζω (LN 57.246) (BDAG p. 679): 'to keep back for oneself' [LN; ESV, NASB, NCV, NET, NIV], 'to keep back' [AB, Bar, BDAG, BECNT, CBC; KJV, NRSV, REB], 'to put aside for oneself' [BDAG], 'to hold back' [GW], 'to keep' [NLT], 'to keep for oneself' [TEV], 'to cheat and keep for themselves' [CEV]. This verb means to misappropriate funds for one's own benefit [LN]. It means to put aside for oneself [BDAG].

d. τιμή (LN 57.161) (BDAG 1. p. 1005): 'proceeds' [BECNT; ESV, NET, NRSV, REB], 'price' [Bar, BDAG, LN; KJV, NASB], 'the price received' [LN], 'value' [BDAG], 'money' [AB; CEV, GW, NCV, NIV, NLT, TEV], 'purchase-money' [CBC]. This noun denotes the amount of money or property regarded as representing the value or price of something [LN]. It denotes the amount at which something is valued [BDAG].

QUESTION—What is indicated by the conjunction δέ 'but' at the beginning of the verse?

The conjunction 'but' indicates the contrast of what Ananias and Sapphira did from what Barnabas did in Acts 4:36–37 [TNTC, TRT]. They too sold a piece of property, pledging the proceeds to the community of believers. But they held back some of the proceeds; and a terrible judgment followed, resulting in both their deaths [NAC].

QUESTION—Why did Ananias lay the money at the feet of the apostles?
It means that he 'turned the money over to the apostles' or 'gave the money to the apostles' [TH]. He gave the money to the apostles as a trust, not as a personal gift [TNTC].

5:3 But Peter said, "Ananias, why has- Satan^a -filled^b your heart to lie to-the Holy Spirit and to-keep-back^c (part) of the price of-the land?

LEXICON—a. Σατανᾶς (LN 93.330) (BDAG p. 916): 'Satan' [AB, Bar, BDAG, BECNT, CBC, LN; all versions]. This noun refers to an adversary and it is used as a title for the Devil [LN]. Literally 'adversary'; it refers to 'Satan', the title or name of the enemy of God and all those who belong to God [BDAG].

b. aorist act. indic. of πληρόω (LN 30.29) (BDAG 1.a. p. 828): 'to fill' [BDAG, LN], 'to take possession of' [BDAG]. The phrase 'filled your heart' [AB, BECNT; ESV, KJV, NASB, NET, NIV, NLT, NRSV] is also translated 'put into your heart' [Bar], 'rule your thoughts' [NCV], 'so possessed your mind' [CBC; REB], 'take control of you' [TEV], 'made you' [CEV], 'fill you with the idea (that you could deceive)' [GW], 'cause you to think as you did' [LN]. The idiom 'to throw into the heart' means: to cause someone to think in a particular manner, often as a means of inducing some behavior. Accordingly, one may translate this 'why did Satan cause you to think as you did so as to lie to the Holy Spirit?' [LN]. This means 'to make full,' and to fill someone's heart is to take full possession of someone's heart [BDAG].

c. aorist mid. infin. of νοσφίζω (LN 57.246) (BDAG p. 679): 'to keep back for oneself' [BDAG, LN]. The phrase 'kept back part of the price' [CBC] is also translated 'to keep back some of the price' [Bar; NASB], 'to-keep/by-keeping back part of the price' [KJV, REB], 'by keeping part of the money you received' [TEV], 'to keep back part of the proceeds' [NRSV], 'to keep back some of the proceeds' [BECNT], 'to keep back for yourself part of the price' [ESV], 'keep back for yourself part of the proceeds from the sale' [NET], 'have kept for yourself some of the money you received' [NIV], 'to keep for yourself part of the money you received' [NCV], 'keep back some of the money from the sale' [CEV], 'to put some of the money aside' [AB], 'You've held back some of the money you received (for the land)' [GW], 'You kept some of the money for yourself' [NLT]. This verb means to misappropriate funds for one's own benefit [LN]. It means to put aside for oneself [BDAG].

QUESTION—Who is this 'Satan' who has filled Ananias' heart?
'Satan' is the devil's Hebrew name which means 'adversary/enemy. Satan was at one time one of God's angels, but he rebelled, was expelled from heaven by God and became the ruler/leader of the evil spirits who rebelled with him [TRT]. Satan is the supernatural power opposed to God [Bar].

ACTS 5:3   139

QUESTION—How did Peter relate a Satan-filled heart to lying to the Holy Spirit?

Peter reasoned that it was because Satan had filled Ananias' heart that Ananias lied to the Holy Spirit. Although influenced by Satan, Ananias was responsible for what he himself had done since he had left himself open to follow Satan and try to deceive the Holy Spirit [BECNT]. Satan filled Ananias' heart just as Satan had filled Judas' heart (Luke 22:3) [AB, NAC]. Like Judas, Ananias was motivated by money (Luke 22:5) [NAC].

5:4 While it-remained[a] (unsold), did-it- not -remain yours? And after-it was-sold, was- not (the money) -under your control[b]? Why (is it) that this deed was-put[c] in your heart? You-did- not -lie to-men, but to-God."

LEXICON—a. pres. act. participle of μένω (LN 13.89) (BDAG 1.b. p. 631): 'to remain' [BDAG, LN], 'to stay' [BDAG], 'to continue' [LN]. The question 'While it remained unsold, did it not remain yours?' is also translated 'While it remained, did it not remain yours?' [Bar, CBC], 'While it remained unsold, did it not remain yours?' [BECNT], 'While it remained, was it not thine own?' [KJV]. 'Before it was sold, did it not belong to you?' [NET], 'Didn't it belong to you before it was sold?' [NIV], 'While it remained unsold, did it not remain your-own/yours?' [ESV, NASB, NRSV, REB], 'was it (the piece of ground) not yours as long as it remained (unsold)?' [BDAG], 'Was it not yours as long as you owned it?' [AB]. It is also translated as a statement: 'While you had the land, it was your own' [GW], 'Before you sold the land/property, it belonged to you' [NCV, TEV], 'The property was yours before you sold it' [CEV], 'The property was yours to sell or not sell, as you wished' [NLT]. This verb means to remain or continue [LN]. It means 'to remain' and here it refers to something continuing in the same state [BDAG].

b. ἐξουσία (LN 37.13) (BDAG 1. p. 352): 'under one's control' [LN], 'at ones disposal' [BDAG]. The question 'was not the money under your control?' is also translated 'was it not under your control?' [NASB], 'was it not under your authority?' [Bar], 'was it not in your authority?' [BECNT], 'was it not at your disposal?' [ESV], 'was it not still at your own disposal?' [CBC; REB], 'wasn't the money at your disposal?' [NIV], 'was the money not at your disposal?' [NET], 'was not the money yours to dispose of?' [AB], 'were not the proceeds at your disposal?' [NRSV], 'was it not in thine own power?' [KJV]. It is also translated as a statement: 'you could have done as you pleased with the money' [GW], 'you could have used the money any way you wanted' [NCV], 'the money was still yours' [CEV], 'the money was yours' [TEV], 'the money was also yours to give away' [NLT], 'the money from the sale remained under your control' [LN]. This noun denotes a state of control over someone or something [LN]. It denotes a state of control over something [BDAG].

c. aorist mid. indic. of τίθημι (LN 30.76) (BDAG 1.b.ε. p. 1003): 'to put, to place' [LN], 'to have (in mind)' [BDAG]. The question 'Why is it that this deed was put in your heart?' is also translated 'Why is it that you contrived this deed in your heart?' [ESV], 'why hast thou conceived this thing in thine heart?' [KJV], 'why is it that you have conceived this deed in your heart?' [NASB], 'why, then, did you decide to do such a thing?' [TEV], 'what made you think of doing such a thing?' [NIV], 'why did you think of doing this?' [NCV], 'how have you thought up this deed in your heart?' [NET], 'how is it that you have contrived this deed in your heart?' [NRSV], 'what made you think of doing this?' [REB], 'what made you think of doing this thing?' [CBC], 'how could you do a thing like this?' [GW, NLT], 'What made you do such a thing?' [CEV], 'Why did you plan this act?' [Bar], 'Why did you devise this deed in your heart?' [BECNT], 'Why did you decide in your heart to act so?' [AB], 'why, then, did you make up your mind that you would do such a thing?' [LN]. The idiom 'to place in the heart, or mind' means to engage in the process of deciding [LN (30.76)]. It means to contrive something in one's mind [BDAG].

QUESTION—What does the term 'this deed' refer to?

'This deed' refers to the lie that Ananias made to Peter [TRT]. Ananias had pretended to give all the money he received to the apostles. This lie is not just a lie that he made to human beings but also to God [EBC, PNTC, TNTC]. The act against the Spirit is an act against God [BECNT, EBC, NAC].

5:5 And when Ananias heard these words, he fell-down^a and died. And great fear^b came upon all who heard (of it). 5:6 And the young-men rose and wrapped- him -up^c and after-carrying-(him)-out, they-buried-(him).

LEXICON—a. aorist act. participle of πίπτω (LN 15.119) (BDAG 1.b.α.ℵ. p. 815): 'to fall down' [Bar, BDAG, BECNT, LN; ESV, KJV, NASB, NCV, NIV, NRSV, TEV], 'to fall to the ground' [BDAG], 'to fall to the floor' [NLT]. The phrase 'fell down and died' is also translated 'collapsed and died' [NET], 'sank to the ground and died' [AB], 'dropped dead' [CBC; CEV, GW, REB]. This verb means to fall from a standing or upright position down to the ground or surface [LN].

b. φόβος (LN 25.251) (BDAG 2.a.α. p. 1062): 'fear' [AB, Bar, BDAG, BECNT, LN; ESV, KJV, NASB, NCV, NET, NIV, NRSV]. The phrase 'great fear came upon all' is also translated 'everyone...was frightened' [CEV], 'all...were terrified' [TEV], 'Everyone...was terrified' [GW, NLT], 'all...were awestruck' [CBC; REB]. This noun denotes a state of severe distress that is aroused by an intense concern for impending pain, danger, evil, etc. [LN]. It denotes the product of an alarming force [BDAG].

c. aorist act. Indic. of συστέλλω (LN 79.119) (BDAG 3. p. 978): 'to wrap up' [BDAG, BECNT, LN; all versions except KJV, NASB, REB], 'to wrap' [AB], 'to wind up' [KJV], 'to cover' [BDAG, CBC; NASB, REB], 'to prepare his body for burial' [Bar]. This verb means to wrap something up in order to get it ready for removal [LN]. It means to wrap something up by winding something around it [BDAG].

QUESTION—What caused the great fear on all who heard about this incident and who were they?

Their great fear was due to the evident act of judgment upon the sudden death of Ananias as a result of his lie and with the understanding that the ultimate causation of God as the agent in his death, judgment began first at the house of God [EBC, NICNT, TNTC]. The great fear involved here is a healthy sense of awe at the supernatural and reverence for God, rather than terror or panic [PNTC], they saw the hand of God in it all [NAC]. Great fear implies the impression that supernatural and dangerous powers were at work [Bar]. They were people other than those who were present and saw what happened. Most probably the reference is to Jesus' followers and non-Jesus' followers alike [PNTC, TH].

QUESTION—Who were the young men mentioned in this verse?

Those young men were probably 20–24 years old. For some languages a good cultural equivalent is 'unmarried men' [TH, TRT]. They were not an official group but active members of the community, quick to relieve their elders of a necessary but unpleasant duty [Bar], the more mundane duties [TNTC]. They were some younger men in the Christian community, not professional buriers [EBC, NICNT].

QUESTION—What was the Jewish burial custom like?

According to Jewish custom, when people died, their bodies were wrapped in cloth and placed in graves or tombs outside of the city walls, normally within 24 hours of their death [TRT]. In hot climates burial had to take place soon after death, on the same day of death [BECNT, EBC, NICNT]. Ananias' burial had proceeded with great haste, and without his wife Sapphira even being informed or involved [EBC, PNTC]. It was an unusually hasty burial [BECNT, NAC].

DISCOURSE UNIT—5:7–11 [NICNT]. The topic is the death of Sapphira.

5:7 And after an-interval-ofᵃ **about three hours his wife came-in, not knowing what had-happened. 5:8 And Peter-(said) to her, "Tell me whether you-sold the land for-so-much.**ᵇ**" And she-said, "Yes, for-so-much."**

LEXICON—a. διάστημα (LN 67.150) (BDAG 4. p. 237): 'interval' [Bar, BDAG, BECNT, LN; ESV, NASB, NET, NRSV]. The phrase 'And after an interval of about three hours' is also translated 'about three hours later' [AB; GW, NCV, NIV, NLT, TEV], 'Three hours later' [CEV], 'And it was about the space of three hours after' [KJV], 'About three hours passed' [CBC; REB]. This noun denotes a unit of time between specified events [LN]. It denotes a space of time between events [BDAG].

b. τοσοῦτος (LN 59.18) (BDAG 4. p. 1012): 'for so much' [AB, Bar, BECNT, LN; ESV, KJV], 'so and so much' [BDAG], 'this much' [NCV], 'for such and such a price' [NASB, NRSV], 'for that price' [GW], 'for this amount' [CEV]. The phrase 'whether you sold the land for so much' is also translated 'were you paid such and such a price for the land?' [CBC; REB], 'were you paid this amount for the land?' [NET], 'is this the price you and Ananias got for the land?' [NIV], 'was this the price you and your husband received for your land?' [NLT], 'was this the full amount you and your husband received for your property?' [TEV]. This adjective pertains to a quantity considerably beyond normal expectations [LN]. It pertains to a limited extent [BDAG].

QUESTION—What is indicated by Sapphira's reply to Peter?

Sapphira's reply confirming the amount indicated that she had agreed with her husband Ananias, and joined him in the conspiracy about the proceeds and lied [BECNT, NAC]. She had a chance to tell the truth and rectify the wrong but she did not. We see from the next verse she experienced the same consequence of divine judgment as Ananias [BECNT, NAC, NICNT, TNTC].

5:9 And Peter (said) to her, "Why-(was-it) that you(pl) have-agreed[a] (together) to-test[b] the Spirit[c] of-(the)-Lord? Behold, the feet[d] of-those who-have-buried your husband (are)-at the door, and they-will-carry- you -out."

LEXICON—a. aorist pass. indic. of συμφωνέω (LN 31.15) (BDAG 3. p. 961): 'to agree' [AB, Bar, BDAG; all versions except NLT, REB, TEV], 'to agree with' [LN], 'to be of one mind' [BDAG]. The phrase 'Why was it that you have agreed' is also translated 'Why is it that you conspired' [BECNT], 'How could the two of you even think of conspiring' [NLT], 'Why did the two of you conspire' [REB], 'Why did you both conspire' [CBC], 'Why did you and your husband decide' [TEV]. This verb means to come to an agreement with someone, often implying a type of joint decision [LN]. It means to have come to an agreement about something [BDAG].

b. aorist act. infin. of πειράζω (LN 27.46) (BDAG 2.c. p. 793): 'to test' [BECNT, LN; CEV, ESV, GW, NCV, NET, NIV, NLT], 'to put to the test' [BDAG, CBC, LN; NASB, NRSV, REB, TEV], 'to tempt' [Bar; KJV], 'to harass' [AB]. This verb means to try to learn the nature or character of someone by submitting such a one to thorough and extensive testing [LN]. Their intent is to put God to the test, to discover whether God really can do some certain thing, especially whether God notices sin and is able to punish it [BDAG].

c. πνεῦμα (LN 12.18) (BDAG 5.a. p. 834): 'Spirit' [LN]. The phrase τὸ πνεῦμα κυρίου 'the Spirit of the Lord' [AB, Bar, BECNT, CBC; all versions except CEV, GW, TEV] is also translated 'the Lord's Spirit' [CEV, GW, TEV]. The phrase 'Spirit of the Lord,' is ambiguous because Lord may either refer to God the Father or to Jesus Christ, but the Spirit in either case is the same: 'why did you decide to put the Lord's Spirit to the test?' [LN]. Here 'Lord' presumably stands for 'God' [TH]. The phrases 'the Spirit of God' and 'the Spirit of the Lord (= God)' denote God's being as a controlling influence, with the focus on his association with humans [BDAG].

d. πούς (LN 8.49) (BDAG 1.b. p. 858): 'foot' [AB, Bar, BDAG, BECNT, LN; ESV, KJV, NASB, NET, NIV, NRSV], 'footstep' [CBC]. The phrase 'the feet of those who have buried your husband' is also translated 'the footsteps of those who buried your husband' [CBC], 'The men who buried Ananias' [CEV], 'Those who buried your husband' [GW, REB], 'The men who buried your husband' [NCV, TEV], 'The young men who buried your husband' [NLT]. The feet represents a person who is in motion, and here it refers to those who have buried her husband [BDAG].

QUESTION—In what way had Sapphira and Ananias tested the Spirit of the Lord?

They had attempted to see if they could lie to the Lord's Spirit and not suffer punishment [TH], to see how far the Spirit would go in his tolerance [NAC], to see how far they could go in presuming on the forbearance of the Spirit of God [NICNT], to see how much they can get away with [TNTC], to test the Spirit's ability to be deceived about what is going on [BECNT]. Sapphira's sudden death shows that the Spirit sees sin and deals with it in a timing that the Spirit determines. In the cases of Sapphira and Ananias, their sins were dealt with immediately [BECNT].

QUESTION—What is indicated by Peter's exclamation ἰδού 'look'?

The use of ἰδού 'look' points to an announcement to be absorbed. It serves as a dramatic narrative note pointing to the importance of what this entire verse says about the consequences of deceiving God [BECNT].

5:10 And immediately she-fell-down[a] at his feet and died. And when, the young-men entered, they-found her dead, and having-carried-(her)-out, they-buried-(her) beside her husband. **5:11** And great fear came upon (the)-whole church and upon all the-ones who-heard-of these-things.

LEXICON—a. aorist act. indic. of πίπτω (LN 15.119) (BDAG 1.b.α. ℵ. p. 815): 'to fall down' [BDAG, BECNT, LN; ESV, KJV, NCV, NIV, NRSV, TEV], 'to fall' [Bar, LN; CEV, NASB, NLV], 'to sink down' [AB]. The phrase 'she fell down at his feet and died' is also translated 'she fell at his feet and expired' [Bar], 'she dropped dead in front of Peter' [GW], 'she dropped dead at his feet' [CBC; REB], 'she collapsed at his feet and died' [NET]. This verb means to fall from a standing or upright position down to the ground or surface [LN]. It refers to a person who had been standing upright falling to the ground [BDAG].

QUESTION—What does the 'whole church' refer to in this context?

Here the 'whole church' refers to the group/community of Jesus' followers who were living there in Jerusalem [TH, TRT], a group of communities bound together by Jesus [BECNT], the community of believers in Jesus [NICNT], the local church of Jerusalem [Bar, EBC], the people of God gathered as a religious community [NAC, TNTC]. It does not refer to a building. The name 'Christians' was not used until Acts 11:26 [TRT]. The adjective 'whole' indicates the inclusion of those not present when the judgment was visited upon Ananias and Sapphira [PNTC].

QUESTION—What is implied by these two verses?

These two verses echo verses 5–6. Sapphira's death is immediate just as Ananias' death. The use of the term 'immediately' heightens the effect and the sense of the supernatural [Bar]. The absence of wrapping the body may reflect Jewish custom, where men do not wrap a woman's dead body [BECNT]. Great fear came upon the whole church as once again an act of divine judgment had happened right away manifesting the awesome presence of God [PNTC]. The implication of the instantaneous and direct judgment against Sapphira as well as Ananias is that sin is serious to God and how gracious God is in often deferring such judgment. Most sin is not treated so harshly, but at this early stage, such a divine act serves to remind the community of its call to holiness, to a path of honesty and integrity and of its loyalty to God [BECNT]. If the church is to have genuine spiritual power in its life and witness, it must be an environment of the Spirit, devoted to maintaining its sanctity and purity [NAC].

DISCOURSE UNIT—5:12–42 [EBC, NICNT]. The topic is the apostles before the Sanhedrin [NICNT] the apostles again before the Sanhedrin [EBC].

DISCOURSE UNIT—5:12b–42 [CBC]. The topic is a second skirmish.

DISCOURSE UNIT—5:12–16 [AB, Bar, BECNT, EBC, NAC, PNTC, TNTC; CEV, ESV, GW, NCV, NET, NIV, NLT, NRSV, TEV]. The topic is the miracles worked by the apostles [NAC], the apostles perform many miracles [GW], the apostles perform miraculous signs and wonders [NET], signs and wonders by the apostles [AB], signs and wonders among the people [PNTC], summary: signs and wonders [BECNT], many signs and wonders done [ESV], signs and wonders [BECNT], miraculous signs and wonders [EBC], miracles and wonders [TEV], miracle-working or supernatural community [Bar], the apostles heal many [NCV, NIV, NLT, NRSV], Peter's unusual power [CEV], the continuing growth of the church [TNTC].

5:12 By the hands[a] of-the apostles many signs[b] and wonders[c] were-being-done among the people. And they-all were of-one-mind[d] in the Portico[e] of-Solomon.

LEXICON—a. χείρ (LN 8.30, 76.3) (BDAG 2.a. p. 1082): 'hand' [Bar, BDAG, BECNT, CBC, LN (8.30); ESV, KJV, NASB, NET]. The clause 'By the hands of the apostles many signs and wonders were being done' is also translated 'The apostles worked many miracles and wonders' [CEV], 'the apostles perform many miracles and do amazing things' [GW], 'The apostles did many signs and miracles' [NCV], 'The apostles performed many miraculous signs and wonders' [NIV], 'The apostles were performing many miraculous signs and wonders' [NLT], 'many signs and wonders were done...through/by the apostles' [NRSV, REB], 'Many miracles and wonders were being performed...by the apostles' [TEV].

The phrase 'by the hands of the apostles' is also translated 'through the ministry of the apostles' [AB]. This noun denotes the hand or any relevant portion of the hand [LN (8.30)] and in a figurative sense it denotes power as an expression of the activity of a person [LN (76.3)]. The hand is the acting agent and in this sense the focus is on the person as the source of an activity. Something is done through or by someone or someone's activity [BDAG].

b. σημεῖον (LN 33.477) (BDAG 2.a. p. 920): 'sign' [AB, Bar, BECNT, LN; all versions except CEV, GW, TEV], 'miracle' [BDAG; CEV, GW, TEV], 'remarkable thing' [CBC]. This noun denotes an event which is regarded as having some special meaning [LN]. It denotes an event that is an indication or confirmation of intervention by transcendent powers [BDAG].

c. τέρας (LN 33.480): 'wonder' [AB, BECNT; all versions except GW, NCV], 'portent' [Bar, BDAG, LN], 'amazing thing' [GW], 'miracle' [NCV], 'wonderful thing' [CBC], 'sign' [LN]. This noun denotes an unusual sign, especially one in the heavens, serving to foretell impending events [LN].

d. ὁμοθυμαδόν (LN 31.23) (BDAG p. 706): 'with one mind' [BDAG, LN], 'by common consent, unanimously' [LN], 'together' [BDAG]. The clause 'they all were of one mind' is also translated 'they were all with one accord' [KJV, NASB], 'they (the apostles) were all gathering together' [BECNT], 'they customarily gathered together' [AB], 'they used to meet by common consent' [CBC], 'they were all together [Bar, ESV, NRSV], 'they would all meet together' [NCV], 'they were all meeting together' [NET], 'all the believers met together' [TEV], 'all the believers used to meet together' [NIV], 'all the believers were meeting regularly' [NLT], all of the Lord's followers often met' [CEV], 'all the believers used to meet by common consent' [REB], 'the believers had a common faith in Jesus' [GW]. This adverb pertains to mutual consent or agreement [LN]. The usual meaning 'with one mind, with one purpose, with one impulse' is probably weakened in this verse and it simply means that they met together [BDAG].

e. στοά (LN 7.40) (BDAG p. 946): 'portico' [Bar, BDAG, BECNT, LN; ESV, NASB, NET, NRSV, RSV], 'porch' [LN; CEV, GW, KJV, NCV, TEV], 'colonnade' [AB, BDAG; NIV, NLT], 'cloister' [BDAG, CBC]. This noun denotes a covered colonnade, open normally on one side, where people could stand, sit, or walk, protected from the weather and the heat of the sun. In many parts of the world the closest equivalent to a portico would be a veranda, an extensive type of porch. Such a porch may be described as a long outside room or a room made with pillars and open [LN]. It is a roofed colonnade open normally on one side [BDAG].

QUESTION—Who were the people who were of one mind in the Portico of-Solomon?

1. These people were the apostles [BECNT].

2. These people were all of the believers and not just the apostles [AB, Bar, EBC, NAC, PNTC, TH, TNTC]. It includes the 5,000 believers who are mentioned in Acts 4:4 [TRT].

5:13 **But none of-the rest dared[a] to-join[b] them, although the people held-them-in-high-esteem.[c]**

LEXICON—a. imperf. act. indic. of τολμάω (LN 25.161) (BDAG a.α. p. 1010): 'to dare' [Bar, BDAG, BECNT, LN; all versions except REB], 'to venture' [AB, CBC; REB], 'to have the courage, to be brave enough' [BDAG]. This verb means to be so bold as to challenge or defy possible danger or opposition [LN]. It means to show boldness or resolution in the face of danger, opposition, or a problem [BDAG].

b. pres. pass. infin. of κολλάω (LN 34.22) (BDAG 2.b.α. p. 556): 'to be joined to' [BDAG, LN; all versions except NASB], 'to be associated with' [BDAG; NASB], 'to join' [AB, Bar, BECNT, CBC], 'to become a part of' [LN]. This verb means to begin an association with someone [LN]. It means to be closely associated with someone [BDAG].

c. imperf. act. indic. of μεγαλύνω (LN 87.15) (BDAG 2. p. 623): 'to hold in high esteem' [BDAG; ESV, NASB, NRSV], 'to hold in high honor' [BECNT; NET], 'to hold in great honor' [LN], 'to hold in respect' [AB], 'to pay special respect to, to regard as important' [LN], 'to like very much' [CEV], 'to speak highly of' [BDAG, CBC; GW, REB, TEV], 'to magnify' [KJV], 'to respect' [NCV], 'to regard highly' [NIV], 'to have high regard for' [NLT], 'to praise' [Bar]. This verb means to show respect to a person on the basis of the importance of such an individual [LN]. It means to cause to be held in high esteem through praise or deeds [BDAG].

QUESTION—What does 'them' refer to?

Here 'them' refers to the same group of people that 'everyone' refers to in the preceding verse [TRT].

QUESTION—Who are 'the rest' who did not dare to join them?

1. 'The rest' refers to the believers other than the apostles [Bar, BECNT].
2. 'The rest' refers to the remainder of the Christians not included by the 'everyone' in v.12 [BECNT, PNTC].
3. 'The rest' refers to non-Christians [AB, Bar, BECNT, TH], unbelieving Jews [EBC, TNTC].

QUESTION—Who were 'the people' who held them in high esteem?

If the expression 'the people' must be more definitely identified, then expressions like 'the nonbelievers' or 'the people in Jerusalem' could be used [TH]. Or likely these were believers who hesitated to join with them in view of the hostile view and actions of the Jewish leadership [BECNT]. They were the responsive Jews [EBC], the people at large [AB], the common people [CBC].

5:14 **And more-than-ever[a] believers in-the Lord were-being-added[b] (to their number), multitudes of-both men and women.** **5:15** **As a result[c] they**

ACTS 5:14-15 147

even carried-out the sick into the streets and laid-(them) on cots^d and mats,^e so-that as Peter came-by at-least (his) shadow might-fall-upon some of-them.

LEXICON—a. μᾶλλον (LN 78.28) (BDAG 1. p. 613), 'more than ever' [BDAG, LN; ESV, GW], 'all the more' [NASB], 'even more' [BDAG, BECNT], 'still more' [AB], 'the more' [KJV], 'more and more' [NCV, NET, NET, NLT, TEV], 'in increasing numbers' [Bar], 'an ever increasing number' [REB], 'yet more than ever' [NRSV], 'many' [CEV] 'more than that' [CBC], 'to a greater degree than before' [BDAG, LN]. This adverb refers to a degree which surpasses in some manner a point on an explicit or implicit scale of extent [LN]. It means to a greater degree than before [BDAG].

b. imperf. pass. indic. of προστίθημι (LN 59.72) (BDAG 1.b. p. 885): 'to be added' [AB, Bar, BDAG, BECNT, CBC, LN; all versions except CEV, GW, NLT]. This verse is also translated 'Many men and women started having faith in the Lord' [CEV], 'More men and women than ever began to believe in the Lord' [GW], 'Yet more and more people believed and were brought to the Lord—crowds of both men and women' [NLT]. This verb means to add something to an existing quantity [LN]. It pertains to persons who are added to a group already existing [BDAG].

c. ὥστε (LN 89.52) (BDAG 2.a.β. p. 1107): 'as a result' [LN; GW, NIV, NLT, REB, TEV], 'so that' [AB, Bar, BECNT, LN; ESV, NRSV], 'insomuch that' [KJV], 'to such an extent that' [NASB], 'that' [BDAG], 'then' [CEV], 'thus' [NET], in the end' [CBC], not explicit [NCV]. This conjunction indicates the actual result [BDAG, LN].

d. κλινάριον (LN 6.107) (BDAG p. 549): 'cot' [LN; CEV, ESV, NASB, NET, NRSV], 'bed' [AB, BDAG, BECNT, CBC; KJV, NCV, NIV, NLT, REB, TEV], 'pallet' [LN], 'stretcher' [LN; GW], 'mattress' [Bar]. This noun denotes a relatively small and often temporary type of object on which a person may lie or recline [LN].

e. κράβαττος (LN 6.107) (BDAG p. 563): 'mat' [CEV, ESV, NCV, NIV, NLT, NRSV, TEV], 'mattress' [BDAG], 'couch' [KJV], 'cot' [LN; GW], 'pallet' [BDAG, BECNT, LN; NASB, NET], 'stretcher' [Bar, CBC; REB], 'litter' [AB]. This noun denotes a relatively small and often temporary type of object on which a person may lie or recline [LN], or a 'poor man's bed' [BDAG].

QUESTION—What does 'as a result' at the beginning of v.15 refer to?

It refers back to the first part of v.12 where the apostles had performed many signs and miracles. [Bar, NAC, TH], and verses 12b–14 are to be understood as a parenthetical statement [TH]. Others relate this result clause to verse 14 [BECNT, PNTC ESV, NASB, NRSV].

QUESTION—Why did the sick want Peter's shadow to fall upon them?

The sick were carried out to the street in the hope of being healed even by Peter's shadow [AB, BECNT, PNTC, TNTC]. It was thought that it mattered little whether a miracle was worked by the shadow, the hands, or the words of the miracle worker. In any case the agent here is God [Bar]. Though Luke does not explicitly state that the people upon whom Peter's shadow fell were healed, healing is implied in this context [NAC, TH]. God used Peter's shadow to effect a cure [EBC]. Peter's shadow was as efficacious as a medium of healing power as the fringe of his Master's cloak had been (Mark 6:56) [NICNT].

5:16 Also a-crowd of people from-the towns around Jerusalem came-together, bringing (the)-sick and (those-who)-were-afflicted[a] by unclean[b] spirits. They were all being-healed.[c]

LEXICON—a. pres. pass. participle of ὀχλέω (LN 22.24) (BDAG p. 746): 'to be afflicted' [AB, Bar, LN; ESV, NASB], 'to be troubled' [BDAG; CEV, GW, NET], 'to be disturbed' [BDAG], 'to be tormented' [BDAG; NIV, NRSV], 'to be vexed' [KJV], 'to be bothered' [NCV], 'to be harassed' [BECNT, CBC; REB]. The phrase 'those who were afflicted by unclean spirits' is also translated 'those possessed by evil spirits' [NLT], 'those who had evil spirits in them' [TEV]. This verb means to cause hardship by continual annoyance [LN]. It means to be caused trouble by harassment [BDAG].
  b. ἀκάθαρτος (LN 12.39) (BDAG 2. p. 34): 'unclean' [AB, Bar, BDAG, BECNT, CBC, LN; ESV, KJV, NASB, NET, NRSV, REB]. The phrase 'unclean spirits' is also translated 'evil spirits' [CEV, GW, NCV, NIV, NLT, TEV]. This adjective, when modifying the word for 'spirit,' describes an evil supernatural spirit which is ritually unclean and which causes persons to be ritually unclean [LN]. It pertains to moral impurity [BDAG].
  c. imperf. pass. indic. of θεραπεύω (LN 23.139) (BDAG 2. p. 453): 'to be healed' [AB, Bar, BDAG, BECNT, LN; all versions except GW, NRSV, REB], 'to be cured' [CBC, LN; GW, NRSV, REB], 'to be taken care of' [LN], 'to be restored' [BDAG]. This verb means to cause someone to recover health, often with the implication of having taken care of such a person [LN].

QUESTION—What does the term 'towns' refer to?
  The term 'towns' refers to the small neighboring communities [BECNT]. They were outlying villages around the city of Jerusalem [EBC, NAC, TH].

QUESTION—What were those who were afflicted by unclean spirits like at that time?
  Those who were afflicted by unclean spirits were considered as unfit to socialize/live with others or worship God with others until they were free from the evil spirit and offered a sacrifice to become 'clean' again. Anyone who touched such a person also became 'unclean' [TH, TRT]. They were demon-possessed people [BECNT], they were tormented by evil spirits [PNTC].

DISCOURSE UNIT—5:17–42 [AB, BECNT, NAC, PNTC, TNTC; CEV, ESV, GW, NCV, NET, NIV, NLT, NRSV, TEV]. The topic is all the apostles before the Council [NAC], the apostles' trial in front of the Jewish Council [GW], the second arrest of the apostles [TNTC], the apostles arrested and freed [ESV], the apostles persecuted [NIV], the apostles are persecuted [NRSV, TEV], the apostles meet opposition [NLT], the public arrest of the twelve apostles and Gamaliel's advice [AB], further trouble for the apostles [NET], trouble for the apostles [CEV], leaders try to stop the apostles [NCV], conflict with the authorities again [PNTC], more persecution [BECNT].

DISCOURSE UNIT—5:17–40 [Bar]. The topic is the arrest and examination of apostles.

DISCOURSE UNIT—5:17–33 [EBC, PNTC]. The topic is the apostles are re-arrested [PNTC], the arrest and trial of the apostles [EBC].

DISCOURSE UNIT—5:17–32 [NASB]. The topic is imprisonment and release.

DISCOURSE UNIT—5:17–26 [BECNT, NAC]. The topic is arrest, escape, and re-arrest [NAC], arrest, divine release, and re-arrest [BECNT].

DISCOURSE UNIT—5:17–21a [NICNT]. The topic is the apostles imprisoned and released.

5:17 But the high-priest[a] rose-up, along with all those with him (that is, the party[b] of-the Sadducees), (and) they-were-filled with-jealousy.[c] **5:18** They-laid[d] hands on the apostles and put them in (the)-public[e] jail.

LEXICON—a. ἀρχιερεύς (LN 53.89): 'high priest' [AB, Bar, BECNT, CBC, LN; all versions except GW], 'chief priest' [GW], 'most important priest' [LN]. This noun denotes the principal member among the chief priests [LN].

b. αἵρεσις (LN 11.50) (BDAG 1.a. p. 28): 'party' [AB, Bar, BDAG, BECNT, CBC; ESV, GW, NIV, REB], 'religious party' [LN; NET], 'sect' [BDAG, LN; KJV, NASB, NRSV], 'school' [BDAG]. The phrase 'all those with him (that is, the party of the Sadducees)' is also translated 'all the other Sadducees' [CEV], 'all his friends (a group called the Sadducees)' [NCV], 'his officials, who were Sadducees' [NLT], 'all his companions, members of the local party of the Sadducees' [TEV]. This noun denotes a division or group based upon different doctrinal opinions and/or loyalties [LN]. It is a group that holds tenets distinctive to it [BDAG].

c. ζῆλος (LN 88.162) (BDAG 2. p. 427): 'jealousy' [BDAG, BECNT, CBC, LN; ESV, NASB, NET, NIV, NLT, NRSV], 'envy' [Bar, BDAG, LN], 'resentment' [LN], 'indignation' [KJV], 'zeal' [AB]. The phrase 'were filled with jealousy' is also translated 'became jealous' [CEV], 'were extremely jealous' [GW], 'became very jealous' [NCV], 'were goaded by jealousy' [REB], 'became extremely jealous' [TEV], 'inflamed with zeal' [AB]. This noun denotes a particularly strong feeling of resentment and

jealousy against someone [LN]. It denotes intense feelings over another's achievements or success [BDAG].
d. aorist act. indic. of ἐπιβάλλω (LN 37.110) (BDAG 1.b. p. 367): 'to lay on' [AB, Bar, BDAG; KJV, NASB, NET], 'to put on' [BDAG], 'to seize, to arrest' [LN]. The phrase 'They laid hands on the apostles' is also translated 'They arrested the apostles' [CEV, ESV, NIV, NLT, TEV], 'the high priest...he and all who were with him...arrested the apostles' [NRSV], 'the high priest and his colleagues...to arrest the apostles' [REB], 'they took action by arresting the apostles' [GW], 'They proceeded to arrest the apostles' [CBC], 'They...seized the apostles' [BECNT], 'to take' [NCV]. This verb means to lay on, to put on [BDAG], and to lay on their hands has the meaning 'to take a person into custody for alleged illegal activity' [LN].
e. δημόσιος (LN 28.66) (BDAG 1. p. 223): 'public' [BDAG, LN; NIV, NLT, TEV]. The phrase 'the public jail' is also translated 'the city jail' [CEV, GW], 'the public prison' [BDAG; ESV, NRSV], 'the common prison' [LN; KJV], 'a common prison' [BECNT], 'a public jail' [NASB, NET], 'jail' [NCV], 'official custody' [CBC; REB], 'in prison publicly' [Bar], 'under public arrest' [AB]. This adjective means being able to be known by the public [LN]. It means that it belongs to the state [BDAG].

QUESTIONS—Who were the apostles mentioned in this verse?
1. Since Peter and John were the focus of attention in Acts 4, it is possible that they were the apostles mentioned here [PNTC].
2. It is likely that the reference is to the apostles more generally and this is a sign of the escalation of opposition in comparison with Acts 4:1–31 [PNTC]. It refers to all of the apostles [AB, Bar, EBC, NAC, NICNT, TNTC].

5:19 But during (the)-night an-angel[a] of-(the)-Lord opened the doors[b] of-the jail and having-led- them -out, he-said, **5:20** "Go stand in the temple and tell the people all the words of-this life.[c]"

LEXICON—a. ἄγγελος (LN 12.28) (BDAG 2.a. p. 8): angel' [BDAG, LN]. The phrase 'an angel of the Lord' [AB, Bar, BECNT, CBC; all versions except CEV, GW] is also translated 'an angel from the Lord' [CEV, GW]. The noun ἄγγελος can denote a person who makes an announcement [LN (33.195)], but here it denotes a supernatural being that attends upon or serves as a messenger of a superior supernatural entity. In many languages a term for 'angels' is borrowed from another dominant language, but in other instances a somewhat descriptive phrase may be employed. The most common expressions for 'angels of God' are 'messengers' and 'messengers from heaven.' Sometimes these angels are called 'spirit messengers' and even 'flying messengers.' [LN (12.28)]. It denotes a transcendent power who carries out various missions or tasks. Here it refers to an angel who is a messenger of God [BDAG]. One commentary thinks that the hand of God was at work in the apostle's release whether

the agent was a supernatural being or a human messenger of God [NICNT].
   b. θύρα (LN 7.49) (BDAG 1.a. p. 462): 'door' [AB, Bar, BDAG, BECNT, CBC, LN; all versions except NASB, NLT, TEV], 'gate' [LN; NASB, NLT, TEV]. This noun denotes the door to a house or building. It often occurs in the plural form to designate double doors or gates [LN].
   c. ζωή (LN 23.88) (BDAG 2.b.α. p. 430): 'life' [BDAG, LN]. The phrase 'all the words of this life' [Bar; ESV, KJV, NET] is also translated 'the words of this life' [BECNT], 'the whole message of/about this Life/life' [NASB, NRSV], 'this message of life' [NLT], 'the full message of this new life' [NIV], 'all about this new life' [REB, TEV], 'about this new life and all it means' [CBC], 'all about this way of life' [AB], 'everything about life in Christ' [GW], 'everything about this new life' [CEV, NCV]. This noun refers to the life of the believer which proceeds from God and Christ [BDAG].
QUESTION—What did the angel of the Lord do?
   The angel of the Lord acted secretly at night to rescue the apostles from prison and re-commission them to speak to the people at the temple about the message of this life [Bar, EBC, NAC, PNTC]. The hand of God was at work in the apostles' release [EBC, NICNT, PNTC]. The angel acted as the spokesman of God in commanding the apostles to go and speak [TNTC]. Notice the two imperative words 'go' and 'speak' in v. 20, the apostles were to obey and take their stand at the very center of Israel's national and religious life, in the temple [PNTC].
QUESTION—What is meant by ζωῆς ταύτης 'this life'?
   'This life' may mean this 'way of life', probably the new life offered by Jesus, the author of life (Act 3:15) [Bar, BECNT]. It refers to the new Christian Life, the new way of living [TH], a new life with life and salvation, life and salvation are understood in the New Testament as being synonymous since both are Greek translations of the Hebrew word 'life' [EBC], an apt term for the message of the salvation [NICNT, TNTC].

DISCOURSE UNIT—5:21b–26 [NICNT]. The topic is the apostles brought before the Sanhedrin.

5:21 And upon-hearing (this), they-entered into the temple about daybreak and began-to-teach. And (when) the high-priest and the-ones with him came, they-called-together the Sanhedrin and all the assembly-of-elders[a] of-the sons of-Israel and sent[b] to the jail-(for-the-apostles) to-be-brought to-them.
LEXICON—a. γερουσία (LN 11.83) (BDAG p. 195): 'assembly of elders' [LN], 'council of elders' [BDAG, LN]. The phrase 'the Sanhedrin and all the assembly of elders of the sons of Israel' is also translated so as to make the assembly of elders a separate group from the Sanhedrin: 'the Sanhedrin and all the Senate of the children of Israel' [Bar], 'the council and the whole body of the elders of Israel' [NRSV], 'the council and all

the senate of the people/children of Israel' [ESV, KJV], 'the Jewish leaders and all the important older Jewish men' [NCV], 'called the Council together, even all the Senate of the sons of Israel' [NASB], 'the council, that is, all the senate of the sons of Israel' [BECNT], 'the Jewish council, that is, all the leaders of Israel' [GW], 'the Sanhedrin, that is, the whole Israelite council of elders' [AB], 'the Sanhedrin, that is, the whole council of elders of the Jewish people' [LN], 'the Sanhedrin—that is, the whole high council of the Israelites' [NET], 'the Sanhedrin—the full assembly of the elders of Israel' [NIV], 'the high council—the full assembly of the elders of Israel' [NLT], 'their council, which included all of Israel's leaders' [CEV], 'the Sanhedrin, the full Council of the Israelite nation' [REB], 'the Sanhedrin, that is, the full senate of the Israelite nation' [CBC], 'all the Jewish elders for a full meeting of the Council' [TEV]. This noun refers to members of the highest council of the Jews (see also 'Sanhedrin, the council of the Jews) 11.80). but it also implies they are mature members of relatively advanced age [LN]. It denotes a council of elders, especially the Sanhedrin in Jerusalem [BDAG]. Most take the assembly of elders to be another designation of the Sanhedrin or part of the Sanhedrin: 'the Sanhedrin, that is, the whole council of elders of the Jewish people' [TH]

b. aorist act. indic. of ἀποστέλλω (LN 15.66) (BDAG 1.b.γ. p. 121): 'to send' [LN], 'to send away, to send out' [BDAG]. The phrase 'sent to the jail for the apostles to be brought to them' is also translated 'sent to the jail to have the apostles brought before them' [NET], 'sent to the prison to have them brought' [BECNT; ESV, KJV, NRSV], 'sent to the gaol that they might be brought' [Bar], 'sent to the jail for the apostles/prisoners' [NIV, REB], 'sent to the jail to fetch the prisoners' [CBC], 'sent orders to the prison to have the apostles brought before them' [TEV], 'sent orders to the prison house for them to be brought' [NASB], 'sent word to the prison that they should be brought before them' [AB], 'sent some men to the prison to bring the apostles to them' [NCV], 'sent men to the prison to get the apostles' [GW], 'they ordered the apostles to be brought to them from the jail' [CEV], 'sent for the apostles to be brought from the jail for trial' [NLT]. This verb means to cause someone to depart for a particular purpose [LN]. It means to dispatch someone for the achievement of some object and with the purpose of the sending indicated by the infinitive [BDAG].

QUESTION—When did the apostles go to the temple and speak?

The apostles did as the angel had told them. They went there at daybreak since the crowds would be gathering in the temple early in the morning in order to observe the morning sacrifice [BECNT, NAC].

QUESTION—How are the Sanhedrin and all the assembly of elders of the sons of Israel connected?

Most think that one group, the Sanhedrin, is referred to in two ways. However some think that two groups are being referred to: the Sanhedrin and either a group of elders within the Sanhedrin or a group of elders that the Sanhedrin is part of [TRT]. The council and 'all the senate of Israel' is a hendiadys, only one body being meant [TNTC]. The high priest and his circle called together the governing council of Israel [BECNT], the full assembly of the elders of Israel [NAC]. The high priest and his colleagues arrived and called the Sanhedrin together—the senate of the people of Israel' [NICNT]. 'All the assembly of elders of the sons of Israel' signifies: the presence of the Pharisees in the Council [EBC].

5:22 But the officers[a] who-came did- not -find them in the prison. So they-returned and reported, **5:23** saying, "We-found the prison[b] securely[c] locked and the guards[d] standing at the doors. But when-we-had-opened-(them), we-found no-one inside."

LEXICON—a. ὑπηρέτης (LN 35.20) (BDAG p. 1035): 'officer' [BECNT; ESV, KJV, NASB, NCV, NET, NIV, REB], 'temple police' [CEV, NRSV], 'temple guard' [GW, NLT], 'official' [TEV], 'servant' [LN], 'attendant' [BDAG], 'agent' [Bar], 'police' [CBC], 'deputy' [AB]. This noun denotes 'a person who renders service' [LN]. In the New Testament, this noun is employed to refer to many diverse types of servants, such as attendants to a king, officers of the Sanhedrin, attendants of magistrates and, especially in the Gospel of John, the Jewish Temple guards [LN]. It denotes one who functions as a helper and here it refers to the attendants of the Sanhedrin [BDAG],

b. δεσμωτήριον (LN 7.24) (BDAG p. 219): 'prison' [AB, BDAG, BECNT, LN; ESV, GW, KJV, NRSV], 'prison house' [NASB], 'jail' [BDAG, CBC, LN; CEV, NCV, NET, NIV, NLT, REB, TEV], 'gaol' [Bar]. This noun denotes a place of detention [LN]. It denotes a place for detention. Prisons in the Roman world were ordinarily used for temporary custody to prevent escape pending sentencing [BDAG].

c. ἀσφάλεια (LN 21.9) (BDAG 3. p. 147): 'security' [BDAG, LN]. The phrase 'securely locked' [AB, BDAG; ESV, GW, NIV, NLT, NRSV] is also translated 'securely locked at every point' [CBC; REB], 'locked quite securely' [NASB], 'locked securely' [NET], 'locked up tight' [TEV], 'locked tight' [CEV], 'closed in all security' [Bar], 'closed and locked' [NCV], 'shut with all safety' [KJV], 'standing locked securely' [BECNT]. This noun denotes detention that restricts movement [LN].

d. φύλαξ (LN 37.121) (BDAG p. 1068): 'guard' [AB, Bar, BDAG, LN; all versions except KJV, REB], 'sentinel' [BDAG, LN], 'keeper' [KJV], 'warder' [CBC; REB], 'sentry' [BECNT]. This noun denotes one who is responsible for guarding an area or a person [LN].

QUESTION—What does οὐδένα 'no one' in 'we found no one inside' mean?
'No one' means no one of those whom they sought, that is, the apostles whom they sought were not found inside the prison house [Bar, TH].

5:24 And, when they-heard these words, both the commander[a] of-the temple (guard) and the chief-priests were-greatly-perplexed[b] about them as to what would come of this.

LEXICON—a. στρατηγός (LN 37.91) (BDAG 2. p. 948): 'commander' [BDAG, LN]. The phrase 'the commander of the temple guard' [NET] is also translated 'the commander of the temple' [AB], 'the captain of the temple/Temple guards/guard' [NASB, NCV, NIV, NLT], 'the captain of the temple police' [CEV], 'the officer of the temple guards' [GW], 'the captain of the temple' [Bar, BECNT; ESV, KJV, NRSV], 'the controller of the temple' [CBC; REB], 'the officer in charge of the Temple' [TEV]. The title στρατηγὸς τοῦ ἱεροῦ is literally 'official of the temple' and it refers to the commander of the Jewish soldiers responsible for guarding and maintaining order in the Jewish Temple [LN]. It denotes the commander responsible for the temple in Jerusalem [BDAG]. This title also occurs in Acts 4:1.

b. imperf. act. indic. of διαπορέω (LN 32.10) (BDAG p. 235): 'to not know what to do, to be very confused' [LN], 'to be greatly perplexed, to be at a loss' [BDAG]. The phrase 'were greatly perplexed about them as to what would come of this' is also translated 'they were greatly perplexed about them as to what would come of this' [NASB], 'they were greatly perplexed about them, wondering what this would come to' [ESV], 'they were very perplexed about them, wondering what this might be' [BECNT], 'they were perplexed, wondering where it would end' [NLT], 'they were perplexed about them, wondering what might be going on' [NRSV], 'they were perplexed about these men as to what might happen' [AB], 'they were wondering what could have become of them' [CBC], 'they were greatly puzzled concerning it, wondering what this could be' [NET], 'they were puzzled about what could have happened' [GW], 'were puzzled, wondering what would come of this' [NIV], 'were confused and wondered what was happening' [NCV], 'but they did not know what to think about this' [CEV], 'they were at a loss concerning them to know what this might mean' [Bar], 'were at a loss to know what could have become of them'[REB], 'they wondered what had happened to the apostles' [TEV], 'they doubted of them whereunto this would grow' [KJV]. This verb means to be thoroughly perplexed [LN]. It means to be greatly perplexed, to be at a loss about something [BDAG].

5:25 And someone came and told them, "Look!"[a] The men whom you-put in the prison are standing in the temple and teaching the people." **5:26** Then the commander went with (his) officers and brought them back without (using) force[b] because they-were-afraid-of the people, that they-might-be-stoned.

LEXICON—a. ἰδού (LN 91.13): 'look' [BECNT, CBC, LN; ESV, NET, NIV, NRSV], 'behold' [KJV], 'see' [Bar, BDAG], 'listen' [AB; NCV, TEV], 'pay attention' [LN], not explicit [CEV, GW, NASB, NLT, REB]. This

particle functions as a prompter of attention, also serving to emphasize the statement which follows [LN].
   b. βία (LN 20.1) (BDAG b. p. 175): 'force' [AB, BDAG, BECNT, CBC, LN; CEV, ESV, GW, NCV, NIV, TEV], 'violence' [Bar, LN; KJV, NASB, NLT, NRSV], 'the use of force' [NET, REB]. This noun denotes a strong, destructive force [LN]. It denotes the strength or energy brought to bear in varying degrees on things or persons [BDAG].
QUESTION—What does the report given in verse 25 tell us?
   It tells us that the apostles had done precisely what the angel of the Lord had told them to do [Bar, PNTC].
QUESTION—Why did the commander fear that he and his men might be stoned?
   Stoning was not a formal legal penalty [Bar, PNTC], but angry crowds sometimes stoned people to death without permission [TRT]. A stoning could either be a non-specific form of protest against the authorities or a way of accusing them of blasphemy because of their treatment of the apostles [PNTC]. In this case no force was used when bringing the apostles back and there was no resistance on the part of the apostles [BECNT, NICNT, TNTC].

DISCOURSE UNIT—5:27-42 [BECNT]. The topic is deliberations and release.

DISCOURSE UNIT—5:27-40 [NAC]. The topic is appearance before the Sanhedrin.

DISCOURSE UNIT—5:27-32 [NICNT]. The topic is the high priest's charge and the apostles' reply.

5:27 And when-they-had-brought them, they-stood-(them)-before[a] the Sanhedrin. And the high-priest questioned[b] them, **5:28** saying, "(Did-we)-not strictly-command[c] you not to-teach in this name[d]? And look, you-have-filled[e] Jerusalem with your teaching and you-intend-to-bring this man's blood[f] upon us."
LEXICON—a. aorist act. indic. of ἵστημι (LN 85.40) (BDAG A.1. p. 482): 'to make (them) stand before' [NCV, REB, TEV], 'to make (them) stand in front of' [GW], 'to stand (them) before' [CBC; NASB, NET], 'to make (them) stand' [LN], 'to set (them)' [AB, Bar, BDAG, BECNT, LN; ESV, KJV], 'to make (them) appear before' [NIV], 'to have (them) stand before' [NRSV], 'to place' [BDAG, LN], 'to put' [LN], 'to bring' [BDAG], not explicit [CEV, NLT]. This verb means to cause someone to be in a place, with or without the accompanying feature of a standing position [LN]. It means to cause someone to be in a certain place or position [BDAG].
   b. aorist act. indic. of ἐπερωτάω (LN 56.14) (BDAG 1.b. p. 362): 'to question' [AB, BECNT, LN; all versions except CEV, KJV, NLT, REB], 'to interrogate, to try to learn' [LN], 'to ask' [Bar, BDAG; KJV], 'to say' [CEV], 'to confront' [NLT]. The phrase 'the high priest questioned them'

is also translated 'the high priest began his examination' [CBC; REB]. This verb means to attempt in a legal or semi-legal procedure to know the truth about a matter by interrogation [LN]. It means to put a question to someone, and here it refers to a judge questioning someone when making an investigation [BDAG].
c. aorist act. indic. of παραγγέλλω (LN 33.327) (BDAG p. 760): 'to command' [BDAG, LN], 'to order' [LN], 'to give orders, to instruct, to direct' [BDAG]. The clause 'Did we not strictly command you' is also translated 'Did not we straitly command you' [KJV], 'Didn't we tell you' [NLT], 'We strictly commanded you' [BECNT], 'We expressly commanded you' [AB], 'We strictly charged you' [ESV], 'We strictly ordered you' [Bar], 'We expressly ordered you' [CBC], 'We gave you strict orders' [GW, NASB, NCV, NET, NIV, NRSV, TEV], 'We gave you explicit orders' [REB], 'We told you plainly' [CEV]. This verb means to announce what must be done [LN]. It means to make an announcement about something that must be done [BDAG].
d. ὄνομα (LN 33.126) (BDAG 1.d.γ.ה. p. 714): 'name' [AB, Bar, BDAG, BECNT, CBC, LN; all versions]. The phrase 'not to teach in this name' [AB, Bar, BECNT] is also translated 'not to teach in the name of this man' [TEV], 'not to teach in the name of Jesus' [CEV], 'not to mention Jesus' name when you teach' [GW], 'not to continue teaching in this name' [NASB], 'not to continue teaching in that name' [NCV], 'never again to teach in this man's name' [NLT], 'to stop teaching in that name' [REB], 'to desist from teaching in that name' [CBC]. This noun denotes the proper name of a person and refers to speaking using this name [LN].
e. perf. act. indic. of πληρόω (LN 59.37) (BDAG 1.a. p. 828): 'to fill' [AB, Bar, BDAG, BECNT, CBC, LN; all versions except CEV, TEV]. The phrase 'you have filled Jerusalem with your teaching' is also translated 'You have been teaching all over Jerusalem' [CEV], 'You have spread your teaching all over Jerusalem' [TEV]. This verb means to cause something to become full [LN]. It means to make full [BDAG].
f. αἷμα (LN 23.107) (BDAG 2.a. p. 26): 'blood' [AB, Bar, BDAG, BECNT, LN; ESV, KJV, NASB, NET, NIV, NRSV], 'death' [CBC, LN; CEV, GW, NCV, NLT, REB, TEV], 'violent death' [LN]. The phrase 'to bring this man's blood upon us' [Bar, BECNT; ESV, KJV, NASB] is also translated 'to bring this man's blood upon our heads' [AB], 'to bring this man's blood on us' [NET, NRSV], 'to take revenge on us for putting that man to death' [GW], 'to make us responsible for this man's death' [NCV], 'to make us guilty of this man's blood' [NIV], 'to make us responsible for his death' [NLT, TEV], 'to make us responsible for that man's death' [CBC], 'to hold us responsible for that man's death' [REB], 'to blame us for his death' [CEV]. This noun denotes the death of a person, generally as a result of violence or execution [LN]. It is a figurative use of 'blood' as constituting the life of an individual [BDAG].

QUESTION—What is meant by 'bringing blood' on someone?

'Bringing blood' on others means to blame them for another's death [PNTC]. This expression is an idiom for being responsible for the man's death [BECNT, TRT]. 'This man' refers to Jesus, whose name the high priest refused to mention [EBC, TNTC, TRT] or was reluctant to pronounce [NICNT]. The high priest meant that the apostles were blaming the Sanhedrin and the high priest for Jesus' death, they were the guilty party responsible for Jesus' death [EBC, NAC, NICNT, PNTC, TH, TNTC].

5:29 And answering Peter and the apostles said, "We must obey God rather than men. 5:30 The God of our ancestors^a raised^b Jesus, whom you had-put-to-death by hanging (him) on (a)-cross.^c

LEXICON—a. πατήρ (LN 10.20): 'ancestor' [LN; CEV, GW, NCV, NLT, NRSV, TEV], 'forefather' [LN; NET], 'father' [AB, Bar, BECNT, CBC; ESV, KJV, NASB, NIV, REB]. This noun denotes a person several preceding generations removed from the reference person [LN].

b. aorist act. indic. of ἐγείρω (LN 23.94) (BDAG 6. p. 271): 'to raise' [BDAG, BECNT; ESV], 'to raise to life' [LN; CEV], 'to make live again' [LN], 'to bring back to life' [GW], 'to raise up' [AB, Bar, BDAG, CBC; KJV, NASB, NET, NRSV, REB], 'to raise up from the dead' [NCV], 'to raise from the dead' [NIV, NLT], 'to raise from death' [TEV]. This verb means to cause someone to live again after having once died [LN]. It means to cause to return to life [BDAG].

c. ξύλον (LN 6.28) (BDAG 2.c. p. 685): 'cross' [BDAG, LN; CEV, GW, NASB, NCV, NLT, TEV], 'tree' [Bar, BECNT, ESV, KJV, NET, NIV, NRSV], 'gibbet' [CBC; REB]. The phrase 'by hanging (him) on a cross' is also translated 'by crucifixion' [AB]. This noun is a figurative extension of meaning of the word for 'wood' and here it refers to an instrument of execution. In the NT contexts it refers to the cross on which Jesus was crucified [LN]. It denotes an object made of wood and here it refers to the cross, a wooden structure used for crucifixion [BDAG].

QUESTION—Does the phrase 'Peter and the apostles said' mean they all spoke in unison?

It means that Peter was the spokesman for the group of apostles on trial and the whole group was in agreement with Peter [BECNT, EBC, NICNT, TRT].

QUESTION—What was Peter's defense?

Peter's response is hardly a reasoned defense. His statement 'We must obey God rather than men' is simply a reaffirmation of their position and principles [EBC, TNTC].

QUESTION—What incident was Peter referring to when he said that the God of our ancestors 'raised' Jesus?

1. He was referring to raising Jesus from the dead [AB, Bar, CBC, NAC, TH, TNTC, TH, TRT; CEV GW, NCV, NIV, NLT, TEV]. The word 'exalt' in the next verse suggests the resurrection [Bar]. The resurrection

is probable since immediately there follows the affirmation that these people had been the ones responsible for killing Jesus [TH].
2. He was referring to the inauguration of Jesus' ministry (NAC, NICNT). As God had once raised up David to be their king, so he had more recently raised up Jesus to be their Messiah [NICNT].

5:31 **He is the-one whom God exalted**[a] **to-his right-(hand)**[b] **(as)-Leader**[c] **and Savior, to-grant repentance**[d] **to-Israel and forgiveness**[e] **of-sins.**

LEXICON—a. aorist act. indic. of ὑψόω (LN 87.20) (BDAG 2. p. 1046): 'to exalt' [AB, Bar, BDAG, BECNT, CBC, LN; ESV, KJV, NASB, NET, NIV, NRSV, REB], 'to lift up, to raise high' [BDAG], 'to give high position to' [LN]. The phrase 'He is the one whom God exalted to his right hand' is translated 'Then God gave him a place at his right side' [CEV], 'God used his power to give Jesus the highest position as leader and savior' [GW], 'Jesus is the One whom God raised to be on his right side' [NCV], 'Then God put him in the place of honor at his right hand' [NLT], 'God raised him to his right side' [TEV]. This verb means to cause someone to have a high status [LN]. It means to cause enhancement in honor, fame, position, and power [BDAG].

b. δεξιός (LN 82.8) (BDAG 1.b. p. 218): 'the right hand' [AB, Bar, BDAG, BECNT, CBC; ESV, KJV, NASB, NET, NIV, NLT, NRSV, REB], 'the right side' [LN; CEV, NCV, TEV], 'the right' [LN]. The phrase 'his right hand' is also translated 'the highest position' [GW]. This noun denotes a position to the right of some point of reference [LN]. The related Greek phrase ἐκ δεξιῶν καθίζω 'to sit on the right side of' means to be in a position of high status [LN 87.34]. To sit at someone's right means to be at the place of honor [BDAG].

c. ἀρχηγός (LN 36.6) (BDAG 1. p. 138): 'leader' [BDAG, BECNT, CBC; CEV, ESV, GW, NCV, NET, NRSV, REB, TEV], 'prince' [AB, BDAG, LN; KJV, NASB, NIV, NLT], 'ruler' [Bar, BDAG], 'pioneer leader, founding leader' [LN]. This noun denotes a person who as originator or a founder of a movement continues as the leader [LN]. It denotes one who has a preeminent position [BDAG].

d. μετάνοια (LN 41.52) (BDAG p. 640): 'repentance' [AB, Bar, BDAG, BECNT, CBC, LN; ESV, KJV, NASB, NET, NIV, NRSV, REB], 'a change of mind' [BDAG]. The phrase 'to grant repentance to Israel' is also translated 'that the people of Israel would turn back to him' [CEV], 'to change the way they think and act' [GW], 'Through him, all Jewish people could change their hearts and lives' [NCV], 'so the people of Israel would repent of their sins' [NLT], 'to give the people of Israel the opportunity to repent' [TEV]. This noun denotes a complete change of thought and attitude with regard to sin and righteousness [LN]. It denotes a change of mind, repentance, turning about, and conversion, and this is mostly concerned with the beginning of a new relationship with God [BDAG].

e. ἄφεσις (LN 40.8) (BDAG 2 p. 155): 'forgiveness' [AB, Bar, BECNT, CBC, LN; ESV, KJV, NASB, NET, NIV, NRSV, REB], 'pardon, cancellation' [BDAG]. The phrase 'forgiveness of sins' is also translated 'to be forgiven' [CEV, NLT], 'to forgive their sins' [GW], 'to have their sins forgiven' [NCV, TEV]. This noun denotes the removal of guilt resulting from wrongdoing [LN]. It is the act of being freed from an obligation, guilt, or punishment [BDAG].

5:32 And we are witnesses[a] to-these things, and (so is) the Holy Spirit, whom God has-given[b] to-those who-obey him."

LEXICON—a. μάρτυς (LN 33.270) (BDAG 2.c. p. 620): 'witness' [AB, Bar, BDAG, BECNT, CBC, LN; all versions except CEV, NCV], 'testifier' [BDAG], 'one who testifies' [LN]. The phrase 'we are witnesses to these things' is also translated 'We are here to tell you about all this' [CEV], 'We saw all these things happen' [NCV]. This noun denotes a person who witnesses [LN]. It denotes one who affirms or attests, and here it refers to a witness who bears a divine message [BDAG].

b. aorist act. indic. of δίδωμι (LN 57.71, 37.98): 'to give' [AB, Bar, BECNT, CBC, LN (57.71); all versions except CEV, TEV], 'to appoint, to assign (on behalf of)' [LN (37.98)]. The phrase 'whom God has given to those who obey him' [Bar, BECNT], is also translated 'which God gives to those who obey him' [AB], 'who is God's gift to everyone who obeys God' [CEV], 'who is God's gift to those who obey him' [TEV], 'is given by God to those who are obedient to him' [CBC]. This verb means to give an object, usually implying value [LN (57.71)] or it means to assign a person to a task as a particular benefit to others [LN (37.98)].

QUESTION—What things are these disciples and the Holy Spirit witnesses to?
They are witnesses to the things Peter has related in verses 30–31 [TRT], that is, the guilt of the Jewish leaders for crucifying Jesus, the resurrection and exaltation, repentance and forgiveness in his name [NAC].

QUESTION—How was the Holy Spirit bearing witness to these things?
The pouring out of the Holy Spirit, so evident in all the miraculous works that were being accomplished, was bearing his own witness [NAC]. The Spirit functions as revealer of the gospel here [BECNT]. Here Peter spoke about the Holy Spirit who was not only once poured upon the believers at Pentecost but was continuously granted to all who obeyed God [Bar, NAC]. Both the apostles and the Holy Spirit bore witness to Jesus whom God exalted and authorized to bless his people with the grace of repentance and the gift of forgiveness [BECNT, NICNT, TH, TNTC]. The apostles were eyewitnesses of things in verses 30–31 and the Holy Spirit confirmed them [CBC].

DISCOURSE UNIT—5:33–42 [NASB]. The topic is Gamaliel's counsel.

DISCOURSE UNIT—5:33–40 [NICNT]. The topic is the court's decision.

5:33 And when-they-heard (this), they-were-enraged[a] and wanted to-kill[b] them.

LEXICON—a. imperf. pass. indic. of διαπρίω (LN 88.181) (BDAG p. 237): 'to be enraged' [LN; ESV, NRSV], 'to be furious' [LN; GW, NIV, NLT, TEV], 'to be infuriated' [BDAG], 'to become angry' [CEV, NCV], 'to be cut (to the heart)' [KJV], 'to be cut to the quick' [BDAG; NASB], 'to become furious' [NET], 'to be incensed' [Bar], 'to be filled with rage' [BECNT], 'to be seized with indignation' [AB], 'to be touched on the raw' [CBC; REB]. This verb means to be angry to the point of rage [LN].
  b. aorist act. infin. of ἀναιρέω (LN 20.71) (BDAG 2. p. 64): 'to kill' [AB, Bar, BECNT, LN; CEV, ESV, NASB, NCV, NLT, NRSV], 'to execute' [LN; GW, NET]. 'to put to death' [CBC; NIV, NRSV, TEV], 'to slay' [KJV], 'to dispose of' [BDAG]. This verb means to get rid of somebody by execution, often with legal or quasi-legal procedures [LN]. It means to get rid of by execution [BDAG].

DISCOURSE UNIT—5:34–40 [EBC, PNTC]. The topic is the moderating influence of Gamaliel [PNTC], Gamaliel's wise counsel of moderation [EBC].

5:34 But a-Pharisee named Gamaliel, (a)-teacher-of-the-law[a] respected[b] by-all the people, stood-up in the Sanhedrin and gave-orders to-put the men outside[c] (for-a)-little-(while).

LEXICON—a. νομοδιδάσκαλος (LN 33.248) (BDAG p. 676): 'teacher of the law' [AB, Bar, BDAG, BECNT, CBC, LN; ESV, NASB, NCV, NET, NIV, NRSV, REB, TEV], 'expert in the law' [LN], 'teacher' [CEV], 'doctor of the law' [KJV]. The phrase 'teacher of the law, respected by all the people' is also translated 'a highly respected expert in Moses' Teachings' [GW], 'an expert in religious law and respected by all the people' [NLT]. This noun denotes a person who is skilled in the teaching and interpretation of the law, and in the NT it refers to the law of the OT [LN]. This refers to a teacher of the Mosaic law [BDAG].
  b. τίμιος (LN 87.6) (BDAG 2. p. 1006): 'respected' [AB, BDAG, LN; NASB, NCV, NET, NLT, NRSV], 'highly respected' [CEV, GW, TEV], 'honored' [BECNT, LN; NIV], 'held in honor' [Bar, BDAG; ESV], 'held in high regard' [BDAG, CBC; REB]. The phrase 'respected by all the people' is also translated 'had in reputation among all the people' [KJV]. This adjective refers to someone who is ascribed high status, involving both honor and respect [LN]. It pertains to high status that merits esteem BDAG].
  c. ἔξω (LN 83.20) (BDAG 2.a. p. 354): 'outside' [AB, Bar, BDAG, BECNT, CBC, LN; ESV, GW, NASB, NET, NIV, NLT, NRSV, REB], 'out' [BDAG; TEV], 'apart from' [LN]. The phrase 'gave orders to put the men outside for a little while' is also translated 'ordered the apostles to be taken out of the room for a little while' [CEV], 'commanded to put the apostles forth a little space' [KJV], 'ordered the apostles to leave the meeting for a little while' [NCV]. This adverb refers to a position not

contained within a particular area [LN]. It pertains to a position outside an area or limits [BDAG].

QUESTION—What is known about the Pharisee named Gamaliel?

Pharisees believed in a coming Messiah, the resurrection, and a life after death, none of which the Sadducees accepted [Bar, BECNT, EBC, NAC]. Such differences contributed to Gamaliel's more tolerant stance toward the apostles than the Sadducees [Bar, NAC]. The Gamaliel here was Gamaliel I [Bar, BECNT, EBC, NAC, TH, TNTC]. He was the greatest Jewish rabbi/teacher of his day [TRT], a noted and highly respected Jewish teacher [Bar, BECNT, PNTC, TH]. Rabbinic tradition gives him the title of Nasi, or president of the high court. His prime influence was from about A.D. 25–50 [NAC]. The apostle Paul had been educated under him (Act 22:3) [AB, Bar, BECNT, CBC, EBC, NAC, NICNT, TRT]. He spoke as a significant representative of the Pharisees in the Council as displayed in the following verses [EBC, TNTC].

5:35 And he-said to them, "Men of-Israel, take-care what you-are-about to-do with these men. **5:36** For before[a] these days, Theudas rose-up,[b] claiming to-be somebody,[c] and a-group of about four-hundred men joined him. He-was-killed and all who followed him were-dispersed[d] and came to nothing.[e]

LEXICON—a. πρό (LN 67.17) (BDAG 2. p. 864): 'before' [BDAG, BECNT, LN; ESV, KJV], 'previous' [LN]. The phrase 'before these days' is also translated 'before these times' [AB], 'some time ago' [Bar, CBC; GW, NASB, NET, NIV, NLT, NRSV, REB, TEV], 'not long ago' [CEV]. The phrase 'For before these days Theudas rose up' is also translated 'Remember when Theudas appeared?' [NCV]. This preposition refers to a point of time prior to another point of time [LN]. It is a marker of a point of time prior to another point of time [BDAG].

b. aorist act. indic. of ἀνίστημι (LN 13.81, 39.34): 'to rise up' [Bar; ESV, KJV, NASB, NET, NRSV], 'to arise' [BECNT, LN (13.81)], 'to appear' [LN (13.81); GW, NCV, NIV, TEV], 'to come forward' [AB, CBC; REB], not explicit [CEV]. The phrase 'before these days Theudas rose up' is also translated 'Some time ago there was that fellow Theudas' [NLT]. This verb means to rise up in open defiance of authority, with the presumed intention to overthrow it or to act in complete opposition to its demands [LN (39.34)], or it means to come into existence, with the implication of assuming a place or position [LN (13.81)].

c. τις (LN 92.13, 87.49) (BDAG 2. p. 1009): 'a great person' [LN (87.49)], 'someone important' [LN (92.13)], 'a person of importance' [BDAG]. The phrase 'claiming to be somebody' [BDAG, CBC; ESV, NASB, NET, NIV, NRSV] is also translated 'claimed to be somebody' [CEV], 'claiming to be somebody great' [TEV], 'claiming to be someone of significance' [BECNT], 'he claimed he was important' [GW], 'making claims for himself' [REB], 'saying that he was somebody' [Bar], 'said that he was somebody' [AB], 'he said he was a great man' [NCV], 'who

pretended to be somebody' [NLT], 'boasting himself to be somebody' [KJV]. The pronominal adjective 'someone' in a predicate position refers to someone of prominence or distinction [LN (92.13)], so the phrase 'to be someone' means to be a person of importance [LN (87.49)]. It refers to someone of prominence [BDAG].
   d. aorist pass. indic. of διαλύω (LN 15.136) (BDAG 3. p. 233): 'to be dispersed' [AB, Bar, BDAG; ESV, NASB, NET, NIV, NRSV], 'to be scattered' [BDAG, BECNT, LN; CEV, GW, KJV, NCV, TEV], 'to be broken up' [CBC], 'to be caused to disperse' [LN]. The phrase 'all who followed him were dispersed' is also translated 'all his followers went their various ways' [NLT], 'his whole movement was destroyed' [REB]. This verb means to cause a group or gathering to disperse or scatter, with a possible emphasis on the distributive nature of the scattering (that is to say, each going in a different direction) [LN]. It means to cause a group to be broken up [BDAG].
   e. οὐδείς (LN 92.23): 'nothing' [AB, Bar, BECNT, LN; ESV, NASB, NCV, NET, NIV, NLT, REB], 'nought' [KJV]. The phrase 'came to nothing' is also translated 'and that was the end of that' [CEV], 'and disappeared' [CBC; NRSV], 'and his movement died out' [TEV], 'was a failure' [GW]. This noun denotes a negative reference to an entity, event, or state [LN].

QUESTION—What is the function of these two verses?

Here Gamaliel made his point to the Council by citing a previous movement led by the man named Theudas. The movement ended in nothing because it was of human origin and was not in the name of heaven [BECNT, NICNT, TNTC], because God was not in them [NAC].

5:37 After this (man), Judas the Galilean[a] rose-up[b] in the days of-the census[c] and incited[d] people (to)-follow-after him. And-that-one perished[e] and all who followed him were-scattered.[f]

LEXICON—a. Γαλιλαῖος (LN 93.445) (BDAG p. 187): 'Galilean' [Bar, BDAG, BECNT, CBC, LN; ESV, NET, NIV, NRSV, REB, TEV]. The phrase 'Judas the Galilean' is also translated 'Judas from Galilee' [CEV, GW], 'Judas of Galilee' [AB; KJV, NASB, NCV, NLT]. This noun denotes a person who is a native of Galilee [LN]. It is the surname of the insurrectionist Judas [BDAG].
   b. aorist act. indic. of ἀνίστημι (BDAG 9. p. 83): 'to rise up' [Bar, BDAG, BECNT; ESV, KJV, NASB, NRSV], 'to arise' [BDAG; NET], 'to appear' [GW, NIV, TEV], 'to show up' [CEV], 'to come' [CBC; NCV, REB], 'to come forward' [AB], 'to be' [NLT]. This verb means to cause/appear to carry out a function or role [BDAG].
   c. ἀπογραφή (LN 33.43) (BDAG p. 108): 'census' [Bar, BDAG, BECNT, CBC, LN; all versions except CEV, KJV, NCV], 'registration' [AB, BDAG; NCV], 'list, inventory' [BDAG], 'taxing' [KJV]. The phrase 'in the days of the census' is also translated 'when the people of our nation were being counted' [CEV]. This noun denotes the event of registering

persons in connection with taking a census [LN]. The verb ἀπογραφω means to enter into a list [BDAG].
d. aorist act. indic. of ἀφίστημι (LN 39.41) (BDAG 1. p. 157): 'to incite people to revolt' [LN], 'to cause people to rebel' [LN], 'to cause people to revolt' [BDAG]. The phrase 'he incited people to follow after him' is also translated 'he got people to follow him' [NLT, NRSV], 'he also led a group of followers' [NCV], 'he drew a crowd after him' [TEV], 'he drew a company after himself' [Bar], 'he drew away some of the people after him' [BECNT; ESV, NASB], 'he drew away much people after him' [KJV], 'he incited a-crowd/people to follow him in revolt' [LN; NET], 'he induced some people to revolt under his leadership' [CBC; REB], 'he led people in a revolt' [GW], 'he led a band of people in revolt' [NIV], 'he gathered a (large) following' [AB], 'a lot of people followed him' [CEV]. This verb means to cause people to rebel against or to reject authority [LN]. It means to cause someone to move from a reference point, and in reference to altering allegiance it means to cause people to revolt [BDAG].
e. aorist mid. indic. of ἀπόλλυμι (LN 20.31) (BDAG 1.b.α. p. 116): 'to perish' [AB, Bar, BDAG, BECNT, CBC; ESV, KJV, NASB, NRSV, REB], 'to die' [BDAG; GW], 'to be ruined, to be destroyed' [LN], 'to be killed' [BDAG; CEV, NCV, NET, NIV, NLT, TEV]. This verb means to destroy or to cause the destruction of persons, objects, or institutions [LN]. In the middle voice it means to perish or to die [BDAG].
f. aorist pass. indic. of διασκορπίζω (LN 15.136) (BDAG 1. p. 236): 'to be scattered' [AB, Bar, BDAG, BECNT, CBC, LN; all versions except KJV, REB], 'to be dispersed' [BDAG, LN; KJV], 'to be broken up' [REB]. This verb means to cause a group or gathering to disperse or scatter, with a possible emphasis on the distributive nature of the scattering, that is to say, each going in a different direction [LN]. It means to scatter or to disperse on the field of battle [BDAG].

QUESTION—What is the function of this verse?
This verse continued Gamaliel's reasoning. He now cites another movement that was led by the man named Judas. This movement also ended in failure because it was not of God [BECNT, NICNT, TNTC], God was not in them [NAC].

5:38 So now I-say to-you, keep-away[a] from these men and leave them-(alone), because if this plan[b] or this undertaking[c] is of men,[d] it-will-fail.[e]
LEXICON—a. aorist act. impera. of ἀφίστημι (LN 34.41) (BDAG 2.b. p. 158): 'to keep away' [BDAG, BECNT, LN; ESV, GW, NRSV], 'to stay away' [CEV, NASB, NCV, NET], 'to stay clear of' [AB], 'to keep clear of' [CBC; REB], 'to steer clear of' [Bar], 'to refrain' [KJV], 'to shun, to avoid, to have nothing to do with' [LN]. The phrase 'keep away from these men and leave them alone' is also translated 'Leave these men alone! Let them go!' [NIV, NLT], 'do not take any action against these

men. Leave them alone!' [TEV]. This verb means to purposely avoid association with someone [LN]. It means to distance oneself from some person [BDAG].
- b. βουλή (LN 30.57) (BDAG 2.a. p. 181): 'plan' [Bar, BECNT, LN; ESV, GW, NASB, NCV, NET, NRSV], 'intention' [LN], 'purpose' [LN; NIV], 'resolution, decision' [BDAG], 'counsel' [KJV], 'idea' [CBC], 'design' [AB]. The phrase 'this plan' is also translated 'what they are planning' [CEV], 'what is being planned' [REB], 'what they have planned' [TEV], 'if they are planning these things' [NLT]. This noun denotes that which has been purposed or planned [LN]. It denotes that which one decides [BDAG].
- c. ἔργον (LN 42.42) (BDAG 4. p. 391): 'undertaking' [ESV, NET, NRSV], 'work' [AB, BECNT, LN; KJV], 'task' [LN], 'action' [NASB], 'activity' [NIV], 'matter, thing' [BDAG], 'something' [CEV], 'deed' [Bar], 'execution' [CBC], not explicit [NCV]. The phrase 'this undertaking' is also translated 'doing these things' [NLT], 'what is being...done' [REB], 'what they have...done' [TEV], '(the plan) they put into action' [GW]. This noun denotes that which one normally does [LN]. It denotes something having to do with what is under discussion [BDAG].
- d. ἄνθρωπος (LN 9.1): 'man' [AB, Bar, BDAG, BECNT; ESV, KJV, NASB], 'human being' [BDAG, LN], 'person' [LN], 'people, mankind' [LN]. The phrase 'is of men' is also translated 'is of human origin' [CBC; GW, NIV, NRSV, REB, TEV], 'originates with people' [NET], 'comes from human authority' [NCV], 'is something of their own doing' [CEV], '(doing these things) merely on their own' [NLT]. This noun denotes a human being [LN].
- e. fut. pass. indic. of καταλύω (LN 13.100) (BDAG 3.b. p. 522): 'to fail' [BDAG; CEV, ESV, GW, NCV, NIV, NRSV], 'to come to nothing' [BDAG, LN; NET], 'to come to nought' [KJV], 'to be overthrown' [NASB, NLT], 'to be destroyed' [AB, Bar], 'to collapse' [CBC; REB], 'to disappear' [TEV], 'to self-destruct' [BECNT], 'to be put to an end' [BDAG, LN]. This verb means to cause to cease to exist [LN]. It means to end the effect or validity of something [BDAG].

QUESTION—What conclusion did Gamaliel draw?

After citing the two failed movements, Gamaliel concluded that if the plan of the apostles was of merely human origin, it would come to nothing. Thus he suggested to the council to leave the apostles alone [AB, Bar, BECNT, CBC, NICNT, PNTC, TH, TNTC].

5:39 **But if it-is of God, you-will- not -be-able to-overthrow[a] them. You- may-even-be-found to-be-fighting-against-God.[b]" So they-were-persuaded[c] by-him.**

LEXICON—a. aorist act. infin. of καταλύω (LN 13.100) (BDAG 3.b. p. 522): 'to overthrow' [ESV, KJV, NASB, NLT, NRSV], 'to stop' [BDAG; GW, NCV, NET, NIV], 'to destroy' [AB, Bar, BECNT], 'to put down' [CBC].

The phrase 'you will not be able to overthrow them' is also translated 'you cannot stop it anyway' [CEV], 'you will never be able to stamp it out' [REB], 'you cannot possibly defeat them' [TEV], 'to cause to come to an end, to cause to become nothing' [LN], 'to do away with, to abolish, to annul, to make invalid' [BDAG]. This verb means to cause to cease to exist [LN]. It means to bring to an end [BDAG].
- b. θεομάχος (LN 39.32) (BDAG p. 449): 'fighting against God' [Bar, BDAG, LN; GW, NASB, NCV, NET, NIV, NLT, NRSV, TEV], 'to fight against God' [LN; CEV, KJV], 'to contend against God' [AB], 'to be against God, to be an enemy of God' [LN], 'to be opponents of God' [BECNT], 'opposing God' [ESV], 'at war with God' [CBC; REB]. This adjective describes someone or something that is opposed to God [LN], or is fighting against God [BDAG, LN].
- c. aorist pass. indic. of πείθω (LN 33.301): 'to be persuaded' [LN; NIV], 'to be convinced' [LN; NET, NRSV, REB]. The clause 'So they were persuaded by him' is also translated 'So he persuaded them' [BECNT], 'The council members agreed with what he said' [CEV], 'So they took his advice' [ESV], 'The council took his advice' [GW], 'And to him they agreed' [KJV], 'They took his advice' [Bar, CBC; NASB], 'They followed his advice' [AB], 'The Jewish leaders agreed with what Gamaliel said' [NCV], 'The others accepted his advice' [NLT], 'The Council followed Gamaliel's advice' [TEV]. This verb means to convince someone to believe something and to act on the basis of what is recommended [LN].

QUESTION—What was the final argument that Gamaliel made?

The final argument that Gamaliel made was a continuation of his conclusion from the last verse and it is clear that this is the most likely option. If the movement is from God, then opposition is futile [BECNT]. Thus, let the apostles alone or they would find themselves fighting against God. The Council was persuaded by Gamaliel [AB, Bar, BECNT, CBC, NICNT, PNTC, TH, TNTC].

5:40 And after-calling-in the apostles (and)-having-(them)-flogged,[a] they-ordered-(them)[b] not to-speak in the name[c] of-Jesus, and (then) released (them).

LEXICON—a. aorist act. participle of δέρω (LN 19.2) (BDAG p. 218): 'to flog' [CBC; NASB, NIV, NLT, NRSV, REB], 'to beat' [AB, Bar, BDAG, BECNT, LN; ESV, GW, KJV, NCV, NET], 'to beat with a whip' [CEV], 'to whip' [BDAG, LN; TEV]. This verb means to strike or beat repeatedly [LN].
- b. aorist act. indic. of παραγγέλλω (LN 33.327) (BDAG p. 760): 'to order' [CBC, LN; GW, NASB, NET, NIV, NLT, NRSV, REB, TEV], 'to give orders, to instruct, to direct' [BDAG], 'to command' [AB, Bar, BDAG, BECNT, LN; KJV], 'to charge' [ESV], 'to tell' [NCV], 'to warn' [CEV].

This verb means to announce what must be done [LN]. It means to make an announcement about something that must be done [BDAG].

    c. ὄνομα (LN 33.126) (BDAG 1.d.γ.ℶ. p. 714): 'name' [AB, Bar, BDAG, BECNT, CBC, LN; all versions]. The phrase 'to speak in the name of Jesus' is also translated 'to speak using this name' [BDAG], 'to speak about the one named Jesus' [GW]. This noun denotes the proper name of a person or object [LN]. This refers to when someone's name is mentioned or called upon [BDAG].

QUESTION—What is known about the punishment of flogging?

Although the Council concurred with Gamaliel's advice, it did not entirely divert their wrath and the ban against teaching in the name of Jesus. They flogged the apostles before releasing them [EBC, NICNT, TNTC]. Flogging was a customary punishment used as a warning not to persist in an offense. It consisted of thirty-nine lashes, often referred to as the forty less one. Based on the provision for forty stripes given in Deut. 25:3, the practice had developed of only giving thirty-nine in the event of miscounting, preferring to err on the side of clemency rather than severity [BECNT, NAC, NICNT, TNTC, TRT].

DISCOURSE UNIT—5:41–42 [Bar, EBC, NAC, NICNT, PNTC]. The topic is release and witness [NAC], rejoicing and witnessing community: final summary [Bar], the apostles' rejoicing and continued ministry [EBC], the apostles continue their public witness [NICNT], the ministry of the apostles continues [PNTC].

5:41 Then they-went-away from (the)-presence[a] of-the Sanhedrin, rejoicing that they-were-considered-worthy[b] to-suffer-shame for the Name.[c]

LEXICON—a. πρόσωπον (LN 85.26) (BDAG 1.b.β.ℵ. p. 888): 'presence' [AB, Bar, BDAG, BECNT, LN; ESV, KJV, NASB], 'face' [BDAG, LN], not explicit [CBC; CEV, GW, NCV, NET, NIV, NLT, NRSV, REB, TEV]. This noun is a figurative extension of meaning of 'face' that refers to the personal presence of an individual at a particular place [BDAG, LN].

    b. aorist pass. indic. of καταξιόω (LN 65.18) (BDAG 1 p. 415): 'to be considered worthy' [BDAG, LN; CEV, GW, NASB, NET, NRSV, TEV], 'to be counted worthy' [Bar, BECNT; ESV, KJV, NIV, NLT], 'to be found worthy' [CBC; REB], 'to be held worthy' [AB]. The phrase 'rejoicing that they were considered worthy' is also translated 'full of joy because they were given the honor of' [NCV]. This verb means to consider something of a comparable merit or worth [LN].

    c. ὄνομα (LN 33.126) (BDAG 1.d.γ.ℶ. p. 714): 'name' [BDAG, LN]. The phrase 'for the Name/name' [ESV, NCV] is also translated 'for his/His name' [KJV, NASB], 'for the name of Jesus' [NLT], 'for the sake of the name' [NET, NRSV, REB], 'for the sake of the Name' [Bar, CBC], 'for the sake of his name' [AB], 'for the sake of Jesus' [CEV, TEV], 'for Jesus' [NCV], 'for speaking about Jesus' [GW], 'because of the name'

[BECNT]. This noun denotes the proper name of a person or object [LN]. When it refers to God or Christ the word frequently stands alone [BDAG].
QUESTION—What is the function of the particle μέν οὖν 'then' in this verse?
Here μέν οὖν 'then' is used as a connective to lead into a conclusion of the apostles' second trial (in the case of Peter and John) before the Sanhedrin [EBC]. The apostles had been flogged before they were released, but they went away rejoicing as they were considered worthy of suffering disgrace/punishment for the name of Jesus, for Jesus' sake. Moreover they had performed miracles through the power of the name of Jesus and witnessed for the name before the people and the Council [BECNT, EBC, NICNT, TH,

5:42 And every day, in the temple and from-house-to-house, they-did- not - stop teaching and preaching-the-good-news-(about)[a] the Messiah[b] Jesus.
LEXICON—a. pres. mid. participle of εὐαγγελίζω (LN 33.215) (BDAG 2.a.β. p. 402): 'to tell the good news' [Bar, CBC, LN; CEV, GW, NCV, REB], 'to announce the gospel' [LN], 'to preach' [ESV, KJV, NASB], 'to proclaim the good news' [NET, NIV], 'to proclaim the gospel' [BDAG], 'to proclaim' [NRSV], 'to preach the Good News' [TEV]. The phrase 'they did not stop teaching and preaching the good news' is also translated 'they continued to teach and preach this message' [NLT], 'they did not cease teaching and preaching' [BECNT], 'they did not cease to teach and proclaim' [AB]. This verb means to communicate good news concerning something and in the NT it is a particular reference to the gospel message about Jesus [LN]. It means to proclaim the divine message of salvation. Here it denotes the object of the proclamation, the Christ [BDAG].
   b. Χριστός (LN 53.82) (BDAG 1. p. 1091): 'Messiah' [AB, BDAG, CBC, LN; CEV, GW, NLT, NRSV, REB, TEV], Christ' [Bar, BDAG, BECNT, LN; ESV, KJV, NASB, NCV, NET, NIV], 'the Anointed One, Jesus the Messiah' [BDAG]. This noun, which means one who has been anointed denotes Jesus as the Messiah [LN]. This refers to the fulfiller of the Israelite expectation of a deliverer: the Anointed One, the Messiah, the Christ, Jesus the Messiah [BDAG].
QUESTION—What did the apostles do daily after they were released?
The apostles continued to obey God rather than men. They did not stop teaching and preaching the good news that Jesus is the Christ in the temple and in various homes [BECNT, EBC, NICNT, TNTC]. Daily they taught the gospel from house to house, that is where they met within the Christian fellowship [Bar, NAC, TNTC], and they preached publicly in the temple grounds [NAC, TNTC].

DISCOURSE UNIT—6:1–12:25 [CBC]. The topic is the church moves outwards.

DISCOURSE UNIT—6:1–9:31 [NICNT, TNTC]. The topic is the church begins to expand [TNTC], persecution and expansion [NICNT].

ACTS 6:1

DISCOURSE UNIT—6:1–8:40 [NAC]. The topic is the Hellenists break through to a wider witness.

DISCOURSE UNIT—6:1–8:3 [Bar]. The topic is problems and persecution lead to the beginning of expansion.

DISCOURSE UNIT—6:1–8:1a [NICNT; REB]. The topic is Stephen [NICNT], the church moves outwards [REB].

DISCOURSE UNIT—6:1–15 [NASB]. The topic is the choosing of the seven.

DISCOURSE UNIT—6:1–7 [AB, Bar, CBC, NAC, PNTC, TNTC; CEV, ESV, GW, NCV, NET, NIV, NLT, NRSV, TEV]. The topic is the appointment of the seven and further prosperity [Bar], the appointment of the first seven deacons [NET], the appointment of the seven [CBC, TNTC], the choosing of the seven [NIV], introduction of the seven [NAC], seven leaders for the church [CEV], seven leaders are chosen [NCV], seven men chosen to serve [NLT], seven chosen to serve [ESV, NRSV], the seven helpers [TEV], the disciples choose seven men to help the apostles [GW], resolution of a significant conflict in the Jerusalem church [PNTC], the widows and their support [AB].

DISCOURSE UNIT—6:1–6 [BECNT, EBC, NICNT]. The topic is community life: the appointment of the seven to help Hellenist widows [BECNT], the appointing of the seven [NICNT], the Hellenists' presence and problem in the church [EBC].

DISCOURSE UNIT—6:1–2 [NAC]. The topic is The Problem.

6:1 Now in these days when the disciples were increasing (in number), there-was (a)-complaint[a] by-the Hellenists[b] against the Hebrews[c] that their widows were-being-overlooked[d] in the daily distribution.

LEXICON—a. γογγυσμός (LN 33.382) (BDAG p. 204): 'complaint' [Bar, BDAG, LN; ESV, NASB, NET], 'a murmuring' [KJV], 'grievance' [REB], 'quarrel' [TEV], 'great dissatisfaction [AB], 'disagreement' [CBC], 'grumbling' [BECNT]. This noun is also translated as a verb: 'complained' [GW, NIV, NLT, NRSV], 'started complaining' [CEV], 'had an argument' [NCV]. This noun denotes one's complaint against others. In a number of languages it may be necessary to restructure the noun 'complaint' to function as a verb: 'Greek-speaking Jews complained against what the local Jews were doing. [LN]. In its negative aspect it denotes a complaint against someone [BDAG].

b. Ἑλληνιστής (LN 11.93) (BDAG p. 319): 'Hellenist' [AB, Bar, BDAG, BECNT; ESV, NRSV], 'Hellenistic Jew' [NASB], 'Greek-speaking Jew' [LN; GW, NET, TEV], 'Grecian' [KJV], 'Grecian Jew' [NIV]. The phrase 'the Hellenists' is also translated 'some of the ones who spoke Greek' [CEV], 'the Greek-speaking followers' [NCV], 'the Greek-speaking believers' [NLT], 'those who spoke Greek' [CBC; REB]. This noun denotes a Greek-speaking Jew in contrast with one who speaks a

Semitic language. The Greek-speaking Jews were basically Jewish in culture and religion, but they had adopted certain customs typical of the larger Greco-Roman world in which many of them lived. This inevitably resulted in certain suspicions and misunderstandings. [LN]. It denotes one who uses the Greek language, specifically a Greek-speaking Israelite in contrast to one speaking a Semitic language [BDAG].
  c. Ἑβραῖος (LN 93.105) (BDAG 2. p. 270): 'Hebrew' [AB, Bar, BDAG, BECNT, LN; ESV, KJV, NRSV], 'Hebrew-speaking Israelite' [BDAG]. The phrase 'the Hebrews' is also translated 'the Hebrew-speaking Jews' [GW], 'the native Hebrews' [NASB], 'the native Hebraic Jews' [NET], 'the Hebraic Jews' [NIV], 'the ones who spoke Aramaic' [CEV], 'the other Jewish followers' [NCV], 'the Hebrew-speaking believers' [NLT], 'those who spoke the language of the Jews' [CBC; REB], 'the native Jews' [TEV]. This noun denotes the oldest ethnic name for a Jew or the Jewish people [LN]. It denotes a Hebrew/Aramaic-speaking Israelite in contrast to a Greek-speaking Israelite [BDAG].
  d. imperf. pass. indic. of παραθεωρέω (LN 30.48) (BDAG p. 764): 'to be overlooked, to be neglected' [BDAG, LN], 'to be disregarded' [LN], 'to be left unnoticed' [BDAG]. The phrase 'were being overlooked in the daily distribution' [CBC; REB] is also translated, 'were being overlooked in the daily distribution of food' [NET, NIV, NCV], 'were being overlooked in the daily ministration of charity' [Bar], 'were neglected in the daily ministration' [KJV], 'were being neglected in the daily distribution' [ESV], 'were being neglected in the ministry of daily distribution' [BECNT], 'were treated unfairly at the daily distribution' [AB], 'were being discriminated against in the daily distribution of food' [NLT], 'were being overlooked in the daily serving of food' [NASB], 'were neglected every day when food and other assistance was distributed' [GW], 'were not getting their share of the food that was given out every day' [NCV], 'were not given their share when the food supplies were handed out each day' [CEV], 'were being overlooked in the daily ministration of charity' [Bar], 'were being neglected in the daily distribution of funds' [TEV]. This verb means to fail to consider something sufficiently, and as a result, fail to respond appropriately [LN]. It means to pay insufficient attention, with a resulting deficiency in response [BDAG].
QUESTION—What 'days' does this refer to?
  There is no attempt at precise chronology. Luke might be thinking of the time when the church was still confined to Jerusalem [Bar], perhaps five years or so after Pentecost [NAC].
QUESTION—What was increasing in number?
  The number of disciples was increasing in number. Note that this is the first time in the book of Acts where the word 'disciples' is used as a designation of the people who were followers/believers of Jesus [AB, BECNT, CBC, EBC, NICNT, PNTC, TH].

QUESTION—Who were the Hellenists?
The term 'Hellenists' refers to Greek-speaking Jews of the Diaspora who were living in Jerusalem [EBC, NAC, PNTC, TH, TNTC]. They were Jews living in Jerusalem whose primary language was Greek and they followed Greek customs [AB, Bar, BECNT, CBC, NICNT, TRT]. It does not mean that they were from the country of Greece [TRT]. They likely had come from the Jewish dispersion to settle in Jerusalem [NAC]. In this verse, the term refers to Jewish Christians who spoke only Greek [PNTC]. They had their own synagogues [NAC]. This term is also used in Acts 9:29 and 11:20 [Bar, BECNT, NAC, PNTC].

QUESTION—Who were the 'Hebrews'?
The term 'Hebrews' refers to Hebrew-speaking Jews. The word 'Hebrew' means 'Jewish' and in the New Testament they were only capable of using the Hebrew or Aramaic Jewish language. They valued the beliefs, traditions, and history of their people [Bar, PNTC, TNTC].

QUESTION—Who were these widows?
Widows were always a vulnerable group, and this may be a special reference to the widows of the Diaspora Jews who had come to spend their last years in Jerusalem in order that they would be buried there when they died. Such widows often would have been left with no nearby family members or friends to care for them [Bar, BECNT, EBC, NAC, TNTC]. The Hellenist widows might have been attracted to the Christian community precisely because of its concern for the material need of its members as described in Acts 2:44; 4:32, 34 [NAC].

QUESTION—What is meant by the 'daily support'?
The 'daily support' refers to distributing food or money or both, whatever way the widows needed help [BECNT, CBC, NAC, NICNT, TRT], whether charity [Bar], money that was given for the widows' needs of each day [TH], or the daily distribution of food [EBC, PNTC].

6:2 **And having-called-together the full-number[a] of disciples, the Twelve said, "It-is not right that we neglect[b] the word of-God to-serve-tables/to-handle-finances.[c]**

LEXICON—a. πλῆθος (LN 11.1) (BDAG 2.b.δ. p. 826): 'multitude, crowd' [LN], 'fellowship, community, church' [BDAG]. The phrase 'the full number of disciples' [ESV] is also translated 'the whole group of the disciples' [NET], 'the multitude of disciples' [BECNT; KJV], 'the whole community of the disciples' [NRSV], 'the whole company of the disciples' [Bar; REB], 'the congregation of the disciples' [NASB], 'the whole body of disciples' [CBC], 'the band of disciples' [AB], 'all the disciples' [GW, NIV], 'the whole group of followers' [CEV, NCV], 'the whole group of believers' [TEV], 'all the believers' [NLT]. This noun denotes a casual non-membership group of people, fairly large in size and assembled for whatever purpose. In a number of languages there is no term corresponding to 'crowd.' One may, however, usually speak of such

a group of people as 'many people' or 'many men and women.' Depending on the context, it may be necessary to indicate some relative difference in size, for example, 'very large crowd' or 'many, many people.' If the crowd is relatively small, one may sometimes speak of 'just some people.' [LN]. It denotes the whole body of the members of a religious community, fellowship, or church [BDAG].
- b. aorist act. participle of καταλείπω (LN 30.51) (BDAG 7.c. p. 521): 'to neglect' [AB, BDAG, CBC, LN; NASB, NET, NIV, NRSV, REB, TEV], 'to no longer be concerned about, to give up one's concern for' [LN], 'to set to one side' [BDAG], 'to forsake' [Bar], 'to give up' [BECNT; CEV, ESV, GW], 'to leave' [KJV], 'to stop one's work of teaching' [NCV], not explicit [NLT]. This verb means to give up or neglect one's concern for something [LN]. It means to set something aside in the interest of something else [BDAG].
- c. pres. act. infin. of διακονέω (LN 57.230) (BDAG 5. p. 230): 'to serve tables' [ESV, KJV, NCV], 'to serve at tables' [Bar; CEV], 'to wait on tables' [NRSV, NET, NIV], 'the daily serving of food' [NASB], 'to distribute food' [GW], 'the ministry of daily distribution' [BECNT], 'in the daily distribution' [CBC], 'to run a food program' [NLT]. Some understand it as an idiom meaning the daily distribution of funds: 'to handle finances' [BDAG. LN], 'to assist in the distribution' [REB, TEV], 'to act as stewards'[AB]. The phrase 'to serve tables' is an idiom that means to be responsible for the financial aspects of an enterprise, and this verse means 'it is not right that we should give up preaching the word of God to handle finances'. It is also possible to interpret the phrase not as an idiom but simply as 'to wait on tables, to serve meals' (see LN 23.26 and LN 46.13), but even so, the context relates to caring for needs [LN 57.230]. This verb can mean to perform obligations (BDAG 2. p. 229) including waiting on someone at table (BDAG 2.b. p. 229), but it can also mean to carry out official duties (BDAG 4. p. 229). The verse in Acts 6:2 poses a special problem (BDAG 5. p. 230) The meanings 'care for, take care of' can be understood as serving food at tables, but it is improbable that some widows would be deprived of food at a communal meal. More probably it refers to administrative responsibility, one of whose aspects is concern for widows, without specifying the kind of assistance that is allotted [BDAG].

QUESTION—Who were 'the Twelve'?

'The twelve' were the original twelve disciples of Jesus except with Judas having been replaced by Matthias [PNTC, TRT]. Instead of simply a number, 'the twelve' should be taken as a title, 'the Twelve' [AB, Bar, BDAG, BECNT, CBC, TH; NIV, NLT, REB], 'the twelve apostles' [CEV, GW. NCV, TEV], 'the twelve disciples' [NCV]. This term occurs only here in the book of Acts [EBC, PNTC, TH].

QUESTION—What is implied by the phrase 'it is not right'?

This phrase really means 'it is not pleasing in God's eyes'. To serve tables would distract them from their primary mission of witness. They were the eye-witnesses of the life, death, and resurrection of Jesus [BECNT, NAC]. It is a priority choice about observing the call of God versus a moral choice of right, wrong, and sin [BECNT, TNTC]. 'It is not right' could be rendered 'it is not acceptable' or 'it is not appropriate' since it was not correct for the twelve to be serving tables instead of preaching [BECNT, PNTC].

QUESTION—What is meant by the phrase 'to serve tables'?

The phrase literally means to serve food to people. However, LN defines the phrase 'to serve tables' as being an idiom meaning 'to handle finances'. Corresponding to 'daily support' in v. 1, it should be broadened to mean something like 'to see that the widows' needs are properly cared for' [TH].

DISCOURSE UNIT—6:3–4 [NAC]. The topic is The Solution.

6:3 Therefore, brothers, select[a] from-among you seven men of-good-reputation,[b] full of-(the)-Spirit and wisdom, whom we-will-appoint[c] to this duty.

LEXICON—a. aorist mid. (deponent = act.) impera. of ἐπισκέπτομαι (LN 30.102) (BDAG 1. p. 378): 'to select' [BDAG; NASB, NLT, NRSV], 'to select carefully' [LN; NET], 'to choose' [AB; CEV, GW, NCV, NIV, TEV], 'to pick out' [ESV], 'to pick' [REB], 'to look out' [Bar, CBC; KJV], 'to look at, to examine, to inspect' [BDAG], 'to look, to select' [BECNT]. This verb means to choose or select on the basis of having investigated carefully [LN]. It means to make a careful inspection [BDAG].

b. pres. pass. participle of μαρτυρέω (LN 33.263) (BDAG 2.b. p. 618): 'to be spoken well of, to be approved' [BDAG, LN]. The phrase 'men of good reputation' [BDAG, BECNT, CBC; NASB] is also translated 'men who have a good reputation' [AB], 'men of good repute' [Bar; ESV, REB], 'men who are well attested' [NET], 'men who are respected' [CEV], 'men who are well respected' [NLT], 'men of honest report' [KJV], 'men of good repute" [REB], 'men who are good' [NCV], 'men of good standing' [NRSV]. Some connect this more closely with the following words 'full of the Spirit and wisdom'): 'men who are known to be full of the Spirit and wisdom' [NIV, TEV], 'men whom the people know are spiritually wise' [GW]. This verb means to speak well of a person on the basis of personal experience [LN]. It means to be well spoken of, to be approved [BDAG].

c. fut. act. indic. of καθίστημι (LN 37.104) (BDAG 2.a. p. 492): 'to appoint' [AB, Bar, BDAG, BECNT, CBC, LN; ESV, KJV, NRSV, REB], 'to assign' [LN], 'to put in charge' [BDAG; CEV, GW, NASB, NCV, NET, TEV], 'to turn over to' [NIV]. The phrase 'whom we will appoint to this duty' is also translated 'We will give them this responsibility' [NLT].

This verb means to assign to someone a position of authority over others [LN]. It means to assign someone a position of authority [BDAG].

QUESTION—What is meant by being 'full of the Spirit and wisdom?

Spirit and wisdom are genitives of content [BECNT]. A man who is filled with the Spirit means that the man is spiritually minded and is directed by the Spirit so that he is spiritually sensitive and able to make good judgments, a sign of spiritual maturity [BECNT, TH]. Such men allow the Spirit to work in them [NAC], and they manifest the Spirit's presence in their lives [PNTC]. A man who is filled with wisdom means that he is very wise or knows things very well [TH] and demonstrates the practical know-how necessary for the proper management of the charity and dealing with the complexity of relationships [EBC, NAC, NICNT, PNTC].

6:4 **But we will-be-devoted**^{a} **to-prayer and to-the ministry**^{b} **of-the word.**^{c}"

LEXICON—a. fut. act. indic. of προσκαρτερέω (LN 68.68) (BDAG 2.a. p. 881): 'to devote oneself to' [BDAG, BECNT, CBC, LN; ESV, GW, NASB, NET, NRSV, REB], 'to give oneself to' [KJV], 'to keep on, to persist in' [LN], 'to continue' [Bar; NCV], 'to be able to continue devoting' [AB], 'to give attention to' [NIV], 'to busy oneself with, to be busily engaged in' [BDAG]. The phrase 'we will be devoted to prayer' is also translated 'We can spend our time praying' [CEV], 'we apostles can spend our time in prayer' [NLT], 'We ourselves, then, will give our full time to prayer' [TEV]. This verb means to continue to do something with intense effort, with the possible implication of doing so despite difficulty [LN]. It means to persist in something [BDAG].

b. διακονία (LN 35.21) (BDAG 2.a. p. 230): 'ministry' [Bar, BECNT, CBC, LN; ESV, KJV, NASB, NET, NIV, REB], 'service' [AB, BDAG], 'task' [LN]. The phrase 'the ministry of the word' is also translated 'serving God by preaching' [CEV], 'serving in ways that are related to the word' [GW], 'to teach the word of God' [NCV], 'teaching the word' [NLT], 'serving the word' [NRSV], 'the work of preaching' [TEV]. This noun denotes the role or position of serving [LN]. It denotes the performance of a service [BDAG].

c. λόγος (LN 33.260) (BDAG 1.a.β. p. 600): 'word' [AB, Bar, BDAG, BECNT, CBC; ESV, GW, KJV, NASB, NET, NIV, NLT, NRSV, REB], 'gospel' [LN], 'what is preached' [LN], 'speaking' [BDAG], 'preaching' [CEV, TEV], 'the word of God' [NCV]. This noun denotes the content of what is preached about Christ or about the good news [LN]. It denotes the Christian message, the gospel [BDAG].

QUESTION—What is meant by 'the ministry of the word'?

This phrase refers to the preaching/proclamation of the word of God [Bar, BECNT, CBC, NAC, NICNT, PNTC, TH, TNTC], and the teaching about its implications [PNTC, TNTC].

DISCOURSE UNIT—6:5–6 [NAC]. The topic is selection and installation.

6:5 And that statement[a] pleased[b] the whole multitude,[c] and they-chose Stephen, (a)-man full of-faith and (of) (the)-Holy Spirit, and Philip, and Prochorus, and Nicanor, and Timon, and Parmenas, and Nicolas, (a)-proselyte[d] of-Antioch. **6:6** These they-placed[e] before the apostles, and they-prayed and laid- their hands -on them.

LEXICON—a. λόγος (LN 33.98) (BDAG 1.a.γ. p. 600): 'statement' [BDAG, LN; NASB], 'pronouncement' [AB], 'saying' [LN; KJV], 'what they said' [ESV, NRSV], 'suggestion' [CEV, GW], 'proposal' [Bar, CBC; NET, NIV, REB, TEV], 'word' [BECNT], 'idea' [NCV, NLT]. This noun denotes that which has been stated or said, with the primary focus upon the content of the communication' [LN]. It denotes an individual declaration or remark [BDAG].

b. aorist act. indic. of ἀρέσκω (LN 25.90) (BDAG 2.b. p. 130): 'to please' [Bar, BDAG, BECNT, LN; CEV, ESV, GW, KJV, NET, NIV, NRSV, TEV], 'to prove acceptable' [CBC; REB], 'to be applauded' [AB], 'to find approval' [NASB]. The phrase 'that statement pleased the whole multitude' is also translated 'The whole group liked the idea' [NCV], 'Everyone liked this idea' [NLT]. This verb means to cause someone to be pleased with someone or something [LN]. It means to give pleasure or satisfaction [BDAG].

c. πλῆθος (LN 11.1) (BDAG 2.b.δ. p. 826): 'multitude' [LN; KJV], 'crowd' [LN], 'fellowship, community, congregation' [BDAG]. The phrase 'the whole multitude' is also translated 'the entire multitude' [BECNT], 'the whole gathering' [ESV], 'the whole group' [GW, NCV, NIV, TEV], 'the whole congregation' [NASB], 'the entire group' [NET], 'the whole community' [NRSV], 'the whole company' [AB, Bar; REB], 'the whole body' [CBC], 'everyone' [CEV, NLT]. This noun denotes a casual non-membership group of people, fairly large in size and assembled for whatever purpose [LN]. In reference to a cultic community it refers to the whole body of their members [BDAG].

d. προσήλυτος (LN 11.54) (BDAG p. 880): 'proselyte' [AB, Bar, BECNT, LN, BDAG; ESV, KJV, NASB, NRSV], 'convert' [BDAG]. The phrase 'Nicolaus, a proselyte of Antioch' is also translated 'Nicolaus, who worshiped with the Jewish people in Antioch' [CEV], 'Nicolas (a man from Antioch who had become a Jew)' [NCV], 'Nicolaus, who had converted to Judaism in the city of Antioch' [GW], 'Nicolas, a Gentile convert to Judaism' [NET], 'Nicolas from Antioch, a convert to Judaism' [NIV], 'Nicolas of Antioch, a former convert to Judaism' [CBC], 'Nicolas of Antioch (an earlier convert to the Jewish faith)' [NLT], 'Nicolas of Antioch, who had been a convert to Judaism' [REB], 'Nicolaus, a Gentile from Antioch who had earlier been converted to Judaism' [TEV]. This noun denotes a Gentile who had converted to Judaism [LN]. It denotes one who has come over from paganism to the Judean religion and practice [BDAG].

e. aorist act. indic. of ἵστημι (LN 85.40) (BDAG A.1. p. 482): 'to place, to put, to set' [BDAG, LN], 'to make stand' [LN]. The phrase 'these they placed before' is also translated 'these they brought before' [NASB], 'these/whom they set before' [AB; ESV, KJV], 'they set these men before' [Bar], 'then they put these men before' [NCV], 'these men were brought to' [CEV], 'they stood these men before' [NET], 'they had these men stand before' [NRSV], 'the disciples had these men stand in front of' [GW], 'these they presented to' [CBC], 'whom the multitude presented before' [BECNT], 'and presented them to' [REB], 'the group presented them to '[TEV], 'they presented these men to' [NIV], 'these seven men were presented to' [NLT]. This verb means to cause someone to be in a place, with or without the accompanying feature of a standing position [LN]. It means to cause to be in a place or position before someone [BDAG].

QUESTION—What did these chosen men have in common?

All seven men had Greek names [AB, Bar, BECNT, CBC, EBC, NICNT, PNTC, TNTC, TRT]. This suggests that they were of Diaspora origin [Bar, EBC]. There was no official 'deacon office' yet, but they had conventionally been considered as the first deacons [BECNT, NICNT, TRT]. Note that this is a different Philip from Jesus' apostle Philip who is mentioned in Acts 1:13 [BECNT, PNTC, TH, TNTC, TRT]. Only two of the seven are mentioned further in Acts: Stephen (Acts 7; 8:2; 11:19; 22:20) and Philip (Acts 8; 21:8) [NAC, TH]. The Antioch from which Nicolas came was probably Antioch in Syria [TH]. He was a proselyte, a Gentile convert to Judaism [Bar, BECNT, CBC, EBC, NICNT, PNTC]. That is, he was a Gentile/non-Jew and had become a Jew and follower of Jesus [TRT].

QUESTION—Why did the apostles lay their hands upon the chosen men?

The laying of hands on the chosen men was a gesture symbolizing the giving of responsibility and the imparting of strength and of the community's blessing to them [Bar, BECNT, EBC, NICNT, TH, TNTC], thus commissioning them to the task [CBC, EBC, NAC, NICNT, PNTC].

DISCOURSE UNIT—6:7 [BECNT, EBC, NAC, NICNT]. The topic is summary of the Jerusalem community [BECNT], summary and transition [NAC], summary statement [EBC], progress report [NINCT].

6:7 And the word[a] of-God was-spreading[b] and the number of-the disciples in Jerusalem was-increasing[c] greatly, and a great many[d] of-the priests were-obeying[e] the faith.

LEXICON—a. λόγος (LN 33.260) (BDAG 1.a.β. p. 599): 'word' [AB, Bar, BDAG, BECNT, CBC; all versions except CEV, NLT], 'message' [CEV, NLT], 'gospel' [LN], 'what is preached' [LN]. This noun denotes the content of what is preached about Christ or about the good news' [LN]. It is the Christian message, the gospel [BDAG].

b. imperf. act. indic. of αὐξάνω (LN 59.62) (BDAG 2.b. p. 151): 'to spread' [CBC, LN; all versions except ESV, KJV], 'to extend' [LN], 'to increase'

[BDAG, LN; ESV, KJV], 'to grow' [Bar, BDAG, BECNT, LN], 'to prosper' [AB]. This verb means to increase in the extent of or in the instances of an activity or state [LN]. It means to become greater in number [BDAG].
   c. imperf. pass. indic. of πληθύνω (LN 59.68) (BDAG 1.b. p. 826): 'to increase' [AB, Bar, CBC, LN; NASB, NCV, NET, NIV, NLT, NRSV, REB], 'to grow' [BDAG, LN], 'to spread, to extend' [LN], 'to increase greatly' [LN], 'to multiply' [BDAG, BECNT, LN; ESV, KJV]. The clause 'the number of the disciples in Jerusalem was increasing greatly' is also translated 'many more people in Jerusalem became followers' [CEV], 'the number of disciples in Jerusalem grew very large' [GW], 'the number of disciples in Jerusalem grew larger and larger' [TEV]. This verb means to increase greatly in number or extent [LN].
   d. ὄχλος (LN 11.1) (BDAG 1.b.β. p. 746): 'a great many' [Bar; ESV, NASB, NRSV], 'a crowd' [LN; CEV. GW, NIV], 'a great crowd' [BECNT], 'a group' [NET], 'a multitude' [LN], 'a large number' [AB, BDAG; TEV], 'a great company' [KJV]. The phrase 'a great many of the priests' is also translated 'a great number of the Jewish priests' [NCV], 'many of the Jewish priests' [NLT], 'very many of the priests' [CBC; REB]. This noun denotes a casual non-membership group of people, fairly large in size and assembled for whatever purpose [LN]. It denotes a group or company of people with common interests or of distinctive status [BDAG].
   e. imperf. act. indic. of ὑπακούω (LN 36.15) (BDAG 1. p. 1029): 'to obey' [BDAG, LN], 'to follow, to be subject to' [BDAG]. The phrase 'were obeying the faith' is also translated 'were obedient to the faith' [KJV], 'were becoming obedient to the faith' [NASB], 'became obedient to the faith' [ESV, NET, NIV, NRSV], 'was being obedient to the faith' [BECNT], 'gave their obedience to the faith [Bar], 'adhered to the faith' [CBC; REB], 'accepted the faith' [AB; GW, TEV], 'believed and obeyed' [NCV], 'were converted' [NLT], 'put their faith in the Lord' [CEV]. This verb means to obey on the basis of having paid attention to [LN]. It means to be in compliance of the thing to which one embraces in full surrender [BDAG].
QUESTION—What is meant by the priests obeying the faith?
   It means that the priests were obedient to the faith [Bar, CBC, TH], that is, obedient to the call for faith contained in the gospel [TNTC]. In this context the word 'faith' is taken as synonymous with 'the Good News'. For a similar use of 'the faith' in Acts, see 13:8; 14:22; 16:5 [TH]. It refers to the content of Christian belief and life [Bar, PNTC]. The priests became believers of Christ [BECNT, EBC, NAC, TNTC], obeyed the apostolic pattern of belief and lifestyle [PNTC], and joined the church community [AB, NICNT].

DISCOURSE UNIT—6:8–9:31 [BECNT, EBC, PNTC]. The topic is the word goes out from Jerusalem [PNTC], persecution in Jerusalem moves the message to Judea and Samaria as a new witness emerges [BECNT], critical events in the lives of three pivotal figures [EBC].

DISCOURSE UNIT—6:8–8:3 [EBC]. The topic is the martyrdom of Stephen.

DISCOURSE UNIT—6:8–8:1a [BECNT]. The topic is the arrest, speech, and martyrdom of Stephen.

DISCOURSE UNIT—6:8–7:53 [CBC]. The topic is the arrest of Stephen.

DISCOURSE UNIT—6:8–7:1 [EBC, NAC]. The topic is Stephen's arrest and trial [NAC], opposition to Stephen's ministry [EBC].

DISCOURSE UNIT—6:8–15 [AB, Bar, BECNT, PNTC, TNTC; CEV, ESV, GW, NCV, NET, NIV, NLT, NRSV, TEV]. The topic is the prophetic ministry of Stephen [PNTC], the controversy over Stephen [TNTC], the arrest of Stephen [BECNT; NRSV, TEV], attack on Stephen [Bar], Stephen is arrested [CEV, GW, NET, NLT], Stephen is seized [ESV], Stephen seized [NIV], Stephen is accused [NCV], Stephen's activities in Jerusalem [AB].

DISCOURSE UNIT—6:8–10 [NAC, NICNT]. The topic is Stephen's debate with the Hellenist synagogue [NAC], Stephen's activity arouses opposition [NICNT].

6:8 **And Stephen, full of-grace**[a] **and power,**[b] **was-doing**[c] **great wonders**[d] **and signs**[e] **among the people.**

TEXT—Earlier texts describe Stephen as 'full of grace' (χάριτος). Later texts, including the text on which the KJV is based, were apparently assimilated to Acts 6:5, where he is said to be 'full of faith' (πίστεως).

LEXICON—a. χάρις (LN 88.66) (BDAG 4. p. 1080): 'grace' [AB, Bar, BECNT, CBC, LN; ESV, NASB, NET, NRSV, REB], 'graciousness, kindness' [LN], 'divine grace' [BDAG]. The phrase 'Stephen, full of grace' is also translated 'Stephen, a man full of God's grace' [NIV, NLT], 'Stephen, a man richly blessed by God (and full of power)' [TEV], 'Steven was a man filled with God's favor' [GW], 'Stephen was richly blessed by God (who gave him the power to do great miracles)' [NCV], 'God gave Stephen the power (to work great miracles)' [CEV], 'Stephen, full of faith and power' [KJV]. This noun refers to the kindness shown to someone, with the implication of graciousness on the part of the one showing such kindness [LN]. It denotes the effect produced by divine beneficence [BDAG].

b. δύναμις (LN 76.1) (BDAG 1.a. p. 263): 'power' [AB, Bar, BDAG, BECNT, CBC, LN; all versions], 'might, strength, force, capability' [BDAG]. This noun denotes the potentiality to exert force in performing some function [LN]. It denotes the potential for functioning in some way, here an apostle is equipped with all power [BDAG].

c. imperf. act. indic. of ποιέω (LN 90.45) (BDAG 2.b. p. 839): 'to do' [BDAG, LN; ESV, GW, KJV, NCV, NIV, NRSV, REB], 'to perform'

[BDAG, BECNT, LN; NASB, NET, NLT, TEV], 'to work' [AB, Bar, CBC; CEV], 'to practice, to make' [LN]. This verb means to undertake or do something that brings about an event, here to perform miracles [BDAG].
- d. τέρας (33.480): 'wonder' [AB, BECNT; ESV, KJV, NASB, NET, NIV, NRSV, REB], 'portent' [Bar, LN], 'sign' [LN], 'amazing thing' [GW], 'miracle' [CBC; CEV, NCV, NLT, TEV]. This noun denotes 'an unusual sign, especially one in the heavens, serving to foretell impending events' [LN].
- e. σημεῖον (LN 33.477) (BDAG 2.a.α. p. 920): 'sign' [AB, Bar, BDAG, BECNT, CBC, LN; ESV, NASB, NCV, NLT, NRSV, REB], 'wonder' [CEV, TEV], 'miracle' [BDAG; GW, KJV], 'miraculous sign' [NET, NIV]. This noun denotes undertaking or doing something that brings about an event which is regarded as having some special meaning [LN]. It denotes an event that is an indication or conformation of intervention by transcendent powers [BDAG].

QUESTION—What was special about Stephen's ministry?

Stephen's ministry had similarities with Jesus' ministry (Luke 2:40, 52; 24:19; Acts 2:22) [BECNT, EBC, PNTC, TRT] and with Jesus' apostles' ministries (Acts 2:43; 4:33) [Bar, BECNT, EBC, PNTC, TRT]. His influence went far beyond the distribution of charity [CBC]. He was the first disciple other than the apostles to be described as working miracles. Faith, wisdom, grace, power, and above all the presence of the Spirit enabled him to perform signs and wonders [BECNT, NAC, NICNT, PNTC].

QUESTION—What does the phrase 'great wonders and signs refer to?

The phrase 'great wonders and signs' is a hendiadys, that is, the two nouns refer to the same thing, not two separate things. It refers to amazing miracles that show God's presence [TRT].

6:9 But some men from what was-called the synagogue of-the Freedmen,[a] (including) both Cyrenians and Alexandrians, and some from Cilicia and Asia, rose-up[b] and disputed[c] with-Stephen.

LEXICON—a. Λιβερτῖνος (LN 87.86) (BDAG p. 594): 'Freedmen' [AB, BDAG, BECNT, CBC; ESV, GW, NASB, NET, NIV, NRSV, REB, TEV], 'Free Men' [LN; CEV, NCV], 'Libertines' [Bar; KJV], 'Freed Slaves' [NLT]. This noun denotes a group of people, presumably Jews, who had been slaves but later obtained their freedom and their synagogue was also known by the same name [LN]. It denotes a person who was released from slavery, a designation for certain Israelites in Jerusalem who had their own synagogue. This name describes these people as former slaves or their descendants. [BDAG].
- b. aorist act. indic. of ἀνίστημι (LN 13.81) (BDAG 9. p. 83): 'to rise up' [Bar, BDAG; ESV, NASB], 'to arise' [BDAG, BECNT, LN; KJV, NIV], 'to stand up' [NET, NRSV], 'to come' [NCV], 'to come forward' [AB, CBC; REB], not explicit [CEV, GW, NLT, TEV]. This verb means to

come into existence, with the implication of assuming a place or position [LN]. It means to come/appear to carry out a function or role [BDAG].
c. pres. act. participle of συζητέω (LN 33.440) (BDAG 2. p. 954: 'to dispute' [AB, Bar, BDAG, BECNT, LN; ESV, KJV], 'to argue' [BDAG, CBC; CEV, NASB, NCV, NET, NIV, NRSV, REB, TEV], 'to debate' [BDAG; NLT]. The phrase 'disputed with Stephen' is also translated 'started an argument with Stephen' [GW]. This verb means to express forceful differences of opinion without necessarily having a presumed goal of seeking a solution [LN]. It means to contend with persistence for a point of view [BDAG].

QUESTION—What was the synagogue mentioned in this verse like?

A synagogue was a place of instruction, worship, prayer, and reading of Scripture (God's word) [Bar, BECNT, TRT]. It was also the place where local court cases were held [TRT]. It was a place of worship on the Sabbath day, and throughout the week the building was used as a school for Jewish children [TH]. It also served as a place where Jews met for social activities [Bar, TH]. Synagogues were plentiful. Each town had a local synagogue which was the center of Jewish community life [BECNT, TRT].

QUESTION—Who were the Freedmen?

The Freedmen were descendants of the Jews who were taken as prisoners of war by the Romans in 63 B.C. [BECNT, NICNT, TRT]. They had been sold as slaves, but later set free [AB, Bar, BECNT, CBC, TH, TRT]. They were formerly slaves or descendants/families of former slaves [EBC, NAC, NICNT, PNTC]. They were formerly Roman prisoners or descendants of such prisoners [TNTC]. They had a synagogue in Jerusalem together with Jews who had moved there from Cyrene, which was the capital city of Cyrenaica Province in North Africa, and Alexandria, the capital of Egypt. Alexandria was the second most important city in the Roman Empire next to the city of Rome [TRT].

QUESTION—Who disputed with Stephen?

There were five groups of men who disputed with Stephen: the group of Jews called Freedmen, groups of Jews from the cities of Cyrene and Alexandria, and groups of Jews from the Cilicia and Asia provinces [CBC]. The structure of the Greek of this verse is complex and has caused discussions about how many synagogues are involved. Possibilities are:
1. Some think that five synagogues are involved, one for each of the groups mentioned [CBC].
2. Some think that probably two synagogues are involved, one for the Freedmen and the Jews of Cyrene and Alexandria, and another for Jews from the provinces of Cilicia and Asia [TRT].
3. Some think that probably only one synagogue is intended, the Synagogue of the freedmen, which was composed of Jews from Cyrene, Alexandria, Cilicia and Asia [Bar].

6:10 But they-were- not -able to-withstand[a] the wisdom[b] and the Spirit[c] with-which he-was-speaking.

LEXICON—a. aorist act. infin. of ἀνθίστημι (LN 39.18) (BDAG 1.b. p. 80): 'to withstand' [Bar; ESV, NRSV], 'to resist' [LN; KJV, NET], 'to cope' [NASB], 'to stand up against' [NIV], 'to stand against' [NLT], 'to hold one's own against' [AB, CBC; REB], 'to refute' [TEV], 'to oppose' [BDAG, BECNT], 'to set oneself against' [BDAG]. The clause 'they were not able to withstand the wisdom and the Spirit with which he was speaking' is also translated 'they were no match for Stephen, who spoke with great wisdom that the Spirit gave him' [CEV], 'They couldn't argue with Stephen because he spoke with the wisdom that the Spirit had given him' [GW], 'the Spirit was helping him to speak with wisdom, and his words were so strong that they could not argue with him' [NCV]. This verb means to resist by actively opposing pressure or power [LN]. It means to be in opposition to [BDAG].

b. σοφία (LN 32.32) (BDAG 1.b.α. p. 934): 'wisdom' [AB, Bar, BDAG, BECNT, CBC, LN; all versions]. It denotes the capacity to understand and, as a result, to act wisely. Here it is the wisdom that God imparts [BDAG].

c. πνεῦμα (LN 12.18): 'Spirit' [Bar, BECNT, LN; all versions except REB], 'Spirit of God, Holy Spirit' [LN. The phrase 'the wisdom and the Spirit with which he was speaking' is also translated 'the inspired wisdom with which he spoke' [AB, CBC; REB]. This noun is a title for the third person of the Trinity' [LN].

QUESTION—What was the result of the dispute against Stephen?

Stephen was filled with the Spirit and wisdom., so the members of the synagogue argued with Stephen in vain [Bar]. They were unable to refute Stephen [BECNT, EBC, NAC, PNTC, TNTC].

DISCOURSE UNIT—6:11–15 [NICNT]. The topic is Stephen accused before the Sanhedrin.

DISCOURSE UNIT—6:11–12 [NAC]. The topic is the frame-up.

6:11 Then they-secretly-induced[a] men (into) saying, "We-have-heard him speak blasphemous[b] words against Moses and God."

LEXICON—a. aorist act. indic. of ὑποβάλλω (LN 57.176) (BDAG p. 1036): 'to secretly induce' [NASB], 'to instigate secretly' [BDAG; ESV, NET, NRSV], 'to instigate' [BECNT], 'to hire' [LN], 'to bribe' [LN; GW, TEV], 'to prompt' [AB], 'to suborn' [Bar, BDAG; KJV], 'to urge secretly' [NCV], 'to persuade secretly' [NIV], 'to persuade' [NLT]. The phrase 'they secretly induced men into saying' is also translated 'they talked some men into saying' [CEV], 'they put up men to allege' [CBC; REB]. This verb means to hire a person to act in a particular way, often involving dishonest activities [LN].

b. βλάσφημος (LN 33.402) (BDAG p. 178): 'blasphemous' [AB, Bar, CBC, LN; ESV, KJV, NASB, NET, NRSV, REB], 'defaming, denigrating, demeaning' [BDAG]. The phrase 'We have heard him speak blasphemous words against Moses and God' is also translated 'We have heard him speaking blasphemy against Moses and God' [BECNT], 'We heard Stephen say terrible things against Moses and God' [CEV], 'We heard him slander Moses and God' [GW], 'We heard Stephen speak against Moses and God' [NCV], 'We have heard Stephen speak words of blasphemy against Moses and against God' [NIV], 'We heard him blaspheme Moses, and even God' [NLT], 'We heard him speaking against Moses and against God' [TEV]. This adjective describes something which is insulting and slanderous [LN].

QUESTION—What would be the consequence if anyone blasphemed God and Moses?

Anyone guilty of blaspheming/dishonoring God was to be stoned to death (Leviticus 24:16) [TRT]. Blasphemy against Moses was a capital crime [BECNT].

6:12 And they-stirred-up[a] the people and the elders[b] and the scribes,[c] and they-came-up-to-(him-and) seized[d] him and brought-(him) before the Sanhedrin.

LEXICON—a. aorist act. indic. of συγκινέω (LN 39.8) (BDAG p. 952): 'to stir up' [AB, Bar, BDAG, BECNT, CBC, LN; ESV, KJV, NASB, NIV, NRSV, REB, TEV], 'to stir up trouble among' [GW], 'to incite' [LN; NET], 'to set in motion, to arouse' [BDAG], 'to turn against' [CEV], 'to rouse' [NLT]. The phrase 'they stirred up the people' is also translated 'this upset the people' [NCV]. This verb means to stir up hostility against someone [LN]. It means to arouse/excite someone with the focus on the emotional aspect [BDAG].

b. πρεσβύτερος (LN 53.77) (BDAG 2.a.β. p. 862): 'elder' [AB, Bar, BDAG, CBC, LN; all versions except CEV, GW, NCV], 'leader' [BECNT; CEV, GW], 'older Jewish leader' [NCV]. This noun denotes a person of responsibility and authority in matters of socio-religious concerns [LN]. It denotes an official. Here it is a group in the Sanhedrin [BDAG].

c. γραμματεύς (LN 53.94): 'scribe' [AB, Bar, BECNT, LN; ESV, GW, KJV, NASB, NRSV, REB], 'teacher' [CEV, NCV], 'expert in the law' [BDAG, LN; NET], 'doctor of the law' [CBC], 'teacher of the law' [NIV, TEV], 'teacher of religious law' [NLT], 'scholar versed in the law' [BDAG], 'one who is learned in the law' [LN]. This noun denotes a recognized expert in Jewish law (including both canonical and traditional laws and regulations) [LN].

d. aorist act. indic. of συναρπάζω (LN 18.5) (BDAG p. 785): 'to seize' [Bar, BDAG, BECNT, CBC, LN; ESV, NET, NIV, NRSV, REB, TEV], 'to take off with' [LN], 'to drag away' [BDAG; NASB], 'to drag' [AB], 'to take by force' [GW], 'to catch' [KJV], 'to grab' [CEV, NCV], 'to arrest' [NLT]. This verb means to seize or snatch by force [LN]. It means to take hold of forcibly [BDAG].

QUESTION—How had Stephen been falsely treated?
Stephen had been falsely accused of being a blasphemer [AB, BECNT, CBC, EBC, NAC, PNTC, TNTC]. The news was spread all over town to the people, elders, and scribes. The elders represented the Sadducees and the scribes represented the Pharisees. Both had their representatives on the Sanhedrin [CBC, EBC, NAC]. Stephen was then brought to the Sanhedrin [BECNT, CBC, EBC, NAC, PNTC, TNTC].

DISCOURSE UNIT—6:13–7:1 [NAC]. The topic is the trial.

6:13 **And they-put-forward false[a] witnesses (who) said, "This man does-not -stop speaking words[b] against this holy place and the law.[c]**

LEXICON—a. ψευδής (LN 33.255) (BDAG a. p. 1096): 'false' [BDAG], 'lying' [BDAG, LN]. The phrase 'they put/brought forward false witnesses' [AB; NASB, NET] is also translated 'they set forward false witnesses' [BECNT], 'they set up false witnesses' [Bar; ESV, KJV, NRSV], 'They produced false witnesses' [CBC; NIV, NRSV], 'They brought in some people/men to tell lies about Stephen/him' [NCV, TEV], 'Some men agreed to tell lies about Stephen' [CEV], 'Some witnesses stood up and lied about Stephen' [GW], 'The lying witnesses (said)' [NLT]. This adjective describes one who utters falsehoods and lies [LN]. It pertains to being contrary to the truth [BDAG].

b. ῥῆμα (LN 33.98) (BDAG 1. p. 905): 'word' [Bar, BDAG, BECNT, LN; ESV, KJV], 'saying' [BDAG, LN], 'statement' [BDAG, LN], 'that which is said' [BDAG], 'message' [LN], not explicit [AB; NASB, NCV, NIV, NLT]. The phrase 'This man does not stop speaking words against this holy place' is also translated 'This man never stops saying bad things about the holy place' [GW], 'This man does not stop saying things against this holy place' [NET], 'This man keeps on saying terrible things about this holy temple' [CEV], 'This man never stops saying things against this holy place' [NRSV], 'This man/fellow is forever saying things against this holy place' [CBC; REB], 'This man...is always talking against our sacred Temple' [TEV]. This noun denotes that which has been stated or said, with primary focus upon the content of the communication' [LN].

c. νόμος (LN 33.55) (BDAG 2.b. p. 677): 'law' [BDAG, BECNT, LN; ESV, KJV, NASB, NET, NIV, NRSV, REB], 'Law' [AB, Bar, CBC], 'Law of Moses' [CEV, NCV, NLT, TEV], 'Moses' Teachings' [GW]. This noun denotes the first five books of the Old Testament called the Torah, often better referred to as 'instruction'. In a number of languages it is not possible to use a singular expression such as 'the Law' since the Torah consisted of five books and included a number of regulations and instructions, so it is necessary in many languages to use 'the laws.' Furthermore, to distinguish this body of laws from common, ordinary customs or legal regulations, it may be necessary to employ a phrase such as 'the laws given to Moses' or simply 'the laws of Moses' [LN]. It refers specifically to the law that Moses received from God and is the standard according to which membership in the people of Israel is determined [BDAG].

QUESTION—What was the 'holy place'?

The 'holy place' refers to the Temple in Jerusalem, which was a consecrated place where people worshiped God [Bar, BECNT, CBC, EBC, NAC, NICNT, TNTC, TRT]. It was the Jerusalem temple [Bar, EBC, TH]. Speaking against this holy place was seen as a direct affront to God himself, the same accusation as in v. 11 [AB, EBC, NAC, NICNT, PNTC].

QUESTION—What does 'the law' refer to?

The law referred to the Law of Moses [Bar, BECNT, CBC, TH, TNTC]. Speaking against the law was the same accusation made against Stephen in v. 11 that he spoke blasphemous words against Moses [AB, EBC, NAC, NICNT, PNTC].

6:14 For we-have-heard him say that this Nazarene,^a Jesus, will-destroy this place and change the customs^b which Moses handed-down^c to-us."

LEXICON—a. Ναζωραῖος (LN 93.538) (BDAG p. 664): 'Nazarene' [BDAG, LN; NASB, NET], 'Nazarean' [BECNT], '(Jesus) from Nazareth' [CEV, GW, NCV], '(Jesus) of Nazareth' [AB, Bar, CBC; ESV, KJV, NIV, NLT, NRSV, REB, TEV]. This noun denotes a person who lives in or is a native of Nazareth [LN].

b. ἔθος (LN 41.25) (BDAG 2. p. 277): 'custom' [BDAG, BECNT, CBC, LN; all versions], 'habit' [LN], 'customary rule' [Bar], 'rule' [AB]. This noun denotes a pattern of behavior more or less fixed by tradition and generally sanctioned by the society [LN]. It denotes a long-established usage or practice common to a group [BDAG].

c. aorist act. indic. of παραδίδωμι (LN 33.237) (BDAG 3. p. 763): 'to hand down' [Bar, BDAG, CBC; NASB, NET, NIV, NLT, REB], 'to hand on' [NRSV], 'to instruct' [LN], 'to pass on' [BDAG, BECNT], 'to teach' [BDAG, LN], 'to transmit, to relate' [BDAG], 'to give' [AB; CEV, GW, NCV], 'to deliver' [ESV, KJV]. The phrase 'which Moses handed down to us' is also translated 'which have come down to us from Moses' [TEV]. This verb means to pass on traditional instruction, often implying over a long period of time [LN]. It means to pass on to another what one knows, of oral or written tradition [BDAG].

QUESTION—What is the hidden meaning when they referred to 'this Nazarene Jesus'?

The word 'this' in 'this Nazarene Jesus' shows their contempt for Jesus [TRT]. 'This Nazarene Jesus' is intended as a derogatory term [TH], a contemptuous term [Bar].

QUESTION—What were the customs handed down?

The customs which Moses handed down covered both written and oral traditions [Bar, BECNT, PNTC, TNTC]. They were laws, not mere customs lacking authority [Bar, TNTC].

6:15 And, looking-intently^a at him, all those sitting in the Sanhedrin saw his face (was) like (the)-face of-an-angel.

LEXICON—a. aorist act. participle of ἀτενίζω (LN 24.49) (BDAG p. 148): 'to look intently' [BDAG; NET, NIV, NRSV], 'to stare' [BDAG, LN; CEV, GW, NLT], 'to look straight at, to keep one's eyes fixed on' [LN], 'to look at' [AB], 'to look steadfastly' [KJV], 'to gaze' [ESV], 'to gaze intently' [BECNT], 'to fix one's gaze' [NASB], 'to watch closely' [NCV], 'to fix one's eyes' [Bar, CBC; REB, TEV]. This verb means to fix one's eyes on some object continually and intensely [LN].

QUESTION—What is meant by Stephen's face being like the face of an angel?

They saw a transfigured face like that of an angel, a picture of a martyr inspired by God [CBC, PNTC, TH, TRT]. Steven stood before the Sanhedrin with his face aglow, as one who stood consciously in the presence of God [NICNT]. His transfigured face was like that of an angel, filled with the Spirit and empowered for fearless testimony before his accusers [NAC]. It is a picture of him, being filled with the Holy Spirit and possessing a genuine spiritual winsomeness, radiating a presence marked by confidence, serenity, and courage [EBC]. Stephen had the appearance of one inspired by and in touch with God. It was Luke's way of saying that Stephen was innocent [BECNT].

DISCOURSE UNIT—7:1–8:1a [NLT]. The topic is Stephen addresses the Council.

DISCOURSE UNIT—7:1–56 [PNTC]. The topic is Stephen's defense.

DISCOURSE UNIT—7:1–53 [AB, Bar, BECNT, TNTC; CEV, ESV, GW, NASB, NCV, NET, NIV, NRSV, TEV]. The topic is the speech of Stephen [BECNT], Stephen's speech [AB, Bar; CEV, ESV, NCV, TEV], Stephen's speech to the Sanhedrin [NIV], Stephen's speech to the Council [NRSV], Stephen's speech in court [TNTC], Stephen speaks in his own defense [GW], Stephen's defense [NASB], Stephen's defense before the Council [NET].

DISCOURSE UNIT—7:1–1 [NICNT]. The topic is the high priest's question.

DISCOURSE UNIT—7:2–53 [EBC, NAC, NICNT]. The topic is Stephen's speech before the Sanhedrin [NAC], Stephen's defense before the Sanhedrin [EBC], Stephen's reply [NICNT].

DISCOURSE UNIT—7:2–36 [EBC]. The topic is on the land.

DISCOURSE UNIT—7:2–8 [NAC, NICNT, PNTC]. The topic is the foundational promises to Abraham [PNTC], the promises to Abraham [NAC], the patriarchal age [NICNT].

7:1 And the high-priest said, "Are these-things so?" **7:2** And (Stephen) said, "Men, brothers and fathers,ᵃ listen. The God of-gloryᵇ appeared to our forefatherᶜ Abraham (when) he-was in Mesopotamia, before he lived in Haran.

LEXICON—a. πατήρ (LN 11.26) (BDAG 4.a. p. 787): 'father' [AB, Bar, BDAG, BECNT, CBC, LN; all versions except CEV], 'elder' [LN], not explicit [CEV]. The phrase 'Men, brothers and fathers, listen' is also translated 'My brothers, fathers of this nation, listen to me' [CBC; REB]. This noun denotes a person belonging to the same socio-religious entity and being of the same age group as the so-called reference person [LN]. 'Father' is used as a title of respectful address [BDAG].
  b. δόξα (LN 79.18) (BDAG 1.b. p. 257): 'glory' [AB, Bar, BECNT, CBC, LN; ESV, GW, KJV, NASB, NET, NIV, NRSV, REB, TEV], 'splendor' [BDAG, LN], 'brightness, radiance' [BDAG]. The phrase 'the God of glory' is also translated 'Our glorious God' [CEV, NCV, NLT], 'The God who reveals his glory' [GW]. This noun denotes the quality of splendid, remarkable appearance [LN]. It denotes the condition of being bright or shining [BDAG].
  c. πατήρ (LN 10.20) (BDAG 2. p. 635): 'forefather' [BDAG, LN; NET], 'father' [AB, Bar, BECNT; ESV, KJV, NASB, NIV], 'ancestor' [BDAG, CBC, LN; CEV, GW, NCV, NLT, NRSV, REB, TEV], 'progenitor' [BDAG]. This noun denotes a person several preceding generations removed from the reference person [LN]. It denotes one from whom one is descended and who is generally at least several generations removed [BDAG].

QUESTION—Who was the high priest at this time?
  Caiaphas was probably the high priest at this time since this is likely still before A.D. 36 [AB, BECNT, PNTC, TRT]. He was the high priest at A.D. 18–36 [TRT].

QUESTION—What things was the high priest referring to?
  'These things' refer to the accusations against Stephen described in the previous chapter 6:13–14 [PNTC]. The question can be understood as 'Are these accusations against you (Stephen) true?' [TH]. 'Are the facts stated in the accusation true?' [Bar], 'Are these charges true?' [NAC, PNTC]. 'Are the charges of speaking against God, Moses, the Law, and the temple true?' [BECNT].

7:3 And he-said to him, 'Go-out from your countryᵃ and from your relatives,ᵇ and come into the landᶜ that I-will-showᵈ you.'

LEXICON—a. γῆ (LN 1.79) (BDAG 3. p. 196): 'country' [LN; AB, BDAG, CBC; all versions except ESV, GW, NLT], 'land' [Bar, BDAG, BECNT, LN; ESV, GW], 'native land' [NLT], 'region' [BDAG, LN]. This noun denotes a region of the earth, normally in relation to some ethnic group or geographical center, but not necessarily constituting a unit of

governmental administration [LN]. It denotes a portion or region of the earth [BDAG].
b. συγγένεια (LN 10.5) (BDAG p. 950): 'relatives' [BDAG, BECNT, LN; CEV, GW, NASB, NCV, NET, NLT, NRSV], 'kinfolks' [CBC, LN], 'kindred' [ESV, KJV], 'kin' [AB], 'people' [NIV], 'kinsfolk' [REB], 'family' [Bar; TEV]. This noun denotes the group of persons who are members of an extended family [LN]. It denotes an extended family system [BDAG].
c. γῆ (LN 1.79) (BDAG 3. p. 196): 'land' [Bar, BDAG, BECNT, CBC, LN; all versions], 'country' [AB, BDAG], 'region' [BDAG, LN], 'territory' [LN]. This noun denotes a region or regions of the earth, normally in relation to some ethnic group or geographical center, but not necessarily constituting a unit of governmental administration [LN].
d. aorist act. subj. of δείκνυμι (LN 28.47) (BDAG 1. p. 214): 'to show' [AB, Bar, BDAG, BECNT, CBC, LN; all versions], 'to make known' [BDAG, LN], 'to point out' [BDAG], 'to demonstrate' [LN]. This verb means to make known the character or significance of something by visual, auditory, gestural, or linguistic means [LN]. It means to exhibit something that can be apprehended by one or more of the senses [BDAG].

7:4 Then, having-gone-out[a] from (the)-land of-(the)-Chaldeans, he-settled[b] in Haran. From-there, after (the)-death-(of) his father, (God) had- him - move[c] to this land in which you now are-living.
LEXICON—a. aorist act. impera. of ἐξέρχομαι (LN 15.40) (BDAG 1.a.α.ℵ. p. 347): 'to go out' [BDAG, BECNT; ESV, NET], 'to leave' [AB, Bar, CBC; all versions except ESV, KJV, NET], 'to come out' [BDAG; KJV], 'to go away' [BDAG], 'to go out of, to depart out of, to leave from within' [LN]. This verb means to move out of an enclosed or well-defined two or three-dimensional area [LN]. It means to move out of or away from an area [BDAG].
b. aorist act. indic. of κατοικέω (LN 85.69) (BDAG 1.a. p. 534): 'to settle-down' [AB, Bar, BDAG, CBC; CEV, NASB, NET, NIV, NRSV, REB], 'to live' [BDAG, BECNT, LN; ESV, GW, NLT], 'to dwell' [BDAG, LN; KJV], 'to go to live' [NCV, TEV], 'to reside' [BDAG, LN]. This verb means to live or dwell in a place in an established or settled manner [LN]. It means to live in a locality for any length of time [BDAG].
c. aorist act. indic. of μετοικίζω (LN 85.83) (BDAG p. 643): 'to have (someone) move' [AB; NASB, NRSV], 'to resettle' [BDAG, LN], 'to move to another place' [LN], 'to make (someone) move' [LN; GW, NET, TEV], 'to settle' [CEV], 'to remove' [BECNT; ESV, KJV], 'to send' [NCV, NIV], 'to bring' [NLT], 'to lead (someone), to migrate' [CBC; REB], 'to transfer (someone)' [Bar]. This verb means to cause someone to change his place of habitation [LN]. It means to remove to another place of habitation [BDAG].

QUESTION—Where was 'the land of the Chaldeans'?

The 'land of the Chaldeans' was another name for the land of Mesopotamia mentioned in verse 2 [NICNT, TRT].

7:5 **Yet he-did- not -give him an-inheritance**[a] **in it, not even (a)-foot of ground**[b] **of it, but he-promised to-give it to-him and to-his descendants after him even when he had no child.**

LEXICON—a. κληρονομία (LN 57.132) (BDAG 2. p. 548): 'inheritance' [Bar, BECNT; ESV, KJV, NASB, NET, NIV, NLT], 'heritage' [NRSV], 'possession' [BDAG, CBC, LN; REB], 'land' [AB], 'part' [CEV, TEV]. The phrase 'he did not give him an inheritance in it' is also translated 'God didn't give Abraham anything in this land to call his own' [GW], 'God did not give Abraham any of this land' [NCV]. This noun denotes a valuable possession which has been received [LN].

b. βῆμα (LN 80.3) (BDAG 2. p. 175): 'step' [BDAG, LN]. The phrase 'not even a foot of ground' [NASB, NET, NIV] is also translated 'not even a foot's length' [BECNT; ESV, NRSV], 'not even a square foot/meter' [BDAG, LN; CEV], 'not so much as a foot of ground' [AB], 'not so much as to set his foot on' [KJV], 'not even a foot of it' [NCV], 'not even one/a square foot of land/ground' [NLT, TEV], 'not one yard' [CBC], 'no foothold in it' [REB], 'not even a place to rest his feet' [GW], 'not even space to plant his foot' [Bar]. The idiom βῆμα ποδός 'a step of a foot' refers to a distance of approximately two and a half feet and it is used to indicate an extremely limited or restricted space [LN]. It denotes a very limited space, less than the space covered by one taking a stride [BDAG].

QUESTION—What had God promised Abraham?

This promise is based on Genesis 17:8 'And I will give to you and to your offspring after you the land of your sojourns, all the land of Canaan, for an everlasting possession, and I will be their God' [BECNT, TH]. God gave Abraham not the land in actual possession but the promise that he would give him the land as a possession [Bar]. The promise of the land was truly a promise, since at the time it was given, Abraham had neither the land nor an heir to possess it [AB, NAC, NICNT, TNTC]. Abraham depended on God's promise [CBC].

7:6 **And God spoke to-this-effect, that his descendants would-be**[a] **strangers in another's land, and they-would-enslave**[b] **(them) and mistreat-(them)**[c] **four-hundred years.**

LEXICON—a. εἰμί [LN 85.1]: 'to be' [LN]. The phrase 'that his descendants would be strangers' is also translated 'that his descendants would be foreigners/aliens/resident-aliens' [GW, NASB, NRSV], 'that his offspring would be sojourners' [ESV], 'that his descendants will live in' [NLT], 'that his seed should sojourn' [KJV], 'that his seed should be sojourners' [Bar], 'that his seed would be foreigners' [BECNT], 'that Abraham's descendants would live for a while' [CEV]. Some translations change this to a direct quote: 'Your descendants will be strangers/foreigners' [NCV,

NET, NIV], 'Your descendants will live (in a foreign country)' [TEV], 'Abraham's descendants shall live as aliens' [CBC; REB], 'His descendants shall live as strangers' [AB]. The verb means to be in a place [LN].
   b. fut. act. indic. of δουλόω (LN 87.82) (BDAG 1. p. 260): 'to enslave' [Bar, BDAG, BECNT, LN; ESV, NASB, NET, NIV, NRSV], 'to make a slave of someone' [AB, BDAG, LN; GW, NCV], 'to bring into bondage' [KJV], 'to subject' [BDAG]. Instead of referring to what the inhabitants of the land will do, the subject of the verb is changed to refer to Abraham's descendants: 'they would/will be slaves' [CEV, TEV], 'they would be oppressed as slaves' [NLT], 'held in slavery' [CBC; REB]. This verb means to make someone a slave [BDAG, LN].
   c. fut. act. indic. of κακόω (LN 20.12) (BDAG 1. p. 502): 'to mistreat' [BDAG; CEV, GW, NASB, NCV, NET, NIV, NRSV], 'to afflict' [ESV], 'to oppress' [NLT], 'to hold in oppression' [CBC; REB], 'to ill-use' [AB, Bar], 'to ill-treat' [BECNT], 'to treat badly' [TEV], 'to entreat (them) evil' [KJV], 'to harm' [BDAG, LN], 'to hurt, to injure' [LN]. This verb means to cause harm to someone [BDAG, LN] and it is a highly generic meaning involving a wide range of harm and injury' [LN]. It means to cause harm to someone [BDAG].

QUESTION—Which Scripture passage did Stephen refer to in this verse?
   The Scripture passage referred to is from Genesis 15:13 [Bar, BECNT, CBC, EBC, PNTC, TH].

7:7 'But I will-judge[a] the nation that they-serve-as-slaves,[b]' said God, 'and after that they-will-come-out and worship[c] me in this place.'

LEXICON—a. fut. act. indic. of κρίνω (LN 56.30) (BDAG 5.b.α. p. 568): 'to judge' [AB, Bar, BDAG, BECNT; ESV, KJV, NASB, NRSV], 'to pass judgment on' [CBC; REB, TEV], 'to punish' [CEV, GW, NCV, NET, NIV, NLT], 'to judge as guilty, to condemn' [LN]. This verb means to judge a person to be guilty and liable to punishment [LN]. It means to engage in a judicial process [BDAG].
   b. fut. act. indic. of δουλεύω (LN 87.79) (BDAG 1.a. p. 259): 'to serve as a slave' [AB, Bar; NET, NIV], 'to serve' [BECNT; ESV, GW, NRSV, TEV], 'to be in bondage' [KJV, NASB], 'to be a slave' [BDAG, CBC, LN; NCV, REB], 'to be subjected' [BDAG], 'to be made a slave' [CEV], 'to enslave' [NLT]. This verb means to be a slave of someone [LN]. It means to be owned by another [BDAG].
   c. fut. act. indic. of λατρεύω (LN 53.14) (BDAG p. 587): 'to worship' [AB, Bar, BECNT, CBC, LN; all versions except KJV, NASB], 'to serve' [BDAG; KJV, NASB], 'to perform religious rites, to venerate' [LN]. This verb means to perform religious rites as a part of worship [LN]. It refers to the carrying out of religious duties [LN]. It means 'to serve' in the sense of 'the carrying out of religious duties, especially of a cultic nature, by human beings' [BDAG].

ACTS 7:7

QUESTION—What does 'they' refer to here?
This 'they' refers to Abraham's descendants, not the people of the nation that had made them slaves [BECNT, TRT].

QUESTION—What Scripture passages was Stephen referring to?
Stephen referred to Genesis 15:14 and Exodus 3:12. To 'worship God on this mountain' (that is, Mount Horeb or Sinai) of Exodus 3:12 has been adapted by Stephen to 'worship in this place'. In this verse, some refer 'this place' to the land of Canaan, that is, Palestine or Jerusalem [BECNT, TH, TNTC], and others refer it more particularly to the temple at Jerusalem [Bar, NAC, PNTC].

7:8 **And he-gave him (the)-covenant[a] of-circumcision.[b] And so he-became-(the)-father-of[c] Isaac, and circumcised him on-the eighth day. And Isaac-(became-the-father-of) Jacob; and Jacob (became the father) (of)-the twelve patriarchs.[d]**

LEXICON—a. διαθήκη (LN 34.44) (BDAG 2. p. 228): 'covenant' [AB, Bar, BDAG, BECNT, CBC, LN; all versions except CEV, GW, NCV], 'pact' [LN], 'agreement' [CEV, NCV], 'promise' [GW]. This noun denotes the verbal content of an agreement between two persons which specifies their reciprocal benefits and responsibilities [LN]. It is a declaration of one person's initiative, and in the case of God's covenants, God alone sets the conditions [BDAG].

b. περιτομή (LN 53.51) (BDAG 1.a. p. 807): 'circumcision' [AB, Bar, BDAG, BECNT, CBC, LN; all versions]. This noun denotes the cutting off of the foreskin of the male genital organ as a religious rite involving consecration and ethnic identification [LN]. It denotes the covenant or decree of circumcision [BDAG].

c. aorist act. indic. of γεννάω (LN 23.58) (BDAG 1.a. p. 193): 'to become the father of' [BDAG; ESV, NASB, NET, NIV, NLT, NRSV], 'to be the father of' [BECNT, LN], 'to beget' [Bar, BDAG, LN; KJV], 'to father' [AB], not explicit [CEV]. The phrase 'so he became the father of Isaac' is also translated 'when Abraham's son Isaac was born' [GW], 'when Abraham had his son Isaac' [NCV], 'when his son Isaac was born' [REB], 'after Isaac was born' [CBC], 'after he was born' [TEV]. This verb means to exercise the male role in causing the conception and birth of a child [LN]. It means to become the parent of by procreation [BDAG].

d. πατριάρχης (LN 10.22) (BDAG p. 788): 'patriarch' [AB, Bar, BDAG, BECNT, CBC, LN; ESV, KJV, NASB, NET, NIV, NLT, NRSV, REB], 'father of a nation' [BDAG], 'ancestor' [CEV, NCV], 'ancestor of our tribes' [GW], 'famous ancestor of our race' [TEV]. This noun denotes a particularly noted male ancestor, either because of his role in initiating an ethnic group or groups, for example, Abraham, Isaac, Jacob and the twelve sons of Jacob, or because of important exploits and accomplishments, for example, David [LN]. It denotes the prime ancestor of a national entity [BDAG].

QUESTION—What is meant by 'the covenant of circumcision'?
This was the covenant agreed upon between God and Abraham and it had circumcision as its external/outward sign [BECNT, NICNT, PNTC, TH]. The covenant of circumcision was made with Abraham in Genesis 17:10–14 [NAC, TNTC]. The covenant meant that every father in every generation must circumcise his male children [AB, Bar, NAC, NICNT]. That would be an intimate sign that would remind the Israelites of their commitment to God and its connection to life [BECNT, TNTC].

DISCOURSE UNIT—7:9–19 [NICNT]. The topic is Israel in Egypt.

DISCOURSE UNIT—7:9–16 [NAC, PNTC]. The topic is Joseph being blessed with grace and wisdom for the salvation of God's people [PNTC], the deliverance through Joseph [NAC].

7:9 And the patriarchs,a becoming-jealous-of Joseph, sold-(him) into Egypt. But God was with him **7:10** and rescuedb him from all his troubles,c and gave him favord and wisdom before Pharaoh, king of-Egypt. And he-appointede him (the-one)-rulingf over Egypt and over all his household.g

LEXICON—a. πατριάρχης (LN 10.22) (BDAG p. 788): 'patriarch' [AB, Bar, BDAG, BECNT, CBC, LN; ESV, KJV, NASB, NET, NIV, NLT, NRSV, REB], 'father of a nation' [BDAG], 'ancestor' [CEV], 'Jacob's sons' [GW, NCV, TEV]. This noun denotes a particularly noted male ancestor, either because of his role in initiating an ethnic group or groups, for example, Abraham, Isaac, Jacob and the twelve sons of Jacob, or because of important exploits and accomplishments, for example, David. The equivalent expression for patriarch in a number of languages is merely 'important forefather' or 'famous forefather' or 'great ancestor' [LN]. It denotes the prime ancestor of a national entity [BDAG].

b. aorist mid. indic. of ἐξαιρέω (LN 21.17) (BDAG 2. p. 344): 'to rescue' [Bar, BDAG, BECNT, CBC, LN; all versions except KJV, NCV, TEV], 'to deliver' [AB, BDAG, LN; KJV], 'to save' [NCV]. The phrase 'rescued him from all his troubles' is also translated 'brought him safely through all his troubles' [TEV]. This verb means to rescue or set someone free from danger [LN]. It means to rescue someone from peril or a confining circumstance [BDAG].

c. θλῖψις (LN 22.2) (BDAG 1. p. 457): 'trouble' [CBC; CEV, NCV, NET, NIV, NLT, REB, TEV], 'affliction' [AB, Bar, BDAG BECNT; ESV, KJV, NASB, NRSV], 'suffering' [LN; GW], 'trouble and suffering, persecution' [LN], 'oppression, tribulation' [BDAG]. This noun denotes trouble involving direct suffering [LN]. It denotes trouble that inflicts distress [BDAG].

d. χάρις (LN 25.89) (BDAG 2.b. p. 1079): 'favor' [BDAG, LN; ESV, KJV, NASB, NET, NLT, NRSV], 'divine favor' [GW], 'grace' [AB, Bar, BDAG, LN], 'good will' [BDAG, LN; NIV], 'acceptance' [BECNT], 'a pleasing manner' [TEV], 'gracious care/help' [BDAG]. The phrase 'gave him favor and wisdom before Pharaoh, king of Egypt' is also translated 'God made him so wise that the Egyptian king thought highly of him' [CEV], 'The king of Egypt liked Joseph and respected him because of the wisdom God gave him' [NCV], 'He gave him wisdom which so commended him to Pharaoh king of Egypt' [REB], 'He also gave him a presence and powers of mind which so commended him to Pharaoh king of Egypt' [CBC]. This noun denotes a favorable attitude toward someone or something [LN]. It denotes a beneficent disposition toward someone [BDAG].

e. aorist act. indic. of καθίστημι (LN 37.104) (BDAG 2.b. p. 492): 'to appoint' [AB, Bar, BDAG, CBC, LN; NLT, NRSV, REB], 'to authorize' [BDAG], 'to put in charge of' [BDAG; CEV], 'to designate' [LN], 'to make' [BECNT]. The phrase 'he appointed him the governor over Egypt' is also translated 'he made him governor over Egypt' [KJV, NASB], 'he made him ruler over Egypt' [ESV, NET, NIV], 'The king even made Joseph governor over Egypt and put him in charge' [CEV], 'The king made him governor of Egypt' [NCV], 'the king made Joseph governor over the country' [TEV], 'he became ruler of Egypt' [GW]. This verb means to assign to someone a position of authority over others [LN].

f. pres. mid./pass. (deponent = act.) participle of ἡγέομαι (LN 37.58) (BDAG 1. p. 434): 'to rule' [LN], 'to rule over, to order, to govern' [LN], 'to lead, to guide' [BDAG]. The phrase 'the one ruling over Egypt' is also translated 'governor over Egypt' [BECNT; CEV, KJV, NASB], 'ruler over Egypt' [Bar; ESV, NET, NIV, NRSV], 'ruler of Egypt' [GW], 'governor of Egypt' [AB; NCV, REB], 'governor over all of Egypt' [NLT], 'governor over the country' [TEV], 'chief administrator for Egypt [CBC]. This verb means to rule over, with the implication of providing direction and leadership [LN]. It refers to being in a supervisory capacity [BDAG].

g. οἶκος (LN 10.8, 57.21) (BDAG 4. p. 699): 'household' [AB, Bar, BECNT, CBC, LN (10.8); ESV, NASB, NET, NRSV, REB, TEV], 'property' [BDAG, LN (57.21)], 'estate' [BDAG], 'possessions' [BDAG, LN (57.21)], 'palace' [GW, NIV, NLT], 'house' [LN (57.21); KJV]. The phrase 'all his household' is also translated 'all the people in his palace' [NCV], 'everything he owned' [CEV]. This noun denotes the family consisting of those related by blood and marriage, as well as slaves and servants, living in the same house or homestead [LN (10.8)] or it denotes possessions associated with a house and household [LN (57.21)]. It denotes a house and what is in it [BDAG].

QUESTION—Who were the patriarchs who became jealous of Joseph?

This is about the patriarchs who were the twelve sons of Jacob. The older sons of Jacob had become very jealous of their younger brother Joseph [BECNT, NAC, PNTC, TH, TRT]. These brothers sold Joseph to some merchants who then took him to Egypt and sold him there as a slave

[BECNT, TH, TRT]. From this verse to v. 16, Stephen summarizes the story of the Patriarchs from Genesis 38–50 [TRT].

QUESTION—What is meant by the phrase 'God was with him'?

This phrase is rendered in many languages as 'God continued to help him' or even 'God caused him to succeed' [TH, TNTC]. For God to be with someone means that God is present and working through that person in an unusual way [BECNT].

QUESTION—Is Pharaoh a title or a name?

Pharaoh is the title of the kings of Egypt. It means something like 'his majesty.' However the Greek text and the Old Testament Hebrew texts seem to treat 'Pharaoh' as a name [TRT].

QUESTION—What do all the pronouns 'he', 'his' and 'him' in this verse represent?

Rewritten to show whom the pronouns represent, the verse says: 'and (God) delivered him (Joseph) from all his (Joseph's) troubles, and gave him (Joseph) favor and wisdom before Pharaoh, king of Egypt. And he (Pharaoh) appointed him (Joseph) the governor over Egypt and over all his (Pharaoh's) household' [Bar, NAC, TRT].

7:11 Now (a)-famine[a] came throughout all Egypt and Canaan, and great suffering,[b] and our ancestors[c] could-find no food.[d]

LEXICON—a. λιμός (LN 23.33) (BDAG 2. p. 596): 'famine' [AB, Bar, BDAG, BECNT, CBC, LN; all versions except CEV, KJV, NCV], 'hunger' [LN], 'dearth' [KJV]. The clause 'a famine came throughout all Egypt and Canaan' is also translated 'Everywhere in Egypt and Canaan the grain crops failed' [CEV], 'all the land of Egypt and Canaan became so dry that nothing would grow' [NCV]. This noun denotes a widespread lack of food over a considerable period of time, and the result was hunger for many of the people [LN].

b. θλῖψις (LN 22.2) (BDAG 1. p. 457): 'suffering' [BECNT, LN; CEV, GW, NET, NIV, NRSV, TEV], 'affliction' [Bar, BDAG; ESV, KJV, NASB], 'misery' [NLT], 'distress' [REB], 'hardship' [AB, CBC], 'trouble and suffering, persecution' [LN], 'tribulation' [BDAG]. The phrase 'great suffering' is also translated 'the people suffered very much' [NCV]. This noun denotes trouble involving direct suffering [LN]. It denotes trouble that inflicts distress [BDAG].

c. πατήρ (LN 10.20): 'ancestor' [CBC, LN; CEV, GW, NCV, NET, NLT, NRSV, REB, TEV], 'forefather' [LN], 'father' [AB, Bar, BECNT; ESV, KJV, NASB, NIV]. This noun denotes a person several preceding generations from the reference person [LN].

d. χόρτασμα (LN 5.1) (BDAG p. 1087): 'food' [Bar, BDAG, BECNT, LN; ESV, GW, NASB, NET, NIV, NLT, NRSV, TEV], 'sustenance' [KJV]. The phrase 'our ancestors could find no food' is also translated 'our ancestors could not find enough to eat' [CEV], 'Jacob's sons, our ancestors, could not find anything to eat' [NCV], 'our ancestors could find nothing to eat' [CBC; REB], 'our fathers could find nothing to eat' [AB]. This noun denotes any kind of food or nourishment [LN].

7:12 But when- Jacob -heard there-was grain[a] in Egypt, he-sent-out[b] our ancestors[c] (on their) first (visit). **7:13** And on the second-(visit) Joseph made-himself-known[d] to his brothers, and Joseph's family became known[e] to-Pharaoh.[f]

LEXICON—a. σιτίον (LN 3.42, 5.2) (BDAG p. 925): 'grain' [AB, BECNT, LN (3.42, 5.2)]; all versions except GW, KJV, REB], 'corn' [Bar; KJV], 'food' [BDAG, CBC, LN (3.42, 5.2); GW, REB]. Here in its plural form, this noun denotes any grain with the evident implication of its relevance as food [LN (3.42)], or occurring primarily in the plural, it refers to food consisting principally of grain products. In this verse it is possible to understand the plural form as grain, but the reference is probably to food made from grain, a common meaning of the term in Classical Greek [LN (5.2)]. This is the word for grain or for food made from grain, but in the plural form it is a general reference to food [BDAG].

b. aorist act. indic. of ἐξαποστέλλω (LN 15.68) (BDAG 1.b. p. 346): 'to send out' [BDAG, LN; ESV, KJV], 'to send' [AB, Bar, CBC, LN; all versions except ESV, KJV], 'to send forth' [BECNT, LN]. This verb means to send out or away from, presumably for some purpose [LN]. It means to send someone off to a locality or on a mission [BDAG].

c. πατήρ (LN 10.20): 'ancestor' [LN; CEV, GW, NET, NLT, NRSV, TEV], 'forefather' [BDAG, LN], 'father' [AB, Bar, BECNT, CBC; ESV, KJV, NASB, NIV, REB], 'progenitor' [BDAG]. The phrase 'Jacob…sent out our ancestors' is also translated 'Jacob…sent his sons there' [NCV]. This noun denotes a person several preceding generations from the reference person [LN].

d. aorist pass. indic. of ἀναγνωρίζω (LN 27.62) (BDAG p. 61): 'to make oneself known' [AB, BECNT; ESV, NASB, NET, NRSV, REB, TEV],'to make known' [Bar; KJV], 'to make known again' [LN], 'to make recognized' [LN], 'to learn to know again, to see again' [BDAG]. The clause 'Joseph made himself known to his brothers' is also translated 'Joseph told his brothers who he was' [CEV, GW, NCV, NIV], 'Joseph revealed his identity to his brothers' [NLT], 'Joseph made himself known to his brothers again' [LN], 'Joseph was recognized by his brothers' [CBC]. This verb means to cause oneself to be recognized or to be known again [LN]. It means to learn to know again [BDAG].

e. φανερός (LN 28.28) (BDAG 1. p. 10.48): 'known' [AB, Bar, BDAG; ESV, KJV, NET, NRSV], 'well known, widely known' [LN], 'disclosed' [NASB, REB], 'visible, plainly to be seen, open, plain' [BDAG], 'clear' [BDAG, BECNT], 'evident' [BDAG]. The phrase 'Joseph's family became known to Pharaoh' is also translated 'the king learned about Joseph's family' [CEV, NCV], 'Pharaoh learned about Joseph's family' [GW, NIV], 'they were introduced to Pharaoh' [NLT], 'the king of Egypt came to know about Joseph's family' [TEV], 'his family connections were disclosed to Pharaoh' [CBC]. This adjective pertains to being widely and well known [LN]. It pertains to being evident so as to be readily known [BDAG].

f. Φαραώ (LN 93.373) (BDAG p. 1049): 'Pharaoh' [AB, Bar, BDAG, BECNT, CBC, LN; all versions except CEV, NCV, TEV], 'the king' [CEV, NCV], 'the king of Egypt' [TEV]. The noun 'Pharaoh' is a title used as a proper name of the Egyptian king [LN]. Actually the title of Egyptian kings, it became a proper name of the Pharaoh of the Exodus [BDAG].

7:14 And-then Joseph sent[a] (and) summoned[b] Jacob his father and all (his) relatives, seventy-five persons (in all). **7:15** And Jacob went-down[c] to Egypt and (there) he died, he and our ancestors.[d]

LEXICON—a. aorist act. participle of ἀποστέλλω (LN 15.67) (BDAG 2.b. p. 121): 'to send word, to send a message' [LN]. The clause 'Joseph sent and summoned Jacob his father' [Bar; ESV] is also translated 'Joseph sent and summoned to him his father Jacob' [AB], 'Joseph sent and called Jacob his father' [BECNT], 'Joseph sent for his father Jacob' [GW, NIV, REB], 'Joseph sent for his father' [CEV], 'Joseph sent word and invited Jacob his father…to come to him' [NASB], 'Joseph sent a message and invited his father…to come' [NET], 'Joseph sent and invited his father Jacob…to come to him' [NRSV], 'Then sent Joseph, and called his father Jacob to him' [KJV], 'Joseph sent for his father, Jacob…to come to Egypt' [NLT], 'Joseph sent messengers to invite Jacob, his father, to come to Egypt' [NCV], 'Joseph sent a message to his father Jacob, telling him… to come to Egypt' [TEV], 'Joseph sent an invitation to his father Jacob' [CBC]. This verb means to send a message, presumably by someone [LN]. It means to dispatch a message. When used with other verbs, it often functions like our verbal auxiliary 'have' and means simply that the action in question has been performed by someone else. In this verse it means 'he had him summoned' [BDAG].

b. aorist mid. indic. of μετακαλέω (LN 33.311) (BDAG p. 639): 'to summon' [AB, Bar, BDAG, LN; ESV], 'to call' [BECNT], 'to call to oneself' [BDAG; KJV], 'to tell to come' [LN; TEV], 'to invite to come' [NASB, NCV, NET, NRSV], not explicit [CBC; CEV, GW, NIV, NLT, REB]. This verb means to summon someone with considerable insistence and authority [LN]. It means to call to oneself [BDAG].

c. aorist act. indic. of καταβαίνω (LN 15.107) (BDAG 1.a.β. p. 514): 'to go down' [AB, Bar, BDAG, BECNT, CBC, LN; ESV, KJV, NASB, NCV, NET, NIV, NRSV, REB], 'to go' [CEV, GW, NLT, TEV], 'to descend, to move down' [LN]. This verb means to move down, irrespective of the gradient [LN]. It means to move downward when going away from Jerusalem [BDAG].

d. πατήρ (LN 10.20): 'ancestor' [LN; CEV, GW, NET, NLT, NRSV], 'forefather' [CBC, LN], 'father' [AB, Bar, BECNT; ESV, KJV, NASB, NIV, REB]. The phrase 'he and our ancestors' is also translated 'he and his sons died' [NCV, TEV]. This noun denotes a person several preceding generations from the reference person [LN].

QUESTION—Who were 'our ancestors'?

Here Stephen refers to the twelve patriarchs and their father Jacob who died in Egypt [BECNT, PNTC]. Stephen called them 'our' ancestors since he still considered himself to be part of Israel's history [BECNT].

7:16 And they-were-moved[a] to Shechem and placed in the tomb[b] that Abraham had-bought for-(a)-sum[c] of silver[d] from the sons of-Hamor in Shechem.

LEXICON—a. aorist pass. indic. of μετατίθημι (LN 15.2) (BDAG 1. p. 642): 'to be moved' [AB, LN; NCV, NET], 'to be transferred' [Bar], 'to be taken' [GW, NLT, TEV], 'to be brought back' [BDAG; NIV, NRSV], 'to be taken back' [CEV], 'to be carried back' [BECNT; ESV],'to be carried over' [KJV], 'to be removed' [CBC; NASB, REB], 'to be moved from one place to another, to change one's location, to depart' [LN], 'to be conveyed to another place, to be put in another place' [BDAG]. This verb means to effect a change of location in space, with the implication that the two locations are significantly different [LN]. It means to convey from one place to another [BDAG].

b. μνῆμα (LN 7.75) (BDAG p. 655): 'tomb' [AB, Bar, BDAG, BECNT, CBC, LN, all versions except KJV, NCV, TEV], 'grave' [BDAG, LN; NCV, TEV], 'sepulcher' [KJV]. This noun denotes a construction for the burial of the dead [LN].

c. τιμή (LN 57.161) (BDAG 1. p. 1005): 'sum' [AB, Bar, BDAG, BECNT; ESV, KJV, NASB, NCV, NRSV, REB, TEV], 'certain sum' [NET, NIV], 'price' [BDAG, LN], 'certain price' [NLT], 'amount, cost' [LN], 'value' [BDAG], not explicit [CBC; CEV, GW]. This noun denotes the amount of money or property regarded as representing the value or price of something [LN]. It denotes the amount at which something is valued [BDAG].

d. ἀργύριον (LN 6.73) (BDAG 2.a. p. 128): 'silver' [BDAG, BECNT; ESV, NRSV], 'silver money, silver coin' [LN], 'money' [AB, Bar; KJV, NASB, NCV, NET, NIV, REB, TEV], not explicit [CBC; CEV, GW, NLT]. The phrase 'Abraham had bought for a sum of silver' is also translated 'Abraham had bought and paid for' [CBC]. This noun denotes silver used as money [BDAG, LN].

QUESTION—Where was the burial place for the ancestors?

Actually it was Jacob who bought land from the sons of Hamor at the town of Shechem (Genesis 33:19). Abraham bought a burial cave near the town of Hebron from Ephron the Hittite (Genesis 23:15–18). Stephen's audience knew that he was combining those two events. They also knew that Jacob was buried in the cave that Abraham bought (Genesis 50:13), and Joseph was buried at Shechem (Joshua 24:32) [AB, Bar, BECNT, CBC, EBC, NAC, TNTC, TRT].

DISCOURSE UNIT—7:17-38 [PNTC]. The topic is Moses blessed with wisdom and power, in words and deeds, for the salvation of God's people.

DISCOURSE UNIT—7:17-34 [NAC]. The topic is the deliverance through Moses.

7:17 But as the time drew-near for-the promise which God had-given[a] to-Abraham, the people[b] increased[c] and multiplied[d] in Egypt **7:18** until there arose[e] over Egypt another king who did-not know Joseph.

LEXICON—a. aorist act. indic. of ὁμολογέω (LN 33.221) (BDAG 1. p. 708): 'to give' [AB], 'to grant' [BECNT; ESV], 'to promise' [BDAG; CEV, GW], 'to assure' [BDAG; NASB], 'to declare' [LN; NET], 'to swear' [KJV]. The phrase 'the promise which God had given to Abraham' is also translated 'the promise God made to Abraham' [Bar, BDAG; NCV], 'the promise God/he had made to Abraham' [CBC; NRSV, REB, TEV], 'his promise to Abraham' [NIV, NLT]. This verb means to make an emphatic declaration which is often made public [LN]. It means to commit oneself to do something for someone [BDAG].

b. λαός (LN 11.12) (BDAG 4.a. p. 586): 'people' [BDAG]. The phrase 'the people' [AB, Bar, BECNT; ESV, KJV, NASB, NET] is also translated 'the number of people' [NCV], 'our people' [CEV, GW, NIV, NLT], 'our people in Egypt' [NRSV, REB, TEV], 'the people of God' [LN], 'the people of Israel' [BDAG], 'our nation' [CBC]. This noun denotes the people who belong to God, whether Jews or Christians [LN]. It denotes the people of God [BDAG].

c. aorist act. indic. of αὐξάνω (LN 59.62) (BDAG 2.b. p. 151): 'to increase' [AB, BDAG, BECNT, LN; ESV, NASB, NRSV], 'to grow' [Bar, BDAG, CBC, LN; KJV, REB], 'to grow large in number' [GW, NCV], 'to increase greatly in number' [CEV, NET, NIV, NLT], 'to grow much larger in number' [TEV]. This verb means to increase in the extent of or in the instances of an activity or state [LN]. It means to become greater [BDAG].

d. aorist pass. indic. of πληθύνω (LN 59.68) (BDAG 1.b. p. 826): 'to multiply' [AB, Bar, BDAG, BECNT, LN; ESV, KJV, NASB, NRSV], 'to increase' [BDAG], 'to increase in numbers' [CBC; REB], 'to increase greatly' [LN], 'to grow' [BDAG, LN], not explicit [CEV, GW, NCV, NET, NIV, NLT, TEV]. This verb means to increase greatly in number or extent [LN]. It means to become greater in number [BDAG].

e. aorist act. indic. of ἀνίστημι (LN 13.81) (BDAG 9. p. 83): 'to arise' [AB, Bar, BDAG, BECNT, LN; ESV, KJV, NASB], 'to come into existence, to appear' [BDAG, LN]. The phrase 'until there arose over Egypt another king' is also translated 'Then a different king…began to rule in Egypt'

[GW], 'Then a new king...began to rule Egypt' [NCV], 'until another king ruled over Egypt' [NET], 'Another king was ruling Egypt' [CEV], 'Then another king became ruler of Egypt' [NIV], 'But then a new king came to the throne of Egypt' [NLT], 'until another king ruled over Egypt' [NRSV], 'At length another king ascended the throne of Egypt' [CBC; REB], 'At last a king began to rule in Egypt' [TEV]. This verb means to come into existence, with the implication of assuming a place or position [LN]. It means to come or to appear in order to carry out a function or role [BDAG].

7:19 This-one dealt-shrewdly[a] with our race[b] and forced our fathers to expose[c] their infants so that they would not be kept-alive.[d]

LEXICON—a. aorist mid. participle of κατασοφίζομαι (LN 88.147) (BDAG p. 527): 'to deal shrewdly with' [ESV], 'to take shrewd advantage of' [NASB], 'to deal subtly with' [KJV], 'to employ cunning' [REB], 'to use cunning' [AB], 'to trick' [Bar; CEV, NCV, TEV], 'to exploit' [NET, NLT], 'to deal treacherously with' [NIV], 'to deal craftily with' [NRSV], 'to make a crafty attack on' [CBC], 'to scheme against' [BECNT], 'to get the better of, to take advantage of by trickery' [BDAG]. The phrase 'dealt shrewdly with our race' is also translated 'was shrewd in the way he took advantage of our people' [GW], 'he cunningly exploited our people' [LN]. This verb means to exploit by means of craftiness and cunning, and it implies the use of false arguments [LN]. It means to get the better of people or take advantage of them by cunning or trickery [BDAG].

b. γένος (LN 10.1) (BDAG 3. p. 194): 'race' [Bar, BECNT, CBC, LN; ESV, NASB, NRSV, REB], 'nation' [BDAG, LN], 'people' [BDAG; GW, NCV, NET, NIV, NLT], 'kindred' [AB; KJV], 'ethnic group' [LN] not explicit [CEV, TEV]. This noun denotes a relatively large group of persons regarded as being biologically related [LN]. It denotes a relatively large people group [BDAG].

c. ἔκθετος (LN 85.47) (BDAG p. 303): 'exposed' [BDAG, LN], 'abandoned' [BDAG, LN]. The phrase 'forced our fathers to expose their infants' [ESV] is also translated 'forced our ancestors to expose their children' [CBC; REB], 'ill-treated our fathers, causing them to expose their infants' [Bar], 'made them leave their babies outside' [CEV], 'made them abandon their newborn babies outdoors' [GW], 'so that they cast out their young children' [KJV], 'so that they would expose their infants' [NASB], 'forcing them to leave their babies outside' [NCV], 'forcing them to abandon their infants' [NET], 'forcing them to expose their infants' [BECNT], 'by forcing them to throw out their newborn babies' [NIV], 'forcing parents to abandon their newborn babies' [NLT], 'forced our ancestors to abandon their infants' [NRSV], 'forcing them to put their babies out of their homes' [TEV], 'they had to expose their newborn sons' [AB]. This adjective pertains to being put out and hence exposed, and here there is a particular reference to abandoned children that were exposed so that they would not live [LN].

d. pres. pass. infin. of ζῳογονέω (LN 23.89) (BDAG 2. p. 431): 'to be kept alive, to be preserved alive' [BDAG, LN]. The phrase 'so that they would not be kept alive' [ESV] is also translated 'so that they might not remain alive' [BECNT], 'that they might not be preserved alive' [Bar], 'in order that they might not live' [AB], 'to the end they might not live' [KJV], 'and they would not survive' [NASB], 'so they would die' [CEV, NET, NLT], 'so that they would die' [NIV, NRSV, REB, TEV], 'so that they should not survive' [CBC], 'where they would die' [GW], 'to die' [NCV]. This verb means to cause to continue to live [LN]. It means to be caused to remain alive [BDAG].

QUESTION—Why did this king of Egypt not want the infants kept alive?

This king of Egypt was afraid that the Israelites were becoming too numerous and too powerful, so he ordered his people to throw the Israelites' newborn baby boys into the Nile River so that they would not stay alive (Exodus 1:8–22) [NAC, TRT]. The adjective ἔκθετα 'exposed' is the meaning here and infanticide is the goal as an order by Pharaoh, as the final phrase 'so they not be kept alive' indicates [BECNT, NAC, NICNT, TNTC].

DISCOURSE UNIT—7:20–29 [NICNT]. The topic is Moses' early days.

7:20 At this time Moses was-born, and he-was beautiful[a] to-God. And he-was-brought-up-(for)[b] three months in his father's[c] house.

LEXICON—a. ἀστεῖος (LN 79.11) (BDAG p. 145): 'beautiful' [ESV, NET, NLT, NRSV], 'very beautiful' [CEV, GW, NCV, TEV], 'exceeding fair' [KJV], 'lovely' [NASB], 'splendid' [Bar], 'attractive' [LN], 'well-bred' [BDAG]. The phrase 'he was beautiful to God' is also translated 'he was no ordinary child' [NIV], 'he was no ordinary child before God' [BECNT], 'he was a fine child, and pleasing to God' [CBC; REB], 'he found favor in the sight of God' [AB]. This adjective pertains to being beautiful or attractive in terms of being well-formed [LN]. Although his shepherd background would be a mark of ill-breeding to Egyptians, God considers him a person of refined status, a perspective developed in the narrative that follows [BDAG].

b. aorist pass.. indic. of ἀνατρέφω (LN 35.51) (BDAG a. p. 74): 'to be brought up' [BDAG, BECNT, LN; ESV, NET, NRSV], 'to be raised' [LN], 'to be reared' [LN], 'to be cared for' [AB, Bar, BDAG; NCV, NIV, NLT, TEV], 'to be taken care of' [CEV, GW], 'to be nourished up' [KJV], 'to be nurtured' [NASB], 'to be nursed' [CBC; REB], 'to be trained' [BDAG]. This verb means to raise a child to maturity by providing for physical and psychological needs [LN]. It means to provide nurture [BDAG].

c. πατήρ (LN 10.14): 'father' [AB, Bar, BECNT, CBC, LN; ESV, KJV, NASB, NCV, NET, NIV, NRSV, REB]. The phrase 'he was brought up for three months in his father's house' is also translated 'for three months his parents took care of him in their home' [CEV], 'His parents took care of him for three months' [GW], 'His parents cared for him at home for three months' [NLT], 'He was cared for at home for three months' [TEV]. This noun denotes one's biological male parent [LN].

QUESTION—What is meant by the phrase 'he was beautiful to God'?

This phrase refers to Moses' appearance, and it means that 'Moses was exceptionally beautiful, a very fine child'. His physical appearance is mentioned in Exodus 2:2 and Hebrews 11:23 [TRT]. It may be a Hebrew idiom meaning that he was a very fine child or it may mean that Moses found favor with God [TNTC]. Moses was well formed or of favored status before God [BECNT]. The addition of the phrase 'to God' or 'before God' was evidently a way of forming a strong superlative [BECNT, TH].

7:21 **And after he-had-been-put-out-of**[a] **(his home), Pharaoh's daughter adopted**[b] **him and raised**[c] **him as her own son.**

LEXICON—a. aorist pass. participle of ἐκτίθημι (LN 85.46) (BDAG 1. p. 310): 'to be put out of' [LN], 'to be abandoned' [BDAG; NET, NLT, NRSV], 'to be abandoned outdoors' [GW], 'to be exposed' [AB, Bar, BDAG, BECNT, CBC; ESV, REB], 'to be left outside' [CEV], 'to be cast out' [KJV], 'to be set outside' [NASB], 'to be put outside' [NCV], 'to be placed outside' [NIV], 'to be put out of one's home' [TEV]. This verb means to put or place something out of an area [LN]. It means to withdraw support or protection [BDAG].
  b. aorist mid. indic. of ἀναιρέω (LN 35.53) (BDAG 3. p. 64): 'to adopt' [CBC, LN; ESV, GW, NCV, NET, NLT, NRSV, REB, TEV], 'to take' [AB; NIV], 'to take up' [Bar, BDAG; KJV], 'to take away' [NASB], 'to carry off' [BECNT], 'to find' [CEV], 'to claim (for oneself)' [BDAG]. This verb means to formally and legally declare that someone who is not one's own child is henceforth to be treated and cared for as one's own child, including complete rights of inheritance [LN]. It means to take up for oneself [BDAG].
  c. aorist mid. indic. of ἀνατρέφω (LN 35.51) (BDAG b. p. 74) 'to raise' [LN; CEV, GW, NCV, NLT], 'to bring up' [AB, BDAG, CBC, LN; ESV, NET, NIV, NRSV, REB, TEV], 'to rear' [BDAG, LN], 'to nourish' [KJV], 'to nurture' [NASB], 'to care for' [Bar, BECNT], 'to train' [BDAG]. This verb means to raise a child to maturity by providing for physical and psychological needs [LN]. It means to provide nurture [BDAG].

7:22 **And Moses was-instructed**[a] **in all (the)-wisdom of-(the)-Egyptians, and he-was powerful**[b] **in his words and deeds.**

LEXICON—a. aorist pass. indic. of παιδεύω (LN 33.226) (BDAG 1. p. 749): 'to be instructed' [BECNT, LN; ESV, NRSV], 'to be taught' [LN; NLT, TEV], 'to be educated' [AB, BDAG; GW, NASB, NIV], 'to be trained' [Bar, CBC, LN; NET, REB]. The phrase 'Moses was instructed in all the wisdom of the Egyptians' is also translated 'Moses was given the best

education in Egypt' [CEV], 'The Egyptians taught Moses everything they knew' [NCV]. 'Moses was learned in all the wisdom of the Egyptians' [KJV]. This verb means to provide instruction with the intent of forming proper habits of behavior [LN]. It means to provide instruction for informed and responsible living [BDAG].
  b. δυνατός (LN 74.4) (BDAG 1.b.α. p. 264): 'powerful' [Bar, BDAG; NET, NIV, NLT, NRSV], 'mighty' [BDAG, BECNT; ESV, KJV], 'skilled' [AB], 'particularly capable, expert, competent' [LN], 'strong, able' [BDAG]. The phrase 'he was powerful in his words and deeds' is also translated 'he was a man of power in words and deeds' [NASB]. 'Moses was...a powerful speaker and a man of action' [CBC; REB], 'he was a strong man and a powerful speaker' [CEV], 'Moses...became a great man in what he said and did' [GW], 'He...became a great man in words and deeds' [TEV], 'he was a powerful man in what he said and did' [NCV], 'he was skilled in planning and doing' [AB], 'he was very effective in speech and action' [BDAG]. This adjective pertains to having special competence in performing some function [LN]. It pertains to being capable or competent [BDAG].

7:23 But when he-had reached[a] the age of forty, it-entered[b] his mind to-visit his countrymen,[c] the sons[d] of-Israel.
LEXICON—a. imperf. pass. indic. of πληρόω (LN 67.70) (BDAG 2. p. 828): 'to complete' [BDAG, LN], 'to come to an end' [LN], not explicit [AB]. The phrase 'when he had reached the age of forty' [BDAG] is also translated 'When he/Moses was forty years old' [BECNT; CEV, ESV, GW, NIV, NLT, NRSV, TEV], 'when he was full forty years old' [KJV], 'when he was approaching the age of forty' [NASB], 'He was approaching the age of forty' [CBC; REB], 'When he/Moses was about forty years old' [NCV, NET], 'when he had completed the span of forty years' [Bar]. This verb means to come to the end of a period of time [LN]. It means to complete a period of time [BDAG].
  b. aorist act. indic. of ἀναβαίνω (LN 30.17): 'to arise' [BDAG, LN], not explicit [AB]. The idiom ἀνέβη ἐπὶ τὴν καρδίαν αὐτοῦ 'it entered his mind' [NASB, NET] is also translated 'it came into his mind' [Bar], 'it came into his heart' [ESV, KJV, NRSV], 'it entered into his heart' [BECNT], 'it occurred to him' [CBC; REB], 'he decided' [GW, NIV, NLT, TEV], 'he thought it would be good' [NCV], 'he wanted to help' [CEV]. The idiom ἀναβαίνω ἐπὶ καρδίαν 'to arise in the heart' means to begin to think, to think, to have a thought occur to someone [LN].
  c. ἀδελφός (LN 11.57) (BDAG 2.b. p. 19): 'countryman' [LN], 'fellow countryman' [CBC; NET, REB], 'brother' [Bar, BDAG, BECNT; ESV, KJV, NASB], 'relative' [NLT, NRSV], not explicit [AB]. The phrase 'his countrymen, the sons of Israel' is also translated 'the Israelites...his own people' [CEV], 'his own people, the Israelites' [GW], 'his own people, the people of Israel' [NCV], 'his fellow Israelites' [NIV, TEV]. This noun

denotes a person who is a member of the same nation [LN]. It denotes a person who is viewed as a brother in terms of a close affinity, in this case a compatriot [BDAG].
   d. υἱός (LN 11.58) (BDAG 1.c. p. 1024): 'son' [BDAG, LN], 'descendant' [BDAG], not explicit [AB]. The phrase 'the sons of Israel' [Bar, BECNT; NASB] is also translated 'the children of Israel' [ESV, KJV], 'the people of Israel' [LN; NCV, NLT], 'the Israelites' [CBC; CEV, GW, NET, NIV, NRSV, REB, TEV]. The Greek phrase υἱοὶ Ἰσραήλ 'sons of Israel' refers to the people of Israel as an ethnic entity [LN]. It denotes a human offspring in an extended line of descent [BDAG].
QUESTION—What is meant by the phrase 'to enter one's mind'?
   'To enter one's mind' is an idiom that suggests that God gives a thought to someone. Here it indicates that God gave a thought to Moses [BECNT, TNTC].
QUESTION—What came to Moses' mind?
   The thought that came to Moses' mind was to visit his fellow Israelites. The word ἐπισκέψασθαι 'to visit' includes more than the conventional sense; Moses intends to come out of his royal environment not only to see but to assist/care for his fellow Israelites [Bar, NAC, NICNT, PNTC, TNTC].

7:24 And seeing one (of them) being-wronged,[a] he-defended[b] the oppressed[c] man and avenged him by-striking-down[d] the Egyptian.
LEXICON—a. pres. pass. participle of ἀδικέω (LN 88.128) (BDAG 1.c. p. 20): 'to be wronged' [BDAG, BECNT; ESV, NRSV], 'to be treated unjustly' [Bar, BDAG; NASB], 'to be treated unfairly' [GW], 'to be mistreated' [LN; CEV, NCV, NIV, NLT, TEV], 'to suffer wrong' [KJV], 'to suffer injustice' [AB], 'to be hurt unfairly' [NET], 'to be ill-treated' [CBC; REB]. This verb means to mistreat by acting unjustly toward someone [LN]. It means to act in an unjust manner and do wrong to someone [BDAG].
   b. aorist mid. (deponent = act.) indic. of ἀμύνομαι (LN 35.3) (BDAG p. 55): 'to defend' [Bar, BDAG, BECNT; ESV, GW, KJV, NASB, NCV, NRSV], 'to help' [AB, BDAG, LN], 'to rescue' [CEV], 'to come to the defense of someone' [NET, NIV, NLT], 'to come to the help of someone' [TEV], 'to come to the aid of someone' [BDAG; REB], 'to go to someone's aid' [CBC]. This verb means to assist by intervening on behalf of, primarily in terms of defense [LN]. It means to help by coming to the aid of someone [BDAG].
   c. pres. pass. participle of καταπονέω (LN 88.126) (BDAG p. 525): 'to be oppressed' [BDAG, BECNT; ESV, KJV, NASB, NRSV], 'to be mistreated' [LN; NET], 'to be wronged' [Bar], 'to be ill-used' [AB], 'to be ill-treated' [LN], not explicit [CEV, GW, NCV, NIV, NLT, TEV]. The phrase 'the oppressed man' is also translated 'the victim' [CBC; REB]. This verb means to cause someone to suffer ill-treatment [LN]. It means to cause distress through oppressive means [BDAG].

d. aorist act. participle of πατάσσω (LN 20.73) (BDAG 1.c. p. 786): 'to strike down' [BDAG, CBC, LN; ESV, NASB, NET, NRSV, REB], 'to strike' [BECNT], 'to slay' [BDAG, LN], 'to kill' [AB; CEV, GW, NCV, NIV, NLT, TEV], 'to smite' [Bar; KJV]. This verb means to slay by means of a mortal blow or disease [LN]. It means to physically strike a blow that kills [BDAG].

QUESTION—Who was 'the oppressed man'?
The oppressed man was one of the Israelites, not an Egyptian [Bar, NAC, TH, TNTC].

7:25 **And he-supposed (that) his countrymen would-understand that God was-giving them deliverance^a by his hand, but they-did- not -understand.**

LEXICON—a. σωτηρία (LN 21.18) (BDAG 1. p. 980): 'deliverance' [BDAG, LN]. The phrase 'God was giving them deliverance by his hand' [Bar, BECNT], is also translated 'God was giving them salvation by his hand' [ESV], 'God was (together) granting them deliverance through him' [NASB], 'God was delivering them through him' [NET], 'God would deliver them by his hand' [AB], 'God was offering them deliverance through him' [CBC; REB], 'God was going to use him to give them freedom' [GW], 'God was using him to save them' [NCV], 'God was using him to rescue them' [NIV], 'God through him was rescuing them' [NRSV], 'God had sent him to rescue them' [NLT], 'God by his hand would deliver them' [KJV], 'God was going to use him to set them free' [CEV, TEV]. This noun denotes the act of being rescued from danger and being restored to a former state of safety and well-being [LN]. It denotes deliverance or preservation with the focus on its physical aspect. Here it refers to the deliverance of the Israelites from Egyptian bondage [BDAG].

7:26 **And on-the next day he-appeared^a to-them-(as they-were) quarreling and he-tried-to-reconcile^b them in peace, saying, 'Men, you-are fellow-countrymen. Why do-you-injure^c one-another?'**

LEXICON—a. aorist pass. indic. of ὁράω (LN 24.1) (BDAG A.1.d. p. 719): 'to appear' [BDAG], 'to be seen' [LN], 'to become visible' [BDAG]. The clause ὤφθη αὐτοῖς μαχομένοις 'he appeared to them as they were quarreling' [BECNT; ESV] is also translated 'he appeared to them as they were fighting' [Bar], 'he appeared to them as they were fighting together' [NASB], 'he visited them again and saw two men of Israel fighting' [NLT], 'he came upon two of them fighting' [CBC; REB], 'he came to some of them as they were quarreling' [NRSV], 'Moses saw two of-his-own-people/Israelites/men-of-Israel/men fighting' [CEV, GW, NCV, NET], 'he saw two Israelites fighting' [TEV], 'he showed himself unto them' [KJV], 'he showed himself to (two of) them while they fought with each other' [AB], 'Moses came upon two Israelites who were fighting' [NIV]. This verb means to see [LN]. It means to become visible or appear [BDAG].

b. imperf. act. indic. of συναλλάσσω (LN 40.1) (BDAG p. 965): 'to reconcile' [AB, BDAG, Bar, BECNT, LN; ESV, NASB, NIV, NRSV], 'to make things right with one another' [LN]. The phrase 'he tried to reconcile them in peace' is also translated 'he tried to make peace between them' [LN; GW, NCV, TEV], 'Moses...tried to make peace between them' [NET], 'he tried to make them stop' [CEV], 'he...would have set them at one again' [KJV], 'he...tried to persuade them to make up their quarrel' [REB], 'He tried to be a peacemaker' [NLT], 'he tried to bring them to make up their quarrel' [CBC]. This verb means to reestablish proper friendly interpersonal relations after these have been disrupted or broken [LN]. He was putting pressure on them to reconcile them so that they would be peaceful [BDAG].

c. pres. act. indic. of ἀδικέω (LN 20.25) (BDAG 1.c. p. 20): 'to injure' [NASB], 'to hurt' [LN; NCV, NET, NIV], 'to harm' [LN], 'to be cruel' [CEV], 'to wrong someone' [Bar; ESV, KJV, NRSV], 'to do wrong to someone' [BDAG], 'to treat unfairly' [GW], 'to treat unjustly' [AB, BDAG], 'to treat unrighteously' [BECNT], 'to ill-treat' [CBC; REB]. The phrase 'Why do you injure one another' is also translated 'Why are you fighting each other' [NLT], 'why are you fighting like this' [TEV]. This verb means to hurt or to harm, with the implication of doing something which is wrong and undeserved [LN]. It means to do wrong to someone [BDAG].

7:27 But the-one who-was-injuring (his) neighbor pushed- him -away, saying, 'Who made[a] you a-ruler and a-judge over us? **7:28** (Do) you want to-kill[b] me as you-killed the Egyptian yesterday?'

LEXICON—a. aorist act. indic. of καθίστημι (LN 37.104) (BDAG 2.b. p. 492): 'to appoint' [BDAG, LN], 'to put in charge of, to designate' [LN], 'to authorize' [BDAG]. The phrase 'Who made you a ruler and a judge over us' [ESV, NRSV] is also translated 'Who made you our ruler and judge' [CEV, GW, NCV], 'Who made thee a ruler and a judge over us' [KJV], 'Who made you a ruler and judge over us' [BECNT; NASB, NET, NLT], 'Who made you ruler and judge over us' [NIV, REB, TEV], 'Who has made you a ruler and judge over us' [AB], 'Who appointed you a ruler and judge over us' [Bar], 'Who set you up as a ruler and judge over us' [CBC]. This verb means to assign someone a position of authority over others [BDAG, LN].

b. aorist act. infin. of ἀναιρέω (LN 20.71) (BDAG 2. p. 64): 'to kill' [AB, Bar, BECNT, CBC, LN; all versions], 'to execute' [LN], 'to do away with, to destroy' [BDAG]. This verb means to get rid of someone by execution, often with legal or quasi-legal procedures [LN]. This verb means to get rid of someone by execution [BDAG, LN], often with legal or quasi-legal procedures [LN].

QUESTION—Why did the man who was injuring his neighbor push Moses away?

This action indicated that the man who was injuring his neighbor rejected Moses' attempt to stop the fight [NAC]. His rejection was both physical and verbal [PNTC]. Others think that probably the phrase 'pushed him away' is an idiom which meant that the man rejected Moses' intervention verbally, not physically [NAC, PNTC, TNTC, TRT].

7:29 And Moses fled^a at this remark^b and he-became an-alien^c in (the)-land of-Midian, where he-became-(the)-father-of two sons.

LEXICON—a. aorist act. indic. of φεύγω (LN 15.61) (BDAG 1. p. 1052): 'to flee' [AB, Bar, BDAG, BECNT, CBC, LN; all versions except CEV, GW, NCV], 'to run away' [LN; CEV], 'to leave quickly' [GW], 'to leave' [NCV]. This verb means to move quickly from a point or area in order to avoid presumed danger or difficulty [LN]. It means to seek safety in flight [BDAG].

b. λόγος (LN 33.98) (BDAG 1.a.γ. p. 600): 'remark' [NASB], 'retort' [BECNT; ESV], 'word, statement' [AB, Bar, LN], 'assertion, declaration, statement' [BDAG], 'saying' [LN; KJV]. The phrase 'Moses fled at this remark' is also translated 'When Moses heard this, he ran away' [CEV], 'After he said that, Moses quickly left' [GW], 'When Moses heard him say this, he left Egypt' [NCV], 'When the man said this, Moses fled' [NET], 'When Moses heard this, he fled' [NIV, TEV], 'When Moses heard that, he fled' [NLT], 'When he heard this, Moses fled' [NRSV], 'At this Moses fled' [CBC; REB]. This noun denotes that which has been stated or said, with primary focus upon the content of the communication [LN]. It denotes an individual declaration or remark [BDAG].

c. πάροικος (LN 11.77) (BDAG p. 779): 'alien' [AB, Bar, LN; NASB], 'stranger' [BDAG, LN; KJV, NCV], 'temporary resident' [LN], 'exile' [BECNT; ESV], 'foreigner' [GW, NET, NIV, NLT], 'resident alien' [NRSV]. The phrase 'Moses fled…and became a stranger in the land of Midian' is also translated 'he ran away to live in the country of Midian' [CEV], 'Moses fled…and settled in Midianite territory' [CBC; REB], 'he fled from Egypt and went to live in the land of Midian' [TEV]. This noun denotes a person who for a period of time lives in a place which is not his normal residence [LN]. It describes being a resident foreigner [BDAG].

QUESTION—Why did Moses flee from Egypt?

Moses fled from Egypt because he was afraid that the Egyptians would soon find out that he had killed an Egyptian and have him executed [CBC, NICNT, TNTC, TRT]. The complete failure of his fellow Israelites to understand his intentions, and their rejection of him, had put his life in danger so that he was forced to flee [AB, Bar, NAC].

QUESTION—Where was the land of Midian?
The land of Midian was located east of the Red Sea, more than 100 miles or 160 kilometers from Egypt [TRT], on the east coast of the Gulf of Aqaba [Bar, BECNT], south of Edom [BECNT].

DISCOURSE UNIT—7:30–34 [NICNT]. The topic is the call of Moses.

7:30 **And after forty years had-passed, an-angel appeared to-him in the wilderness[a] of Mount Sinai, in (a)-flame of-fire[b] in-a-bush.[c]**

- LEXICON—a. ἔρημος (LN 1.86) (BDAG 2. p. 392): 'wilderness' [Bar, BDAG, BECNT, LN; ESV, KJV, NASB, NRSV], 'desert' [BDAG, CBC, LN; CEV, GW, NCV, NET, NIV, NLT, REB, TEV], not explicit [AB]. This noun denotes a largely uninhabited region [BDAG, LN], normally with sparse vegetation [LN]. It denotes an uninhabited region or locality. Here it refers to the Arabian Desert [BDAG].
- b. πῦρ (LN 2.3) (BDAG 1.b. p. 898): 'fire' [BDAG, LN]. The phrase 'in a flame of fire in a bush' [BECNT; ESV, KJV] is also translated 'in the flame of a burning bush' [CBC; NET, NLT, NRSV, REB], 'in the flames of a burning bush' [GW, NCV, NIV, TEV], 'in the flame of a burning thorn bush' [AB; NASB], 'in a fiery flame in a bush' [Bar], 'from a burning bush' [CEV]. This noun denotes fire or something that is on fire and therefore burning [LN]. It denotes a fire that is heavenly in origin and nature [BDAG].
- c. βάτος (LN 3.16) (BDAG p. 137): 'bush' [Bar, BECNT, CBC, LN; all versions except NASB], 'thorn bush' [AB, BDAG, LN; NASB]. This noun denotes any type of thorn bush or shrub [LN]. It denotes a spiny or thorny shrub [BDAG].

QUESTION—Why was Moses in the wilderness?
According to Exodus 3:1, Moses was tending a flock and led the flock to the far side of the wilderness/desert where he came to Horeb, the mountain of God [TRT]. In Biblical accounts Mount Horeb and Mount Sinai are identified as the same mountain [AB, BECNT, TH, TRT]. Sinai was not in Midianite territory but on the other side of the Gulf of Aqaba [Bar]. A wilderness is a large dry area where few plants grow and few people live. Although the wilderness could not be farmed, people did take their livestock there to graze [TRT] in that uninhabited area [TH].

QUESTION—Who appeared to Moses?
An angel appeared to Moses. It is understood that the angel is God's messenger [AB, BECNT, NAC, NICNT, TNTC]. Angels appear in God's service and for the benefit of his people but it is God who speaks [Bar].

7:31 And when Moses saw-(it), he-was-amazed-at[a] the sight. And as-he-approached to-look-(more)-closely,[b] (there) came (the)-voice of-(the)-Lord: **7:32** 'I-(am) the God of-your fathers,[c] the God of-Abraham and Isaac and Jacob.' And Moses trembled[d] and did- not -dare[e] to-look.

LEXICON—a. imperf. act. indic. of θαυμάζω (LN 25.213) (BDAG 1.b.α. p. 444): 'to be amazed at' [CBC, LN; ESV, NET, NIV, NLT, NRSV, REB], 'to be amazed by' [TEV], 'to be amazed' [LN; NCV], 'to wonder at' [AB, BDAG, BECNT, LN; KJV], 'to marvel at' [Bar, BDAG, LN, NASB], 'to admire' [BDAG], 'to be surprised' [CEV, GW]. This verb means to wonder or marvel at some event or object [LN]. It means to be extraordinarily impressed or disturbed by something, to wonder [BDAG].

    b. aorist act. infin. of κατανοέω (LN 30.4, 32.12) (BDAG 2. p. 522): 'to look more closely' [NASB, NIV, REB], 'to look closely' [Bar, CBC], 'to look closer' [NCV], 'to take a closer look' [NLT], 'to get a better look' [CEV, TEV], 'to look' [AB; ESV, GW, NRSV], 'to see' [BECNT], 'to behold' [KJV], 'to investigate' [NET], 'to consider closely, to think about very carefully' [LN (30.4)], 'to look at (with reflection), to consider, to contemplate' [BDAG]. This verb means to give very careful consideration to some matter' [LN (30.4)]. This verb means to come to a clear and definite understanding of something [LN (32.12)]. It means to look at in a reflective manner [BDAG].

    c. πατήρ (LN 10.20): 'father' [AB, Bar, BECNT, CBC; ESV, KJV, NASB, NIV, REB], 'forefather' [LN; NET], 'ancestor' [LN; CEV, GW, NCV, NLT, NRSV, TEV. This noun denotes a person several preceding generations removed from the reference person [LN].

    d. ἔντρομος (LN 16.6) (BDAG p. 341): 'trembling' [BDAG, LN], 'shaking, quivering' [LN]. The word 'trembled' [ESV, KJV] is also translated 'began to tremble' [AB; GW, NET, NRSV], 'trembled with fright' [Bar], 'trembled with fear' [NIV, TEV], 'shook with fear' [NASB], 'shook with terror' [NLT], 'started shaking all over' [CEV], 'began to shake with fear' [NCV], 'became terrified' [BECNT], 'was terrified' [CBC; REB]. This adjective describes one who is shaking or trembling, often with the implication of fear and/or consternation [LN]. It pertains to being in a quivering condition because of exposure to an overwhelming circumstance [BDAG].

    e. imperf. act. indic. of τολμάω (LN 25.161) (BDAG a.α. p. 1010): 'to dare' [AB, Bar, BDAG, BECNT, CBC, LN; all versions except NASB, NCV], 'to have the courage, to be brave enough' [BDAG], 'to venture' [NASB]. The phrase 'did not dare to look' is also translated 'was afraid to look' [NCV]. This verb means to be so bold as to challenge or defy possible danger or opposition [LN].

7:33 And the Lord said to-him, 'Untie[a] the sandal(s) from-your feet, for the place on which you-are-standing is holy[b] ground. **7:34** I-have seen the oppression[c] of my people in Egypt and have-heard their groaning,[d] and I-have-come-down to-deliver[e] them. And now come, I-will-send you to Egypt.'

LEXICON—a. aorist act. impera. of λύω (LN 18.18) (BDAG 2.a. p. 607): 'to untie' [BDAG, LN], 'to loosen' [LN]. The phrase 'untie the sandals from your feet' is also translated 'Take off the sandals from your feet' [ESV, NASB, NRSV], 'Loosen the sandals on your feet' [BECNT], 'Take off your sandals' [CEV, GW, NCV, NIV, NLT, REB], 'Take the sandals off your feet' [NET], 'Take your sandals off' [TEV], 'Take off the shoes you are wearing' [Bar], 'Take off your shoes' [AB, CBC], 'Put off thy shoes from thy feet' [KJV]. This verb means to reverse the result of tying by untying [LN]. It means to set free something tied or similarly constrained [BDAG].

b. ἅγιος (LN 88.24) (BDAG 1.a.α. p. 10): 'holy' [BDAG, LN], 'sacred, dedicated to God' [BDAG], 'pure, divine' [LN], [BDAG]. The phrase 'holy ground' [AB, Bar, BECNT, CBC; all versions except CEV] is also translated 'holy' [CEV]. This adjective pertains to being holy in the sense of superior moral qualities and possessing certain essentially divine qualities in contrast with what is human [LN]. It pertains to being dedicated or consecrated to the service of God [BDAG].

c. κάκωσις (LN 20.12) (BDAG p. 502): 'oppression' [BDAG; NASB, NIV, NLT], 'affliction' [ESV, KJV], 'suffering' [CEV, NET, TEV], 'trouble' [NCV], 'persecution' [AB], 'mistreatment' [BDAG; NRSV], 'ill-treatment' [Bar, BECNT], 'harm' [LN]. The phrase 'I have seen the oppression of my people in Egypt' is also translated 'I've seen how my people are mistreated in Egypt' [GW], 'I have…seen how my people are oppressed in Egypt' [CBC; REB], 'I have seen the harming of my people in Egypt, I have seen the harm done to my people in Egypt, I have seen how the people in Egypt harmed my people' [LN]. This noun denotes the harm or injury inflicted on someone or something [LN].

d. στεναγμός (LN 25.143) (BDAG p. 942): 'groaning' [Bar, BDAG, BECNT; ESV, GW, KJV, NET, NIV, NRSV], 'groan/groans' [AB, BDAG, CBC, LN; CEV, NASB, NLT, REB, TEV], 'sigh' [BDAG, LN], 'cry' [NCV]. This noun denotes groaning or sighing resulting from deep concern or stress [LN]. It denotes an involuntary expression of great concern or stress [BDAG].

e. aorist mid. infin. of ἐξαιρέω (LN 21.17) (BDAG 2. p. 344): 'to deliver' [AB, BDAG, LN; ESV, KJV], 'to rescue' [Bar, BDAG, CBC, LN; CEV, GW, NASB, NET, NLT, NRSV, REB], 'to set free' [BDAG, LN; NIV, TEV], 'to lead out' [BECNT], 'to save' [NCV]. This verb means to rescue or set someone free from danger [LN]. It means to deliver someone from peril or confining circumstance [BDAG].

QUESTION—Why was Moses told to untie his sandals?

To 'untie' the sandals means to take off the sandals, and doing that would show his respect and humbleness before God [TRT]. As God is holy and the place where God makes his presence known is holy [EBC, NICNT, PNTC,

TNTC]. The removal of shoes (probably as bearing uncleanness) on approaching a holy place was (and is) a common religious rite [Bar].

DISCOURSE UNIT—7:35–50 [NAC]. The topic is the apostasy of Israel.

DISCOURSE UNIT—7:35–43 [NICNT]. The topic is the wilderness wanderings.

7:35 **This Moses, whom they-had-rejected,ᵃ saying, 'Who madeᵇ you a-ruler and a-judge?' is the-one whom God appointed (to be) both ruler and delivererᶜ through (the)-handᵈ of-(the)-angel who-appeared to-him in the thorn-bush.**

LEXICON—a. aorist mid. (deponent = act.) indic. of ἀρνέομαι (LN 36.43) (BDAG 3. p. 132): 'to reject' [BECNT, CBC, LN; all versions except KJV, NASB], 'to disown' [Bar, BDAG; NASB], 'to refuse' [KJV], 'to refuse to follow' [LN], 'to refuse to obey' [LN], 'to deny' [AB, BDAG], 'to repudiate' [BDAG]. This verb means to refuse to follow someone as a leader [LN]. It means to disclaim association with a person or event [BDAG].

b. aorist act. indic. of καθίστημι (LN 37.104) (BDAG 2.b. p. 492): 'to make' [AB, BECNT, CBC; all versions], 'to appoint' [Bar, BDAG, LN], 'to designate' [LN]. This verb means to assign to someone a position of authority over others [LN]. It means to assign someone a position of authority [BDAG].

c. λυτρωτής (LN 37.129) (BDAG p. 606): 'deliverer' [AB, BECNT, LN; KJV, NASB, NET, NIV], 'redeemer' [Bar, BDAG; ESV], 'savior' [NCV, NLT], 'liberator' [CBC, LN; NRSV, REB]. The phrase 'both a ruler and a deliverer' is also translated 'as one who is to rule over you and to set you free' [LN], '(as one sent to) rescue the people and be their leader' [CEV], 'the one God sent to free them' [GW], 'the one whom God sent to rule the people and set them free' [TEV]. This noun denotes a person who liberates or releases others [LN].

d. χείρ (LN 90.2) (BDAG 2.b.δ. p. 1083): 'hand' [AB, BDAG, BECNT, LN; ESV, KJV, NET], 'help' [BDAG, LN; GW, NASB, NCV, TEV], 'aid' [Bar]. The phrase 'through the hand of the angel' is also translated 'with the help of an angel' [BDAG], 'with the aid of the angel [Bar], 'through the angel' [NIV, NLT, NRSV], '(speaking) through the angel' [CBC; REB], '(God had even sent) the angel to help' [CEV]. The Greek phrase σὺν χειρί (literally, 'with (the) hand (of))' means with the help of [LN]. It denotes an acting agent [BDAG].

QUESTION—Who was the one who is now speaking?

Stephen had finished quoting what God said in vv. 33–34 and was now speaking his own words again in this verse [TH, TNTC, TRT].

7:36 This-one led- them -out,ᵃ performing wondersᵇ and signsᶜ in (the)-land (of)-Egypt and at (the)-Red Sea and in the wildernessᵈ (for) forty years.
LEXICON—a. aorist act. indic. of ἐξάγω (LN 15.174) (BDAG 1. p. 343): 'to lead out' [AB, BDAG, BECNT, CBC, LN; all versions except CEV, KJV], 'to bring out' [Bar, BDAG; KJV], 'to bring forth' [LN]. The phrase 'This one led them out' is also translated 'Moses rescued the people' [CEV]. This verb means to lead or bring out of a structure or area [LN]. Here and in verse 40 it means to conduct from an area [BDAG].
    b. τέρας (LN 33.480) (BDAG p. 999): 'wonder' [AB, BDAG; ESV, KJV, NASB, NET, NIV, NLT, NRSV], 'miracle' [CBC; CEV, NCV, TEV], 'amazing thing' [GW], 'sign' [BECNT, LN; REB], 'portent' [Bar, BDAG, LN]. This noun denotes an unusual sign, especially one in the heavens, that serves to foretell impending events' [LN]. It denotes something that astounds because of a transcendent association [BDAG].
    c. σημεῖον (LN 33.477) (BDAG 2.a.α. p. 920): 'sign' [AB, Bar, CBC, LN; ESV, KJV, NASB, NCV, NRSV], 'miracle' [BDAG, LN; GW], 'miraculous sign' [NET, NIV, NLT], 'wonder' [BECNT; CEV, REB, TEV]. This noun denotes an event which is regarded as having some special meaning, and in a number of contexts it may be rendered as 'miracle' [LN]. It denotes an event that is an indication or confirmation of intervention by transcendent powers [BDAG].
    d. ἔρημος (LN 1.86) (BDAG 2. p. 392): 'wilderness' [AB, Bar, BDAG, BECNT, LN; ESV, KJV, NASB, NET, NLT, NRSV], 'desert' [BDAG, CBC, LN; CEV, GW, NCV, NIV, REB, TEV], 'lonely place' [BDAG, LN], 'grassland' [BDAG]. This noun denotes a largely uninhabited region, normally with sparse vegetation [LN]. It denotes an uninhabited region or locality [BDAG].
QUESTION—What does the phrase 'for forty years' modify?
The phrase 'for forty years' modifies 'in the wilderness' and not 'in the land of Egypt' or 'at the Red Sea' [PNTC, TH, TRT].

DISCOURSE UNIT—7:37–43 [EBC]. The topic is on the law.

7:37 This is the Moses, who said to-the sons of-Israel, 'God will-raise-upᵃ for-you (a)-prophetᵇ like me from your brothers.ᶜ'
LEXICON—a. fut. act. indic. of ἀνίστημι (LN 17.7): 'to raise up' [Bar, BECNT, CBC, LN; ESV, KJV, NASB, NET, NLT, NRSV, REB], 'to cause to arise' [AB], 'to cause to stand up' [LN]. The phrase 'God will raise up for you a prophet' is also translated 'God will choose...a prophet' [CEV], 'God will send you a prophet' [GW, NIV, TEV], 'God will give you a prophet' [NCV]. This verb means to cause someone to stand up [LN].
    b. προφήτης (LN 53.79) (BDAG 3. p. 890): 'prophet' [AB, Bar, BDAG, BECNT, CBC, LN; all versions], 'inspired preacher' [LN]. This noun

denotes one who proclaims inspired utterances on behalf of God [LN]. It denotes a person inspired to proclaim or reveal divine will or purpose [BDAG].
  c. ἀδελφός (LN 11.25): 'brother' [AB, Bar, BECNT, LN; ESV, KJV, NASB, NET], 'fellow countryman' [LN], 'fellow Jew, associate' [LN]. The phrase 'your brothers' is also translated 'your people' [CEV], 'your own people' [NCV, NIV, NLT, NRSV, TEV], 'yourselves' [CBC; REB], 'an Israelite' [GW]. This noun denotes a person belonging to the same socio-religious entity and being of the same age group as the so-called reference person [LN].

QUESTION—Who is the prophet like Moses that God will raise up for the sons of Israel?

The prophet that God will raise up to save is Jesus [AB, BECNT, NAC, NICNT, PNTC, TNTC]. Jesus is the promised prophet like Moses because he brings the ultimate revelation of God's will and leads God's people to final salvation [EBC, PNTC].

QUESTION—What is being emphasized by using the term οὗτός 'this' in each of the verses 35–38?

The fivefold repetition of the term οὗτός 'this' emphasizes that it was this Moses whom God had singled out to deliver God's people. Almost like a refrain in a hymn, Stephen speaks of this one whom God chose, thus prepares a reference to Jesus, another one like him [BECNT, EBC, TNTC].

7:38 **This is the-one who-was- in the assembly[a] in the wilderness with the angel who-spoke to-him at Mount Sinai, and (with) our ancestors. He received living[b] words to-give to-us.**

LEXICON—a. ἐκκλησία (LN 11.78) (BDAG 3. p. 303): 'assembly' [BDAG, BECNT, LN; GW, NIV, REB], 'congregation' [AB, BDAG; ESV, NASB, NET, NRSV], 'church' [KJV], 'gathering' [LN; NCV], 'assembly of God's people' [Bar; NLT]. The phrase 'the assembly in the wilderness' is also translated 'the people of Israel assembled in the desert' [TEV], 'they were assembled there in the desert' [CBC], 'brought our people together in the desert' [CEV]. This noun denotes a group of citizens assembled for socio-political activities [LN]. This noun denotes the congregation of the Israelites, especially when gathered for religious purposes [BDAG].
  b. ζάω (LN 23.88) (BDAG 5. p. 426): 'to live, to be alive' [LN], 'to offer life' [BDAG]. The phrase 'living words' [AB; NIV] is also translated, 'living utterances' [CBC; REB], 'living messages' [TEV], 'living oracles' [Bar, BECNT; ESV, NASB, NET, NRSV], 'life-giving messages' [GW], 'life-giving words' [CEV, NLT], 'words that meant life' [BDAG], 'lively oracles' [KJV], 'commands from God that give life' [NCV]. This verb means to be life productive [BDAG].

QUESTION—What is meant by λόγια ζῶντα 'living words'?
Stephen identifies the Law of Moses received on Mount Sinai as being living words of God [BECNT, NAC, NICNT, PNTC, TNTC].
1. It refers to words that give people eternal life [BDAG, TRT; GW].
2. It refers to words that are from God that tell people how to live before God [AB, EBC, NICNT, TRT].
3. It refers to words that endure and never go out of effect [TH].

DISCOURSE UNIT—7:39–53 [PNTC]. The topic is Jesus rejected as part of a continuing pattern of disobedience to God.

7:39 Our ancestors were-unwilling to-be-obedient to-him. Instead they rejected-(him)[a] and in their hearts[b] they-turned-back[c] to Egypt, **7:40** saying to-Aaron, 'Make for-us gods[d] who will-go-before[e] us. As for this Moses who led- us -out from (the)-land of-Egypt, we-do- not -know what has-happened to-him.'

LEXICON—a. aorist mid. indic. of ἀπωθέω (LN 31.63) (BDAG 2. p. 126): 'to reject' [AB, BDAG, LN; CEV, NCV, NIV, NLT], 'to thrust aside' [Bar, BECNT, CBC; ESV, REB], 'to push aside' [GW, NET, NRSV, TEV], 'to thrust from' [KJV], 'to repudiate' [BDAG; NASB], 'to refuse to listen to' [LN]. This is a figurative extension of the verb 'to push away' and means to no longer pay attention to previous beliefs [LN].
  b. καρδία (LN 26.3) (BDAG 1.b.ε. p. 509): 'heart' [AB, Bar, BDAG, BECNT, LN; ESV, GW, KJV, NASB, NET, NIV, NRSV], 'inner self, mind' [LN], 'wishes, desires' [BDAG]. The phrase 'in their hearts they turned back to Egypt' is also translated 'wanted to go back to Egypt' [CEV, NCV], 'wanted to return to Egypt' [NLT], 'wished themselves back in Egypt' [CBC; REB], 'wished that they could go back to Egypt' [TEV]. This noun denotes the causative source of a person's psychological life in its various aspects, but with special emphasis upon thoughts [LN]. It denotes the center and source of the emotions [BDAG].
  c. aorist pass. indic. of στρέφω (LN 16.14) (BDAG 1.b.β. p. 948): 'to turn back' [AB, BDAG; GW, NASB, NET, NIV, NRSV], 'to turn back again' [KJV], 'to turn' [LN; ESV], 'to turn to' [BECNT], 'to return' [Bar]. The phrase 'in their hearts they turned back to Egypt' is also translated 'wanted to go back to Egypt' [CEV, NCV], 'wanted to return to Egypt' [NLT], 'wished themselves back in Egypt' [CBC; REB], 'wished that they could go back to Egypt' [TEV]. This verb means to cause something to turn [LN]. It refers to a change of mind and direction [BDAG].
  d. θεός (LN 12.22) (BDAG 1. p. 450): 'god' [AB, Bar, BDAG, BECNT, CBC, LN; all versions]. This noun denotes any one of many different supernatural beings regarded as having authority or control over some aspect of the universe or human activity [LN]. It denotes a transcendent being who exercises extraordinary control in human affairs BDAG].
  e. fut. mid. (deponent = act.) indic. of προπορεύομαι (LN 15.181) (BDAG p. 873): 'to go before' [AB, Bar, BECNT, CBC; ESV, KJV, NASB, NIV,

REB], 'to go on before' [BDAG], 'to lead' [LN; CEV, GW, NCV, NLT, TEV], 'to go in front to lead' [LN], 'to go in front' [NET], 'to show the way' [LN], 'to lead the way' [NRSV]. This verb means to go in front of others in order to show the way [LN].

QUESTION—What does the phrase 'in their hearts they turned back to Egypt' mean?

It means 'they started wanting to go back to Egypt' as in Exodus 14:12, 16:3, 17:3 [TH, TRT]. They were not grateful for their salvation and they were unwilling to obey God. They were still attracted to the relative ease and comfort of Egypt and continued to be captivated by the idolatry they had known there, so they asked Aaron to make them idols that would be their gods [NICNT, PNTC]. It was an inward turning to the ways of Egypt. Their minds were already set on other gods and they turned to idolatry [EBC, NAC, NICNT, TNTC]. In their hearts, slavery in Egypt was better than freedom coupled with the service of God and the rigor of life in the desert [Bar].

QUESTION—What does the phrase 'go before us' mean?

The phrase 'go before us' is an idiom which means 'lead us and protect us' [TRT].

7:41 And they-made-(a)-calf-idol[a] in those days, and offered[b] a-sacrifice[c] to-the idol[d] and were-rejoicing in the works[e] of-their hands.

LEXICON—a. aorist act. indic. of μοσχοποιέω (LN 6.101) (BDAG p. 660): 'to make a calf-idol' [LN], 'to make an idol in the form of a calf' [LN; NET, NIV], 'to shape an idol in the form of a calf' [LN], 'to make an idol in the shape of a calf' [CEV], 'to make a calf' [AB, Bar, BDAG, BECNT; ESV, GW, KJV, NASB, NRSV], 'to make the bull-calf' [CBC; REB], 'to make an idol that looks like a calf' [NCV], 'to make an idol shaped like a calf' [NLT], 'to make an idol in the shape of a bull' [TEV]. This verb means to make an idol in the form of a calf [LN]. It means to manufacture a calf [BDAG].

b. aorist act. indic. of ἀνάγω (LN 15.211) (BDAG 3. p. 61): 'to offer' [Bar, BDAG, BECNT, CBC, LN; CEV, ESV, GW, KJV, NRSV, REB, TEV], 'to bring' [AB; NASB, NCV, NET, NIV]. The phrase 'offered a sacrifice' [Bar] is also translated 'they sacrificed to (it)' [NLT], 'they presented a sacrifice to (it)' [LN]. This verb means to bring an offering to something [BDAG, LN].

c. θυσία (LN 53.20) (BDAG 2.a.α. p. 462): 'a sacrifice' [Bar, BDAG, BECNT, CBC; CEV, GW, ESV, NASB, NET, NRSV, REB, TEV], 'sacrifices' [CEV, NCV, NIV], 'an offering' [AB, BDAG]. This noun is also translated as a verb: 'they sacrificed to it' [NLT]. This noun denotes that which is offered as a sacrifice [BDAG, LN]. They had to kill an animal and present it to the idol that they had made [TH]

d. εἴδωλον (LN 6.97) (BDAG 1. p. 281): 'idol' [AB, Bar, BDAG, BECNT, CBC, LN; CEV, ESV, KJV, NASB, NET, NRSV, REB], 'image'

[BDAG, LN], 'false god' [GW], not explicit [NCV, NIV, NLT, TEV]. This noun denotes an object which resembles a person, animal, god, etc. and which is an object of worship [LN]. It denotes a cultic image or representation of an alleged transcendent being [BDAG].
  e. ἔργον (LN 42.12) (BDAG 3. p. 391): 'work' [AB, Bar, BDAG, BECNT; ESV, KJV, NASB, NET, NRSV], 'workmanship, result of what has been done' [LN]. The phrase 'the works of their hands' is also translated 'what they had done' [CEV], 'what they had made' [GW], 'what they had made with their own hands' [NCV], 'this thing they had made' [NLT], 'what they themselves had made' [TEV]. The phrase 'were rejoicing in the works of their hands' is also translated 'They...held a celebration in honor of what their hands had made' [NIV], 'they...held festivities in honor of what their hands had made' [REB], 'they held a feast in honor of the thing their hands had made' [CBC]. This noun denotes the result of someone's activity or work [LN]. It denotes that which is brought into being by work [BDAG].

QUESTION—Why were the people rejoicing?
The people were rejoicing in the works of their hands. 'The works of their hands' is a Hebraic expression which here refers to idols, as it often does in the Old Testament [PNTC, TH]. Here it refers to the calf as a man-made and thus idolatrous object [Bar, EBC, NAC, NICNT].

QUESTION—What was wrong with what they had done?
The making and worshipping of the idol is a sinful act. The Jews considered this act to be their ancestors' worst sin, especially since God had just delivered them from slavery in Egypt and had forbidden them to make or worship idols (Exodus 20:4–5, 23) [EBC, TRT]. The ancestors were disobedient and unfaithful to God [BECNT, TNTC]. Sacrifice and celebration before such an idol indicated their abandonment of God's holy calling (Ex. 19:5–6) [PNTC].

7:42 But God turned-away[a] and gave-them-over[b] to-worship the stars[c] of-heaven just-as it-is-written in (the)-book of-the prophets: 'It was not to me that you offered sacrifices and offerings[d] during the forty years in the wilderness (was it), house[e] of Israel?

LEXICON—a. aorist act. indic. of στρέφω (LN 34.28) (BDAG 4. p. 948): 'to turn away' [AB, BDAG; ESV, NASB, NIV], 'to turn away (from them)' [CBC, LN; GW, NET, NLT, NRSV, REB, TEV], 'to turn' [Bar, BDAG, BECNT; KJV], 'to turn one's back on' [CEV], 'to turn against' [NCV], 'to reject' [LN]. This verb means to reject an existing relation of association [LN]. It means to turn away so as to dissociate oneself [BDAG].
  b. aorist act. indic. of παραδίδωμι (LN 37.111) (BDAG 1.b. p. 762): 'to give over' [BDAG, BECNT, CBC; ESV, NET, NIV, REB, TEV], 'to hand over' [Bar, BDAG, LN; NRSV], 'to turn over to' [BDAG, LN], 'to give (them) up' [BDAG; KJV], 'to deliver up' [NASB], 'to abandon'

[NLT], 'to consign' [AB]. The phrase 'God turned away and gave them over' is also translated 'God turned his back on his people and left them' [CEV], 'God turned away from them and let them' [GW], 'God turned against them and did not try to stop them' [NCV]. This verb means to deliver a person into the control of someone else, involving either the handing over of a presumably guilty person for punishment by authorities or the handing over of an individual to an enemy who will presumably take undue advantage of the victim [LN]. It means to convey something in which one has a relatively strong personal interest [BDAG].

c. στρατιά (LN 12.45) (BDAG 1. p. 948): 'stars' [LN; CEV, NLT, TEV], 'army' [BDAG]. The phrase 'the stars of heaven' is also translated 'the host of heaven' [AB, Bar, BDAG, BECNT, CBC; ESV, KJV, NASB, NET, NRSV, REB], 'the heavenly bodies' [BDAG; NIV], 'the sun, moon, and stars' [GW, NCV]. The idiom στρατιὰ τοῦ οὐρανοῦ 'the army of heaven' denotes the stars of heaven as symbols of various supernatural powers [LN]. The idiom 'the host of heaven' refers to the heavenly bodies [BDAG].

d. σφάγιον (LN 53.20) (BDAG 2.a. p. 979): 'offering' [BDAG], 'sacrifice' [LN]. The phrase σφάγια καὶ θυσίας 'sacrifices and offerings' [Bar; CEV, NCV, NIV, NLT] is also translated 'victims and offerings' [CBC; REB], 'victims and sacrifices' [NASB], 'slain victims and sacrifices' [NRSV], 'slain beasts and sacrifices' [BECNT; ESV, KJV], 'slain animals and sacrifices' [LN; NET], 'sacrifices and grain offerings' [GW], 'sacrifices and (other) offerings' [AB]. The question is also translated as a statement: 'It was not to me that you slaughtered and sacrificed animals' [TEV]. This noun denotes that which is offered as a sacrifice. The terms σφάγια and θυσίας 'sacrifices and offerings' semantically reinforce one another and are combined here for emphasis [LN]. This noun denotes something that is offered as a sacrifice, the victim to be sacrificed [BDAG].

e. οἶκος (LN 11.58) (BDAG 3. p. 699): 'house' [AB, Bar, BDAG, BECNT, CBC, LN; ESV, KJV, NASB, NET, NIV, NRSV], 'nation' [BDAG, LN; GW], 'people' [LN; CEV, NCV, REB, TEV], 'descendants' [BDAG]. The phrase 'house of Israel' is also translated 'Israel' [NLT]. The phrase 'house of Israel' denotes the people of Israel as an ethnic entity [LN]. It denotes a whole clan or tribe of people descended from a common ancestor [BDAG].

QUESTION—What is meant by God 'turning away'?

It means that God turned away from those disobedient ancestors, and it implies that God was angry with them and stopped blessing them [TRT]. God handed them over to the consequences of their sins [TH]. He gave them over to their own choice [Bar, BECNT, EBC]. He allowed his people to become captive to the consequences of their own evil choices [AB, NAC, PNTC] and abandoned them to the worship of the host of heaven [NICNT, TNTC]. God let them go their own way [CBC].

QUESTION—What do 'the stars of heaven' refer to?
The worship of stars is another idolatry in which the creation is worshipped instead of the Creator [BECNT]. This refers to the sun, moon, planets, and stars which the nations living next to the Israelites worshipped as gods (Deuteronomy 4:19) [Bar, NAC, TNTC, TRT]. The pagans regarded them to be either deities or the dwelling place of deities [PNTC, TNTC].

QUESTION—What was 'the book of the prophets'?
It refers to the scroll that contained the twelve books written by the twelve so-called Minor Prophets including Amos [Bar, NAC, PNTC, TRT]. The quotation in verses 42–43 is from the Greek Septuagint version of Amos 5:25–27 [AB, Bar, BECNT, CBC, EBC, NAC, NICNT, PNTC, TH, TNTC]. Stephen used these verses to prove that the Israelites were idolatrous all during the time of their wilderness wanderings [TH].

QUESTION—What do the 'offerings and sacrifices' refer to?
They both refer to the animals that were slaughtered and then burnt as sacrifices [TRT].

QUESTION—What is implied by the question 'It was not to me that you offered sacrifices and offerings during the forty years in the wilderness, was it?'
In Greek the quotation from Amos is a rhetorical question that expects the answer to be 'No' [Bar, NICNT, PNTC, TH, TNTC]. The question indicates that the people of Israel had not offered sacrifices to God but to other gods during the forty years in the wilderness [NAC, PNTC, TRT].

7:43 And you-took-along the tent of-Moloch and the star/constellation^a of-your god Rephan, the images^b that you-made to-worship.^c And I-will-deport^d you beyond Babylon.'

LEXICON—a. ἄστρον (LN 1.30, 1.31) (BDAG p. 146): 'star' [AB, Bar, BDAG, BECNT, CBC, LN (1.30); all versions], 'constellation' [BDAG, LN (1.31)]. This singular noun denotes a group of stars, a constellation, here it refers to the constellation of the god Rephan [BDAG, LN (1.31)]. Normally a constellation may be described as 'a group of stars' or 'a family of stars' or 'stars that travel together' or even 'stars that live together.' It is possible, however, to interpret the occurrence of ἄστρον in Acts 7:43 as being a reference to a particular planet (namely, Saturn) rather than a constellation [LN (1.31)].

   b. τύπος (LN 6.96) (BDAG 3. p. 1020): 'image' [AB, Bar, BDAG, BECNT, CBC, LN; ESV, NASB, NET, NLT, NRSV, REB, TEV], 'idol' [LN; CEV, NCV, NIV], 'figure' [KJV], 'likeness' [LN], 'statue' [BDAG; GW], 'that which is formed' [BDAG]. This noun denotes an object (not necessarily three-dimensional) which has been formed to resemble a person, god, animal, etc. [LN]. It denotes an object formed to resemble some entity [BDAG].

   c. pres. act. indic. of προσκυνέω (LN 53.56) (BDAG b.β. p. 883): 'to worship' [AB, Bar, BECNT, LN; all versions except REB], 'to prostrate oneself in worship, to bow down and worship' [LN], 'to (fall down and) worship, to do obeisance to, to prostrate oneself before, to do reverence to, to welcome respectfully' [BDAG]. The phrase 'the images that you made to worship' is also translated 'the images which you had made for your adoration' [CBC; REB]. This verb means to express by attitude and possibly by position one's allegiance to and regard for deity [LN]. It means to express in attitude one's complete dependence on or submission to a high authority figure. In this verse it refers to image worship [BDAG].

d. fut. act. indic. of μετοικίζω (LN 85.83) (BDAG p. 643): 'to deport' [BDAG, LN; NET],'to send into exile' [ESV, GW, NIV, NLT, TEV], 'to send away' [NCV], 'to banish' [CBC; REB], 'to carry away' [KJV], 'to carry off' [CEV], 'to transport' [Bar], 'to remove' [AB, BECNT; NASB, NRSV], 'to move to another place of habitation, to resettle' [BDAG]. This verb means to cause someone to change the place of habitation [LN]. It means remove someone to another place of habitation [BDAG].

QUESTION—What does 'Moloch' refer to?

'Moloch' is the Greek spelling of the name 'Molech/Molek'. Molech is the planet Venus which was worshipped by the Canaanites and Phoenicians as the sky and sun god [BECNT, PNTC, TH, TRT]. Children were offered to it as sacrifices [TNTC, TRT].

QUESTION—What does 'Rephan' refer to?

'Rephan' refers to the planet Saturn which was worshipped as a god by the Egyptians [BECNT, CBC, NICNT, TH, TNTC, TRT]. It refers to the worship of the Egyptian god Repa [PNTC].

QUESTION—What does 'I will deport you beyond Babylon' mean?

It means that under God's judgment, the people of Israel would be forced to leave their country and live somewhere else against their will. Babylon was the capital city of the country of Babylonia. Stephen combines the Assyrian and Babylonian captivities/exiles by quoting from the book of Amos (which is about the Assyrian captivity/exile) and substituting the city of Babylon for the city of Damascus [AB, Bar, CBC, EBC, NAC, NICNT, PNTC, TRT]. By such substitution, Stephen might want to reflect the judgment that God executed on Israel. The point is that such idolatry is a pattern of Israelite behavior and that it results in national judgment [AB, BECNT, CBC, EBC, NAC, NICNT]. Stephen's only concern is that idolatry is to be punished by exile [Bar].

DISCOURSE UNIT—7:44–50 [EBC, NICNT]. The topic is the temple [EBC], tabernacle and temple [NICNT].

7:44 Our fathers had the Tent of-the Testimony[a] in the wilderness, just-as the-one who-spoke to-Moses directed[b] (him) to-make it, according-to the pattern[c] that he-had-seen. **7:45** And having-received-(it), our fathers under Joshua brought it with them when they took[d] the land from the nations

God drove-out before[e] them. It remained in the land until the time of David.

LEXICON—a. μαρτύριον (LN 33.264) (BDAG 2. p. 619): 'testimony' [BDAG, LN]. The phrase 'Tent of the Testimony' [CBC; REB] is also translated 'tent of testimony' [AB, Bar, BDAG; NRSV], 'tabernacle of testimony' [NASB, NET], 'tabernacle of the Testimony' [NIV], 'tabernacle of witness' [KJV], 'tent of witness' [ESV], 'tent of God's promise' [GW], 'tent of God's presence' [LN; TEV], 'tent of the meeting' [BECNT], 'tent where our ancestors worshiped God' [CEV], 'Holy Tent' [NCV], 'Tabernacle' [NLT]. This noun denotes the content of what is witnessed or said [LN]. It denotes that which serves as testimony or proof [BDAG].

b. aorist mid. indic. of διατάσσω (LN 33.325) (BDAG 2. p. 238): 'to direct' [BDAG; ESV, NASB, NIV, NRSV], 'to command' [AB, BECNT, CBC, LN; CEV, REB], 'to order' [LN; NET], 'to instruct, to tell' [LN; GW, NCV, TEV], 'to appoint' [KJV], 'to show' [NLT], 'to charge' [Bar]. This verb means to give detailed instructions as to what must be done [BDAG, LN].

c. τύπος (LN 58.58) (BDAG 6.a. p. 1020): 'pattern' [AB, Bar, BDAG, BECNT, CBC; ESV, NASB, NIV, NRSV, REB, TEV], 'model' [BDAG, LN; CEV, GW], 'design' [BDAG; NET], 'fashion' [KJV], 'plan' [NCV, NLT]. This noun denotes a visual form designed to be imitated or copied [LN]. It is an archetype serving as a model [BDAG].

d. κατάσχεσις (LN 57.57) (BDAG 1. p. 528): 'to take possession of' [BDAG, LN], 'into the possession of' [BDAG; KJV], 'dispossessing' [NASB], 'taking in possession' [BDAG]. The phrase 'they took the land from the nations' is also translated 'they took possession of the land of/from the Gentiles' [AB, BDAG], 'they took possession of what belonged to the Gentiles' [LN], 'they took possession of the land from the nations' [GW], 'they took over the land from those people' [CEV], 'they dispossessed the nations' [CBC; ESV, NET, NRSV, REB], 'they dispossessed the Gentiles' [Bar], 'to dispossess the nations' [BECNT], 'to capture the lands of the other nations' [NCV], 'they took the land from the nations' [NIV], 'in battle against the nations that God drove out' [NLT], 'they took over the land from the nations' [TEV]. This noun denotes the act of taking possession of something [BDAG, LN].

e. πρόσωπον (LN 83.33) (BDAG 1.b.β.ℵ. p. 888): 'before' [Bar, BECNT, CBC, LN; ESV, KJV, NASB, NET, NIV, NRSV, REB], 'presence' [BDAG, LN], 'face, in front of' [LN], not explicit [CEV, NCV, NLT]. The phrase 'drove out before them' is also translated 'drove out in front of our ancestors' [LN], 'forced out of our ancestors' way' [GW], 'drove out as they advanced' [TEV], 'drove back from the face of our fathers' [AB]. This noun denotes a position in front of an object, whether animate or inanimate, which is regarded as having a spatial orientation of front and back [LN]. It denotes a personal presence [BDAG].

QUESTION—What was the Tent of Testimony?
This was the tent that contained the two stones on which the Ten Commandments were written and given to Moses by God for the people of Israel to obey. The stones were referred to as 'the Testimony' (see Exodus 25:16, 21), a testimony to God's covenant with his people. The stones were kept inside the ark that was inside the tent. That is why the tent is called the tent of testimony [NAC, NICNT, PNTC, TRT]. 'Our fathers' were those of the Exodus. The tent was also called a tabernacle. God commanded Moses to make the tabernacle in the wilderness as a place to worship Him [AB, Bar, BECNT, CBC, EBC, NICNT, TNTC].

QUESTION—Who was it who spoke to Moses'?
The 'he' who spoke to Moses refers to God [Bar, BECNT, TH, TRT, and that is made explicit in the translations of CBC; CEV, GW, NCV, NET, NIV, NLT, NRSV, REB, TEV].

QUESTION—Who are referred to as 'our fathers' in verse 45?
The 'fathers' are now the next generation of Israelite ancestors who took up their turn in the use of the tabernacle up to the time of David [Bar, TNTC]. In its mobile character, the tabernacle was a figure of God's presence in the midst of Israel, his never-ceasing, never-halted appointment for his people's salvation [CBC, NICNT].

7:46 (David) found^a favor in God's sight and asked that he-might-find/build^b (a)-dwelling-place^c for-the God/house-of-Jacob. **7:47** But it was Solomon who built (a)-house for-him.

TEXT—Rather than οἴκῳ Ἰακώβ 'house of Jacob' [NET, NRSV], 'family of Jacob' [GW], some manuscripts read θεῷ Ἰακώβ 'God of Jacob', as preferred by ESV, KJV, NASB, NCV, NIV, NLT, REB, TEV.

LEXICON—a. aorist act. indic. of εὑρίσκω (LN 90.70) (BDAG 3. p. 412): 'to find' [AB, Bar, BECNT, CBC; ESV, KJV, NASB, NET, NLT, NRSV, REB], 'to obtain' [BDAG, LN], 'to win' [GW, TEV], 'to enjoy' [NIV], 'to begin to experience, to come into an experience' [LN]. The phrase 'found favor in God's sight' is also translated 'pleased God' [CEV, NCV], 'attained favor in the sight of God' or 'on whom God looked with favor' [LN]. This verb means to begin to experience an event or state [LN]. It means to attain a state or condition [BDAG].

b. aorist. act. infin. of εὑρίσκω (LN 13.17) (BDAG 3. p. 412): 'to find' [AB, BECNT; ESV, KJV, NASB, NET, NRSV], 'to discover' [LN], 'to maintain' [BDAG], 'to build' [CEV, NCV], 'to provide' [Bar, CBC; GW, NIV, REB, TEV]. The phrase 'asked that he might build a dwelling-place' is also translated 'asked that he might provide a sacred dwelling-place' [Bar], 'David...asked for the privilege of building a permanent Temple' [NLT], 'to maintain a dwelling for God' [BDAG], 'asked to be allowed to provide a dwelling place' [CBC]. This verb means to attain a state, with the supplementary implication of discovery [LN]. It means to attain some state or condition [BDAG].

c. σκήνωμα (LN 7.8, 85.77) (BDAG a. p. 929): 'dwelling place' [Bar, CBC, LN (7.8, 85.77); ESV, NASB, NET, NIV, NRSV, REB, TEV], 'temporary dwelling place' [LN (85.77)], 'house' [LN (85.77); NCV], 'habitation' [BDAG, BECNT], 'dwelling' [AB, LN (7.8)], 'house of worship' [CEV], 'permanent place' [GW], 'tabernacle' [KJV], 'permanent Temple' [NLT]. This noun denotes a dwelling, with the implication that it is a temporary duration [LN (7.8)]. It is a lodging or dwelling in which one may dwell, and it could imply that it is something that is of temporary duration. It would mean 'to provide a dwelling place for the people of Jacob'. The alternative reading has θεῷ 'God' instead of οἴκῳ 'house' and the consequent translation is 'a house for the God of Jacob. It is only with this latter form of the text that σκήνωμα 'dwelling' would refer to an actual construction or dwelling. But if one adopts the form of the critical text, then δελλινγ 'dwelling' would point to 'a place to dwell,' in other words, an area or region [LN (85.77)].

QUESTION—Is the dwelling place to be built for τῷ θεῷ Ἰακώβ 'the God of Jacob' or for τῷ οἴκῳ Ἰακώβ 'the house of Jacob'?

In Acts 7:46 there is a complex textual problem in which the critical text has τῷ οἴκῳ Ἰακώβ 'for the house of Jacob' (but in the figurative sense of 'house' referring to people). But the Byzantine text reads τῷ θεῷ Ἰακώβ 'for the God' of Jacob'. It is only with this latter form of the text that σκήνωμα 'dwelling place' would mean an actual construction or dwelling. If one adopts the meaning 'house' in the critical text, then σκήνωμα would point to 'a place to dwell', in other words, an area or region [LN (7.8)].

1. The dwelling place is to be built for the God of Jacob [CBC; ESV, KJV, NASB, NCV, NIV, NLT, NRSV, REB, TEV].

2. The dwelling place is to be built for the house of Jacob [AB, Bar, BECNT, TNTC; CEV, GW, NET].

The two readings have substantially the same meaning. A dwelling for the God of Jacob is a temple for him to dwell in; a dwelling for the house of Jacob (the people of Israel) is a place that the house of Jacob (the people of Israel) may use as a temple, that is, as a dwelling for their God [Bar]. The two readings imply the same thing – a dwelling place for God for the house of Jacob to worship God in [AB, NAC, TNTC]. The prophet Nathan at first approved David's desire, later forbade it, with the promise that David's son should build a house for God's name [Bar, EBC, NAC, NICNT, TNTC].

7:48 However, the Most-High[a] does not dwell[b] in (houses)-made-by-human-hands.[c] As the prophet[d] says,

LEXICON—a. ὕψιστος (LN 12.4) (BDAG 2. p. 1045): 'Most High' [AB, Bar, BDAG, BECNT, CBC, LN; all versions except CEV, TEV], 'Highest, Supreme One' [LN], 'Most High God' [CEV, TEV]. This noun is literally 'highest' and is used as a title for God as being the one who is supreme [LN]. It pertains to being the highest in status [BDAG].

b. pres. act. indic. of κατοικέω (LN 85.69) (BDAG 1.a. p. 534): 'to dwell' [AB, Bar, BDAG, BECNT, LN; ESV, KJV, NASB, NRSV], 'to live' [BDAG, CBC, LN; CEV, GW, NCV, NET, NIV, NLT, REB, TEV], 'to reside' [BDAG, LN]. This verb means to live or dwell in a place in an established or settled manner [LN]. It means to live in a locality for any length of time [BDAG].
c. χειροποίητος (LN 42.32) (BDAG p. 1083): 'made by human hands' [Bar, BDAG, BECNT, LN; NASB, NET, NLT], 'built by human hands' [BDAG, LN; TEV], 'built by the hands of men' [AB], 'man-made' [LN], 'made by humans' [CEV], 'made by hands' [ESV], 'built by humans' [GW], 'made with hands' [KJV], 'made by men' [CBC; NIV, REB], 'made with human hands' [NRSV]. The phrase 'houses made by human hands' is also translated 'houses that people build with their hands' [NCV]. This adjective pertains to what has been made by someone [LN].
d. προφήτης (LN 53.79) (BDAG 1.a. p.890): 'prophet' [AB, Bar, BDAG, BECNT, CBC, LN; all versions], 'inspired preacher' [LN]. This noun denotes one who proclaims inspired utterances on behalf of God [LN].

QUESTION—Who does 'the Most High' refer to?

In the Old Testament, 'the Most High' is a common name or description of God. It was also used of Zeus and was thought by the heathen to be a suitable term for the solitary Jewish deity [Bar]. It is the greatest God who is in a position on top of other gods [TH].

QUESTION—Is there any specific meaning about the term χειροποιήτοις 'a house/place/thing made by human hands'?

In Greek, 'a house/place/thing made by human hands' is in one compound word which is used in the Greek Septuagint (LXX) in a uniformly bad sense and connected with idolatry [Bar]. It is a term frequently used to describe temples devoted to idols [TH].

7:49 'Heaven (is)-my throne, and the earth (is-the)-footstool[a] of my feet. What-kind-of house will-you-build for-me', says (the)-Lord, 'or what is the place of-my rest[b]? **7:50** (Did)-not my hand[c] make all these-things?'

LEXICON—a. ὑποπόδιον (LN 6.117) (BDAG p. 1040): 'footstool' [AB, Bar, BDAG, BECNT, CBC, LN; all versions]. This noun denotes a piece of furniture on which one may rest one's feet [LN].
b. κατάπαυσις (LN 23.81) (BDAG 1. p. 523): 'rest' [BDAG, BECNT, LN; ESV, KJV, NRSV], 'repose' [NASB]. The phrase 'what is the place of my rest' is also translated 'what place where I will rest' [Bar], 'In what place will I rest' [CEV], 'Where will I rest' [GW], 'Do I need a place to rest' [NCV], 'what is my resting place' [NET], 'where will my resting place be' [NIV], 'Could you build me such a resting place' [NLT], 'where is my resting-place' [CBC], 'where shall my resting-place be' [REB], 'what kind of sanctuary for my rest' [AB], 'Where is the place for me to live in' [TEV]. This noun denotes a cessation of one's work or activity'

[LN]. It denotes a state of cessation of work or activity, and 'the place of rest' is where one rests and lives [BDAG].
   c. χείρ (LN 76.3) (BDAG 2.b.α. p. 1083): 'hand' [AB, Bar, BDAG, BECNT, LN; ESV, KJV, NASB, NCV, NET, NIV, NLT, NRSV], 'power' [BDAG, LN]. The phrase 'Did not my hand make all these things?' [Bar, BECNT] is also translated 'Didn't I make all these things?' [GW], 'Did not I myself make all these things?' [TEV], 'Are not all these things of my own making?' [CBC; REB], 'I have made everything' [CEV], 'did not my power do all these things?' or 'did not I use my power to do all these things?' [LN]. This noun is a figurative extension of meaning of 'hand' and denotes power as an expression of the activity of a person or supernatural being [LN]. The hand of deity denotes his divine power as Creator [BDAG].

QUESTION—Where are these two verses quoted from?

Stephen quoted verses 49–50 from Isaiah 66:1–2 [AB, Bar, BECNT, CBC, EBC, NAC, NICNT, PNTC, TH]. The message conveyed is that God is much greater than anything mankind can make. God is everywhere and so He can be worshipped anywhere. The leaders of the Jews put too much emphasis on worship at the temple and in that way put false limits on God. Mankind cannot cage or restrain God [EBC, NAC, PNTC, TRT]. The questions are merely rhetorical. God is not asking for information, but by means of the question form he is emphasizing his independence upon what man has built [TH]. The God of creation will not find abode or rest in a single locale that is merely a place made by humans [AB, BECNT, NAC, NICNT, TNTC]. If God has a home on earth, it is with his people that he lives. According to his covenant promise, wherever they are, there he is also [NICNT, PNTC].

QUESTION—What is meant by the words 'the earth is the footstool of my feet'?

Footstool is used here as an illustration of the greatness of God, for whom the earth/whole world is merely a small footstool [TH]. The earth is merely the place where God sets his feet [BECNT].

DISCOURSE UNIT—7:51–53 [EBC, NAC, NICNT]. The topic is the rejection of the Messiah [NAC], the indictment [EBC], a personal application [NICNT].

7:51 "(You)-stubborn-(people),[a] uncircumcised[b] in hearts and ears, you always resist[c] the Holy Spirit. You are doing just as your fathers did.

LEXICON—a. σκληροτράχηλος (LN 88.223) [BDAG p. 930]: 'stubborn' [BDAG, CBC, LN; CEV, GW, NCV, NET, NLT, REB, TEV], 'stiff-necked' [Bar, BDAG, BECNT; ESV, KJV, NASB, NIV, NRSV], 'obstinate' [AB], 'completely unyielding' [LN]. This adjective pertains to being obdurate and obstinate [LN].
   b. ἀπερίτμητος (LN 88.224) (BDAG 2. p. 102): 'uncircumcised' [AB, BDAG, LN], 'obstinate' [LN], 'obdurate' [BDAG]. The idiom ἀπερίτμητοι καρδίαις καὶ τοῖς ὠσίν 'uncircumcised in/of hearts and

ears' [AB, Bar, BECNT; ESV, KJV, NASB, NRSV] is also translated 'with uncircumcised hearts and ears' [NET, NIV], 'stubborn and obstinate in your thinking and understanding' [LN], 'be so heartless and disobedient' [GW], 'heathen still at heart and deaf to the truth' [CBC; REB], 'you have not given your hearts to God, nor will you listen to him' [NCV], 'you are heathen at heart and deaf to the truth' [NLT], 'How heathen your hearts, how deaf you are to God's message' [TEV], 'hardheaded people' [CEV]. Literally 'uncircumcised in heart and ears' means 'obstinate in your thinking and understanding' [LN].
  c. pres. act. indic. of ἀντιπίπτω (LN 39.18) (BDAG p. 90): 'to resist' [AB, BDAG, BECNT, LN; ESV, KJV, NASB, NET, NIV, NLT, REB, TEV], 'to oppose' [BDAG; GW, NRSV], 'to contradict' [Bar], 'to fight against' [CBC; CEV], 'to be against' [NCV]. This verb means to resist by actively opposing pressure or power [LN].

QUESTION—What is meant by the phrase 'uncircumcised in hearts and ears'?
  In Old Testament times, God had told the Jews to circumcise their hearts (Deuteronomy 10:16, 30:6; Jeremiah 4:4). That meant they should listen to God and obey Him [EBC, TNTC, TRT]. By telling the Jewish leaders that they had uncircumcised hearts and ears, Stephen was calling them heathens (people who do not know God). That would have been a big insult to the Jewish leaders who prided themselves in their knowledge about God [TRT]. Being circumcised, they are no more responsive to God than uncircumcised pagans [NICNT, PNTC].

QUESTION—What is meant by 'resisting the Holy Spirit'?
  The phrase 'resist the Holy Spirit' may be rendered as 'refuse to listen to the Holy Spirit' or 'will not obey the Holy Spirit' [TH, TNTC]. Stephen uses the word ἀεί 'always' to describe their resistance, that is, they are opposing God again and again [BECNT]. Stephen has been willing to speak about 'our ancestors/fathers' up to this point. Now he distances himself from them, accusing his audience of being 'just as your fathers' in resisting God [BECNT, NAC, PNTC].

7:52 Which of-the prophets did- your fathers not -persecute[a]? And they-killed those who had-previously-announced the coming of-the Righteous-One,[b] whose betrayers[c] and murderers you have now become, **7:53** you-who received the Law[d] as directions[e] of-angels and you-did- not -keep-(it)."

LEXICON—a. aorist act. indic. of διώκω (LN 39.45) (BDAG 2. p. 254): 'to persecute' [AB, Bar, BDAG, BECNT, CBC, LN; all versions except CEV, NCV], 'to harass people' [LN], 'to mistreat' [CEV], 'to try to hurt' [NCV]. This verb means to systematically organize a program to oppress and harass people [LN]. It means to harass someone, especially because of beliefs [BDAG].
  b. δίκαιος (LN 88.12) (BDAG 1. p. 246): 'righteous, just' [BDAG, LN]. The phrase 'the Righteous One' [AB, Bar, BECNT, CBC; ESV, NASB, NET, NIV, NLT, NRSV, REB] is also translated 'the Just One' [KJV],

'the One who is good' [NCV], 'the One Who Obeys God' [CEV], 'a man with God's approval' [GW], 'his righteous Servant' [TEV]. This adjective pertains to being in accordance with what God requires [LN]. It refers to Jesus who as the ideal of an upright person is called simply 'the upright one' [BDAG].

c. προδότης (LN 37.113) (BDAG p. 867): 'betrayer' [AB, Bar, BDAG, LN; NASB, KJV, NET, NRSV], 'traitor' [BDAG]. The phrase 'whose betrayers and murderers you have now become' is also translated 'whom you betrayed and murdered' [NLT], 'now you have betrayed and murdered him' [NIV, TEV], 'now you have betrayed him and murdered him' [CBC; REB], 'whom you have now betrayed and murdered' [BECNT; ESV], 'You have now become the people who betrayed and murdered that man' [GW], 'now you have turned against him and killed him' [CEV], 'now you have turned against and killed the One who is good' [NCV]. This noun denotes one who delivers without justification a person into the control of someone else [LN].

d. νόμος (LN 33.55) (BDAG 2.b. p. 677): 'Law' [AB, Bar, BDAG, CBC, LN; ESV, KJV, NASB, NET, NIV, NRSV, REB], 'God's Law' [CEV, NLT, TEV], 'Moses' Teachings' [GW], 'law of Moses' [NCV], 'law' [BECNT]. This noun denotes the first five books of the Old Testament called the Torah [LN]. It is the legal system that Moses received from God and which is the standard according to which membership in the people of Israel is determined [BDAG].

e. διαταγή (LN 33.326) (BDAG p. 237): 'direction' [BDAG], 'decree' [LN; NET], 'command, instruction' [LN], 'ordinance' [Bar, BDAG, LN]. The phrase 'as directions of angels' [BDAG], is also translated 'at the direction of angels' [BECNT], 'by the disposition of angels' [KJV], 'as ordained by angels' [NASB, NRSV], 'as delivered by angels' [ESV], 'which were put into effect by angels' [GW], 'that was put into effect through angels' [NIV], 'which God gave you through his angels' [NCV], 'as God's angels gave it to you' [CBC], 'from the hands of angels' [NLT], 'given by God's angels' [REB], 'that was handed down by angels' [TEV], 'by the mediation of angels' [AB]. The phrase 'you who received the Law as directions of angels' is also translated 'Angels gave you God's Law' [CEV], 'you who received the law on the basis of instructions given by angels' or '... on the basis of decrees delivered by angels' [LN]. This noun denotes that which has been specifically ordered or commanded [LN]. It denotes 'that which has been ordered or commanded', and in this verse it means 'you received the law by directions of angels' that is, 'by angels under God's direction to transmit it' [BDAG].

QUESTION—What is the purpose of the question 'Which of the prophets did your fathers not persecute?

This question is obviously rhetorical since Stephen is not asking for information. In a number of languages it is necessary to render this as an emphatic statement, such as, 'your ancestors persecuted every prophet' or 'there was not one prophet that your ancestors did not cause to suffer' [TH].

QUESTION—Who is 'the Righteous One'?

'The Righteous One' is a title which refers to the Messiah (Isaiah 53:11; Jeremiah 23:5, 33:15) [Bar, CBC, NAC, NICNT, PNTC, TRT].

QUESTION—What was Stephen accusing these members of the Sanhedrin of doing?

Stephen accused them of being betrayers and murderers since they had secured Jesus' death by handing Jesus over to Pilate [Bar, CBC, NICNT], and by failing to obey the laws [TNTC].

DISCOURSE UNIT—7:54–8:2a [CEV]. The topic is Stephen is stoned to death.

DISCOURSE UNIT—7:54–8:1a [AB, Bar, BECNT, CBC, EBC, NAC, NICNT, TNTC; NCV, NET, NIV, NRSV, TEV]. The topic is the martyrdom of Stephen [BECNT], Stephen's martyrdom [Bar, NAC], the stoning of Stephen [EBC, NICNT; NIV, NRSV TEV], the death of Stephen [AB, TNTC], persecution has begun [CBC], Stephen is killed [NCV, NET].

DISCOURSE UNIT—7:54–60 [ESV, GW, NASB]. The topic is the stoning of Stephen [ESV], Stephen is executed [GW], Stephen put to death [NASB].

DISCOURSE UNIT—7:54–56 [NICNT, PNTC]. The topic is Stephen's final witness [NICNT], Jesus as the glorified son of man [PNTC].

7:54 And when they heard this, they-were-enraged[a] in-their hearts and they-ground[b] their teeth at him.

LEXICON—a. imperf. pass. indic. of διαπρίω (LN 88.181) (BDAG p. 235): 'to be enraged' [LN; ESV], 'to be infuriated' [BDAG, LN], 'to be cut to the quick' [Bar, BDAG; NASB], 'to become furious' [BECNT], 'to become very angry' [AB]. The phrase 'they were enraged in their hearts' is also translated 'they were cut to the heart' [KJV], 'this touched them on the raw' [CBC; REB], 'they became enraged' [NRSV], 'they were infuriated' [NLT], 'they were furious' [NIV], 'they became furious' [BECNT; NCV, NET, TEV], 'they became very angry' [AB]. The phrase 'they were enraged in their hearts and they ground their teeth at him' is also translated 'they were angry and furious' [CEV], 'they became noticeably furious' [GW]. This is a figurative extension of meaning of διαπρίομαι 'to be sawn through' and it means to be angry to the point of rage [LN]. This is a figurative use of the phase 'be cut to the quick' and it means to be infuriated [BDAG].

b. imperf. act. indic. of βρύχω (LN 23.41, 88.184) (BDAG p. 184): 'to grind' [BECNT, CBC, LN (23.41); ESV, NCV, NET, NRSV, REB, TEV], 'to gnash' [Bar, BDAG, LN (23.41); KJV, NASB, NIV], 'to grit' [AB], 'to be furious' [LN (88.184)]. The phrase 'they were enraged in their hearts and they ground their teeth at him' is also translated 'they were angry and furious' [CEV], 'they became noticeably furious' [GW], 'The Jewish leaders were infuriated by Stephen's accusation, and they shook their fists at him in rage' [NLT]. This verb means to grind or gnash the teeth, either involuntarily as in the case of certain illnesses, or as an expression of an emotion such as anger or of pain and suffering. In translating 'they ground their teeth at him' it may be necessary to indicate the type of emotion which is involved in such an action. For example, 'in anger they ground their teeth at him' or 'they showed their anger by grinding their teeth.' It is essential to avoid an expression such as 'to grit the teeth,' which in English is a symbol of determination, not of anger. [LN (23.41)]. The idiom 'to grind one's teeth' means to express and manifest intense anger [LN (88.184)]. To grind one's teeth is a sign of violent anger [BDAG].

QUESTION—What does the reaction of the audience imply?

Stephen's speech had provoked the audience to an even greater rage [AB, Bar, EBC, NICNT, TNTC]. They were enraged in their hearts and ground their teeth at him. In the Old Testament, grinding one's teeth is a sign of hostility and rage (e.g., Psa. 35:16; 37:12; 112:10). In the Gospels it is the response of those excluded from the kingdom of God (e.g., Matt. 8:12; 13:42, 50; Luke 13:28). Here the implication is that the members of the Sanhedrin felt exposed and condemned by Stephen's argument [PNTC, TNTC].

7:55 **But he, full of-(the)-Holy Spirit, gazed^a into heaven^b and saw (the)-glory^c of-God, and Jesus standing at (the)-right-hand^d of-God.**

LEXICON—a. aorist act. participle of ἀτενίζω (LN 24.49) (BDAG p. 148): 'to gaze' [AB, Bar, BECNT; ESV, NRSV], 'to gaze intently' [CBC; NASB, REB], 'to gaze steadily' [NLT], 'to look' [CEV, GW, NCV, NIV, TEV], 'to look steadfastly' [KJV], 'to look intently' [BDAG; NET], 'to look straight at, to stare at' [BDAG, LN]. This verb means to fix one's eyes on some object continually and intensely [LN].

b. οὐρανός (LN 1.11) (BDAG 2.b. p. 738): 'heaven' [AB, Bar, BDAG, BECNT, CBC, LN; all versions]. This noun denotes the abode of the divine, the dwelling-place (or throne) of God [BDAG]. This noun denotes the supernatural dwelling place of God and other heavenly beings. In a number of languages precisely the same term is used to designate both 'sky' and 'heaven' (as the abode of God). But in many instances a completely separate term must be employed in speaking of the dwelling place of God, for example, 'where God lives' or 'where God is' or 'from where God governs.' In some languages the term referring to 'heaven' is simply 'the home above,' and in one instance a designation of heaven refers primarily to a state, for example, 'the life above.' [LN]. It is the transcendent abode that is the dwelling place or throne of God [BDAG].

c. δόξα (LN 79.18) (BDAG 1.b. p. 257): 'glory' [AB, Bar, BECNT, CBC, LN; all versions except CEV], 'splendor' [BDAG, LN], 'brightness,

radiance' [BDAG]. The phrase 'the glory of God' is also translated 'our glorious God' [CEV]. This noun denotes the quality of splendid, remarkable appearance [LN]. It refers to the condition of being bright or shining [BDAG].
  d. δεξιός (LN 82.8) (BDAG 1.b. p. 218): 'right hand' [AB, Bar, BECNT, CBC; ESV, KJV, NASB, NET, NIV, NLT, NRSV, REB], 'right' [LN], 'right side' [BDAG; CEV, NCV, TEV]. The phrase 'at the right hand of God' is also translated 'in the position of authority that God gives' [GW], 'in the place of honor at God's right hand' [NLT]. This adjective pertains to being to the right of some point of reference [LN]. To stand on the right is at the place of honor [BDAG].

QUESTION—What does 'the glory of God' refer to?

'The glory of God' refers to the brightness from God's presence. Stephen probably did not see God himself [TRT]. Stephen remains calm in the face of such anger and is granted a special vision of God's glory and to see Jesus [CBC, NAC, NICNT, PNTC]. The Spirit enabled Stephen to see a vision of heaven and face death [Bar, TNTC].

7:56 **And he-said, "Look,ᵃ I-see the heavensᵇ opened, and the Son of-Man standing at (the)-right-hand of-God."**

LEXICON—a. ἰδού (LN 91.13): 'look' [Bar, CBC, LN; GW, NCV, NET, NIV, NLT, NRSV, REB, TEV], 'pay attention' [LN], 'behold' [AB, BECNT; ESV, KJV, NASB], not explicit [CEV]. This word serves to draw attention to the statement that follows [LN].
  b. οὐρανός (LN 1.11): 'heaven' [AB, Bar, BECNT, LN; all versions], 'sky' [CBC]. This noun denotes the supernatural dwelling place of God and other heavenly beings. There seems to be no semantic distinction in NT literature between the singular and plural forms of this word [LN].

QUESTION—Stephen said to the audience around him that he saw the heavens opened. How did this happen?

The perfect passive participle διηνοιγμένους 'having been opened' expresses the present phenomenon of being open and it indicates that God himself had taken the initiative and drawn back the veil, so that heavenly realities could be seen by Stephen [PNTC].

QUESTION—Who does the phrase 'the Son of Man' refer to?

'The Son of Man' is a Messianic title that Jesus used to refer to himself [AB, NICNT, TNTC, TRT]. It is Jesus' favorite self-designation [BECNT]. This is the only place outside of the Gospels that this title is used in the New Testament [AB, Bar, BECNT, CBC, NICNT, TNTC]. Stephen is the only person in the New Testament apart from Jesus who specifically uses the title 'Son of Man' [AB, PNTC]. The description of Jesus as 'the Son of Man standing at the right hand of God' recalls Daniel 7:13 and Psa. 110:1—two texts that were linked by Jesus in his prophecy before the same Sanhedrin (Matt. 26:64; Mk. 14:62; Luke 22:69) [BECNT, NICNT, PNTC].

QUESTION—What is significant about the Son of Man being at God's right hand?
>   The presence of the Son of Man at God's right hand means that for his people a way of access to God had been opened up more immediate and heart-satisfying than the temple could provide. The sovereignty of the Son of Man was to embrace all nations and races without distinction [NICNT].

QUESTION—Why is the Son of Man revealed to Stephen as standing rather than sitting?
>   Verse 7:55 and 56 are the only places in the Bibles where Jesus is said to stand, rather than sit, at the right hand of God [Bar]. This posture has been variously interpreted. It could symbolize Jesus' readiness to welcome Stephen as a persecuted prophet, soon to enter his presence. Perhaps the vision serves to give assurance of Jesus' supportive witness in the heavenly court. Perhaps it implies a personal coming to the martyr at the time of his death, in the same way that he will come to all at the end [Bar, CBC, EBC, NICNT, PNTC, TNTC]. In this context, it is more likely to be a way of asserting the readiness of the Son of Man to act in judgment against those who deny him (Isa. 3:13, where standing is the posture for judgment). Here it is a specific warning to those who have rejected Jesus and his witnesses in the past and who are about to reject him again by killing Stephen [BECNT, NAC, NICNT, PNTC].

DISCOURSE UNIT—7:57–60 [NICNT, PNTC]. The topic is Stephen's martyrdom [PNTC], death of Stephen [NICNT].

7:57 But they-cried-out[a] with-(a)-loud voice, and covered[b] their ears and rushed[c] together[d] at him.

LEXICON—a. aorist act. participle of κράζω (LN 33.83) (BDAG 1. p. 563): 'to cry out' [BDAG, BECNT, LN; ESV, KJV, NASB], 'to shout' [Bar, LN; CEV, GW, NCV], 'to shout out' [NET], 'to yell' [NIV], 'to shriek' [AB, BDAG], 'to scream' [BDAG, LN]. The phrase 'they cried out with a loud voice' is also translated 'began shouting' [NLT], 'with a loud shout' [NRSV], 'gave a great shout' [CBC; REB], 'with a loud cry' [TEV]. This verb means to shout or cry out, with the possible implication of the unpleasant nature of the sound [LN]. It means to make a vehement outcry [BDAG].
>   b. aorist act. indic. of συνέχω (LN 24.70) (BDAG 2. p. 971): 'to cover' [AB; CEV, NASB, NCV, NET, NIV, NRSV, TEV], 'to shut' [BDAG], 'to hold closed' [LN], 'to close by holding' [BDAG], 'to stop' [Bar, BDAG, BECNT, CBC; ESV, KJV, REB]. The phrase 'they...covered their ears' is also translated 'they refused to listen' [LN; GW], 'they put their hands over their ears' [NLT]. The idiom 'hold the ears closed' means to refuse to listen to what is being said [BDAG, LN].
>   c. aorist act. indic. of ὁρμάω (LN 15.222) (BDAG p. 724): 'to rush' [AB, Bar, BDAG, BECNT, LN; ESV, GW, NASB, NET, NIV, NLT, NRSV, TEV], 'to run' [LN; KJV, NCV]. The phrase 'rushed together at him' is

also translated 'they made one rush at him' [CBC], 'they made a concerted rush at him' [REB], 'at once they all attacked Stephen' [CEV]. This verb refers to a fast movement from one place to another [LN]. It means to make a rapid movement from one place to another [BDAG].
   d. ὁμοθυμαδόν (LN 31.23) (BDAG p. 706): 'together' [Bar, BECNT; ESV], 'with one impulse' [BDAG; NASB], 'with one mind' [BDAG, LN], 'with one purpose' [BDAG], 'all' [CEV, NCV, NIV], 'with one purpose in mind' [GW], 'with one accord' [KJV], 'with one intent' [NET], 'all together' [NRSV], 'all at once' [TEV], 'one' [CBC], 'all' [AB], 'concerted' [REB], 'by common consent, unanimously' [LN], not explicit [NLT]. This adverb means with mutual consent or agreement [LN]. It means with one mind/purpose/impulse [BDAG].
QUESTION—Who were the 'they' in this verse?
   They could be the members of the Sanhedrin, or the crowd which was last mentioned in Acts 6:12, or both of them [TRT].
QUESTION—What caused such a reaction from the audience?
   By saying that he saw the Son of Man standing at the right hand of God (previous verse), Stephen was claiming that Jesus is God. In the view of the Jews, no one has the right to be at the side of God's heavenly presence, so they considered what Stephen said to be blasphemy, an insult against God. This made them angry and triggered their reaction against Stephen [BECNT, NAC, NICNT, TNTC, TRT]. Anyone who blasphemed God was to be stoned to death (Leviticus 24:16), that's what happened next (next verse) [TRT].

7:58 And when-they-had-driven-(him)-out[a] of the city, they-(began)-stoning-(him).[b] And the witnesses[c] laid-aside[d] their robes at the feet of-(a)-young-man named Saul.
LEXICON—a. aorist act. participle of ἐκβάλλω (LN 15.44) (BDAG 1. p. 299): 'to drive out' [AB, BDAG, LN; NASB, NET], 'to throw out' [Bar; GW, REB, TEV], 'to drag out' [CEV, NIV, NLT, NRSV], 'to cast out' [BECNT; ESV, KJV], 'to take out' [NCV], 'to fling out' [CBC]. This verb means to cause to go out and leave, often, but not always, involving force [LN]. It means to force to leave [BDAG].
   b. imperf. act. indic. of λιθοβολέω (LN 20.79) (BDAG 2. p. 595): 'to stone' [AB, Bar, BECNT, CBC; ESV, KJV, TEV], 'to stone to death' [BDAG, LN]. The phrase 'they began stoning him' [NASB] is also translated 'they started throwing stones at him' [CEV], 'they began to throw stones at him to kill him' [NCV], 'they began to stone him' [NET, NIV, NLT, NRSV], 'they…set about stoning him' [CBC; REB], 'they began to stone him to death' [GW]. This verb means to kill or attempt to kill by means of hurling stones, normally carried out by angry mobs [LN].
   c. μάρτυς (LN 33.270) (BDAG 1. p. 619): 'witness' [AB, Bar, BDAG, BECNT, CBC, LN; all versions except CEV, NCV, NLT], 'accuser' [NLT]. The phrase 'the witnesses' is also translated 'the men who had

brought charges against him' [CEV], 'those who told lies against Stephen' [NCV]. This noun denotes a person who witnesses [LN]. It denotes one who testifies in legal matters [BDAG].

d. aorist mid. indic. of ἀποτίθημι (LN 85.44) (BDAG 1.a. p. 123): 'to take off' [BDAG], 'to put out of the way, to put away, to remove' [LN]. The phrase 'laid aside their robes' [NASB] is also translated 'laid down their garments' [ESV], 'set their garments' [BECNT], 'laid their outer garments' [AB], 'put/laid their coats' [CBC; CEV, NET, NIV, NRSV, REB], 'laid down their clothes' [Bar; KJV], 'took off their coats and laid them' [NLT], 'left their cloaks in the care of' [TEV], 'left their coats with' [GW, NCV]. This verb means to put or take something away from its normal location and here they put their clothes at a young man's feet [LN].

QUESTION—Who were these witnesses?

The witnesses were probably the ones mentioned in Acts 6:13 [AB, TRT]. They took off their garments, probably outer garments only, so that it would be easier for them to throw stones at Stephen [TH, TRT].

QUESTION—Who was the man named Saul?

This Saul was the same one who later was known as Paul (starting in Acts 13:9) and became one of Jesus' greatest apostles/messengers. He was described as a young man at this time, probably around 30 or about 24-40 years old [AB, Bar, BECNT, CBC, EBC, NICNT, TNTC, TRT]. The fact that the witnesses laid their clothes at Saul's feet suggests that he was already the acknowledged leader in the opposition to the early church [PNTC].

7:59 And as they-were-stoning Stephen, he called-out,[a] saying, "Lord Jesus, receive my spirit.[b]"

LEXICON—a. pres. mid. participle of ἐπικαλέω (LN 33.131) (BDAG 1. p. 373): 'to call out' [BDAG, BECNT, CBC; ESV, GW, CEV], 'to call upon' [BDAG], 'to call' [LN]. The phrase 'he called out' is also translated 'Stephen called out' [REB], 'he called on the Lord' [NASB], 'he called upon God/the-Lord' [Bar; KJV], 'as he called out to the Lord' [TEV], 'Stephen/he prayed' [NCV, NIV, NLT, NRSV], 'Stephen, who prayed' [AB], 'while he prayed' [NET]. This verb means to use an attribution in speaking of a person' [LN]. It means to call upon deity for any purpose [BDAG].

b. πνεῦμα (LN 26.9) (BDAG 2. p. 832): 'spirit' [AB, Bar, BDAG, BECNT, CBC, LN; all versions except CEV], 'spiritual nature, inner being' [LN], 'breath' [BDAG]. The phrase 'receive my spirit' is also translated 'please welcome me' [CEV]. This noun denotes the non-material, psychological faculty which is potentially sensitive and responsive to God [LN]. It denotes that which animates or gives life to the body [BDAG].

QUESTION—What was the first thing Stephen did when he was being stoned?
The first thing Stephen did was to call out to the Lord Jesus to receive his spirit [AB, Bar, BECNT, NAC, PNTC, TNTC]. The term ἐπικαλούμενον 'calling out' is no accident. It recalls the exhortation of Peter that to receive salvation one must call out to the Lord (Acts 2:21). In the moment when Stephen was truly alone and his life was at an end, he turned to God and asked that his spirit be received. He explicitly called out to the Lord Jesus, his mediator to the Father, to receive him [AB, BECNT, NICNT, PNTC]. Stephen committed himself to the Lord Jesus, he articulates his belief in the divinity of Christ [PNTC, TNTC].

7:60 And falling-to[a] (his) knees he-cried-out with (a)-loud voice, "Lord, do-not -hold this sin (against)-them!" And when he had-said this, he-fell-asleep.[b]

LEXICON—a. aorist act. participle of τίθημι (LN 17.19, 85.32) (BDAG 1.b.γ. p. 1003): 'to fall' [CBC; ESV, NASB, NCV, NET, NIV, NLT, REB], 'to place, to put' [BDAG, LN]. The phrase 'falling to his knees' is also translated, 'he knelt' [AB], 'he knelt down' [Bar; CEV, GW, KJV, NRSV, TEV], 'kneeling down' [BECNT]. This verb means to put or place in a particular location [LN (85.32)]. The idiom τίθημι τὰ γόνατα 'to place the knees' means to kneel down before someone as an act of worship. In a number of cultures, kneeling does not imply either reverence or an act of supplication. In some instances translators have used a functional substitute involving a similar type of stance, namely, 'to bow low before,' but it may be necessary to use a more or less literal description of 'kneeling before' and then to place in a marginal note an indication of the implications of such an act [LN (17.19)]. To bend the knee or to kneel down is an act that shows deference to someone [BDAG].

b. aorist (deponent = pass.) indic. of κοιμάομαι (LN 23.104) (BDAG 2.a. p. 551): 'to fall asleep' [AB, Bar, BDAG, BECNT; ESV, KJV, NASB, NIV], 'to die' [BDAG, CBC, LN; CEV, GW, NCV, NET, NLT, NRSV, REB, TEV], 'to sleep, to be dead, to have died' [LN], 'to pass away' [BDAG]. This is a figurative extension of meaning of καθεύδω and κοιμάομαι, respectively, 'to sleep,' as a euphemistic expression for the state of being dead—'to be dead, to have died.' Some translators have attempted to preserve this figure of speech by translating it 'to sleep' rather than 'to have died' or 'to be dead.' Such a practice, however, has resulted in misunderstanding in a number of instances and has sometimes led to the doctrine of so-called 'soul-sleep' [LN]. It is a figurative extension of meaning in which 'to be asleep' means 'to be dead' [BDAG].

QUESTION—What was Stephen's attitude as he faced his persecutors?
Stephen knew that he was going to die from the stoning. After he asked the Lord Jesus to receive his spirit, he ended up on his knees in prayer asking the Lord Jesus' forgiveness of the persecutors who were stoning him. His words in vv. 59–60 are similar to Jesus' words from the cross in Luke 23:34 and 46

except Jesus' words were directly addressed to God the Father [AB, BECNT, CBC, NAC, NICNT, PNTC, TH, TNTC, TRT]. 'He fell asleep' is a soft way of saying that he died, not just went to sleep [TH, TRT]. To fall asleep' is an unexpectedly peaceful description of such a brutal death, but one which fits the spirit in which Stephen accepted his martyrdom [NICNT]. He was the first Christian who died for the sake of Jesus [TNTC]. The early Christians often used the concept of 'sleep' for death, an indication of their assurance of resurrection [BECNT, NAC]. Calling death a sleep occurs elsewhere in the New Testament, in the Old Testament, and in post-biblical Judaism [Bar].

DISCOURSE UNIT—8:1–3 [PNTC; ESV, NASB]. The topic is Saul ravages the church [ESV], Saul persecutes the church [NASB], persecution leads to expansion [PNTC].

DISCOURSE UNIT—8:1b–12:25 [REB]. The topic is the church in Judea and Samaria.

DISCOURSE UNIT—8:1b–40 [NICNT]. The topic is Philip.

DISCOURSE UNIT—8:1b–25 [CBC]. The topic is 'And Samaria' (1:8).

DISCOURSE UNIT—8:1b–4 [BECNT; NCV]. The topic is Saul the persecutor and the spread of the word [BECNT], troubles for the believers [NCV].

DISCOURSE UNIT—8:1b–3 [AB, Bar, EBC, NAC, NICNT, TNTC; NET, NIV, NLT, NRSV, TEV]. The topic is persecution of the whole church [AB], persecution [Bar], the immediate aftermath [EBC], persecution and dispersal of the Hellenists [NAC], Saul begins to persecute the church [NET], persecution and dispersion [NICNT], the church persecuted and scattered [NIV], persecution scatters the believers [NLT], Saul persecutes the church [NRSV, TEV], the sequel to Stephen's death [TNTC].

8:1 **And Saul approved[a] of-his killing.[b] And on that day (a)-great persecution[c] began against the church in Jerusalem, and all except the apostles were-scattered throughout the regions of-Judea and Samaria.**

LEXICON—a. pres. act. participle of συνευδοκέω (LN 31.17) (BDAG p. 970): 'to give approval to' [NIV], 'to consent to' [BDAG, BECNT, LN; KJV], 'to agree to' [AB; LN], 'to agree with' [BDAG], 'to agree completely with' [NET, NLT], 'to approve (of)' [BDAG, CBC; CEV, ESV, GW, NRSV, TEV], 'to sympathize with' [BDAG]. The phrase 'Saul approved of his killing' is also translated 'Saul was in hearty agreement with putting him to death' [NASB], 'Saul agreed that the killing of Stephen was good' [NCV], 'Saul was among those who approved of his execution' [REB], 'Saul was in full agreement with his killing' [Bar]. This verb means to decide with someone else that something is preferable or good [LN]. It means to join in approval [BDAG].

b. ἀναίρεσις (LN 20.71) (BDAG p. 64): 'killing' [Bar, BDAG, BECNT, LN; NCV, NET, NLT, NRSV], 'death' [KJV, NIV], 'putting to death' [BDAG; GW, NASB], 'murder' [AB, BDAG, CBC, LN; TEV], 'stoning' [CEV], 'execution' [ESV, REB]. This noun denotes the act of getting rid of someone by execution, often with legal or quasi-legal procedures [LN].

c. διωγμός (LN 39.45) (BDAG p. 253): 'persecution' [AB, Bar, BDAG, BECNT, CBC, LN; all versions except CEV, NCV]. The phrase 'on that day a great persecution began against the church in Jerusalem' is also translated 'At that time the church in Jerusalem suffered terribly' [CEV], 'On that day the church of Jerusalem began to be persecuted' [NCV]. This noun denotes a systematic, organized program to oppress and harass people [LN]. It denotes a program or process designed to harass and oppress someone [BDAG].

QUESTION—Who were 'all' those who were scattered?

This refers to all of the fleeing Christians who scattered throughout Judea and Samaria. The fact that the apostles remained in Jerusalem may mean that the persecution was directed primarily against the Hellenist believers whom Stephen represented [AB, BECNT, EBC, NAC, NICNT, PNTC, TNTC]. The apostles remained the leaders of the Jerusalem church in order to preserve the continuity of the community [AB, EBC, NICNT, PNTC]. The Hebrew believers may have felt a greater loyalty to Jerusalem [BECNT]. The reference to 'all' the believers being scattered is probably hyperbolic, but it shows that when a significant portion of the church is persecuted, the whole is attacked and affected [BECNT, PNTC].

DISCOURSE UNIT—8:2b–3 [CEV]. The topic is Saul makes trouble for the church.

8:2 And devout[a] men buried Stephen and made loud lamentation[b] over him.

LEXICON—a. εὐλαβής (LN 53.8) (BDAG p. 407): 'devout' [AB, Bar, BDAG, CBC; all versions except CEV, NCV, NIV], 'reverent' [LN], 'pious' [BECNT; LN], 'godly' [NIV], 'God-fearing' [BDAG]. The phrase 'devout men' is also translated 'faithful followers' [CEV], 'religious people' [NCV]. This adjective describes someone who is reverent toward God [LN]. It denotes a religious attitude [BDAG].

b. κοπετός (LN 52.1) (BDAG p. 558): 'lamentation' [Bar, BDAG, CBC, LN; ESV, KJV, NASB, NET, NRSV, REB], 'mourning' [BDAG, LN; NLT]. The phrase 'made loud lamentation over him' is also translated 'made a great lament for/over him' [AB, BECNT], 'mourned loudly for him' [GW], 'mourned very much for him' [CEV], 'mourned deeply for him' [NIV], 'mourning for him with loud cries' [TEV], 'cried loudly for him' [NCV]. This noun denotes lamentation, including the beating of the breast as an expression of sorrow [LN].

QUESTION—Who were the 'devout men' who buried Stephen?

In the New Testament, 'devout men' usually refer to Jews who carefully obeyed the Laws that God gave to Moses for the Israelites to obey [TNTC, TRT], They were worshippers of God [TH], Jewish-Christians [EBC, NAC, NICNT, TNTC], good Jews who, if not already Christians, were ready to be persuaded [Bar].

QUESTION—What did the adjective 'loud' testify about the lamentation?

It was illegal for Jews to mourn the death of a condemned criminal and this 'loud' mourning testified that Stephen was an innocent man [TRT]. Sanhedrin judgment limited the degree of mourning for executed criminals, so this loud lamentation is an indication that Stephen's death was due to lynching, not to a court decision [Bar]. It took considerable risk and real courage for these devout men to mourn for Stephen with loud lamentation [NAC, TNTC]. Mourning usually included beating the chest and wailing loudly [BECNT, TRT].

8:3 But Saul was-destroying^a the church,^{b} and entering house-after-house, he-dragged-off^c both men and women and put-(them)^d in-prison.

LEXICON—a. imperf. mid. indic. of λυμαίνω (LN 20.31) (BDAG p. 604): 'to destroy' [AB, BDAG, LN; GW, NCV, NET, NIV, NLT, TEV], 'to ravage' [BECNT; ESV, NASB, NRSV], 'to ruin' [BDAG, LN], 'to work for the destruction of' [LN], 'to harm, to injure, to damage, to spoil' [BDAG], 'to make trouble for' [CEV], 'to make havoc of' [KJV], 'to harry' [CBC; REB], 'to violently attack' [Bar]. This verb means to destroy or to cause the destruction of persons, objects, or institutions [LN].

b. ἐκκλησία (LN 11.32) (BDAG 3.b.β. p. 304): 'church' [AB, Bar, BDAG, BECNT, CBC, LN; all versions]. This noun denotes a congregation of Christians, implying interacting membership [LN]. It denotes the totality of Christians living together and meeting in a particular area, but not necessarily limited to one meeting place. Here it refers to the Christians in Jerusalem [BDAG].

c. pres. act. participle of σύρω (LN 15.178) (BDAG p. 977): 'to drag off' [AB, Bar, BECNT, LN; all versions except CEV, KJV, REB], 'to seize' [CBC], 'to pull, to draw, to drag away' [BDAG], 'to lead by force' [LN]. The phrase 'he dragged off both men and women' is also translated 'He went...arresting men and women' [CEV], 'he...haling men and women' [KJV], 'he...seizing men and women' [REB]. This verb means to drag or pull by physical force, often implying resistance [LN]. It means to drag someone away by force [BDAG].

d. imperf. act. indic. of παραδίδωμι (LN 37.111) (BDAG 1.b. p. 762): 'to put (in prison or jail)' [BDAG; CEV, NASB, NCV, NET, NIV], 'to hand over, to turn over' [Bar, BDAG, LN], 'to give up' [BDAG], 'to commit (to prison)' [BECNT; ESV, KJV, NRSV], 'to throw (into prison or jail)' [AB; GW, NLT, TEV], 'to send (to prison)' [CBC; REB], 'to betray'

[LN]. This verb means to deliver a person into the control of someone else, involving either the handing over of a presumably guilty person for punishment by authorities or the handing over of an individual to an enemy who will presumably take undue advantage of the victim [LN]. It means to hand over or turn over into custody [BDAG].

QUESTION—What is indicated by the beginning conjunction δέ 'but'?

The conjunction 'but' contrasts the activity of those who wept for Stephen with the behavior of Saul who was determined to destroy the church [TH]. The imperfect tense of the word λυμαίνω 'was destroying' highlights Saul's act as an ongoing act [BECNT].

QUESTION—Who were the men and women whom Paul dragged off?

These men and women were believers [TH], people who had responded to Jesus as Messiah [PNTC], Christians [Bar, EBC, NAC], members of the church [NICNT]. That Paul did this from house to house indicates the significant influence of house meetings of the believers at that time [PNTC].

DISCOURSE UNIT—8:4–40 [Bar, EBC, NAC]. The topic is the gospel reaches Samaria: Philip in Samaria and beyond [Bar], the early ministries of Philip [EBC], the witness of Philip [NAC].

DISCOURSE UNIT—8:4–25 [AB, Bar, EBC, NAC, PNTC, TNTC; CEV, GW, NET, NLT, NRSV, TEV]. The topic is Philip's mission to Samaria [AB], evangelization of Samaria; Simon Magus [Bar], the good news is preached in Samaria [CEV], the evangelization of Samaria [EBC], some Samaritans become believers [GW], the mission in Samaria, [NAC], Philip preaches in Samaria [NET, NLT, NRSV], the word goes to Samaria [PNTC], the gospel is preached in Samaria [TEV], the gospel spreads to Samaria [TNTC].

DISCOURSE UNIT—8:4–24 [NASB]. The topic is Philip in Samaria.

DISCOURSE UNIT—8:4–8 [NICNT; ESV, NIV]. The topic is Philip proclaims Christ in Samaria [ESV], Philip in Samaria [NICNT; NIV].

DISCOURSE UNIT—8:5–40 [BECNT]. The topic is Philip in Samaria and with a eunuch from Ethiopia.

DISCOURSE UNIT—8:5–25 [BECNT; NCV]. The topic is Philip in Samaria [BECNT], Philip preaches in Samaria [NCV].

DISCOURSE UNIT—8:5–13 [PNTC]. The topic is some Samaritans find their true deliverer.

8:4 Therefore, those who had-been-scattered went-about[a] preaching the word.[b] **8:5** And Philip, went-down[c] to the city of-Samaria and proclaimed[d] the Messiah to-them.

LEXICON—a. aorist act. indic. of διέρχομαι (LN 15.21) (BDAG 1.a. p. 244): 'to travel around through, to journey all through' [LN], 'to move within or through an area' [BDAG]. The phrase 'went about' [BECNT; ESV, NASB] is also translated 'went about from place to place' [BDAG], 'went from place to place' [CEV, GW, NRSV], 'went through the country' [CBC; REB], 'traveled through the country' [AB], 'went everywhere' [KJV, TEV], 'went around' [NET], 'went on their way' [Bar], 'wherever they went' [NIV, NLT], 'wherever (they were scattered)' [NCV]. This verb means to travel around through an area, with the implication of both extensive and thorough movement throughout an area [LN]. It means to travel or move about from place to place through an area [BDAG].

b. λόγος ([LN 33.260) (BDAG 1.a.β. p. 600): 'the word' [BDAG, LN], 'what is preached, the gospel' [LN]. The phrase 'preaching the word' [AB, Bar, BECNT, CBC; ESV, KJV, NASB, REB] is also translated 'proclaiming the word' [NRSV], 'proclaiming the good news of the word' [NET], 'preached the word' [NIV], 'preached the Good News about Jesus' [NLT], 'preaching the message' [TEV], 'they spread the word' [GW], 'they told people the Good News' [NCV], 'telling the good news' [CEV]. In many places this 'word' is 'the Christian message'. This noun denotes the content of what is preached about Christ or about the good news [LN]. Since the divine word is brought to humanity through Christ, 'his word' is used in the same sense, or it is called simply 'the word' since no misunderstanding would be possible among Christians [BDAG].

c. aorist act. participle of κατέρχομαι (LN 15.107) (BDAG 1. p. 531): 'to go down' [Bar, BECNT, LN; ESV, KJV, NASB, NET, NIV, NRSV], 'to come down' [BDAG, CBC, LN; REB], 'to go' [CEV, GW, NCV, NLT, TEV], 'to travel down' [AB]. This verb means to move down, irrespective of the gradient [LN]. It means to move in a direction considered the opposite of up [BDAG].

d. imperf. act. indic. of κηρύσσω (LN 33.256) (BDAG 2.b.β. p. 544): 'to proclaim' [Bar, BDAG, BECNT, CBC; ESV, NASB, NET, NIV, NRSV, REB], 'to preach' [AB, LN; KJV, NCV, TEV], 'to tell' [CEV, GW, NLT]. This verb means to publicly announce religious truths and principles while urging acceptance and compliance [LN]. It means to make a public declaration [BDAG].

QUESTION—Who was this Philip?

Here Philip was one of the seven men chosen like Stephen in Acts 6:5 [AB, CBC, EBC, NAC, NICNT, TH, TNTC, TRT], not the apostle Philip [Bar].

QUESTION—What is the deeper meaning of the phrase 'preaching the word'?

The phrase 'preaching the word' has an inclusive meaning of winning people to Christ, as all who were scattered were proclaiming the good news of the word [PNTC].

QUESTION—What is meant by 'going down' to the city of Samaria?

Here 'down' refers to the fact that Samaria Province is lower than Jerusalem in elevation, not south in direction. Samaria is north of Jerusalem [TRT]. In Acts, Samaria generally denotes the territory, not the city of that name [PNTC].

8:6 And the crowds with-one-accord[a] were-paying-attention[b] to-what was-being-said by Philip when they heard-(him) and saw the signs[c] which he-was-doing.

LEXICON—a. ὁμοθυμαδόν (LN 31.23) (BDAG p. 706): 'with one accord' [Bar, BECNT; ESV, KJV, NASB, NRSV], 'with one mind' [BDAG, LN; NET], 'by common consent, unanimously' [LN], 'with one purpose or impulse' [BDAG], not explicit [CEV, GW, NLT, TEV]. The phrase 'with one accord were paying attention' is also translated 'all listened carefully' [NCV], 'listened all together' [AB], 'to a man, listened eagerly' [CBC], 'all paid close attention' [NIV], 'everyone paid close attention' [REB]. This adjective pertains to mutual consent or agreement [LN].

b. imperf. act. indic. of προσέχω (LN 30.35) (BDAG 2.b. p. 880): 'to pay attention' [Bar, BDAG; ESV, NET], 'to pay close attention to' [LN; GW, NIV, REB, TEV], 'to give attention to' [NASB], 'to consider carefully' [LN], 'to give heed to' [BDAG, BECNT; KJV], 'to listen carefully to' [NCV], 'to listen intently' [NLT], 'to listen eagerly' [CBC; NRSV], 'to listen' [AB], 'to be eager to hear' [CEV]. This verb means to pay close attention to something, with the possible implication of agreement [LN]. It means to pay close attention to something [BDAG].

c. σημεῖον (LN 33.477) (BDAG 2.a.α. p. 920): 'sign' [Bar, BECNT, LN; ESV, NASB, NIV, NRSV, REB], 'miracle' [BDAG, CBC, LN; CEV, GW, KJV, NCV, TEV], 'miraculous sign' [NET, NLT], 'act' [AB]. This noun denotes an event which is regarded as having some special meaning [LN]. It denotes an event that is an indication or confirmation of intervention by transcendent powers [BDAG].

QUESTION—Who were the crowds in this verse?

They were the people who lived in the city of Samaria. In the book of Acts the Samaritans were the first non-Jews to hear the message about Christ. In 722 B.C. the Assyrians had taken most of the people of Israel's northern kingdom to their country as captives, but they had left some behind in Israel. Those who were left behind intermarried with Gentiles whom the Assyrians had brought to Israel. That resulted in the Samaritan race (2 Kings 17:24), a mixed race with mixed cultural heritage. The pure-blooded Jews hated the Samaritans and considered them to be 'unclean/impure' [BECNT, CBC, EBC, NICNT, TRT]. The Jews put the Samaritans on a level with Gentiles and had restricted dealings with them, even though the Samaritans claimed to worship the same God and follow the Law of Moses [PNTC].

8:7 For unclean[a] spirits, crying-out[b] with-(a)-loud voice, came-out of many who had them, and many who were-paralyzed[c] or lame were-healed.[d] **8:8** And there-was great joy[e] in that city.

LEXICON—a. ἀκάθαρτος (LN 12.39) (BDAG 2. p. 34): 'unclean' [Bar, BDAG, BECNT, CBC, LN; ESV, KJV, NASB, NET, NRSV, REB], 'impure' [BDAG; NIV], 'evil' [CEV, GW, NCV, NLT, TEV], 'vicious' [BDAG]. The phrase 'unclean spirits' is also translated 'spirits' [AB]. The

phrase 'unclean spirit' denotes an evil supernatural spirit which is ritually unclean and causes persons to be ritually unclean [LN]. This pertains to moral impurity [BDAG].
   b. pres. act. participle of βοάω (LN 33.81) (BDAG 1.b. p. 180): 'to cry out' [BDAG, BECNT, LN; ESV], 'to shout' [BDAG, LN; NASB], 'to cry' [Bar; KJV, NET, NRSV], 'to scream' [LN; GW, NLT]. The phrase 'crying out with a loud voice, were coming out' is also translated 'went out of them with a shout' [CEV], 'shrieked with a loud voice and left' [AB], 'made a loud noise when they came out' [NCV], 'with shrieks…came out' [NIV], 'came out with a loud cry' [REB, TEV], 'came out with a great outcry' [CBC]. This verb means to cry or shout with unusually loud volume [LN]. It means to use one's voice at high volume for uttering anguished outcries [BDAG].
   c. perf. pass. participle of παραλύω (LN 23.170) (BDAG p. 760): 'to be paralyzed' [Bar, BECNT, CBC, LN; all versions except CEV, NCV, KJV], 'to be made lame' [LN], 'to be disabled' [BDAG], 'to be weakened' [BDAG; NCV], 'to be crippled' [AB], 'to cripple' [CEV]. The phrase 'many who were paralyzed' is also translated 'many taken with palsies' [KJV]. This verb means to cause to suffer paralysis in one or more limbs, especially in the leg or foot [LN]. It means to cause to be feeble, to weaken, to disable [BDAG].
   d. aorist pass. indic. of θεραπεύω (LN 23.129) (BDAG 2. p. 453): 'to be healed' [BDAG, BECNT, LN; all versions except GW, NRSV, REB], 'to be cured' [AB, Bar, CBC, LN; GW, NRSV, REB], 'to be restored' [BDAG], 'to be taken care of' [LN]. This verb means to cause someone to recover health, often with the implication of having taken care of such a person [LN].
   e. χαρά (LN 25.123) (BDAG 1.a. p. 1077): 'joy' [AB, Bar, BDAG, BECNT, CBC, LN; ESV, KJV, NET, NIV, NLT, NRSV, TEV], 'gladness' [LN], 'rejoicing' [NASB, REB], 'great happiness' [LN]. The phrase 'there was great joy in that city' is also translated 'Everyone in that city was very glad' [CEV], 'that city was extremely happy' [GW], 'the people in that city were very happy' [NCV]. This noun denotes a state of joy and gladness [LN]. It denotes the experience of gladness [BDAG].
QUESTION—What is meant by the clause 'there was great joy in that city'?
   It means that the people in the city of Samaria were very joyful or were glad in their hearts [TH]. God's work through Philip's preaching and signs filled the city of Samaria with great joy [BECNT, CBC, EBC, NICNT, PNTC, TNTC].

DISCOURSE UNIT—8:9–25 [ESV, NIV]. The topic is Simon the sorcerer [NIV], Simon the Magician believes [ESV].

DISCOURSE UNIT—8:9–13 [NICNT]. The topic is Simon Magus believes and is baptized.

8:9 Now there-was a-man named Simon who-had-formerly practiced-magic[a] in the city and amazed[b] the people of-Samaria, saying-that he himself was someone great.[c]

LEXICON—a. pres. act. participle of μαγεύω (LN 53.96) (BDAG p. 608): 'to practice magic' [BDAG, BECNT, LN; ESV, GW, NASB, NCV, NET, NRSV], 'to practice magical arts' [AB], 'to practice as a magus' [Bar], 'to practice witchcraft' [CEV], 'to employ witchcraft' [LN], 'to use sorcery' [KJV], 'to practice sorcery' [NIV], 'to be a sorcerer' [NLT]. The phrase 'who had formerly practiced magic…and amazed the people of Samaria' is also translated 'for some time…had captivated the Samaritans with his magical arts' [REB], 'for some time, and had swept the Samaritans off their feet with his magical arts' [CBC], 'had astounded the Samaritans with his magic' [TEV]. This verb means to practice magic [BDAG, LN], presumably by invoking supernatural powers [LN].

b. pres. act. participle of ἐξίστημι (LN 25.220) (BDAG 1. p. 350): 'to amaze' [BDAG, BECNT; CEV, ESV, GW, NET, NCV, NIV, NLT, NRSV], 'to astonish' [NASB], 'to astonish greatly' [LN], 'to astound' [Bar, BDAG; TEV], 'to bewitch' [KJV], 'to captivate' [REB], 'to fascinate' [AB], 'to greatly astound, to astound completely' [LN], 'to sweep someone off their feet' [CBC], 'to confuse, to drive out of one's senses' [BDAG]. This verb means to cause someone to be so astounded as to be practically overwhelmed [LN].

c. μέγας (LN 87.22) (BDAG 4.a. p. 624): 'great' [AB, Bar, BDAG, BECNT, CBC, LN; all versions except REB], 'important' [LN]. The phrase 'saying that he himself was someone great' is also translated 'making large claims for himself' [REB]. This adjective pertains to being great in terms of status [LN]. It pertains to being relatively superior in importance and here it refers to people who are prominent for any reason [BDAG].

QUESTION—What did Simon claim for himself?

Simon claimed that he was someone great, and drew attention to himself and his work by practicing magic. He portrayed himself as being divine [AB, BECNT, PNTC, TNTC].

8:10 They-all paid-attention to-him, from (the)-unimportant[a] to (the)-important,[b] saying, "This (man) is the power[c] of-God that is-called Great." **8:11** And they-were-paying-close-attention to-him because for-(a)-long time he-had-amazed them with-his-magic.[d]

LEXICON—a. μικρός (LN 87.58) (BDAG 1.b. p. 651): 'unimportant' [LN], 'least important' [NCV], 'least' [Bar, BECNT, LN; ESV, KJV, NET, NLT, NRSV], 'low' [CBC, LN; NIV, REB], 'poor' [CEV], 'small' [AB], 'smallest' [NASB]. The phrase 'from the unimportant to the important' is also translated 'from all classes of society' [TEV], 'from children to adults' [GW]. This adjective describes someone of low or unimportant status in contrast with μέγας 'great, important' [LN]. Another view is that

it pertains to a relatively limited size and here it is a designation of all the members of a group who are like little ones, children [BDAG].
b. μέγας (LN 87.22) (BDAG 1.d. p. 623): 'important' [LN], 'most important' [NCV], 'great' [AB, BDAG, LN], 'greatest' [Bar, BECNT; ESV, KJV, NASB, NET, NLT, NRSV], 'rich' [CEV], 'high' [CBC; NIV, REB]. The phrase 'from the unimportant to the important' is also translated 'from children to adults' [GW], 'from all classes of society' [TEV]. This adjective describes someone or something great in terms of status [LN]. Another view is that it pertains to age, and when used with μικρός describes young and old alike [BDAG].
c. δύναμις (LN 12.44) (BDAG 5. p. 264): 'power' [Bar, BDAG, CBC LN; CEV, GW, NCV, NIV, REB, TEV], 'miracle, wonder' [BDAG]. The phrase 'is the power of God that is called Great' [BECNT; ESV, NET, NRSV] is also translated 'is the so-called great power of God' [AB], 'is what is called the Great Power of God' [BDAG; NASB], 'is the great power of God' [KJV], 'spoke of him as "the Great One—the Power of God"' [NLT]. This noun denotes supernatural power having some particular role in controlling the destiny and activities of human beings [LN]. It denotes an entity or being, whether human or transcendent, that functions in a remarkable manner [BDAG]. It is not clear in the Greek text whether the people of Samaria think Simon is actually God, a representative of God, a manifestation of God's power, or another god [TRT].
d. μαγεία (LN 53.96) (BDAG p. 608): 'magic' [AB, BDAG, BECNT, CBC, LN; ESV, NET, NCV, NLT, NRSV, REB, TEV], 'practice of magic' [GW], 'magic arts' [NASB], 'magical practices' [Bar], 'witchcraft' [CEV], 'sorceries' [KJV], 'sorcery' [NIV]. This noun denotes the practice of magic, presumably by invoking supernatural powers [LN]. It denotes a rite ordinarily using incantations and is designed to influence/control transcendent powers [BDAG].

QUESTION—Why did the people pay such attention to Simon?

These people considered Simon to be a bearer of God's great power [BECNT, CBC, TNTC]. They accepted what Simon apparently claimed for himself. because he had gained credence by his magic powers [CBC, EBC, TNTC]. Simon did not presume to be the supreme God, but he inculcated the belief that with all of his God-like powers he was the great one [PNTC].

QUESTION—What was it that the people paid close attention to?

In verses 10 and 11 Luke uses the verb 'pay close attention to' to describe the Samaritans' reaction to Simon's magic practices. They gave him their attention and followed him about. In v. 6, the same word had been used to describe the reaction of the crowds to the preaching of Philip. The Samaritans who had previously been captivated by Simon were now captivated by Philip [PNTC].

QUESTION—What is the function of verse 11?
Verse 11 does not add any new information that is not already contained in the two preceding verses. It is simply an emphatic repetition of the essential information [Bar, TH]. The repetition might point to a mixing of sources or to Luke's own stitching together of oral reports [BECNT].

8:12 But when they-believed^a Philip as-he-preached-the-good-news^b about the kingdom of-God and the name^c of-Jesus Christ, they-were-baptized, both men and women.

LEXICON—a. aorist act. indic. of πιστεύω (LN 31.85) (BDAG 1.b. p. 816): 'to believe' [Bar, BDAG, BECNT; all versions], 'to come to believe' [CBC], 'to have faith in' [AB, LN], 'to believe in, to have confidence in, to trust' [LN], 'to give credence to' [BDAG]. This verb means to believe to the extent of complete trust and reliance [LN]. It means to consider something to be true, and therefore worthy of one's trust [BDAG].

b. pres. mid. participle of εὐαγγελίζω (LN 33.215) (BDAG 2.a.β. p. 402): 'to preach the good news' [Bar, BECNT; ESV, NASB, NIV], 'to tell the good news, to announce the gospel' [LN], 'to proclaim the gospel' [BDAG], 'to proclaim the good news' [NET, NRSV], 'to tell about the Good News' [NCV], 'to spread the Good News' [GW], 'to preach' [KJV]. The phrase 'they believed Philip as he preached the good news' is also translated 'the people believed Philip's message of Good News' [NLT], 'they came to believe Philip with his good news' [CBC; REB], 'they believed Philip's message about the good news' [TEV], 'they had faith in Philip, with his preaching (of the kingdom of God)' [AB], 'they believed what Philip was saying (about God's kingdom)' [CEV]. This verb means to communicate good news concerning something, and in the NT it refers to the gospel message about Jesus [LN]. It means to proclaim the divine message of salvation [BDAG].

c. ὄνομα (LN 33.126) (BDAG1.d.γ.ⁱ. p. 714): 'name' [BDAG, LN]. The phrase καὶ τοῦ ὀνόματος Ἰησοῦ Χριστοῦ 'and (about) the name of Jesus Christ' [AB, Bar, BECNT, CBC; CEV, ESV, NASB, NET, NRSV, REB] is also translated 'and (about) the one named Jesus Christ' [GW], 'and (his message) about Jesus Christ' [TEV], 'and (concerning) the name of Jesus Christ' [NLT], 'and (the things concerning) the name of Jesus Christ' [KJV], 'and (the good news) of the name of Jesus Christ' [NIV], 'and (about) the power of Jesus Christ' [NCV]. This noun denotes the proper name of a person or object [LN].

QUESTION—What is meant by the statement 'they believed Philip'?
It means that the Samaritans believed that what Philip had told them was true [Bar]. They believed the good news about Christ that Philip had preached [NICNT, PNTC]. The verb εὐαγγελίζω 'preaching the good news' is used five times in this chapter: 8:4, 12, 25, 35, 40. Out of a genuine conviction that the good news about Christ was true, both men and women were baptized [PNTC].

ACTS 8:12

QUESTION—What was the good news about the kingdom of God that Philip preached?

The topic of the kingdom of God had been the focus of Jesus' teachings in the Gospels (e.g., Luke 4:43; 6:20). Now in Acts, the kingdom remains the theological context in which to proclaim Christ. The term βασιλεία 'kingdom' has been mentioned eight times: 1:3–6 (2x); 8:12; 14:21–22; 19:8; 20:25; 28:23, 30–31 [BECNT, PNTC].

QUESTION—What was the good news about the name of Jesus Christ?

Here the good news was that Jesus is the Messiah [TH]. Believing in the name of Jesus refers to responding to Jesus' power, and this wording occurs in Acts 2:38; 3:6; 4:8–10; 8:12; 10:48; 16:18 [BECNT].

8:13 Even Simon himself believed, and after-being-baptized he stayed-close-to[a] Philip. And, seeing signs[b] and great miracles[c] happening, he-was-amazed.[d]

LEXICON—a. pres. act. participle of προσκαρτερέω (LN 34.2) (BDAG 1. p. 881): 'to stay close to' [LN; CEV, NET, TEV], 'to stay very close to' [NCV], 'to stay with' [NRSV], 'to continue with' [BECNT; ESV, KJV], 'to continue on with' [NASB], 'to continue in one's company' [Bar], 'to be with one continually' [AB], 'to be constantly in one's company' [CBC, REB], 'to attach oneself to someone' [BDAG], 'to follow everywhere' [NIV], 'to follow wherever' [NLT], 'to become devoted to' [GW], 'to associate closely with' [LN]. This verb means to associate closely and continuously with someone [LN]. It means to stick by or be close at hand [BDAG].

b. σημεῖον (LN 33.477) (BDAG 2.a.α. p. 920): 'sign' [AB, Bar, BECNT, CBC, LN; ESV, NASB, NET, NIV, NLT, NRSV, REB], 'miracle' [BDAG, LN; CEV, GW, KJV, NCV, TEV]. This noun denotes an event which is regarded as having some special meaning [LN]. It denotes an event that is an indication or confirmation of intervention by transcendent powers [BDAG].

c. δύναμις (LN 76.7) (BDAG 3. p. 264): 'miracle' [BDAG, BECNT, CBC, LN; ESV, NASB, NET, NIV, NLT, NRSV, REB, TEV], 'wonder' [BDAG; CEV], 'sign' [KJV], 'impressive thing' [GW], 'powerful thing' [NCV], 'act of power' [AB], 'mighty work' [Bar], 'mighty deed' [LN], 'deed of power' [BDAG]. This noun denotes a deed manifesting great power, with the implication of some supernatural force [LN]. It denotes a deed that exhibits ability to function powerfully [BDAG].

d. imperf. mid. indic. of ἐξίστημι (LN 25.220) (BDAG 2.b. p. 350): 'to be amazed' [BDAG, BECNT; ESV, GW, NCV, NET, NLT, NRSV], 'to be astonished' [Bar, BDAG; NIV], 'to be constantly amazed' [NASB], 'to marvel' [CEV], 'to wonder' [KJV], 'to be captivated' [REB], 'to be astounded' [TEV], 'to be overwhelmed' [AB], 'to be carried away' [CBC], 'to be astonished greatly, to be greatly astounded, to be astounded completely' [LN]. This verb means to cause someone to be so astounded as to be practically overwhelmed [LN]. It refers to the feeling of astonishment mingled with fear caused by events which are miraculous, extraordinary, or difficult to understand [BDAG].

QUESTION—How did Simon react to the signs and great miracles performed by Philip?

Simon was amazed [AB, BECNT, CBC, TNTC] and the imperfect tense of the word ἐξίστημι 'to be amazed' points to his ongoing amazement [BECNT]. This same verb is used in v. 11 to describe how the Samaritans reacted to Simon. Now this magician is amazed while beholding Philip's signs and great miracles [BECNT, CBC, PNTC].

QUESTION—How did Simon react?

Luke uses the word καὶ with the meaning 'also, even'. This suggests that Simon was a special and unexpected person in making a public commitment to Christ like the rest of the Samaritan converts [PNTC]. Luke adds that Simon attached himself to Philip and followed him everywhere. Such behavior of a personal attachment seems unusual [BECNT, NICNT, PNTC]. Simon's belief in Jesus might be based only on seeing the miraculous signs, and therefore inferior to a true commitment to Jesus [EBC, NAC, TNTC].

DISCOURSE UNIT—8:14–17 [NICNT, PNTC]. The topic is Peter and John visit Samaria [NICNT], Jerusalem witnesses Samaria's reception of the Holy Spirit [PNTC].

8:14 And when the apostles in Jerusalem heard that Samaria had-received[a] the word[b] of-God, they-sent to them Peter and John, **8:15** who came-down (and) prayed for them that they-might-receive[c] (the)-Holy Spirit,

LEXICON—a. perf. mid./pass. (deponent = act.) indic. of δέχομαι (LN 31.51) (BDAG 5. p. 221): 'to receive' [AB, Bar, BECNT, LN; ESV, KJV, NASB, TEV], 'to receive readily' [LN], 'to accept' [BDAG, CBC, LN; CEV, GW, NCV, NET, NIV, NLT, NRSV, REB], 'to believe' [LN], 'to be receptive of, to be open to, to approve' [BDAG]. This verb means to readily receive information and to regard it as being true [LN]. It means to indicate approval or conviction by accepting the teaching [BDAG].

b. λόγος (LN 33.260) (BDAG 1.a.β. p. 599): 'word' [AB, Bar, BDAG, BECNT, CBC; all versions except CEV, NLT], 'message' [CEV, NLT], 'gospel, what is preached' [LN]. This noun denotes the content of what is preached about Christ or about the good news [LN]. It denotes the divine revelation through Christ and his messengers [BDAG].

c. aorist act. subj. of λαμβάνω (LN 57.125): 'to receive' [AB, Bar, BECNT, CBC, LN; all versions except CEV], 'to be given' [CEV], 'to accept' [LN]. This verb means to receive or accept an object or benefit for which the initiative rests with the giver, but the focus of the attention in the transfer is upon the receiver [LN].

QUESTION—What is meant by 'Samaria' receiving the word of God?

The location 'Samaria' is the subject of the verb 'had received', so here Samaria refers to 'people living in Samaria' and it may have to be translated as 'the people of Samaria' [NCV, NLT], 'some people in Samaria' [CEV]. Saying that some had received the word of God means that they had believed and accepted the word of God [Bar, BECNT, TH].

QUESTION—What was the purpose for Peter and John being sent to Samaria?
Peter and John were sent to Samaria to verify the surprising news that Samaria had accepted the word of God because of the work of Philip. After they witnessed the results, they were convinced that the Samaritans were truly included in the messianic salvation [Bar, BECNT, CBC, NAC, NICNT, PNTC, TNTC] and the new converts in Samaria would therefore be accepted by the mother church at Jerusalem [Bar, EBC, NICNT].

8:16 for he-had not-yet fallen[a] upon any of-them, they-had- only -been baptized in the name[b] of-the Lord Jesus. **8:17** Then they-laid their hands on them, and they-received (the)-Holy Spirit.

LEXICON—a. perf. act. participle of ἐπιπίπτω (LN 13.122) (BDAG 2. p. 377): 'to fall upon/on' [Bar, BECNT, LN; ESV, KJV, NASB], 'to come upon' [AB, CBC; NCV, NET, NLT, NRSV, REB], 'to come on' [NIV], 'to come down on' [TEV], 'to come to' [GW], 'to be given to' [CEV], 'to befall' [BDAG]. This verb means to happen suddenly to someone [LN]. It means to happen to and here it refers to the Holy Spirit coming upon someone [BDAG].

b. ὄνομα (LN 33.126) (BDAG 1.d.γ.ב. p. 713): 'name' [AB, Bar, BDAG, BECNT, CBC, LN; all versions]. This noun denotes the proper name of a person or object [LN]. Through baptism those who are baptized become the possession of and come under the dedicated protection of the one whose name they bear. [BDAG].

QUESTION—Who do all the pronouns in these two verses refer to?
These two verses are re-written to show whom the pronouns represent: 'For he (the Holy Spirit) had not yet fallen upon any of them (the Samaritans), they (the Samaritans) had only been baptized in the name of the Lord Jesus. Then they (Peter and John) began laying their (Peter and John's) hands on them (the Samaritans), and they (the Samaritans) were receiving the Holy Spirit' [TRT].

QUESTION—Why did they lay their hands on these people?
This was a way of asking God's blessing on someone. Probably the Holy Spirit had not yet fallen on these Samaritan believers so that there would be unity in the Church between the Jews and Samaritans who had hated each other for hundreds of years. It was important for the Jews and the Holy Spirit to welcome the Samaritans into the Church at the same time [TRT]. The laying on of hands and the confirmation of the Spirit were actions that indicated fellowship and identification with the new believers in Samaria. The result was the unity of the church as all participated in the expansion to Samaria [Bar, BECNT, EBC, NAC, NICNT]. As representatives from the Jerusalem church, Peter and John had witnessed what God had done in Samaria and would report this upon their return to Jerusalem [PNTC].

DISCOURSE UNIT—8:18-25 [PNTC]. The topic is a pretender is exposed.
DISCOURSE UNIT—8:18-24 [NICNT]. The topic is Peter and Simon Magus.

8:18 Now when Simon saw that the Spirit was-given through the laying-on[a] of-the apostles' hands, he-offered them money, **8:19** saying, "Give this power[b] to-me-also, so-that everyone on-whom I-lay my hands may-receive (the)-Holy Spirit."

LEXICON—a. ἐπίθεσις (LN 85.51) (BDAG p. 371): 'laying on' [AB, BDAG, BECNT, CBC, LN; ESV, KJV, NASB, NET, NIV, NRSV, REB], 'placing on' [LN]. The phrase 'the laying on of the apostles' hands' is also translated 'when the apostles placed their hands on people' [CEV], 'when the apostles placed their hands on them' [GW, TEV], 'when the apostles laid their hands on them' [NCV], 'when the apostles laid their hands on people' [NLT], 'the imposition of the apostles' hands' [Bar]. This noun denotes the placing of something on something else [LN]. It denotes the superimposing of something on something [BDAG].
  b. ἐξουσία (LN 76.12) (BDAG 2. p. 352): 'power' [AB, Bar, BDAG, CBC, LN; all versions except NASB, NIV], 'authority' [BECNT, LN; NASB], 'ability' [BDAG; NIV], 'capability, might' [BDAG]. This noun denotes the power to do something, with or without an added implication of authority [LN]. It denotes the potential or resource to command, control, or govern [BDAG].

8:20 But Peter said to him, "May your silver perish[a] with you, because you-thought you could obtain[b] the gift of-God with money!

LEXICON—a. ἀπώλεια (LN 20.31) (BDAG 2. p. 127): 'destruction' [BDAG, LN], 'annihilation, ruin' [BDAG]. The clause 'May your silver perish with you' [AB; ESV, NASB, NET, NRSV] is also translated 'May your money be destroyed with you' [GW, NLT], 'May your money perish with you' [Bar; NIV], 'Thy money perish with thee' [KJV], 'You and your money should both be destroyed' [NCV], 'Your money can go with you to damnation' [REB], 'May your silver go with you into destruction' [BECNT], 'May you and your money go to hell' [TEV], 'To hell with you and your money' [BDAG], 'You and your money will both end up in hell' [CEV], 'You and your money, may you come to a bad end' [CBC]. This noun denotes the destruction of persons, objects, or institutions [LN]. It denotes the destruction that one experiences [BDAG].
  b. pres. mid./pass. (deponent = act.) inf. of κτάομαι (LN 57.58) (BDAG 1. p. 572): 'to obtain' [BECNT, LN; ESV, NASB, NRSV], 'to buy' [AB; CEV, GW, NCV, NIV, NLT, REB], 'to acquire' [Bar, BDAG, LN; NET], 'to get' [BDAG, LN], 'to gain' [LN], 'to purchase' [KJV], 'to procure for oneself' [BDAG]. The clause 'you thought you could obtain the gift of God with money' is also translated 'You thought God's gift was for sale?' [REB], 'for thinking God's gift is for sale' [CBC]. This verb means to

acquire possession of something [LN]. It means to gain possession of something [BDAG].

QUESTION—What was the 'gift of God'?

In this context the gift does not refer to an object but to the power or ability to cause the Holy Spirit to come upon people through the laying on of hands [EBC, TH]. It refers to the act of distributing the Holy Spirit, and only God gives the Holy Spirit to people as a benevolent and gracious act [BECNT, CBC].

8:21 You have neither part[a] nor share[b] in this matter, for your heart[c] is not right before God. **8:22** Therefore repent[d] of this wickedness[e] of-yours, and pray to-the Lord that, if possible,[f] the intention of-your heart may be-forgiven you.

LEXICON—a. μερίς (LN 63.13) (BDAG 2. p. 633): 'part' [AB, Bar, BECNT, CBC, LN; CEV, ESV, KJV, NASB, NIV, NLT, NRSV, REB, TEV], 'share' [BDAG, LN; NET], 'portion' [BDAG, LN], not explicit [GW, NCV]. This noun denotes a share or portion, with the possible implication of a division of significant distinction [LN]. It denotes a portion of a whole that has been divided [BDAG].

b. κλῆρος (LN 63.18) (BDAG 2. p. 548): 'share' [BDAG, LN; GW, NIV, NRSV, REB, TEV], 'portion' [BDAG, BECNT; NASB], 'part' [AB, LN; NET], 'right' [AB], 'lot' [Bar, CBC; ESV, KJV], 'that which is assigned by lot' [BDAG], 'to share' [NCV], not explicit [CEV, NLT]. This noun denotes a share or portion which has been assigned or granted [BDAG, LN].

c. καρδία (LN 26.3) (BDAG 1.b.δ. p. 509): 'heart' [BDAG, LN], 'inner self, mind' [LN]. The phrase 'your heart is not right before God' [BECNT; ESV, NASB, NCV, NET, NIV, NRSV] is also translated 'your heart is not right with God' [NLT], 'your heart is not right in the-sight-of-God/God's-sight' [KJV, TEV], 'your heart is not straight in the sight of God' [Bar], 'your heart is not true with God' [AB], 'you are corrupt in the eyes of God' [REB], 'you are dishonest with God' [CBC], 'God sees that your heart isn't right' [CEV], 'God can see how twisted your thinking is' [GW]. This noun is a figurative extension of meaning of 'heart' and it denotes the causative source of a person's psychological life in its various aspects, but with special emphasis upon thought [LN]. It refers to the heart as the center of moral decisions, the inner life of vices and virtues [BDAG].

d. aorist act. impera. of μετανοέω (LN 41.52) (BDAG 2. p. 640): 'to repent' [Bar, BDAG, BECNT, CBC, LN; all versions except CEV, GW, NCV], 'to turn away' [AB], 'to change one's way' [LN]. The phrase 'repent of this wickedness of yours' is also translated 'Get rid of these evil thoughts' [CEV], 'change your wicked thoughts' [GW], 'Change your heart! Turn away from this evil thing you have done' [NCV]. This verb means to change one's way of life as the result of a complete change of thought and

attitude with regard to sin and righteousness [LN]. It means to feel remorse, to repent [BDAG].
e. κακία (LN 88.105) (BDAG 1. p. 500): 'wickedness' [AB, Bar, BDAG, BECNT, CBC, LN; ESV, KJV, NASB, NET, NIV, NLT, NRSV, REB], 'evil, badness' [LN], 'depravity, vice' [BDAG], 'evil thoughts' [CEV], 'wicked thoughts' [GW], 'evil thing' [NCV], 'evil plan' [TEV]. This noun denotes the quality of wickedness, with the implication of that which is harmful and damaging [LN]. It denotes the quality or state of wickedness [BDAG].
f. ἄρα (LN 71.19) (BDAG 3. p. 127): 'if possible' [BECNT; ESV, NASB, NRSV], 'perhaps' [Bar, BDAG, LN; KJV, NET, NLT], 'maybe' [NCV], 'in the hope of' [NIV], not explicit [AB, CBC; CEV, GW, REB, TEV]. This particle indicates a degree of uncertainty [LN]. It is a marker that expresses something tentative [BDAG].

QUESTION—Why did Simon have no part or share in this matter?

It means that he is not really one with them in this matter' [TH]. In the Old Testament 'part or share' refers to the privilege of belonging to God's people and sharing the inheritance he has granted. Simon's behavior betrayed that he had no real portion in God's people [NAC]. The term 'part' has the same meaning as 'share'. Using two terms for the idea makes the point emphatic. Simon's faith is deficient at this point; there is no blessing for him [BECNT, TNTC].

QUESTION—What is the proper interpretation of 'if possible' here?

It does not show doubt that God has the ability to forgive Simon's sin. God no doubt can, only if he will [TNTC, TRT]. The indefinite construction 'if possible' highlights the seriousness of Simon's wicked situation in which he is greedy and has not truly responded to the gospel [Bar, NAC, PNTC, TNTC]. The only thing for Simon to do is to repent [Bar, EBC, NAC, PNTC].

8:23 For I-see (that) you are in (the) gall^a of bitterness and (in-the)-bond^b of-iniquity." 8:24 And answering, Simon said, "Pray to the Lord for me, that nothing of-what you-have-said may-happen to me."

LEXICON—a. χολή (LN 8.75, 88.166) (BDAG 2. p. 1086): 'gall' [BDAG, LN (8.75)]. The idiom 'you are in the gall of bitterness' [BECNT, LN; ESV, KJV, NASB, NRSV] is also translated 'you are bitter with jealousy' [GW], 'you are bitterly envious' [NET], 'you are full of bitter poison' [Bar], 'you are full of bitterness' [NIV], 'you are full of bitter envy' [TEV], 'you are full of bitter jealousy' [NCV, NLT], 'you are headed for bitterness' [AB], 'you are doomed to taste the bitter fruit of sin' [CBC], 'bitter gall will be your fate' [REB],'you are jealous' [CEV]. This noun denotes the bitter yellowish liquid secreted by the liver and stored in the gall bladder [LN (8.75)], and the idiom εἰς χολὴν πικρίας εἰμί 'to be in the gall of bitterness' means to be particularly envious or resentful of someone [LN (88.166)]. It is a figurative use of gall, a substance with an

unpleasant taste and means 'gall of bitterness' or 'bitter gall'. Here this bitter poison refers to Simon's state of sin and not to an emotional condition [BDAG].
  b. σύνδεσμος (LN 18.17) (BDAG 3. p. 966): 'bond' [BDAG, LN], 'fetter' [BDAG]. The phrase 'in the bond/bondage of iniquity' [BECNT; ESV, KJV, NASB] is also translated 'bound by your evil ways' [CEV], 'bound by unrighteousness' [Bar], 'wrapped up in your evil ways' [GW], 'in bondage to sin' [NET], 'are captive to sin' [NIV, NLT], 'the chains of sin' [AB; REB], 'in the chains of wickedness' [NRSV], 'are ruled by sin' [NCV], 'are a prisoner of sin' [TEV], 'doomed to wear the fetters of sin' [CBC]. This noun denotes that which ties something together [LN]. It denotes a bond that confines or hinders, and here it refers to a fetter that consists in unrighteousness [BDAG].

QUESTION—Why did Peter rebuke Simon?

Simon was full of bitterness and a captive to sin [Bar, EBC, PNTC]. The rebuke is about his condition and position. It points more to the risk it entails than the attitude that has brought him there. Simon's response in v. 24 that what Peter says may not happen to him shows that his condition and its great risk are in view [BECNT].

DISCOURSE UNIT—8:25 [NICNT]. The topic is the Apostles return to Jerusalem.

DISCOURSE UNIT—8:25-40 [NASB]. The topic is an Ethiopian receives Christ.

8:25 Then when they had-testified^a and spoken the word of-the Lord, they started-back^b to Jerusalem, preaching-the-good-news^c to-many villages^d of-the Samaritans.

LEXICON—a. aorist mid. (deponent = act.) participle of διαμαρτύρομαι (LN 33.223) (BDAG 1. p. 233): 'to testify (of)' [BDAG, BECNT, LN; ESV, KJV, NIV, NLT, NRSV], 'to testify solemnly' [NASB, NET], 'to declare, to assert' [LN], 'to bear testimony' [Bar], 'to bear witness (to) solemnly' [BDAG], 'to give witness' [AB]. The phrase 'when they had testified and spoken the word of the Lord' is also translated 'After Peter and John had preached about the Lord' [CEV], 'After they had boldly spoken about the message of the Lord' [GW], 'After Peter and John told the people what they had seen Jesus do and after they had spoken the message of the Lord' [NCV], 'After giving their testimony and speaking the word of the Lord' [CBC; REB], 'After they had given their testimony and proclaimed the Lord's message' [TEV]. This verb means to make a serious declaration on the basis of presumed personal knowledge [LN]. It means to make a solemn declaration about the truth of something [BDAG].
  b. imperf. act. indic. of ὑποστρέφω (LN 15.88) (BDAG p. 1041): 'to start back' [NASB, NET], 'to take the road back' [CBC; REB], 'to return' [AB, Bar, BDAG, BECNT, LN; CEV, ESV, KJV, NIV, NLT, NRSV], 'to

go back' [LN; NCV, TEV], 'to come back' [LN], 'to turn back' [BDAG]. The phrase 'they started back to Jerusalem, preaching the good news' is also translated 'they spread the Good news...on their way back to Jerusalem' [GW]. This verb means to move back to a point from which one has previously departed [LN].

c. imperf. mid. indic. of εὐαγγελίζω (LN 33.215) (BDAG 2.a.γ. p. 402): 'to preach the Good News' [NCV, NLT, TEV], 'to proclaim the good news' [NET, NRSV], 'to proclaim the gospel' [BDAG], 'to tell the good news' [LN; CEV], 'to announce the gospel' [LN], 'to preach the gospel' [AB, BECNT; ESV, KJV, NASB, NIV], 'to spread the Good News' [GW], 'to bring the good news' [CBC; REB], 'to evangelize' [Bar]. This verb means to communicate good news concerning something and in the NT it refers to the gospel message about Jesus [LN]. It means to proclaim the divine message of salvation [BDAG].

d. κώμη (LN 11.62) (BDAG 2. p. 580): 'village' [AB, Bar, BECNT, CBC; all versions except NCV], 'the people of a village' [LN], 'the inhabitants of a village' [BDAG]. The phrase 'they...preaching the good news to many villages of the Samaritans' is also translated 'they went through many Samaritan towns and preached the Good News to the people' [NCV]. This noun denotes the inhabitants of a village [BDAG, LN].

QUESTION—Who were the 'they' in this verse?

The 'they' are the apostles Peter and John [Bar, CBC, EBC, NAC, NICNT, PNTC, TH, TNTC]; Philip, Peter and John [BECNT, EBC, NAC, TH, TNTC].

DISCOURSE UNIT—8:26–40 [AB, Bar, BECNT, CBC, EBC, NAC, NICNT, PNTC, TNTC; CEV, ESV, GW, NCV, NET, NIV, NLT, NRSV, TEV]. The topic is Philip and the Ethiopian treasurer [AB], Philip and the Ethiopian [Bar, NICNT; NIV], Philip and the eunuch [BECNT], Philip and an Ethiopian official [CEV], Philip and the Ethiopian official [TEV], Philip in the south [CBC], an Ethiopian eunuch converted [EBC], Philip and the Ethiopian eunuch [ESV, NET, NLT, NRSV], Philip tells an Ethiopian about Jesus [GW], the witness to the Ethiopian treasurer [NAC], Philip teaches an Ethiopian [NCV], the word goes to Ethiopia [PNTC], the conversion of an Ethiopian [TNTC].

DISCOURSE UNIT—8:26–31 [PNTC]. The topic is a divinely arranged encounter.

8:26 Now an-angel of-(the)-Lord spoke to Philip saying, "Get-up[a] and go[b] toward (the)-south to the road that-goes-down from Jerusalem to Gaza." It is (a)-desert[c] (road).

LEXICON—a. aorist act. impera. of ἀνίστημι (LN 17.6) (BDAG 10. p. 83): 'to get up' [AB, Bar, BDAG; GW, NASB, NET, NRSV], 'to rise' [BDAG, BECNT; ESV], 'to arise' [KJV], 'to get ready' [BDAG; NCV, TEV], 'to set out, to stand up' [BDAG], 'to start out' [CBC; REB], 'to raise up' [LN], not explicit [CEV, NIV, NLT]. This verb means to assume a

standing position [LN]. It indicates the beginning of an action (usually a motion) expressed by another verb [BDAG].
   b. pres. mid./pass. (deponent = act.) impera. of πορεύομαι (LN 15.18) (BDAG 1. p. 853): 'to go' [AB, BDAG, BECNT, CBC; all versions], 'to travel' [Bar, BDAG, LN], 'to journey, to be on one's way' [LN], 'to proceed' [BDAG]. This verb means to move a considerable distance, either with a single destination or from one destination to another in a series [LN]. It means to move over an area, generally with a point of departure or destination specified [BDAG].
   c. ἔρημος (LN 1.86) (BDAG 1.a. p. 309): 'desert' [LN; all versions except NRSV, TEV], 'deserted' [BDAG], 'wilderness' [LN; NRSV], 'lonely place' [LN]. The phrase 'it/this is a desert road' [AB, BECNT, CBC] is also translated 'this is deserted' [Bar], 'this road is not used nowadays' [TEV]. This adjective describes a largely uninhabited region, normally with sparse vegetation [LN]. It describes being in a state of isolation [BDAG].
QUESTION—What is meant by a 'desert road'?
It is a road that is located in a desolate area [Bar, BECNT].
QUESTION—What is known about Gaza?
Gaza was the southernmost of the five chief Philistine cities in southwest Palestine [Bar, CBC, EBC, NICNT]. It was the last town before the desert that stretched on to Egypt [CBC]. It was the last watering place before the desert on the route to Egypt [BECNT, NAC].

8:27 **And he-got-up and went. And look!**[a] **There-was (an)-Ethiopian, (a)-eunuch,**[b] **(a)-court-official**[c] **of-(the)-Candace/of-Candace,**[d] **queen of-(the)-Ethiopians, who was in-charge of-all her treasury.**[e] **He-had-come to Jerusalem to-worship,**
LEXICON—a. ἰδού (LN 91.13) (BDAG 2. p. 468): 'look!' [BDAG, LN], 'behold' [BECNT; KJV], 'catch sight of' [CBC], 'listen, pay attention' [LN], not explicit [AB, Bar; all versions except KJV]. This particle is one of several words used as prompters of attention which serve to emphasize the following statement [LN]. It is a marker of strong emphasis [BDAG].
   b. εὐνοῦχος (LN 9.25) (BDAG 1. p. 409): 'eunuch' [AB, Bar, BDAG, BECNT, CBC, LN; all versions except CEV], not explicit [CEV]. This noun denotes a castrated male person. Since in many societies castration of human males is not known, any attempt to employ a descriptive explanation within the text might seem unnecessarily crude and even vulgar. A number of translators have therefore preferred to borrow a term for eunuch and then place the explanation of its meaning in a glossary or word list [LN]. In this verse the word 'eunuch' refers primarily to his physical state [BDAG].
   c. δυνάστης (LN 37.62) (BDAG 2. p. 264): 'a court official' [BDAG, LN; ESV, NASB, NET, NRSV], 'an official at the court' [AB], 'an important official' [CEV, NIV, TEV], 'an important officer' [NCV], 'a high-ranking

official' [GW], 'a high official' [CBC; REB], 'a minister' [Bar, BECNT], 'a ruler' [LN]. The phrase 'a eunuch, a court official' is also translated 'a eunuch of great authority' [KJV, NLT]. This noun is a derivative of δύναμις 'ruler' and denotes one who is in a position of authority to command others [LN]. It denotes one who is in a relatively minor position [BDAG].

d. Κανδάκη (LN 37.77, 93.209) (BDAG p. 507). 'Some take this word to be the title for any queen of Ethiopia: 'the Candace' [BDAG, LN (37.77); NRSV], 'the Kandake' [CBC; NLT, REB]. Others apparently take this word to be the personal name of this particular queen of Ethiopia: 'Candace' [AB, Bar, BECNT, LN (93.209); CEV, ESV, GW, KJV, NASB, NCV, NET, NIV], not explicit [TEV]. This noun denotes the title of the queen of Ethiopia: 'the Candace' who is the female ruler of Ethiopia [LN (37.77)], or it denotes the particular name of this queen of Ethiopia: 'Candace' [LN (93.209)]. It is the title of the queen of Ethiopia [BDAG].

e. γάζα (LN 57.36) (BDAG p. 186): 'treasury' [AB, BDAG, LN; NET, NIV, NRSV, TEV], 'treasure' [BECNT, CBC; ESV, KJV, NASB, REB], 'treasures' [GW], 'money' [NCV], 'wealth' [Bar]. The phrase 'of all her treasury' is also translated 'chief treasurer' [BDAG; CEV], 'treasurer' [NLT]. This noun denotes a number of possessions and valuables constituting an important and official asset of a political entity [LN].

QUESTION—What is a eunuch?

A eunuch is a man who has been castrated [BECNT, NAC, PNTC, TH, TNTC, TRT]. It was done so that his master does not have to worry about him sleeping with his wife or daughters [TRT]. Jewish Law did not allow eunuchs to become a full convert to Judaism and therefore they were not allowed to fully participate in Jewish worship (Deut. 23:1) [BECNT, NAC, TH, TNTC, TRT]. The word 'eunuch' was often used in the Old Testament as a synonym for a high political or military official [EBC, NICNT, TH, TNTC].

QUESTION—What is known about this eunuch?

This eunuch was the treasurer to the queen of Ethiopia called Candace. Therefore he was an important person who had much power. Being an Ethiopian, he probably was black, which indicates that the gospel was expanding to a new ethnic group. Since he had gone to Jerusalem to worship, he probably was a Diaspora God-fearer, a non-Jew who worshiped the Jewish God. He would have been limited to the Court of the Gentiles at the temple or perhaps only allowed to go to a synagogue [BECNT, NAC, NICNT, PNTC, TNTC]. Ethiopia is known as the land of Cush in the earlier books of the Old Testament. Its population consisted of blacks (e.g., Genesis 2:13) [BECNT, NAC, PNTC]. It is in what today is known as the Sudan [AB, Bar, BECNT, CBC, PNTC, TNTC].

8:28 and he-was returning,[a] sitting in his chariot, and he-was-reading the prophet[b] Isaiah. **8:29** And the Spirit said to-Philip, "Go-over[c] and join[d] this chariot."

LEXICON—a. pres. act. participle of ὑποστρέφω (LN 15.88) (BDAG p. 1041): 'to return' [Bar, BDAG, BECNT, LN; ESV, KJV, NASB, NLT], 'to return home' [NET, NRSV, REB], 'to go back' [LN]. The phrase 'was returning' is also translated 'was on his way back' [AB], 'was on his way home' [CEV, NCV, TEV], 'as the official rode along' [GW], 'on his way home' [CBC; NIV]. This verb means to move back to a point from which one has previously departed [LN]. It means to return [BDAG].
  b. προφήτης (LN 53.79) (BDAG 1. p. 891): 'prophet' [BDAG, LN], 'inspired preacher' [LN]. The phrase 'reading the prophet Isaiah' [AB, Bar, BECNT; ESV, KJV, NASB, NET, NRSV] is also translated 'reading the prophet Isaiah out loud' [GW], 'reading aloud the prophet Isaiah' [CBC], 'reading aloud from the prophet Isaiah' [REB], 'reading the book of Isaiah the prophet' [NIV], 'reading aloud from the book of the prophet Isaiah' [NLT], 'reading from the Book of Isaiah, the prophet' [NCV], 'reading from the book of the prophet Isaiah' [TEV], 'reading the book of the prophet Isaiah' [CEV]. This noun denotes one who proclaims inspired utterances on behalf of God [LN]. It is a metonymy in which the name of the prophet refers to the writings of that prophet [BDAG].
  c. aorist act. impera. of προσέρχομαι (LN 15.77) (BDAG 1. p. 878): 'to go over' [ESV, NET, NLT], 'to go over to' [NRSV, TEV], 'to go to' [BDAG; GW, NCV, NIV], 'to go near' [KJV], 'to go up' [Bar; NASB], 'to go' [AB, BECNT, CBC; REB], 'to approach' [BDAG, LN], 'to come near to, to move toward' [LN], not explicit [CEV]. This verb means to move toward a reference point, with a possible implication in certain contexts of a reciprocal relationship between the person approaching and the one who is approached [LN]. It means to move towards something [BDAG].
  d. aorist pass. impera. of κολλάω (LN 34.22) (BDAG 2.b.α. p. 556): 'to join' [Bar, BDAG, BECNT, CBC, LN; ESV, NASB, NET, NRSV], 'to join oneself to' [BDAG, LN; KJV], 'to catch up with' [CEV], 'to stay close to' [GW, TEV], 'to stay near' [NCV, NIV], 'to get near' [AB], 'to walk along beside' [NLT], 'to meet' [REB], 'to associate with' [BDAG], 'to become a part of' [LN]. This verb means to begin an association with someone, whether temporary or permanent. Although the Greek text says literally 'join this carriage'…the association is not directly with the carriage, but with the man riding in the carriage [LN]. It means to join oneself to something, and a rendering like 'stick to this chariot' suggests the imagery [BDAG].

QUESTION—What was a chariot like at that time?
  A chariot was a horse-drawn cart. Normally, it had two wheels and would hold two or three people, including the driver. Some had four wheels and

could hold more people [TRT]. It was either a carriage, a wagon, or a two-wheeled cart used in war [TH], a slow-moving wagon [NAC]. An ox-drawn wagon moves at not much more than a walking pace [Bar, PNTC, TNTC]. It was a traveling vehicle that could hold at least three people. (Verse 13 indicates it held the driver, the eunuch, and Philip) [BECNT].

QUESTION—What is meant by the expression 'reading the prophet Isaiah'?

It means reading the book that contained the words of the prophet Isaiah, or reading the book written by the prophet Isaiah [TH]. This eunuch was wealthy enough to have his own copy of Isaiah [Bar, BECNT, PNTC]. He was probably reading aloud, since that was the ancient custom to help one's memory [AB, Bar, BECNT, EBC, NAC, PNTC, TNTC]. It would likely have been a scroll [BECNT, NAC, NICNT, TNTC].

8:30 So Philip ran-up[a] and heard him reading Isaiah the prophet, and said, "Do-you-understand what you-are-reading?" **8:31** And he-said, "How could-I unless someone guides[b] me?" And he-invited[c] Philip to-come-up and sit with him.

LEXICON—a. aorist act. participle of προστρέχω (LN 15.234) (BDAG p. 886): 'to run up to someone' [BDAG, LN]. The phrase 'ran up' [Bar, CBC; NASB, REB] is also translated 'ran up close' [CEV], 'ran' [BECNT], 'ran over' [NLT, TEV]. Some specify his destination to be the chariot: 'ran over to it' [AB], 'ran up to it' [NET, NRSV], 'ran to the carriage' [GW], 'ran toward the chariot' [NCV], 'ran up to the chariot' [NIV]. Others specify his destination to be the Ethiopian 'ran to him' [ESV], 'ran thither to him' [KJV]. This verb means to run into the presence of someone [LN]. It means to run to or towards something [BDAG].

b. fut. act. indic. of ὁδηγέω (LN 27.17) (BDAG 2. p. 690): 'to guide' [AB, Bar, BDAG, BECNT, LN; ESV, GW, KJV, NASB, NET, NRSV, REB], 'to lead' [BDAG, LN], 'to explain' [NCV, NIV, TEV], 'to instruct' [NLT], 'to give the clue' [CBC], 'to lead someone to know, to guide someone in learning' [LN], 'to guide, to conduct' [BDAG]. The clause 'How could I unless someone guides me' is also translated 'How can I understand unless someone helps me' [CEV]. This verb means to guide someone in acquiring information [LN]. It means to assist someone in acquiring information or knowledge [BDAG].

c. aorist act. indic. of παρακαλέω (LN 33.315) (BDAG 1.b. p. 764): 'to invite' [AB, BDAG, BECNT, LN; all versions except KJV, NLT], 'to urge' [NLT], 'to ask' [Bar, CBC], 'to call to one's side' [BDAG]. The phrase 'he invited Philip to come up and sit with him' is also translated 'he desired Philip that he would come up and sit with him' [KJV]. This verb means to ask a person to accept an offered hospitality [LN]. It means to ask to come and be present where the speaker is [BDAG].

QUESTION—What is meant by understanding what he was reading?
The question can be stated as 'Do you understand the meaning of' or 'do you know the interpretation of' what he was reading? [Bar, BECNT, NAC, NICNT, PNTC, TH, TNTC].

DISCOURSE UNIT—8:32–38 [PNTC]. The topic is finding Christ in the Scriptures.

8:32 Now, the passage[a] of-the Scripture that he-was-reading was this: "Like (a)-sheep he-was-led to slaughter,[b] and like (a)-lamb before the-one who-shears[c] it (is)-silent, so he-does- not -open his mouth.
LEXICON—a. περιοχή (LN 33.10) (BDAG 2. p. 803): 'passage' [AB, Bar, BECNT, CBC, LN; CEV, ESV, NASB, NET, NIV, NLT, NRSV, REB, TEV], 'portion' [NCV], 'part' [LN; GW], 'place' [KJV]. This noun denotes a particular portion or unit of discourse [LN]. It denotes a portion of written scripture [BDAG].
  b. σφαγή (LN 20.72) (BDAG p. 979): 'slaughter' [AB, Bar, BDAG, BECNT, CBC, LN; all versions except CEV, NCV]. The phrase 'like a sheep he was led to slaughter' is also translated 'like a sheep on its way to be killed' [CEV], 'like a sheep being led to be killed' [NCV]. This noun denotes the slaughter of either animals or persons [LN].
  c. aorist act. participle of κείρω (LN 19.23) (BDAG p. 538): 'to shear' [BDAG, LN], 'to cut hair' [LN]. The phrase 'a lamb before the one who shears it' [Bar] is also translated 'a lamb…before the man who shears it' [AB], 'a lamb…before…its shearer' [ESV, NASB, NET, NIV, NRSV], 'a lamb before…his shearer' [KJV], 'a lamb…before the shearer' [CBC; REB], 'a lamb…before the shearers' [NLT], 'a lamb before its shearers' [BECNT], 'a lamb…when its wool is cut off' [LN; TEV], 'a lamb whose wool is being cut off' [CEV], 'a sheep…when its wool is cut off' [GW], 'a lamb…while its wool is being cut' [NCV]. This verb means to cut the hair of a person or animal [LN]. It means to have one's hair cut off [BDAG].
QUESTION—Where is the passage of Scripture that the eunuch is quoting?
The passage in verses 32–33 is from Isaiah 53:7b–8 in the Greek Septuagint [BECNT], 53:7–8 [Bar, CBC, EBC, NAC, NICNT, PNTC, TH, TNTC]. It is the first time in the book of Acts that the 'suffering servant' passage is applied to our Lord Jesus Christ [TH]. Isaiah 53:7 looks at the innocent, silent suffering of the servant and compares the figure to a sacrificial lamb that is unjustly slain as verse 33 makes clear [BECNT].

8:33 In his humiliation[a] justice/judgment[b] was-denied him. Who can describe his descendants/generation[c]? For his life is taken-away[d] from the earth."
LEXICON—a. ταπείνωσις (LN 87.60) (BDAG 1. p. 990): 'humiliation' [AB, Bar, BDAG, BECNT; ESV, KJV, NASB, NET, NIV, NRSV], 'humility, low status, low estate' [LN]. The phrase 'in his humiliation' is also

translated 'when he humbled himself' [GW], 'he was treated like a nobody' [CEV], 'he was shamed' [NCV], 'he was humiliated' [NLT, TEV], 'he has been humiliated' [CBC; REB]. This noun denotes the state of low status, with the probable implication of humility [LN]. It denotes the experience of a reversal in fortunes [BDAG].

b. κρίσις (LN 56.25) (BDAG 1.a.β. or 3. p. 569): 'justice' [BDAG (3. p. 569), LN], 'judgment' [BDAG (1.a.β. p. 569)]. The interpretation 'justice was denied him' [BECNT; ESV, NRSV, TEV] is also translated 'he did not receive a fair trial' [CEV], 'he was not judged fairly' [GW], 'he received no justice' [NLT], 'he was deprived of justice' [NIV], 'he was treated unfairly' [NCV]. The alternative interpretation 'judgment was denied him' is also translated 'his judgment was taken away' [Bar; KJV, NASB, NET], 'his conviction was quashed' [AB], 'he has no redress' [CBC; REB]. This noun denotes the administration of justice [LN]. It denotes the administration of what is right and fair [BDAG (3. p. 569)], or it denotes the legal procedure of judgment and here it refers to a judgment of condemnation that goes against a person and the sentence that follows [BDAG (1.a.β. p. 569)].

c. γενεά (LN 10.28, 11.4) (BDAG 4. p. 192): 'descendants, offspring, posterity' [LN (10.28)], 'generation' [LN (11.4)]. The phrase 'Who can describe his descendants?' is also translated 'Who can speak of his descendants?' [NIV, NLT], 'Who can describe his posterity?' [NET], 'Who will be able to speak of his posterity?' [CBC; REB], 'No one will be able to tell about his descendants' [TEV]. 'He died without children to continue his family' [NCV], 'How can he have children (if his life is snatched away?)' [CEV]. The phrase 'Who can describe his generation?' [BECNT; ESV] is also translated 'Who shall recount his generation?' [Bar], 'who shall declare his generation?' [KJV], 'Who will relate/describe his generation?' [NASB, NRSV], 'Who from his generation will talk about (his life on earth being cut short?)' [GW], 'Who will be able to tell of the span of his life?' [AB]. This noun denotes the successive following generations of those who are biologically related to a reference person [LN (10.28)], or it denotes the people living at the same time and belonging to the same reproductive age-class [LN (11.4)]. It probably is to be taken in the sense of family history and denotes those descended from a common ancestor [BDAG].

d. pres. pass. indic. of αἴρω (LN 20.43) (BDAG 4. p. 28): 'to be taken away' [AB, Bar, BDAG; ESV, NET, NRSV], 'to be taken up' [BECNT], 'to be taken' [KJV, NIV, NLT], 'to be removed' [BDAG; NASB], 'to be destroyed, to be done away with' [LN], 'to be snatched away' [CEV]. The phrase 'his life is taken away from the earth' is also translated 'His life on earth has ended' [NCV], 'he is cut off from the world of the living' [REB], 'his life is cut off and he is gone from the earth' [CBC],'his life on earth being cut short' [GW], 'his life on earth has come to an end' [TEV].

This verb means to destroy, with the implication of removal and doing away with [LN]. It means to take away, remove, or seize control [BDAG].
QUESTION—What was denied the man in this verse?
1. The man was denied justice from those who said that he was guilty and executed him [Bar, BECNT, NAC; CEV, ESV, GW, NIV, NCV, NLT, NRSV, TEV]. Most commentaries think it means that he was treated unjustly or unfairly [TRT]. Here it is justice that is removed as the unjust death of an innocent man takes place [BECNT]. Being deprived of justice reminds one of the false accusations of blasphemy leveled at Christ and the equivocation of Pilate [NAC].
2. The man was denied a legal trial by those who said that he was guilty and executed him [AB, Bar, CBC, NICNT; ESV, KJV, NASB, NET, REB]. His rights were taken away [NICNT].

QUESTION—What is meant by the rhetorical question 'Who can describe his descendants/generation'?
There are two views on this rhetorical question. One is rendered as no one will be able to tell about his descendants since he was put to death without leaving any posterity [PNTC, TH]. Another view is that the word translated descendants may mean 'contemporary generation'. If this is the case, the question can mean 'who can relate the evil of his contemporaries?' [TH]. 'what kind of generation can take a life like this' [BECNT].

QUESTION—What does the phrase 'for his life was taken away from the earth' mean?
It refers to 'his death' [BECNT].

8:34 And the eunuch said-to Philip, "I-ask you, about whom does- the prophet -say this? About himself or about someone else?" **8:35** Then Philip opened[a] his mouth, and beginning with this Scripture he-told- him -the-good-news-(about)[b] Jesus. **8:36** And as they-were-going along the road they-came to some water, and the eunuch said, "Look! Water! What prevents[c] me from-being-baptized?"

LEXICON—a. aorist act. participle of ἀνοίγω (LN 79.110, 33.29) (BDAG 5.a. p. 84): 'to open' [BDAG, LN (79.110)]. The phrase 'Philip opened his mouth' [Bar, BECNT; ESV, KJV, NASB] is also translated 'Philip began to speak' [NCV, NRSV, TEV], 'Philip started speaking' [NET], 'Philip spoke' [AB; GW], 'Philip' [CBC; CEV, NIV, NLT, REB]. This verb means to cause something to open [LN (79.110)]. The phrase ἀνοίγω τὸ στόμα 'to open the mouth' means to begin to speak in a somewhat formal and systematic manner [LN (33.29)]. It means to cause to function, and here it means to open one's own mouth to speak [BDAG].

b. aorist mid. indic. of εὐαγγελίζω (LN 33.215) (BDAG 2.a.α. p. 402): 'to tell the good news' [CBC, LN; ESV, GW, NCV, NIV, NLT, REB, TEV], 'to proclaim the good news' [Bar, BECNT; NET, NRSV], 'to proclaim the gospel' [BDAG], 'to announce the gospel' [LN], 'to bring the gospel' [AB], 'to explain the good news' [CEV], 'to preach' [KJV, NASB]. This

verb means to communicate good news concerning something, and in the NT it is a particular reference to the gospel message about Jesus [LN]. It means to proclaim the divine message of salvation [BDAG].
- c. pres. act. indic. of κωλύω (LN 13.146) (BDAG 1. p. 580): 'to prevent' [AB, Bar, BDAG, BECNT, CBC, LN; ESV, NASB, NRSV, REB], 'to hinder' [BDAG, LN; KJV], 'to keep from' [GW, TEV], 'to stop' [NCV, NET], 'to stand in the way of' [NIV]. The phrase 'What prevents me to be baptized?' is also translated 'Why can't I be baptized?' [CEV, NLT]. This verb means to cause something not to happen [LN]. It means to keep something from happening [BDAG].

QUESTION—What is meant by the expression 'opened his mouth'?

In Judaism, to open one's mouth often refers to lecturing on Scripture [Bar, BECNT]. It is used when a significant or weighty utterance follows [TNTC]. In this context, it refers to Philip beginning to preach the gospel about Jesus [Bar, BECNT, PNTC].

QUESTION—Is there anything that prevented the eunuch from being baptized?

The answer is 'No.' All barriers have been removed. A eunuch Gentile who was black was baptized and received into full membership in the people of Jesus Christ [BECNT, NAC]. 'What prevents?' is a fairly common idiom for 'Why not?' [Bar].

8:37 [[Omitted]]

TEXT—Manuscripts omitting this verse are given an A rating by GNT to indicate the omission was regarded to be certain. A variant reading is "And Philip said, 'If thou believest with all thine heart, thou mayest.' And he answered and said, 'I believe that Jesus Christ is the Son of God'" and it is followed by KJV. This verse is included in parentheses by NASB.

8:38 And (Philip)-ordered the chariot to-stop, and they-both went-down into the water, both Philip and the eunuch, and he-baptized him.

DISCOURSE UNIT—8:39–40 [PNTC]. The topic is Philip's continuing ministry.

8:39 And, when they-came-up out-of the water, (the)-Spirit of-(the)-Lord carried-away[a] Philip, and the eunuch saw him no-more,[b] and went (on) his way[c] rejoicing.

LEXICON—a. aorist act. indic. of ἁρπάζω (LN 18.4) (BDAG 2.b. p. 134): 'to carry away' [BDAG; ESV], 'to take away' [BDAG, LN; CEV, GW, NCV, TEV], 'to snatch (away)' [CBC, LN; NASB, NET, NLT, NRSV, REB], 'to catch away' [Bar; KJV], 'to catch up' [BECNT], 'to take away suddenly' [NIV], 'to seize' [AB, LN]. This verb means to grab or seize by force, with the purpose of removing someone [LN]. It means to grab or seize suddenly so as to carry away someone in such a way that no resistance is offered [BDAG].
- b. οὐκέτι (LN 67.130) (BDAG 1. p. 736): 'no more' [Bar, BDAG, BECNT, CBC; ESV, KJV, NRSV], 'not any more' [NET], 'no longer' [BDAG,

LN; NASB], 'not again' [AB; GW, NIV, REB, TEV], 'never again' [CEV, NCV, NLT]. This adverb describes the extension of time up to a point but not beyond [LN]. It refers to the extension of time up to a point but not beyond it [BDAG].
   c. ὁδός (LN 15.19) (BDAG 2. p. 691): 'way' [AB, Bar, BDAG, BECNT, CBC; all versions], 'journey' [BDAG, LN]. The phrase 'on his way' is also translated 'on his way home' [NCV]. This noun denotes the process of traveling, presumably for some distance [LN]. It denotes the action of traveling [BDAG].
QUESTION—Why did the Spirit carry Philip away'?
   This means that the Spirit 'seized' or 'took hold of' Philip and moved him on to a new place [NAC, PNTC]. The verb 'carried away' connotes both a forceful and sudden action by the Spirit and a lack of resistance from Philip [EBC]. His instant removal makes clearer still that God is at work [BECNT].
QUESTION—What was the eunuch rejoicing about?
   The eunuch was rejoicing about his being saved by God, not because Philip disappeared [TRT], at his newfound relationship to God [BECNT], at his receiving of the Spirit [CBC, NICNT, TNTC], a genuine manifestation of the Spirit's work in his life [NAC]. His conversion was a significant episode in the advance of the gospel [EBC].

8:40 **But Philip found-himself[a] at Azotus, and as-he-went-about-from-place-to-place he-preached-the-good-news[b] in-all the towns until he came to Caesarea.**

LEXICON—a. aorist pass. indic. of εὑρίσκω (LN 27.27) (BDAG 1.b. p. 411): 'to find, to come upon' [BDAG, LN], 'to discover, to happen to find, to learn the whereabouts of something' [LN]. The phrase 'found himself at/in Azotus' [BECNT; ESV, KJV, NASB, NET, NRSV, TEV] is also translated 'found himself in the city of Azotus' [GW], 'found himself farther north at the town of Azotus' [NLT], 'appeared at Azotus' [CBC; NIV, REB], 'later appeared in Azotus' [CEV], 'appeared in a city called Azotus' [NCV], 'was then found on the way to Azotus' [AB], 'arrived at Azotus' [Bar]. This verb means to learn the location of something, either by intentional searching or by unexpected discovery [LN]. It means to find, to come upon, and here it means that he found himself or was present at Azotus [BDAG].
   b. imperf. mid. indic. of εὐαγγελίζω (LN 33.215) (BDAG 2.a.γ. p. 402): 'to preach the good news' [NCV, NLT, TEV], 'to proclaim the good news' [NET, NRSV], 'to tell the good news, to announce the gospel' [LN], 'to preach' [BDAG, CBC; KJV, REB], 'to proclaim' [BDAG], 'to proclaim the gospel' [BECNT], 'to tell people about Jesus' [CEV], 'to preach the gospel' [AB; ESV, NASB, NIV], 'to spread the Good News' [GW], 'to evangelize' [Bar]. This verb means to communicate good news concerning something and in the NT it refers to the gospel message about

Jesus [LN]. It means to proclaim the divine message of salvation [BDAG].

QUESTION—Where was the city Azotus?

Azotus is the Greek name of the city of Ashdod that is mentioned in the Old Testament when it was one of the five major Philistine cities like Gaza (Joshua 13:3) [Bar, BECNT, CBC, NAC, NICNT, PNTC, TRT]. It was about 22 miles (35 kilometers) north of the city of Gaza [Bar, BECNT, NICNT, PNTC, TRT] and about 56 miles (90 kilometers) south of Caesarea [PNTC, TRT].

QUESTION—What does 'until he came to Caesarea' indicate?

It means that Philip stayed at Caesarea when he got there. It does not mean that Philip stopped preaching when he got to Caesarea [TRT].

QUESTION—What was special about Caesarea at that time?

Caesarea was a major seaport city [BECNT, TH, TRT]. It was on the coast, 55 miles northwest of Jerusalem [BECNT, TH]. It may have been Philip's hometown or he may have settled there, some twenty years after the events of this chapter (Acts 21:8) [AB, Bar, CBC, NAC, NICNT, PNTC, TH, TNTC, TRT]. Herod the Great had built the city in honor of Caesar Augustus in 13 B.C. After A.D. 6, Roman governors over Judea Province had their headquarters in Caesarea [BECNT, TH, TRT].

DISCOURSE UNIT—9:1–12:25 [NAC]. The topic is Peter joins the wider witness.

DISCOURSE UNIT—9:1–31 [NAC, NICNT; GW]. The topic is Saul becomes a follower of Jesus [GW], Paul's new witness to Christ [NAC], conversion of Saul of Tarsus [NICNT].

DISCOURSE UNIT—9:1–30 [BECNT, CBC, EBC]. The topic is Saul [CBC], the conversion and early reception of Saul [BECNT], the conversion of Saul of Tarsus [EBC].

DISCOURSE UNIT—9:1–22 [NAC; NET]. The topic is Paul the converted [NAC], the conversion of Saul [NET].

DISCOURSE UNIT—9:1–19a [AB, Bar, BECNT, PNTC, TNTC; CEV, ESV, NASB, NCV, NIV, NLT, NRSV, TEV]. The topic is Paul's call [AB], Saul's conversion [Bar; NIV, NLT], the conversion of Saul [BECNT; NASB, NRSV, TEV], Saul becomes a follower of the Lord [CEV], the conversion of Paul [ESV], Saul is converted [NCV], Saul's conversion and commissioning [PNTC], the conversion and call of Paul [TNTC].

DISCOURSE UNIT—9:1–9 [EBC, PNTC]. The topic is the Christ-encounter on the Damascus Road [EBC], meeting the ascended Lord [PNTC].

DISCOURSE UNIT—9:1–2 [NICNT]. The topic is Saul's expedition to Damascus.

9:1 But[a] Saul, still breathing[b] threats and murder against the disciples of the Lord, went-to the high-priest **9:2** and asked him for letters to the synagogues[c] at Damascus, so that if he found any belonging to the Way,[d] men or women, he-might-bring (them) bound to Jerusalem.

LEXICON—a. δὲ (LN 89.124): 'but' [AB, BECNT, LN; ESV], 'meanwhile' [CBC; NET, NIV, NLT, NRSV], 'in the meantime' [TEV], 'now' [NASB], 'and' [KJV], not explicit [Bar; CEV, GW, NCV, REB]. This conjunction indicates a contrast [LN].

   b. pres. act. participle of ἐμπνέω (LN 33.293) (BDAG 1. p. 324): 'to breathe' [Bar, BDAG, BECNT, CBC; ESV, KJV, NASB, NET, NIV, NRSV, REB], 'to utter' [NLT]. The phrase 'still breathing threats' is also translated 'kept-on/kept threatening' [CEV, GW], 'still threatening' [NCV], 'breathed murderous threats' [BDAG], 'kept up his violent threats' [TEV], 'was still set on threats' [AB]. The phrase 'to breathe out threats' is an idiom meaning to express dire threats. In this verse it means to threaten strongly, to make firm threats [LN]. It means to emit breath [BDAG].

   c. συναγωγή (LN 11.45) (BDAG 3.a. p. 963): 'synagogue' [AB, BDAG, BECNT, CBC, LN; all versions except CEV], 'congregation' [LN], 'their leaders' [CEV], not explicit [Bar]. This noun denotes a congregation of Jews. Since the borrowed term 'synagogue' in receptor languages so frequently refers only to a building rather than to a congregation, it may be necessary in Acts 9:2 to say he asked for letters of introduction to 'leaders of the synagogues' or 'leaders of the congregations of Jews' [LN]. This noun denotes localized synagogues [BDAG].

   d. ὁδός (LN 41.35) (BDAG 3.c. p. 692): 'Way' [AB, Bar, BDAG, BECNT, CBC, LN; ESV, NASB, NET, NIV, NRSV], 'Christian way of life' [LN]. The phrase 'belonging to the Way' is also translated 'of this way' [KJV], 'followed the way' [GW], 'followers of Christ's Way' [NCV], 'followers of the Way' [NLT, TEV], 'followers of the new way' [REB], 'had accepted the Lord's Way' [CEV]. This noun denotes behavior in accordance with Christian principles and practices [LN]. It denotes the whole way of life from a moral and spiritual viewpoint [BDAG].

QUESTION—Why does it say that Saul was 'still' breathing out threats?

The account of Saul's persecution of the church in 8:1–4 is now resumed [Bar, BECNT, CBC, EBC, NAC, NICNT, PNTC, TH, TNTC, TRT]. This is the only time in the New Testament that the term ἐμπνέων for 'breathe' is used. It is part of the idiom ἐμπνέων ἀπειλῆς 'to breath out threat, threaten strongly.' This expression reflects Saul's highly hostile attitude toward believers [BECNT].

QUESTION—Why did Saul go to the high priest?

At that time, the Roman government had given the Jewish Council authority over the Jews living in foreign cities and the high priest was the head of the Jewish Council. For this reason, Saul went to the high priest to ask for authority over the persons whom he wanted to arrest [TH].

QUESTION—What kind of city was Damascus?
Damascus was one of the ten main Greek cities in Decapolis Province (Mark 5:20) [Bar, EBC, NAC, TNTC, TRT]. It had thousands of Jews living in it, and it is the oldest continually-inhabited city in the world [TRT]. It was a prosperous commercial center in the Roman province of Syria, with a large Jewish population and several synagogues [Bar, EBC, NICNT, PNTC, TNTC]. The Jewish Christians there had mostly fled from Jerusalem and had taken refuge there [NAC, TH]. It is an important city 135 miles north-northeast of Jerusalem [Bar, BECNT, TNTC]; the first city outside the land of Israel to be noted as having Christians [BECNT].

QUESTION—Who would be anticipated in the synagogues?
At that time, most Christians were Jews who continued worshipping God at synagogues [TRT]. Jewish Christians considered belief in Christ the fulfillment of their Jewish hopes [TH].

QUESTION—What does τῆς ὁδοῦ ὄντας 'belonging to the Way' refer to?
'Belonging to the Way' refers to the followers of Jesus. It focuses on the way of salvation or the way to eternal life, namely Jesus. In John 14:6 Jesus called himself 'the Way' [NICNT, TRT]. The phrase refers to Christians, disciples, and those calling on the name of the Lord [Bar, CBC, PNTC, TH]. 'The Way' was an early name for Christianity [AB, TNTC]. It was sometimes referred to as 'the way of the Lord' or 'the way of God [BECNT, TNTC].

QUESTION—What is meant by δεδεμένους ἀγάγῃ εἰς Ἰερουσαλήμ 'might bring them bound to Jerusalem'?
The phrase 'bring them bound to Jerusalem' refers to arresting them and taking them back to Jerusalem [TH].

DISCOURSE UNIT—9:3–7 [NICNT]. The topic is the light and voice from heaven.

9:3 Now as (he)-was-traveling, it-happened-(that) he was-approaching Damascus, and suddenly (a)-light from heaven/the-sky[a] flashed-around him. **9:4** And falling[b] to the ground he-heard (a) voice saying to-him, "Saul, Saul, why are-you-persecuting[c] me?"

LEXICON—a. οὐρανός (LN 1.5, 1.11) (BDAG 2.b. p. 739): 'heaven' [AB, Bar, BDAG, BECNT, LN (1.11); all versions except REB, TEV], 'sky' [CBC, LN (1.5); REB, TEV]. This noun denotes heaven, the supernatural dwelling place of God and other heavenly beings [LN (1.11)] or it denotes the sky above the earth, including the vault arching high over the earth from one horizon to another, as well as the sun, moon, and stars [LN (1.5)]. It denotes the transcendent abode that is the dwelling place or throne of God [BDAG].

b. aorist act. participle of πίπτω (LN 15.119) (BDAG 1.b.α. p. 815):'to fall' [BDAG, BECNT; all versions], 'to fall down' [AB, Bar, BDAG, CBC, LN]. This verb means to fall from a standing or upright position down to the ground or surface [LN].

c. pres. act. indic. of διώκω (LN 39.45) (BDAG 2. p. 254): 'to persecute' [AB, Bar, BDAG, BECNT, CBC, LN; all versions except CEV], 'to harass' [LN]. The clause 'why are you persecuting me?' is also translated 'why are you so cruel to me?' [CEV]. This verb means to systematically organize a program to oppress and harass people [LN]. It means to harass someone, especially because of beliefs [BDAG].

QUESTION—What was the light from heaven that Paul saw?

Verses 3-9 are the first description of Paul's conversion (the others are 22:3-16; 26:4-18) [AB, BECNT, CBC]. In Acts 22:6, this supernatural light outshone the noonday sun, suggesting a glorious epiphany [BECNT, EBC, PNTC]. Subsequent references in Acts (22:14-15; 26:16) make it clear that Saul saw the exalted Messiah, not just a light from heaven. The light in this context appears to be a manifestation of Christ's heavenly glory. There is also a symbolic aspect to this light. Saul is 'forced by the Messiah's light to recognize his own blindness and to receive his sight through him.' Having seen the light of Christ himself, Saul was then required to bear witness to what he had seen and heard (22:14-15; 26:16). Jesus appointed Saul to fulfill the Servant's role outlined in Isaiah 49:6 and become 'a light for the Gentiles' [PNTC]. For Luke, light is a physical representation of the divine glory of Christ [AB, Bar, TNTC].

QUESTION—What caused Saul to fall on the ground?

As always happened at revelations, men were overwhelmed by the heavenly reality and fell to the ground [AB].

QUESTION—Whose voice did Saul hear?

Saul heard the voice of Jesus [NICNT, TNTC, TRT]. The double calling out of the name of Saul indicates intense emotion from Jesus [BECNT].

QUESTION—Why did Jesus say that Saul was persecuting him?

The relationship between Jesus and his followers was so close that when Saul persecuted Jesus' followers, it was as if he was persecuting Jesus (Luke 10:16) [TRT]. Jesus closely identified himself with his own [BECNT], with his church [AB]. Any leader is injured if his followers are attacked [Bar].

9:5 And he-said, "Who are-you, Lord?" And-(the-voice-said), "I am Jesus, whom you are-persecuting. 9:6 But stand-up[a] and enter the city, and you will-be-told what you have[b] to-do."

LEXICON—a. aorist act. impera. of ἀνίστημι (LN 17.6) (BDAG 10. p. 83): 'to stand up' [AB, Bar, BECNT, CBC, LN; all versions except ESV, KJV], 'to rise' [BDAG, BECNT; ESV], 'to arise' [KJV], 'to set out' [BDAG], 'to get ready' [BDAG]. This verb means to assume a standing position [LN]. It means to initiate an action [BDAG].

b. pres. act. indic. of δεῖ (LN 71.21) (BDAG 1.d. p. 214]: 'to have to do' [AB, Bar, BDAG, BECNT, CBC, LN; all versions except CEV, GW], 'should do' [LN; GW]. The phrase 'what you have to do' is also translated 'what to do' [CEV]. This verb means to be something which should be done as the result of compulsion, whether internal (as a matter of duty) or external (law, custom, and circumstances) [LN]. It means to be of compulsion caused by the necessity of attaining a certain result [BDAG].

QUESTION—Why did Saul address the speaker 'Lord'?

Although Saul did not yet know that he was talking to Jesus, he probably realized that he was in God's presence, and so he addressed the person of the voice with respect and used the term 'Lord' which means master here [EBC, TRT]. His use of 'Lord' here is not a Christological confession but indicates his high respect for the heavenly one in the vision, an expression more than 'sir' but less than an expression of a Christological understanding [BECNT, EBC, NAC, TNTC].

QUESTION—What is implied by the clause 'what you have to do'?

The clause 'what you must do' implies a 'divine necessity' inherent in the calling [BECNT, PNTC]. Saul must now begin walking by faith in Jesus, obedient to the heavenly vision and the revelation to follow [PNTC].

9:7 The men who were traveling with-him stood speechless,[a] on-the-one-(hand)[b] hearing the voice but-on-the-other-(hand) seeing no-one.

LEXICON—a. ἐνεός (LN 33.108) (BDAG p. 335): 'speechless' [BDAG, BECNT, CBC, LN; all versions except NCV, TEV], 'dumbfounded' [AB, LN]. The phrase 'stood speechless' is also translated 'stood there but said nothing' [NCV], 'had stopped, not saying a word' [TEV], 'stood still, struck dumb' [Bar]. This adjective pertains to an incapacity to speak, whether temporary or permanent, but in the NT only temporary and associated with fright or amazement [LN]. It pertains to lacking ability to speak [BDAG].

b. μέν...δέ (LN 89.136): This combination of conjunctions means 'on the one hand...but on the other hand' [LN]. The words 'hearing on the one hand..., but on the other (hand)...' is also translated 'on the one hand, hearing the voice but on the other...' [BECNT], 'hearing the voice but seeing no one' [ESV, NASB], 'heard the voice but saw no one' [Bar, CBC; CEV, GW, NCV, NET, NRSV, REB, TEV], 'hearing a voice, but seeing no man' [KJV], 'heard the sound but did not see anyone' [NIV], 'heard the sound of someone's voice but saw no one' [NLT], 'heard the voice, they saw no one' [AB]. The combination of conjunctions 'on the one hand..., but...' marks one set of items in contrast with another set [LN].

QUESTION—What is meant by the statement that they heard the voice but they saw no one?

The men saw the light but did not see anyone. This tells that Saul saw what his companions did not see (Acts 9:17, 27). This encounter was for Saul alone [AB, Bar, BECNT, CBC, NAC, PNTC, TNTC].

DISCOURSE UNIT—9:8–9 [NICNT]. The topic is Saul enters Damascus.

9:8 Saul got-up[a] from the ground, and although his eyes were-opened,[b] he-could-see nothing. So they led-him-by-(the)-hand[c] and brought him into Damascus. **9:9** And for three days he-was without sight, and neither ate nor drank.

LEXICON—a. aorist pass. indic. of ἐγείρω (LN 17.9) (BDAG 4. p. 271): 'to get up' [AB, Bar, BDAG, CBC, LN; CEV, NASB, NCV, NET, NIV, NRSV, REB, TEV], 'to stand up' [LN], 'to rise' [BDAG, BECNT; ESV, KJV]. The phrase 'Saul got up' is also translated 'Saul was helped up' [GW], 'Saul picked himself up' [NLT]. This verb means to get up, normally from a lying or reclining position but possibly from a seated position [LN]. It means to move to a standing position [BDAG].
  b. perf. pass. participle of ἀνοίγω (LN 79.110) (BDAG 5.b. p. 84): 'to be opened' [AB, Bar, BDAG, BECNT, CBC, LN; CEV, ESV, GW, KJV, NCV, NIV, NLT, REB, TEV], 'to be made open' [LN]. This verb is also translated 'were open' [NASB, NET, NRSV]. This verb means to cause something to be open [LN]. It means to cause to function [BDAG].
  c. pres. act. participle of χειραγωγέω (LN 15.184) (BDAG p. 1083): 'to take/lead by the hand' [AB, Bar, BDAG, BECNT, CBC, LN; all versions except GW], not explicit [GW]. This verb means to lead or guide by taking by the hand [LN].

QUESTION—What is the significance of Saul becoming blind?
  The blindness is the outcome of having seen such glory and it shows that Saul has been reduced to powerlessness and helplessness before the Lord [Bar, BECNT, NAC].

QUESTION—Why did Saul neither eat nor drink for three days?
  This implies that Paul was fasting [Bar, BECNT, CBC, PNTC, TNTC]. Fasting in Scripture can be an expression of repentance, but it is also a way of preparing to receive further revelation from the Lord [PNTC].

DISCOURSE UNIT—9:10–19a [EBC, PNTC]. The topic is Ananias's ministry to Saul [EBC], accepted into the fellowship of the persecuted church [PNTC].

DISCOURSE UNIT—9:10–16 [NICNT]. The topic is Ananias sent to Saul.

9:10 Now there-was a disciple at Damascus named Ananias. The Lord said to him in (a)-vision,[a] "Ananias." And he-said, "(Here)-I-(am), Lord."

LEXICON—a. ὅραμα (LN 33.488) (BDAG 2. p. 718): 'vision' [AB, Bar, BDAG, BECNT, CBC, LN; all versions]. This noun denotes an event in which something appears vividly and credibly to the mind, although not actually present, but implying the influence of some divine or supernatural power or agency [LN]. It denotes the act by which the recipient of a vision is granted a vision, or the state of being in which the person receives a vision [BDAG].

QUESTION—Who was this 'Lord'?
  Verse 17 confirms that 'the Lord' was Jesus [Bar, BECNT, NAC, PNTC, TNTC, TRT].

QUESTION—What is a vision?

A vision indicates a supernatural experience in which a divine revelation is given to a person [TH].

QUESTION—What is indicated by Ananias' response?

Ananias' response 'Here I am Lord' indicates both his presence and his readiness to obey and carry out the Lord's will [BECNT, PNTC].

9:11 And the Lord (said) to him, "Rise[a] and go to the street called Straight, and at (the)-house of-Judas look[b] for (a)-man-from-Tarsus named Saul, for behold, he-is-praying, 9:12 and he has seen in a vision a man named Ananias come in and lay his hands on him so that he might regain his sight."

TEXT—Some manuscripts include [ἐν ὁράματι] 'in a vision'. The GNT includes this phrase in the text in brackets with a C rating indicating that the Committee had difficulty making the decision. All versions except RSV include this phrase.

LEXICON—a. aorist act. participle of ἀνίστημι (LN 17.6) (BDAG 10. p. 83): 'to rise' [BDAG, BECNT; ESV, KJV], 'to stand up' [LN], 'to get up' [AB, Bar; CEV, GW, NASB, NCV, NET, NRSV], 'to get ready' [BDAG; TEV], not explicit [CBC; NIV, NLT, REB]. This verb means to assume a standing position [LN]. It means to initiate an action [BDAG].

b. aorist act. impera. of ζητέω (LN 27.41): 'to look' [ESV, NET, NRSV], 'to inquire' [BECNT; KJV, NASB], 'to ask' [CBC; GW, NCV, NIV, NLT, REB, TEV], 'to seek' [AB, Bar], 'to find' [CEV]. This verb means to try to learn the location of something, often by movement from place to place in the process of searching [LN].

QUESTION—Where was this Straight Street?

Straight Street was one of the two main streets that ran the length of the city of Damascus from east to west [BECNT, EBC, NAC, NICNT, PNTC, TH, TRT]. It was very long and very straight [CBC]. Today the road is known as Derb el-Mustaqim or Darb el-Mostakim [BECNT, EBC, NAC, NICNT, PNTC].

QUESTION—Who was this Judas?

Judas was probably a Jewish acquaintance of Saul or one of his companions [PNTC]. He is unknown, but he was presumably a Jew [Bar].

QUESTION—What does the word 'Tarsus' refer to?

It refers to the city of Tarsus [TH]. Tarsus, was an important Hellenistic city [Bar]. It was the major city of Cilicia [BECNT, CBC]. It was a great commercial and educational center, a seat for the Roman governor [BECNT].

QUESTION—What does the clause 'for behold, he is praying' suggest?

The fact that Saul is praying suggests that Saul has been humbled and was now seeking God's help. It is introduced by the words ἰδού γάρ 'for behold' which suggest something worthy of special attention [PNTC]. He was serious in embracing Christianity [AB], and needed the help that Ananias could bring [Bar].

QUESTION—What is indicated by the use of a double vision?

In v. 10 the Lord said to Ananias in a vision to look for Saul and now in v. 12 Saul has seen in a vision in which a man named Ananias came to him. By means of a double vision, with very specific directions, the Lord brings Saul and Ananias together [PNTC, TNTC]. This reassures both parties of God's will in the situation [PNTC]. Double vision means that an event is fixed by God (Gen. 41:32) [BECNT]. It emphasizes the centrality of the divine leading in the entire episode [NAC].

9:13 But Ananias answered, "Lord, I have heard from many about this man, how much evil he has done to your saints[a] at Jerusalem. **9:14** And here he-has authority[b] from the chief-priests to-bind[c] all who call-on your name."

LEXICON—a. ἅγιος (LN 11.27): 'saints' [AB, Bar, BECNT; ESV, KJV, NASB, NET, NIV, NRSV], 'God's people' [LN], 'followers' [CEV], 'people' [CBC; GW, REB, TEV], 'holy people' [NCV], 'believers' [NLT]. This adjective occurs in the plural as a substantive that refers to persons who belong to God, and as such constitute a religious entity [LN].
  b. ἐξουσία (LN 37.35): 'authority' [AB, Bar, BECNT, CBC, LN; all versions except CEV, NCV, NLT], 'power' [CEV, NCV]. The phrase 'he has authority' is also translated 'he is authorized' [NLT]. This noun denotes the right to control or govern over others [LN].
  c. aorist act. infin. of δέω (LN 37.114) (BDAG 1.b. p. 221): 'to bind' [BDAG, BECNT; ESV, KJV, NASB, NRSV], 'to tie' [BDAG], 'to imprison' [LN; NET], 'to put in prison' [GW], 'to arrest' [AB, Bar, CBC; CEV, NCV, NIV, NLT, REB, TEV]. This verb means to confine someone in prison [LN]. It means to bind and imprison someone [BDAG].

QUESTION—Who were these ἁγίοις 'saints'?

The word 'saints' used here in the Greek text literally means 'holy ones.' It refers to God's people as people who are set apart (that is, chosen by God) to serve Him [Bar, CBC, TH, TNTC, TRT]. Here the saints are specifically Jewish believers in Jesus [BECNT, NAC, PNTC]. It is a common Pauline term for Christians [TH].

QUESTION—Who were the ones that Saul had authority to bind?

Saul had the authority to bind all who called on Jesus' name, those who were followers of Jesus [NICNT]. Those believers who called on Jesus' name for salvation [BECNT], depended on Jesus to provide for them and help them. They also worshipped Jesus and prayed to Him [TRT]. The phrase 'call on your name' is equivalent to 'worship you' [TH].

9:15 But the Lord said to him, "Go, for he is (a)-chosen instrument[a] of mine to-carry[b] my name before the Gentiles and kings and (the)-people[c] of-Israel.
LEXICON—a. σκεῦος (LN 9.21) (BDAG 3. p. 927): 'instrument' [BDAG, CBC; ESV, NASB, NET, NIV, NLT, NRSV, REB], 'person' [LN], 'vessel' [Bar, BDAG, BECNT; KJV], 'agent' [AB]. The phrase 'he is a chosen instrument' is also translated 'I have chosen him' [CEV, TEV], 'I've chosen this man' [GW], 'I have chosen Saul' [NCV]. This noun is a figurative extension of meaning of the word 'instrument' or 'thing' and it denotes a person in relation to a particular function or role [LN]. It denotes a human being exercising a function [BDAG].
   b. aorist act. infin. of βαστάζω (LN 33.210) (BDAG 2.c. p. 171): 'to carry' [AB, BDAG, BECNT; ESV, NET, NIV], 'to take' [NLT], 'to bear' [Bar, BDAG; KJV, NASB], 'to tell' [CEV, NCV], 'to bring' [CBC; GW, NRSV, REB]. The phrase 'to carry my name' is also translated 'to make my name known' [LN; TEV], 'to inform people about me' [LN]. The idiom 'to carry a name' means to spread information extensively about a person [LN]. It means to sustain a burden without the idea of outward or inward stress [BDAG].
   c. υἱός (LN 11.58) (BDAG 1.c. p. 1024): The idiom 'sons of Israel' [Bar, BECNT; NASB] denotes 'the people of Israel' [CBC; CEV, GW, NCV, NET, NIV, NLT, NRSV, REB, TEV], 'the children of Israel' [ESV, KJV], 'his countrymen, the people of Israel' [LN], 'the Israelites' [AB]. The Greek idiom 'sons of Israel' refers to the people of Israel as an ethnic entity. In translating the expression 'the people of Israel' it may be necessary to use an appositional phrase, for example, 'the people, namely, Israel' or a relative clause which also serves an appositional function, for example, 'the people who are Israel.' In some languages it may be preferable to use a term such as 'nation' followed by some expression which will indicate that Israel is simply the name of the nation, for example, 'the nation called Israel' [LN]. This noun denotes human offspring in an extended line of descent [BDAG].
QUESTION—What does 'carry my name' mean?
   'Carry my name' means 'bear witness to what Saul has seen and heard of the risen Jesus and preach in Jesus' name' [PNTC, TNTC]. Saul was selected as a vessel and he was given a ministry of taking the name of Jesus to Gentiles, kings, and Israel, throughout the world [Bar, BECNT].

9:16 For I-(myself) will-show[a] him how-much he must suffer for the sake of my name.[b]"
LEXICON—a. fut. act. indic. of ὑποδείκνυμι (LN 28.47) (BDAG 2. p. 1037): 'to show' [AB, Bar, BDAG, BECNT, CBC, LN; all versions], 'to make known' [LN], 'to demonstrate' [LN], 'to prove' [BDAG], 'to set forth' [BDAG]. This verb means to make known the character or significance of

something by visual, auditory, gestural, or linguistic means [LN]. It means to give instruction or moral direction. [BDAG].
b. ὄνομα (LN 33.126): 'name' [AB, Bar, BECNT, CBC, LN; all versions except TEV]. The phrase 'for the sake of my name' is also translated 'for my sake' [TEV]. This noun denotes the proper name of a person or object [LN].

QUESTION—What is the function of the beginning conjunction γάρ 'for'?
The use of γάρ 'for' shows that this verse explains the chosen-instrument and bearing-the-name remark of v. 15 [BECNT].

QUESTION—In Greek, the pronoun subject ἐγώ 'I' is placed at the beginning of the verse before the verb ὑποδείξω 'I will show' which already includes a suffix that indicates that its subject is 'I'. What is the purpose of beginning the verse with this emphatic word 'I'?
Such usage indicates that the subject 'I' is to be stressed. If one wishes to bring out the intended emphasis, one can translate the subject as 'I myself' [TH]. The emphatic 'I' explains the unexpected 'for'. You, Ananias, need not hesitate to perform the task I am giving you, for I myself will be personally engaged in it [Bar]. It is also translated 'I myself' by TH, TRT; NCV, NRSV, REB, TEV.

DISCOURSE UNIT—9:17–19a [NICNT]. The topic is Ananias visits Saul.

9:17 **So Ananias departed**[a] **and entered the house. And laying his hands on him he-said, "Brother**[b] **Saul, the Lord Jesus who appeared**[c] **to-you on the road by-which you-came**[d] **has sent me so that you-may-regain-your-sight and be-filled**[e] **with-(the)-Holy Spirit."**

LEXICON—a. aorist act. indic. of ἀπέρχομαι (LN 15.37): 'to depart' [BECNT, LN; ESV, NASB, NET], 'to go away' [LN; KJV], 'to leave' [LN; CEV, GW], not explicit [AB, Bar, CBC; NCV, NIV, NLT, NRSV, REB, TEV]. This verb means to move away from a reference point with emphasis upon the departure [LN].
b. ἀδελφός (LN 11.23): 'brother' [AB, Bar, BECNT, CBC, LN; all versions except CEV], 'fellow believer' [LN], not explicit [CEV]. This noun denotes a close associate of a group of persons having a well-defined membership. In the NT ἀδελφός 'brother' refers specifically to fellow believers in Christ [LN].
c. aorist pass. participle of ὁράω (LN 24.1) (BDAG A.1.d. p. 719): 'to appear' [Bar, BDAG, BECNT, CBC; all versions except NCV], 'to be seen' [LN]. The phrase 'who appeared to you' is also translated 'who revealed himself to you' [AB], 'the one you saw' [NCV]. This verb means to see [LN]. In the passive voice it means to appear, to become visible [BDAG].
d. imperf. mid./pass. (deponent = act.) indic. of ἔρχομαι (LN 15.81): 'to come' [AB, Bar, BECNT, LN; ESV, KJV, NASB, NET, NIV, TEV], not explicit [CBC; CEV, GW, NCV, NLT, NRSV, REB]. This verb means to

move toward or up to the reference point of the viewpoint character or event [LN].
  e. aorist pass. subj. of πίμπλημι (LN 59.38) (BDAG 1.a.β. p. 813): 'to be filled' [AB, Bar, BDAG, BECNT, CBC LN; all versions]. This verb means to cause something to be completely full [BDAG, LN], and here it refers to a person's inner life in regard to the Holy Spirit [BDAG].

QUESTION—Why is the Greek word δὲ at the beginning of 9:17 translated as 'So'?

It is important to translate δὲ 'So' as a transitional particle, a marker of result. It marks the conclusion of the preceding paragraph and introduces the result stated in this paragraph [TH]. It also reflects the obedience of Ananias to the divine command (vv. 11–12) [PNTC].

9:18 And immediately (something)-like scales fell from his eyes and he-regained-his-sight. And when-he-arose[a] he-was-baptized.[b] **9:19a** And he-took food and was strengthened.[c]

LEXICON—a. aorist act. participle of ἀνίστημι (LN 17.6): 'to arise' [AB, BECNT; ESV, KJV], 'to get up' [Bar; CEV, NASB, NCV, NET, NIV, NLT, NRSV, REB], 'to stand up' [LN; GW, TEV], not explicit [CBC]. This verb means to assume a standing position [LN].
  b. aorist pass. indic. of βαπτίζω (LN 53.41) (BDAG 2.c. p. 164): 'to be baptized' [AB, Bar, BDAG, BECNT, CBC, LN; all versions], 'to be plunged, to be dipped, to be washed' [BDAG]. This verb means to employ water in a religious ceremony designed to symbolize purification and initiation on the basis of repentance [LN]. It means to use water in a rite for the purpose of renewing or establishing a relationship with God [BDAG].
  c. aorist act. indic. of ἐνισχύω (LN 79.65) (BDAG 1. p. 337): 'to regain strength' [AB, BDAG, BECNT, LN; ESV, KJV, NASB, NIV, NLT, NRSV], 'to grow strong' [Bar, BDAG]. This verb is also translated 'his strength came back' [GW, TEV], 'his strength returned' [CBC; NCV, NET, REB], 'felt much better' [CEV]. This verb means to regain one's physical strength after a temporary loss of it [LN]. It means to recover from loss of strength [BDAG].

QUESTION—What was it that fell from his eyes so that he could see again?

It was a thin layer or peel, something like fish scales or small flakes of skin [LN (8.57)]. It was thin flaky pieces like scales that were falling from his eyes [BDAG (2. p. 592)]. They were flaky substances [BECNT, NICNT], a kind of a film [TNTC], Translations call it flakes [NAC]. scaly substances [NASB, EBC], scales [KJV, NCV, NET, NIV, NLT, NRSV, REB] or something like fish scales [CEV, GW, TEV].

DISCOURSE UNIT—9:19b–31 [PNTC, TNTC; NASB, NIV, NLT]. The topic is Saul begins to preach Christ [NASB], Saul in Damascus and Jerusalem [NIV, NLT], Saul preaches in Damascus and Jerusalem [PNTC], Paul begins to preach [TNTC].

DISCOURSE UNIT—9:19b–30 [AB, Bar]. The topic is Paul in Damascus and Jerusalem [AB], Saul from Damascus to Jerusalem [Bar].

DISCOURSE UNIT—9:19b–25 [BECNT, EBC, PNTC; CEV, NCV, TEV]. The topic is Saul preaches in Damascus [BECNT], Saul preaches in Damascus [CEV, NCV, TEV], Saul's conversion evidenced in Damascus [EBC], proclaiming the son of God in Damascus [PNTC].

DISCOURSE UNIT—9:19b–22 [NICNT; ESV, NRSV]. The topic is Saul proclaims Jesus in Synagogues [ESV], Saul preaches in Damascus [NICNT; NRSV].

9:19b For some days he was with the disciples in Damascus. **9:20** And immediately he-was-proclaiming[a] Jesus in the synagogues,[b] saying, "He is the Son of-God."

LEXICON—a. imperf. act. indic. of κηρύσσω (LN 33.256) (BDAG 2.b.β. p. 544): 'to proclaim' [Bar, BDAG, BECNT, CBC; ESV, NASB, NET, NRSV, REB], 'to preach' [AB, LN; KJV, NCV, NIV, NLT, TEV], 'to tell' [CEV], 'to spread the word' [GW]. This verb means to publicly announce religious truths and principles while urging acceptance and compliance [LN]. It means to make public declarations [BDAG].
  b. συναγωγή (LN 7.20) (BDAG 2.a. p. 963): 'synagogue' [AB, Bar, BECNT, CBC, LN; all versions except CEV], 'Jewish meeting place' [CEV], 'Christian assembly place' [LN]. This noun denotes a building of assembly, associated with religious activity. Normally it was a building in which Jewish worship took place and in which the Law was taught [LN]. It denotes a place of assembly [BDAG].

QUESTION—Who do the pronouns 'he' represent in verse 20?
  It means: And immediately Saul was proclaiming Jesus in the synagogues, saying, "Jesus is the son of God" [TRT]. Note that 'He is the son of God' is a direct discourse reflected by the conjunction ὅτι 'that' in front of the clause οὗτός ἐστιν ὁ υἱὸς τοῦ θεοῦ 'this one is the son of God' [BECNT].

9:21 And all those hearing him were-amazed[a] and were-saying, "Is not this the-man who destroyed those who called-upon[b] this name in Jerusalem? And has he not come here for the-(purpose) of bringing such-people bound before the chief-priests?[c]"

LEXICON—a. imperf. indic. of ἐξίστημι (LN 25.220) (BDAG 2.b. p. 350): 'to be amazed' [BDAG, BECNT; all versions except NIV, REB], 'to be astounded' [CBC; REB], 'to be astonished' [AB, Bar, BDAG; NIV], 'to be astonished greatly, to be greatly astounded, to be astounded completely' [LN]. This verb means to cause someone to be so astounded as to be practically overwhelmed [LN]. It means to have the feeling of astonishment mingled with fear caused by events which are miraculous, extraordinary, or difficult to understand [BDAG].
  b. pres. mid. participle of ἐπικαλέω (LN 33.131) (BDAG 1. p. 373): 'to call upon' [BDAG; ESV], 'to call on' [BECNT; KJV, NASB, NET, NIV], 'to

call out to' [BDAG], 'to call' [LN], 'to invoke' [AB, Bar, CBC; NRSV, REB], not explicit [NLT]. The phrase 'who called upon this name' is also translated 'who worship in the name of Jesus' [CEV], 'who worshiped the one named Jesus' [GW], 'who trust in this name' [NCV], 'who worship that man Jesus' [TEV]. This verb means to use an attribution in speaking of a person [LN]. It means to call upon deity for any purpose [BDAG].
   c. ἀρχιερεύς (LN 53.88): 'chief priest' [AB, Bar, BECNT, CBC, LN; all versions except NCV, NLT], 'leading priest' [NCV, NLT]. This noun denotes a principal priest, in view of belonging to one of the high-priestly families. In a number of languages 'chief priests' are referred to simply as 'big priests' or 'important priests' [LN].

QUESTION—What kind of questions are these?

These questions are rhetorical questions that clearly indicate that a positive answer is implied [TH]. The negative interrogative οὐχ 'not' means that the question expects a positive reply [BECNT].

9:22 But Saul kept increasing-in-strength^a and confounding^b the Jews who lived in Damascus by proving^c that this Jesus is the Messiah.^d

LEXICON—a. imperf. pass. indic. of ἐνδυναμόω (LN 74.7) (BDAG 2. p. 333): 'to become strong' [AB, Bar, BDAG, BECNT, CBC; all versions except CEV, NET], 'to become able' [LN], 'to become capable' [LN; NET], not explicit [CEV]. This verb means to become able to do something [LN]. It means to become able to function or to do something [BDAG].
   b. imperf. act. indic. of συγχέω (LN 25.221) (BDAG p. 953): 'to confound' [Bar, BDAG, BECNT, LN; ESV, KJV, NASB, NRSV, REB], 'to confuse' [CEV, GW], 'to cause consternation' [BDAG, LN; NET], 'to baffle' [NIV], 'to silence' [AB, CBC], not explicit [NCV, NLT, TEV]. This verb means to cause such astonishment as to bewilder and dismay [LN]. It means to cause dismay [BDAG].
   c. pres. act. participle of συμβιβάζω (LN 28.46) (BDAG 3. p. 957): 'to prove' [AB, BDAG, BECNT; ESV, GW, KJV, NASB, NET, NIV, NRSV], 'to make known' [LN], 'to demonstrate' [BDAG, LN], 'to show' [LN; CEV], 'to teach' [Bar]. This verb is also translated as a noun: 'proofs' [CBC; NCV, NLT, REB, TEV]. This verb means to make known the character or significance of something by visual, auditory, gestural, or linguistic means [LN]. It means to present a logical conclusion [BDAG].
   d. Χριστός (LN 53.82) (BDAG 1. p. 1091): 'Messiah' [AB, BDAG, CBC, LN; CEV, GW, NLT, NRSV, REB, TEV], 'Christ' [Bar, BDAG, BECNT, LN; ESV, KJV, NASB, NCV, NET, NIV], 'the Anointed One' [BDAG]. Literally 'one who has been anointed' it is a title for Jesus as the Messiah [LN]. It is the name for the fulfiller of Israelite expectation of a deliverer and it is also translated 'the Messiah, the Anointed One, the Christ' [BDAG]. This title occurs in verses 3:31, 36; 9:22; 17:3; 18:5, 28; 26:23.

QUESTION—What is meant by 'Saul kept increasing in strength'?

The phrase refers to Saul's knowledge and his ability in preaching about Jesus, not his physical strength or health, and not the loudness or length of his preaching [BECNT, TH, TRT]. The term ἐνεδυναμοῦτο 'was being strengthened, became capable' suggests the empowerment of the Spirit [PNTC].

DISCOURSE UNIT—9:23-31 [NAC]. The topic is Paul the persecuted.

DISCOURSE UNIT—9:23-25 [NICNT; ESV, NET, NRSV]. The topic is Saul's escape from Damascus [NET], Saul escapes from Damascus [NICNT; ESV], Saul escapes from the Jews [NRSV].

9:23 **When many days had-passed,[a] the Jews plotted[b] to-kill him, 9:24 but their plot became-known to-Saul. They-were- also -watching[c] the gates day and night so that they-might-kill him, 9:25 but his disciples took him during-(the)-night and let him down through an opening in the wall, lowering him in (a)-basket.**

LEXICON—a. imperf. pass. indic. of πληρόω (LN 67.70) (BDAG 2. p. 828): 'to pass' [BECNT; ESV, NET, NRSV, REB], 'to elapse' [NASB], 'to be fulfilled' [KJV], 'to be completed' [Bar, BDAG, LN], 'to come to an end' [BDAG, LN]. The phrase 'when many days had passed' is also translated 'after many days' [NCV], 'after many days had gone by' [NIV, TEV], 'after a while' [NLT], 'after some time' [AB], 'as the days mounted up' [CBC], 'later' [CEV, GW]. This verb means to come to the end of a period of time, with the implication of the completion of an implied purpose or plan [LN]. It means to complete a period of time [BDAG].

b. aorist mid. indic. of συμβουλεύω (LN 30.74) (BDAG 2. p. 957): 'to plot' [AB, Bar, BDAG, BECNT, LN; ESV, NASB, NET, NLT, NRSV], 'to hatch a plot' [CBC; REB], 'to consult' [BDAG, LN], 'to confer' [LN], 'to counsel' [KJV], 'to conspire' [NIV], 'to make plans against' [LN; CEV, GW, NCV, TEV]. This verb means to engage in joint planning so as to devise a course of common action, often one with a harmful or evil purpose [LN]. It means to be involved with others in plotting a course of action [BDAG].

c. imperf. mid. indic. of παρατηρέω (LN 24.48) (BDAG 2.b. p. 771): 'to watch' [AB, Bar, BDAG, BECNT, CBC; all versions except CEV, NIV], 'to watch closely' [LN; NIV], 'to guard' [BDAG, LN; CEV]. This verb means to watch closely or diligently [LN]. It means to stand guard [BDAG].

QUESTION—Where were the gates?

The city of Damascus was surrounded by a tall thick stone wall that had gates in it. At that time most cities had walls around them for protection [TRT].

272   ACTS 9:23–25

QUESTION—Who were Saul's disciples?
They were possibly his converts, Christians who owed their faith to Saul and stood particularly close to him; but no answer to this question is entirely satisfactory [Bar]. They were his converts, and calling them his disciples would give the impression that already a group of supporters had risen [CBC]. That Saul had disciples at this point is somewhat surprising. Perhaps they were converts from the synagogues who had responded to his preaching and scriptural argumentation (vv. 20, 22) [NAC]. Saul apparently ministered long enough to have his own band of disciples [BECNT]. They were Saul's followers who had responded favorably to his new proclamation about Christ and wanted to help him [EBC]. They were the disciples, the Christians of that town (Damascus) [AB].

QUESTION—What kind of basket was used to lower Saul?
The word σπυρίς 'basket' refers to a large container that was often used to collect excess food, such as at the feeding of the multitudes (Matt. 15:37; 16:10). It was like a hamper basket. Such escape was not unusual (Josh. 2:15; 1 Sam. 19:12) [BECNT].

DISCOURSE UNIT—9:26–31 [PNTC; CEV, ESV, NRSV, TEV]. The topic is Saul in Jerusalem [CEV, ESV, NRSV, TEV], Saul preaches in Jerusalem [NCV], disputing with Hellenists in Jerusalem [PNTC].

DISCOURSE UNIT—9:26–30 [BECNT, EBC, NICNT]. The topic is Saul in Jerusalem [BECNT], Saul's reception at Jerusalem [EBC], Saul in Jerusalem: He is sent to Tarsus [NICNT].

9:26 And when he had-come to Jerusalem he-attempted to-join[a] the disciples. But they were all afraid of him, for they did not believe that he-was (a)-disciple. 9:27 But Barnabas took-hold-of him and brought-(him) to the apostles and described to them how on the road he-had-seen the Lord,[b] who-spoke to-him, and how at Damascus he-had-spoken-out-boldly in the name[c] of-Jesus.

LEXICON—a. pres. pass. infin. of κολλάω (LN 34.22) (BDAG 2.b.α. p. 556): 'to join' [AB, Bar, BECNT, CBC, LN; CEV, ESV, GW, KJV, NCV, NIV, NRSV, REB, TEV], 'to associate with' [BDAG; NASB, NET], 'to meet with' [NLT], 'to become a part of' [LN]. This verb means to begin an association with someone, whether temporary or permanent [LN]. It means to be closely associated with someone [BDAG].
  b. κύριος (LN 12.9): 'Lord' [AB, Bar, BECNT, CBC, LN; all versions], 'Ruler' [LN], 'One who commands' [LN]. This noun denotes a title for God and for Christ. It indicates one who exercises supernatural authority over mankind [LN].
  c. ὄνομα (LN 33.126) (BDAG 1.d.γ. p. 713): 'name' [AB, Bar, BDAG, BECNT, CBC, LN; all versions except GW]. The clause 'he had spoken out boldly in the name of Jesus' is also translated 'how boldly Saul had

spoken about the one named Jesus' [GW]. This noun denotes the proper name of a person [LN].

QUESTION—Who was Barnabas?

This Barnabas is the same Barnabas mentioned in Acts 4:36–37 [TRT]. Here Barnabas had taken the mediating role, securing Saul's acceptance in the apostolic circle in Jerusalem [NAC]. Only someone of Barnabas's stature and respect could bring the church to lay aside its fears [BECNT].

QUESTION—How did Barnabas describe Saul's preaching?

The verb used for Saul's teaching is παρρησιάζομαι 'to speak freely, openly, or fearlessly.' Only someone of Barnabas's stature and respect could bring the church to lay aside its fears [BECNT]. To speak in the name of Jesus is more than to speak about him; it is to speak on his behalf, almost in his person [Bar].

9:28 So he-went in and out among them at Jerusalem, speaking-boldly in the name[a] of-the Lord.[b] **9:29** And he-was-speaking and disputing[c] with the Hellenists.[d] But they-were-trying to-kill him.

LEXICON—a. ὄνομα (LN 33.126) (BDAG 1.d.γ. p. 713): 'name' [AB, Bar, BDAG, BECNT, CBC, LN; all versions except CEV, GW], not explicit [CEV]. The phrase 'in the name of the Lord' is also translated 'with the power and authority of the Lord' [GW]. This noun denotes the proper name of a person or object [LN]. In many passages it seems to be a formula [BDAG].

b. κύριος (LN 12.9): 'Lord' [AB, Bar, BECNT, CBC, LN; all versions], 'Ruler' [LN], 'One who commands' [LN]. This noun is a title for God and for Christ and denotes one who exercises supernatural authority over mankind [LN].

c. imperf. act. indic. of συζητέω (LN 33.440) (BDAG 2. p. 954): 'to dispute' [AB, BECNT, LN; ESV, KJV, TEV], 'to debate' [Bar, BDAG, CBC; NET, NIV, NLT, REB], 'to argue' [BDAG; CEV, GW, NASB, NCV, NRSV]. This verb means to express forceful differences of opinion without necessarily having a presumed goal of seeking a solution [LN]. It means to contend with persistence for a point of view [BDAG].

d. Ἑλληνιστής (LN 11.93) (BDAG p. 319): 'Hellenist' [AB, Bar, BDAG, BECNT; ESV, NRSV], 'Hellenistic Jew' [NASB], 'Greek-speaking Jew' [CBC, LN; GW, NET, NLT, REB, TEV], 'Grecian' [KJV], 'Grecian Jew' [NIV]. The phrase 'the Hellenists' is also translated 'the Jews who spoke Greek' [CEV], 'the Jewish people who spoke Greek' [NCV]. This noun denotes a Greek-speaking Jew in contrast to one speaking a Semitic language. The Greek-speaking Jews were basically Jewish in culture and religion, but they had adopted certain customs typical of the larger Greco-Roman world in which many of them lived. This inevitably resulted in certain suspicions and misunderstandings [LN]. It denotes one who uses the Greek language, and here it refers to a Greek-speaking Israelite in contrast to one speaking a Semitic language [BDAG].

QUESTION—Who were the people Saul went in and out among?

Saul was not only with the apostles but he shared their activities [Bar]. He was fully accepted into the apostolic circle. He too was a witness for Christ [NAC].

QUESTION—Who were the Hellenists?

They were the Greek-speaking Jews [Bar, BECNT, CBC, NAC, PNTC, TH], the group with whom Stephen had been in conflict [Bar, PNTC, TNTC]. They had earlier slain Stephen [BECNT, CBC, NAC].

9:30 But when the brothers[a] learned-(of it),[b] they brought him down to Caesarea and sent- him -away[c] to Tarsus.

LEXICON—a. ἀδελφός (LN 11.23) (BDAG 2.a. p. 18): 'brother' [Bar, BDAG; ESV, NET, NIV], 'fellow believer, a Christian brother' [LN], 'fellow member, associate' [BDAG]. The phrase 'the brothers' is also translated 'the brethren' [AB, BECNT, CBC; KJV, NASB, REB], 'the followers' [CEV, NCV], 'the disciples' [GW], 'the believers' [NLT, NRSV, TEV]. This noun denotes a close associate of a group of persons having a well-defined membership and in the NT it refers specifically to fellow believers in Christ [LN]. It denotes a person viewed as a brother in terms of a close affinity. It was used by Christians in their relations with each other [BDAG].

b. aorist act. participle of ἐπιγινώσκω (LN 27.8) (BDAG 2.c. p. 369): 'to learn about' [BDAG, Bar, CBC, LN; ESV, KJV, NASB, NCV, NIV, NRSV], 'to find out about' [LN; CEV, GW, NET, TEV], 'to hear about' [AB; NLT], 'to discover' [BECNT; REB]. This verb means to acquire information, probably in a somewhat more exact or detailed form and perhaps with focus upon what is learned [LN]. It means to ascertain or gain information about something [BDAG].

c. aorist act. indic. of ἐξαποστέλλω (LN 15.68) (BDAG 1.a. p. 346): 'to send away' [AB, BDAG; NASB, NET, NLT, REB, TEV], 'to send off' [Bar, BDAG, BECNT, CBC; ESV, NIV, NRSV], 'to send out' [BDAG, LN], 'to send forth' [LN; KJV], 'to send' [LN; CEV, GW, NCV]. This verb means to send out or away from, presumably for some purpose [LN]. It means to send someone off to a locality or on a mission [BDAG].

QUESTION—Who were the brothers mentioned here?

In this context, 'brothers' is a title for 'followers of Jesus'. It should not sound like these men are Saul's natural brothers [TRT].

QUESTION—Where was Caesarea?

The city of Caesarea was about 62 miles (100 km.) by road northwest from the city of Jerusalem [TRT]. It was the principal port city of the Herodian kingdom [BECNT].

QUESTION—Where was Tarsus?

Tarsus was the capital city of Cilicia Province [NAC, NICNT, TNTC, TRT]. It came under the Roman provincial administration of Syria [NAC]. It was on the southern coast of what is now called Turkey [PNTC]. Tarsus was famous for its universities and competed with the cities of Alexandria and Athens as one of the greatest education/learning centers in the world [NICNT, TNTC, TRT]. Saul was born in Tarsus (Acts 22:3) [TRT], his former home [BECNT].

DISCOURSE UNIT—9:31–11:18 [CBC]. The topic is back to Peter and the Church in Palestine: 'to the Gentiles also' (11:18).

DISCOURSE UNIT—9:31–43 [AB, CBC]. The topic is Peter's pastoral visit to Lydda and Joppa [AB], Peter's general tour through Lydda to Joppa [CBC].

DISCOURSE UNIT—9:31 [Bar, BECNT, EBC, NICNT]. The topic is the church in Judaea, Galilee, and Samaria: a summary [Bar], closing summary [BECNT], summary statement [EBC], the church enjoys peace and prosperity [NICNT].

9:31 So the church throughout all Judea and Galilee and Samaria had peace and was being-built-up.ᵃ And livingᵇ in-the fearᶜ of-the Lord and in-the comfortᵈ of-the Holy Spirit, it-continued-to-increase.ᵉ

LEXICON—a. pres. pass. participle of οἰκοδομέω (LN 74.15) (BDAG 3. p. 696): 'to be built up' [Bar, BDAG, BECNT, CBC, LN; ESV, NASB, NRSV, REB], 'to be strengthened' [AB, BDAG, LN; NET, NIV, TEV], 'to be made more able' [BDAG, LN], 'to be edified' [KJV], not explicit [CEV, GW]. The phrase 'was being built up' is also translated 'became stronger' [NCV, NLT]. This verb means to increase the potential of someone or something, with focus upon the process involved [LN]. It means to help improve ability to function in living responsibly and effectively [BDAG].

b. pres. mid./pass. (deponent = act..) participle of πορεύομαι (LN 41.11) (BDAG 2. p. 853): 'to live' [BDAG, LN; GW, NCV, NET, NIV, NLT, NRSV, REB, TEV], 'to behave' [LN], 'to walk' [AB, Bar; ESV, KJV], 'to proceed' [BECNT], 'to go on' [NASB], 'to keep on' [CEV], 'to go about doing' [LN], not explicit [CBC]. This verb means to live or behave in a customary manner, with a possible focus upon continuity of action [LN]. It means to conduct oneself [BDAG].

c. φόβος (LN 53.59) (BDAG 2.b. p. 1062): 'fear' [AB, Bar, BECNT, CBC; ESV, GW, KJV, NASB, NET, NIV, NLT, NRSV, REB], 'reverence' [BDAG, LN; TEV], 'awe' [LN], 'respect' [BDAG; NCV]. This noun is also translated as a verb: 'worshiping' [CEV]. This noun denotes a profound respect and awe for deity [LN]. It denotes the product of an intimidating or alarming force [BDAG].

d. παράκλησις (LN 25.150) (BDAG 3. p. 766): 'comfort' [BDAG, BECNT; ESV, GW, KJV, NASB, NRSV], 'consolation' [BDAG], 'encouragement' [LN; NET, NLT], 'help' [TEV], 'strength' [AB], 'influence' [Bar]. This noun is also translated as a verb: 'encouraged' [CEV, NCV, NIV, REB], 'upheld' [CBC]. This noun denotes encouragement either by verbal or

non-verbal means [LN]. It refers to the lifting of another's spirits [BDAG].
e. imperf. pass. indic. of πληθύνω (LN 59.68) (BDAG 1.b. p. 826): 'to increase' [Bar, BDAG; GW, NASB, NET, NRSV], 'to increase greatly' [LN], 'to multiply' [BDAG, BECNT, LN; ESV, KJV], 'to grow' [BDAG, CBC, LN; CEV, NCV, NIV, NLT, REB, TEV], 'to be strengthened' [AB]. This verb means to increase greatly in number or extent [LN]. It means to be multiplied [BDAG].

QUESTION—What does the term ἐκκλησία 'church' refer to here?

Here 'the church' refers to the sum of Jewish believers over a large area corresponding to the boundaries of ancient Israel rather than just one congregation in a given place [NICNT, PNTC, TNTC]. The term here is singular; referring to one community in three regions in view (Judea, Galilee and Samaria). The sense of the church in many locales appears only here and in 20:28. Usually the word refers to a specific local gathering [BECNT, NAC].

QUESTION—What is meant by 'the comfort of the Holy Spirit'?

This expression refers to the 'encouragement and help of the Holy Spirit' rather than the notion of relief from sorrow [BECNT, PNTC, TH].

QUESTION—What does it mean by saying that the church increased?

It means that it increased in numbers [EBC, PNTC, TH, TNTC, TRT], it grew in size and maturity [PNTC]. The church experienced peace and growth with the encouragement and support of the Holy Spirit given to the community even in the midst of persecution [BECNT, NAC]. Note that this verse is a summary statement which concludes the narrative from Acts 6:8 [PNTC]. It concludes the Pauline conversion narrative and completes the entire persecution story that began in 8:1b [NAC, NICNT].

DISCOURSE UNIT—9:32–12:25 [BECNT, PNTC, TNTC]. The topic is the gospel to the Gentiles and more persecution in Jerusalem [BECNT], the word advances in Judea and Syria [PNTC], the beginning of the Gentile mission [TNTC].

DISCOURSE UNIT—9:32–12:24 [EBC]. The topic is advances of the gospel in Palestine-Syria.

DISCOURSE UNIT—9:32–43 [Bar, BECNT, EBC, NAC, NICNT, PNTC, TNTC; NASB, NIV, NLT, TEV]. The topic is Peter's miracles on the way to Caesarea [Bar], Peter performs two miracles at Lydda and Joppa [BECNT], the ministry of Peter in the Maritime Plain [EBC], Peter's witness in the coastal towns [NAC], Peter's ministry [NASB], Peter in Western Judaea [NICNT], Aeneas and Dorcas [NIV], Peter heals Aeneas and raises Dorcas [NLT], Peter's pastoral and evangelistic ministry in Western Judea [PNTC], Peter in Lydda and Joppa [TEV], Peter's mighty works [TNTC].

DISCOURSE UNIT—9:32–35 [EBC, NAC, NICNT, PNTC; CEV, ESV, GW, NCV, NET, NRSV]. The topic is Peter heals Aeneas [CEV, GW, NCV, NET],

Aeneas healed at Lydda [EBC], the healing of Aeneas [ESV, NAC, NRSV], Peter at Lydda: the healing of Aeneas [NICNT], healing Aeneas in Lydda [PNTC].

9:32 Now as Peter was-traveling through all-those-regions, he came-down[a] also to the saints[b] who lived at-Lydda. **9:33** There he-found[c] a-man named Aeneas, who had-been-bedridden for eight years, for he was paralyzed.[d]

LEXICON—a. aorist act. infin. of κατέρχομαι (LN 15.107) (BDAG 1. p. 53): 'to come down' [Bar, BDAG, BECNT, LN; ESV, KJV, NASB, NET, NLT, NRSV], 'to go down' [CBC, LN; REB], 'to move down' [LN], 'to descend' [LN], not explicit [AB; CEV, GW, NCV, NIV, TEV]. This verb means to move down, irrespective of the gradient [LN]. It means to move in a direction considered the opposite of up, but not necessarily with suggestion of a gradient [BDAG].

b. ἅγιος (LN 11.27) (BDAG 2.d.β. p. 11): 'saints' [AB, Bar, BDAG, BECNT; ESV, KJV, NASB, NET, NIV, NRSV], 'the Lord's followers' [CEV], 'God's people' [CBC, LN; NCV, REB, TEV], 'believers' [BDAG; NLT], 'loyal followers' [BDAG]. This noun is also translated 'those' referring to 'God's people' in the first clause [GW]. This adjective refers to persons who belong to God, and as such constitute a religious entity [LN].

c. aorist act. indic. of εὑρίσκω (LN 27.27): 'to find' [AB, Bar, BECNT, CBC, LN; ESV, GW, KJV, NASB, NET, NIV, NRSV, REB], 'to discover, to come upon, to happen to find' [LN], 'to meet' [CEV, NCV, NLT, TEV], 'to learn the whereabouts of something' [LN]. This verb means to learn the location of something, either by intentional searching or by unexpected discovery [LN].

d. perf. pass. participle of παραλύω (LN 23.170) (BDAG p. 769): 'to be paralyzed' [Bar, BECNT, LN; ESV, GW, NASB, NCV, NET, NLT, NRSV, TEV], 'to be lame' [LN], 'to be weakened, to be disabled' [BDAG]. The phrase 'was paralyzed' is also translated 'could not move' [CEV], 'was sick of the palsy' [KJV]. This verb is also translated as a noun: 'a paralytic' [NIV]. The phrase 'bedridden..., for he was paralyzed' is also translated 'bedridden with paralysis' [AB, CBC; REB]. This verb means to suffer paralysis in one or more limbs, especially in the leg or foot [LN]. It means to cause to be feeble [BDAG].

QUESTION—Where was Lydda?

The city of Lydda was located in Judea Province about 25 miles (40 km.) northwest of Jerusalem [BECNT, CBC, EBC, PNTC, TH, TNTC, TRT]. It was located in the fertile coastal plain of Sharon, which extends north from Joppa to Mt. Carmen [NAC]. The city was lower in elevation than Jerusalem and the surrounding area [TRT].

QUESTION—Who were the saints in Lydda?

These saints were Christians [Bar]. They were Jewish Christians who either came from Jerusalem because of persecution (8:1), or turned to Christ because of the preaching of Philip when he journeyed from Azotus to Caesarea (8:40) [NAC, NICNT, PNTC].

9:34 **And Peter said to-him, "Aeneas, Jesus Christ heals you; get-up**[a] **and make-your-bed.**[b]**" And immediately he-got-up.** **9:35** **And all who lived at-Lydda and Sharon saw him, and they turned**[c] **to the Lord.**

LEXICON—a. aorist act. impera. of ἀνίστημι (LN 17.6) (BDAG 10. p. 83): 'to get up' [Bar, CBC; CEV, GW, NASB, NET, NIV, NLT, NRSV, REB, TEV], 'to stand up' [LN; NCV], 'to rise' [AB, BDAG, BECNT; ESV, KJV], 'to set out' [BDAG], 'to get ready' [BDAG]. This verb means to assume a standing position [LN]. It means to initiate an action [BDAG].

b. aorist act. impera. of στρωννύω (LN 46.10) (BDAG 1. p. 949): 'to make one's bed' [AB, Bar, BDAG, BECNT, CBC, LN; CEV, ESV, KJV, NASB, NCV, NET, NRSV, REB, TEV], 'to spread' [BDAG]. This verb is also translated 'pick up your cot' [GW], 'take care of your mat' [NIV], 'roll up your sleeping mat' [NLT]. This verb means to prepare a bed, either for sleeping or making it up after it has been used [LN]. It means to distribute something over a surface [BDAG].

c. aorist act. indic. of ἐπιστρέφω (LN 31.60) (BDAG 4.a. p. 382): 'to turn to' [AB, Bar, BECNT, CBC, LN; all versions except CEV], 'to come to believe' [LN], 'to come to accept' [LN], 'to turn' [BDAG]. The phrase 'turned to the Lord' is also translated 'became followers of the Lord' [CEV]. This verb means to change one's belief, with focus upon that to which one turns [LN]. It means to change one's mind or course of action, for better or worse [BDAG].

QUESTION—What was involved in making his bed?

At Peter's time making ones bed meant to take care of his mat [EBC]. to arrange the bed or roll up the mat [NAC, NICNT, PNTC, TH, to pack it up and take it away [Bar], to tidy it up after sleep [TNTC].

QUESTION—Where was Sharon?

Sharon was a plain known as the Plain of Sharon, a coastal plain [Bar, TNTC]. It was a strip of fertile flat land about 10 miles (16 km.) wide and 50 miles (80 km.) long located next to the Mediterranean Sea. The City of Lydda was located on the southeast edge of the plain [TRT]. The Sharon Plain extended thirty miles along the sea from Joppa to Caesarea [CBC, EBC, TH].

QUESTION—What is meant by them turning to the Lord?

The expression 'turned to the Lord' is an idiom that means they 'started believing in the Lord' or 'they became believers in the Lord' [TH, TRT]. The unbelievers in Lydda and Sharon turned to Jesus as their Lord, acknowledging Jesus' divine authority and saving power through the actions and words of his apostle Peter [PNTC].

DSCOURSE UNIT—9:36–43 [EBC, NAC, NICNT, PNTC; CEV, ESV, NCV, NET, NRSV]. The topic is Peter brings Dorcas back to life [CEV], Dorcas raised at Joppa [EBC], Dorcas restored to life [ESV], Peter brings Tabitha back to life [GW], the raising of Dorcas [NAC], Peter heals Tabitha [NCV], Peter raises Dorcas [NET], Peter at Joppa: the raising of Dorcas [NICNT], Peter in Lydda and Joppa [NRSV], raising Tabitha/Dorcas in Joppa [PNTC].

9:36 **Now in Joppa there-was a disciple named Tabitha, which, translated (in Greek), means Dorcas. She was-full[a] of-good works and charity[b] which she-was-doing.**

LEXICON—a. πλήρης (LN 59.53) (BDAG 1.b. p. 827): 'full' [AB, BDAG, BECNT, LN; ESV, KJV], 'filled' [BDAG]. The phrase 'was full of good works' is also translated 'was abounding with deeds of kindness' [NASB], 'was always doing kind things for others' [NLT], 'was always doing good things for people' [CEV], 'always helped people' [GW], 'was continually doing good deeds' [NET], 'spent all her time doing good' [TEV], 'filled her days with acts of kindness' [CBC; NCV, REB], 'was devoted to good works' [NRSV], 'was always doing good' [NIV], 'was constantly practicing good works' [Bar]. This adjective pertains to a particularly large number of objects or events [LN]. It pertains to containing within itself all that it can hold, and in this verse it refers to a person being rich in good deeds [BDAG].

b. ἐλεημοσύνη (LN 57.111) (BDAG 1. p. 315): 'charity' [CBC; NASB, REB], 'acts of charity' [BDAG; ESV, NET, NRSV], 'charitable giving' [BDAG], 'acts of mercy' [BECNT], 'alms' [AB, Bar, BDAG, LN], 'almsdeeds' [KJV], 'giving to the needy' [LN], not explicit [NCV]. This noun is also translated as a verb phrase: 'had given much to the poor' [CEV], 'gave things to the poor' [GW], 'helping the poor' [NIV, NLT, TEV]. This noun denotes giving to those in need as an act of mercy [LN]. It denotes the exercise of benevolent goodwill [BDAG].

QUESTION—Where was Joppa?

Joppa was a Greek city [Bar, PNTC]. It was the main port city of Judea located on the Philistine coast, about 10 miles northwest of Lydda [NAC, NICNT, TH, TNTC]. It is now the modern city of Jaffa, the most important port in southern Palestine [TH, TNTC].

QUESTION—What is the meaning of the name Tabitha?

Tabitha is an Aramaic name and Dorcas is its Greek name. Both names mean 'Gazelle/Antelope/Deer' [AB, Bar, BECNT, CBC, EBC, NAC, NICNT, PNTC, TH, TNTC, TRT]. 'Gazelle' was the metaphor for 'beloved' in Song 2:9 and 8:14. In this case, the name fits her character [BECNT].

QUESTION—What were the ἐλεημοσυνῶν 'acts of charity'?

'Acts of charity' refers to providing alms through charitable giving. Almsgiving was highly regarded in Judaism [BECNT].

9:37 In those days she became-ill and died, and when they had-washed-(her), they-laid her in (an)-upper-room.ᵃ **9:38** Since Lydda was near Joppa, the disciples, having-heard that Peter was there, sent two men to him, urgingᵇ (him), "Please come to us without delay."
LEXICON—a. ὑπερῷον (LN 7.27) (BDAG p. 1034): 'upper room' [AB, Bar, BECNT; ESV, NASB], 'upstairs room' [LN; CEV, GW, NET, NIV, NLT], 'upper chamber' [KJV], 'room upstairs' [BDAG, CBC; NCV, NRSV, REB, TEV], 'upper story' [BDAG]. This noun denotes a room on the level above the ground floor (second story in American usage and first story in most other languages) [LN].
    b. pres. act. participle of παρακαλέω (LN 33.168) (BDAG 1.b. p. 764): 'to urge' [ESV, NET, NIV], 'to request, to plead, to appeal' [LN], 'to entreat' [BECNT], 'to implore' [NASB], 'to beg' [GW, NCV, NLT[, 'to desire' [KJV], 'to call to one's side, to invite' [BDAG]. The phrase 'urging him' is also translated 'with the urgent request' [REB], 'with the message' [TEV], 'to say to him' [CEV], 'with the/this request' [AB, Bar, CBC; NRSV]. This verb means to ask for something earnestly and with propriety [LN]. It means to ask to come and be present where the speaker is, and the content of the invitation follows in direct discourse [BDAG].
QUESTION—What is the purpose of washing a dead body?
    The washing of a dead body was a preparation for burial [Bar, BECNT, PNTC]. The placing of the body in an upper room is unusual [BECNT, NAC]. Although the body was washed but not anointed for burial, and her good deeds were told to Peter when he arrived, they apparently wanted Jesus to restore her to life [EBC]. It suggests the faith and hope that she can be raised from the dead [BECNT, NAC, TNTC].
QUESTION—How near was Lydda to Joppa?
    The city of Lydda was about 10 miles (16 km.) southeast of the city of Joppa, about a three-hour walk [TH, TRT].

9:39 So Peter roseᵃ and went-with them. When he arrived, they-brought him into the upper-room. And all the widows stood-beside him weeping and showing (the)-tunics and garments that Dorcas made while she was with them. **9:40** But Peter put them all outside and knelt-downᵇ and prayed. And turning to the body he-said, "Tabitha, arise." And she-opened her eyes, and when she saw Peter she-sat-up.
LEXICON—a. aorist act. participle of ἀνίστημι (LN 17.6): 'to rise' [AB, BECNT; ESV, KJV, NASB], 'to stand up' [LN], 'to get up' [Bar; NET, NRSV], 'to get ready' [NCV, TEV], not explicit [CBC; CEV, GW, NIV, NLT, REB]. This verb means to assume a standing position [LN].
    b. aorist act. participle of τίθημι (LN 17.19): 'to kneel down' [Bar, BECNT, CBC, LN; CEV, ESV, KJV, NASB, NET, NRSV, REB, TEV], 'to kneel' [AB, LN; GW, NCV, NLT], 'to get down' [NIV]. The idiom 'to place the knees' means to kneel down before someone as an act of worship. This

verb means to kneel down before, with the implication of an act of reverence or of supplication [LN].

QUESTION—What was a tunic?

A tunic was a short-sleeved garment that reached to the knees. It was held in at the waist by a cloth belt. Both men and women normally wore a tunic. Although it was optional, people would often wear over the tunic a long robe that reached down to the hands and feet [TRT].

QUESTION—How did Peter bring Dorcas back to life?

Peter got down on his knees and prayed. He totally depended on God for the resuscitation of the dead. Then he said the Greek word ἀνάστηθι 'get up, rise, arise' to Dorcas. This same word was used in v. 34. It is a verb frequently associated with the resurrection of Jesus. In dependence upon the risen Lord, Peter called upon a dead person to rise [NAC, PNTC].

9:41 And he gave her (his)-hand and raised- her -up.[a] Then having-called the saints[b] and widows, he-presented[c] her alive. **9:42** And it-became[d] known throughout all Joppa, and many believed[e] in the Lord.[f]

LEXICON—a. aorist act. indic. of ἀνίστημι (LN 17.7): 'to raise up' [Bar, LN; ESV, NASB], 'to help up' [AB, CBC; CEV, GW, NCV, NET, NIV, NLT, NRSV, REB, TEV], 'to lift up' [BECNT; KJV], 'to cause to stand' [LN]. This verb means to cause someone to stand up [LN].
  b. ἅγιος (LN 11.27): 'saints' [AB, Bar, BECNT; ESV, KJV, NASB, NCV, NET, NRSV], 'followers' [CEV], 'believers' [GW, NIV, NLT, TEV], 'God's people' [LN], 'members of the church' [REB], 'members of the congregation' [CBC]. This adjective refers to persons who belong to God, and as such constitute a religious entity [LN].
  c. aorist act. indic. of παρίστημι (LN 85.14) (BDAG 1.b.α. p. 778): 'to present' [Bar, BDAG, BECNT, LN; ESV, GW, KJV, NASB, NET, NIV, NLT, TEV], 'to show' [CBC; CEV, NCV, NRSV, REB], 'to set before' [AB]. This verb means to cause to be in a place [LN]. It means to cause to be present in any way [BDAG].
  d. aorist mid. (deponent = act.) indic. of γίνομαι (LN 13.48) (BDAG 5.b. p. 198): 'to become' [AB, Bar, BDAG, BECNT, LN; ESV, NASB, NET, NIV, NRSV], 'was' [KJV], 'to learn about' [NCV]. The clause 'And it became known throughout all Joppa' is also translated 'Everyone in Joppa heard what had happened' [CEV], 'The news about this spread throughout the city of Joppa' [GW], 'The news about this spread all over Joppa' [TEV], 'The news spread through the whole town' [NLT], 'News of it spread all over Joppa' [REB], 'The news spread all over Joppa' [CBC]. This verb means to come to acquire or experience a state [LN]. It means to experience a change in nature and so indicate entry into a new condition [BDAG].
  e. aorist act. indic. of πιστεύω (LN 31.85) (BDAG 2.a.δ. p. 817): 'to believe in' [AB, Bar, BDAG, BECNT, CBC, LN; all versions except CEV], 'to trust' [BDAG], 'to have faith in' [CEV]. This verb means to believe to the

extent of complete trust and reliance [LN]. It means to entrust oneself to an entity in complete confidence [BDAG].

f. κύριος (LN 12.9) (BDAG 2.b.γ. p. 577): 'Lord' [AB, Bar, BDAG, BECNT, CBC, LN; all versions], 'Ruler' [LN], 'master' [BDAG], 'one who commands' [LN]. This noun denotes (a title for God and for Christ) one who exercises supernatural authority over mankind [LN]. It means one who is in a position of authority [BDAG].

9:43 And (he)-stayed[a] in Joppa for many days with (a)-tanner named Simon.

LEXICON—a. aorist act. infin. of μένω (LN 85.55) (BDAG 1.a. p. 630): 'to stay' [AB, Bar, BDAG, BECNT, CBC, LN; all versions except KJV], 'to remain' [LN], 'to tarry' [KJV]. This verb means to remain in the same place over a period of time [LN]. It means to remain [BDAG].

QUESTION—What did a tanner do?

A tanner made leather by tanning animal skins. A leather maker was considered 'unclean' by the Jews and was despised because he touched the skins of dead animals (Leviticus 11:39–40) [Bar, BECNT, NICNT, PNTC, TH, TNTC, TRT]. Peter was apparently not troubled by such concerns [PNTC]. The fact that Peter stayed with a leather maker showed that he was ready to separate himself from Jewish legalism and work among the Gentiles [TRT].

DISCOURSE UNIT—10:1–11:18 [BECNT, EBC, NAC, TNTC]. The topic is Peter and Cornelius: the gospel to the Gentiles [BECNT], the conversion of Cornelius at Caesarea [EBC], Peter's witness to a Gentile God-fearer [NAC], the conversion of Cornelius [TNTC].

DISCOURSE UNIT—10:1–48 [AB, Bar, BECNT, CBC, NICNT, PNTC; CEV, NCV]. The topic is the baptism of Cornelius [AB], Peter and Cornelius: Caesarea [Bar], Peter and Cornelius [BECNT; CEV], Cornelius [CBC], Peter teaches Cornelius [NCV], the story of Cornelius [NICNT], Peter's role in the evangelization of the Gentiles [PNTC].

DISCOURSE UNIT—10:1–43 [NET]. The topic is Peter visits Cornelius.

DISCOURSE UNIT—10:1–33 [NRSV, TEV]. The topic is Peter and Cornelius [NRSV, TEV].

DISCOURSE UNIT—10:1–23a [NASB]. The topic is Cornelius' vision.

DISCOURSE UNIT—10:1–16 [PNTC]. The topic is two significant visions.

DISCOURSE UNIT—10:1–8 [EBC, NAC, NICNT; ESV, GW, NIV, NLT]. The topic is Cornelius' vision [EBC], Peter and Cornelius [ESV], Cornelius has a vision [GW], the vision of Cornelius [NAC], Cornelius the Centurion sees a vision [NICNT], Cornelius calls for Peter [NIV, NLT].

10:1 Now there was a man at Caesarea named Cornelius, (a)-centurion[a] of what was-called (the)-Italian cohort,[b]

LEXICON—a. ἑκατοντάρχης (LN 55.16) (BDAG p. 299): 'centurion' [AB, Bar, BDAG, BECNT, CBC, LN; ESV, KJV, NASB, NET, NIV, NRSV, REB], 'captain' [BDAG, LN; CEV, NLT, TEV], 'officer' [GW, NCV]. This noun denotes a Roman officer in command of about one hundred men [LN]. It denotes a Roman officer commanding about a hundred men [BDAG].

b. σπεῖρα (LN 55.9): 'cohort' [AB, Bar, BECNT, CBC, LN; ESV, NASB, NET, NRSV, REB], 'Unit' [CEV], 'Regiment' [GW, NIV, NLT, TEV], 'band of soldiers' [LN], 'band' [KJV], 'group' [NCV]. This noun denotes a Roman military unit of about six hundred soldiers, though only a part of such a cohort was often referred to as a cohort [LN].

QUESTION—What was Caesarea?

Caesarea was the city which had been rebuilt by Herod the Great in honor of Caesar Augustus [EBC, TH]. It was the headquarters of the Roman governor and of the Roman garrison [AB, BECNT, CBC, EBC, NAC, PNTC, TH, TNTC]. Its population consisted mainly of Gentiles [BECNT, NAC, PNTC]. Philip had previously gone as far as Caesarea in his evangelistic ministry (Acts 8:40) [Bar, PNTC].

QUESTION—What was Cornelius' job?

Cornelius was a centurion, an officer in the Roman army who was in command of one hundred men. In most languages there is an equivalent word such as 'captain', one who commands soldiers [AB, Bar, BECNT, EBC, NAC, NICNT, PNTC, TH, TNTC, TRT]. His name and occupation indicate that Cornelius was a Roman citizen [PNTC].

QUESTION—What was a cohort?

A cohort was one of the basic divisions in the Roman army, consisting of six hundred men (one tenth of a legion), and it was commanded by an officer of higher rank than the centurion. There is an equivalent word 'regiment', a term for group of soldiers [AB, Bar, BECNT, EBC, NAC, TH, TRT]. The title 'the Italian Cohort' can be translated as 'the cohort from Italy' [TH, TNTC]. The Italian Cohort was probably an auxiliary force, not part of the regular army [BECNT]. Such a cohort would have been made up of freedmen who were enrolled only in periods of great need [CBC, EBC, PNTC].

10:2 a devout[a] man who feared[b] God with all his household,[c] and gave alms[d] generously to-the people, and prayed to-God continually.

LEXICON—a. εὐσεβής (LN 53.6) (BDAG p. 413): 'devout' [AB, BDAG, LN; ESV, GW, KJV, NASB, NET, NIV, NLT, NRSV, REB], 'pious' [Bar, BDAG, BECNT, LN], 'religious' [CBC, LN; CEV, NCV, TEV], 'reverent' [BDAG], 'godly' [BDAG]. This adjective pertains to being devoted to a proper expression of religious beliefs [LN]. It pertains to being profoundly reverent or respectful [BDAG].

b. pres. pass. participle of φοβέω (LN 53.58) (BDAG 2.a. p. 1061): 'to fear' [AB, Bar, BECNT; ESV, KJV, NASB, NET, NIV, NLT, NRSV], 'to reverence' [BDAG, LN], 'to worship' [LN; CEV, NCV, TEV], 'to respect' [BDAG; GW]. The phrase 'feared God' is also translated 'joined in the worship of God' [CBC; REB]. This is a figurative extension of meaning of the verb 'to fear' and it means to have a profound reverence and respect for deity, with the implication of awe bordering on fear [LN]. It means to have a profound measure of respect for with special reference to fear of offending [BDAG].

c. οἶκος (LN 10.8) (BDAG 2. p. 699): 'household' [AB, Bar, BDAG, BECNT, LN; ESV, NASB, NET, NLT, NRSV], 'family' [BDAG, CBC, LN; NIV, REB, TEV], 'house' [KJV]. This noun is also translated with the phrase 'everyone...who lived in his house' [CEV], 'all the other people who lived in his house' [NCV], 'everyone in his home' [GW]. This noun denotes the family consisting of those related by blood and marriage, as well as slaves and servants, living in the same house or homestead [LN].

d. ἐλεημοσύνη (LN 57.111) (BDAG 1. p. 316): 'alms' [BDAG, BECNT, LN; ESV, KJV, NASB, NRSV], 'money' [CEV, NCV], 'gifts' [GW], 'charitable giving' [BDAG], 'charitable gifts' [Bar], 'acts of charity' [LN; NET], 'giving to the needy' [CBC, LN; NIV, NLT, REB, TEV], 'contributions' [AB]. This noun denotes giving to those in need as an act of mercy [LN]. It denotes the exercise of benevolent goodwill [BDAG].

QUESTION—What would be considered as Cornelius' household?

Cornelius' household would include his wife, all his children and other close relatives who were living with him, as well as all of his slaves and their children [EBC, TRT].

QUESTION—What kind of a man was Cornelius?

Cornelius prayed to God regularly, following the Jewish hours of prayer. The Jewish Christians recognized a truly biblical piety in him [AB, Bar, CBC, EBC, NAC, PNTC]. He was generous in giving alms [AB, Bar, BECNT, CBC, EBC, NAC]. Cornelius was a devout, religious man. He and his family were Gentiles but they worshipped God as the Jews did. Such Gentiles were sometimes called 'the God-fearers' [AB, Bar, BECNT, CBC, EBC, NAC, NICNT, TNTC, TRT]. The God-fearers were the first ones to become Christians in many of the cities where Paul traveled [TRT]. God-fearers were a specific class of persons who were not Jews nor had they fully embraced Judaism with all its rituals. They were Gentiles who were attached to the synagogues and were sympathetic to Jewish theology and ethics [Bar, BECNT, CBC, EBC, NICNT, PNTC, TNTC].

QUESTION—Who were τῷ λαῷ 'the people' referred to here?

'The people' refers to the Jews here [PNTC, TH, TRT].

10:3 About (the)-ninth[a] hour of-the day he-saw clearly in (a)-vision[b] an-angel[c] of-God come-in and say to-him, "Cornelius."
LEXICON—a. ἔνατος (LN 60.56) (BDAG p. 331): 'ninth' [AB, Bar, BDAG, BECNT, LN; ESV, KJV, NASB]. The phrase 'the ninth hour' is also translated 'One afternoon at about three o'clock' [CEV, NRSV], 'about three in the afternoon' [CBC; GW, NIV, REB], 'One afternoon about three o'clock' [NCV, NLT], 'about three o'clock one afternoon' [NET, TEV]. The adjective 'ninth' refers to 'the ninth hour' or 'three o'clock in the afternoon [LN].
  b. ὅραμα (LN 33.488) (BDAG 2. p. 718): 'vision' [AB, Bar, BDAG, BECNT, CBC, LN; all versions]. This noun denotes an event in which something appears vividly and credibly to the mind, although not actually present, but implying the influence of some divine or supernatural power or agency [LN]. It denotes the act by which the recipient of a vision is granted a vision or the state of being in which the person receives a vision [BDAG].
  c. ἄγγελος (LN 12.28): 'angel' [AB, Bar, BECNT, CBC, LN; all versions]. This noun denotes a supernatural being that attends upon or serves as a messenger of a superior supernatural entity. In many languages a term for 'angels' is borrowed from another dominant language, but in other instances a somewhat descriptive phrase may be employed. The most common expressions for 'angels of God' are 'messengers' and 'messengers from heaven.' Sometimes these angels are called 'spirit messengers' and even 'flying messengers.' [LN].
QUESTION—When was the ninth hour of the day?
The ninth hour of the day was three o'clock in the afternoon which was the regular hour that the Jews prayed. Cornelius was praying at this time [AB, Bar, BECNT, CBC, EBC, NAC, NICNT, PNTC, TH, TNTC, TRT].

10:4 And he stared[a] at-him and having-become afraid he-said, "What is-it, lord?[b]" And he-said to-him, "Your prayers and your alms[c] have-ascended as (a)-memorial[d] before[e] God.
LEXICON—a. aorist act. participle of ἀτενίζω (LN 24.49) (BDAG p. 148): 'to stare at' [Bar, BDAG, BECNT, CBC, LN; all versions except KJV, NASB], 'to look straight at' [LN], 'to keep one's eyes fixed on' [LN; NASB], 'to look intently at' [BDAG], 'to look at' [KJV], 'to gaze at' [AB]. This verb means to fix one's eyes on some object continually and intensely [LN].
  b. κύριος (LN 87.53) (BDAG 2.b.ε. p. 578): 'Lord' [AB, BECNT, CBC; ESV, KJV, NASB, NET, NIV, NRSV], 'my lord' [NCV, REB], 'sir' [Bar, LN; GW, NLT, TEV], not explicit [CEV]. This noun denotes a title of respect used in addressing a man [LN]. It is used in reference to an angel [BDAG].
  c. ἐλεημοσύνη (LN 57.111) (BDAG 1. p. 316): 'alms' [BDAG, BECNT, LN; ESV, KJV, NASB, NRSV], 'acts of charity' [CBC, LN; NCV, NET,

REB], 'giving to the needy' [LN], 'charitable giving' [BDAG], 'charitable gifts' [Bar], 'gifts to the poor' [CEV, GW, NIV, NLT], 'works of charity' [TEV], 'generosity' [AB]. This noun denotes that which is given to help the needy [LN]. It denotes the exercise of benevolent goodwill [BDAG].

d. μνημόσυνον (LN 29.12) (BDAG 3. p. 655): 'memorial' [LN; ESV, KJV, NASB, NET, NRSV], 'in memory of' [LN], 'a memorial offering' [BDAG; NIV], 'remembrance' [Bar], 'tribute' [BECNT], not explicit [AB, CBC; CEV, NLT, REB, TEV]. This noun is also translated as a verb phrase: 'he has remembered' [GW], 'he remembers' [NCV]. This noun denotes an instrument or means designed to cause to remember [LN]. It denotes an offering that presents a worshiper to God [BDAG].

e. ἔμπροσθεν (LN 83.33) (BDAG 1.b.γ. p. 325): 'before' [Bar, BDAG, BECNT, CBC, LN; ESV, KJV, NASB, NET, NIV, NRSV, REB], not explicit [AB; CEV, GW, NCV, NLT, TEV]. This preposition denotes a position in front of an object, whether animate or inanimate, which is regarded as having a special orientation of front and back [LN]. It denotes a position in front of an object [BDAG].

QUESTION—Who was Cornelius addressing when he said 'Lord'?

He was addressing the angel who had spoken to him in the vision [BDAG, TH]. The word κύριος can be translated either as 'sir' or 'Lord.' The problem is that the word 'sir' may mean too little, and the word 'Lord' may be taken to mean too much. Cornelius recognized that this was a heavenly messenger, though it is doubtful if he would address him in the same way that one addresses God, that is, 'Lord'. In many languages there is simply no equivalent for the term 'sir' as merely a polite means of addressing a person and one is justified in omitting such an expression of polite, direct address [TH].

QUESTION—How did his prayers and alms-giving ascend as a memorial before God?

The language used here is that of sacrifices whose smoke ascends to God, and the implication is that God will respond to the prayer uttered by Cornelius [TNTC]. This was a biblical and traditional way of saying that he was commended before God and that God was attentive to his situation [EBC]. God was aware of his piety [NAC]. It means that God has accepted his prayers and works of charity, and has remembered him' [TH]. The picture is of God responding to Cornelius's effort to know him [BECNT].

10:5 And now send[a] (some)-men to Joppa and send-for[b] a man named Simon, who is-(also)-called[c] Peter.

TEXT—Manuscripts reading τινα 'a certain' are given a B rating by GNT to indicate it was regarded to be almost certain. The NRSV, TEV follow this reading.

LEXICON—a. aorist act. impera. of πέμπω (LN 15.66) (BDAG 1. p. 794): 'to send' [AB, Bar, BDAG, BECNT, CBC, LN; all versions except NASB], 'to dispatch' [NASB]. This verb means to cause someone to depart for a

particular purpose [LN]. It means to dispatch someone, whether a human or transcendent being, usually for the purposes of communication [BDAG].
b. aorist mid. impera. of μεταπέμπω (LN 15.73) (BDAG p. 641): 'to send for' [Bar, BDAG, LN; NASB], 'to call for' [KJV], 'to summon' [BDAG, LN; GW, NET, NLT], 'to bring' [AB, BECNT; ESV, NCV, NIV]. The phrase 'send for a man named Simon' is also translated 'for a man named Simon Peter' [CEV], 'for a man named Simon' [CBC; REB], 'for a certain Simon' [NRSV], 'for a certain man whose full name is Simon Peter' [TEV]. This verb means to send someone to obtain something or someone [LN].
c. pres. pass. indic. of ἐπικαλέω (LN 33.131) (BDAG 2. p. 373): 'to be called' [BDAG, BECNT, CBC, LN; ESV, NASB, NCV, NET, NIV, NRSV, REB], 'to be named' [LN], 'to be surnamed' [AB, Bar], 'to be given a surname' [BDAG], not explicit [CEV, NLT]. This verb is also translated with the phrase 'whose name/surname is' [GW, KJV], 'whose full name is' [TEV]. This verb means to use an attribution in speaking of a person [LN]. It means to address or characterize someone by a special term [BDAG].

QUESTION—Where was Joppa?

Joppa was about 30 miles (50 km.) from Caesarea [AB, NAC, PNTC, TNTC], south of Caesarea [NAC, TH, TRT]. The information given in 9:43 about Peter's location is repeated (he was staying with Simon the tanner), with additional detail that the house is by the sea in the following verse [PNTC].

10:6 He is-staying[a] with a-certain Simon, (a)-tanner whose house is by (the)-sea."

LEXICON—a. pres. pass. indic. of ξενίζω (LN 34.57) (BDAG 1. p. 684): 'to stay with' [AB, BECNT; NASB, NCV, NET, NIV, NLT], 'to lodge with' [Bar, CBC; ESV, KJV, NRSV, REB], 'to visit with' [CEV], 'to show hospitality' [LN], 'to receive a stranger as a guest' [LN], 'to receive as a guest' [BDAG], 'to entertain' [BDAG]. This verb is also translated with the phrase 'is a guest' [GW, TEV]. This verb means to receive and show hospitality to a stranger, that is, someone who is not regarded as a member of the extended family or a close friend [LN]. It means to show hospitality [BDAG].

QUESTION—What is meant by παρά τινι Σίμωνι 'a certain Simon'?

It should be made clear that this Simon is different from Simon Peter [TRT]. This Simon was not the same person as the apostle Simon Peter in v. 5. This Simon was a tanner who lived by the Mediterranean Sea [EBC].

10:7 When the angel who was speaking to-him had departed,ᵃ he calledᵇ two of his servantsᶜ and (a)-devoutᵈ soldier of-those who attendedᵉ him, **10:8** and after he had-explained everything to-them, he-sentᶠ them to Joppa.

LEXICON—a. aorist act. indic. of ἀπέρχομαι (LN 15.37) (BDAG 1.a. p. 102): 'to depart' [AB, BDAG, BECNT, LN; ESV, KJV, NET], 'to go away' [Bar, BDAG, CBC, LN; NIV, NLT, REB, TEV], 'to leave' [LN; CEV, GW, NASB, NCV, NRSV]. This verb means motion away from a reference point with emphasis upon the departure, but without implications as to any resulting state of separation or rupture [LN]. It means to move from a reference point [BDAG].

b. aorist act. participle of φωνέω (LN 33.307) (BDAG 3. p. 1071): 'to call' [AB, Bar, BECNT, LN; all versions except NASB, REB], 'to summon' [BDAG, CBC, LN; NASB, REB]. This verb means to communicate directly or indirectly to someone who is presumably at a distance, in order to tell such a person to come [LN]. It means to call to oneself [BDAG].

c. οἰκέτης (LN 46.5) (BDAG p. 694): 'servant' [Bar, BECNT, CBC; CEV, ESV, NASB, NCV, NIV, REB], 'house servant' [LN; TEV], 'household servant' [LN; GW, KJV, NLT], 'personal servant' [BDAG; NET], 'house slave' [AB, BDAG], 'slave' [BDAG; NRSV]. This noun denotes a servant in a household [LN].

d. εὐσεβής (LN 53.6): 'devout' [AB, LN; ESV, GW, KJV, NASB, NET, NIV, NLT, NRSV], 'pious' [Bar, BECNT, LN], 'religious' [LN]. The phrase 'a devout soldier' is also translated 'one of his soldiers who worshiped God' [CEV], 'a military orderly who was a religious man' [CBC; REB], 'a soldier, a religious man' [NCV, TEV]. This adjective pertains to being devoted to a proper expression of religious beliefs [LN].

e. pres. act. participle of προσκαρτερέω (LN 35.28) (BDAG 1. p. 881): 'to attend to' [Bar; ESV], 'to serve' [GW, NET, NRSV], 'to serve personally' [LN], 'to wait on' [BDAG, BECNT; KJV], 'to work for' [NCV], 'to attach oneself to' [BDAG], 'to be faithful to someone' [BDAG], not explicit [CBC; CEV, REB]. The phrase 'of those who attended him' is also translated 'from among his men' [AB], 'of those who were his personal attendants' [NASB], 'who was one of his attendants' [NIV, TEV], 'one of his personal attendants' [NLT]. This verb means to serve in a close personal relationship [LN]. It means to stick by or be close at hand [BDAG].

f. aorist act. indic. of ἀποστέλλω (LN 15.66): 'to send' [AB, Bar, BECNT, CBC, LN; all versions except REB]. This verb is also translated 'ordered' [REB]. This verb means to cause someone to depart for a particular purpose [LN].

QUESTION— What was a 'house servant'?

The term 'house servant' refers to a rather special category of servants that were closely related to the affairs of the household. It might be expressed as 'personal servants' [TH]. They were obviously trusted individuals [NAC, PNTC, TH], men with whom their master could share confidential matters [Bar].

QUESTION—How did they travel to Joppa?

The Greek text does not specify whether Cornelius' men walked or rode to Joppa [TRT]. This was a full day's journey, so probably they were traveling with horses [BECNT], probably riding them [TNTC].

DISCOURSE UNIT—10:9–33 [ESV, NLT]. The topic is Peter's vision [ESV], Peter visits Cornelius [NLT].

DISCOURSE UNIT—10:9–23a [GW, NIV]. The topic is Peter has a vision [GW], Peter's vision [NIV].

DISCOURSE UNIT—10:9–16 [EBC, NAC, NICNT]. The topic is Peter's vision [EBC], the vision of Peter [NAC], Peter sees a vision [NICNT].

10:9 **On-the next-day, (as)-they were-traveling and approaching the-city, Peter went-up on the housetop[a] about (the)-sixth[b] hour to-pray.**

LEXICON—a. δῶμα (LN 7.51) (BDAG p. 266): 'housetop' [BDAG, BECNT, LN; ESV, KJV, NASB], 'roof' [AB, Bar, BDAG, CBC; CEV, GW, NCV, NET, NIV, NLT, NRSV, REB, TEV]. This noun denotes the area on the top of a flat-roof house [LN]. It denotes the level surface of a flat roof [BDAG].

b. ἕκτος (LN 60.53) (BDAG p. 310): 'sixth' [AB, Bar, BDAG, BECNT, LN; ESV, KJV, NASB]. The phrase 'the sixth hour' is also translated 'noon' [CBC; CEV, GW, NCV, NET, NIV, NLT, NRSV, REB, TEV] This adjective refers to the sixth in a series involving either time, space, or set [LN].

QUESTION—When was the sixth hour of the day?

The sixth hour of the day was noon/mid-day [AB, Bar, BECNT, CBC, EBC, NAC, NICNT, PNTC, TH, TNTC, TRT]. This was not normally a time to pray, but a time to eat [Bar, BECNT, EBC, PNTC].

QUESTION—What is meant by 'Peter went up on the housetop'?

The Jews built houses that had flat roofs. Each house had a stairway outside that went up to the roof [BECNT, EBC, NICNT, TH, TRT]. The roof was a private place where people frequently spent time visiting, resting or praying undisturbed [BECNT, TNTC, TRT]. It means that Peter went up onto the flat rooftop [NICNT, TRT].

10:10 **And he-became[a] hungry and wanted something to eat, but[b] (while)-they-were making-preparations, he fell into (a)-trance[c]**

LEXICON—a. aorist mid. (deponent = act.) indic. of γίνομαι (LN 13.48): 'to become' [AB, BECNT, LN; CEV, ESV, GW, KJV, NASB, NET, NIV, NRSV, TEV], 'to be' [NCV, NLT], 'to grow' [CBC; REB], 'to feel' [Bar]. This verb means to come to acquire or experience a state [LN].

b. δέ (LN 89.124): 'but' [BECNT, LN; ESV, KJV, NASB, NCV, NET, NLT, REB], 'and' [NIV, NRSV], not explicit [AB, Bar, CBC; CEV, GW, TEV]. This conjunction indicates a contrast [LN].
c. ἔκστασις (LN 33.489) (BDAG 2. p. 309): 'trance' [Bar, BDAG, BECNT, CBC; ESV, GW, KJV, NASB, NET, NIV, NLT, NRSV, REB], 'ecstasy' [AB, BDAG], 'ecstatic vision' [LN], 'vision' [NCV, TEV]. The clause 'he fell into a trance' is also translated 'he fell sound asleep and had a vision' [CEV]. This noun denotes a vision accompanied by an ecstatic psychological state [LN]. It denotes a state of being in which consciousness is wholly or partially suspended, frequently associated with divine action [BDAG].

QUESTION—What is meant by falling into a trance?

'He fell into a trance' means that he was awake and semi-conscious, not asleep. The Greek term ἔκστασις 'trance' is another expression for 'vision'. With this sense it refers to a trance where God communicates directly with someone [BECNT]. Peter's physical condition (being hungry) and his prayerfulness made him receptive to the vision [CBC, EBC, NICNT, PNTC, TNTC].

10:11 and he-saw heaven^a opened^b and an object^c like (a)-great sheet coming-down, being-let-down^d by-(its)-four corners upon the earth.^e **10:12** In it were all kinds of four-footed-animals and reptiles of-the earth and birds of-the air.

TEXT—Manuscripts reading καὶ καταβαῖνον σκεῦός τι ὡς ὀθόνην μεγάλην τέσσαρσιν ἀρχαῖς καθιέμενον 'and coming down a certain object like a large linen cloth being let down by four corners' are given a C rating by GNT to indicate that the Committee had difficulty making the decision. All versions follow this except GW, KJV, NLT.

LEXICON—a. οὐρανός (LN 1.5, 1.11): 'heaven' [AB, Bar, BECNT, LN (1.11); CEV, ESV, KJV, NCV, NET, NIV, NRSV, REB, TEV], 'sky' [CBC, LN (1.5); GW, NASB, NLT]. This noun denotes heaven, the supernatural dwelling place of God and other heavenly beings [LN (1.11)] or it denotes the sky above the earth, including the vault arching high over the earth from one horizon to another, as well as the sun, moon, and stars [LN (1.5)].
b. perf. pass. participle of ἀνοίγω (LN 79.110) (BDAG 2. p. 84): 'to be opened' [AB, Bar, BDAG, BECNT, LN; all versions], 'to be made open' [LN]. The clause 'he saw heaven opened' is also translated 'He saw a rift in the sky' [CBC]. This verb means to cause something to be open [LN]. It means to render something readily accessible [BDAG].
c. σκεῦος (LN 6.1) (BDAG 1. p. 927): 'object' [BDAG, LN; NASB, NET], 'thing' [BDAG, CBC, LN], 'something' [AB; CEV, ESV, GW, NCV, NIV, NLT, NRSV, REB, TEV], 'sort of vessel' [Bar], 'vessel' [BECNT], 'certain vessel' [KJV]. This noun denotes any kind of instrument, tool, weapon, equipment, container, or property [LN]. It denotes a material

object used to meet some need in an occupation or other responsibility [BDAG].
d. pres. pass. participle of καθίημι (LN 15.111) (BDAG p. 492): 'to be let down' [Bar, BDAG, BECNT, LN; ESV, KJV, NET, NIV, NLT], 'to be lowered' [AB, CBC, LN; all versions except CEV], not explicit [CEV]. This verb means to cause something to move down gradually [LN].
e. γῆ (LN 1.39): 'earth' [AB, Bar, BECNT, LN; ESV, KJV, NCV, NET, NIV, REB, TEV], 'ground' [CBC; GW, NASB, NRSV], 'world' [LN], not explicit [CEV, NLT]. This noun denotes the surface of the earth as the dwelling place of mankind, in contrast with the heavens above and the world below [LN].

QUESTION—What is meant by 'being let down by its four corners'?
'Being let down' is a passive expression. However, it does not imply that people were actually doing this. It was only 'as though people were doing it' [TH].

QUESTION—What does the word τετράποδα 'four-footed animals' include?
Four-footed animals would include both domestic and wild animals [TH, TRT].

QUESTION—What does the phrase πετεινὰ τοῦ οὐρανοῦ 'birds of the sky' refer to?
'Birds of the sky' is an idiom that refers to wild birds contrasted with domesticated birds such as chickens [TH, TRT].

10:13 And there-came (a)-voice to him, "Get-up,ᵃ Peter, kill and eat."
LEXICON—a. aorist act. impera. of ἀνίστημι (LN 17.6): 'to get up' [AB, Bar; all versions except ESV, KJV], 'to stand up' [LN], 'to rise' [BECNT; ESV, KJV]. This verb is also translated 'up' [CBC]. This verb means to assume a standing position [LN].

QUESTION—What is meant by the command 'kill and eat'?
The verb θῦσον 'kill' is also regularly used with reference to sacrifice and it may imply a ritual killing before eating [Bar, PNTC], a religious act [Bar, BECNT]. In the present context the word simply means 'kill' and not 'offer as a sacrifice' [TH].

QUESTION—Whose voice was this?
It is not clear whose voice this was. The title 'Lord' that Peter uses in v. 14 showed that it could be God, Jesus, or the Holy Spirit. It is probably best, if possible, not to specify who the speaker was [TRT]. Peter took what the voice said as a message from God [EBC] It was obviously God who spoke to Peter [TH].

10:14 Butᵃ Peter said, "By-no-means,ᵇ Lord,ᶜ for I have never eaten anything that is commonᵈ and unclean.ᵉ"
LEXICON—a. δέ (LN 89.124): 'but' [AB, Bar, BECNT, CBC, LN; CEV, ESV, KJV, NASB, NCV, NET, NRSV, REB, TEV], 'on the other hand' [LN], not explicit [GW, NIV, NLT]. This conjunction indicates a contrast [LN].

b. μηδαμῶς (LN 69.6) (BDAG p. 647): 'by no means' [AB, BDAG, LN; ESV, NASB, NRSV], 'no indeed' [LN], 'most certainly not' [LN], 'certainly not' [Bar, BDAG; NET, TEV], 'surely not' [NIV], 'no' [BDAG, CBC; NCV, NLT, REB], 'not so' [KJV], 'no way' [BECNT]. This adverb is also translated 'I can't do that' [CEV, GW]. This adverb indicates a strong emphatic negation [LN]. It indicates a negative reaction [BDAG].
c. κύριος (LN 12.9): 'Lord' [AB, Bar, BECNT, CBC, LN; all versions], 'Ruler' [LN], 'One who commands' [LN]. This noun denotes a title for God and for Christ. It indicates one who exercises supernatural authority over mankind [LN].
d. κοινός (LN 53.39) (BDAG 2.b. p. 552): 'common' [BDAG, BECNT; ESV, KJV], 'defiled' [LN; NET], 'ritually unclean' [LN; TEV], 'unholy' [NASB, NCV], 'impure' [GW, NIV, NLT], 'ritually impure' [AB], 'ordinary' [BDAG], 'profane' [Bar, BDAG, CBC; NRSV, REB], 'not fit' [CEV]. This adjective pertains to being ritually unacceptable, either as the result of defilement or because of the very nature of the object itself (for example, ritually unacceptable animals) [LN]. It pertains to being of little value because of being common, specifically of that which is ceremonially impure [BDAG].
e. ἀκάθαρτος (LN 53.39) (BDAG 1. p. 34): 'unclean' [AB, Bar, BDAG, BECNT, CBC; all versions except NET, TEV], 'ritually unclean' [LN; NET], 'defiled' [LN; TEV], 'impure' [BDAG]. This adjective pertains to being ritually unacceptable, either as the result of defilement or because of the very nature of the object itself (for example, ritually unacceptable animals) [LN]. It pertains to that which may not be brought into contact with the divinity [BDAG].

QUESTION—What is meant by the word Μηδαμῶς 'by no means'?

The word 'by no means' in Greek is a very strong expression meaning certainly not, surely not, no indeed [Bar, EBC, TH].

QUESTION—What is meant by the word κοινὸν 'common'?

The word κοινὸν 'common' is equivalent to 'defiled', 'unclean', 'impure'. The same word was used in v. 15 [Bar, BECNT, EBC, NAC, TH].

QUESTION—What caused Peter to claim that the animals, reptiles, and birds were unclean?

Peter had always observed the basic dietary restrictions of Leviticus 11, and there it identifies which animals are 'clean' and which are 'unclean'. Many of the animals that Peter saw here were 'unclean', which means they were not to be eaten by Jews. 'Unclean' refers to being spiritually or ritually 'impure' or, in this context, 'unfit/wrong to eat' [EBC, TH, TRT]. It does not refer to being physically dirty or to having bad behavior [TH, TRT].

QUESTION—Why did Peter refuse to kill and eat the animals, reptiles and birds?

It is because if a Jew touched or ate an 'unclean/impure animal', they became ceremonially/spiritually 'unclean/impure (Leviticus 11). That means they could not socialize or worship God with others until they offered a sacrifice to become 'clean/pure' again [TRT]. Also for being faithful to texts such as Leviticus 11 and obedient to God, Peter refused to kill and eat [Bar, BECNT, EBC, NAC, NICNT, PNTC].

10:15 And (the)-voice (came)- to him again -(a)-second-(time), "What God has made-clean,[a] do- not -call-common.[b]"

LEXICON—a. aorist act. indic. of καθαρίζω (LN 53.28) (BDAG 3.a. p. 488): 'to make clean' [BDAG; ESV, GW, NCV, NET, NIV, NLT, NRSV], 'to cleanse' [Bar, BECNT, LN; KJV, NASB], 'to purify' [LN], 'to declare clean' [BDAG; TEV], 'to count clean' [CBC; REB], 'to declare ritually pure' [AB]. The clause 'what God has made clean' is also translated 'when God says that something can be used for food' [CEV]. This verb means to cleanse from ritual contamination or impurity [LN]. It means to purify through ritual cleansing [BDAG].

b. pres. act. impera. of κοινόω (LN 53.40) (BDAG 3. p. 552): 'to call something common' [LN; ESV, KJV], 'to regard something as defiled' [LN], 'to consider/declare (ritually) unclean' [BDAG]. The phrase 'do not call common' is also translated 'you shall not regard as common' [BECNT], 'no longer consider unholy' [NASB], 'don't call them unholy' [NCV], 'you must not consider ritually unclean' [NET], 'Do not consider anything unclean' [TEV], 'do not call something unclean' [NLT], 'Don't say that the things...are impure' [GW], 'do not call anything impure' [NIV], 'you shall not call impure' [AB], 'you must not call profane' [NRSV], 'it is not for you to call profane' [CBC; REB], 'do not treat as profane' [Bar], 'don't say it isn't fit to eat' [CEV]. This verb means to call or to regard something as common or defiled [LN]. It means to consider/declare (ritually) unclean [BDAG].

QUESTION—Is there anywhere in the Bible where God has declared all foods are clean, not defiled?

The passage in Mark 7:14–23 implies that all foods are clean. There Jesus says that nothing that enters a man from the outside can make him 'unclean' [Bar, EBC, NAC, NICNT, TNTC, TRT].

10:16 This happened three-times, and immediately the object was-taken-up[a] into heaven/the-sky.[b]

TEXT—Manuscripts reading εὐθὺς ἀνελήμφθη 'immediately was taken up' are given a B rating by GNT to indicate that it was regarded to be almost certain. This is followed by all versions except KJV, NLT, REB, TEV.

LEXICON—a. aorist pass. indic. of ἀναλαμβάνω (LN 15.203) (BDAG 1. p. 66): 'to be taken up' [AB, Bar, BDAG, BECNT, CBC, LN; ESV, NASB, NET, NRSV, REB], 'to be taken back' [CEV, NCV, NIV], 'to be taken' [GW], 'to be taken back up' [TEV], 'to be received up' [KJV], 'to be pulled up' [NLT]. This verb means to lift up and carry (away) [BDAG, LN].

b. οὐρανός (LN 1.5, 1.11): 'heaven' [AB, Bar, BECNT, LN (1.11); all versions except GW, NASB], 'sky' [CBC, LN (1.5); GW, NASB]. This noun denotes heaven, the supernatural dwelling place of God and other heavenly beings [LN (1.11)] or it denotes the sky above the earth, including the vault arching high over the earth from one horizon to another, as well as the sun, moon, and stars [LN (1.5)].

QUESTION—What does the clause 'this happened three times' indicate?
The clause 'this happened three times' indicates that this message from God to Peter is important and is true [BECNT, PNTC, TRT]. Here 'this' may refer to the conversion between Peter and the voice [Bar, EBC, NICNT, TRT]. 'This' may refer to the command of God or to the entire event, including God's statement and Peter's reply [TH].

DISCOURSE UNIT—10:17–29 [PNTC]. The topic is two significant journeys.

DISCOURSE UNIT—10:17–23 [NAC]. The topic is Peter's visit to Cornelius.

DISCOURSE UNIT—10:17–23a [EBC, NICNT]. The topic is the messengers from Cornelius arrive at Joppa [EBC, NICNT].

10:17 Now while Peter was- inwardly -perplexed[a] as to what the vision[b] which he-had-seen might-mean,[c] behold,[d] the men who had-been-sent[e] by Cornelius, having-made-inquiry[f] for Simon's house, stood at the gate

LEXICON—a. imperf. act. indic. of διαπορέω (LN 32.10) (BDAG p. 235): 'to be perplexed' [BECNT; ESV], 'to be very perplexed' [LN; NLT], 'to be greatly perplexed' [BDAG; NASB], 'to be very confused' [LN], 'to be puzzled/puzzling' [CBC; GW, NET, REB], 'to be greatly puzzled' [NRSV], 'to not know what to do' [LN], 'to be at a loss' [BDAG], 'to doubt' [Bar; KJV], 'to wonder' [CEV, NCV, NIV, TEV], 'to be uncertain' [AB]. This verb means to be thoroughly perplexed [LN].

b. ὅραμα (LN 33.488) (BDAG 1. p. 718): 'vision' [AB, Bar, BDAG, BECNT, CBC, LN; all versions except CEV], 'something seen' [BDAG]. The phrase 'what the vision which he had seen might mean' is also translated 'what all of this meant' [CEV]. This noun denotes an event in which something appears vividly and credibly to the mind, although not actually present, but implying the influence of some divine or supernatural power or agency [LN]. It denotes something that is viewed with one's eye [BDAG].

c. pres. act. opt. of εἰμί (LN 58.68): 'to mean' [AB, Bar, BECNT; CEV, ESV, KJV, NCV, NLT], 'to be' [NASB], 'to signify' [NET], 'to correspond to, to stand for, to be a figure of, to represent' [LN], not explicit [NRSV]. This verb is also translated as a noun: 'the meaning' [CBC; GW, NIV, REB, TEV]. This verb means to correspond to something else in certain significant features [LN].

d. ἰδού (LN 91.13): 'behold' [Bar, BECNT; ESV, KJV, NASB], 'pay attention, look, listen' [LN], not explicit [AB, CBC; CEV, GW, NCV, NET, NIV, REB, TEV]. The phrase 'behold, the men who had been sent

by Cornelius' is also translated 'suddenly the men sent by Cornelius' [NRSV], 'just then the men sent by Cornelius' [NLT]. This particle functions as a prompter of attention, also serving to emphasize the statement which follows [LN].
  e. perf. pass. participle of ἀποστέλλω (LN 15.66): 'to be sent' [AB, Bar, BECNT, LN; all versions except REB], not explicit [CBC; REB]. This verb means to cause someone to depart for a particular purpose [LN].
  f. aorist act. participle of διερωτάω (LN 27.11) (BDAG p. 244): 'to make inquiry' [AB; ESV, KJV], 'to ask' [Bar, CBC; NASB, NRSV, REB], 'to ask about' [BDAG], 'to seek out' [BECNT], 'to learn about' [LN; NET, TEV], 'to find' [GW, NCV, NLT], 'to find out' [NIV], 'to find out about by inquiry' [LN], 'to find by inquiry' [BDAG], not explicit [CEV]. This verb means to acquire information by questioning [LN].

QUESTION—Who is the man Simon in this verse?

The Simon who owns the house is Simon, the tanner, not Simon Peter [BECNT, TRT].

QUESTION—What is the πυλῶνα 'gate'?

The word 'gate' or door when applied to a house indicates the gateway leading to the inner court [TH].

10:18 **and called-out[a] to-ask[b] whether Simon, who was-called[c] Peter, was-staying[d] there.**

LEXICON—a. aorist act. participle of φωνέω (LN 33.77a) (BDAG 3. p. 1071): 'to call out' [BECNT, CBC, LN; ESV, NASB, NET, REB, NRSV, NIV, TEV], 'to call' [AB, Bar; KJV], 'to cry out' [LN], 'to shout' [LN], 'to speak loudly' [LN], 'to summon' [BDAG], not explicit [CEV, GW, NCV, NLT]. This verb means to speak with considerable volume or loudness [LN]. It means to call to oneself [BDAG].
  b. imperf. mid./pass. (deponent = act.) indic. of πυνθάνομαι (LN 33.181) (BDAG 1. p. 897): 'to ask' [AB, Bar, BDAG, CBC, LN; all versions], 'to inquire' [BDAG, BECNT, LN], 'to make an inquiry' [LN]. This verb means to inquire about something [LN]. It means to seek to learn by inquiry [BDAG].
  c. pres. pass. participle of ἐπικαλέω (LN 33.131) (BDAG 2. p. 373): 'to be called' [BDAG, BECNT, LN; ESV, NASB, NRSV], 'to be named' [LN; NLT], 'to be surnamed' [AB, Bar; KJV], 'to be given a surname' [BDAG], 'to be known as' [NET, NIV]. The phrase 'Simon, who is called Peter' is also translated 'Simon Peter' [CBC; CEV, GW, NCV, REB, TEV]. This verb means to use an attribution in speaking of a person [LN]. It means to address or characterize someone by a special term [BDAG].
  d. pres. pass. indic. of ξενίζω (LN 34.57) (BDAG 1. p. 683): 'to be staying' [AB; CEV, GW, NASB, NCV, NET, NRSV, NLT, NIV], 'to be lodging' [Bar, BECNT, CBC; ESV, REB], 'to be lodged' [KJV], 'to show hospitality' [LN], 'to receive a stranger as a guest' [LN], 'to receive as a guest' [BDAG], 'to entertain' [BDAG], not explicit [TEV]. This verb

means to receive and show hospitality to a stranger, that is, someone who is not regarded as a member of the extended family or a close friend [LN]. It means to show hospitality [BDAG].

10:19 While Peter was-pondering[a] the vision,[b] the Spirit[c] said to-him, "Behold,[d] three men (are)-looking-for[e] you.

TEXT—Manuscripts reading τρεῖς 'three' are given a B rating by GNT to indicate that it was regarded to be almost certain. All versions except REB follow this.

LEXICON—a. pres. mid. or pass. participle of διενθυμέομαι (LN 30.2) (BDAG p. 244): 'to be pondering' [AB, BDAG, BECNT, LN; ESV], 'to be reflecting on' [Bar; NASB], 'to be thinking seriously about' [LN; NET], 'to be thinking about' [CBC; CEV, GW, KJV, NCV, NIV, NRSV, REB], 'to be puzzling over' [NLT]. The clause 'while Peter was pondering the vision' is also translated 'Peter was still trying to understand what the vision meant' [TEV]. This verb means to think about something thoroughly and/or seriously [LN]. It means to give serious thought to something [BDAG].
  b. ὅραμα (LN 33.488) (BDAG 1. p. 718): 'a vision' [AB, Bar, BDAG, BECNT, CBC, LN; all versions], 'something seen, a sight' [BDAG]. This noun denotes an event in which something appears vividly and credibly to the mind, although not actually present, but implying the influence of some divine or supernatural power or agency [LN]. It denotes something that is viewed with one's eye [BDAG].
  c. πνεῦμα (LN 12.18) (BDAG 5.d.α. p. 835): 'Spirit' [AB, Bar, BDAG, BECNT, CBC, LN; all versions except CEV, NLT], 'Spirit of God' [LN], 'Holy Spirit' [LN; CEV, NLT]. This noun denotes a title for the third person of the Trinity' [LN]. It denotes God's being as controlling influence, with focus on association with humans [BDAG].
  d. ἰδού (LN 91.13): 'behold' [AB, BECNT; ESV, KJV, NASB], 'look' [LN; NET, NRSV], 'listen' [LN; NCV, TEV], 'pay attention, come now, then' [LN], not explicit [Bar, CBC; CEV, GW, NIV, NLT, REB]. This word serves as a prompter of attention, which serves also to emphasize the following statement [LN].
  e. pres. act. participle of ζητέω (LN 27.41) (BDAG 1.b. p. 428): 'to look for' [Bar, BDAG, BECNT, CBC, LN; all versions except KJV, NRSV], 'to try to find' [LN], 'to seek' [AB, BDAG; KJV], 'to search for' [NRSV], 'to try to learn where something is' [LN]. This verb means to try to learn the location of something, often by movement from place to place in the process of searching [LN]. It means to try to find what one desires somehow to bring into relation with oneself or to obtain without knowing where it is to be found [BDAG].

QUESTION—Who were the three men?
  The three men were the two house servants and the soldier of Cornelius mentioned in verse 7 [Bar, TH].

10:20 But rise[a] and go-down[b] and accompany them without hesitating,[c] because I have-sent them."

LEXICON—a. aorist act. participle of ἀνίστημι (LN 17.6) (BDAG 10. p. 83): 'to rise' [BDAG, BECNT; ESV, KJV], 'to stand up' [LN], 'to get up' [AB, Bar; GW, NASB, NCV, NET, NIV, NLT, NRSV, REB], 'to set out' [BDAG], 'to get ready' [BDAG; TEV], 'to make haste' [CBC], not explicit [CEV]. This verb means to assume a standing position [LN]. It means to initiate an action [BDAG].
- b. aorist act. impera. of καταβαίνω (LN 15.107) (BDAG 1.a.β. p. 514): 'to go down' [AB, Bar, BDAG, BECNT, LN; ESV, KJV, NET, NRSV, TEV], 'to hurry down' [CEV], 'to go downstairs' [CBC; GW, NASB, NCV, NIV, NLT, REB], 'to move down' [LN], 'to come down' [BDAG, LN], 'to climb down' [BDAG], 'to descend' [LN]. This verb means to move down, irrespective of the gradient [LN]. It means to move downward [BDAG].
- c. pres. mid. participle of διακρίνω (LN 31.37) (BDAG 6. p. 231): 'to hesitate' [GW, NIV, TEV], 'to doubt' [BDAG, LN; KJV, NCV], 'to waver' [BDAG], 'to be uncertain about' [LN], 'to be at odds with oneself' [BDAG], 'to worry' [CEV]. This verb is also translated as a noun: 'hesitation' [AB, Bar; ESV, NET, NLT, NRSV], 'misgiving/s' [CBC; NASB, REB], 'concern' [BECNT]. This verb means to think that something may not be true or certain [LN]. It means to be uncertain [BDAG].

QUESTION—Why does this verse begin with ἀλλά 'but'?
The use of 'but' may suggest, 'You may object, but go without refusing.' The most important point the Son tells him is to go without trying to understand what was going on. Peter was to go with the men because the Spirit had sent them [BECNT]. The Spirit told Peter to go 'without doubting' [Bar, EBC, NICNT, PNTC, TNTC].

10:21 And Peter went-down[a] to the men and said, "Behold,[b] I am the-one you-are-looking-for.[c] What (is)-the reason for which you-have-come?[d]"

LEXICON—a. aorist act. participle of καταβαίνω (LN 15.107) (BDAG 1.a.δ. p. 514): 'to go down' [AB, Bar, BDAG, BECNT, LN; all versions except GW, REB], 'to move down' [LN], 'to come down' [BDAG, CBC, LN; REB], 'to climb down' [BDAG], 'to descend' [LN], 'to go' [GW]. This verb means to move down, irrespective of the gradient [LN]. It means to move downward with the indication of the place to which one goes or comes down [BDAG].
- b. ἰδού (LN 91.13): 'behold' [KJV, NASB], 'look, listen, pay attention, come now, then' [LN], not explicit [AB, Bar, BECNT, CBC; all versions except KJV, NASB]. This particle functions as a prompter of attention, also serving to emphasize the statement which follows [LN].
- c. pres. act. indic. of ζητέω (LN 27.41) (BDAG 1.b. p. 428): 'to look for' [AB, Bar, BDAG, BECNT, CBC, LN; all versions except KJV], 'to seek'

[BDAG; KJV], 'to try to learn where something is, to try to find' [LN]. This verb means to try to learn the location of something, often by movement from place to place in the process of searching [LN]. It means to try to find what one desires somehow to bring into relation with oneself or to obtain without knowing where it is to be found [BDAG].

d. pres. act. indic. of πάρειμι (LN 85.23) (BDAG 1.a. p. 773): 'to come' [AB, Bar; CEV, KJV, NASB, NCV, NET, NIV, NLT, TEV], 'to be present' [BDAG, LN], 'to be here' [LN; GW], 'to be there, to be at hand' [LN]. This verb is also translated as a noun: 'coming' [BECNT; ESV, NRSV]. The clause 'What is the reason for which you have come?' is also translated 'What brings you here?' [CBC; REB]. This verb means to be present at a particular time and place [LN].

10:22 And they-said, "Cornelius, (a)-centurion,[a] (a)-righteous[b] and God fearing[c] man, who-is-well- spoken-of[d] by the entire nation of-the Jews, was-directed[e] by (a)-holy[f] angel to-send-for[g] you to come to his house and to-hear a-message[h] from you." **10:23a** So he invited- them -in[i] to be his guests.

LEXICON—a. ἑκατοντάρχης (LN 55.16) (BDAG p. 299): 'centurion' [AB, BDAG, BECNT, CBC, LN; ESV, KJV, NASB, NET, NIV, NRSV, REB], 'captain' [BDAG, LN]. This noun is also translated as a phrase: 'a Roman army officer' [GW], 'a Roman officer' [NLT], 'an army officer' [NCV]. The phrase 'Cornelius, a centurion' is also translated 'Captain Cornelius' [CEV, TEV], 'Centurion Cornelius' [Bar]. This noun denotes a Roman officer in command of about one hundred men [LN]. It denotes a Roman officer commanding about a hundred men [BDAG].

b. δίκαιος (LN 88.12) (BDAG 1.a.α. p. 246): 'righteous' [Bar, BECNT, LN; NASB, NET, NIV], 'just' [AB, BDAG, LN; KJV], 'upright' [BDAG; ESV, NRSV], 'fair' [BDAG], 'good' [CBC; CEV, NCV, REB, TEV], 'devout' [NLT]. The phrase 'Cornelius,..., a righteous...man' is also translated 'Cornelius...He's a man who has God's approval' [GW]. This adjective pertains to being in accordance with what God requires [LN]. It pertains to being in accordance with high standards of rectitude [BDAG].

c. pres. pass. participle of φοβέω (LN 53.58) (BDAG 2.a. p. 1061): 'to fear' [Bar; KJV], 'to have reverence' [BDAG, LN], 'to worship' [LN], 'to respect' [BDAG]. This verb is also translated as an adjective: 'God-fearing' [AB, BECNT; ESV, NASB, NET, NIV, NLT, NRSV], 'religious' [CBC; REB]. The phrase 'God fearing man' is also translated 'a... man who worships God' [CEV, TEV], 'he worships God' [NCV], 'a...man who respects God' [GW]. This verb means to have profound reverence and respect for deity, with the implication of awe bordering on fear [LN]. It means to have a profound measure of respect for with special reference to fear of offending [BDAG]. This is the same verb that is used in verse 2.

d. pres. pass. participle of μαρτυρέω (LN 33.263) (BDAG 2.b. p. 618): 'to be spoken well of' [BDAG, LN; ESV, NASB, NET, NRSV], 'to be approved of' [BDAG, LN], 'to be liked' [CEV], 'to be respected' [NIV, NLT, TEV], 'to be acknowledged' [CBC; REB]. This verb is also translated with the phrase 'of good report/repute/reputation' [AB, Bar, BECNT; KJV]. The clause 'who is well spoken of by the entire nation of the Jews' is also translated 'the Jewish people respect him' [GW, NCV]. This verb means to speak well of a person on the basis of personal experience [LN]. It means to affirm in a supportive manner [BDAG].

e. aorist pass. indic. of χρηματίζω (LN 28.39) (BDAG 1.b.α. p. 1089): 'to be directed' [CBC; ESV, NASB, NET, NRSV, REB], 'to be instructed' [Bar, BECNT], 'to be warned' [KJV], 'to be commanded' [AB], 'to make known God's message' [LN], 'to reveal a message from God' [LN], 'to make known a divine injunction/warning' [BDAG]. The phrase 'was directed by a holy angel' is also translated 'One of God's holy angels told' [CEV], 'a holy angel told' [GW, NIV], 'The angel told' [NCV], 'A holy angel instructed' [NLT], 'An angel of God told' [TEV]. This verb means to make known a divine revelation [LN]. It means to impart a divine message [BDAG].

f. ἅγιος (LN 88.24) (BDAG 1.a.β. p. 11): 'holy' [AB, Bar, BDAG, BECNT, CBC, LN; all versions except TEV], 'sacred, dedicated to God' [BDAG], 'pure, divine' [LN], not explicit [TEV]. This adjective pertains to being holy in the sense of superior moral qualities and possessing certain essentially divine qualities in contrast with what is human [LN]. It pertains to being dedicated or consecrated to the service of God [BDAG].

g. aorist mid. infin. of μεταπέμπω (LN 15.73) (BDAG p. 641): 'to send for' [Bar, BDAG, BECNT, CBC, LN; CEV, ESV, KJV, NASB, NRSV, REB], 'to summon' [LN, BDAG; GW, NET, NLT], 'to ask' [NCV], 'to invite' [TEV]. The phrase 'to send for you to come' is also translated 'to have you come' [NIV], 'to have you brought' [AB]. This verb means to send someone to obtain something or someone [LN].

h. ῥῆμα (LN 33.98) (BDAG 1. p. 905): 'message' [LN; NASB, NET, NLT], 'word' [Bar, BDAG, LN; KJV], 'saying' [BDAG, LN], 'statement', [BDAG, LN]. The phrase 'a message from you' is also translated 'what you have to say' [AB, BECNT, CBC; CEV, ESV, GW, NCV, NIV, NRSV, REB, TEV]. This noun denotes that which has been stated or said, with primary focus upon the content of the communication [LN]. It denotes that which is said [BDAG].

i. aorist mid. participle of εἰσκαλέομαι (LN 33.316) (BDAG p. 294): 'to invite in/into' [BDAG, LN; ESV, NASB, NET, NIV, NRSV, TEV], 'to invite' [CEV, NLT], 'to ask in/into' [AB, CBC, Bar; GW, NCV, REB], 'to call in' [BECNT; KJV]. This verb means to invite a person in as a guest [LN]. It means to invite in as a guest [BDAG].

QUESTION—What does 'a holy angel' refer to?

'Holy' is used in the sense of 'belonging to God'; thus 'a holy angel' refers to God's angel [TH].

DISCOURSE UNIT—10:23b–48 [GW, NIV]. The topic is Peter speaks with Cornelius [GW], Peter at Cornelius' house [NIV].

DISCOURSE UNIT—10:23b–33 [EBC, NICNT; NASB]. The topic is Peter's reception by Cornelius [EBC], Peter at Caesarea [NASB], Peter enters the house of Cornelius [NICNT].

10:23b **And on the next-day he rose[a] and went-away[b] with them, and some of-the brothers[c] from Joppa accompanied[d] him.**

LEXICON—a. aorist act. participle of ἀνίστημι (LN 17.6): 'to rise' [Bar, BECNT; ESV], 'to get up' [NASB, NET, NRSV], 'to stand up' [LN], 'to get ready' [NCV, TEV], not explicit [AB, CBC; CEV, GW, KJV, NIV, NLT, REB]. This verb means to assume a standing position [LN].

b. aorist act. indic. of ἐξέρχομαι (LN 15.40): 'to go away' [ESV, KJV, NASB], 'to go' [AB, Bar; NCV, NLT, NRSV, TEV], 'to go off' [BECNT], 'to leave' [CEV, GW], 'to set out' [CBC; NET, REB], 'to start out' [NIV], 'to go out of, to depart out of, to leave from within' [LN]. This verb means to move out of an enclosed or well defined two or three-dimensional area [LN].

c. ἀδελφός (LN 11.23) (BDAG 2.a. p. 18): 'brother' [Bar, BDAG; ESV, NET, NIV, NLT], 'fellow believer, a Christian brother' [LN], 'fellow member, associate' [BDAG]. The phrase 'the brothers' is also translated 'the/certain brethren' [AB, BECNT; KJV, NASB], 'the Lord's followers' [CEV], 'the followers' [NCV], 'the believers' [NRSV, TEV], 'some disciples' [GW], 'some members' [CBC; REB]. This noun denotes a close associate of a group of persons having a well-defined membership and in the NT 'brothers' refers specifically to fellow believers in Christ [LN]. It denotes a person viewed as a brother in terms of a close affinity. It was used by Christians in their relations with each other [BDAG].

d. aorist act. indic. of συνέρχομαι (LN 15.148) (BDAG 2. p. 970): 'to accompany' [Bar, BECNT, LN; ESV, KJV, NASB, NET, NRSV], 'to come with' [LN], 'to go with' [LN; GW, NIV], 'to go along with' [TEV], 'to travel with' [AB], 'to travel together with' [BDAG], 'to join with' [NCV], not explicit [CEV]. This verb is also translated as a passive verb: 'accompanied by some' [CBC; NLT, REB]. This verb means to come/go together with one or more other persons [LN]. It means to come/go with one or more persons [BDAG].

QUESTION—Did the men accept Peter's invitation?

This first half of v. 23 can be rendered as 'Peter said to the men, come in and spend the night here' [TH]. With the context in the next half of v. 23, apparently the men had accepted Peter's invitation and stayed there for the night [TRT]. Peter hosted them overnight because the journey back would take more than the day remaining [BECNT, NICNT, TNTC]. This gesture of invitation indicates Peter's new attitude toward the Gentiles and already the idea of fellowship is implied [AB, Bar, BECNT, EBC, NAC, NICNT].

10:24 And on-the following-day he-entered[a] Caesarea. Cornelius was expecting them and had-called-together[b] his relatives and close friends.
LEXICON—a. aorist act. indic. of εἰσέρχομαι (LN 15.93) (BDAG 1.a.α. p. 293): 'to enter' [Bar, BDAG, BECNT, LN; ESV, KJV, NASB, NET], 'to arrive' [CBC; CEV, GW, NIV, NLT, REB, TEV], 'to come to' [AB; NCV, NRSV], 'to move into, to come into, to go into' [LN]. This verb means to move into a space, either two-dimensional or three-dimensional [LN]. It means to move into a space of geographical and other types of localities and areas [BDAG].
  b. aorist mid. participle of συγκαλέω (LN 33.309) (BDAG 2. p. 951): 'to call together' [AB, CBC, LN; all versions except CEV, TEV], 'to summon' [BDAG], 'to invite' [BECNT; CEV, TEV], 'to gather' [Bar]. This verb means to call persons together, presumably at the reference point of the one who calls [LN]. It means to call to one's side [BDAG].
QUESTION—What does the term 'close friends' refer to?
  The term ἀναγκαίους φίλους 'close friends' refers to intimate friends [BECNT, NAC], friends who are so close as to be almost like relatives [Bar].

10:25 When Peter entered,[a] Cornelius met him and fell[b] at his feet and worshiped-(him).[c]
LEXICON—a. aorist act. infin. of εἰσέρχομαι (LN 15.93) (BDAG 1.a.δ. p. 294): 'to enter' [AB, Bar, BDAG, BECNT, LN; ESV, GW, NASB, NCV, NIV, NLT], 'to arrive' [CBC; CEV, NRSV, REB], 'to come in' [KJV, NET], 'to go into' [LN; TEV], 'to move into, to come into' [LN]. This verb means to move into a space, either two-dimensional or three-dimensional [LN]. It means to move into a space of geographical and other types of localities and areas [BDAG].
  b. aorist act. participle of πίπτω (LN 17.22) (BDAG 1.b.α. p. 815): 'to fall' [Bar; NASB, NCV, NET, NIV, NLT, NRSV, TEV], 'to fall down' [AB, BDAG, BECNT; ESV, KJV], 'to prostrate oneself before, to fall down before' [LN], 'to throw oneself to the ground' [BDAG], 'to kneel' [CEV], 'to bow down' [GW], 'to bow to the ground' [CBC; REB]. This verb means to prostrate oneself before someone, implying supplication [LN].
  c. aorist act. indic. of προσκυνέω (LN 53.56) (BDAG a. p. 882): 'to worship' [LN; CEV, ESV, GW, KJV, NASB, NCV, NET, NLT, NRSV], 'to prostrate oneself in worship, to bow down and worship' [LN], 'to (fall down and) worship, to do obeisance to, to prostrate oneself before, to welcome respectfully' [BDAG], 'to do reverence to' [Bar, BDAG], not explicit [TEV]. This verb is also translated as a noun: 'reverence' [CBC; NIV, REB]. The phrase 'worshiped him' is also translated 'greeted him as one divine' [AB], 'gave him homage' [BECNT]. This verb means to express by attitude and possibly by position one's allegiance to and regard for deity [LN]. It means to express in attitude one's complete dependence on or submission to a high authority figure [BDAG].

QUESTION—What is meant by 'Cornelius met him'?
'Cornelius met him (Peter)' meant that Cornelius greeted Peter or welcomed Peter [Bar, BECNT, TH].

QUESTION—What is meant by Peter falling down at his feet?
Cornelius met Peter and out of his respect to Peter, he intentionally knelt at Peter's feet and worshipped Peter [Bar, BECNT, EBC, NAC, PNTC, TH, TNTC, TRT]. A translation should not imply that he tripped and fell down accidentally [TH, TRT].

10:26 But[a] **Peter raised- him -up,**[b] **saying, "Stand-up;**[c] **I too am (a)-man."**

LEXICON—a. δέ (LN 89.124): 'but' [AB, Bar, BECNT, CBC, LN; all versions], 'on the other hand' [LN]. This conjunction indicates a contrast [LN].
  b. aorist act. indic. of ἐγείρω (LN 17.10) (BDAG 3. p. 271): 'to raise up' [Bar; NASB], 'to raise' [BDAG, CBC; REB], 'to help to rise' [BDAG], 'to get up, to cause to stand up' [LN], 'to lift up' [BECNT; ESV], 'to take up' [KJV], 'to help up' [NCV, NET], 'to pull up' [NLT], not explicit [AB; CEV, GW, NIV, NRSV, TEV]. This verb means to cause to stand up, with a possible implication of some previous incapacity [LN]. It means to cause to stand up from a position lower than that of the person rendering assistance [BDAG].
  c. aorist act. impera. of ἀνίστημι (LN 17.6): 'to stand up' [BECNT, CBC, LN; all versions], 'to get up' [AB, Bar]. This verb means to assume a standing position [LN].

QUESTION—What caused Peter to respond that he too was a man?
Peter asked Cornelius to stand up and stop kneeling to worship him as he was only human himself; that is, he was not God, not divine [Bar, BECNT, EBC, NAC, NICNT, PNTC, TNTC, TRT]. He does not merit any kind of special regard or worship such as Cornelius gave him [BECNT, NICNT, TH]. In both Old and New Testaments, there are teachings/instructions in which God commanded men to only worship Him not any others (Ex. 20:3–5; Deut. 5:7–9; Luke 4:5–8; Rev. 19:10, 22:8–9) [TRT].

10:27 **And as he talked with-him, he-entered**[a] **and found**[b] **many people assembled.**[c]

LEXICON—a. aorist act. indic. of εἰσέρχομαι (LN 15.93): 'to enter' [AB, LN; CEV, GW, NASB], 'to go in' [Bar, BECNT, CBC; ESV, KJV, NET, NRSV, REB], 'to move into, to come into' [LN], 'to go into' [LN; TEV], 'to go inside' [NCV, NIV, NLT]. This verb means to move into a space, either two-dimensional or three-dimensional [LN].
  b. pres. act. indic. of εὑρίσκω (LN 27.27) (BDAG 1.c.α. p. 411): 'to find' [AB, Bar, BDAG, BECNT, CBC, LN; ESV, GW, KJV, NASB, NET, NIV, NRSV, REB, TEV], 'to see' [NCV], 'to learn the whereabouts of something, to discover, to come upon, to happen to find' [LN], not explicit [CEV, NLT]. This verb means to learn the location of something, either by intentional searching or by unexpected discovery [LN]. It means

to come upon something, either through purposeful search or accidentally [BDAG].
c. perf. act. participle of συνέρχομαι (LN 15.123) (BDAG 1. p. 969): 'to assemble' [Bar, BDAG, LN; NASB, NLT, NRSV], 'to gather' [AB, BDAG, BECNT; ESV, GW, NCV, TEV], 'to come together' [LN; KJV], 'to gather together' [LN; NET], 'to go together, to meet' [LN]. The phrase 'many people assembled' is also translated 'Many people were there' [CEV], 'a large gathering of people' [NIV], 'a large gathering' [CBC; REB]. This verb means the movement of two or more objects to the same location [LN]. It means to come together with others as a group [BDAG].

QUESTION—What do the pronouns 'he' and 'him' represent?

This verse is rewritten to indicate who the pronouns represent: And as Peter talked with Cornelius, Peter went in and found many persons gathered [TRT] and similarly CEV, GW, and TEV.

10:28 And he-said to them, "You-yourselves know how unlawful it-is for-(a)-man-who-is-a-Jew to-associate-with[a] or to-visit (a)-foreigner,[b] and yet God has-shown[c] me that I should not call[d] any-man common[e] or unclean.[f]

LEXICON—a. pres. pass. infin. of κολλάω (LN 34.22) (BDAG 2.b.α. p. 556): 'to associate with' [AB, BECNT, CBC; all versions except CEV, KJV], 'to join' [BDAG, LN], 'to join oneself to, to become a part of' [LN]. This verb is also translated 'to have anything to do with' [CEV], 'to keep company' [KJV], 'to attach himself to' [Bar]. This verb means to begin an association with someone, whether temporary or permanent [LN]. It means to associate with on intimate terms [BDAG].

b. ἀλλόφυλος (LN 11.43) (BDAG p. 48): 'foreigner' [LN; NASB], 'Gentile' [AB, LN; NET, NIV, NLT, NRSV, TEV], 'heathen, pagan' [LN], 'alien, foreign' [BDAG]. This adjective is also translated 'anyone/one of another nation' [BECNT; ESV, KJV], 'other people' [CEV], 'anyone/man of another race' [Bar, CBC; GW, REB], 'anyone who is not Jewish' [NCV]. This adjective refers to a person not belonging to the ethnic group in question (from the specifically Jewish point of view, one who is not a Jew, but a Gentile) [LN].

c. aorist act. indic. of δείκνυμι (LN 28.47) (BDAG 2. p. 215): 'to show' [Bar, BECNT, CBC, LN; all versions], 'to make known, to demonstrate' [LN], 'to explain, to prove' [BDAG], 'to command' [AB]. This verb means to make known the character or significance of something by visual, auditory, gestural, or linguistic means [LN]. It means to prove or make clear by evidence or reasoning [BDAG].

d. pres. act. infin. of λέγω (LN 33.131) (BDAG 4. p. 590): 'to call' [AB, Bar, BDAG, CBC, LN; ESV, GW, KJV, NASB, NCV, NET, NIV, NRSV, REB], 'to name' [BDAG, LN], 'to consider' [TEV], 'to regard' [BECNT], 'to think of' [NLT], not explicit [CEV]. This verb means to use an attribution in speaking of a person [LN]. It means to identify in a specific manner [BDAG].

e. κοινός (LN 53.39) (BDAG 2.b. p. 552): 'common' [BDAG, BECNT; ESV, KJV], 'ordinary' [BDAG], 'profane' [Bar, BDAG, CBC; NRSV, REB], 'defiled' [LN; NET, TEV], 'ritually unclean' [LN], 'ritually impure' [AB], 'unholy' [NASB, NCV], 'unfit' [CEV], 'impure' [GW, NIV, NLT]. This adjective pertains to being ritually unacceptable, either as the result of defilement or because of the very nature of the object itself (for example, ritually unacceptable animals) [LN]. It pertains to being of little value because of being common, specifically, of that which is ceremonially impure [BDAG].
   f. ἀκάθαρτος (LN 53.39) (BDAG 1. p. 34): 'unclean' [Bar, BDAG, BECNT, CBC; all versions except NET, TEV], 'impure' [BDAG], 'defiled' [LN], 'ritually unclean' [LN; NET, TEV], 'ritually impure' [AB]. This adjective pertains to being ritually unacceptable, either as the result of defilement or because of the very nature of the object itself (for example, ritually unacceptable animals) [LN]. It pertains to that which may not be brought into contact with the divinity [BDAG].

QUESTION—Who does the phrase 'anyone of another nation' refer to?
   The phrase 'anyone of another nation' refers to a Gentile, not a Jew [TH, TRT].
QUESTION—What does the term ἀθέμιτόν 'unlawful' mean?
   The term 'unlawful' means that something is not permitted or allowed [BECNT].
QUESTION—Why was it unlawful for a Jew to associate with a Gentile?
   The main reason that Jews avoided associating with Gentiles is that Gentiles ate many foods that the Jews considered 'unclean', especially, meat from 'unclean' animals, meat that had been offered to idols, and meat that had its blood still in it. For an explanation about 'unclean', see v. 14 [TRT]. It was unlawful in the more general sense of being against Jewish custom that the Gentiles did not observe the biblical rules about food [EBC, PNTC].

10:29 So when I was-sent-for,[a] I-came[b] without raising-any-objection. I-ask then for-what reason you-sent-for me."

LEXICON—a. aorist pass. participle of μεταπέμπω (LN 15.73) (BDAG p. 641): 'to be sent for' [AB, Bar, BDAG, BECNT, LN; ESV, KJV, NASB, NIV, NLT, NRSV], 'to be summoned' [BDAG, LN], 'to be asked to come' [NCV], not explicit [CEV]. This verb is also translated as an active verb: 'you sent for me' [CBC; GW, NET, REB, TEV]. This verb means to send someone to obtain something or someone [LN].
   b. aorist act. indic. of ἔρχομαι (LN 15.81) (BDAG 1.a. p. 393): 'to come' [AB, Bar, BDAG, BECNT, CBC, LN; all versions except NCV], not explicit [NCV]. This verb means to move toward or up to the reference point of the viewpoint character or event [LN]. It means the movement from one point to another, with the focus on approach from the narrator's perspective [BDAG].

DISCOURSE UNIT—10:30-48 [PNTC]. The topic is salvation for Gentiles in the fellowship of the Spirit.

10:30 And Cornelius said, "Four days ago, about this hour, I-was praying in my house at-the ninth[a] hour, and behold,[b] a-man stood before me in shining clothing **10:31** and he-said, 'Cornelius, your prayer has-been-heard and your alms[c] have-been-remembered before God.

TEXT—Manuscripts reading τὴν ἐνάτην 'at the ninth' are given a B rating by GNT to indicate that it was regarded to be almost certain. The ESV, KJV, NASB follow this.

LEXICON—a. ἔνατος (LN 60.56) (BDAG p. 331): 'ninth' [AB, Bar, BDAG, BECNT, LN; ESV, KJV, NASB]. The phrase 'at the ninth hour' is also translated 'at about three o'clock in the afternoon' [CEV], 'three o'clock in the afternoon' [GW, NCV, NET, NLT, TEV], 'at three o'clock' [NRSV], 'at three in the afternoon' [NIV], not explicit [CBC; REB]. The adjective 'ninth' refers to 'the ninth hour' or 'three o'clock in the afternoon [LN].

b. ἰδού (LN 91.13): 'behold' [Bar, BECNT; ESV, KJV, NASB], 'look, listen, pay attention, come now, then' [LN], not explicit [AB]. The phrase 'behold, a man' is also translated 'Suddenly, a man' [CBC; CEV, GW, NET, NIV, NLT, NRSV, REB, TEV], 'Suddenly, there was a man' [NCV]. This particle functions as a prompter of attention, which serves also to emphasize the following statement [LN].

c. ἐλεημοσύνη (LN 57.111) (BDAG 1. p. 316): 'alms' [AB, BDAG, BECNT, LN; ESV, KJV, NASB, NRSV], 'charitable gifts' [Bar], 'charitable giving' [BDAG], 'acts of charity' [CBC, LN; NET, REB], 'works of charity' [TEV], 'giving to the needy' [LN], 'gifts to the poor' [CEV, GW, NIV, NLT]. This noun is also translated as a verb phrase: 'give to the poor' [NCV]. This noun denotes giving to those in need as an act of mercy [LN]. It denotes the exercise of benevolent goodwill [BDAG].

QUESTION—What is meant by 'four days ago'?

Cornelius reviewed the sequence of events beginning four days ago, counting inclusively; it was three days ago by our counting of elapsed time. The chronology is this (with our way of counting in parentheses): day 1 (start), Cornelius saw the angel; day 2 (day 1), the emissaries arrived in Joppa; day 3 (day 2), they set out for Caesarea; day 4 (day 3), they arrived [BECNT, NICNT].

QUESTION—When was the ninth hour of the day?

Refer to the QUESTION for v. 3.

QUESTION—Who was the man in bright clothing?

What Cornelius referred to as a man in this verse is called an angel in v. 3 [AB, Bar, BECNT, NAC, PNTC, TH, TNTC, TRT]. In Acts 1:10, the two angels who appeared were said to have been men also.

10:32 **Therefore send**[a] **to Joppa and ask-for**[b] **Simon, who is-called Peter. He is-staying**[c] **in (the)-house of-Simon, (the)-tanner, by (the)-sea.'**

LEXICON—a. aorist act. impera. of πέμπω (LN 15.67) (BDAG 1. p. 794): 'to send' [AB, Bar, BDAG, BECNT, CBC; all versions], 'to send a message, to send word' [LN]. This verb means to send a message, presumably by someone [LN]. It means to dispatch someone, whether human or transcendent being, usually for the purposes of communication [BDAG].
- b. aorist mid. impera. of μετακαλέω (LN 33.311) (BDAG p. 639): 'to ask for' [ESV, NRSV], 'for' [CEV, NIV, TEV], 'to summon' [Bar, BDAG, LN; NET, NLT, GW], 'to invite' [NASB], 'to ask to come' [CBC; NCV, REB], 'to tell to come' [LN], 'to call to oneself' [BDAG], 'to call' [KJV], 'to seek out' [BECNT], 'to have (him) brought' [AB]. This verb means to summon someone, with considerable insistence and authority [LN]. It means to call to oneself [BDAG].
- c. pres. pass. indic. of ξενίζω (LN 34.57): 'to be staying' [AB; NASB, NCV, NET, NLT, NRSV], 'to be lodging' [Bar, BECNT, CBC; ESV, REB], 'to be lodged' [KJV], 'to be visiting' [CEV], 'to be a guest' [GW, NIV, TEV], 'to show hospitality, to receive a stranger as a guest' [LN]. This verb means to receive and show hospitality to a stranger, that is, someone who is not regarded as a member of the extended family or a close friend [LN].

10:33 **So I-sent**[a] **for you at-once, and you have been kind enough to come. Now then, we all are-present**[b] **before God to-hear all that you have-been-commanded**[c] **by the Lord.**[d]**"**

TEXT—Manuscripts reading τοῦ κυρίου 'the Lord' are given a C rating by GNT to indicate that the Committee had difficulty making the decision. The ESV, GW, NASB, NCV, NET, NIV, NLT, NRSV, REB, TEV follow this. Some Manuscripts have θεοῦ 'God'. The KJV follows this.

LEXICON—a. aorist act. indic. of πέμπω (LN 15.67) (BDAG 1. p. 794): 'to send' [Bar, BDAG, BECNT, CBC; all versions], 'to send a message' [LN], 'to send word' [AB, LN]. This verb means to send a message, presumably by someone [LN]. It means to dispatch someone, whether human or transcendent being, usually for the purposes of communication [BDAG].
- b. pres. act. indic. of πάρειμι (LN 85.23) (BDAG 1.a. p. 773): 'to be present' [BDAG, LN; KJV, NASB], 'to be here' [Bar, BDAG, BECNT; CEV, ESV, GW, NCV, NET, NIV, NLT, NRSV, TEV], 'to be at hand' [LN], 'to be met here' [CBC; REB], 'to be assembled' [AB]. This verb means to be present at a particular time and place [LN]. It means to be present, and in this verse it means 'we are here in the presence of God' [BDAG].
- c. perf. pass. participle of προστάσσω (LN 33.325) (BDAG p. 885): 'to be commanded' [AB, BDAG, BECNT, LN; ESV, KJV, NASB], 'to be ordered' [BDAG, LN], 'to be laid upon' [Bar], 'to be instructed, to be

told, to be given instruction, to determine' [BDAG], not explicit [CEV]. This verb is also translated as an active verb: 'the Lord has commanded/instructed/ordered you' [CBC; GW, NCV, NET, NIV, NRSV, REB, TEV]. The phrase 'to hear all that you have been commanded by the Lord' is also translated 'to hear the message the Lord has given you' [NLT]. This verb means to give detailed instructions as to what must be done [LN]. It means to issue an official directive or make a determination [BDAG].
- d. κύριος (LN 12.9): 'Lord' [AB, Bar, BECNT, CBC, LN; all versions except KJV], 'God' [KJV], 'Ruler, One who commands' [LN], not explicit [CEV]. This noun denotes a title for God and for Christ. It indicates one who exercises supernatural authority over mankind [LN].

QUESTION—What is meant by being in the presence of God?
'In the presence of God' means that God is with us [TH]. God is also a witness to what is taking place [BECNT].

DISCOURSE UNIT—10:34–48 [NASB]. The topic is the Gentiles hear good news.

DISCOURSE UNIT—10:34–43 [EBC, NAC, NICNT; ESV, NLT, NRSV, TEV]. The topic is Peter's sermon in Cornelius' house [EBC], Peter's witness [NAC], Gentiles hear the good news [NICNT; ESV, NRSV], the Gentiles hear the good news [NLT], Peter's speech [TEV].

10:34 So Peter opened[a] his mouth and said: "Truly I-understand that God is not one-to-show-partiality, **10:35** but in every nation anyone who fears[b] him and does what is right is acceptable to-him.

LEXICON—a. aorist act. participle of ἀνοίγω (LN 33.29) (BDAG 5.a. p. 84): 'to open' [Bar, BDAG, BECNT, LN; ESV, KJV, NASB], 'to address' [LN], 'to start speaking' [LN; NET], 'to begin to speak' [LN; NCV, NIV, NRSV, TEV], 'to utter' [LN], not explicit [CEV, GW, NLT]. The phrase 'Peter opened his mouth' is also translated 'Peter began:' [CBC; REB], 'Peter then spoke thus' [AB]. The idiom 'to open the mouth' means to begin to speak in a somewhat formal and systematic manner [LN]. It means to cause to function, and here it means to open one's own mouth to speak [BDAG].
- b. pres. pass. participle of φοβέω (LN 53.58) (BDAG 2.a. p. 1061): 'to fear' [AB, Bar, BECNT; ESV, KJV, NASB, NET, NIV, NLT, NRSV, TEV], 'to reverence' [BDAG, LN], 'to worship' [LN; CEV, NCV], 'to respect' [BDAG; GW]. This verb is also translated 'god-fearing' [CBC; REB]. This verb is a figurative extension of meaning of the verb 'to fear' and it means to have a profound reverence and respect for deity, with the implication of awe bordering on fear. In Acts 13:16 the phrase 'those who fear God' is essentially a technical phrase to identify the non-Jews who worshiped the God of the Jews. These would have been Gentiles who were 'God fearers' or 'worshipers of God' [LN]. It means to have a

profound measure of respect for someone, with special reference to a fear of offending [BDAG].

QUESTION—What is meant by Peter 'opened his mouth'?

The expression 'opened his mouth' is an idiom that means 'he started teaching' [TRT].

QUESTION—What is meant by the expression 'God shows no partiality'?

It means that God treats all people on the same basis [NAC, TH, TNTC]. God looks at a person's heart [TH, TRT]. Jews are as accountable to God for sin as are the Gentiles, there is no distinction [BECNT]. A Gentile may be as good as an Israelite, and be treated by God with equal favor [Bar].

QUESTION—What is meant by 'every nation'?

'Every nation' refers either to 'every race/tribe' or 'every ethnic/people group', and not to geographical or political boundaries [TRT]. This affirms God's impartiality in judgment and salvation. What counts with God is not outward appearance, race, nationality, or class, since in every nation whoever fears God and works righteousness is acceptable to Him [Bar, CBC, EBC, NAC, NICNT, PNTC, TNTC].

10:36 (Concerning) the word[a] that he-sent to-the sons[b] of-Israel, preaching-the-good-news[c] (about) peace through Jesus Christ (the one who is Lord[d] of-all), **10:37** you yourselves know what happened throughout all Judea, beginning from Galilee after the baptism which John proclaimed.[e]

TEXT—Some manuscripts read ὅν 'which'. GNT includes this word in the text in brackets with a C rating to indicate that the Committee had difficulty making the decision. This is followed by CEV, ESV, KJV, NASB, NCV. Some manuscripts omit this word. This is followed by GW, NET, NIV, NLT, NRSV, REB, TEV.

LEXICON—a. λόγος (LN 33.211a) (BDAG 1.a.β. p. 600): 'word' [Bar, BDAG, BECNT, CBC, LN; ESV, GW, KJV, NASB, REB], 'message' [AB; CEV, NCV, NET, NIV, NRSV, NLT, TEV], 'report, news, information' [LN]. This noun denotes information concerning a person or an event [LN]. It denotes a communication whereby the mind finds expression [BDAG].

b. υἱός (LN 11.58) (BDAG 1.c. p. 1024): 'son' [BDAG, LN; NASB], 'descendant' [BDAG]. The phrase 'the sons of Israel' is also translated 'the people of Israel' [CEV, GW, NCV, NET, NIV, NLT, NRSV, TEV], 'the children of Israel' [Bar, BECNT; KJV], 'the Israelites' [AB, CBC; REB], 'Israel' [ESV]. The Greek phrase υἱοὶ Ἰσραήλ 'sons of Israel' refers to the people of Israel as an ethnic entity [LN]. It denotes a human offspring in an extended line of descent [BDAG].

c. pres. mid. participle of εὐαγγελίζω (LN 33.215) (BDAG 2.a.β. p. 402): 'to preach the good news' [ESV], 'to tell the good news' [LN; NIV], 'to announce the gospel' [LN], 'to proclaim the gospel' [BDAG], 'to proclaim the good news' [NET, TEV], 'to preach' [BECNT; KJV, NASB, NRSV], 'to proclaim' [AB], not explicit [CEV, NCV, NLT]. This verb is

also translated 'brought them the Good News' [GW], 'bringing the good news' [Bar], 'gave the good news' [CBC; REB]. This verb means to communicate good news concerning something and in the NT a particular reference to the gospel message about Jesus [LN]. It means to proclaim the divine message of salvation. Here it denotes the object of the proclamation, the Christ [BDAG].
- d. κύριος (LN 12.9) (BDAG 2.b.γ. p. 577): 'Lord' [AB, Bar, BDAG, BECNT, CBC, LN; all versions], 'Ruler, One who commands' [LN], 'master' [BDAG]. This noun denotes a title for God and for Christ. It indicates one who exercises supernatural authority over mankind [LN]. It denotes one who is in a position of authority, and is used in reference to Jesus [BDAG].
- e. aorist act. indic. of κηρύσσω (LN 33.256) (BDAG 2.b.β. p. 543): 'to proclaim' [Bar, BDAG, CBC; ESV, NASB, REB], 'to preach' [AB, BECNT, LN; KJV, NCV, NIV, NLT, TEV], 'to tell' [CEV], 'to announce' [NET, NRSV]. The phrase 'the baptism which John proclaimed' is also translated 'John spread the news about baptism' [GW]. This verb means to publicly announce religious truths and principles while urging acceptance and compliance [LN]. It means to make public declarations [BDAG].

QUESTION—What does 'Jesus is Lord of all' imply?

What made Jesus important is what God was doing through him. Since Jesus is Lord of all, the gospel can go to all, including the Gentiles of the nations such as Cornelius [BECNT, CBC, EBC, NAC, PNTC]. Jesus is the one with authority to deliver the peace that comes from God to those of every nation [BECNT, CBC, EBC, NAC, TNTC].

QUESTION—What does 'Judea' refer to in this context?

In this context, Judea probably refers to the entire land of Israel, not just the Roman Province of Judea [TRT].

QUESTION—What does 'after the baptism that John proclaimed' refer to?

'After the baptism that John proclaimed' refers to the specific baptism of Jesus Christ by John, as described in the following verse how the Holy Spirit came upon Jesus [Bar, BECNT, NAC, TH].

10:38 **(You know about) Jesus of Nazareth, how God anointed[a] him with-(the)-Holy Spirit and with-power. He went-about[b] doing-good[c] and healing all who were oppressed[d] by the devil, for God was with him.**

LEXICON—a. aorist act. indic. of χρίω (LN 37.107) (BDAG b. p. 1091): 'to anoint' [AB, Bar, BDAG, BECNT, CBC, LN; ESV, GW, KJV, NASB, NET, NIV, NLT, NRSV, REB], 'to assign, to appoint' [LN]. The clause 'God anointed Jesus of Nazareth with the Holy Spirit and with power' is also translated 'God gave the Holy Spirit and power to Jesus from Nazareth' [CEV], 'God gave him the Holy Spirit and power' [NCV], 'God poured out on him the Holy Spirit and power' [TEV]. This verb is a figurative extension of meaning of 'to anoint' and it means to assign a person to a task, with the implication of supernatural sanctions, blessing, and endowment. A strictly literal rendering of anoint such as 'to pour oil upon' is likely to be interpreted either as an insult or as an event preparatory to setting a person on fire and thus to destroy or to torture. Accordingly, in place of a literal rendering of anoint, it is often necessary to employ some such expression as 'to be appointed by God' or 'to be given a special task by God' [LN]. It means to anoint in a figurative sense of an anointing by God to set a person apart for special service under divine direction, and here Jesus is anointed for his work or mission [BDAG].

b. aorist act. indic. of διέρχομαι (LN 15.21) (BDAG 1.a. p. 244): 'went about' [Bar, BECNT, CBC; ESV, KJV, NASB, NRSV, REB], 'went around' [CEV, NET, NIV, NLT], 'went everywhere' [GW, NCV, TEV], 'to travel through' [AB], 'to travel around through, to journey all through' [LN], 'to move within or through an area' [BDAG]. This verb means to travel around through an area, with the implication of both extensive and thorough movement throughout an area [LN]. It means to travel or move about from place to place through an area [BDAG].

c. pres. act. participle of εὐεργετέω (LN 88.7) (BDAG p. 405): 'to do good' [AB, Bar, BDAG, BECNT, CBC, LN; all versions], 'to benefit' [BDAG]. This verb means to do that which is good and beneficial to someone [LN]. It means to render exceptional service, especially to a community [BDAG].

d. pres. pass. participle of καταδυναστεύω (LN 22.22) (BDAG p. 516): 'to be oppressed' [BDAG, BECNT, CBC, LN; ESV, KJV, NASB, NET, NLT, NRSV, REB], 'to be overwhelmed' [LN], 'to be exploited' [BDAG], 'to be dominated' [BDAG], 'to be ruled' [NCV], 'to be overpowered' [Bar]. The phrase 'who were oppressed' is also translated 'who was/were under the power' [CEV, NIV, TEV], 'who was/were under/in the devil's power' [AB; GW]. This verb means to cause serious trouble to, with the implication of dire consequences and probably a weakened state [LN]. It means to be dominated [BDAG].

QUESTION—What is the interpretation for 'God anointed Jesus of Nazareth with the Holy Spirit'?

'God anointed Jesus of Nazareth with the Holy Spirit' can be interpreted as 'God chose Jesus and caused the Holy Spirit to come into him' [TH], and gave Jesus power to do good and to heal those oppressed by the devil [BECNT, TNTC].

QUESTION—What is meant by doing good?

'Doing good' may be rendered as 'doing good to people, causing good to come to people' [TH], 'pointing to a benefactor, someone who does good for society' [BECNT].

10:39 And we (are)-witnesses[a] of-all-the-(things) that he-did both in the country[b] of-the Jews and in Jerusalem. They- also -put- him -to-death[c] by hanging-(him)[d] on (a)-tree.[e]

LEXICON—a. μάρτυς (LN 33.270) (BDAG 2.c. p. 620): 'witness' [AB, Bar, BDAG, BECNT, CBC, LN; ESV, KJV, NASB, NET, NIV, NLT, NRSV, REB, TEV], 'testifier' [BDAG], 'one who testifies' [LN]. The phrase 'we are witnesses of all the things that he did' is also translated 'we all saw what Jesus did' [CEV, NCV], 'we can testify to what Jesus did' [GW]. This noun denotes a person who witnesses [LN]. It denotes one who affirms or attests, and here it refers to a witness who bears a divine message [BDAG].
  b. χώρα (LN 1.79) (BDAG 2.b. p. 1094): 'country' [BECNT; ESV, NIV], 'region' [BDAG, LN], 'territory' [LN], 'land' [AB, Bar, LN; GW, KJV, NASB, TEV], 'place' [BDAG]. The phrase 'both in the country of the Jews' is also translated 'both in Israel' [CEV], 'both in Judea' [NET, NRSV], 'in Judea' [NCV], 'throughout Judea' [NLT], 'in the Jewish countryside' [CBC; REB]. This noun denotes a region of the earth, normally in relation to some ethnic group or geographical center, but not necessarily constituting a unit of governmental administration [LN]. It denotes a portion of land area [BDAG].
  c. aorist act. indic. of ἀναιρέω (LN 20.71) (BDAG 2. p. 64): 'to put to death' [CBC; CEV, ESV, NASB, NLT, NRSV, REB, TEV], 'to kill' [AB, Bar, BECNT, LN; GW, NCV, NET, NIV], 'to execute' [LN], 'to do away with, to destroy' [BDAG], 'to slay' [KJV]. This verb means to get rid of someone by execution, often with legal or quasi-legal procedures [LN]. It means to get rid of by execution [BDAG].
  d. aorist act. participle of κρεμάννυμι (LN 20.76) (BDAG 1. p. 566): 'to hang' [Bar, BDAG, BECNT, CBC; all versions except CEV, TEV], 'to crucify' [AB, LN], 'to nail' [TEV], not explicit [CEV]. This verb means to execute by nailing to a cross [LN]. It means to cause to hang [BDAG].
  e. ξύλον (LN 6.28) (BDAG 2.c. p. 685): 'tree' [Bar, BECNT; ESV, KJV, NET, NIV, NRSV], 'cross' [BDAG, LN; CEV, GW, NASB, NCV, NLT, TEV], 'gibbet' [CBC; REB], not explicit [AB]. This noun is a figurative extension of meaning of the word for 'wood' and here it refers to an instrument of execution. In the NT contexts it refers to the cross on which Jesus was crucified [LN]. It denotes an object made of wood and here it refers to the cross, a wooden structure used for crucifixion [BDAG].

QUESTION—Where was Jerusalem?
  Jerusalem was in the country of the Jews. Thus it can be understood that Peter meant witnessing in the city of Jerusalem and in the rest of the country of the Jews [TH, TRT].

10:40 God raised[a] him on the third day and allowed[b] him to-become visible, **10:41** not to-all the people, but to-witnesses who were-chosen-

beforehand^c by God, that is, to-us who ate and drank with-him after he arose^d from (the)-dead.

TEXT—Some manuscripts read ἐν τῇ τρίτῃ ἡμέρᾳ 'on the third day'. GNT includes the word ἐν in the text in brackets with a C decision, indicating that the Committee had difficulty making the decision. All versions follow this except CEV, KJV, NLT, TEV.

LEXICON—a. aorist act. indic. of ἐγείρω (LN 23.94) (BDAG 6. p. 271): 'to raise' [AB, BECNT; ESV, NRSV], 'to raise up' [Bar, BDAG; KJV, NASB, NET], 'to raise to life' [CBC, LN; CEV, NCV, NLT, REB]. The phrase 'raised him' is also translated 'raised him from the dead' [NIV], 'raised him from death' [TEV], 'brought him back to life' [GW], 'to make live again' [LN]. This verb means to cause someone to live again after having once died. In a number of languages there is a difficulty involved in formulating some expression for 'resurrection' or 'living again' since such a phrase may refer to what is technically known as metempsychosis, that is to say, the rebirth of the soul in another existence, a belief which is widely held in a number of areas of south Asia. This problem may be avoided in some languages by speaking of 'his body will live again' or 'his body will come back to life' or 'he will be the same person when he lives again.' [LN]. It means to cause to return to life [BDAG].

b. aorist act. indic. of δίδωμι (LN 13.142) (BDAG 13. p. 243): 'to allow' [BDAG, CBC, LN; NLT, NRSV, REB], 'to grant' [Bar, BDAG, LN; NASB], not explicit [GW]. The phrase 'allowed him to become visible,' is also translated 'let him be seen' [CEV], 'let him appear visible' [AB], 'made him to appear' [ESV], 'showed him openly' [KJV], 'caused him to be visible' [BECNT], 'caused him to be seen' [NCV, NET, NIV], 'caused him to appear' [TEV]. This verb means to grant someone the opportunity or occasion to do something [LN]. It means to grant by formal action [BDAG].

c. perf. pass. participle of προχειροτονέω (LN 30.89) (BDAG p. 892): 'to be chosen beforehand' [AB, BDAG, BECNT; NASB], 'to be appointed beforehand' [Bar, BDAG], 'to be chosen in advance' [LN], 'to be selected beforehand, to be designated in advance' [LN], 'to be chosen' [ESV, KJV, NRSV]. The phrase 'who had been chosen beforehand' is also translated 'apostles he had already chosen' [GW], 'witnesses God had already chosen' [NCV, NET], 'witnesses that God had already chosen' [TEV], 'witnesses whom God had already chosen' [NIV], 'witnesses whom God had chosen in advance' [CBC; REB], 'us whom God had chosen in advance' [NLT], 'the ones God chose' [CEV]. This verb means to choose for a particular purpose in advance [LN]. It means to choose/appoint beforehand [BDAG].

d. aorist act. infin. of ἀνίστημι (LN 23.93): 'to rise' [Bar, BECNT, CBC; ESV, KJV, NASB, NET, NIV, NLT, NRSV, REB, TEV], 'to come back to life' [LN; GW], 'to live again' [LN]. This verb is also translated as a passive verb: 'he was raised' [CEV, NCV]. This verb is also translated as a noun: 'his resurrection' [AB]. This verb means to come back to life after having once died [LN].

QUESTION—Who does τῷ λαῷ 'the people' refer to here?

This is a reference to the Jewish people [TH]. These appearances were not made to the people at large but to a select group of witnesses whom he had chosen beforehand for the purpose [BECNT, TNTC].

10:42 And he-commanded^a us to-preach^b to-the people and to-testify^c that he is the-one appointed^d by God (to be) judge of-(the)-living and (the)-dead.

LEXICON—a. aorist act. indic. of παραγγέλλω (LN 33.327) (BDAG p. 760): 'to command' [AB, BDAG, BECNT, CBC, LN; ESV, KJV, NET, NIV, NRSV, REB, TEV], 'to order' [LN; GW, NASB, NLT], 'to tell' [CEV, NCV], 'to charge' [Bar], 'to give orders, to instruct, to direct' [BDAG]. This verb means to announce what must be done [LN]. It means to make an announcement about something that must be done [BDAG].

b. aorist act. infin. of κηρύσσω (LN 33.256) (BDAG 2.b.β. p. 544): 'to preach' [AB, BECNT, LN; ESV, KJV, NASB, NCV, NET, NIV, NLT, NRSV, TEV], 'to proclaim' [Bar, BDAG, CBC; REB], 'to announce' [CEV], 'to warn' [GW]. This verb means to publicly announce religious truths and principles while urging acceptance and compliance [LN]. It means to make public declarations [BDAG].

c. aorist mid. (deponent = act.) infin. of διαμαρτύρομαι (LN 33.223) (BDAG 1. p. 233): 'to testify (of)' [Bar, BDAG, BECNT, LN; ESV, KJV, NASB, NIV, NLT, NRSV, TEV], 'to declare, to assert' [LN], 'to bear witness (to)' [BDAG], 'to tell' [NCV], 'to warn' [NET], 'to affirm' [CBC; REB], 'to witness' [AB], not explicit [GW]. The phrase 'to preach…and to testify' is also translated 'to announce clearly' [CEV]. This verb means to make a serious declaration on the basis of presumed personal knowledge [LN]. It means to make a solemn declaration about the truth of something [BDAG].

d. perf. pass. participle of ὁρίζω (LN 37.96) (BDAG 2.b. p. 723): 'to be appointed' [BDAG, LN; ESV, NASB, NET, NLT], 'to be designated' [BDAG, CBC, LN; REB], 'to be ordained' [BECNT; KJV, NRSV], 'to be marked out' [Bar], 'to be assigned, to be given a task' [LN]. The clause 'he is the one having been appointed by God' is also translated 'Jesus is the one he has chosen' [CEV], 'he is the one whom God chose/appointed' [NCV, NIV], 'he is the one whom God has appointed' [AB; TEV]. This verb is also translated as an active verb: 'God has appointed Jesus' [GW]. This verb means to assign someone to a particular task, function, or role [LN]. It means to make a determination about a person [BDAG].

QUESTION—What is meant by 'to be judge of the living and the dead'?

'To be judge' means to be the one to decide who is good and who is evil, that is, to decide who are God's people and who are not. It does not mean to accuse or blame someone here [TRT]. 'The living and the dead' is a comprehensive term for all people, past and present [TH]. Jesus has been appointed by God to be a universal judge [PNTC], to be the judge of all people [BECNT].

10:43 To-him all the prophets[a] bear-witness[b] that everyone who believes[c] in him receives[d] forgiveness[e] of-sins through his name."

LEXICON—a. προφήτης (LN 33.60): 'the prophets' [AB, Bar, BECNT, CBC, LN; all versions], 'the writings of the prophets' [LN]. This noun denotes the writings of the prophets, including both the earlier and the later prophets [LN].

b. pres. act. indic. of μαρτυρέω (LN 33.262) (BDAG 1.a.α. p. 618): 'to bear witness' [Bar, BDAG; ESV, NASB], 'to witness' [AB, LN; KJV], 'to testify' [BECNT, CBC; GW, NCV, NET, NIV, NLT, NRSV, REB]. The phrase 'the prophets bear witness' is also translated 'every one of the prophets has said' [CEV], 'the prophets spoke about him' [TEV]. This verb means to provide information about a person or an event concerning which the speaker has direct knowledge [LN]. It means to offer testimony [BDAG].

c. pres. act. participle of πιστεύω (LN 31.102) (BDAG 2.a.β. p. 817): 'to believe' [AB, Bar, BECNT; all versions except CEV, REB], 'to believe (in)' [BDAG], 'to trust' [BDAG, CBC; REB], 'to be a believer' [LN]. The phrase 'who believes in him' is also translated 'who have faith in Jesus' [CEV]. This verb means to believe in the good news about Jesus Christ and to become a follower [LN]. It means to entrust oneself to an entity in complete confidence [BDAG].

d. aorist act. infin. of λαμβάνω (LN 57.125) (BDAG 10.b. p. 584): 'to receive' [AB, Bar, BDAG, CBC, LN; ESV, GW, KJV, NASB, NET, NIV, NRSV, REB], 'to have' [CEV, NLT, TEV]. This verb is also translated with a passive verb 'is received' (by everyone) [BECNT]. The phrase 'receives forgiveness' is also translated 'will be forgiven' [NCV]. This verb means to receive or accept an object or benefit for which the initiative rests with the giver, but the focus of attention in the transfer is upon the receiver [LN].

e. ἄφεσις (LN 40.8) (BDAG 2. p. 155): 'forgiveness' [AB, Bar, BECNT, CBC, LN; ESV, GW, NASB, NET, NIV, NRSV, REB], 'pardon, cancellation' [BDAG], 'remission' [KJV]. The phrase 'receives forgiveness of sins' is also translated 'will have their sins forgiven' [CEV, NLT, TEV], 'will be forgiven of their sins' [NCV]. This noun denotes the removal of guilt resulting from wrongdoing [LN]. It is the act of being freed from an obligation, guilt, or punishment [BDAG].

QUESTION—What is meant by 'through his name'?

'Through his name' is an idiom that focuses on who the Messiah/Christ is and what he did, namely dying on the cross to pay for mankind's sins and then rising from the dead [TRT]. In this context 'through his name' refers to Jesus himself. That is, a person believes in Jesus and it is through Jesus that God forgives his sins [TH]. This idiom focuses on who Christ is and what he did, namely he died on the cross to pay for mankind's sins and then rose from the dead. If 'through his name' is not meaningful, it could be stated 'through him' or 'because of what he did;' or 'because of who Christ is and what he did' [TRT].

DISCOURSE UNIT—10:44-48 [EBC, NAC, NICNT; ESV, NET, NLT, NRSV, TEV]. The topic is the Gentiles receive the Holy Spirit [EBC, NICNT; NRSV], the Holy Spirit falls on the Gentiles [ESV], the impartiality of the Spirit [NAC], the Gentiles receive the Holy Spirit [NET, NLT, TEV].

10:44 While Peter was still speaking these words,[a] the Holy Spirit fell[b] upon all who heard[c] the word.[d]

LEXICON—a. ῥῆμα (LN 33.9) (BDAG 1. p. 905): 'word' [AB, BDAG, BECNT, LN; KJV, NASB, NET, NIV], 'saying' [BDAG, LN], 'expression, statement' [BDAG], not explicit [CBC; CEV, GW, NRSV, REB, TEV]. The phrase 'speaking these words' is also translated 'saying/speaking these things' [Bar; ESV, NLT], 'saying this' [NCV]. This noun denotes a minimal unit of discourse, often a single word [LN]. It denotes that which is said [BDAG].
  b. aorist act. indic. of ἐπιπίπτω (LN 13.122) (BDAG 2. p. 377): 'to fall' [Bar, BECNT; ESV, KJV, NASB, NET, NLT, NRSV], 'to happen to' [BDAG, LN], 'to fall upon' [LN], 'to come down' [NCV, TEV], 'befall' [BDAG]. The phrase 'the Holy Spirit fell upon all' is also translated 'the Holy Spirit took control of everyone' [CEV], 'the Holy Spirit came to everyone' [GW], 'the Holy Spirit came on/upon all' [AB, CBC; NIV, REB]. This verb means to happen suddenly to someone [LN].
  c. pres. act. participle of ἀκούω (LN 31.56): 'to hear' [AB, BECNT; ESV, GW, KJV, NET, NIV, NRSV], 'to listen' [CEV, NCV], 'to accept' [LN], 'to listen to' [Bar, CBC, LN; NASB, NLT, REB, TEV], 'to listen and respond, to pay attention and respond, to heed' [LN]. This verb means to believe something and to respond to it on the basis of having heard it [LN].
  d. λόγος (LN 33.98) (BDAG 1.a.β. p. 599): 'message' [BDAG, BECNT, CBC, LN; GW, NET, NASB, NCV, NIV, NLT, REB, TEV], 'word' [BDAG, LN; ESV, KJV, NRSV], 'preaching' [AB], 'proclamation, instruction, teaching' [BDAG], 'speech' [Bar], not explicit [CEV]. This noun denotes that which has been stated or said, with primary focus upon the content of the communication [LN]. It denotes a communication whereby the mind finds expression [BDAG].

QUESTION—What is of special importance about the conversion of Cornelius and his household?

Cornelius and his household had not yet openly professed faith in Jesus as Lord and Christ, but the Spirit enabled them to respond appropriately to the gospel. They experienced the benefits of Jesus' saving work and articulated their response to him in 'tongues' with praise (v. 46), and then in baptism (v. 47–48; contrast to the pattern in 2:37–41). In this way it is shown that

Gentiles belong to the renewed people of God, on the same basis as believing Israelites [PNTC]. The arrival of the Spirit is the sign of a new age. It confirms that Gentiles can be saved as the following verse also suggests [BECNT].

10:45 And those of (the)-circumcision[a] who had-come-with[b] Peter were-amazed,[c] because the gift of-the Holy Spirit has-been-poured-out[d] on the Gentiles also.

LEXICON—a. περιτομή (LN 11.51) (BDAG 2.a. p. 807): 'circumcision' [LN]. The phrase οἱ ἐκ περιτομῆς πιστοί literally 'the faithful of the circumcision' is also translated 'the believers from among the circumcised' [BECNT; ESV], 'the circumcised believers' [Bar; NASB, NET, NIV, NRSV], 'all the believers who were circumcised' [GW], 'some Jewish followers of the Lord' [CEV], 'the Jewish believers' [NLT, TEV], 'the believers, men of Jewish birth' [NCV], 'men of Jewish birth' [CBC; REB], 'the believers who belonged to the circumcision party' [AB], 'the believers from among the circumcised' [BECNT], 'they of the circumcision' [KJV], 'those who insisted on circumcision' [LN]. This noun denotes those who insisted on circumcising Gentiles if they were to be regarded as true believers in Jesus Christ [LN]. It denotes those of the 'circumcised' who believe, that is, the Judean (Jewish) Christians [BDAG].

b. aorist act. indic. of συνέρχομαι (LN 15.148) (BDAG 2. p. 970): 'to come with' [BECNT, CBC, LN; all versions except NET], 'to go with' [LN], 'to accompany' [Bar, LN; NET], 'to travel with' [AB], 'to travel together with' [BDAG]. This verb means to come/go together with one or more other persons [LN]. It means to come/go with one or more persons [BDAG].

c. aorist act. indic. of ἐξίστημι (LN 25.220) (BDAG 2.b. p. 350): 'to be amazed' [BDAG; ESV, GW, NASB, NCV, NLT, REB, TEV], 'to be astonished' [Bar, BDAG, BECNT, CBC; KJV, NIV], 'to be greatly astonished' [NET], 'to be surprised' [AB; CEV], 'to be astounded' [NRSV], 'to astonish greatly, to greatly astound, to astound completely' [LN]. This verb means to cause someone to be so astounded as to be practically overwhelmed [LN]. It refers to the feeling of astonishment mingled with fear caused by events which are miraculous, extraordinary, or difficult to understand [BDAG].

d. perf. pass. indic. of ἐκχέω (LN 59.50) (BDAG 2. p. 312): 'to be poured out' [AB, Bar, BDAG, BECNT, CBC; ESV, GW, KJV, NASB, NET, NIV, NLT, NRSV, REB], 'to be given' [CEV, NCV], 'to give in abundance, to bestow generously' [LN]. This verb is also translated as an active verb: 'God had poured out' [TEV]. This verb means to cause to exist in an abundance [LN]. It means to cause to fully experience something [BDAG].

QUESTION—What is meant by the expression 'those of the circumcision'?
This refers to Jewish believers [TH, TRT]. The Gentiles/non-Jews were often referred to as uncircumcised (see Acts 11:3 as an example) [TRT].

10:46 For they-were-hearing them speaking in-tongues^a and exalting^b God. Then Peter answered,^c

LEXICON—a. γλῶσσα (LN 33.2) (BDAG 3. p. 201): 'tongues' [AB, Bar, BDAG, BECNT, CBC; ESV, KJV, NASB, NET, NIV, NLT, NRSV, REB, TEV], 'language, dialect, speech' [LN], 'ecstatic language, ecstatic speech' [BDAG]. This noun is also translated 'unknown language' [CEV], 'other languages' [GW], 'different languages' [NCV]. This noun denotes a language, with the possible implication of its distinctive form [LN]. It denotes an utterance outside the normal patterns of intelligible speech and therefore requiring special interpretation [BDAG].
b. pres. act. participle of μεγαλύνω (LN 33.358) (BDAG 2. p. 623): 'to exalt' [BDAG; NASB], 'to extol' [ESV, NRSV], 'to praise' [AB; CEV, GW, NCV, NET, NIV, NLT, TEV], 'to magnify' [Bar, BDAG, BECNT; KJV], 'to acclaim' [CBC], 'to praise the greatness of' [LN], 'to glorify, to speak highly' [BDAG]. The phrase 'exalting God' is also translated 'acclaiming the greatness of God' [REB]. This verb means to praise a person in terms of that individual's greatness [LN]. It means to cause to be held in greater esteem through praise or deeds [BDAG].
c. aorist pass. indic. of ἀποκρίνομαι (LN 33.28): 'to answer' [KJV, NASB], 'to say' [AB, LN; CEV, GW, NCV, NET, NIV, NRSV], 'to speak' [Bar, CBC, LN; REB, TEV], 'to declare' [BECNT, LN; ESV], 'to ask' [NLT]. This verb means to introduce or continue a somewhat formal discourse [LN].

QUESTION—What was the outward sign of the Spirit's coming on the Gentiles?
The speaking in tongues was the outward sign that was a distinctive feature of the apostolic experience of receiving the Spirit of God at Pentecost [AB, Bar, CBC, EBC, NAC, NICNT, PNTC, TNTC]. We do not know the exact meaning of 'tongues' in this context and in Acts 19:6. Luke does not specify whether the Gentiles spoke in foreign languages as Jesus' followers did in Acts 2:4, or in ecstatic unintelligible speech. Many Bible scholars follow each interpretation. However, there is no evidence that these gentiles spoke in a way that was different from the way Jesus' followers spoke at Pentecost. [TRT]. This was the same sign of tongues as at Pentecost. It refers to distinguishable languages because they were immediately recognized as dialects then current [EBC].

10:47 "Surely no-one can refuse^a the water for these to-be-baptized who have-received^b the holy Spirit just as we did, can he?"

LEXICON—a. aorist act. infin. of κωλύω (LN 13.146) (BDAG 2. p. 580): 'to refuse' [BDAG; NASB], 'to withhold' [BDAG, CBC; ESV, NCV, NET, NRSV, REB],'to deny' [AB, BDAG], 'to keep back' [BDAG], 'to forbid'

[Bar, BECNT; KJV], 'to prevent, to hinder' [LN]. The phrase 'refuse the water for these to be baptized' is also translated 'refuse to baptize these people with water' [GW], 'keep these people from being baptized with water' [NIV], 'stop them from being baptized with water' TEV], 'stop us from baptizing them' [CEV], 'object to their being baptized' [NLT]. This verb means to cause something not to happen [LN]. It means to keep something back [BDAG].
  b. aorist act. indic. of λαμβάνω (LN 57.125): 'to receive' [AB, Bar, BECNT, CBC, LN; all versions except CEV], ' to accept' [LN]. This verb is also translated as a passive verb: 'have been given' [CEV]. This verb means to receive or accept an object or benefit for which the initiative rests with the giver, but the focus of attention in the transfer is upon the receiver [LN].

QUESTION—Is an answer expected to Peter's question?
  Peter's question starts with the interrogative 'surely no one can refuse the water,' which indicates that the expected answer is 'No, nothing should prevent this'. So baptism in the name of Jesus occurs in the following verse [BECNT].

QUESTION—What is the function of this verse?
  This verse shows that water baptism is closely connected in Acts with the bestowal of the Holy Spirit, though the gift sometimes precedes and sometimes follows baptism (cf. 8:12, 14–17; 9:17–18; 10:44–48; 19:5–6). Even after the gift of the Spirit, baptism remains an important means of calling upon the name of Jesus with repentance and faith and identifying with the community of believers [PNTC].

10:48 **And he-ordered[a] them to-be-baptized in the name of-Jesus Christ.[b] Then they-asked him to-remain[c] for some days.**
  TEXT—Manuscripts reading ἐν τῷ ὀνόματι Ἰησοῦ Χριστοῦ βαπτισθῆναι 'to be baptized in the name of Jesus Christ' are given a B rating by GNT to indicate that it was regarded to be almost certain. All versions follow this except the KJV. Some manuscripts read 'the Lord'. The KJV follows this.
  LEXICON—a. aorist act. indic. of προστάσσω (LN 33.325) (BDAG p. 885): 'to order' [BDAG, CBC, LN; CEV, GW, NASB, NCV, NIV, NRSV, REB, TEV], 'to command' [AB, BDAG, BECNT, LN; ESV, KJV], 'to instruct, to tell' [LN], 'to give instructions, to determine' [BDAG]. The phrase 'he commanded' is also translated 'he gave orders' [Bar; NET, NLT]. This verb means to give detailed instructions as to what must be done [LN]. It means to issue an official directive or make a determination [BDAG].
    b. Χριστός (LN 93.387): 'Christ' [AB, Bar, BECNT, CBC, LN; all versions except KJV]. The phrase 'in the name of Jesus Christ' is also translated 'in the name of the Lord' [KJV]. This is the Greek translation of the Hebrew and Aramaic word 'Messiah' used as a proper name for Jesus [LN].

c. aorist act. infin. of ἐπιμένω (LN 85.55) (BDAG 1. p. 375): 'to remain' [AB, BDAG, BECNT, LN; ESV]. The phrase 'to remain for some days' is also translated 'to stay for several days' [NET, NRSV], 'to stay on for a few days' [CEV, NASB], 'to stay with them for a few days' [NCV, NIV, TEV], 'to stay with them for several days' [GW, NLT], 'to stay on with them for a time' [CBC; REB], 'to stay on for some days' [Bar], 'to tarry certain days' [KJV]. This verb means to remain in the same place over a period of time [LN]. It means to remain at or in the same place for a period of time [BDAG].

QUESTION—What is indicated by the fact that Peter remained with them for several days?

This indicates that Peter had recognized Cornelius and his household to be fellow Christians who were in the same relationship with the Lord Jesus, now truly 'made clean' by faith [Bar, EBC, NAC, PNTC]. The new era has arrived, table fellowship and full hospitality between Jews and Gentiles ensues [BECNT, TNTC].

DISCOURSE UNIT—11:1-18 [AB, Bar, BECNT, CBC, EBC, NAC, NICNT, PNTC; CEV, ESV, GW, NASB, NCV, NET, NIV, NLT, NRSV, TEV]. The topic is Peter's defense of his relations with Cornelius [AB], Peter and Cornelius debated [Bar], Peter reports to Jerusalem about Gentiles [BECNT], Peter's action is confirmed [CBC], Peter reports to the church in Jerusalem [CEV], the response of the Jerusalem church [EBC], Peter reports to the church [ESV], Peter reports that non-Jewish people can belong to the church [GW], endorsement of the witness to the Gentiles [NAC], Peter reports at Jerusalem [NASB], Peter returns to Jerusalem [NCV], Peter defends his actions to the Jerusalem church [NET], Peter's action endorsed at Jerusalem [NICNT], Peter explains his actions [NIV, NLT], Peter's report to the church at Jerusalem [NRSV, TEV], Peter's report to the church in Jerusalem [PNTC].

DISCOURSE UNIT—11:1-3 [NICNT, PNTC]. The topic is Peter called to account [NICNT], Peter is called to account [PNTC].

11:1 Now the apostles and the brothers[a] who were throughout Judea heard that the Gentiles also had received[b] the word[c] of-God.

LEXICON—a. ἀδελφός (LN 11.23): 'brother' [Bar, BECNT; ESV, NET, NIV], 'fellow believer, a Christian brother' [LN]. The phrase 'the brothers' is also translated 'the brethren' [AB; KJV, NASB], 'the followers' [CEV], 'the/other believers' [GW, NCV, NLT, NRSV, TEV], 'the members' [CBC; REB]. This noun denotes a close associate of a group of persons having a well-defined membership. In the NT ἀδελφός 'brother' refers specifically to fellow believers in Christ [LN].

b. aorist mid. (deponent = act.) indic. of δέχομαι (LN 31.51) (BDAG 5. p. 221): 'to receive' [AB, Bar, BECNT; ESV, KJV, NASB, NIV, NLT, TEV], 'to accept' [BDAG, CBC, LN; CEV, GW, NCV, NET, NRSV,

REB], 'to receive readily, to believe' [LN], 'to be receptive of, to be open to, to approve' [BDAG] . This verb means to readily receive information and to regard it as true [LN]. It means to indicate approval or conviction by accepting [BDAG].

c. λόγος (LN 33.260) (BDAG 1.b.β. p. 599): 'word' [AB, Bar, BDAG, BECNT, CBC; all versions except CEV, NCV], 'what is preached, gospel' [LN], 'message' [CEV], 'teaching' [NCV]. This noun denotes the content of what is preached about Christ or about the good news [LN]. It denotes a communication whereby the mind finds expression [BDAG].

QUESTION—What is meant by 'the brothers'?

As in so many other contexts, 'brothers' refers to believers [EBC, TH], ordinary members of the church [AB, CBC].

QUESTION—What is meant by 'to receive the word of God'?

'To receive the word of God' is to welcome the gospel message with one's heart [BECNT], to become believers [Bar].

11:2 But^a when Peter went-up^b to Jerusalem, those of (the) circumcision^c (party) criticized^d him, saying, 11:3 "You went to uncircumcised men and ate with-them."

LEXICON—a. δέ (LN 89.124): 'but' [LN; NCV, NLT], 'on the other hand' [LN], 'so' [BECNT; CEV, ESV, NET, NIV, NRSV], 'and' [CBC; KJV, NASB, REB], 'however' [GW], not explicit [AB, Bar; TEV]. This conjunction indicates a contrast [LN].

b. aorist act. indic. of ἀναβαίνω (LN 15.101) (BDAG 1.a.α. p. 58): 'to go up' [Bar, BECNT, LN; ESV, NET, NIV, NRSV], 'to come up' [AB, CBC, LN; KJV, NASB, REB], 'to ascend' [LN]. This verb is also translated 'came' [CEV, NCV], 'went' [GW, TEV], 'arrived back' [NLT]. This verb means to move up [LN]. It means to be in motion upward of living beings [BDAG].

c. περιτομή (LN 11.51) (BDAG 2.a. p. 807): The phrase οἱ ἐκ περιτομῆς 'those of the circumcision party' [AB] is also translated 'they that were of the circumcision' [KJV], 'those from the circumcision' [BECNT], 'those who represented circumcision' [Bar], 'the circumcision party' [ESV], 'the circumcised believers' [NET, NIV, NRSV], 'the believers who insisted on circumcision' [GW], 'those who were circumcised' [NASB], 'those who were of Jewish birth' [CBC; REB], 'the Jewish believers' [NLT], 'some Jewish believers' [NCV], 'those who were in favor of circumcising Gentiles' [LN; TEV], 'they wanted Gentile followers to be circumcised' [CEV]. The set phrase, literally 'those of circumcision') denotes those who insisted on circumcising Gentiles if they were to be regarded as true believers in Jesus Christ [LN]. It denotes those of the 'circumcised' who believe, that is, the Judean (Jewish) Christians [BDAG].

d. imperf. mid. indic. of διακρίνω (LN 33.412) (BDAG 5.b. p. 231): 'to criticize' [LN; ESV, NIV, NLT, NRSV, TEV], 'to take issue' [BDAG; NASB, NET, REB]. The phrase 'the circumcision party criticized him' is also translated 'some of the Jewish followers started arguing with him' [CEV], 'the believers...began to argue with him' [GW], 'some Jewish believers argued with him' [NCV], 'they that were of the circumcision contended with him' [KJV], 'those of the circumcision party attacked him' [AB], 'those who represented circumcision debated with him' [Bar], 'those from the circumcision complained to him' [BECNT], 'those who were of Jewish birth raised the question with him' [CBC]. The set phrase 'those of circumcision' denotes those who insisted on circumcising Gentiles if they were to be regarded as true believers in Jesus Christ [LN]. It means to be at variance with someone by maintaining a firm opposing position or adverse judgment [BDAG].

QUESTION—Why is the verb 'went up' used to describe Peter's travel to Jerusalem?

Peter went up to Jerusalem reflects the geographical position of Jerusalem which was higher than most of the surrounding area. Jerusalem was built on top of several hills [TH, TRT]. Most of the surrounding area is lower than it is. For example, Jerusalem is about 2,600 feet (800 m.) above sea level while the town of Jericho, which is about 15 miles (24 km.) northeast of Jerusalem, is about 800 feet (244 m.) below sea level [TRT].

QUESTION—Who were 'those of the circumcision'?

This refers to those (they were Jewish believers) who insisted on circumcising Gentiles if they were to be regarded as true believers in Jesus Christ. It can be interpreted as 'those who insisted on circumcision' [TRT]. The circumcision group's (they were Jewish believers) understanding would be that Gentiles need to observe the law, keep away from unclean food, and be circumcised to show their participation in the covenant (Gen. 17:9–14; on clean and unclean, see the discussion of Acts 10:13–15) [BECNT, TNTC].

QUESTION—What message was intended to be conveyed in v. 3?

Whether v. 3 is a statement or a rhetorical question, the meaning is basically the same: the people were criticizing Peter and wanted an explanation [BECNT, NICNT, TRT].

DISCOURSE UNIT—11:4–17 [NICNT, PNTC]. The topic is Peter's defense [NICNT], Peter recalls God's direction and control [PNTC].

11:4 And Peter began and explained it to-them in-order, saying, **11:5** "I was in (the)-city of-Joppa praying, and in (a)-trance[a] I-saw (a)-vision,[b] an object like (a)-great sheet coming-down,[c] being-let-down[d] from heaven[e] by-its -four corners, and it-came[f] down-to me.

LEXICON—a. ἔκστασις (LN 33.489) (BDAG 2. p. 309): 'trance' [Bar, BDAG, BECNT, CBC; ESV, GW, KJV, NASB, NET, NIV, NLT, NRSV, REB], 'ecstasy' [BDAG], 'ecstatic vision' [LN], not explicit [CEV, NCV, TEV]. The phrase 'in a trance' is also translated 'in a state of ecstasy' [AB]. This noun denotes a vision accompanied by an ecstatic psychological state [LN]. It denotes a state of being in which

consciousness is wholly or partially suspended, frequently associated with divine action [BDAG].
b. ὅραμα (LN 33.488) (BDAG 1. p. 718): 'vision' [AB, Bar, BDAG, BECNT, CBC, LN; all versions except GW], 'something seen, sight' [BDAG], not explicit [GW]. This noun denotes an event in which something appears vividly and credibly to the mind, although not actually present, but implying the influence of some divine or supernatural power or agency [LN]. It denotes something that is viewed with one's eye [BDAG].
c. pres. act. participle of καταβαίνω (LN 15.107) (BDAG 1.b. p. 514): 'to come down' [Bar, CBC, LN; NASB, NRSV, REB, TEV], 'to move down' [BDAG, LN], 'to go down' [LN], 'to descend' [AB, BECNT, LN; ESV, KJV, NET], not explicit [CEV, GW, NCV, NIV, NLT]. This verb means to move down, irrespective of the gradient [LN]. It means to move downward [BDAG].
d. pres. pass. participle of καθίημι (LN 15.111) (BDAG p. 492): 'to be let down' [Bar, BDAG, BECNT; ESV, KJV, NET, NIV, NLT], 'to be lowered' [AB, CBC; GW, NASB, NCV, NRSV, REB, TEV], not explicit [CEV]. This verb means to cause something to move down gradually [LN].
e. οὐρανός (LN 1.5, 1.11) (BDAG 2.a. p. 738): 'heaven' [AB, Bar, BDAG, BECNT, LN (1.11); CEV, ESV, KJV, NCV, NET, NIV, NRSV, REB, TEV], 'sky' [CBC, LN (1.5); GW, NASB, NLT]. This noun denotes heaven, the supernatural dwelling place of God and other heavenly beings [LN (1.11)] or it denotes the sky above the earth, including the vault arching high over the earth from one horizon to another, as well as the sun, moon, and stars [LN (1.5)]. It is the transcendent abode that is the dwelling place or throne of God [BDAG].
f. aorist act. indic. of ἔρχομαι (LN 15.81) (BDAG 1.a.γ. p. 394): 'to come' [AB, Bar, BDAG, BECNT, LN; all versions except REB, TEV], not explicit [CBC; REB, TEV]. This verb means to move toward or up to the reference point of the viewpoint character or event [LN]. It means movement from one point to another, with the focus on approach from the narrator's perspective [BDAG].

QUESTION—Why does the following explanation (vv. 4–17) so closely follow the wording of the account already given in Chapter 10?

Luke has summarized chapter 10 by using the device of repetition to underscore the significance of the event. His condensed account contains only a slight difference from the account given in chapter 10 [AB, Bar, BECNT, CBC, EBC, NAC, NICNT]. Peter does not respond directly to the criticism of v. 3, but recounts how God brought him to preach to Cornelius and his household and to stay with them (chapter 10). He told this in the first person from his point of view [EBC, PNTC, TNTC]. This happened first through a series of divine revelations (vv. 4–14). Then, the coming of the Holy Spirit upon the Gentiles recalled for him both the experience of the first

Jewish believers at Pentecost and the promise of the Lord about its significance (vv. 15–17). Finally, Peter's own conviction about not standing in God's way becomes an implied challenge to his audience about the attitude towards Gentiles which at least some of them have expressed (v. 3) [EBC, PNTC].

11:6 Looking-at-it-closely,[a] I-saw four-footed-animals of-the earth and beasts of prey and reptiles and birds of-the air. **11:7** And also I-heard (a)-voice saying to-me, 'Rise,[b] Peter; kill and eat.'

LEXICON—a. imperf. act. indic. of κατανοέω (LN 30.4) (BDAG 2. p. 522): 'to look at closely' [ESV, NRSV], 'to consider' [Bar, BDAG; KJV], 'to think about very carefully, to consider closely' [LN], 'to look at (with reflection), to contemplate' [BDAG], 'to observe' [NASB], 'to look' [CEV, NCV, NET, NIV, NLT], 'to look intently' [CBC; REB], 'to look closely' [TEV]. The phrase 'looking at it closely' is also translated 'looked into the sheet very closely' [GW], 'looked at it more closely' [AB], 'gazing at it closely' [BECNT]. This verb means to give very careful consideration to some matter [LN]. It means to look at in a reflective manner [BDAG].

b. aorist act. participle of ἀνίστημι (LN 17.6): 'to rise' [BECNT; ESV, KJV], 'to stand up' [LN], 'to get up' [AB, Bar; all versions except ESV, KJV]. The phrase 'rise, Peter' is also translated 'up, Peter' [CBC]. This verb means to assume a standing position [LN].

11:8 But I-said, 'By-no-means,[a] Lord, for nothing common[b] or unclean[c] has ever entered my mouth.'

LEXICON—a. μηδαμῶς (LN 69.6) (BDAG p. 647): 'by no means' [AB, BDAG, LN; ESV, NASB, NRSV], 'no indeed' [Bar, LN], 'most certainly not' [LN], 'certainly not' [BDAG; NET, TEV], 'surely not' [NIV], 'no' [BDAG, CBC; NCV, NLT, REB], 'not so' [KJV], 'no way' [BECNT]. The phrase 'By no means, Lord' is also translated 'Lord, I can't do that' [CEV], 'I can't do that, Lord' [GW]. This adverb indicates a strong emphatic negation [LN]. It indicates a negative reaction [BDAG].

b. κοινός (LN 53.39) (BDAG 2.b. p. 552): 'common' [BDAG, BECNT; ESV, KJV], 'defiled' [LN; NET], 'ritually unclean' [LN; TEV], 'ritually impure' [AB], 'ordinary' [BDAG], 'profane' [Bar, BDAG, CBC; NRSV, REB], 'unholy' [NASB, NCV], 'impure' [GW, NIV, NLT], 'not fit' [CEV]. This adjective pertains to being ritually unacceptable, either as the result of defilement or because of the very nature of the object itself (for example, ritually unacceptable animals) [LN]. It pertains to being of little value because of being common, specifically of that which is ceremonially impure [BDAG].

c. ἀκάθαρτος (LN 53.39) (BDAG 1. p. 34): 'unclean' [Bar, BDAG, BECNT, CBC; all versions except NET, TEV], 'impure' [BDAG], 'defiled' [LN; TEV], 'ritually unclean' [LN; NET], not explicit [AB]. This adjective pertains to being ritually unacceptable, either as the result of defilement or because of the very nature of the object itself (for example, ritually unacceptable animals) [LN]. It pertains to that which may not be brought into contact with the divinity [BDAG].

11:9 But^a (the)-voice answered (a)-second-(time) from heaven, 'What God has-made-clean, do- not -call-common.^b' **11:10** This happened three times, and everything was-drawn-up^c again into heaven.

LEXICON—a. δέ (LN 89.124): 'but' [BECNT, LN; ESV, KJV, NASB, NCV, NET, NLT, NRSV], 'on the other hand' [LN], not explicit [AB, Bar, CBC; CEV, GW, NIV, REB, TEV]. This conjunction indicates a contrast [LN].

    b. pres. act. impera. of κοινόω (LN 53.40) (BDAG 3. p. 552): 'to call something common' [LN; ESV, KJV], 'to regard as common' [BECNT], 'to call something unclean' [NLT], 'to consider anything unclean' [TEV], 'to consider ritually unclean' [BDAG; NET], 'to declare ritually unclean' [BDAG], 'to call ritually impure' [AB], 'to call anything impure' [NIV], 'to regard something as defiled' [LN], 'to consider unholy' [NASB], 'to call profane' [CBC; NRSV, REB], 'to treat as profane' [Bar], not explicit [CEV]. The phrase 'do not call common' is also translated 'Don't say that the things…are impure' [GW], 'don't call them unholy' [NCV]. This verb means to call or to regard something as common or defiled [LN]. It means to consider/declare (ritually) unclean [BDAG].

    c. aorist pass. indic. of ἀνασπάω (LN 15.213) (BDAG p. 71): 'to be drawn up' [AB, Bar, BDAG, CBC, LN; ESV, KJV, NASB, REB, TEV], 'to be pulled up' [BDAG, LN; NET, NIV, NRSV], 'to be taken up' [BECNT], 'to be taken back' [CEV, NCV], 'to be pulled back' [GW], 'to be pulled back up' [NLT]. This verb means to pull or draw something in an upward direction [LN].

11:11 And behold,^a at-that-very-moment three men arrived at the house in which we-were, having-been-sent to me from Caesarea. **11:12** And the Spirit^b told me to-go-with them, making- no -distinction.^c These six brothers^d also went with me, and we-entered the man's house.

TEXT—Manuscripts reading ἦμεν 'we were' are given a C rating by GNT to indicate that the Committee had difficulty making the decision. Some manuscripts have 'I was'. This is followed by CEV, KJV, NCV, NIV, NLT, REB, TEV.

LEXICON—a. ἰδού (LN 91.13): 'behold' [ESV, KJV, NASB], 'look, listen, pay attention, then' [LN], not explicit [AB, Bar, BECNT, CBC; CEV, GW, NCV, NET, NIV, NLT, NRSV, REB, TEV]. This particle functions as a prompter of attention, which serves also to emphasize the following statement [LN].

    b. πνεῦμα (LN 12.18) (BDAG 5.d.α. p. 835): 'Spirit' [AB, Bar, BDAG, BECNT, CBC, LN; all versions except CEV, NLT], 'Spirit of God' [LN], 'Holy Spirit' [LN; CEV, NLT]. This noun is a title for the third person of the Trinity [LN]. It denotes God's being as the controlling influence, with

focus on association with humans [BDAG]. See the explanation of the meaning and translation of 'the Spirit' at 1:2.
  c. aorist act. participle of διακρίνω (LN 30.113) (BDAG 2. p. 231): 'to make a distinction' [Bar, BDAG, LN; ESV, NRSV], 'to judge that there is a difference' [LN], 'to differentiate' [BDAG], not explicit [CBC; REB]. The phrase 'making no distinction' is also translated 'without misgivings' [NASB], 'not to worry' [CEV, NLT], 'without any hesitation' [GW], 'without hesitation' [NET, TEV], 'have no hesitation' [NIV], 'making no hesitation' [BECNT], 'nothing doubting' [KJV], 'without doubting' [NCV], 'without discrimination' [AB]. This verb means to judge that there is a difference or distinction [LN]. It means to conclude that there is a difference [BDAG].
  d. ἀδελφός (LN 11.23): 'brother' [Bar; ESV, NET, NIV, NLT, NRSV], 'fellow believer' [LN; TEV], 'a Christian brother' [LN], 'believer' [GW, NCV], 'companion' [CBC; REB]. The phrase 'six brothers' is also translated 'six brethren' [BECNT; KJV, NASB], 'six of the Lord's followers' [CEV], 'six men' [AB]. This noun denotes a close associate of a group of persons having a well-defined membership and in the NT it refers specifically to fellow believers in Christ [LN].
QUESTION—What is meant by going with the three men 'making no distinction'?
It means that Peter should exercise no partiality against the three men just because those men were gentiles [BECNT].

11:13 And he-told us how he-had-seen the angel stand in his house and say, 'Send^a to Joppa and summon^b Simon who is-called^c Peter.
LEXICON—a. aorist act. impera. of ἀποστέλλω (LN 15.66): 'to send' [BECNT, LN]. The phrase 'send to Joppa' [Bar, CBC; CEV, ESV, NASB, NCV, NIV, NRSV, REB] is also translated 'send word to Joppa' [AB], 'send someone to Joppa' [TEV], 'send men to Joppa' [KJV], 'send messengers to Joppa' [GW, NET, NLT]. This verb means to cause someone to depart for a particular purpose [LN].
  b. aorist mid. impera. of μεταπέμπω (LN 15.73) (BDAG p. 641): 'to summon' [BDAG, LN]. The phrase 'and summon Simon' is also translated 'and have Simon brought here' [NASB], 'and bring Simon' [BECNT; ESV], '(to send to Joppa) for someone named Simon' [CEV], 'and summon Simon' [Bar; NET], 'send to Joppa for Simon' [NIV], 'and summon a man whose name is Simon' [GW], 'and summon a man named Simon' [NLT],'and call for Simon' [KJV], 'and invite Simon' [NCV], '(send to Joppa) for Simon' [CBC; REB], 'and bring Simon' [NRSV], 'let Simon...be brought' [AB], 'Send someone to Joppa for a man whose full name is Simon Peter' [TEV].
  c. pres. pass. participle of ἐπικαλέω (LN 33.131) (BDAG 2. p. 373): 'to be called' [BDAG, BECNT, CBC, LN; ESV, NASB, NET, NIV, NRSV], 'to be named' [LN; CEV, NLT], 'to be surnamed' [AB, Bar], 'to be given a

surname' [BDAG]. The phrase 'Simon who is called Peter' is also translated 'whose name/surname is' [GW, KJV], 'whose full name is' [TEV]. The phrase 'Simon who is called Peter' is also translated 'Simon Peter' [NCV, REB]. This verb means to use an attribution in speaking of a person [LN]. It means to address or characterize someone by a special term [BDAG].

11:14 He will-speak words[a] to you by which you will-be-saved,[b] you and all your household.[c]'

LEXICON—a. ῥῆμα (LN 33.98) (BDAG 1. p. 905): 'word' [AB, Bar, BDAG, CBC, LN; KJV, NASB, NCV, REB, TEV], 'message' [BECNT, LN; ESV, GW, NET, NIV, NRSV], 'saying' [BDAG, LN], 'expression, statement of any kind' [BDAG]. The phrase 'he will speak words to you' is also translated 'Peter would tell him' [CEV], 'He will tell you' [NLT]. This noun denotes that which has been stated or said, with primary focus upon the content of the communication [LN]. It denotes that which is said [BDAG].
  b. fut. pass. indic. of σῴζω (LN 21.27) (BDAG 2.b. p. 983): 'to be saved' [AB, Bar, BDAG, BECNT, LN; all versions except GW, REB], 'to attain salvation' [BDAG]. This verb is also translated with an active verb 'a message that will save you' [GW]. This verb is also translated as a noun: 'salvation' [CBC; REB]. This verb means to cause someone to experience divine salvation [LN].
  c. οἶκος (LN 10.8) (BDAG 2. p. 699): 'household' [AB, Bar, BDAG, BECNT, CBC, LN; ESV, NASB, NET, NIV, NLT, NRSV, REB], 'family' [BDAG, LN]. The phrase 'all your household' is also translated 'everyone in his house' [CEV], 'everyone in your home' [GW], 'all thy house' [KJV], 'all your family' [NCV, TEV]. This noun denotes the family consisting of those related by blood and marriage, as well as slaves and servants, living in the same house or homestead [LN].

11:15 And as I began to-speak, the Holy Spirit fell[a] upon them just-as he did upon us at (the)-beginning. **11:16** And I-remembered the word[b] of-the Lord,[c] how he-said, 'John baptized with-water, but you will-be-baptized with (the)-Holy Spirit.'

LEXICON—a. aorist act. indic. of ἐπιπίπτω (LN 13.122) (BDAG 2. p. 377): 'to fall' [Bar, BECNT; ESV, KJV, NASB, NET, NLT, NRSV], 'to happen to' [BDAG, LN], 'to fall upon' [LN], 'to befall' [BDAG]. The phrase 'the Holy Spirit fell upon them' is also translated 'the Holy Spirit was given to them' [CEV], 'the Holy Spirit came to these people' [GW], 'the Holy Spirit came on/upon them' [AB, CBC; NCV, NIV, REB], 'the Holy Spirit came down on them' [TEV]. This verb means to happen suddenly to, with the connotation of something bad and adverse [LN].
  b. ῥῆμα (LN 33.98) (BDAG 1. p. 905): 'word' [AB, Bar, BDAG, BECNT, LN; ESV, KJV, NASB, NCV, NET, NLT, NRSV], 'saying' [BDAG, LN], 'message, statement' [LN], 'expression, statement of any kind' [BDAG],

not explicit [CBC; CEV, GW, NIV, REB, TEV]. This noun denotes that which has been stated or said, with primary focus upon the content of the communication [LN]. It denotes that which is said [BDAG].
  c. κύριος (LN 12.9): 'Lord' [AB, Bar, BECNT, CBC, LN; all versions], 'Ruler, One who commands' [LN]. This noun denotes a title for God and for Christ. It indicates one who exercises supernatural authority over mankind [LN].

11:17 **If then God gave the same gift to-them as he also gave to-us when we believed[a] in the Lord Jesus Christ, who was I to hinder[b] God?"**
LEXICON—a. aorist act. participle of πιστεύω (LN 31.102) (BDAG 2.a.γ. p. 817): 'to believe' [AB, Bar, BDAG, BECNT; all versions except CEV], 'to trust' [BDAG], 'to be a believer' [LN]. The phrase 'when we believed in the Lord' is also translated 'when we put our faith/trust in the Lord' [CBC; CEV]. This verb means to believe in the good news about Jesus Christ and to become a follower [LN]. It means to entrust oneself to an entity in complete confidence [BDAG].
  b. aorist act. infin. of κωλύω (LN 13.146) (BDAG 1.a. p. 580): 'to hinder' [BDAG, LN], 'to prevent' [BDAG, LN], 'to stand in the way' [BDAG]. The question 'Who was I-to/that-I-could hinder God? [BECNT; NET, NRSV] is also translated 'who was I that I could stand in God's way?' [ESV, NASB], 'who was I to stand in God's way?' [NLT], 'who was I to be able to stand in God's way?' [Bar], 'who then was I to stand in the way of God?' [AB], 'How could I stand in God's way?' [REB], 'how could I possibly stand in God's way?' [CBC], 'how could I stop the work of God?' [NCV], 'So who was I to interfere with God?' [GW], 'So how could I have gone against God?' [CEV], 'who was I to think that I could oppose God?' [NIV], 'what was I, that I could withstand God?' [KJV], 'who was I, then, to try to stop God?' [TEV]. This verb means to cause something not to happen [LN]. It means to keep something from happening [BDAG].
QUESTION—What was the same gift that God had given them?
  That gift was the Holy Spirit [TRT]. Jesus' prediction of a baptism with the Holy Spirit was fulfilled for the apostles at Pentecost, and now for Cornelius and his fellow Gentiles it was fulfilled with the coming of the Spirit at Cornelius's house [NAC].
QUESTION—What is the point of the rhetorical question asked in this verse?
  Opposition to the Gentiles' baptism would be opposition to God, for God's leading of Peter and Cornelius proved his intention to include them in his people. Who could object? [NAC, NICNT]. Anyone who stands in the way of the full incorporation of others into the church, when they genuinely trust in the Lord Jesus Christ for their salvation, stands in opposition to God himself [PNTC].

DISCOURSE UNIT—11:18 [NICNT, PNTC]. The topic is Peter's defense accepted [NICNT], the church acknowledges God's leading [PNTC].

11:18 When they heard these-things they-remained-silent and glorified[a] God, saying, "Then to-the Gentiles also God has-granted[b] repentance[c] that leads to life.[d]"

LEXICON—a. aorist act. indic. of δοξάζω (LN 33.357) (BDAG 1. p. 258): 'to glorify' [Bar, BECNT, LN; ESV, KJV, NASB], 'to praise' [AB, BDAG, LN; CEV, GW, NCV, NET, NIV, NLT, NRSV, TEV], 'to honor, to extol' [BDAG]. This verb is also translated as a noun: '(to give) praise' [CBC; REB]. This verb means to speak of something as being unusually fine and deserving honor [LN]. It means to influence one's opinion about another so as to enhance the latter's reputation [BDAG].
  b. aorist act. indic. of δίδωμι (LN 57.71a): 'to grant' [AB, BECNT, CBC; ESV, KJV, NASB, NET, NIV, REB], 'to give' [Bar; NLT, NRSV, TEV], 'to allow' [NCV], 'to impart' [LN]. The phrase 'to the Gentiles also God has granted repentance' is also translated 'God has now let Gentiles turn to him' [CEV], 'God has also led people who are not Jewish to turn to him' [GW]. This verb means to impart something intangible [LN].
  c. μετάνοια (LN 41.52) (BDAG p. 640): 'repentance' [Bar, BECNT, CBC, LN; ESV, KJV, NASB, NET, NIV, NRSV, REB], 'conversion' [AB, BDAG], 'a change of mind' [BDAG]. The phrase 'to the Gentiles also God has granted repentance' is also translated 'God has given to the Gentiles also the opportunity to repent' [TEV], 'God has also given the Gentiles the privilege of repenting of their sins' [NLT], 'God has also led people who are not Jewish to turn to him so that they can change the way they think and act' [GW], 'God has now let Gentiles turn to him' [CEV], 'God is allowing even those who are not Jewish to turn to him' [NCV]. This noun denotes a complete change of thought and attitude with regard to sin and righteousness [LN].
  d. ζωή (LN 23.88) (BDAG 2.b.α. p. 430): 'life' [AB, Bar, BDAG, BECNT, LN; CEV, ESV, GW, KJV, NASB, NET, NIV, NLT, NRSV]. This noun is also translated as a verb: 'live' [NCV, TEV]. This noun is also translated as an adjective: 'life-giving' [CBC; REB]. This noun refers to the life of the believer which proceeds from God and Christ [BDAG].

QUESTION—What is meant by 'they remained silent'?
It means that they stopped their criticism of Peter, no further objections. The next portion of the same verse says that they then changed their attitude and glorified God, praised God [EBC, NAC, NICNT, TH].

QUESTION—What is meant by the 'repentance that leads to life'?
This repentance is not simply a repentance of particular sins, but is a rejection of everything that hinders the reception of salvation through faith in Jesus Christ [PNTC]. Repentance is the response of men to the gospel and life is the salvation as a gift to men [BECNT]. The opportunity of repenting of sins was granted and thus the obtaining of eternal life [NICNT, TNTC].

DISCOURSE UNIT—11:19–30 [BECNT, CBC, EBC, NAC, NICNT, PNTC, TNTC; CEV, ESV, GW, NASB, NCV, NIV, NLT, NRSV, TEV]. The topic is the church at Antioch: Barnabas, Saul, and Agabus [BECNT], Barnabas in Antioch is joined by Saul [CBC], the church in Antioch [CEV, ESV, NIV, NRSV], the church at Antioch of Syria [EBC], the new church in Antioch [GW], Antioch's witness to Gentiles [NAC], the good news comes to Antioch [NCV], Antioch becomes a Christian base [NICNT], the church in Antioch of Syria [NLT], the word goes to Antioch in Syria [PNTC], the church at Antioch [TNTC; NASB, TEV].

DISCOURSE UNIT—11:19–26 [AB, Bar, EBC, NAC; NET]. The topic is the mission to the Gentiles begins in Antioch [AB], foundation of the church at Antioch [Bar], founding of the church at Antioch [EBC], establishing a church in Antioch [NAC], activity in the church at Antioch [NET].

DISCOURSE UNIT—11:19–21 [NICNT, PNTC]. The topic is Gentile evangelization in Antioch [NICNT], the planting of a new church [PNTC].

11:19 So then those who were-scattered[a] because of the persecution[b] that occurred[c] in connection with Stephen went[d] to Phoenicia and Cyprus and Antioch, speaking the word[e] to-no-one except Jews.

LEXICON—a. aorist pass. participle of διασπείρω (LN 15.136) (BDAG p. 236): 'to be scattered' [Bar, BDAG, BECNT, CBC, LN; all versions], 'to be caused to disperse' [LN]. The phrase 'those who were scattered' is also translated 'Those who had been put to flight' [AB]. This verb means to cause a group or gathering to disperse or scatter, with a possible emphasis on the distributive nature of the scattering (that is to say, each going in a different direction) [LN].

b. θλῖψις (LN 22.2) (BDAG 1. p. 457): 'persecution' [AB, Bar, BECNT, CBC, LN; ESV, KJV, NASB, NET, NIV, NLT, NRSV, REB, TEV], 'trouble' [CEV, GW], 'trouble and suffering, suffering' [LN], 'oppression, affliction, tribulation' [BDAG]. This noun is also translated as a passive verb: 'they were persecuted' [NCV]. This noun denotes trouble involving direct suffering [LN]. It denotes trouble that inflicts distress [BDAG].

c. aorist mid. (deponent = act.) participle of γίνομαι (LN 13.107) (BDAG 3.b. p. 197): 'to occur' [LN; NASB], 'to arise' [AB, Bar, BDAG, CBC; ESV, KJV, REB], 'to start' [CEV], 'to come about' [BDAG, BECNT], 'to break out' [GW], 'to take place' [NET, NRSV, TEV], 'to happen, to come to be' [LN],'to develop' [BDAG], not explicit [NCV, NIV, NLT]. This verb means to happen, with the implication that what happens is different from a previous state [LN]. It means to come into being as an event or phenomenon from a point of origin [BDAG].

d. aorist act. indic. of διέρχομαι (LN 15.17) (BDAG 1.b.β. p. 244): 'to go' [Bar, BDAG; CEV, GW, NCV, NET, TEV], 'to move on to, to go on to' [LN], 'to travel' [AB, BECNT; ESV, KJV, NIV, NLT, NRSV]. This verb is also translated 'made their way' [CBC; NASB, REB]. This verb means

to complete one's movement in a particular direction [LN]. It means to move toward a destination [BDAG].
e. λόγος (LN 33.260): 'word' [AB, Bar, BECNT; ESV, GW, KJV, NASB, NLT, NRSV], 'message' [CBC; CEV, NCV, NET, NIV, REB, TEV], 'what is preached, gospel' [LN]. This noun denotes the content of what is preached about Christ or about the good news [LN].

QUESTION—Who were 'those who were scattered'?
They were the Hellenists, that is, the Greek-speaking Jewish Christian associates of Stephen and Philip [EBC, NAC, NICNT, PNTC].

QUESTION—Where was Phoenicia?
Phoenicia was part of Syria Province under the Roman rule [TRT]. Its principal cities were Tyre [Bar, BECNT, CBC, NAC, PNTC, TNTC, TRT], Sidon [Bar, BECNT, CBC, NAC, PNTC, TNTC] and Biblos [Bar, PNTC], Zarephath [NAC, TNTC]. It was a long, narrow strip of land on the east coast of the Mediterranean Sea [BECNT, TRT], and it extended some 75 miles along the coast of middle Syria from Mt. Carmel north to the river Eleutheros [NAC].

QUESTION—Where was Cyprus?
Cyprus was a large island lying off the coast of Asia Minor and Syria [BECNT, PNTC, TH], the easternmost island of the Mediterranean and some 100 miles off the Syrian coast [BECNT, NAC].

QUESTION—Where was Antioch?
Antioch was the capital city of Syria Province, was the third most important city in the Roman Empire, next to Rome and Alexandria [AB, BECNT, CBC, NICNT, PNTC, TH, TNTC, TRT]. Paul set off on his three missionary journeys from the church in this city (see Acts 13:1–4; 15:35, 40 and 18:23). Luke, the author of Acts, was a Gentile who was born in this city. Antioch was over 300 miles (480 km.) north of Jerusalem [TRT], was 15 miles from the coast [TH]. Note that there was another city called Antioch in Galatia Province [TRT].

11:20 But[a] there-were some of them, men of-Cyprus and Cyrene, who on-coming to Antioch spoke to the Greeks also, preaching-the-good-news[b]-(about) the Lord Jesus.

LEXICON—a. δέ (LN 89.124): 'but' [AB, Bar, BECNT, CBC, LN; ESV, GW, NASB, NET, NRSV, REB, TEV], 'on the other hand' [LN], 'and' [KJV], 'however' [NLT], not explicit [CEV, NCV, NIV]. This conjunction indicates a contrast [LN].
b. pres. mid. participle of εὐαγγελίζω (LN 33.215) (BDAG 2.a.β. p. 402): 'to tell the good news' [Bar, CBC, LN; CEV, NCV, NIV, REB, TEV], 'to spread the Good News' [GW], 'to proclaim the good news' [BECNT; NET], 'to announce the gospel' [LN], 'to proclaim the gospel' [BDAG], 'to preach' [AB; ESV, KJV, NASB, NLT], 'to proclaim' [NRSV]. This verb means to communicate good news concerning something and in the

NT it is a particular reference to the gospel message about Jesus [LN]. It means to proclaim the divine message of salvation [BDAG].
QUESTION—Where was Cyrene?
Cyrene was a city in North Africa [BECNT, TRT]. The Simon who carried Jesus' cross was from this city [TRT].

11:21 And (the)-hand[a] of-(the)-Lord was with them, and (the)-large number who believed[b] turned[c] to the Lord.
LEXICON—a. χείρ (LN 76.3) (BDAG 2.b.β. p. 1083): 'hand' [AB, Bar, BDAG, BECNT; ESV, KJV, NASB, NET, NIV, NRSV], 'power' [CBC, LN; CEV, GW, NLT, REB, TEV]. The phrase 'the hand of the Lord was with them' is also translated 'The Lord was helping the believers' [NCV]. This noun is a figurative extension of meaning of χείρ 'hand' and denotes power as an expression of the activity of a person or supernatural being [LN]. The hand of deity denotes God's divine power as ruler, helper, worker of wonders, and regulator of the universe [BDAG].
  b. aorist act. participle of πιστεύω (LN 31.102) (BDAG 2.b. p. 817): 'to believe' [AB, Bar, BECNT; ESV, GW, KJV, NASB, NCV, NET, NIV, NLT, TEV], 'to be a believer'[LN], 'to become a believer' [CBC; NRSV, REB], 'to be a Christian' [LN], 'to believe in, to trust' [BDAG], 'to have faith in' [CEV]. This verb means to believe in the good news about Jesus Christ and to become a follower [LN]. It means to entrust oneself to an entity in complete confidence [BDAG].
  c. aorist act. indic. of ἐπιστρέφω (LN 41.51) (BDAG 4.a. p. 382): 'to turn' [AB, Bar, BDAG, BECNT, CBC; all versions], 'to change one's ways, to turn to God' [LN]. This verb means to change one's manner of life in a particular direction, with the implication of turning back to God [LN]. This verb means to change one's mind or course of action, for better or worse [BDAG].
QUESTION—What is meant by 'the hand of the Lord?
The hand of the Lord refers to the Lord's power [BECNT, CBC, NICNT]. The hand of the 'Lord' probably refers to God the Father rather than to Jesus. However in the phrase 'turned to the Lord,' the Lord Jesus is meant [TH].

DISCOURSE UNIT—11:22–26 [NICNT, PNTC]. The topic is Barnabas and Saul's ministry at Antioch [NICNT], the encouraging ministry of Barnabas and Saul [PNTC].

11:22 The report[a] of this was-heard[b] in the ears of-the church in Jerusalem, and they-sent Barnabas to Antioch.
TEXT—Some manuscripts omit the word διελθεῖν 'to go'. GNT includes this word in the text in brackets with a C rating, indicating that the Committee had difficulty making the decision. The KJV follows this.
LEXICON—a. λόγος (LN 33.211a) (BDAG 1.a.β. p. 599): 'report' [Bar, LN; ESV, NET], 'news' [AB, CBC, LN; CEV, GW, NASB, NIV, NRSV,

REB, TEV], 'information' [LN], 'word' [BDAG, BECNT, LN], 'tidings' [KJV], not explicit [NCV, NLT]. This noun denotes information concerning a person or an event [LN]. It denotes a communication whereby the mind finds expression [BDAG].
  b. aorist pass. indic. of ἀκούω (LN 24.52) (BDAG 1.b.α. p. 37): 'to be heard' [BDAG, LN]. This verb is also translated as an active verb: 'The church in/at Jerusalem heard' [NCV, NLT]. The phrase 'was heard in the ears of the church' is also translated 'came to the ears of the church' [AB, Bar, BECNT; ESV, KJV, NRSV], 'reached the ears of the church' [CBC; NASB, NIV, REB], 'reached the church' [CEV, GW, TEV], 'came to the attention of the church' [NET]. This verb means to be heard [LN]. It means to have or exercise the faculty of hearing [BDAG].

QUESTION—Who was Barnabas?

This Barnabas was an important leader in the early church (Acts 4:36; 9:27) although he was not one of Jesus' twelve apostles [TRT]. He was from the island of Cyprus, the same island that some of the people in Antioch were from (v. 20) [BECNT, NAC, TNTC, TRT]. He was a Cypriot Jew by birth [CBC, NICNT].

11:23 **When he came and saw the grace^a of-God, he rejoiced^b and encouraged^c them-all to-remain^d faithful to-the Lord with steadfast^e purpose,^f**

LEXICON—a. χάρις (LN 25.89) (BDAG 3.b. p. 1080): 'grace' [Bar, BECNT, CBC; ESV, KJV, NASB, NET, NIV, NRSV, REB], 'favor, good will' [LN], 'blessing' [NLT], '(a sign of) favor, gracious deed/gift, benefaction' [BDAG]. The phrase 'saw the grace of God' is also translated 'saw what God had been kind enough to do for them' [CEV], 'see what God had done for them' [GW], 'saw how God had blessed the people' [NCV, TEV]. The phrase 'grace of God' is also translated 'God's gracious work' [AB]. It denotes a favorable attitude toward someone or something [LN]. It denotes a practical application of goodwill on the part of God and Christ [BDAG].
  b. aorist pass. (deponent = act.) indic. of χαίρω (LN 25.125) (BDAG 1. p. 1075): 'to rejoice' [Bar, BDAG, CBC, LN; NASB, NET, NRSV, REB], 'to be glad' [AB, BDAG, BECNT, LN; CEV, ESV, KJV, NCV, NIV, TEV], 'to be pleased' [GW], 'to be filled with joy' [NLT]. This verb means to enjoy a state of happiness and well-being [LN]. It means to be in a state of happiness and well-being [BDAG].
  c. imperf. act. indic. of παρακαλέω (LN 25.150) (BDAG 2. p. 765): 'to encourage' [BDAG, CBC, LN; GW, NASB, NCV, NET, NIV, NLT, REB], 'to urge' [BDAG; TEV], 'to exhort' [AB, Bar, BDAG, BECNT; ESV, KJV, NRSV], 'to beg' [CEV]. This verb means to cause someone to be encouraged or consoled, either by verbal or non-verbal means [LN]. It means to urge strongly [BDAG].

d. pres. act. infin. of προσμένω (LN 68.11) (BDAG 1.a.β. and b. p. 883): 'to remain' [AB, BECNT; CEV, ESV, GW, NASB, NET, NIV, NRSV], 'to continue' [Bar, LN], 'to remain in, to keep on' [LN], 'to remain/stay with' [BDAG], 'to cleave' [KJV]. The phrase 'to remain faithful to the Lord' is also translated 'to obey the Lord' [NCV], 'to stay true to the Lord' [NLT], 'to hold fast to the Lord' [CBC; REB], 'to be faithful and true to the Lord' [TEV]. It means to continue in an activity or state [LN]. It means to be steadfast in association [BDAG].

e. καρδία (LN 26.3) (BDAG 1.b.γ. p. 509): 'steadfast' [BECNT; ESV, NRSV], 'heart' [BDAG, LN], 'inner self, mind' [LN], 'solidly committed' [GW], not explicit [NLT]. The phrase 'with steadfast purpose' is also translated 'with resolute heart/hearts' [CBC; NASB, REB], 'with devoted hearts' [NET], 'with all their hearts' [CEV, NCV, NIV, TEV], 'with purpose of heart' [KJV], 'with all their heart and will' [AB], 'in the purpose of their hearts' [Bar]. This noun is a figurative extension of meaning of καρδία 'heart,' and denotes the causative source of a person's psychological life in its various aspects, but with special emphasis upon thoughts [LN]. It denotes the heart as the center and source of the will and its decisions [BDAG].

f. πρόθεσις (LN 30.63) (BDAG 2.a. p. 869): 'purpose' [Bar, BECNT, LN; ESV, KJV], 'plan, proposal' [LN], not explicit [AB, CBC; all versions except ESV, KJV]. This noun denotes that which is planned or purposed in advance [LN]. It denotes that which is planned in advance by humans [BDAG].

11:24 for he-was (a)-good man, and full of-(the)-Holy Spirit and of faith.[a] And (a)-great-many people were-added[b] to-the Lord.

LEXICON—a. πίστις (LN 31.102) (BDAG 2.d.α. p. 819): 'faith' [AB, Bar, BDAG, BECNT, CBC; all versions], 'trust, confidence' [BDAG], 'Christian faith' [LN]. This noun denotes the belief in the good news about Jesus Christ and becoming a follower [LN]. It denotes the state of believing on the basis of the reliability of the one trusted [BDAG].

b. aorist pass. indic. of προστίθημι (LN 59.72) (BDAG 1.b. p. 885): 'to be added' [Bar, BDAG, BECNT, LN; ESV, KJV], 'to be brought' [AB; NASB, NET, NIV, NLT, NRSV, TEV], 'to be won over' [CBC; REB], 'to be put to, to be associated' [BDAG]. The phrase 'were added to the Lord' is also translated 'turned to the Lord' [CEV], 'believed in the Lord' [GW], 'became followers of the Lord' [NCV]. This verb means to add something to an existing quantity [LN]. It means to add to something that is already present or exists. Here it pertains to persons who are added to a group already existing, or who are attached to an individual, to whom they henceforth belong [BDAG].

11:25 So he-went to Tarsus to-look-for Saul. **11:26** And when-he-had-found (him), he-brought (him) to Antioch. And for an-entire year they met[a] with the church and taught (a)-large number of people. And in Antioch the disciples were first called Christians.

LEXICON—a. aorist pass. infin. of συνάγω (LN 15.125) (BDAG 1.b. p. 962): 'to meet' [Bar, BECNT; CEV, ESV, GW, NASB, NCV, NET, NIV, NRSV, TEV], 'to be gathered together' [LN], 'to be gathered (in), to be brought together' [BDAG], 'to be called together' [BDAG, LN]. The phrase 'they met with the church' is also translated 'they assembled themselves with the church' [KJV], 'Both of them stayed there with the church' [NLT], 'the two of them lived in fellowship with the church/congregation' [CBC; REB], 'they were together in the church' [AB]. This verb means to cause to come together, whether of animate or inanimate objects [LN]. It means to cause to come together with the congregation [BDAG].

QUESTION—What is meant by the word 'Christian'?

The word 'Christian' basically means 'one who is a follower of Christ, belonging to Christ.' The word is only used here, Acts 26:28, and 1 Peter 4:16 [Bar, BECNT, EBC, NAC, PNTC, TH, TNTC]. In all three instances it is a term used by outsiders to designate Christians, and it was not originally used by Christians of themselves [EBC, NAC, PNTC, TNTC]. Probably the intransitive passive expression 'were called' suggests that the name was given to believers by others [BECNT, TNTC]. The term mixes the Greek for 'Christ' with the Latin ending for a group, -ianus. It is formed in the same way as the reference to Herodians or Augustinians [AB, Bar, BECNT, TNTC]. In Antioch the adherents of Jesus the Christ first came to be popularly known as Christians [NICNT]. The naming showed that Christ, really the Messiah, was understood to be a proper name [AB, TNTC].

DISCOURSE UNIT—11:27–30 [AB, Bar, EBC, NAC, NICNT, PNTC; NET]. The topic is a general famine and a collection for its victims [AB], the church at Antioch independent [Bar], famine relief for Jerusalem [EBC], sending famine relief to Jerusalem [NAC], famine relief for Judea [NET], famine relief [NICNT], generosity in ministry to Christians in Jerusalem [PNTC].

11:27 Now in these days prophets[a] came-down[b] from Jerusalem to Antioch.

LEXICON—a. προφήτης (LN 53.79) (BDAG 1.e. p. 891): 'prophet' [AB, Bar, BDAG, BECNT, CBC, LN; all versions], 'inspired preacher' [LN]. This noun denotes one who proclaims inspired utterances on behalf of God [LN]. It denotes a person inspired to proclaim or reveal divine will or purpose [BDAG].

b. aorist act. indic. of κατέρχομαι (LN 15.107) (BDAG 1. p. 531): 'to come down' [Bar, BDAG, BECNT, CBC, LN; ESV, NASB, NET, NIV, NRSV, REB], 'to move down, to go down, to descend' [LN], 'to come' [AB; CEV, GW, KJV, NCV], 'to travel' [NLT], 'to go' [TEV]. This verb means to move down, irrespective of the gradient [LN]. It means to move in a direction considered the opposite of up but not necessarily with the suggestion of a gradient [BDAG].

QUESTION—Why is the verb 'came down' used to describe the prophets' travel from Jerusalem to Antioch?

In this context, 'down' refers to elevation, not compass direction. Antioch was north of Jerusalem and lower in elevation [TRT].

11:28 And one of them named Agabus stood-up[a] and foretold[b] by the Spirit that there would be (a)-great famine[c] all over the world (this took-place[d] in the days of-Claudius).

LEXICON—a. aorist act. participle of ἀνίστημι (LN 17.6): 'to stand up' [Bar, BECNT, CBC, LN; ESV, KJV, NASB, NCV, NIV, NLT, NRSV, REB, TEV], 'to get up' [NET], not explicit [CEV, GW]. This verb is also translated 'came forward' [AB]. This verb means to assume a standing position [LN].

b. aorist act. indic. of σημαίνω (LN 33.153) (BDAG 2. p. 920): 'to foretell' [BECNT; ESV], 'to tell' [CEV], 'to speak' [NCV], 'to declare' [Bar], 'to indicate clearly, to make clear' [LN], 'to indicate' [BDAG; NASB], 'to predict' [AB, CBC; GW, NET, NIV, NLT, NRSV, REB, TEV], 'to signify' [KJV], 'to suggest, to intimate' [BDAG]. This verb means to cause something to be both specific and clear [LN]. It means to intimate something respecting the future [BDAG].

c. λιμός (LN 23.33) (BDAG 2. p. 596): 'famine' [AB, Bar, BDAG, BECNT, CBC, LN; all versions except KJV, NCV], 'hunger' [LN], 'dearth' [KJV], 'hard time' [NCV]. This noun denotes a widespread lack of food over a considerable period of time and resulting in hunger for many people [LN].

d. aorist mid. (deponent = act.) indic. of γίνομαι (LN 13.107) (BDAG 3.b. p. 197): 'to take place' [BECNT; ESV, NASB, NET, NRSV], 'to happen' [AB, Bar, LN; CEV, GW, NCV, NIV], 'to occur' [CBC, LN; REB], 'to come to be' [LN], 'to come to pass' [KJV], 'to be fulfilled' [NLT], 'to come' [TEV], 'to arise, to come about, to develop' [BDAG]. This verb means to happen, with the implication that what happens is different from a previous state [LN]. It means to come into being as an event or phenomenon from a point of origin [BDAG].

QUESTION—Why is the verb 'came down' used to describe the prophets' travel from Jerusalem to Antioch?

In this context, 'down' refers to elevation, not compass direction. Antioch was north of Jerusalem and lower in elevation [TRT].

QUESTION—What famine was this that went all over the world?

During Claudius' rule, there were several famines scattered throughout the Roman Empire (all the world) [AB, Bar, BECNT, CBC, EBC, NAC, NICNT, PNTC, TH, TNTC, TRT]. However, since the Christians in Antioch decided to send money to Judea (v. 29), it appears that Antioch (which was part of the Roman Empire) was not expected to suffer from the famine.

Therefore it seems likely that Agabus was referring to the land of Israel [TRT]. Moreover, Claudius ruled the Roman Empire in A.D. 41–54 [AB, Bar, BECNT, CBC, EBC, NAC, PNTC, TH, TNTC, TRT]. There was a particularly severe famine in Judea Province around A.D. 46 [CBC, EBC, NAC, TH, TNTC, TRT], extended to A.D. 47 [PNTC], in A.D. 44–48 [BECNT], in A.D. 45–48 [NICNT], in A.D. 46–48 [AB, Bar].

11:29 So the disciples determined,[a] everyone according to having-(financial)-means, to-send a contribution to-the brothers[b] living in Judea.

LEXICON—a. aorist act. indic. of ὁρίζω (LN 30.83) (BDAG 2.a.β. p. 723): 'to determine' [Bar, BDAG, BECNT, LN; ESV, KJV, NASB, NRSV], 'to decide' [AB, LN; CEV, GW, NCV, NET, NIV, NLT, TEV], 'to resolve' [LN], 'to appoint, to fix, to set' [BDAG], 'to agree' [CBC; REB]. This is a figurative extension of meaning of ὁρίζω 'to set limits on' and it means to come to a definite decision or firm resolve [LN]. It means to make a determination about an entity [BDAG].

b. ἀδελφός (LN 11.23): 'brother' [Bar, BECNT; ESV, NET, NIV, NLT], 'fellow believer' [LN; TEV], 'a Christian brother' [LN]. The phrase 'to the brothers' is also translated 'to the believers' [NRSV], 'to the followers' [CEV], 'to/unto the brethren' [AB; KJV], 'the brethren' [NASB], 'the believers' [GW], 'the followers' [NCV], 'fellow-Christians' [CBC; REB]. This noun denotes a close associate of a group of persons having a well-defined membership. In the NT ἀδελφός 'brother' refers specifically to fellow believers in Christ [LN].

QUESTION—What did 'So' in the beginning of v. 29 relate to?

'So' relates back to Agabus' prophecy of the coming great famine all over the world, not to Luke's comment that the famine came while Claudius was ruling [TRT].

QUESTION—Who were 'the brothers'?

In this context, 'brothers' referred to fellow Christians, including both men and women [CBC, EBC, NAC, TRT], believers [PNTC], church members [NICNT]. The sending of a gift from the mixed Jewish-Gentile church in Antioch to the more established Jewish Christian communities in Judea was an important expression of solidarity across social and cultural boundaries [PNTC]. The famine relief portrays the oneness and caring of the church. The church was one despite being in different locales [BECNT, CBC].

11:30 And they-did so, sending[a] it to the elders[b] by (the)-hand(s)[c] of-Barnabas and Saul.

LEXICON—a. aorist act. participle of ἀποστέλλω (LN 15.67): 'to send' [AB, Bar, BECNT, CBC; ESV, GW, KJV, NASB, NET, NIV, NRSV, REB, TEV], 'to send a message, to send word' [LN], not explicit [CEV]. The phrase 'sending it…by the hands of Barnabas and Saul' is also translated 'gave it to Barnabas and Saul, who brought it' [NCV], 'entrusting their gifts to Barnabas and Saul to take' [NLT]. This verb means to send a message, presumably by someone [LN].

b. πρεσβύτερος (LN 53.77) (BDAG 2.b.α. p. 862): 'elder' [AB, Bar, BDAG, BECNT, CBC, LN; all versions except CEV, GW], 'presbyter' [BDAG], 'leader' [CEV, GW]. This noun denotes a person of responsibility and authority in matters of socio-religious concerns, both in Jewish and Christian societies [LN]. It denotes an official among the Christians [BDAG].

c. χείρ (LN 9.17) (BDAG 2.a. p. 1082): 'the hands (of)' [Bar, BDAG, BECNT; ESV, KJV] 'person, agent' [LN]. The phrase 'by the hands of Barnabas and Saul' is also translated 'in charge of Barnabas and Saul' [CBC; NASB], 'with Barnabas and Saul' [GW], 'by Barnabas and Saul' [NET, NIV, NRSV, TEV], 'entrusting their-gift/it to Barnabas and Saul' [NLT, REB], 'in the care of Barnabas and Saul' [AB], 'they had Barnabas and Saul take their gifts' [CEV], 'gave it to Barnabas and Saul, who brought it to the elders' [NCV]. This is a figurative extension of meaning of χείρ 'hand' and it denotes a human as an agent in some activity [LN]. It denotes an acting agent [BDAG].

QUESTION—Who were 'the elders'?

These elders were the church leaders, not political leaders [CBC, EBC, NAC, NICNT, TH, TNTC, TRT]. They were those who held office in the primitive church [AB]. They worked alongside the apostles and took care of administrative and daily matters in the church [BECNT, PNTC, TNTC].

DISCOURSE UNIT—12:1–25 [AB, CBC, NAC, PNTC, TNTC; NET]. The topic is King Agrippa I persecutes the church and dies [AB], Peter and Herod [CBC], persecution again in Jerusalem [NAC], James is killed and Peter imprisoned [NET], Peter's deliverance in Jerusalem [PNTC], the imprisonment and escape of Peter [TNTC].

DISCOURSE UNIT—12:1–24 [NICNT]. The topic is Herod Agrippa I and the church.

DISCOURSE UNIT—12:1–23 [Bar, BECNT, EBC]. The topic is James, Peter and Herod [Bar], persecution in Jerusalem [BECNT], divine intervention on behalf of the Jerusalem Church [EBC].

DISCOURSE UNIT—12:1–19 [NASB]. The topic is Peter's arrest and deliverance.

DISCOURSE UNIT—12:1–19a [EBC; GW, NIV]. The topic is deliverance of Peter [EBC], an angel frees Peter from prison [GW], Peter's miraculous escape from prison [NIV].

DISCOURSE UNIT—12:1–5 [NAC, PNTC; CEV, ESV, NCV, NLT, NRSV, TEV]. The topic is Herod causes trouble for the church [CEV], James killed and Peter imprisoned [ESV, NRSV], Herod Agrippa's persecution of the apostles [NAC], Herod Agrippa hurts the church [NCV], James is killed and Peter is imprisoned [NLT], persecution and arrest [PNTC], more persecution [TEV].

DISCOURSE UNIT—12:1–4 [NICNT]. The topic is the martyrdom of James and imprisonment of Peter.

DISCOURSE UNIT—12:1–2 [NET]. The topic is James is killed and Peter imprisoned.

12:1 **Now about that time Herod the king laid- hands -on^a some who belonged to the church to-harm^b them.**
LEXICON—a. aorist act. indic. of ἐπιβάλλω (LN 37.110) (BDAG 1.b. p. 367): 'to lay on/upon' [Bar, BDAG, BECNT; ESV, NASB, NET, NRSV], 'to put on' [BDAG], 'to seize' [LN], 'to arrest' [LN; NIV], 'to stretch forth' [KJV], not explicit [AB, CBC; CEV, GW, NCV, NLT, REB, TEV]. The idiom 'to lay hands on' means to take a person into custody for alleged illegal activity [LN].
  b. aorist act. infin. of κακόω (LN 20.12) (BDAG 1. p. 502): 'to harm' [Bar, BDAG, LN; NET], 'to hurt, to injure' [LN], 'to mistreat' [BDAG; GW, NASB, NCV], 'to cause terrible suffering' [CEV], 'to vex' [KJV], 'to persecute' [NIV, NLT, TEV], 'to attack' [CBC; REB]. The phrase 'laid hands on some…to harm them' is also translated 'laid violent hands on/upon some' [BECNT; ESV, NRSV], 'took violent action against some' [AB]. This verb means to cause harm or injury to someone or something. It is a highly generic meaning involving a wide range of harm and injury [LN]. It means to cause harm to [BDAG].
QUESTION—What is meant by the expression 'laid violent hands on someone'?
  This means that he persecuted someone [NAC, TH, TRT]. He laid violent hands on them in order to do evil [BECNT].

12:2 **And he-killed^a James the brother of-John with-(a)-sword,**
LEXICON—a. aorist act. indic. of ἀναιρέω (LN 20.71) (BDAG 2. p. 64): 'to kill' [Bar, BECNT, LN; ESV, KJV, NLT, NRSV], 'to execute' [AB, LN; GW, NET], 'to do away with, to destroy' [BDAG], 'to put to death' [NASB, NIV, TEV]. This verb is also translated with a passive verb 'to be killed' [NCV]. The phrase 'he killed James' is also translated 'He ordered soldiers to cut off the head of James' [CEV], 'He beheaded James' [CBC; REB]. This verb means to get rid of someone by execution, often with legal or quasi-legal procedures [LN]. It means to get rid of someone by execution [BDAG].
QUESTION—Who was this James?
  This James was the brother of John, the son of Zebedee, and one of the twelve apostles [Bar, BECNT, EBC, NAC, NICNT, PNTC, TNTC, TRT]. He was the first apostle to suffer martyrdom [BECNT, NICNT].
QUESTION—How was James killed?
  Herod executed James 'with the sword' in the Roman fashion of having him beheaded [AB, BECNT, EBC, NAC, TRT]. If Herod used the Jewish mode

of execution, which forbade beheading as a desecration to the body, he had 'the edge of the sword' thrust through James' body [NAC].

12:3 **and when he saw^a that it pleased^b the Jews, he-proceeded^c to-arrest^d Peter also. (This)-was-(during) the days of Unleavened-Bread.**
LEXICON—a. aorist act. participle of εἶδον (LN 32.11) (BDAG 3. p. 279): 'to see' [AB, Bar, BDAG, BECNT, CBC, LN; all versions], 'to understand, to perceive, to recognize' [LN], 'to notice, to note' [BDAG]. This verb means to come to understand as the result of perception [LN]. It means to take special note of something [BDAG].
  b. ἀρεστός (LN 25.92) (BDAG p. 130): 'pleasing' [Bar, BDAG, LN]. This adjective is also translated as a verb: 'it/this pleased the Jews' [AB, BECNT; ESV, GW, KJV, NASB, NET, NIV, NRSV, TEV], 'this pleased the Jewish people' [CEV, NLT]. The phrase 'he saw that it pleased the Jews' is also translated 'Herod saw that the Jewish people liked this' [NCV], 'he saw that the Jews approved' [CBC; REB]. This adjective pertains to that which pleases someone [LN]. It pertains to being satisfying [BDAG].
  c. aorist mid. indic. of προστίθημι (LN 89.89) (BDAG 1.c. p. 885): 'to proceed to' [BECNT, CBC, LN; ESV, KJV, NASB, NET, NIV, NRSV, REB], 'to decide to' [NCV], 'to add to, to put to' [BDAG], not explicit [CEV, GW, NLT]. The phrase 'he proceeded to arrest Peter' is also translated 'he went ahead and had Peter arrested' [TEV], 'he went on to arrest Peter' [AB, Bar]. This verb means to mark an immediately following event [LN]. It means to add to something that is already present or exists [BDAG].
  d. aorist act. infin. of συλλαμβάνω (LN 37.109) (BDAG 1.a. p. 955): 'to arrest' [AB, Bar, BECNT, CBC, LN; all versions except KJV, NIV], 'to seize' [BDAG, LN; NIV], 'to catch' [LN], 'to take' [LN; KJV], 'to grasp, to apprehend' [BDAG]. This verb means to seize and to take along with [LN]. It means to take into custody [BDAG].
QUESTION—By whom was Peter arrested?
Herod was responsible for ordering Peter to be arrested and his soldiers were the ones who actually arrested Peter [TRT].
QUESTION—When were the days of Unleavened Bread?
The days of Unleavened Bread is also known as the festival/feast of Unleavened Bread. The festival began the evening that the Passover lamb was eaten on the 14th of the month of Nisan (around March or April). That was followed by seven days of eating unleavened/flat bread (that is, bread made without yeast), ending on Nisan 21 [NAC, NICNT, TH, TRT]. Luke used the term 'Passover' for the entire period [Bar, CBC, NAC, NICNT, TH, TNTC, TRT]. This was the very same season of the year during which Jesus was executed (Luke 22:1) [BECNT, CBC].

12:4 And when he had-seized[a] him, he-put him in prison, delivering- (him) -over[b] to-four squads-of soldiers to-guard him, intending after the Passover to-bring[c] him out (before)-the people.

LEXICON—a. aorist act. participle of πιάζω (LN 37.110) (BDAG 2.a. p. 812): 'to seize' [AB, Bar, BDAG, BECNT, LN; ESV, NASB, NET, NRSV], 'to arrest' [BDAG, LN; NCV, NIV], 'to take into custody' [BDAG], 'to capture' [GW], 'to apprehend' [KJV], 'to secure' [CBC; REB], not explicit [CEV, NLT]. This verb is also translated as a noun: 'his arrest' [TEV]. This verb means to take a person into custody for alleged illegal activity [LN]. It means to seize humans with the intent to overpower or gain control [BDAG].
  b. aorist act. participle of παραδίδωμι (LN 37.111) (BDAG 1.b. p. 762): 'to deliver over to' [ESV], 'to deliver to' [BECNT; KJV, NASB], 'to hand over to' [Bar, BDAG, LN; NCV, NET, NIV, NRSV], 'to turn over to' [BDAG, LN], 'to give up a person' [BDAG], 'to betray' [LN], not explicit [AB, CBC; CEV, GW, NLT, REB]. This verb is also translated as a passive verb: 'he was handed over' [TEV]. This verb means to deliver a person into the control of someone else, involving either the handing over of a presumably guilty person for punishment by authorities or the handing over of an individual to an enemy who will presumably take undue advantage of the victim [LN]. It means to convey something in which one has a relatively strong personal interest [BDAG].
  c. aorist act. infin. of ἀνάγω (LN 15.176) (BDAG 2. p. 61): 'to bring' [AB, BECNT; ESV, GW, KJV, NASB, NCV, NET, NIV, NLT, NRSV], 'to bring up' [Bar, LN], 'to lead up' [LN], 'to bring before' [BDAG]. The phrase 'intending…to bring him out before the people' is also translated 'Herod planned to put him on trial in public' [CEV, TEV], 'meaning to produce him in public' [CBC; REB]. This verb means to bring or lead up [LN]. It means to bring up for judicial process [BDAG].

QUESTION—How was Peter being guarded?
  Peter was guarded by four squads of four soldiers each [AB, Bar, BECNT, CBC, EBC, NAC, NICNT, PNTC, TH, TNTC]. This was the usual Roman practice of changing guards every three hours throughout the twelve night hours in order to assure maximum alertness [AB, BECNT, EBC, NAC, NICNT, PNTC, TH, TNTC].

QUESTION—What was Herod's intention for bringing Peter out to the people?
  Herod intended to put Peter on public trial so that he could be judged and executed by the people [Bar, BECNT, CBC, EBC, NICNT, PNTC, TH, TNTC].

DISCOURSE UNIT—12:5–11 [NICNT]. The topic is Peter's escape from prison.

12:5 So Peter was-kept[a] in the prison, but earnest prayer for him was being-made[b] to God by the church.

LEXICON—a. imperf. pass. indic. of τηρέω (LN 37.122) (BDAG 1. p. 1002): 'to be kept' [Bar, BECNT, CBC; all versions except NLT, REB], 'to be held' [REB], 'to be guarded' [BDAG, LN], 'to keep watch' [LN], 'to keep watch over' [BDAG], not explicit [NLT]. The phrase 'Peter was kept' is also translated 'Peter was now under guard' [AB]. This verb means to continue to hold in custody [LN]. It means to retain in custody [BDAG].

    b. pres. mid. (deponent = act.) participle of γίνομαι (LN 13.107): 'to be made' [AB; ESV, KJV, NASB], 'to happen, to occur, to come to be' [LN], not explicit [CBC; CEV, GW, NCV, NET, NIV, NLT, NRSV, REB, TEV]. The phrase 'was being made to God' is also translated 'was being...offered to God' [Bar], 'was coming to God' [BECNT]. This verb means to happen, with the implication that what happens is different from a previous state [LN].

QUESTION—How did the church pray for Peter?

The church had prayed earnestly to God for Peter. The same Greek adverb ἐκτενῶς 'earnestly, eagerly, continuously' used here is also used of the praying of Jesus in Gethsemane (Luke 22:44) [BECNT, NAC, PNTC, TH, TNTC].

DISCOURSE UNIT—12:6–19a [NAC, NCV]. The topic is Peter's miraculous deliverance from prison [NAC], Peter leaves the jail [NCV].

12:6 Now when Herod was-about to-bring- him -out,[a] on that very night, Peter was sleeping between two soldiers, bound with-two chains, and guards before the door were-watching-over[b] the prison.

LEXICON—a. aorist act. infin. of προάγω (LN 15.171) (BDAG 1. p. 864): 'to bring out' [BDAG, BECNT; ESV, NET, NRSV, TEV], 'to bring forward' [Bar, CBC, LN; NASB], 'to lead forth' [LN], 'to lead forward, to lead' [BDAG], 'to bring forth' [KJV]. The phrase 'Herod was about to bring him out' is also translated 'Herod was going to bring Peter to trial' [GW], 'Herod was to bring him to trial' [NCV, NIV], 'Herod to bring him to trial' [AB], 'Peter was to be put on trial' [CEV], 'Peter was to be placed on trial' [NLT], 'Herod had planned to produce him' [REB]. This verb means to lead or bring forward or forth [LN]. It means to take a lead from one position to another by taking charge [BDAG].

    b. imperf. act. indic. of τηρέω (LN 37.122) (BDAG 1. p. 1002): 'to watch over' [NASB], 'to guard' [AB, BDAG, BECNT, CBC, LN; CEV, ESV, NCV], 'to keep watch' [LN], 'to keep watch over' [BDAG; NET, NRSV], 'to watch' [GW], 'to keep' [Bar; KJV], 'to stand guard' [NIV, NLT], 'to keep guard' [REB]. The phrase 'guards before the door were watching over the prison' is also translated 'there were guards on duty at the prison gate' [TEV]. This verb means to continue to hold in custody [LN]. It means to retain in custody [BDAG].

QUESTION—How was Peter being guarded by the squad of four soldiers?
Peter was chained to two of the soldiers, one on each side [Bar, BECNT, EBC, NAC, TH, TNTC, TRT], and the prison door was guarded by the other two soldiers [BECNT, NAC, TH, TNTC]. Herod had done a great deal to make sure that Peter was secure and well-guarded [BECNT].

12:7 And behold,[a] an-angel[b] of-(the)-Lord[c] stood next to him, and a light shone in the cell. He struck Peter's side and woke- him -up,[d] saying, "Get-up[e] quickly." And the chains fell-off his hands.

LEXICON—a. ἰδού (LN 91.13) (BDAG 1.b.β. p. 468): 'behold' [Bar, BDAG, BECNT; ESV, KJV, NASB], 'look' [BDAG, LN], 'listen, pay attention, come now, then' [LN], 'see' [BDAG], not explicit [AB, CBC; CEV, GW, NCV, NET, NIV, NLT, NRSV, REB, TEV]. This particle functions as a prompter of attention, also serving to emphasize the statement which follows [LN]. It is a prompter of attention [BDAG].
  b. ἄγγελος (LN 12.28) (BDAG 2.a. p. 8): 'angel' [AB, Bar, BDAG, BECNT, CBC, LN; all versions], 'messenger' [BDAG]. This noun denotes a supernatural being that attends upon or serves as a messenger of a superior supernatural entity. In many languages a term for 'angels' is borrowed from another dominant language, but in other instances a somewhat descriptive phrase may be employed. The most common expressions for 'angels of God' are 'messengers' and 'messengers from heaven.' Sometimes these angels are called 'spirit messengers' and even 'flying messengers.' [LN]. It denotes a transcendent power who carries out various missions or tasks. Here it refers to an angel who is a messenger of God [BDAG].
  c. κύριος (LN 12.9) (BDAG 2.b.α. p. 578): 'Lord' [AB, Bar, BDAG, BECNT, CBC, LN; all versions], 'Ruler, One who commands' [LN], 'master' [BDAG]. This noun denotes a title for God and for Christ. It indicates one who exercises supernatural authority over mankind [LN]. It denotes one who is in a position of authority. Here it is a designation of God [BDAG].
  d. aorist act. indic. of ἐγείρω (LN 23.77) (BDAG 1. p. 271): 'to wake' [AB, BDAG, BECNT, CBC; all versions except KJV, NLT], 'to raise' [KJV], 'to awaken' [Bar; NLT], 'to cause to wake up' [LN], 'to awaken someone' [LN], 'to wake up someone' [LN], 'to rouse' [BDAG]. This verb means to cause someone to awaken [LN]. It means to cause someone to wake from sleep [BDAG].
  e. aorist act. impera. of ἀνίστημι (LN 17.6) (BDAG p. 83): 'to get up' [AB, Bar, BECNT, CBC; all versions except KJV], 'to stand up' [LN], 'to rise up' [KJV]. This verb means to assume a standing position [LN].

QUESTION—What does 'a light shone in the cell' point to?
The mention of light points to a heavenly visit (Luke 2:9; Acts 9:3; 22:11) [BECNT]. Obedience was made possible when the chains fell off Peter's

hands. Everything turned upon God's gracious initiative, exercised through an angel [PNTC].

12:8 And the angel said to him, "Gird[a] yourself and put-on your sandals." And he-did so. And he-said to-him, "Wrap your cloak[b] around you and follow[c] me."

LEXICON—a. aorist mid. impera. of ζωννύω (LN 49.14) (BDAG p. 431): 'to gird' [BDAG, LN; KJV, NASB], 'to fasten one's belt' [Bar, LN; NET, NRSV], 'to wear a narrow band of cloth around the waist' [LN]. The phrase 'Gird yourself' is also translated 'Dress yourself' [BECNT; ESV], 'Get dressed' [AB; CEV, NCV, NLT], 'get ready to go' [GW], 'Put on your clothes' [NIV], 'Do up your belt' [CBC; REB], 'Tighten your belt' [TEV]. This verb means to tuck up or hold a garment firmly in place by wrapping a belt, girdle, or piece of cloth around it [LN].

b. ἐπενδύτης (LN 6.173) (BDAG p. 361): 'cloak' AB, Bar, CBC; ESV, NASB, NET, NIV, NRSV, REB, TEV], 'coat' [BDAG, LN; CEV, GW, NCV, NLT], 'garment' [KJV], 'outer garment' [BDAG], 'mantle' [BECNT]. This noun denotes a loose outer garment worn by Roman soldiers and travelers. In some parts of the world the closest equivalent is a poncho [LN]. It denotes a garment put on over another garment [BDAG].

c. pres. act. impera. of ἀκολουθέω (LN 15.144): 'to follow' [AB, BECNT, CBC, LN; all versions except TEV], 'to come behind, to go behind' [LN]. The phrase 'follow me' is also translated 'come with me' [Bar; TEV]. This verb means to come/go behind or after someone else [LN].

12:9 And he went-out[a] and followed (him). He-did- not -know[b] that what was-being-done by the angel was real, but thought he was-seeing (a)-vision.[c]

LEXICON—a. aorist act. participle of ἐξέρχομαι (LN 15.40) (BDAG 1.a.α. p. 348): 'to go out' [AB, Bar, BDAG, BECNT; ESV, KJV, NASB, NET, NRSV], 'to come out, to go away' [BDAG], 'to go out of, to depart out of, to leave from within' [LN]. The clause 'And he went out and followed him' is also translated 'So Peter left the cell, following the angel' [NLT], 'Peter followed the angel out of the cell' [GW], 'Peter followed him out of the prison' [NIV,TEV], 'Peter followed him out' [NCV, REB], 'He followed him out' [CBC], 'Peter left with the angel' [CEV]. This verb means to move out of an enclosed or well defined two or three-dimensional area [LN]. It means to move out of or away from an area [BDAG].

b. pluperfect act. indic. of οἶδα (LN 32.4): 'to know' [AB, Bar, BECNT; ESV, NASB, NCV, TEV], 'to realize' [GW, NET, NLT, NRSV], 'to understand, to comprehend' [LN], not explicit [CEV]. The phrase 'He did not know' is also translated 'he had no idea' [NIV], 'he wist not' [KJV], 'with no idea' [CBC; REB]. This verb means to comprehend the meaning of something, with the focus upon the resulting knowledge [LN].

c. ὅραμα (LN 33.488) (BDAG 1. p. 718): 'a vision' [AB, Bar, BDAG, BECNT, CBC, LN; all versions except CEV]. The phrase 'thought he was seeing a vision' is also translated 'thought everything was only a dream' [CEV]. This noun denotes an event in which something appears vividly and credibly to the mind, although not actually present, but implying the influence of some divine or supernatural power or agency [LN]. It denotes something that is viewed with one's eye [BDAG].

12:10 When they had-passed/passed-through (the) first and (the) second guards/guard-posts,[a] they-came to the iron gate leading into the city. It opened for them by-itself, and they went-outside and went-along one street, and immediately the angel left[b] him.

LEXICON—a. φυλακή (LN 37.123) (BDAG 2. p. 1067): 'guard' [BDAG], 'guard post, guard station' [LN]. This verse refers to the guards who were posted at two places in the prison [AB, Bar, BECNT; CEV, ESV, NASB, NCV, NET, NIV, NRSV]. This verse refers to the first and second guard-posts [CBC, LN; GW, KJV, NLT, REB, TEV]. This noun is a derivative of φυλάσσω 'to guard closely' and denotes a place or post for guarding. Here 'they passed by the first guard post, then the second' [LN]. This noun denotes the act of guarding embodied in a person [BDAG]. The first guard station can be rendered as 'the first group of soldiers who were guarding.' The second can, of course, be rendered 'the second group of soldiers who were guarding' [TH].

b. aorist act. indic. of ἀφίστημι (LN 15.51) (BDAG 2.a. p. 157): 'to leave' [AB, Bar, BECNT, CBC, LN; ESV, GW, NCV, NET, NIV, NLT, NRSV, REB, TEV], 'to go away' [BDAG, LN], 'to depart' [LN; KJV, NASB], 'to withdraw' [BDAG]. The phrase 'the angel left him' is also translated 'the angel disappeared' [CEV]. This verb means to move away from, with emphasis upon separation and possible lack of concern for what has been left [LN]. It means to distance oneself from some person or thing [BDAG].

QUESTION—What is meant by the iron gate opening by itself?

It means that the iron gate opened automatically as they approached [EBC, NICNT]. The gate became open although no one had moved it [TH].

QUESTION—What is meant by 'they went along one street'?

They went down the length of the first street from the prison and perhaps when they came to a corner they turned into a side street to get out of sight of the prison [NAC]. The phrase 'one street' may possibly mean that they went along a certain street [TH], perhaps the main street [Bar].

12:11 When Peter came[a] to himself, he said, "Now I-know[b] for sure that the Lord has sent his angel and rescued[c] me from (the)-hand[d] of-Herod and from-all that the Jewish people were expecting."

LEXICON—a. aorist mid. participle of γίνομαι (LN 13.48) (BDAG 5.c. p. 198): 'to come' [AB, Bar, BECNT, CBC; ESV, GW, KJV, NASB, NET, NIV, NLT, NRSV, REB], 'to become' [LN], 'to become

something' [BDAG]. The phrase 'Peter came to himself' is also translated 'Peter now realized what had happened' [CEV], 'Peter realized what had happened' [NCV, TEV]. This verb means to come to acquire or experience a state [LN]. It means to experience a change in nature and so indicate entry into a new condition. Here it means to come to one's senses [BDAG].
b. perf. act. indic. of οἶδα (LN 28.1, 32.4): 'to know' [AB, Bar, CBC, LN (28.1); KJV, NASB, NCV, NET, NIV, REB, TEV], 'to know about, to have knowledge of, to be acquainted with' [LN (28.1)], 'to understand, to comprehend' [LN (32.4)], not explicit [NLT]. The phrase 'Now I know for sure' is also translated 'Now I am sure' [BECNT; ESV, NRSV], 'Now I'm sure' [GW], 'I am certain' [CEV]. This verb means to possess information about [LN (28.1)]. It means to comprehend the meaning of something, with focus upon the resulting knowledge [LN (32.4)].
c. aorist mid. indic. of ἐξαιρέω (LN 21.17) (BDAG 2. p. 344): 'to rescue' [Bar, BDAG, CBC, LN; all versions except KJV, NLT], 'to set free' [BDAG, LN], 'to deliver' [BDAG, BECNT, LN; KJV], 'to save' [NLT], 'to release' [AB]. This verb means to rescue or set someone free from danger [LN]. It means to deliver someone from peril or confining circumstance [BDAG].
d. χείρ (LN 37.14) (BDAG 2.c. p. 1083): 'hand (of)' [AB, Bar, BDAG, BECNT; ESV, KJV, NASB, NET, NRSV], 'to be in the control of, to be in the power of' [LN], not explicit [CEV, GW, NCV, NLT]. The phrase 'from the hand of Herod' is also translated 'from Herod's clutches' [CBC, NIV, REB], 'from Herod's power' [TEV]. This noun is a figurative extension of meaning of χείρ 'hand' and denotes a state of control exercised by a person [LN]. It denotes an acting agent. In this sense the focus is on the person or thing as the source of an activity. Here it refers to a hostile power [BDAG].

QUESTION—What is meant by 'Peter came to himself'?
The phrase means that Peter realized what had actually been happening [AB, EBC, NAC, NICNT, PNTC, TH]. What happened to him was really true, not a vision [Bar, CBC, TH, TNTC].

QUESTION—What is meant by Peter being rescued from the hand of Herod'?
It means that Peter was rescued from King Herod's power and clutches [EBC, NAC, PNTC, TH], so that Herod could not harm him [TH].

QUESTION—What is meant by Peter being rescued from all that the Jewish people were expecting'?
The phrase means that Peter was rescued from what the Jewish people wanted him to suffer [PNTC, TH]. The people expected him to be put to death [NAC].

DISCOURSE UNIT—12:12–17 [NICNT]. The topic is Peter reports his escape.

12:12 And when he realized-(this), he-went[a] to the house of-Mary, the mother of-John who was- also -called Mark, where many were-gathered-together[b] and were praying.

LEXICON—a. aorist act. indic. of ἔρχομαι (LN 15.81) (BDAG 1.a.β. p. 393): 'to go' [AB, Bar, BECNT; all versions except KJV, REB], 'to come' [BDAG, LN; KJV]. The phrase 'he went to the house' is also translated 'he made for the house' [CBC; REB]. This verb means to move toward or up to the reference point of the viewpoint character or event [LN]. It means movement from one point to another, with focus on approach from the narrator's perspective [BDAG].
   b. perf. pass. participle of συναθροίζω (LN 15.130) (BDAG 1. p. 964): 'to be gathered together' [BECNT, LN; ESV, KJV, NASB], 'to be gathered' [NCV, NLT], 'to be brought together' [BDAG], 'to be assembled' [Bar], 'to gather together' [NET], 'to gather' [AB, BDAG; GW, NIV, NRSV, TEV], 'to come together' [CEV], not explicit [CBC; REB]. This verb means to assemble together, with emphasis on the element of togetherness [LN]. It means to cause to gather together as a group [BDAG].

QUESTION—Who was this John who was also called Mark?
John was his Jewish name and Mark was his Gentile Roman name [BECNT, NICNT, TRT]. He was the cousin of Barnabas (Colossians 4:10) [CBC, EBC, NICNT, TNTC, TRT].

12:13 And when he- knocked -(at) the door of-the gateway, (a)-servant-girl named Rhoda came to-answer.[a] **12:14** Recognizing[b] Peter's voice, because of her joy she-did- not -open the gate, but[c] ran-in and reported-(that) Peter was-standing at the gate.

LEXICON—a. aorist act. infin. of ὑπακούω (LN 46.11) (BDAG 3. p. 1029): 'to answer' [Bar, BECNT, CBC; CEV, ESV, GW, NASB, NCV, NET, NRSV, REB, TEV], 'to hearken' [KJV], 'to answer the door' [LN; NIV], 'to open' [AB; NLT]. This verb means to respond to someone knocking or calling at a door [LN]. It means to answer a knock at the door [BDAG].
   b. aorist act. participle of ἐπιγινώσκω (LN 27.61) (BDAG 3. p. 369): 'to recognize' [AB, Bar, BDAG, BECNT, CBC, LN; all versions except CEV, KJV], 'to acknowledge acquaintance with, to know again' [BDAG], 'to know' [KJV], not explicit [CEV]. This verb means to identify newly acquired information with what had been previously learned or known [LN]. It means to connect present information or awareness with what was known before [BDAG].
   c. δέ (LN 89.124) (BDAG 2. p. 213): 'but' [AB, Bar, BECNT, LN; ESV, KJV, NASB, NET], 'on the other hand' [LN], 'now, then, and, so, that is' [BDAG], not explicit [CEV, NIV, TEV]. The phrase 'but ran in' is also translated 'Instead, she ran inside' [NCV]. The phrase 'she did not open the door, but ran in' is also translated 'instead of opening the door, she ran back inside' [GW, NLT], 'instead of opening the gate, she ran in' [NRSV], 'instead of opening the door she ran in' [CBC; REB]. This

conjunction indicates a contrast [LN]. It is a marker linking narrative segments [BDAG].

12:15 They said to her, "You-are-out-of-your-mind.ᵃ" Butᵇ she-kept-insisting-(that it)ᶜ was so, and they-kept-saying, "It-is his angel!ᵈ"
LEXICON—a. pres. mid./pass. (deponent = act.) indic. of μαίνομαι (LN 30.24) (BDAG p. 610): 'to be out of one's mind' [BDAG, LN; ESV, NASB, NIV, NLT, NRSV], 'to not be in one's right mind, to be insane' [LN], 'to be mad' [AB, Bar, BDAG, BECNT, LN; KJV], 'to be crazy' [CBC; CEV, GW, NCV, REB, TEV]. The phrase 'You are out of your mind' is also translated 'You've lost your mind' [NET]. This verb means to think or reason in a completely irrational manner [LN].
  b. δέ (LN 89.124) (BDAG 2. p. 213): 'but' [AB, BECNT, CBC, LN; CEV, ESV, GW, KJV, NASB, NCV, NET, NRSV, REB, TEV], 'on the other hand' [LN], not explicit [Bar; NIV, NLT]. This conjunction indicates a contrast [LN]. It indicates a marker linking narrative segments [BDAG].
  c. imperf. mid./pass. (deponent = act.) indic. of διϊσχυρίζομαι (LN 33.321) (BDAG p. 246): 'to insist' [AB, BDAG, BECNT, CBC, LN; ESV, GW, NASB, NET, NIV, NLT, NRSV, REB, TEV], 'to insist firmly' [LN], 'to maintain firmly' [BDAG], 'to persist' [Bar]. The phrase 'she kept insisting' is also translated 'she kept saying' [CEV], 'she kept on saying' [NCV], 'she constantly affirmed' [KJV]. This verb means to state something with firmness and certainty [LN]. It means to be emphatic or resolute about something [BDAG].
  d. ἄγγελος (LN 12.28) (BDAG 2.a. p. 8): 'angel' [Bar, BDAG, BECNT, CBC, LN; all versions], 'messenger' [AB, BDAG]. This noun denotes a supernatural being that attends upon or serves as a messenger of a superior supernatural entity [LN]. It denotes a transcendent power who carries out various missions or tasks as a messenger of God [BDAG].
QUESTION—Why did the people inside the house think that Peter could not have been standing at the gate?
  These people knew that Peter had been securely chained and guarded in prison and they did not believe that he could have escaped from there [Bar, BECNT, NAC, PNTC, TNTC]. The Jews believed that God assigned angels to guard his people and that a guardian angel was able to take on the appearance of the person he was protecting [AB, Bar, CBC, NAC, NICNT, PNTC, TH, TNTC, TRT]. They might have thought that Peter's angel had come to tell them that Peter had now died [AB, TRT].

12:16 But Peter continued knocking, and when they opened (the door), they-saw him and were-amazed.ᵃ **12:17** But motioning to-them with-(his) hand to-be-silent, he-described to them how the Lord had-led- him -outᵇ of the prison. And he said, "Report these-things to-James and to-the brothers.ᶜ" Then he departedᵈ and went to another place.
LEXICON—a. aorist act. indic. of ἐξίστημι (LN 25.220) (BDAG 2.b. p. 350): 'to be amazed' [BDAG, BECNT; CEV, ESV, NASB, NCV, NLT, NRSV,

TEV], 'to be astonished' [Bar, BDAG; KJV, NIV], 'to be greatly astonished' [NET], 'to be astounded' [CBC; REB], 'to be overcome with awe' [AB], 'to be astonished greatly, to be greatly astounded, to be astounded completely' [LN]. The phrase 'they saw him and were amazed' is also translated 'they were shocked to see him' [GW]. This verb means to cause someone to be so astounded as to be practically overwhelmed [LN]. It refers to the feeling of astonishment mingled with fear caused by events which are miraculous, extraordinary, or difficult to understand [BDAG].

   b. aorist act. indic. of ἐξάγω (LN 15.174) (BDAG p. 343): 'to lead out' [BDAG, LN; CEV, NASB, NCV, NLT], 'to bring out' [AB, Bar, BDAG, BECNT, CBC; ESV, KJV, NET, NIV, NRSV, REB, TEV], 'to take out' [GW]. This verb means to lead or bring out of a structure or area [LN]. It means to conduct from an area [BDAG].

   c. ἀδελφός (LN 11.23): 'brother' [Bar, BECNT; ESV, NET, NIV, NLT], 'fellow believer, a Christian brother' [LN]. The phrase 'the brothers' is also translated 'the brethren' [AB; KJV, NASB], 'the believers' [NRSV], 'the others' [CEV], 'the other believers' [GW, NCV], 'the rest of the believers' [TEV], 'the members of the church' [CBC; REB]. This noun denotes a close associate of a group of persons having a well-defined membership. In the NT ἀδελφός 'brother' refers specifically to fellow believers in Christ [LN].

   d. aorist act. participle of ἐξέρχομαι (LN 15.40) (BDAG 1.a.α. p. 348): 'to depart' [AB, BECNT; ESV, KJV], 'to leave' [CBC; CEV, GW, NASB, NCV, NET, NIV, NRSV, REB, TEV], 'to go' [NLT], 'to go out of, to depart out of, to leave from within' [LN], 'to go out' [Bar, BDAG], 'to come out, to go away' [BDAG]. This verb means to move out of an enclosed or well defined two or three-dimensional area [LN]. It means to move out of or away from an area [BDAG].

QUESTION—Who were James and the brothers whom Peter mentioned?

James was Jesus' brother who was a leader of the church in Jerusalem at that time [AB, Bar, BECNT, CBC, EBC, NAC, NICNT, PNTC, TH, TNTC, TRT]. The brothers that they were to tell were the other Christians, not natural brothers and sisters [Bar, TRT]. Here the 'brothers' refer to the elders [NAC, NICNT], and to other Christian leaders [TNTC].

QUESTION—Where did Peter go to?

This verse tells that Peter went to another place without specifying exactly where. He probably moved out of Jerusalem to avoid danger [BECNT, CBC, NICNT]. He wanted to avoid re-arrest by Herod and his officials [Bar, EBC, NAC, PNTC].

DISCOURSE UNIT—12:18–19 [NICNT]. The topic is Peter's escape discovered.

12:18 Now when day came,[a] there-was no little disturbance[b] among the soldiers over what had become[c] of-Peter.
  LEXICON—a. aorist mid. (deponent = act.) participle of γίνομαι (LN 13.48) (BDAG 3.c. p. 197): 'to come' [AB, BECNT, CBC; ESV, NASB, NRSV, REB, TEV], 'to become' [LN], 'to arise, to come about, to develop' [BDAG], 'to break' [Bar]. The phrase 'Now when day came' is also translated 'The next morning' [CEV], 'In the morning' [GW, NIV], 'Now as soon as it was day' [KJV], 'The next day' [NCV], 'At daybreak' [NET], 'At dawn' [NLT]. This verb means to come to acquire or experience a state [LN]. It means to come into being as an event or phenomenon from a point of origin and here it pertains to the various divisions of a day [BDAG].
  b. τάραχος (LN 25.243) (BDAG 1. p. 991): 'disturbance' [BECNT; ESV, NASB] 'anxiety.[LN], 'consternation' [CBC; NET, REB], 'commotion' [AB; NIV. NLT, NRSV], 'uproar' [GW], 'confusion' [Bar; TEV], 'stir' [KJV], 'distress' [LN]. It is also translated as a verb: 'were worried' [CEV], 'were very upset' [NCV], This noun denotes a state of acute distress and great anxiety [LN]. It denotes a state of mental agitation [BDAG].
  c. aorist mid. (deponent = act.) indic. of γίνομαι (LN 13.107) (BDAG 4.d. p. 198): 'to become' [AB, Bar, CBC; ESV, KJV, NASB, NET, NIV, NRSV, REB], 'to happen' [LN; CEV, GW, NCV, NLT, TEV], 'to come about' [BECNT], 'to occur' [LN], 'to turn out, to take place' [BDAG. This verb means to happen, with the implication that what happens is different from a previous state [LN]. It means to occur as a process or result [BDAG].
QUESTION—What is meant by 'no little' disturbance?
  'No little' is a litotes, that is, a negative phrase that has a positive meaning. It is used to increase the prominence of this phrase and means 'great' [TRT]. This is a rhetorical device that Luke used in Acts 14:28, 15:2 and 19:23–24 too [BECNT, TH].

12:19a And after Herod searched[a] for him and did- not -find-(him),[b] he examined[c] the guards and ordered- that -(they)[d] be-led-away[e] (to execution).
  LEXICON—a. aorist act. participle of ἐπιζητέω (LN 27.42) (BDAG 1.a. p. 371): 'to search' [AB, LN; CEV, ESV, GW, NASB, NET, NRSV, TEV], 'to seek' [BECNT, LN; KJV], 'to try to find out by looking for' [LN], 'to search for, to seek after' [BDAG], 'to look' [Bar; NCV]. The phrase 'Herod searched for him' is also translated 'Herod had a thorough search made for him' [NIV], 'Herod Agrippa ordered a thorough search for him' [NLT], 'Herod made close/careful search' [CBC; REB]. This verb means to try to learn the location of something by searching for it, presumably somewhat more emphatic or goal-directed than in the case of

ζητέω 'to try to learn where something is' [LN]. It means to try to find out something [BDAG].
b. aorist act. participle of εὑρίσκω (LN 27.27): 'to find' [AB, Bar, BECNT, CBC, LN; all versions except NLT], 'to learn the whereabouts of something, to discover, to come upon, to happen to find' [LN]. This verb is also translated as a passive verb: 'he couldn't be found' [NLT]. This verb means to learn the location of something, either by intentional searching or by unexpected discovery [LN].
c. aorist act. participle of ἀνακρίνω (LN 56.12) (BDAG 2. p. 66): 'to examine' [AB, Bar, BECNT; ESV, KJV, NASB, NRSV], 'to cross-examine' [NIV], 'to question' [BDAG, LN; CEV, GW, NCV, NET] 'to interrogate' [CBC, LN; NLT, REB]. This verb is also translated as a passive verb: 'he had the guards questioned' [TEV]. This verb means to conduct a judicial inquiry [LN]. It means to conduct a judicial hearing [BDAG].
d. aorist act. indicative of κελεύω (LN 33.323) (BDAG p. 538): 'to order' [Bar, BDAG, BECNT, CBC, LN; ESV, NASB, NCV, NIV, NRSV, REB, TEV], 'to command' [AB, BDAG, LN; KJV, NET], 'to sentence' [NLT], not explicit [CEV]. The phrase 'he…ordered' is also translated 'he…gave orders' [GW]. This verb means to state with force and/or authority what others must do [LN]. It means to give a command, ordinarily of an official nature [BDAG].
e. aorist pass. infin. of ἀπάγω (LN 20.65, 56.38) (BDAG 2.c. p. 95) 'to lead away' [BDAG, LN (56.38)]. In this context it means 'to lead away to execution' [BDAG], 'to be led off to punishment [LN (56.38)], 'to be executed' [LN (20.65)]. The phrase 'ordered that they be led away to execution' [NASB] is also translated 'ordered that they should be led away (for execution)' [BECNT], 'commanded that they be led away to execution' [NET], 'gave orders to have them executed' [GW], 'ordered that they be executed' [NIV], 'ordered their execution' [CBC; REB], 'ordered that they should be put to death' [ESV], 'ordered them to be put to death' [NRSV], 'ordered them put to death' [TEV], 'ordered that they be killed' [NCV], 'ordered them to be led off for punishment' [Bar], 'commanded that they should be put to death'[KJV], 'had them put to death' [CEV], 'sentenced them to death' [NLT], 'commanded them to be removed' [AB]. In this context the verb 'to lead away' means to lead a person away for punishment after being sentenced, frequently employed in a context of putting a condemned person to death [LN (56.38)]. It means to deprive a person of life, with the implication of this being the result of condemnation by legal or quasi-legal procedures [LN (20.65)]. It means to conduct a person from one point to another in a legal process. Here it refers to leading a person to execution [BDAG].

QUESTION—What happened to the soldiers when Peter could not be found?
Herod ordered the soldiers to be put to death. The death penalty for allowing prisoners to escape was the norm in the Roman Empire [AB, NAC, NICNT,

PNTC, TH, TNTC], and Herod applied this rule to his own kingdom [NICNT, PNTC].

DISCOURSE UNIT—12:19b–25 [NCV, NIV]. The topic is the death of Herod Agrippa [NCV], Herod's death [NIV].

DISCOURSE UNIT—12:19b–24 [GW]. The topic is Herod's death.

DISCOURSE UNIT—12:19b–23 [EBC, NAC]. The topic is the death of Herod Agrippa I [EBC], Herod's self-destructive arrogance [NAC].

12:19b Then he went-down[a] from Judea to Caesarea and was-spending-time-(there).
LEXICON—a. aorist act. participle of κατέρχομαι (LN 15.107) (BDAG 1. p. 531): 'to go down' [AB, Bar, BECNT, LN; ESV, KJV, NASB, NET, NRSV], 'to move down' [LN], 'to come down' [BDAG, LN], 'to descend' [LN], not explicit [CBC; CEV, GW, NCV, NIV, NLT, REB, TEV]. This verb means to move down, irrespective of the gradient [LN]. It means to move in a direction considered the opposite of up but not necessarily with the suggestion of a gradient [BDAG].
QUESTION—What is meant by Herod going down from Judea to Caesarea?
The expression 'went down from Judea' referred to Herod's departure from Jerusalem [AB, Bar, EBC, NICNT, PNTC, TNTC] to his home in Caesarea down on the coast [BECNT. Caesarea was actually the Roman capital of Judea [BECNT, NCINT, PNTC, TNTC, TRT].

DISCOURSE UNIT—12:20–25 [CEV, ESV, NASB, NLT, NRSV, TEV]. The topic is Herod dies [CEV], the death of Herod [ESV, NRSV, TEV], death of Herod [NASB], the death of Herod Agrippa [NLT].

DISCOURSE UNIT—12:20–23 [NICNT, PNTC]. The topic is the death of Herod Agrippa I [NICNT], divine judgment on Herod Agrippa I [PNTC].

12:20 Now (Herod) was very-angry with the people of Tyre and Sidon, and they-came[a] to him with-one-accord,[b] and having-won-over[c] Blastus, the king's chamberlain, they-were-asking for peace, because their country was-fed by the king's-(country).
LEXICON—a. imperf. act. indic. of πάρειμι (LN 15.86) (BDAG 1.a. p. 773): 'to come' [AB, BECNT, LN; ESV, KJV, NASB, NCV, NRSV], 'to arrive, to come to be present' [LN], 'to be present' [BDAG], 'to go' [CEV, GW, TEV]. The phrase 'they came to him' is also translated 'they presented themselves before him' [Bar; NET], 'presented themselves at his court' [CBC; REB], 'sought an audience with him' [NIV], not explicit [NLT]. This verb means to come to be present at a particular place [LN].
    b. ὁμοθυμαδόν (LN 31.23) (BDAG p. 706): 'with one accord' [ESV, KJV, NASB], 'with one mind' [BDAG, LN], 'by common consent, unanimously' [LN], 'by common agreement' [CBC; REB], 'with one purpose/impulse' [BDAG], not explicit [NLT]. The phrase 'they

came...with one accord' is also translated 'they came...jointly' [AB], 'they came...as a group' [BECNT], 'a group of them went' [CEV], 'they came...in a body' [NRSV], 'They had agreed on what they wanted to do' [GW], the people...all came in a group' [NCV], 'they joined together and presented themselves' [NET], 'they now joined together' [NIV], 'they went in a group' [TEV], 'Together they presented themselves' [Bar]. This adverb pertains to mutual consent or agreement [LN].
  c. aorist act. participle of πείθω (LN 33.301) (BDAG 1.c. p. 791): 'to win over' [BDAG, CBC; NASB, NRSV, REB], 'to persuade' [BECNT, LN; ESV], 'to convince' [LN; CEV, NCV, NET, TEV], 'to strive to please' [BDAG]. The phrase 'having won over Blastus' is also translated 'having made Blastus...their friend' [KJV], 'Having secured the support of Blastus' [NIV], 'had won the support of Blastus' [AB; NLT], 'having got Blastus....on their side' [Bar], 'They enlisted the help of Blastus' [GW]. This verb means to convince someone to believe something and to act on the basis of what is recommended [LN]. It means to cause to come to a particular point of view or course of action [BDAG].

QUESTION—Who were the people who came to see Herod?
  In this context, 'they came' refers to a delegation of citizens from the cities of Tyre and Sidon [PNTC, TH].
QUESTION—What is meant by 'having persuaded Blastus'?
  This probably means that the people from Tyre and Sidon had bribed/paid Blastus to help them [NAC, NICNT, TRT].
QUESTION—What was the role of Blastus?
  Blastus was the king's chamberlain, that is, he was the official who managed the household of the king. In other words, he was the most trusted official of the king [NAC, PNTC, TH, TRT], a personal chief of staff/servant [BECNT, EBC].

12:21 On-(an)-appointed day Herod put on his royal robes, took his seat on the throne, and delivered-(an)-address to them. **12:22** And the people were shouting, "The voice of a god and not of a man!" **12:23** Immediately an-angel[a] of-(the)-Lord struck- him -down[b] because he-did- not -give[c] God the glory,[d] and he was eaten-by-worms and died.

LEXICON—a. ἄγγελος (LN 12.28) (BDAG 2.a. p. 8): 'angel' [AB, Bar, BDAG, BECNT, CBC, LN; all versions], 'messenger' [BDAG]. This noun denotes a supernatural being that attends upon or serves as a messenger of a superior supernatural entity. In many languages a term for 'angels' is borrowed from another dominant language, but in other instances a somewhat descriptive phrase may be employed. The most common expressions for 'angels of God' are 'messengers' and 'messengers from heaven.' Sometimes these angels are called 'spirit messengers' and even 'flying messengers.' [LN]. It denotes a transcendent power who carries out various missions or tasks. Here it refers to an angel who is a messenger of God [BDAG].

b. aorist act. indic. of πατάσσω (LN 20.73) (BDAG 2. p. 786): 'to strike' [AB, Bar, BDAG, BECNT, CBC; CEV, ESV, NASB, NET, NIV, NLT, NRSV, REB, TEV], 'to slay, to strike down' [LN], 'to smite' [KJV], 'to kill' [GW]. The phrase 'an angel of the Lord struck him down' is also translated 'an angel of the Lord immediately caused him to become sick' [NCV]. This verb means to slay by means of a mortal blow or disease [LN]. It means to inflict something disastrous [BDAG].
c. aorist act. indic. of δίδωμι (LN 57.71a) (BDAG 3. p. 242): 'to give' [AB, Bar, BDAG, BECNT; all versions except CEV, REB], 'to impart' [LN]. The phrase 'because he did not give God the glory' is also translated 'because he took the honor that belonged to God' [CEV], 'because he had usurped the honor due to God' [CBC; REB]. This verb means to impart something tangible [LN]. It means to express devotion [BDAG].
d. δόξα (LN 33.357) (BDAG 3. p. 257): 'glory' [AB, Bar, BECNT; ESV, GW, KJV, NASB, NCV, NET, NLT, NRSV], 'honor' [BDAG, CBC; CEV, REB, TEV], 'praise' [LN; NIV], 'fame, recognition, renown, prestige' [BDAG]. This noun denotes speaking of something as being unusually fine and deserving honor [LN]. It denotes honor as enhancement or recognition of status or performance [BDAG].

QUESTION—What is meant by 'an appointed day'?
'On an appointed day' can be rendered 'on a chosen day, the day that Herod had especially selected [TH].

QUESTION—Who were the people that Herod addressed??
Herod gave a public speech to the peoples of Tyre and Sidon. They had come to seek reconciliation with him [Bar, BECNT, NAC, TNTC]. He might commemorate the new arrangement and agreement between them [BECNT, NAC].

QUESTION—What caused Herod to be struck down by an angel of the Lord?
Herod did not give God the glory in the way that he accepted the praise and he did not rebuke the people's flattery [AB, BECNT, CBC, EBC, NAC, NICNT, PNTC, TNTC].

QUESTION—What worms are mentioned here?
In this context, the worms referred to some kind of intestinal worms [EBC, TH, TRT]. It was a sever disease that led to his painful death [BECNT]. It suggests an infection of internal roundworms which grow as long as ten to sixteen inches and feed on the nutrient fluids in the intestines [EBC].

DISCOURSE UNIT—12:24–25 [Bar, BECNT, NAC, PNTC]. The topic is a connecting link [Bar], summary [BECNT], peace for the church [NAC], the word continues to grow [PNTC].

DISCOURSE UNIT—12:24 [EBC, NICNT]. The topic is a summary statement [EBC], continued progress of the gospel [NICNT].

12:24 But[a] the word[b] of-God increased[c] and was-multiplied.[d]

LEXICON—a. δέ (LN 89.124): 'but' [AB, BECNT, LN; ESV, GW, KJV, NASB, NET, NIV, NRSV], 'on the other hand' [LN], 'meanwhile' [CBC; NLT, REB, TEV], not explicit [Bar; CEV, NCV]. This conjunction indicates a contrast [LN].
  b. λόγος (LN 33.260) (BDAG 1.a.β. p. 599): 'word' [AB, Bar, BDAG, BECNT, CBC; all versions except CEV, NCV], 'message' [CEV, NCV], 'what is preached, gospel' [LN]. This noun denotes the content of what is preached about Christ or about the good news [LN]. It denotes a communication whereby the mind finds expression [BDAG].
  c. imperf. act. indic. of αὐξάνω (LN 59.62) (BDAG 2.b. p. 151): 'to increase' [AB, BDAG, LN; ESV, NET, NIV], 'to grow' [Bar, BDAG, BECNT, CBC, LN; KJV, NASB, REB], 'to spread' [LN; CEV, GW, NCV, NLT, TEV], 'to extend' [LN], 'to advance' [NRSV]. This verb means to increase in the extent of or in the instances of an activity or state [LN]. It means to become greater [BDAG].
  d. imperf. pass. indic. of πληθύνω (LN 59.68) (BDAG 1.b. p. 826): 'to multiply' [Bar, BECNT, LN; ESV, KJV, NASB, NET], 'to grow' [BDAG, LN; TEV], 'to increase' [BDAG], 'to increase greatly' [LN], 'to spread' [AB, CBC; NIV, REB], not explicit [CEV]. The phrase 'and was multiplied' is also translated 'and win many followers' [GW], 'and reach people' [NCV], 'and there were many new believers' [NLT], 'and gain adherents' [NRSV]. This verb means to be increased greatly in number or extent [LN]. It means to be multiplied, grow, increase. Here it refers to the growth of Christian preaching expressed in the number of converts [BDAG].

QUESTION—What is the purpose of the brief summary given in verses 24–25?
  There are three purposes in this summary. First, it concludes Luke's focus on the church in Jerusalem. Second, it connects us back to the mission that concluded Acts 11, which is the link between Jerusalem and Antioch. Third, it shifts attention from Peter to Barnabas and Saul [BECNT].

QUESTION—What is meant by the word of God increasing and multiplying?
  It means that more and more people heard the word of God and believed [CBC, PNTC, TH]. The word about the good news and Jesus continued to spread [Bar, BECNT, NICNT, TNTC]. The word of God flourished just as the seed that fell on good ground in Jesus' parable of the sower [NAC].

DISCOURSE UNIT—12:25–28:31 [EBC]. The topic is Part II: The Christian mission to the Gentile world.

DISCOURSE UNIT—12:25–16:5 [EBC]. The topic is the first missionary journey and Jerusalem Council.

DISCOURSE UNIT—12:25–15:35 [NICNT]. The topic is church extension from Antioch and apostolic decree at Jerusalem.

DISCOURSE UNIT—12:25–13:12 [GW]. The topic is Barnabas and Saul travel to Cyprus.

DISCOURSE UNIT—12:25–13:3 [EBC, NICNT]. The topic is the missionaries sent out [EBC], Barnabas and Paul [NICNT].

DISCOURSE UNIT—12:25 [NICNT]. The topic is the envoys from Antioch return.

12:25 **And Barnabas and Saul returned from/to Jerusalem when they had-finished their mission,**[a] **taking-along with them John, who was- also -called**[b] **Mark.**

TEXT—Manuscripts reading εἰς Ἰερουσαλήμ 'to Jerusalem' are given a C rating by GNT to indicate that the Committee had difficulty making the decision. The CEV, NET, NLT, NRSV follow this. Some manuscripts have 'from Jerusalem'. The ESV, GW, KJV, NASB, NIV, REB, TEV follow this.

LEXICON—a. διακονία (LN 35.21) (BDAG 4. p. 230): 'ministry, task' [LN], 'aid, support' [BDAG]. The phrase 'had finished their mission' [NIV, NLT, TEV] is also translated 'had fulfilled their mission' [BECNT; NASB], 'had completed their mission' [NET], 'had completed their service' [ESV], 'had fulfilled their ministry' [KJV], 'had completed their ministry' [AB], 'having fulfilled their service' [Bar], 'finished their task' [NCV], 'had done the work they were sent to do' [CEV], 'after completing their mission' [NRSV], 'their task fulfilled' [CBC; REB], 'After Barnabas and Saul delivered the contribution to the leaders in Jerusalem' [GW]. This noun denotes the role or position of serving [LN]. It denotes rendering of specific assistance [BDAG].

b. aorist pass. participle of ἐπικαλέω (LN 33.131) (BDAG 2. p. 373): 'to be called' [Bar, BDAG, BECNT, LN; NASB, NIV], 'to be named' [LN], 'to be surnamed' [AB], 'to give a surname' [BDAG], not explicit [CBC; GW, NCV, NET, NLT, REB, TEV]. The phrase 'who was also called' is also translated 'whose other name was' [CEV, ESV, NRSV], 'whose surname was' [KJV]. This verb means to use an attribution in speaking of a person [LN]. It means to address or characterize someone by a special term [BDAG].

QUESTION—Did Barnabas and Saul return 'from Jerusalem' or 'to Jerusalem'?

Here there is a severe textual problem that divides the translations (TH).

1. They returned from Jerusalem [AB, BECNT. TNTC, EBC, NICNT, TH, TRT; GW, ESV, KJV, NASB, NCV NIV, NLT, REB, TEV]. Since 11:30 records their arrival in Jerusalem, it is more natural to assume that 12:25 records their departure from Jerusalem to be in Antioch for 13:1 [TH].
2. They returned to Jerusalem [CEV, NET, NRSV].

QUESTION—What service had Barnabas and Saul completed in Jerusalem?

Acts 11:30 says that Saul and Barnabas were taking a gift of money from the Christians in Antioch to help the Christians in Jerusalem who would be suffering from a famine. They had probably completed that task and are now returning to Antioch. Barnabas and Saul had completed their mission in Jerusalem [AB, Bar, BECNT, EBC, NAC, NICNT, TH, TNTC], that is, the sending of money to the elders as recorded in Acts 11:30 [AB, CBC, EBC, NAC, NICNT, TH, TNTC].

QUESTION—Who was this John Mark?
This John Mark was the same person mentioned in v. 12 [Bar, TRT].

DISCOURSE UNIT—13:1–21:26 [REB]. The topic is Paul's work among the Gentiles.

DISCOURSE UNIT—13:1–16:5 [PNTC]. The topic is the word goes to Cyprus and Asia Minor.

DISCOURSE UNIT—13:1–15:35 [BECNT, CBC, NAC, TNTC]. The topic is the mission from Antioch and the full incorporation of Gentiles [BECNT], the church breaks barriers [CBC], Paul turns to the Gentiles [NAC], the mission to Asia Minor and its aftermath [TNTC].

DISCOURSE UNIT—13:1–14:28 [BECNT]. The topic is the first missionary journey.

DISCOURSE UNIT—13:1–43 [NASB]. The topic is first missionary journey.

DISCOURSE UNIT—13:1–12 [AB, CBC]. The topic is Paul and Barnabas on Cyprus [AB], first, in Cyprus [CBC].

DISCOURSE UNIT—13:1–3 [Bar, BECNT, NAC, NICNT, PNTC, TNTC; CEV, ESV, NCV, NET, NIV, NLT, NRSV, TEV]. The topic is Barnabas and Saul commissioned from Antioch [Bar], Barnabas and Saul commissioned [BECNT; NRSV], Barnabas and Saul are chosen and sent [CEV, TEV], Barnabas and Saul sent off [ESV, NIV], Paul and Barnabas commissioned [NAC], Barnabas and Saul are chosen [NCV], the church at Antioch commissions Barnabas and Saul [NET], Barnabas and Saul sent out from Antioch [NICNT], Barnabas and Saul are commissioned [NLT], the release of Barnabas and Saul from Antioch in Syria [PNTC], the call to mission [TNTC].

13:1 Now there-were in the church[a] at Antioch prophets[b] and teachers, Barnabas, Simeon who was-called[c] Niger, Lucius of Cyrene, Manaen (the)-foster-brother[d] of-Herod the tetrarch, and Saul.

LEXICON—a. ἐκκλησία (LN 11.32) (BDAG 3.b.β. p. 304): 'church' [AB, Bar, BDAG, BECNT, LN; all versions], 'congregation' [BDAG, CBC, LN]. This noun denotes a congregation of Christians, implying interacting membership [LN]. It denotes the totality of Christians living together and meeting in a particular area, but not necessarily limited to one meeting place [BDAG].

b. προφήτης (LN 53.79) (BDAG 1.e. p. 891): 'prophet' [AB, Bar, BDAG, BECNT, CBC, LN; all versions], 'inspired preacher' [LN]. This noun denotes one who proclaims inspired utterances on behalf of God [LN]. It

denotes a person inspired to proclaim or reveal divine will or purpose [BDAG].
  c. pres. pass. participle of καλέω (LN 33.129) (BDAG 1.c. p. 503): 'to be called' [AB, Bar, BDAG, BECNT, CBC, LN; all versions], 'to be named' [BDAG, LN], 'to be called by name' [BDAG]. This verb means to speak of a person or object by means of a proper name [LN]. It means to identify by name or attribute [BDAG].
  d. σύντροφος (LN 10.51, 34.15) (BDAG p. 976): 'foster brother' [BDAG, LN (10.51)], 'close friend' [LN (34.15); CEV, GW, NET, REB], 'intimate friend' [Bar, LN (34.15)], 'friend since childhood' [LN (34.15)], 'childhood companion' [NLT], 'companion' [BDAG]. The phrase 'Manaen the foster brother of Herod' is also translated 'Manaen a member of the court of Herod' [BECNT; ESV, NRSV], 'Manaen, who/which had been brought up with…Herod' [AB; KJV, NASB, NIV, TEV], 'Manaen who had grown up with Herod [NCV], 'Manaen who had been at the court of Prince Herod' [CBC]. This adjective pertains to a person offered parental care and/or adoption along with the reference person, though not related by blood [LN (10.51)]. It pertains to a close friend on the basis of having been brought up together [LN (34.15)]. It pertains to being brought up with someone, either as a foster-brother or as a companion/friend [BDAG].

QUESTION—What was the 'church at Antioch'?

This refers to the local church of the Christians in Antioch [PNTC, TH]. It does did not refer to a church building [TH].

QUESTION—Who were the 'prophets'?

In this context, the prophets were those who spoke for God [TRT]. They preached the good news [TH]. They spoke inspired words from God for the edification and direction of the community [NAC]. Their prophecy was 'forth telling' [EBC]. Probably the first three mentioned, Barnabas, Simeon, and Lucas, were the prophets [EBC].

QUESTION—Who were the 'teachers'?

These teachers were Christians who taught the other Christians more about Christ and how to serve Him. They were not school teachers [TRT]. Probably the other two, Manaen and Saul were the teachers [EBC]. These men instructed the Christian converts in the beliefs and duties of the Christian faith [TH]. They taught by identifying logical and thematic relationships, explicating Old Testament foundations, and spelling out practical implications [EBC]. In this way the church was taught its doctrines before there were books that later became a part of the New Testament. Short doctrinal summaries, hymns, and rites like baptism as well as the Lord's Table taught people the core doctrines [BECNT]. The word 'teachers' is only mentioned here in Acts, but cognate words like 'to teach' and 'teaching' are frequent [Bar, BECNT, PNTC].

QUESTION—Who was this Simeon?
The Simeon mentioned here was Simon of Cyrene who carried Jesus' cross (Matthew 27:32; Luke 23:26) [EBC, TNTC, TRT]. The Latin name Niger means 'black' [BECNT, EBC, NAC, PNTC, TH, TRT] and it referred to a dark complexion [TH, TNTC]. Simeon might have been named that because he had dark skin [NICNT, TRT].

QUESTION—Who was Lucius?
The Lucius mentioned here might be the same person Paul sent greetings to in Romans 16:21 [TRT], but others think that he should not be confused with that Lucius [BECNT, EBC, NAC, NICNT, TH].

QUESTION—Who was Manaen?
The Manaen mentioned here was raised as a lifelong friend or a foster brother who had been brought up as a companion of Herod the tetrarch [AB, Bar, BECNT, CBC, EBC, NAC, NICNT, PNTC, TH, TNTC, TRT].

QUESTION—Who was Herod the tetrarch?
This Herod was Herod Antipas [AB, BECNT, CBC, EBC, NAC, NICNT, PNTC, TNTC, TRT], the ruler of Galilee when Jesus was born (Luke 3:1) [CBC, NAC, NICNT, PNTC], and the ruler who beheaded John the Baptist in Matthew 14:3–12 [TRT]. The Greek word τετραάρχου 'Tetrarch' literally means 'ruler of a fourth part' [TH]. It refers to a ruler who rules over a region or a province [TH], a dependent prince of a rank lower than that of king [AB].

13:2 **While they were-worshiping^a the Lord^b and fasting, the Holy Spirit said, "Set-apart^c for-me Barnabas and Saul for the work (to)-which I-have-called^d them."**

LEXICON—a. pres. act. participle of λειτουργέω (LN 35.22) (BDAG 1.a., b. p. 591): 'to worship' [AB, BECNT; CEV, ESV, GW, NCV, NIV, NLT, NRSV], 'to serve' [BDAG, LN; NET, TEV], 'to render service' [BDAG], 'to minister' [KJV, NASB], 'to offer worship' [CBC; REB], 'to wait upon' [Bar]. This verb means to serve, with the implication of more formal or regular service [LN]. It means to render special formal service [BDAG].

b. κύριος (LN 12.9): 'Lord' [AB, Bar, BECNT, CBC, LN; all versions], 'Ruler, One who commands' [LN]. This noun denotes a title for God and for Christ. It indicates one who exercises supernatural authority over mankind [LN].

c. aorist act. impera. of ἀφορίζω (LN 37.97) (BDAG 2. p. 158): 'to set apart' [AB, Bar, BDAG, BECNT, CBC; ESV, GW, NASB, NCV, NET, NIV, NRSV, REB, TEV], 'to separate' [KJV], 'to appoint' [BDAG, LN; CEV], 'to dedicate' [NLT]. This verb means to set aside a person for a particular task or function [LN]. It means to select one person out of a group for a purpose [BDAG].

d. perf. mid. indic. of προσκαλέω (LN 33.312) (BDAG 2.b. p. 881): 'to call' [AB, Bar, BDAG, BECNT, CBC, LN; all versions except CEV,

NCV], 'to call to a task' [LN], 'to choose' [CEV, NCV]. This verb means to urgently invite someone to accept responsibilities for a particular task, implying a new relationship to the one who does the calling [LN]. It means to call in a legal or official sense [BDAG].

QUESTION—Who were the people the Holy Spirit was speaking to?
'They' could be either the five men who are mentioned in v. 1 or the entire church of Antioch [PNTC, TH, TRT]. 'They' probably refers to the entire congregation, but the directive of the Holy Spirit was probably mediated through the inspiration of the prophet-teachers. Acts 14:26–27 shows that it was the entire church of Antioch [Bar, EBC, NAC, NICNT, PNTC, TRT].

QUESTION—What was the work to which Barnabas and Saul were called?
This work involved telling people about Jesus and the Kingdom of God [TRT]. It referred to a similar work that Barnabas and Paul had contributed to in the church in Antioch [BECNT]. It was missionary work [TNTC]. It was Barnabas and Paul's whole mission which occurred from here and concluded at Acts 14:26 [BECNT, NAC].

QUESTION—What is meant by the Holy Spirit 'calling' them to a work?
In this context 'called' means that God chose and appointed Barnabas and Saul to do His work. It does not mean that God shouted to them [TH, TRT]. The tense of the verb 'I have called' suggests that God had already made the decision, and it was the church's responsibility to carry out his will [PNTC, TH].

13:3 **Then after fasting and praying they laid[a] their hands-on them and sent-(them)-away.[b]**

LEXICON—a. aorist act. participle of ἐπιτίθημι (LN 85.51) (BDAG 1.a.α. p. 384): 'to lay' [AB, Bar, BECNT, CBC; ESV, KJV, NASB, NCV, NLT, NRSV, REB], 'to place' [CEV, GW, NET, NIV, TEV], 'to put on, to place on, to lay on' [LN], 'to lay/put upon' [BDAG]. This verb means to place something on something [LN]. It means to place something on or transfer to a place or object [BDAG].

b. aorist act. indic. of ἀπολύω (LN 15.66): 'to send' [AB, Bar, BECNT, LN; all versions except GW]. The phrase 'sent them away' is also translated 'released them' [GW], 'let them go' [CBC]. This verb means to cause someone to depart for a particular purpose [LN].

QUESTION—Who laid their hands on Barnabas and Saul?
It could have been the three men who were not being sent out or else the entire church at Antioch [TH, TRT]. As in v. 2, it probably was the entire church at Antioch [Bar, CBC, EBC, NICNT, TNTC].

QUESTION—Why did they lay their hands on them?
The 'laying on of hands' was an act of commissioning [BECNT, CBC, PNTC, TNTC]. It expressed both a blessing and identification with the two in the work to which God had called them [CBC, PNTC, TNTC]. It commissioned and released the two to their new service [NICNT]. It was a

gesture showing the congregation's endorsement of the work of the two [NAC]. It committed the two to the grace of God for the work ahead [Bar].

DISCOURSE UNIT—13:4-13 [EBC]. The topic is the mission on Cyprus and John Mark's departure.

DISCOURSE UNIT—13:4-12 [Bar, BECNT, NAC, NICNT, PNTC, TNTC; CEV, ESV, NCV, NET, NIV, NLT, NRSV, TEV]. The topic is Barnabas and Saul in Cyprus [Bar; CEV, NCV], Barnabas and Saul's mission in Cyprus [BECNT], Barnabas and Saul on Cyprus [ESV], Sergius Paulus' conversion on Cyprus [NAC], Paul and Barnabas preach in Cyprus [NET], Cyprus [NICNT], on Cyprus [NIV], Paul's first missionary journey [NLT], the apostles preach in Cyprus [NRSV], the word in Cyprus [PNTC], in Cyprus [TEV], evangelism in Cyprus [TNTC].

DISCOURSE UNIT—13:4-5 [NICNT]. The topic is the missionaries arrive in Cyprus.

13:4 So, being-sent-out[a] by the Holy Spirit, they went-down[b] to Seleucia and from-there they-sailed to Cyprus.

LEXICON—a. aorist pass. participle of ἐκπέμπω (LN 15.68) (BDAG p. 307): 'to be sent out' [Bar, BDAG, BECNT, CBC, LN; ESV, NASB, NCV, NET, NLT, NRSV, REB], 'to be sent' [LN; CEV, GW, TEV], 'to be sent forth' [AB, LN; KJV], 'to be sent on their way' [NIV]. This verb means to send out or away from, presumably for some purpose [LN]. It means to cause someone to go away for a purpose [BDAG].

b. aorist act. indic. of κατέρχομαι (LN 15.107) (BDAG 1. p. 531): 'to go down' [BECNT, LN; ESV, NASB, NET, NIV, NLT, NRSV], 'to move down' [LN], 'to come down' [Bar, BDAG, CBC, LN; REB], 'to travel down' [AB], 'to descend' [LN], 'to go' [CEV, GW, NCV, TEV], 'to depart' [KJV]. This verb means to move down, irrespective of the gradient [LN]. It means to move in a direction considered the opposite of up but not necessarily with the suggestion of a gradient [BDAG].

QUESTION—To whom does 'they' refer?

This refers to Barnabas and Saul [Bar, EBC, NAC, NICNT, TH].

QUESTION—Where was Seleucia?

Seleucia was 16 miles (26 km.) west of Antioch [AB, BECNT, CBC, EBC, NAC, PNTC, TH, TRT], and it was at a lower elevation than Antioch [TRT]. It was the port city that served Antioch [AB, Bar, BECNT, CBC, EBC, NAC, PNTC, TNTC, TRT].

QUESTION—Where was Cyprus?

The island of Cyprus was less than a day's sail from Seleucia [TRT], about 60 miles (96 km.) away [NAC, PNTC, TNTC].

13:5 **When they arrived[a] at Salamis, they-proclaimed[b] the word[c] of-God in the synagogues[d] of-the Jews. And they- also -had John (as)-an-assistant.**

LEXICON—a. aorist mid. (deponent = act.) participle of γίνομαι (LN 85.6) (BDAG 10.a. p. 199): 'to arrive' [Bar, BECNT, CBC; CEV, ESV, GW, NET, NIV, NRSV, REB, TEV], 'to reach' [NASB], 'to be (in a place)' [LN], 'to be in, to be there' [BDAG], not explicit [NLT]. The phrase 'When they arrived at Salamis' is also translated 'when they were at Salamis' [KJV], 'When they came to Salamis' [AB; NCV]. This verb means to be in a place, with the possible implication of having come to be in such a place [LN]. It means to be in or at a place [BDAG].

b. imperf. act. indic. of καταγγέλλω (LN 33.204) (BDAG a. p. 515): 'to proclaim' [Bar, BDAG, BECNT; ESV, NASB, NET, NIV, NRSV], 'to preach' [AB; CEV, KJV, NCV, NLT, TEV], 'to declare' [CBC; REB], 'to proclaim throughout' [LN], 'to announce' [BDAG, LN], 'to speak out about' [LN]. The phrase 'they proclaimed the word of God' is also translated 'they began to spread God's word' [GW]. This verb means to announce, with focus upon the extent to which the announcement or proclamation extends [LN]. It means to make known in public, with the implication of broad dissemination [BDAG].

c. λόγος (LN 33.260) (BDAG 1.a.β. p. 599): 'word' [AB, Bar, BDAG, BECNT, CBC; all versions except CEV, NCV], 'message' [CEV], 'Good News' [NCV], 'what is preached, gospel' [LN]. This noun denotes the content of what is preached about Christ or about the good news [LN]. It denotes a communication whereby the mind finds expression [BDAG].

d. συναγωγή (LN 7.20) (BDAG 2.a. p. 963): 'synagogue' [AB, Bar, BECNT, CBC, LN; all versions except CEV], 'Christian assembly place' [LN], 'meeting place' [CEV]. This noun denotes a building of assembly, associated with religious activity. Normally a building in which Jewish worship took place and in which the Law was taught [LN]. It denotes a place of assembly for the Jews [BDAG].

QUESTION—Where was Salamis?

Salamis was the chief city of the island of Cyprus and it was on the eastern coast of Cyprus [AB, BECNT, CBC, EBC, NICNT, PNTC, TH]. It had been the capital of Cyprus but it had been superseded by Paphos in about 200 B.C. [Bar, PNTC]. The city had a rather large Jewish population [AB, CBC, EBC, NAC, NICNT, TH, TNTC].

QUESTION—What were the synagogues of the Jews?

They were the worship houses of the Jews, the buildings where the Jews worshipped God [TH]. Besides worship and scripture reading they were gathering places of teaching and prayer [BECNT].

QUESTION—Who was this John who assisted Barnabas and Saul?

He was the John Mark who is mentioned in Acts 12:12, 25 [AB, Bar, BECNT, CBC, EBC, NAC, NICNT, PNTC, TH, TNTC].

DISCOURSE UNIT—13:6–12 [NICNT]. The topic is confrontation at Paphos.

13:6 When they had-gone-through^a (the)-whole island as-far-as Paphos, they-came-upon^b a-certain magician,^c (a)-Jewish false-prophet^d whose name was Bar-Jesus.

LEXICON—a. aorist act. participle of διέρχομαι (LN 15.21) (BDAG 1.a. p. 244): 'to go through' [BECNT, CBC; ESV, GW, KJV, NASB, NRSV, REB], 'to travel through' [AB; NIV], 'to travel around through, to journey all through' [LN], 'to pass through' [Bar], 'to go across' [NCV], 'to cross over' [NET], 'to travel…across' [NLT], 'to go…across' [TEV]. The clause 'they had gone through the whole island as far as Paphos' is also translated 'Barnabas and Saul went all the way to the city of Paphos' [CEV]. This verb means to travel around through an area, with the implication of both extensive and thorough movement throughout an area [LN]. It means to travel or move about from place to place through an area [BDAG].

b. aorist act. indic. of εὑρίσκω (LN 27.27) (BDAG 1.b. p. 411): 'to come upon' [BDAG, BECNT, CBC, LN; ESV, REB], 'to meet' [AB; CEV, GW, NCV, NIV, NLT, NRSV, TEV], 'to find' [Bar, BDAG, LN; KJV, NASB, NET], 'to learn the whereabouts of something, to discover, to happen to find' [LN]. This verb means to learn the location of something, either by intentional searching or by unexpected discovery [LN]. It means to come upon something accidentally without seeking [BDAG].

c. μάγος (LN 53.97) (BDAG 2. p. 608): 'magician' [AB, BDAG, BECNT, LN; ESV, NASB, NCV, NET, NRSV, TEV], 'astrologer' [GW], 'sorcerer' [CBC; KJV, NIV, NLT, REB], 'magus' [Bar], not explicit [CEV]. This noun denotes one who practices magic and witchcraft [LN].

d. ψευδοπροφήτης (LN 53.81) (BDAG p. 1097): 'false prophet' [Bar, BDAG, BECNT, LN; CEV, ESV, KJV, NASB, NCV, NET, NIV, NLT, NRSV], 'charlatan' [AB]. The phrase 'a Jewish false prophet' is also translated 'a Jew who posed as a prophet' [CBC; REB], 'a Jew who claimed to be a prophet' [TEV], 'an astrologer who claimed to be a prophet' [GW]. This noun denotes one who claims to be a prophet and is not and thus proclaims what is false [LN]. It denotes one who falsely claims to be a prophet of God or who prophesies falsely [BDAG].

QUESTION—Where was Paphos?

Paphos was the capital city of the island of Cyprus [AB, Bar, BECNT, CBC, EBC, NAC, NICNT, PNTC, TH, TNTC, TRT]. It was about 90 miles (145 km.) southwest of the city of Salamis (v. 5) [BECNT, NAC, TH, TRT].

QUESTION—What is the meaning of the name 'Bar-Jesus'?

Bar-Jesus is an Aramaic name which means 'Son of Joshua', and the Greek equivalent of Joshua is 'Jesus' [Bar, BECNT, EBC, NICNT, PNTC, TH, TNTC, TRT]. This adds a note of irony, since the first opponent of Paul and Barnabas is a false prophet named 'Bar-Jesus' [BECNT].

QUESTION—What was a 'false prophet'?

A false prophet refers to any person who spoke a message that was contrary to the Christian preaching [TH]. Bar-Jesus is called a false prophet since he claimed to be a prophet of God although he wasn't [TH]. He was one of a long line of pretenders who opposed God's revealed truth and its messengers [PNTC].

13:7 He was with the proconsul,[a] Sergius Paulus, an-intelligent man. This-man summoned[b] Barnabas and Saul and sought[c] to-hear the word[d] of-God.
LEXICON—a. ἀνθύπατος (LN 37.82) (BDAG p. 82): 'proconsul' [AB, Bar, BDAG, BECNT, LN; ESV, NASB, NET, NIV, NRSV], 'deputy' [KJV], 'governor' [CBC; CEV, GW, NCV, NLT, REB, TEV], 'important official' [LN]. This noun denotes an official ruling over a province traditionally under the control of the Roman senate [LN]. It denotes the head of the government in a senatorial province [BDAG].
- b. aorist mid. participle of προσκαλέω (LN 33.308): 'to summon' [AB, Bar, BECNT; ESV, NASB, NET, NRSV], 'to call' [LN; TEV], 'to call to' [LN], 'to send for' [CBC; CEV, GW, NIV, REB], 'to call for' [KJV], 'to ask to come' [NCV], 'to invite' [NLT]. This verb means to call to, with a possible implication of a reciprocal relation [LN].
- c. aorist act. indic. of ἐπιζητέω (LN 25.9) (BDAG 2.a. p. 371): 'sought' [Bar, BECNT; ESV, NASB], 'to desire' [LN; KJV], 'to want to' [CBC, LN; CEV, GW, NCV, NET, NIV, NLT, NRSV, REB, TEV], 'to wish, to wish for' [BDAG]. The phrase 'sought to hear the word' is also translated 'was very eager to hear the word' [AB]. This verb means to desire to have or experience something, with the probable implication of making an attempt to realize one's desire [LN]. It means to be seriously interested in or have a strong desire for [BDAG].
- d. λόγος (LN 33.260) (BDAG 1.a.β. p. 599): 'word' [AB, Bar, BDAG, BECNT, CBC; all versions except CEV, NCV], 'message' [CEV, NCV], 'what is preached, gospel' [LN].This noun denotes the content of what is preached about Christ or about the good news [LN]. It denotes a communication whereby the mind finds expression [BDAG].

QUESTION—Who was Sergius Paulus?
Sergius Paulus was the proconsul or governor of the island of Cyprus [AB, CBC, NICNT, TNTC, TRT]. Proconsul was the title given to one who was in charge of a Roman senatorial province where no troops were required [AB, Bar, BECNT, CBC, NAC, NICNT, TH, TNTC, TRT]. Cyprus had been a senatorial province of the Roman Empire since 22 B.C. [AB, Bar, BECNT, CBC, NAC, NICNT, PNTC, TH].

QUESTION—What is meant by 'he (Bar-Jesus) was with the proconsul, Sergius Paulus?
It could either mean that Bar-Jesus was a friend of Sergius Paulus [TH, TRT], or that Bar-Jesus was one of Sergius Paulus' attendants as a member of his court [Bar, EBC, NICNT, PNTC, TH, TRT], a court astrologer [BECNT, CBC].

13:8 But[a] Elymas the magician (for so his name is-translated) was-opposing[b] them, seeking[c] to-turn- the proconsul -away[d] from the faith.[e]

LEXICON—a. δέ (LN 89.124): 'but' [AB, Bar, BECNT, LN; all versions except GW, REB], 'on the other hand' [LN], not explicit [CBC; GW, REB]. This conjunction indicates a contrast [LN].
- b. imperf. mid. indic. of ἀνθίστημι (LN 39.1) (BDAG 1.a. p. 80): 'to oppose' [BDAG, BECNT, CBC, LN; ESV, GW, NASB, NET, NIV, NRSV, REB], 'to withstand' [KJV], 'to interfere' [NLT], 'to resist' [AB, Bar], 'to be against' [CEV, NCV], 'to be hostile toward, to show hostility' [LN], 'to set oneself against' [BDAG]. This verb is also translated as a passive verb: 'they were opposed by the magician' [TEV]. This verb means to oppose someone, involving not only a psychological attitude but also a corresponding behavior [LN]. It means to be in opposition to [BDAG].
- c. pres. act. participle of ζητέω (LN 68.60) (BDAG 3.d. p. 428): 'to seek' [Bar, BECNT; ESV, KJV, NASB], 'to try' [AB, CBC, LN; CEV, GW, NCV, NET, NIV, NLT, NRSV, REB, TEV], 'to seek to do' [LN], 'to strive for, to aim (at), to try to obtain, to desire, to wish (for)' [BDAG]. This verb means to seek to do something, but without success [LN]. It means to devote serious effort to realize one's desire or objective [BDAG].
- d. aorist act. infin. of διαστρέφω (LN 13.46) (BDAG 3. p. 237): 'to turn away' [Bar, BECNT, CBC; ESV, KJV, NASB, NET, NRSV, REB, TEV], 'to turn' [NIV], 'to turn away from, to divert from' [LN], 'to mislead' [BDAG]. The phrase 'seeking to turn the proconsul away from the faith' is also translated 'tried to keep the governor from having faith in the Lord' [CEV], 'tried to distort the meaning of the faith so that the governor wouldn't believe' [GW], 'tried to stop the governor from believing in Jesus' [NCV], 'trying to keep the governor from believing' [NLT], 'tried to prevent the proconsul from believing' [AB]. This verb means to cause a state to cease by a diversion to some other state, usually with the implication of a wrong state [LN]. It means to cause to be uncertain about a belief or to believe something different [BDAG].
- e. πίστις (LN 31.102) (BDAG 2.d.α. p. 819): 'faith' [Bar, BDAG, BECNT, CBC; all versions except NCV, NLT], 'Christian faith' [LN], 'trust, confidence' [BDAG]. The phrase 'seeking to turn the proconsul away from the faith' is also translated 'tried to stop the governor from believing in Jesus' [NCV], 'trying to keep the governor from believing' [NLT], 'tried to prevent the proconsul from believing' [AB]. This noun denotes the belief in the good news about Jesus Christ and becoming a follower [LN]. It denotes the state of believing on the basis of the reliability of the one trusted [BDAG].

QUESTION—Who was Elymas?
Elymas was Bar-Jesus. Elymas is the Greek form of an Arabic word that means sorcerer/magician/fortune-teller [CBC, EBC, NICNT, TNTC, TRT], sage [BECNT, NAC]. A sorcerer is someone who uses the power of evil spirits to do things [TRT]. The magician's work would involve healing and looking for signs by using formulas, incantations, amulets, and other forms of inducing discernment [BECNT]. He probably offered Paulus his services to divine future events for him [NAC].

QUESTION—Who were the 'them' whom the magician opposed?
It refers to Barnabas and Saul. The sorcerer opposed Barnabas and Saul as they shared the gospel with Sergius Paulus [PNTC]. He tried to divert Sergius from the gospel [AB, EBC, NAC, NICNT], and prevent Sergius from embracing the truth [BECNT].

13:9 But[a] Saul, who was also-(called) Paul, filled[b] with-(the)-Holy Spirit,[c] looked[d] intently at him

LEXICON—a. δέ (LN 89.124): 'but' [AB, Bar, BECNT, CBC, LN; ESV, GW, NASB, NCV, NET, NRSV, REB], 'on the other hand' [LN], 'then' [CEV, KJV, NIV, TEV], not explicit [NLT]. This conjunction indicates a contrast [LN].
  b. aorist pass. participle of πίμπλημι (LN 59.38) (BDAG 1.a.β. p. 813): 'to be filled' [AB, Bar, BDAG, BECNT, CBC; all versions], 'to be filled completely, to be filled up' [LN]. This verb means to cause something to be completely full [LN]. It means to cause to be completely full of the Holy Spirit [BDAG].
  c. πνεῦμα (LN 12.18) (BDAG 5.c.β. p. 834): 'Spirit' [AB, Bar, BDAG, BECNT, CBC, LN; all versions except KJV], 'Ghost' [KJV]. This noun denotes the third person of the Trinity whose titles are 'Spirit, Spirit of God, and Holy Spirit' [LN]. It denotes God's being as controlling influence, with focus on association with humans [BDAG].
  d. aorist act. participle of ἀτενίζω (LN 24.49) (BDAG p. 148): 'to look intently at' [BDAG; ESV, NRSV], 'to look straight at' [LN; CEV, NCV, NIV, TEV], 'to look at' [AB], 'to look' [NLT], 'to stare at' [BDAG, BECNT, LN; GW], 'to stare straight at' [NET], 'to keep one's eyes fixed on' [LN]. The phrase 'looked intently at him' is also translated 'fixed his gaze/eyes on/upon him' [Bar, CBC; NASB, REB], 'set his eyes on him' [KJV]. This verb means to fix one's eyes on some object continually and intensely [LN].

QUESTION—Why did Saul have another name?
Saul's other name was Paul and is first introduced here [AB, Bar, CBC, EBC, NAC, NICNT, PNTC, TNTC, TRT]. 'Saul' was a Hebrew name stressing his Jewish root while 'Paul' was his Roman/Greek name [AB, BECNT, EBC, NAC, NICNT, PNTC, TH, TNTC, TRT].

13:10 and said, "You son of-(the) devil,[a] you enemy of-all righteousness,[b] full of-all deceit and fraud, will-you- not -stop making-crooked[c] the straight paths[d] of-the Lord[e]?

LEXICON—a. διάβολος (LN 12.34) (BDAG 2. p. 226): 'devil' [AB, Bar, BDAG, BECNT, CBC; all versions except TEV], 'Devil' [LN; TEV], 'Satan' [LN], 'adversary' [BDAG]. This noun refers to a slanderer and it is used as a title for the Devil [LN]. It denotes one who engages in slander. It is a title of the principal transcendent evil being [BDAG].
   b. δικαιοσύνη (LN 88.13) (BDAG 3.a. p. 248): 'righteousness' [BDAG, BECNT, LN; ESV, KJV, NASB, NET, NRSV], 'goodness' [CBC; REB], 'uprightness' [Bar, BDAG], 'doing what God requires, doing what is right' [LN]. The phrase 'you enemy of all righteousness' is also translated 'You are...an enemy of everything that is right' [CEV, NCV, NIV], 'you enemy of all that is righteous' [AB], 'You hate everything that has God's approval' [GW], 'You...enemy of all that is good' [NLT], 'You are the enemy of everything that is good' [TEV]. This noun denotes the act of doing what God requires [LN]. It denotes the quality or characteristic of upright behavior [BDAG].
   c. pres. act. participle of διαστρέφω (LN 88.264) (BDAG 2. p. 237): 'to make crooked' [BDAG, BECNT; ESV, NASB, NET, NRSV], 'to lead astray' [LN], 'to pervert' [Bar, BDAG, LN; KJV, NIV, NLT, REB], 'to twist' [AB], 'to distort' [GW], 'to mislead' [LN], 'to falsify' [CBC], 'to change' [NCV], 'to turn' [TEV]. The clause 'will you not stop making crooked the straight paths of the Lord?' is also translated 'When will you stop speaking against the true ways of the Lord?' [CEV]. This verb means to cause someone to depart from correct behavior and thus engage in serious wrongdoing [LN]. It means to cause to depart from an accepted standard of oral or spiritual values [BDAG].
   d. εὐθύς (LN 88.18) (BDAG 2.a. p. 406): 'path' [AB, BECNT; ESV, NET, NRSV], 'way' [Bar, CBC; CEV, GW, KJV, NASB, NIV, NLT, REB], 'right way, correct manner of life, just way of life' [LN], 'proper, right' [BDAG]. The phrase 'the straight paths of the Lord' is also translated 'the Lord's truths' [NCV, TEV]. The idiom 'a straight road' means the right or correct pattern of behavior [LN].
   e. κύριος (LN 12.9): 'Lord' [AB, Bar, BECNT, CBC, LN; all versions], 'Ruler, One who commands' [LN]. This noun denotes a title for God and for Christ. It indicates one who exercises supernatural authority over mankind [LN].

QUESTION—What is meant by 'son of the devil'?

'Son of the devil' is an idiom that describes one who is working for the devil or is evil like the devil, and not one who was literally the devil's son [TH, TRT]. It means he is like the devil himself [TH]. It refers to an enemy of everything that is right, one who is full of all kinds of deceit and trickery, one who is always perverting the right ways of the Lord [EBC].

QUESTION—What is meant by 'the straight paths of the Lord'?
'The straight paths of the Lord' is an idiom that can either mean 'the right/good way that the Lord does things' or 'the Lord's truths', or both [Bar, BECNT, EBC, TRT], 'the Lord's truths' [TH].

13:11 And now, behold,[a] (the)-hand[b] of-(the)-Lord (is)-upon[c] you, and you-will-be blind and not see the sun for a-time." Immediately mist and darkness fell[d] upon him, and he went-about[e] seeking[f] people-to-lead-(him)[g] by the hand.

LEXICON—a. ἰδού (LN 91.13) (BDAG 1.b.δ. p. 468): 'behold' [BDAG, BECNT; ESV, KJV, NASB], 'look' [BDAG, CBC, LN; NET, REB], 'watch' [NLT], 'see' [Bar, BDAG], 'listen' [AB, LN; NRSV], 'pay attention' [LN], not explicit [CEV, GW, NCV, NIV, TEV]. This particle functions as a prompter of attention, also serving to emphasize the statement which follows [LN]. It functions as a prompter of attention [BDAG].

b. χείρ (LN 76.3) (BDAG 2.b.γ. p. 1083): 'hand' [AB, Bar, BDAG, BECNT, CBC; ESV, KJV, NASB, NET, NIV, NLT, NRSV, REB, TEV], 'power' [LN]. The clause 'the hand of the Lord is upon you' is also translated, 'the Lord is against you' [GW], 'the Lord will touch you' [NCV], 'the Lord is going to punish you' [CEV]. This noun is a figurative extension of meaning of χείρ 'hand' and it denotes power as an expression of the activity of a person or supernatural being [LN]. It denotes an acting agent as punisher. In this sense the focus is on the person or thing as the source of the activity [BDAG].

c. ἐπί (LN 90.57) (BDAG 14.b.β. p. 366): 'upon' [AB, Bar, BECNT; ESV, KJV, NASB, NLT], 'on' [BDAG, LN; TEV], 'to' [BDAG, LN], 'at' [LN], 'against' [GW, NET, NIV, NRSV]. The clause 'the hand of the Lord is upon you' is also translated 'The Lord is going to punish you' [CEV], 'the Lord will touch you' [NCV], 'the hand of the Lord strikes' [CBC; REB]. This preposition is a marker of the experiencer, often with the implication of an action by a superior force or agency [LN]. It is a marker indicating the one to whom, for whom, or about whom something is done. Here it is a marker of unpleasant or startling experiences [BDAG].

d. aorist act. indic. of πίπτω (LN 13.122, 24.40) (BDAG 1.a. p. 815): 'to fall' [AB, Bar, BDAG, BECNT; ESV, KJV, NASB], 'to fall upon' [LN (13.122)], 'to come over' [CBC; NET, NIV, NLT, NRSV, REB], 'to happen to' [LN (13.122)], 'dark mistiness occurs (to someone), to become blind' [LN (24.40)]. The clause 'mist and darkness fell upon him' is also translated 'the man's eyes were covered by a dark mist' [CEV], 'Elymas couldn't see a thing' [GW], 'everything went dark for Elymas' [NCV], 'Elymas felt a dark mist cover his eyes' [TEV]. This verb means to happen suddenly to, with the connotation of something bad and adverse [LN (13.122)]. This is a possible idiom, literally 'mistiness and darkness

fall' and means a serious impairment of sight, possibly involving total blindness [LN (24.40)]. It means to fall down from a higher point [BDAG].
e. pres. act. participle of περιάγω (LN 15.23) (BDAG 2. p. 798): 'to go about' [Bar, BDAG, BECNT; ESV, KJV, NASB, NRSV], 'to travel about, to wander about' [LN], 'to go around' [BDAG; CEV, NET], 'to walk around' [NCV, TEV], 'to grope about' [AB, CBC; NIV, REB], 'to grope around' [NLT], not explicit [GW]. This verb means to move about from place to place, with significant changes in direction [LN]. It means to travel about in various directions. Here it refers to a blind man feeling his way [BDAG].
f. imperf. act. indic. of ζητέω (LN 57.59): 'to seek' [Bar, BECNT, LN; ESV, KJV, NASB, NET, NIV], 'to beg' [NLT], 'to try to get' [CEV], 'to try to find' [GW, NCV, TEV], 'to look for' [AB], 'to try to obtain, to attempt to get' [LN], 'to grope' [NRSV], not explicit [CBC; REB]. This verb means to try to obtain something from someone [LN].
g. χειραγωγός (LN 15.185) (BDAG p. 1083): 'one who leads' [Bar, BECNT, CBC; all versions], 'one who leads by the hand' [LN], 'a guide' [AB, LN], 'leader' [BDAG]. This noun denotes a person who leads another by the hand [LN]. It denotes one who leads another by the hand [BDAG].

13:12 Then the proconsul believed[a] when he saw what had-happened,[b] for he was-astonished[c] at the teaching of-the Lord.
LEXICON—a. aorist act. indic. of πιστεύω (LN 31.102) (BDAG 2.a.α. p. 817): 'to believe' [AB, BECNT; ESV, GW, KJV, NASB, NCV, NET, NIV, NRSV, TEV], 'to believe in, to trust' [BDAG], 'to be a believer' [LN]. The phrase 'the proconsul believed' is also translated 'he put his faith in the Lord' [CEV], 'he became a believer' [Bar, CBC; NLT, REB]. This verb means to believe in the good news about Jesus Christ and to become a follower [LN]. It means to entrust oneself to an entity in complete confidence [BDAG].
b. perf. act. participle of γίνομαι (LN 13.107): 'to happen' [AB, Bar, CBC, LN; CEV, GW, NASB, NET, NIV, NLT, NRSV, REB, TEV], 'to occur' [BECNT, LN; ESV], 'to be done' [KJV], 'to come to be' [LN]. The phrase 'when he saw what had happened' is also translated 'When the governor saw this' [NCV]. This verb means to happen, with the implication that what happens is different from a previous state [LN].
c. pres. pass. participle of ἐκπλήσσω (LN 25.219) (BDAG p. 308): 'to be astonished' [ESV, KJV, NLT, NRSV], 'to be greatly astounded' [LN; NET], 'to be amazed' [BDAG, BECNT; CEV, NASB, NCV, NIV], 'to be greatly amazed' [TEV], 'to be astounded, to be overwhelmed' [BDAG], 'to be deeply impressed' [AB, CBC; REB], 'to be surprised' [Bar]. This verb is also translated as an active verb: 'The Lord's teachings amazed him' [GW]. This verb means to be so amazed as to be practically

overwhelmed [LN]. It means to cause to be filled with amazement to the point of being overwhelmed [BDAG].

DISCOURSE UNIT—13:13–52 [Bar, BECNT, CBC, NAC, NICNT, PNTC, TNTC; CEV, ESV, GW, NCV, NET, NIV, NRSV, TEV]. The topic is through Pamphylia to Pisidian Antioch: Paul's speech [Bar], Paul and Barnabas in Pisidian Antioch [BECNT], Paul and Barnabas in Antioch of Pisidia [CEV, NRSV], Paul and Barnabas at Antioch in Pisidia [ESV], Paul and Barnabas go to Antioch near Pisidia [GW], Paul's address to the synagogue at Pisidian Antioch [NAC], Paul and Barnabas leave Cyprus [NCV], Paul and Barnabas at Pisidian Antioch [NET], the other Antioch [CBC], Pisidian Antioch [NET, NICNT], in Pisidian Antioch [NIV], the word in Pisidian Antioch [PNTC], in Antioch in Pisidia [TEV], evangelism in the synagogue at Pisidian Antioch [TNTC].

DISCOURSE UNIT—13:13–43 [NLT]. The topic is Paul preaches in Antioch of Pisidia.

DISCOURSE UNIT—13:13–41 [AB]. The topic is Paul's speech in Pisidian Antioch.

DISCOURSE UNIT—13:13–15 [NICNT]. The topic is Paul's speech in Pisidian Antioch.

13:13 **Now Paul and his companions set sail from Paphos and came to Perga in Pamphylia. And John left[a] them and returned[b] to Jerusalem.**
LEXICON—a. aorist act. participle of ἀποχωρέω (LN 15.51) (BDAG p. 125): 'to leave' [AB, BDAG, BECNT, CBC, LN; all versions except GW, KJV], 'to go away' [LN], 'to depart' [LN; KJV], 'to desert' [BDAG; GW], 'to separate' [Bar]. This verb means to move away from, with emphasis upon separation and possible lack of concern for what has been left [LN]. It means to move away from a point [BDAG].
  b. aorist act. indic. of ὑποστρέφω (LN 15.88) (BDAG p. 1041): 'to return' [AB, Bar, BDAG, BECNT, CBC, LN; ESV, KJV, NASB, NCV, NET, NIV, NLT, NRSV, REB], 'to go back' [LN; CEV, GW, TEV], 'to come back' [LN], 'to turn back' [BDAG]. This verb means to move back to a point from which one has previously departed [LN].
QUESTION—Where was Perga?
Perga was a city in the province of Pamphylia. It was near but not on the coast of Asia Minor [AB, Bar, CBC, EBC, NICNT, TNTC]. It could be reached by ship on the Cestrus River and then by traveling overland [AB, Bar, NAC, NICNT, TNTC, TRT]. Perga was an important center for the worship of the goddess Artemis [Bar, TNTC, TRT].

DISCOURSE UNIT—13:14–52 [EBC]. The topic is at Antioch of Pisidia.

DISCOURSE UNIT—13:14–43 [PNTC]. The topic is ministry in the synagogue.

370 ACTS 13:14

DISCOURSE UNIT—13:14–15 [EBC]. The topic is a welcome extended at Antioch.

13:14 **But[a] they went-on[b] from Perga and came to Antioch-(in) Pisidia. And on-the Sabbath day they went into the synagogue[c] and sat-down.**
LEXICON—a. δέ (LN 89.124): 'but' [Bar, BECNT, LN; ESV, KJV, NASB, NLT, NRSV], not explicit [AB, CBC; CEV, GW, NCV, NET, NIV, REB, TEV]. This conjunction indicates a contrast [LN].
   b. aorist act. participle of διέρχομαι (LN 15.21) (BDAG 1.b.β. p. 244): 'to go on' [Bar; CEV, ESV, NASB, NIV, NRSV, TEV], 'to move on' [NET], 'to pass on' [BECNT], 'to travel through' [AB], 'to come, to go, to go through' [BDAG], 'to travel around through, to journey all through' [LN], 'to leave' [GW], 'to depart' [KJV], 'to continue' [CBC; NCV, REB], not explicit [NLT]. This verb means to travel around through an area, with the implication of both extensive and thorough movement throughout an area [LN]. It means to move within or through an area toward a destination [BDAG].
   c. συναγωγή (LN 7.20) (BDAG 2.a. p. 963): 'synagogue' [AB, Bar, BECNT, CBC, LN; all versions except CEV], 'Christian assembly place' [LN], 'Jewish meeting place' [CEV]. This noun denotes a building of assembly, associated with religious activity. Normally it was a building in which Jewish worship took place and in which the Law was taught [LN]. It denotes a place of assembly [BDAG].
QUESTION—Was this Antioch a different city from the Antioch mentioned in previous verses?
   This Antioch was an important city about 110 miles (177 km.) north of the city of Perga [BECNT, TRT]. It was located near the region of Pisidia in the Roman province of Galatia [AB, Bar, BECNT, CBC, EBC, NICNT, PNTC, TH, TNTC, TRT]. It was actually in Phrygia [Bar, BECNT, CBC, EBC, NAC, NICNT, PNTC, TNTC]. Paul and Barnabas started their missionary journey from the Antioch in Syria Province [TRT].
QUESTION—Which day was the Sabbath day?
   The Sabbath day was each Saturday, the day when Jews rested from work and worshipped God. God established the seventh day of each week as a day of rest for mankind, because He himself worked for six days creating the world and then rested the seventh day (Exodus 20:8–11) [TRT].

13:15 **After the reading of-the Law[a] and the Prophets,[b] the rulers-of-the-synagogue sent a message to them, saying, "Brothers,[c] if you have any word of-encouragement[d] for the people, say-(it)."**
LEXICON—a. νόμος (LN 33.58) (BDAG 3.a. p. 678): 'Law' [AB, Bar, BECNT, CBC; CEV, ESV, KJV, NASB, NET, NIV, NRSV, REB], 'Moses' Teachings' [GW], 'the law of Moses' [NCV, TEV], 'the books of Moses' [NLT], 'the sacred writings, the Law and the Prophets' [LN], 'sacred ordinance' [BDAG]. The idiom 'the Law and the Prophets' denotes all of the sacred writings of the OT, including the Law, the

Prophets, and the Writings [LN]. It denotes a collection of holy writings precious to God's people. In the strict sense the law=the Pentateuch, the work of Moses the lawgiver [BDAG].
b. προφήτης (LN 33.58) (BDAG 2. p. 891): 'Prophets' [AB, Bar, BECNT, CBC; all versions except NCV, TEV], 'the writings of the prophets' [NCV, TEV], 'the sacred writings, the Law and the Prophets' [LN]. The idiom 'the Law and the Prophets' denotes all of the sacred writings of the OT, including the Law, the Prophets, and the Writings [LN]. It denotes the writings of prophets [BDAG].
c. ἀδελφός (LN 11.25): 'brother' [AB, Bar, BECNT, LN; ESV, GW, KJV, NASB, NCV, NET, NIV, NLT, NRSV], 'friend' [CBC; CEV, REB, TEV], 'fellow countryman, fellow Jew' [LN]. This noun denotes a person belonging to the same socio-religious entity and being of the same age group as the so-called reference person [LN].
d. παράκλησις (LN 25.150) (BDAG 1. p. 766): 'encouragement' [BDAG, LN; ESV, GW, NIV, NLT, TEV], 'exhortation' [AB, Bar, BDAG, BECNT, CBC; KJV, NASB, NET, NRSV, REB]. The phrase 'if you have any word of encouragement for the people' is also translated 'if you have anything to say that will help the people' [CEV]. This noun is also translated as a verb: 'any message that will encourage the people' [NCV]. This noun denotes encouragement or consolation, either by verbal or non-verbal means [LN]. It denotes the act of emboldening another in belief or course of action [BDAG].

QUESTION—What is meant by 'the Law and the Prophets'?

The Law refers to the Law of Moses which is the law given through/by Moses [TH]. It was the Pentateuch [NICNT], the first five books of the Old Testament [TNTC]. The Prophets refers to the writings of the Prophets which are the books that the Prophets wrote [TH].

QUESTION—Who were the rulers of the synagogue?

The rulers of the synagogue were the elders who were elected to lead worship services in the synagogue [CBC, EBC, TNTC, TRT].

QUESTION—What is meant by 'the rulers of the synagogue sent a message to them'?

To send a message implies that the rulers of the synagogue sent someone over to Paul and his companions with the following message [NICNT, TRT]. It did not mean that the message was sent a long distance [TRT].

QUESTION—Who were the 'brothers' that the message was sent to?

In this context, 'brothers' did not refer to fellow believers but to fellow Jews [Bar, PNTC, TH].

DISCOURSE UNIT—13:16–41 [EBC, NICNT]. The topic is Paul's sermon in the synagogue at Antioch [EBC], Paul's synagogue address in Pisidian Antioch [NICNT].

13:16 So Paul stood-up, and motioning with-(his) hand said: "Men of Israel and you who fear^a God, listen.

LEXICON—a. pres. pass. participle of φοβέω (LN 53.58) (BDAG 2.a. p. 1061): 'to fear' [AB, Bar, BECNT; ESV, KJV, NASB, NET, NRSV], 'to reverence' [BDAG, LN], 'to worship' [CBC, LN; CEV, NCV, NIV, REB, TEV], 'to respect' [BDAG], not explicit [GW]. This verb is also translated as an adjective: 'God-fearing' [NLT]. This is a figurative extension of meaning of the verb 'to fear' and it means to have a profound reverence and respect for deity, with the implication of awe bordering on fear. In Acts 13:16 the phrase 'those who fear God' is essentially a technical phrase to identify the non-Jews who worshiped the God of the Jews. These would have been Gentiles who were 'God fearers' or 'worshipers of God' [LN]. It means to have a profound measure of respect for, with special reference to fear of offending [BDAG].

QUESTION—What was the reason that Paul had to motion with his hand?

The wave of one's hand was a typical Jewish gesture for inviting people to listen to him [EBC, NICNT]. Paul was calling for silence and attempting to get the attention of the people [BECNT, TH]. The people were probably talking to each other during this break in the worship service, so that Paul had to motion for silence [TRT].

QUESTION—Who were the people in the audience that were addressed as 'you who fear God?

This refers to the non-Jews/Gentiles who had put their trust in the God of Israel, worshipped God in synagogues, obeyed the Jewish Law but refused to be circumcised [AB, Bar, BECNT, EBC, NAC, PNTC, TRT]. They were known as the God-fearers [Bar, CBC, NICNT].

13:17 The God of-this people Israel chose our fathers^a and made- the people -great^b during their stay in (the)-land of-Egypt, and with an-uplifted^c arm he-led^d them out-of it.

LEXICON—a. πατήρ (LN 10.20): 'father' [AB, Bar, BECNT, CBC; ESV, KJV, NASB, NIV], 'ancestor' [LN; CEV, GW, NCV, NET, NLT, NRSV, TEV], 'forefather' [LN; REB]. This noun denotes a person several preceding generations removed from the reference person [LN].

b. aorist act. indic. of ὑψόω (LN 87.20) (BDAG 2. p. 1046): 'to make great' [ESV, NASB, NCV, NET, NRSV], 'to make multiply and grow strong' [NLT], 'to give high position to' [LN], 'to exalt' [Bar, BDAG, LN; KJV], 'to lift up' [BECNT], 'to make prosper' [NIV]. The clause 'The God...made the people great' is also translated 'he let our people prosper' [CEV], 'The God...made them a strong nation' [GW], 'he made them into a great people' [REB], 'The God...made the people a great nation' [TEV], 'he raised up the people (from their low estate)' [AB], 'he made them into a nation' [CBC]. This verb means to cause someone to have high status [LN]. It means to cause enhancement in honor, fame, position, power, or fortune. [BDAG].

c. ὑψηλός (LN 76.5) (BDAG 1. p. 1044): 'uplifted' [Bar, BECNT; ESV, NASB, NET, NRSV], 'powerful' [GW, NLT], 'high' [BDAG; KJV], 'outstretched' [CBC; REB], 'mighty power' [AB; CEV, NIV], 'great power' [LN; NCV, TEV], 'exalted power, marvelous power' [LN], 'tall' [BDAG]. The idiom 'exalted arm' or 'lifted up arm' pertains to great power, with the implication of an exalted quality [LN]. It pertains to considerable extension upward [BDAG].
d. aorist act. indic. of ἐξάγω (LN 15.174) (BDAG 1. p. 343): 'to lead out' [BDAG, BECNT, LN; CEV, ESV, NASB, NET, NIV, NLT, NRSV], 'to bring out' [AB, Bar, BDAG, CBC; KJV, GW, NCV, REB, TEV], 'to bring forth' [LN]. This verb means to lead or bring out of a structure or area [LN]. It means to conduct from an area [BDAG].

QUESTION—Who were the ones referred to as 'our fathers'?
Paul was talking to an audience that included Jews and Gentiles, but here 'our fathers' referred to the Israelites' fathers, not the Gentiles' [TRT].
QUESTION—What is meant by 'with an uplifted arm'?
'With uplifted arm' means 'with great power' [TH, TRT].

13:18 **And for about forty-years he-put-up-with**[a] **them in the wilderness.**[b]
TEXT—Manuscripts reading ἐτροποφόρησεν 'he put up with' are given a C rating by GNT to indicate that the Committee had difficulty making the decision. Some manuscripts have ἐτροφοφόρησεν 'he cared for'. This is followed by CEV.
LEXICON—a. aorist act. indic. of τροποφορέω (LN 25.173) (BDAG p. 1017): 'to put up with' [LN; ESV, GW, NASB, NET, NLT, NRSV], 'to be patient with' [NCV], 'to bear with, to be very patient with' [LN]. The phrase 'he put up with them' is also translated 'he took care of Israel/them' [AB; CEV], 'he nourished them' [Bar], 'suffered he their manners' [KJV], 'he endured their conduct' [NIV], 'he bore with them' [BECNT], 'he bore with their conduct' [CBC; REB], 'he endured them' [TEV]. This verb means to put up with someone or something, implying extensive patience [LN]. It means to bear with or put up with someone's manner, moods [BDAG].
b. ἔρημος (LN 1.86) (BDAG 2. p. 392): 'wilderness' [AB, Bar, BDAG, BECNT, LN; ESV, KJV, NASB, NET, NLT, NRSV], 'desert' [BDAG, CBC, LN; CEV, GW, NCV, NIV, REB, TEV], 'lonely place' [LN], 'grassland' [BDAG]. This noun denotes a largely uninhabited region, normally with sparse vegetation [LN]. It denotes an uninhabited region or locality. Here it refers to the Arabian Desert [BDAG].

13:19 **And after destroying**[a] **seven nations in (the)-land of-Canaan, he-gave- them their land -as-an-inheritance.**[b]
LEXICON—a. aorist act. participle of καθαιρέω (LN 20.42) (BDAG 2.a.β. p. 488): 'to destroy' [AB, BDAG, BECNT, LN; all versions except NIV, REB], 'to conquer' [BDAG, LN], 'to tear down, to overpower' [BDAG], 'to overthrow' [Bar, CBC; NIV, REB]. This verb means to destroy by

conquering and overpowering [LN]. It means to destroy by tearing down [BDAG].
   b. aorist act. indic. of κατακληρονομέω (LN 57.135) (BDAG 1. p. 518): 'to give/distribute for/as an/their inheritance' [AB, Bar, BECNT; ESV, GW, NASB, NET, NIV, NLT, NRSV], 'to make someone the recipient of a valuable gift' [LN], 'to give over as rightful possession' [BDAG]. The clause 'he gave them their land as an inheritance' is also translated 'He...gave their land to our people' [CEV], 'he divided their land to them by lot' [KJV], 'God...gave the land to his people' [NCV], 'whose lands he gave them to be their heritage' [CBC; REB], 'He...made his people the owners of the land' [TEV]. This verb means to cause someone to receive something of value as a gift [LN]. It means to assign possession of a country [BDAG].

QUESTION—Which were the seven nations?

The names of the seven nations are listed in Deuteronomy 7:1 [AB, Bar, BECNT, CBC, NICNT, PNTC, TNTC, TRT].

13:20 **All of this took about four-hundred and fifty years. And after these-things he-gave^a them judges until Samuel the prophet.^b** **13:21** **Then they-asked-for (a)-king, and God gave them Saul (the)-son of-Kish, (a)-man of (the)-tribe of-Benjamin, for forty years.**

LEXICON—a. aorist act. indic. of δίδωμι (LN 37.98) (BDAG 7. p. 242): 'to give' [AB, Bar, BECNT; all versions except REB], 'to appoint' [BDAG, CBC, LN; REB], 'to assign on behalf of' [LN]. This verb means to assign a person to a task as a particular benefit to others [LN]. It means to appoint to special responsibility. Here it refers to judges [BDAG].
   b. προφήτης (LN 53.79) (BDAG 1.a. p. 890): 'prophet' [AB, Bar, BDAG, BECNT, CBC, LN; all versions], 'inspired preacher' [LN]. This noun denotes one who proclaims inspired utterances on behalf of God [LN]. It denotes a person inspired to proclaim or reveal divine will or purpose [BDAG].

QUESTION—What events made up the 450 years?

The 450 years referred to the time Israel spent in Egypt (400 years), plus the time they travelled in the wilderness (40 years) and plus the time it took to take over Canaan, from the entry into Canaan to the dividing of the land among the tribes (10 years) [CBC, PNTC, TH, TNTC, TRT].

QUESTION—What was the role of these judges?

These judges were leaders that God raised up to help the people of Israel to defeat their enemies. It does not refer to people who sit in court rooms and judge cases in the contemporary sense of the word [TH, TRT].

QUESTION—What is meant by 'until Samuel the prophet'?

'Until Samuel the prophet' can be rendered as 'until the prophet Samuel was leader.' Samuel is regarded as the beginning point of a new period in the history of God's dealings with Israel [TH]. Samuel had been a priest, the first prophet/spokesman of God since Moses, and the last judge of Israel. He anointed Saul as the first king of Israel (1 Samuel 2:35; 3:20; 7:15–17) [Bar, CBC, TNTC, TRT].

QUESTION—What is meant by 'God gave them Saul'?

It means that God appointed Saul to be their king' [TH].

13:22 And (after)- he had-removed[a] him, he-raised-up[b] David to be their king, of-whom he also testified[c] and said, 'I-have-found David the-(son) of-Jesse (a)-man after my heart,[d] who will-do all my will.'

LEXICON—a. aorist act. participle of μεθίστημι (LN 15.9) (BDAG 1.b. p. 625): 'to remove' [AB, Bar, BDAG, BECNT, CBC, LN; all versions except NCV], 'to take away' [NCV], 'to depose' [BDAG]. This verb means to cause something to be moved from one place to another [LN]. It means to remove someone from his place [BDAG].

b. aorist act. indic. of ἐγείρω (LN 13.83) (BDAG 5. p. 271): 'to raise up' [Bar, BDAG, BECNT, LN; ESV, KJV, NASB, NET], 'to set up' [CBC], 'to raise' [AB], 'to cause to exist, to provide' [LN], 'to bring into being' [BDAG], 'to appoint' [REB]. The phrase 'he raised up David to be their king' is also translated 'God…let David rule' [CEV], 'God/he…made David their king' [GW, NCV, NIV, NRSV, TEV], 'God…replaced him with David [NLT]. This verb means to cause to come into existence [BDAG, LN].

c. aorist act. participle of μαρτυρέω (LN 33.263) (BDAG 2.a. p. 618): 'to testify' [BECNT; ESV, NASB, NET, NIV], 'to speak favorably' [GW], 'to speak well of' [BDAG, LN], 'to testify favorably, to approve' [BDAG], 'to approve of' [LN]. The phrase 'of whom he also testified' is also translated 'God said about him' [CEV, NCV, TEV], 'a man about whom God said' [NLT]. This verb is also translated as a noun: 'he…gave him this testimony' [AB], 'of whom he said by way of testimony' [Bar], 'In his testimony about him' [NRSV], 'to whom also he gave testimony' [KJV], 'with this commendation' [REB], 'giving him his approval' [CBC]. This verb means to speak well of a person on the basis of personal experience [LN]. It means to affirm in a supportive manner [BDAG].

d. καρδία (LN 26.3) (BDAG 1.b.ε. p. 509): 'heart' [AB, Bar, BDAG, BECNT, CBC, LN; ESV, GW, KJV, NASB, NET, NIV, NLT, NRSV, REB], 'inner self, mind' [LN], 'wishes, desires' [BDAG]. The clause 'David the son of Jesse a man after my heart' is also translated 'David the son of Jesse is the kind of person who pleases me most' [CEV], 'David son of Jesse the kind of man I want' [NCV], 'David son of Jesse is the kind of man I like' [TEV]. This noun is a figurative extension of meaning of 'heart' and denotes the causative source of a person's psychological life in its various aspects, but with special emphasis upon thoughts [LN]. It denotes the center and source of the emotions [BDAG].

QUESTION—What is meant by 'after he had removed him'?

It means when God had caused Saul to no longer to be king [TH].

13:23 From this man's offspring, according-to (the)-promise, God has brought to-Israel (a)-Savior, Jesus. **13:24** Before his coming, John had proclaimed[a] a baptism of repentance[b] to all the people of Israel.

LEXICON—a. aorist act. participle of προκηρύσσω (LN 33.257) (BDAG p. 871): 'to proclaim' [Bar, CBC; ESV, NASB, NET, NRSV, REB], 'to preach' [AB, BECNT; KJV, NCV, NIV, NLT, TEV], 'to preach beforehand' [LN], 'to proclaim publicly' [BDAG], 'to tell' [CEV, GW]. This verb means to preach in anticipation or in advance [LN].

  b. μετάνοια (LN 41.52) (BDAG p. 640): 'repentance' [AB, Bar, BDAG, BECNT, CBC, LN; ESV, GW, KJV, NASB, NET, NIV, NRSV, REB], 'conversion' [BDAG]. The clause 'John had proclaimed a baptism of repentance to all the people of Israel' is also translated 'John was telling everyone in Israel to turn back to God and be baptized' [CEV], 'John…preached that all the people of Israel needed to repent of their sins and turn to God and be baptized' [NLT], 'John preached to all the people of Israel that they should turn from their sins and be baptized' [TEV]. The phrase 'a baptism of repentance' is also translated 'a baptism of changed hearts and lives' [NCV]. This noun denotes a complete change of thought and attitude with regard to sin and righteousness [LN].

QUESTION—What was Jesus' role as a 'Savior'?

His role was being a deliverer, the one who saves the people of Israel [BECNT, TH].

QUESTION—When had Jesus made this promise?

Jesus had long ago made this promise to the ancestors of the Israelites [TH].

QUESTION—What does 'his coming' refer to?

Here 'his coming' referred to the beginning of Jesus' ministry, not his birth [TRT].

QUESTION—What is meant by the Greek construction 'a baptism of repentance'?

This is essentially a noun phrase which has been constructed by what grammarians call transformations from a verb expression 'repent and be baptized' [PNTC, TH]. The closest equivalent of 'repentance' is 'to change and turn from one's sins' [TH].

QUESTION—What is meant by 'all the people of Israel'?

This does not mean that John preached to each and every Israelite. It means that his message was directed to all of them [TH]. 'All the people' is emphatic [Bar], and it is frequently used in the Old Testament with the meaning 'many people.' In most languages a term for 'all' is also used in the relative sense to mean 'very many' [TH, TRT].

13:25 And as John was-finishing his course, he-said, 'What do-you-suppose that I am? I am- not -(he). But behold,[a] after me one-is-coming, the sandals of-whose feet I-am not worthy[b] to-untie.[c]'

LEXICON—a. ἰδού (LN 91.13): 'behold' [ESV, KJV, NASB], 'look' [LN; NET], 'see' [Bar], 'listen' [LN; TEV], 'pay attention, come now' [LN],

not explicit [AB, BECNT, CBC; CEV, GW, NCV, NIV, NLT, NRSV, REB]. This particle functions as a prompter of attention, also serving to emphasize the statement which follows [LN].
  b. ἄξιος (LN 65.17) (BDAG 2.a. p. 94): 'worthy' [AB, Bar, BDAG, BECNT, LN; ESV, KJV, NASB, NCV, NET, NIV, NLT, NRSV, REB], 'fit' [BDAG, CBC], 'deserving' [BDAG], 'comparable, of comparable value' [LN], 'good enough' [CEV, GW, TEV]. This adjective pertains to having a relatively high degree of comparable merit or worth [LN]. It pertains to being correspondingly fitting or appropriate [BDAG].
  c. aorist act. infin. of λύω (LN 18.18) (BDAG 2.a. p. 607): 'to untie' [AB, BDAG, BECNT, LN; CEV, ESV, GW, NASB, NCV, NET, NIV, NLT, NRSV], 'to unfasten' [CBC; REB], 'to loosen' [LN], 'to loose' [Bar, BDAG; KJV]. The phrase 'the sandals of whose feet I am not worthy to untie' is also translated 'I am not good enough to take his sandals off his feet' [TEV]. This verb means to reverse the result of tying by untying [LN]. It means to set free something tied or similarly constrained [BDAG].
QUESTION—What is meant by 'his course'?
  In this context 'course' is an idiom that refers to his career, not an actual course or a class at school [TRT]. It refers to his mission/task [BECNT, TH], his work for God [TRT].
QUESTION—Since untying someone's sandals was regarded to be a menial task of a slave [BECNT, TH], why did John say that he was unworthy to untie Jesus' sandals?
  The focus was on how great the Messiah was, not on how lowly John was. John meant 'The Messiah is so great that I (John) am less than a slave compared to Him!' [PNTC, TRT]. It does not imply that John had done something wrong [TRT].

13:26 "Men, brothers,[a] sons of-(the)-family of-Abraham, and those among you who fear[b] God, to-us has-been-sent the message[c] of-this salvation.[d]
TEXT—Manuscripts reading ἡμῖν 'to us' are given a B rating by GNT to indicate it was regarded to be almost certain. Some manuscripts have 'to you'. This is followed by KJV.
LEXICON—a. ἀδελφός (LN 11.25): 'brother' [AB, Bar, BECNT, CBC, LN; all versions except CEV, TEV], 'fellow Israelite' [TEV], not explicit [CEV], 'fellow countryman, fellow Jew, associate' [LN]. This noun denotes a person belonging to the same socio-religious entity and being of the same age group as the so-called reference person [LN].
  b. pres. pass. participle of φοβέω (LN 53.58) (BDAG 2.a. p. 1061): 'to fear' [AB, Bar, BECNT; ESV, KJV, NASB, NET, NRSV], 'to reverence' [LN], 'to worship' [LN; CEV, NCV, REB, TEV], 'to respect' [BDAG], 'to revere' [CBC], not explicit [GW]. This verb is also translated as an adjective: 'God-fearing' [NIV, NLT]. This verb is a figurative extension of meaning of φοβέομαι 'to fear' and means to have profound reverence

and respect for deity, with the implication of awe bordering on fear [LN]. It means to have a profound measure of respect for, with special reference to fear of offending [BDAG].
  c. λόγος (LN 33.260) (BDAG 1.a.β. p. 600): 'message' [Bar, BECNT, CBC; all versions except KJV, NCV], 'word' [AB, BDAG; KJV], 'news' [NCV], 'what is preached, gospel' [LN]. This noun denotes the content of what is preached about Christ or about the good news [LN]. It denotes a communication whereby the mind finds expression [BDAG].
  d. σωτηρία (LN 21.26) (BDAG 2. p. 986): 'salvation' [AB, Bar, BDAG, BECNT, CBC, LN; all versions except CEV, GW]. This noun is also translated as a verb: 'this message about how to be saved' [CEV], 'the message that God saves people' [GW]. This noun denotes the process of being saved [LN]. It denotes salvation with focus on transcendent aspects [BDAG].

QUESTION—Who were the 'brothers' being addressed?
  In this context, 'brothers' referred to his fellow Jews, the sons of the family of Abraham' [BECNT, NAC, TRT]. The plural word 'brothers' refers to both the brothers and sisters of the children of Abraham [PNTC].

QUESTION—Who are included in the reference to 'us' to whom the message of this salvation has been sent?
  It refers to both the Jews and the God-fearing Gentiles to whom the message of salvation had been sent [AB, BECNT, EBC, NICNT, PNTC, TH].

QUESTION—What is meant by 'the message of this salvation'?
  It is the message concerning how God saves people [TH], a message of deliverance and enablement as vv. 23, 34–49 show [BECNT].

13:27 For those who live[a] in Jerusalem and their rulers, because they did-not-recognize[b] him nor understand the utterances of-the prophets,[c] which are-read every Sabbath, fulfilled-(them)[d] by condemning[e] him.

LEXICON—a. pres. act. participle of κατοικέω (LN 85.69) (BDAG 1.a. p. 534): 'to live' [AB, BDAG, BECNT, LN; ESV, GW, NASB, NCV, NET, TEV], 'to dwell' [BDAG, LN; KJV], 'to reside' [BDAG, LN], 'to settle down' [BDAG]. The phrase 'those who live in Jerusalem' is also translated 'The people of/in Jerusalem' [CBC; CEV, NIV, NLT, REB]. This verb is also translated as a noun: 'the inhabitants/residents' [Bar; NRSV]. This verb means to live or dwell in a place in an established or settled manner [LN]. It means to live in a locality for any length of time [LN].
  b. aorist act. participle of ἀγνοέω (LN 30.38) (BDAG 1.b. p. 13): 'to not recognize' [Bar, BECNT, CBC; ESV, NASB, NET, NIV, NLT, NRSV, REB], 'to not know' [AB, BDAG; GW, KJV, TEV], 'to be ignorant of' [BDAG], 'to not realize' [CEV, NCV], 'to pay no attention to, to ignore' [LN]. This verb means to refuse to think about or pay attention to [LN]. It means to be uninformed about [BDAG].

c. προφήτης (LN 53.79): 'prophet' [AB, Bar, BECNT, CBC, LN; all versions], 'inspired preacher' [LN]. This noun denotes one who proclaims inspired utterances on behalf of God [LN].
d. aorist act. indic. of πληρόω (LN 13.106) (BDAG 4.a. p. 829): 'to fulfill' [Bar, BDAG, BECNT, CBC, LN; ESV, GW, KJV, NASB, NET, NIV, NLT, NRSV, REB], 'to cause to happen, to make happen' [LN], not explicit [CEV]. The phrase 'they...fulfilled them' is also translated 'they made them come true' [NCV], 'they made the prophets' words come true' [TEV], 'they caused the words of the prophets...to be proved true' [AB]. This verb means to cause to happen, with the implication of fulfilling some purpose [LN]. It means to bring to a designed end, here referring to the fulfillment of divine predictions or promises [BDAG].
e. aorist act. participle of κρίνω (LN 56.30) (BDAG 5.a.α. p. 568): 'to condemn' [AB, BDAG, BECNT, CBC, LN; all versions except NCV], 'to judge as guilty' [LN], 'to judge, to decide, to hale before a court, to hand over for judicial punishment' [BDAG]. The phrase 'they...fulfilled them by condemning him' is also translated 'they made them come true when they said Jesus was guilty' [NCV]. This verb is also translated as a noun: 'sat in judgement' [Bar]. This verb means to judge a person to be guilty and liable to punishment [LN]. It means to engage in a judicial process [BDAG].

QUESTION—What is meant by 'they did not recognize him'?
It means that they had not recognized that Jesus was the Savior/Messiah sent by God [BECNT, NAC, NICNT, TH, TNTC], and they did not recognize Jesus' work [BECNT].

QUESTION—What is meant by those people in Israel 'fulfilling' the utterances of the prophets?
It means that those people and rulers in Jerusalem condemned Jesus to death just as the prophets had said they would [TRT].

13:28 **And though they found^a in him no guilt worthy of-death, they-asked Pilate to have him executed.^b**

LEXICON—a. aorist act. participle of εὑρίσκω (LN 27.1) (BDAG 2. p. 412): 'to find' [AB, Bar, BDAG, BECNT, CBC; all versions], 'to learn, to find out' [LN], to discover' [BDAG, LN]. This verb means to learn something previously not known, frequently involving an element of surprise [LN]. It means to discover intellectually through reflection, observation, examination, or investigation [BDAG].
b. aorist pass. infin. of ἀναιρέω (LN 20.71) (BDAG 2. p. 64): 'to be executed' [AB, CBC, LN; ESV, GW, NASB, NET, NIV, REB], 'to be killed' [Bar, BECNT, LN; CEV, NCV, NLT, NRSV], 'to be done away with, to be destroyed' [BDAG], 'to be slain' [KJV], 'to be put to death' [TEV]. This verb means to get rid of someone by execution [BDAG, LN], often with legal or quasi-legal procedures [LN].

13:29 And when they-had-carried-out[a] all that was-written of him, they took-(him)-down[b] from the tree[c] and laid-(him)[d] in (a)-tomb.[e]

LEXICON—a. aorist act. indic. of τελέω (LN 13.126) (BDAG 2. p. 998): 'to carry out' [BDAG, CBC; ESV, NASB, NIV, NRSV, REB], 'to fulfill' [AB, BDAG, BECNT, LN; KJV], 'to finish' [GW], 'to accomplish' [BDAG, LN; NET], 'to complete' [Bar], 'to make happen, to bring to fruition' [LN], 'to perform, to keep' [BDAG], 'to do' [NCV, NLT, TEV]. The clause 'they had carried out all that was written' is also translated 'They did exactly what the Scriptures said they would' [CEV]. This verb means to cause to happen for some end result [LN]. It means to carry out an obligation or demand [BDAG].
- b. aorist act. participle of καθαιρέω (LN 15.199) (BDAG 1. p. 488): 'to take down' [Bar, BDAG, CBC, LN; all versions except CEV], 'to bring down' [BDAG, LN], 'to lower' [BDAG]. This verb is also translated as a passive verb: 'he was taken down' [AB; CEV], 'taking him down' [BECNT]. This verb means to bring something down from one point to another [LN]. It means to bring down from one level to another [BDAG].
- c. ξύλον (LN 6.28) (BDAG 2.c. p. 685): 'tree' [Bar, BECNT; ESV, KJV, NIV, NRSV], 'cross' [AB, BDAG, LN; CEV, GW, NASB, NCV, NET, NLT, TEV], 'gibbet' [CBC; REB]. This noun is a figurative extension of meaning of the word for 'wood' and here it refers to an instrument of execution. In the NT contexts it refers to the cross on which Jesus was crucified [LN]. It denotes an object made of wood and here it refers to the cross, a wooden structure used for crucifixion [BDAG].
- d. aorist act. indic. of τίθημι (LN 85.32) (BDAG 1.a.β. p. 1003): 'to lay' [AB, Bar, BDAG, BECNT, CBC; ESV, KJV, NASB, NCV, NIV, NRSV, REB], 'to put' [BDAG, LN], 'to place' [LN; CEV, GW, NET, NLT, TEV]. This verb means to put or place in a particular location. Here it refers to laying something in a tomb [BDAG, LN].
- e. μνημεῖον (LN 7.75) (BDAG 2. p. 656): 'tomb' [AB, Bar, BDAG, BECNT, CBC, LN; all versions except KJV], 'grave' [BDAG, LN], 'sepulchre' [KJV]. This noun denotes a construction for the burial of the dead [LN].

QUESTION— Who do the pronouns 'they' refer to?

The first 'they' referred to the Jews and their leaders who condemned Jesus to death. The second 'they' referred to Jesus' followers like Joseph of Arimathea who asked for Jesus' body for burial [AB, Bar, BECNT, NAC, PNTC, TH].

13:30 But[a] God raised[b] him from (the)-dead, **13:31** and for many days he appeared[c] to-those who had-come-up[d] with-him from Galilee to Jerusalem, who are now his witnesses[e] to the people.

LEXICON—a. δέ (LN 89.124): 'but' [AB, Bar, BECNT, CBC, LN; all versions], 'on the other hand' [LN]. This conjunction indicates a contrast [LN].

b. aorist act. indic. of ἐγείρω (LN 23.94) (BDAG 6. p. 271): 'to raise' [AB, Bar, BECNT, CBC; all versions except GW, NCV], 'to raise up' [BDAG; NCV], 'to raise to life, to make live again' [LN]. The clause 'God raised him from the dead' is also translated 'God brought him back to life' [GW]. This verb means to cause someone to live again after having once died [LN]. It means to cause to return to life [BDAG].
c. aorist pass. indic. of ὁράω (LN 24.1) (BDAG A.1.d. p. 719): 'to appear' [AB, Bar, BDAG, BECNT, CBC; CEV, ESV, GW, NASB, NET, NLT, NRSV, REB, TEV], 'to be seen' [LN; KJV, NIV]. The phrase 'for many days he appeared to those' is also translated 'for many days, those...saw him' [NCV]. This verb means to see [LN]. In the passive voice it means to appear, to become visible [BDAG].
d. aorist act. participle of συναναβαίνω (LN 15.153) (BDAG p. 965): 'to come up' [Bar, BECNT, CBC; ESV, KJV, NASB, NRSV, REB], 'to go' [CEV, NCV, NLT], 'to come' [AB; GW], 'to travel' [NIV, TEV], 'to come/go up with' [BDAG], 'to travel with, to go or come up together with' [LN], 'to accompany' [LN; NET]. This verb means to accompany in going up to [LN].
e. μάρτυς (LN 33.270) (BDAG 2.c. p. 620): 'witness' [AB, Bar, BDAG, BECNT, CBC, LN; all versions except CEV], 'testifier' [BDAG], 'one who testifies' [LN]. The phrase 'who are now his witnesses to the people' is also translated 'they are telling our people about him' [CEV]. This noun denotes a person who witnesses [LN]. It denotes one who affirms or attests. Here it refers to witnesses who bear a divine message [BDAG].

QUESTION—What is meant by 'God raised him from the dead'?
It refers to Jesus' physical resurrection [NAC, PNTC]. It means that God raised Jesus from the state of being dead, he brought him back to life, he caused him to live again [TH, TRT].

QUESTION—Who were the people who had come up with Jesus?
'The people' normally referred to the people of Israel. However, here it probably referred to all of God's people including Jews and Gentiles. A similar case as found in Acts 10:41–42 [TNTC, TRT].

13:32 And we preach- to-you -the-good-news[a]-(about) the promise made to the fathers,[b]

LEXICON—a. pres. mid. participle of εὐαγγελίζω (LN 33.215) (BDAG 2.a.α. p. 402): 'to preach the good news' [NASB], 'to tell the good news' [LN; CEV, GW, NCV, NIV], 'to announce the gospel' [LN], 'to proclaim the gospel' [BDAG], 'to proclaim the good news' [BECNT; NET], 'to bring the/this good news' [Bar; ESV, NLT, NRSV, TEV], 'to give the good news' [CBC; REB], 'to tell' [AB]. The phrase 'we preach to you the good news' is also translated 'we declare unto you glad tidings' [KJV]. This verb means to communicate good news concerning something and in the NT it is a particular reference to the gospel message about Jesus [LN]. It means to proclaim the divine message of salvation [BDAG].

b. πατήρ (LN 10.20): 'father' [AB, Bar, BECNT, CBC; ESV, KJV, NASB, NIV, REB], 'ancestor' [LN; CEV, GW, NCV, NET, NLT, NRSV, TEV], 'forefather' [LN]. This noun denotes a person several preceding generations removed from the reference person [LN].

13:33 this God has-fulfilled[a] to-us their children[b] by raising[c] Jesus, as also it-is-written in the second Psalm, "'You are my Son, today I have-begotten[d] you.'

LEXICON—a. perf. act. indic. of ἐκπληρόω (LN 13.106) (BDAG p. 308): 'to fulfill' [AB, Bar, BDAG, BECNT, CBC, LN; ESV, GW, KJV, NASB, NET, NIV, NLT, NRSV, REB], 'to cause to happen, to make happen' [LN]. The phrase 'this God has fulfilled to us' is also translated 'he has kept this promise to us' [CEV], 'God has made this promise come true for us' [NCV], 'what God promised...he has now done for us' [TEV]. This verb means to cause to happen, with the implication of fulfilling some purpose [LN]. It means to cause to happen, with the implication that something is brought to fruition [BDAG].

b. τέκνον (LN 10.28) (BDAG 2. p. 994): 'children' [AB, Bar, BECNT, CBC; ESV, KJV, NASB, NCV, NET, NIV, NRSV, REB], 'descendants' [BDAG, LN; GW, NLT, TEV], 'posterity' [BDAG, LN], 'offspring' [LN], not explicit [CEV]. This noun denotes successive following generations of those who are biologically related to a reference person [LN]. It denotes descendants from a common ancestor [BDAG].

c. aorist act. participle of ἀνίστημι (LN 23.94) (BDAG 2. p. 83): 'to raise' [AB, BDAG, BECNT; ESV, NET, NLT, NRSV], 'to raise up' [Bar, BDAG; KJV, NASB, NIV], 'to raise to life' [LN; TEV], 'to make live again' [LN], 'to bring back to life' [GW], 'to raise from the dead' [CBC; NCV, REB], not explicit [CEV]. This verb means to cause someone to live again after having once died [LN]. It means to raise up by bringing back to life [BDAG].

d. perf. act. indic. of γεννάω (LN 23.58) (BDAG 1.b. p. 193): 'to beget' [Bar, BDAG, BECNT, CBC, LN; ESV, KJV, NASB, NRSV, REB], 'to father' [NET], 'to be the father of, to procreate' [LN]. The clause 'I have begotten you' is also translated 'I have become your Father' [CEV, GW, NCV, NIV, NLT, TEV], 'I have brought you into the world' [AB]. This verb means the male role in causing the conception and birth of a child [LN]. It means to become the parent of by exercising the role of a parental figure [BDAG].

QUESTION—In the quote from the second Psalm, who are being referred to by the words 'you', 'my' and 'I'?

In this quote, 'you' refers to Jesus while 'my' and 'I' refer to God [Bar, BECNT, CBC, EBC, NAC, NICNT, PNTC, TH, TNTC, TRT].

QUESTION—In what way had Jesus been begotten in this Psalm?
Psalm 2 was written to celebrate that God has appointed someone to be king over his people. The Psalm also applies to the Christ/Messiah who will rule God's people forever [TRT].
1. It refers to the day on which God anointed Jesus with the Holy Spirit and power and called him to his messianic mission [NICNT]. It is highly unlikely that the early church saw the resurrection as a begetting and then used this idea to argue that Jesus became God's Son at the resurrection. On the contrary, it was because he was known to be God's Son that Psalm 2 could be applied to him and then seen as foreshadowing the resurrection [TNTC].
2. Paul seems to have been implying that 'today' refers to the day when Jesus' was resurrected [AB, BECNT, NAC]. Here Paul appeals to the promise in Isa. 55:3 that refers to the raising up of Jesus to be his people's Messiah rather than his being raised from the dead [NICNT].

13:34 And as for the fact that he-raised him from (the)-dead, no-longer^a to-return^b to decay,^{c} he-has-spoken in this way, "'I-will-give^d you the holy^e and sure^f blessings of-David.'

LEXICON—a. μηκέτι (LN 67.130) (BDAG c. p. 647): 'no longer' [BDAG, LN; NASB], 'not from now on' [BDAG], 'no more' [Bar, BECNT; ESV, KJV, NRSV], 'never' [GW, NCV, NIV, REB, TEV], 'never again' [CBC; NET]. The clause 'he raised him from the dead, no longer to return to decay' is also translated 'God raised Jesus from death and will never let his body decay' [CEV], 'God had promised to raise him from the dead, not leaving him to rot in the grave' [NLT]. The phrase 'no longer to return' is also translated 'he shall not later return' [AB]. This adverb pertains to the extension of time up to a point but not beyond [LN].
b. pres. act. infin. of ὑποστρέφω (LN 13.24) (BDAG p. 1041): 'to return' [AB, Bar, BDAG, BECNT; ESV, KJV, NASB, NRSV], 'to return to again, to again be in' [LN], 'to turn back' [BDAG], 'to go back' [NCV], 'to revert' [CBC], not explicit [CEV, GW, NIV, NLT, REB, TEV]. The phrase 'no longer to return' is also translated 'never again to be in' [NET]. This verb means to be again in a former state [LN].
c. διαφθορά (LN 23.205) (BDAG p. 239): 'decay' [LN; NASB, NET], 'corruption' [AB, Bar, BDAG, BECNT, CBC; ESV, KJV, NRSV, REB], 'destruction' [BDAG], 'dust' [NCV]. This noun is also translated as a verb: 'never let his body decay' [CEV], 'Jesus' body never decayed' [GW], 'never to decay' [NIV], 'never to rot' [TEV], 'not leaving him to rot' [NLT]. This noun denotes the state of rotting or decaying, in reference to organic matter [LN]. It is the condition or state of rotting or decaying [BDAG].
d. fut. act. indic. of δίδωμι (LN 57.71): 'to give' [Bar, BECNT, CBC, LN; all versions except CEV]. The phrase 'I will give you' is also translated 'I

will make to you' [CEV], 'For you I will fulfill' [AB]. This verb means to give an object, usually implying value [LN].
  e. ὅσιος (LN 33.290): 'holy' [AB, Bar, BECNT, CBC; CEV, ESV, NASB, NCV, NET, NIV, NRSV, REB], 'sacred' [NLT, TEV], 'divine promises, promises from God' [LN], not explicit [KJV]. The clause 'I will give you the holy and sure blessing of David' is also translated 'I will give you the enduring love promised to David' [GW]. This adjective pertains to the divine matters which have been promised [LN].
  f. πιστός (LN 71.17) (BDAG 1.b. p. 821): 'sure' [Bar, BECNT, CBC, LN; ESV, KJV, NASB, NCV, NIV, REB, TEV], 'trustworthy' [BDAG; NET], 'faithful, dependable, inspiring trust/faith' [BDAG], not explicit [CEV, NLT, NRSV]. The clause 'I will give you the holy and sure blessing of David' is also translated 'I will give you the enduring love promised to David' [GW], 'For you I will fulfill the holy and solemn pledges to David' [AB]. This adjective pertains to being sure, with the implication of being fully trustworthy [LN]. It pertains to being worthy of belief or trust of things, especially of words [BDAG].

QUESTION—What is meant by him 'no longer to return to decay'?
  It means that Jesus will never die again [PNTC, TH]. This quote is from the Septuagint (the Old Testament in Greek) of Isaiah 55:3. The 'you' in 'I will give you …' is plural and emphatic; it refers to those who put their trust in Jesus [Bar, BECNT, CBC, EBC, NAC, NICNT, PNTC, TH, TNTC]. The last two sentences don't seem to apply to the question.

13:35 Therefore he-says also in another-(psalm), "'You-will- not -let[a] your Holy-One[b] experience decay.'
LEXICON—a. fut. act. indic. of δίδωμι (LN 13.142) (BDAG 13. p. 243): 'to let' [BECNT, CBC; CEV, ESV, NCV, NIV, NRSV, REB], 'to allow' [AB, Bar, BDAG, LN; GW, NASB, NLT, TEV], 'to permit' [NET], 'to suffer' [KJV], 'to grant' [BDAG, LN]. This verb means to grant someone the opportunity or occasion to do something [LN]. It means to grant by formal action [BDAG].
  b. ὅσιος (LN 88.24) (BDAG 1.b. p. 728): 'Holy One' [AB, Bar, BECNT; all versions except REB, TEV], 'faithful servant' [REB, TEV], 'loyal servant' [CBC], 'holy' [BDAG, LN], 'pure, divine' [LN], 'devout, pious, pleasing to God' [BDAG]. This adjective pertains to being holy in the sense of superior moral qualities and possessing certain essentially divine qualities in contrast with what is human [LN]. It pertains to being without fault relative to deity and here refers to the qualities of Christ. [BDAG].

QUESTION—In the quotation, who does 'You and 'your' refer to?
  In this quote from Psalm 16:10, 'You' and 'your' referred to God [Bar, BECNT, CBC, EBC, NAC, NICNT, PNTC, TH, TNTC, TRT].

QUESTION—Who is God's Holy One'?
  'God's Holy One' is a Christological title [PNTC], another title applied to Jesus in this speech alongside 'Savior' and 'Son' [Bar, BECNT, TNTC].

13:36 For David, after he had-served[a] the purpose[b] of-God in-his-own generation,[c] fell-asleep[d] and was-laid[e] with his fathers[f] and experienced decay,

LEXICON—a. aorist act. participle of ὑπηρετέω (LN 35.19) (BDAG p. 1035): 'to serve' [AB, Bar, BDAG, BECNT, CBC, LN; ESV, GW, KJV, NASB, NET, NIV, NRSV, REB, TEV], 'to render service, to help' [LN], 'to be helpful' [BDAG]. The phrase 'he had served the purpose of God' is also translated 'he obeyed God' [CEV], 'David did God's will' [NCV], 'David had done the will of God' [NLT]. This verb means to render assistance or help by performing certain duties, often of a humble or menial nature [LN]. It means to render service [BDAG].
  b. βουλή (LN 30.57) (BDAG 2.b. p. 182): 'purpose' [CBC, LN; ESV, NASB, NET, NIV, NRSV, REB, TEV], 'will' [AB, Bar; GW, KJV, NCV, NLT], 'counsel' [BECNT], 'plan, intention' [LN], 'resolution, decision' [BDAG], not explicit [CEV]. This noun denotes that which has been purposed and planned [LN]. It denotes that which is of the divine will [BDAG].
  c. γενεά (LN 11.4) (BDAG 2. p. 192): 'generation' [AB, Bar, BDAG, BECNT, CBC; ESV, KJV, NASB, NET, NIV, NLT, NRSV, REB], 'contemporaries' [BDAG], 'the people of his time' [GW], 'those of the same time, those of the same generation' [LN], not explicit [CEV, NCV]. The phrase 'in his own generation' is also translated 'in his own time' [TEV]. This noun denotes people living at the same time and belonging to the same reproductive age [LN]. This noun denotes the sum total of those born at the same time, expanded to include all those living at a given time and frequently defined in terms of specific characteristics [BDAG].
  d. aorist pass. (deponent = act.) indic. of κοιμάομαι (LN 23.104) (BDAG 2.a. p. 551): 'to fall asleep' [AB, Bar, BECNT; ESV, NASB, NIV], 'to die' [CBC; CEV, GW, NCV, NET, NLT, NRSV, REB, TEV], 'to be dead' [BDAG, LN], 'to have died' [LN], 'to sleep' [BDAG]. This verb is also translated 'fell on sleep' [KJV]. This verb is a figurative extension of the meaning of 'to sleep', and is a euphemistic expression for the state of being dead [LN]. The Greek word κοιμάω means to be dead [BDAG].
  e. aorist pass. indic. of προστίθημι (LN 52.7) (BDAG 1.b. p. 885): 'to be laid' [AB, BECNT; ESV, GW, KJV, NASB, NRSV], 'to be buried' [LN; CEV, NCV, NET, NIV, NLT, TEV], 'to be gathered' [CBC; REB], 'to be added' [Bar, BDAG], 'to be put' [BDAG]. The idiom 'to place with his fathers' means to carry out a burial procedure [LN]. It means to add to something that is already present or exists and here it refers to persons who are added to a group already existing or who are attached to an individual to whom they henceforth belong [BDAG].
  f. πατήρ (LN 52.7): 'father' [AB, Bar, BECNT, CBC; ESV, KJV, NASB, NIV, REB], 'ancestor' [GW, NCV, NET, NLT, NRSV, TEV], 'to bury' [LN]. The phrase 'was laid with his fathers' is also translated 'was buried

in the family grave' [CEV]. The idiom 'to place with his fathers' means to carry out a burial procedure [LN].

13:37 but he whom God raised-up^a did- not -experience decay.
LEXICON—a. aorist act. indic. of ἐγείρω (LN 23.94) (BDAG 6. p. 271): 'to raise up' [Bar, BDAG, BECNT, CBC; ESV, NET, NRSV, REB], 'to raise' [AB; NASB, NLT], 'to raise again' [KJV], 'to raise from death' [CEV, TEV], 'to raise from the dead' [NCV, NIV], 'to bring back to life' [GW], 'to raise to life, to make live again' [LN]. This verb means to cause someone to live again after having once died [LN]. It means to cause to return to life [BDAG].
QUESTION—Who does 'he' whom God raised refer to?
In this verse 'he' refers to Jesus [AB, Bar, BECNT, TH, TRT].

13:38 Therefore let-it-be known^a to-you, brothers,^b that through this-man forgiveness^c of-sins is-proclaimed^d to-you,
LEXICON—a. γνωστός (LN 28.21) (BDAG 1.a. p. 204): 'known' [AB, Bar, BDAG, BECNT, LN; ESV, KJV, NASB, NET, NRSV], not explicit [CEV, GW, NLT]. The phrase 'let it be known to you, men, brothers' is also translated 'Brothers, understand what we are telling you' [NCV], 'my brothers, I want you to know' [NIV], 'you must understand, my brothers' [CBC; REB], 'All of you, my fellow Israelites, are to know for sure' [TEV]. This adjective pertains to that which is known [LN]. It pertains to being familiar or known [BDAG].
b. ἀδελφός (LN 11.25): 'brother' [AB, Bar, BECNT, CBC, LN; all versions except CEV, TEV], 'fellow Israelite' [TEV], 'fellow countryman, fellow Jew, associate' [LN], 'friend' [CEV]. This noun denotes a person belonging to the same socio-religious entity and being of the same age group as the so-called reference person [LN].
c. ἄφεσις (LN 40.8) (BDAG 2. p. 155): 'forgiveness' [AB, Bar, BECNT, CBC, LN; all versions except CEV, GW], 'pardon, cancellation' [BDAG]. The phrase 'through this man forgiveness of sins is proclaimed to you' is also translated 'the message is that Jesus can forgive your sins' [CEV], 'I'm telling you that through Jesus your sins can be forgiven' [GW]. This noun denotes the removal of guilt resulting from wrongdoing [LN]. It denotes the act of freeing from an obligation, guilt, or punishment [BDAG].
d. pres. pass. indic. of καταγγέλλω (LN 33.204) (BDAG a. p. 515): 'to proclaim' [Bar, BDAG, BECNT, CBC; ESV, NASB, NET, NIV, NLT, NRSV, REB], 'to announce' [BDAG], 'to tell' [GW, NCV], 'to preach' [AB; KJV, TEV], 'to proclaim throughout, to announce, to speak out about' [LN], not explicit [CEV]. This verb means to announce, with focus upon the extent to which the announcement or proclamation extends [LN]. It means to make known in public, with the implication of broad dissemination [BDAG].

ACTS 13:38

QUESTION— Who are the 'brothers' being addressed?
Here the 'brothers' were the Jews and Gentiles, male and female whom he was addressing [BECNT, EBC, PNTC, TH, TNTC, TRT].

13:39 and by him everyone who believes[a] is-freed[b] from all-(things) from-which you-could not be-freed by (the)-law[c] of-Moses.
LEXICON—a. pres. act. participle of πιστεύω (LN 31.102) (BDAG 2.b. p. 817): 'to believe' [AB, Bar, BECNT; all versions except CEV, REB], 'to believe (in), to trust' [BDAG], 'to be a believer' [LN]. The phrase 'everyone who believes' is also translated 'everyone who has faith' [CBC; REB], 'everyone who has faith in Jesus' [CEV]. This verb means to believe in the good news about Jesus Christ and to become a follower [LN]. It means to entrust oneself to an entity in complete confidence [BDAG].
b. aorist pass. infin. of δικαιόω (LN 56.34) (BDAG 2.b.β., 3. p. 249): 'to be freed' [ESV, NASB, NCV], 'to be set free' [BDAG (3. p. 249), LN; CEV, NRSV, TEV], 'to be justified' [Bar, BECNT; KJV, NET, NIV], 'to be acquitted' [CBC, LN; REB], 'to be vindicated' [AB, BDAG (2.b.β p. 249)]. The phrase 'everyone who believes is freed' is also translated 'everyone who believes in Jesus receives God's approval' [GW], 'everyone who believes in him is declared right with God' [NLT]. This verb refers to the act of clearing someone of transgression [LN]. It means to render a favorable verdict. Here it means to be found in the right, to be free of charges, [BDAG (2.b.β. p. 249)] or perhaps it means to cause someone to be released from personal or institutional claims that are no longer to be considered pertinent or valid [BDAG (3. p. 249)].
c. νόμος (LN 33.55) (BDAG 2.b. p. 677): 'law' [AB, Bar, BDAG, BECNT, CBC, LN; all versions except GW]. The phrase 'the law of Moses' is also translated 'Moses' Teachings' [GW]. This noun denotes the first five books of the OT called the Torah, often better referred to as 'instruction.' In a number of languages it is not possible to use a singular expression such as 'the Law' since the Torah consisted of five books and included a number of regulations and instructions, so it is necessary in many languages to use 'the laws.' [LN]. It refers specifically to the law that Moses received from God and is the standard according to which membership in the people of Israel is determined [BDAG].

13:40 Beware,[a] therefore, so that what is-said in the Prophets may not come-upon[b] (you):
LEXICON—a. pres. act. impera. of βλέπω (LN 27.58) (BDAG 5. p. 179): 'to beware' [Bar, BECNT, CBC; ESV, KJV, NRSV, REB], 'to take heed' [NASB], 'to take care' [AB; NIV, TEV], 'to be careful' [GW, NCV, NLT], 'to watch out' [LN; NET], 'to beware' [BDAG, LN]. The phrase 'Beware, therefore, so that what is said in the Prophets' is also translated 'Make sure that what the prophets have said' [CEV]. This is a figurative extension of the verb 'to see' and means to be ready to learn about future

dangers or needs, with the implication of preparedness to respond appropriately [LN]. It means to be ready to learn about something that is needed or is hazardous [BDAG].
  b. aorist act. subj. of ἐπέρχομαι (LN 13.119) (BDAG 2.b.β. p. 362): 'to come upon' [Bar, BECNT, LN; KJV, NASB], 'to come about' [BDAG; ESV], 'to happen to' [AB, LN; CEV, GW, NCV, NET, NIV, NRSV, TEV], 'to overtake' [LN], 'to happen' [BDAG]. The phrase 'what is said in the Prophets may not come upon you' is also translated 'Don't let the prophets' words apply to you' [NLT], 'lest you bring down upon yourselves the doom proclaimed by the prophets' [CBC; REB]. This verb means to happen to someone or something, with the implication of an event which is undesirable [LN]. It means to occur as an event or process [BDAG].

13:41 "'Look,a you scoffers,b marvelc and perish;d for I am-doing (a)-work in your days, (a)-work which you-will- not -believe,e even if someone tells it to you.'"

LEXICON—a. aorist act. impera. of εἶδον (LN 30.45): 'look' [CEV, ESV, GW, NET, NIV, NLT, NRSV, TEV], 'see' [Bar], 'behold' [AB, BECNT; KJV, NASB], 'listen' [NCV], 'to take notice of, to consider, to pay attention to, to concern oneself with' [LN]. This verb is also translated 'see this' [CBC; REB]. This verb means to take special notice of something, with the implication of concerning oneself [LN].
  b. καταφρονητής (LN 88.193) (BDAG p. 529): 'scoffer' [AB, BDAG, BECNT, CBC, LN; ESV, NASB, NET, NIV, NRSV, REB, TEV], 'mocker' [GW, NLT], 'despiser' [Bar, BDAG; KJV]. This noun is also translated 'you people who make fun of God' [CEV], 'you people who doubt' [NCV]. This noun is a derivative of καταφρονέω 'to despise' and denotes one who customarily feels contempt for something or someone [LN].
  c. aorist act. impera. of θαυμάζω (LN 25.213) (BDAG 1.a.α. p. 444): 'to marvel' [Bar, LN; NASB, REB], 'to be astounded' [ESV], 'to be astonished' [AB; TEV], 'to wonder' [BECNT, CBC, LN; KJV, NCV, NIV], 'to be amazed' [LN; CEV, GW, NET, NLT, NRSV]. This verb means to wonder or marvel at some event or object [LN]. It means to be extraordinarily impressed or disturbed by something [BDAG].
  d. aorist pass. impera. of ἀφανίζω (LN 13.98) (BDAG 1.b. p. 154): 'to perish' [AB, BDAG, BECNT; ESV, KJV, NASB, NET, NIV, NRSV], 'to disappear' [BDAG, LN; CEV], 'to die' [LN; GW, NCV, NLT, TEV], 'to cease to exist' [LN], 'to be gone' [CBC; REB], 'to fade away' [Bar], 'to be destroyed' [BDAG]. This verb means to cease to exist, with the implication of no longer being evident or visible [LN]. It means to cause something to disappear [BDAG].
  e. aorist act. subj. of πιστεύω (LN 31.35) (BDAG 1.a.α. p. 816): 'to believe' [AB, Bar, BDAG, BECNT, CBC, LN; all versions], 'to think to

be true, to regard as trustworthy' [LN]. This verb means to believe something to be true and, hence, worthy of being trusted [LN]. It means to consider something to be true and therefore worthy of one's trust [BDAG].

QUESTION—Who does the pronoun 'I' refer to?
   In this quote from Habakkuk 1:5, the pronoun 'I' referred to God [Bar, BECNT, CBC, EBC, NAC, NICNT, PNTC, TH, TNTC].

QUESTION—What is meant by 'you-scoffers'?
   The expression means 'you who scoff at what God has said' or 'you who speak bad about what God has said' [TH], It means 'you who have not believed God' [BECNT].

QUESTION—What is meant by 'in your days'?
   The phrase refers to the time while they were still alive [TH].

QUESTION—What work was God doing?
   The work that God was doing was to fulfill the messianic promises achieved by Christ in his death and resurrection [PNTC]. It was the work that God has done in Christ [Bar, BECNT] and the message about it [BECNT].

DISCOURSE UNIT—13:42–52 [AB]. The topic is the issue of the missionary work in Pisidian Antioch.

DISCOURSE UNIT—13:42–45 [EBC]. The topic is the varying responses to Paul's sermon.

DISCOURSE UNIT—13:42–43 [NICNT]. The topic is the response to Paul's address.

13:42 As they were going-out,[a] the people begged[b] that these things might be-spoken to-them the next Sabbath.

LEXICON—a. pres. act. participle of ἔξειμι (LN 15.40) (BDAG p. 347): 'to go out' [Bar, BDAG, BECNT; ESV, KJV, NASB, NET, NRSV], 'to leave' [AB, CBC; CEV, GW, NCV, NIV, NLT, REB, TEV], 'to go out of, to depart out of, to leave from within' [LN], 'to depart from an area, to go away' [BDAG]. This verb means to move out of an enclosed or well defined two or three-dimensional area [LN]. It means to depart from an area [BDAG].

b. imperf. act. indic. of παρακαλέω (LN 33.168) (BDAG 3. p. 765): 'to beg' [Bar, BECNT; CEV, ESV, NASB, NLT], 'to request' [BDAG, LN], 'to beseech' [KJV], 'to ask' [NCV], 'to earnestly ask' [AB], 'to urge' [NET, NRSV], 'to ask for earnestly, to plead for, to appeal to' [LN], 'to implore, to entreat' [BDAG]. This verb is also translated as a passive verb: 'they were asked' [CBC; REB]. The phrase 'the people begged that these things might be spoken to them' is also translated 'the people invited them to speak on the same subject' [GW], 'the people invited them to speak further about these things' [NIV], 'the people invited them...and tell them more about these things' [TEV]. This verb means to ask for something earnestly and with propriety [LN]. It means to make a strong request for something [BDAG].

QUESTION—Who was the subject of 'they' in 'they were going out'?
'They' refers to Paul and Barnabas [BECNT, NAC, TH, TNTC, TRT].

QUESTION—What does 'these things' refer to?
'These things' refers back to the content of the message that Paul had spoken at the synagogue [TH].

13:43 And after the meeting of the synagogue broke-up,ᵃ many Jews and devout converts to Judaism followed Paul and Barnabas, who, as they spoke with-them, were-urgingᵇ them to-continueᶜ in-the graceᵈ of-God.

LEXICON—a. aorist pass. participle of λύω (LN 15.139) (BDAG 3. p. 607): 'to break up' [Bar, BECNT; ESV, GW, KJV, NASB, NET, NRSV], 'to disperse' [CBC, LN; REB], 'to be dismissed' [LN; NIV], 'to be sent away' [AB], not explicit [CEV, NLT]. The phrase 'the meeting of the synagogue broke up' is also translated 'the meeting was over' [NCV], 'the people had left the meeting' [TEV]. This verb means to cause a gathering to be dismissed or dispersed [LN]. It means to reduce something by violence into its components [BDAG].

b. imperf. act. indic. of πείθω (LN 33.301) (BDAG 1.b. p. 791): 'to urge' [Bar, BECNT, CBC; ESV, NASB, NIV, NLT, NRSV, REB], 'to beg' [CEV], 'to persuade' [AB, BDAG, LN; GW, KJV, NCV, NET], 'to convince' [LN], 'to appeal to' [BDAG], 'to encourage' [TEV]. This verb means to convince someone to believe something and to act on the basis of what is recommended [LN]. It means to cause to come to a particular point of view or course of action [BDAG].

c. pres. act. infin. of προσμένω (LN 68.11) (BDAG 1.b. p. 883): 'to continue' [Bar, LN; ESV, GW, KJV, NASB, NCV, NET, NIV, NLT, NRSV], 'to remain' [BECNT; CEV], 'to remain in' [LN], 'to keep on' [LN; TEV], 'to remain with, to stay with' [BDAG], 'to hold fast' [AB, CBC; REB]. This verb means to continue in an activity or state [LN]. It means to be steadfast in association [BDAG].

d. χάρις (LN 88.66) (BDAG 3.b. p. 1080): 'grace' [AB, Bar, BECNT, CBC, LN; all versions except CEV, GW], 'kindness, graciousness' [LN], 'favor, gracious deed, gracious gift, benefaction' [BDAG], 'good will' [GW]. The phrase 'to continue in the grace of God' is also translated 'to remain faithful to God, who had been so kind to them' [CEV]. This noun denotes the kindness shown to someone, with the implication of graciousness on the part of the one showing such kindness [LN]. It denotes the practical application of goodwill [BDAG].

QUESTION—What is meant by the meeting of the synagogue breaking up?
It means that the meeting of the synagogue was over/dismissed [NICNT, PNTC, TRT] or the people had left the meeting [TH].

QUESTION—What is meant by 'devout converts to Judaism'?
'Devout converts to Judaism' refers to the Gentiles who had converted to Judaism (the Jewish religion) [Bar, CBC, NICNT, TRT], Gentiles who had made themselves Jews including men underwent a circumcision and their families underwent a ceremonial cleansing similar to baptism [AB, BECNT, NAC, PNTC, TH]. They are different from God-fearers who were Gentiles who had not fully converted to Judaism. Cornelius was an example of one in Acts 10:2, [AB, Bar, BECNT, CBC, NAC, NICNT, TH, TRT].

QUESTION—What is meant by continuing in the grace of God?
It means to continue to rely on the goodness of God [TH], to remain faithful in God's salvation that only God can give by His grace [BECNT, PNTC], to remain open in the grace of God [NAC]. In this context, the term 'grace' is not to be understood in any special technical sense in contrast with the Law. It is simply a reference to the nature of the Good News which comes to men as an expression of God's grace or goodness, His favor to men even though they do not deserve it [TH].

DISCOURSE UNIT—13:44–52 [NICNT, PNTC; NASB, NLT]. The topic is the Gentile interest arouses Jewish opposition [NICNT], Paul turns to the Gentiles [NASB, NLT], turning to the Gentiles: fulfilling the servant's role [PNTC].

13:44 The next Sabbath almost the whole city gathered[a] to-hear the word[b] of-the Lord.[c]

TEXT—Manuscripts reading τὸν λόγον τοῦ κυρίου 'the word of the Lord' are given a C rating by GNT to indicate that the Committee had difficulty making the decision. Some manuscripts have τὸν λόγον τοῦ θεοῦ 'the word of God'. The KJV and REB follow this.

LEXICON—a. aorist pass. indic. of συνάγω (LN 15.125) (BDAG 1.b. p. 962): 'to gather' [AB, CBC; ESV, GW, NIV, NRSV, REB], 'to assemble' [NASB], 'to assemble together' [NET], 'to gather together' [BECNT], 'to be gathered together' [Bar, LN], 'to be called together' [BDAG, LN], 'to be gathered, to be brought together' [BDAG], 'to come together' [KJV], 'to come' [CEV, NCV, TEV]. The phrase 'the whole city gathered' is also translated 'the entire city turned out' [NLT]. This verb means to cause to come together, whether of animate or inanimate objects [LN]. It means to cause to come together with the city [BDAG].

b. λόγος (LN 33.260) (BDAG 1.a.β. p. 599): 'word' [AB, Bar, BDAG, BECNT, CBC; ESV, GW, KJV, NASB, NCV, NET, NIV, NLT, NRSV, REB, TEV], 'message' [CEV], 'what is preached, gospel' [LN]. This noun denotes the content of what is preached about Christ or about the good news [LN]. It denotes a communication whereby the mind finds expression [BDAG].

c. κύριος (LN 12.9): 'Lord' [Bar, BECNT, LN; all versions except KJV, REB], 'God' [AB, CBC; KJV, REB], 'Ruler, One who commands' [LN].

This noun denotes a title for God and for Christ. It indicates one who exercises supernatural authority over mankind [LN].

QUESTION—What does the 'word of the Lord' refer to?

It refers to the 'word of God' [BECNT, TNTC, TRT].

13:45 **But when the Jews saw the crowds, they-were-filled-with[a] jealousy[b] and began to contradict[c] what was spoken by Paul, blaspheming[d] him.**

LEXICON—a. aorist pass. indic. of πίμπλημι (LN 59.38) (BDAG 1.a.β. p. 813): 'to be filled' [AB, Bar, BDAG, BECNT, CBC; ESV, KJV, NASB, NET, NIV, NRSV, REB, TEV], 'to be filled completely, to be filled up' [LN]. The phrase 'they were filled with jealousy' is also translated 'they were/became very jealous' [CEV, GW], 'the Jewish people became very jealous' [NCV], 'they were jealous' [NLT]. This verb means to cause something to be completely full [LN]. It means to cause to be completely full. Here it refers to a person's inner life [BDAG].

b. ζῆλος (LN 88.162) (BDAG 2. p. 427): 'jealousy' [AB, BDAG, BECNT, LN; ESV, NASB, NET, NIV, NRSV, TEV], 'envy' [Bar, BDAG, LN; KJV], 'resentment' [LN]. This noun is also translated as an adjective: 'they were/became very jealous' [CEV, GW], 'the Jewish people became very jealous' [NCV], 'they were jealous' [NLT], 'jealous resentment' [CBC; REB]. This noun denotes a particularly strong feeling of resentment and jealousy against someone [LN]. It denotes intense negative feelings over another's achievements or success [BDAG].

c. imperf. act. indic. of ἀντιλέγω (LN 33.455) (BDAG 1. p. 89): 'to contradict' [AB, Bar, BDAG, BECNT, CBC; ESV, GW, KJV, NASB, NET, NRSV, REB], 'to dispute' [TEV], 'to speak against' [BDAG; CEV], 'to argue against' [NCV, NLT], 'to talk abusively against' [NIV], 'to oppose, to speak in opposition to' [LN]. This verb means speak against something or someone [LN]. It means to speak against, contradict someone or something [BDAG].

d. pres. act. participle of βλασφημέω (LN 33.400) (BDAG a. p. 178): 'to blaspheme' [Bar, LN; KJV, NASB, NRSV], 'to revile' [BDAG, LN; ESV, NET], 'to defame' [BDAG, LN], 'to slander' [BDAG, BECNT; NLT], 'to insult' [CEV, TEV], not explicit [NIV]. The phrase 'blaspheming him' is also translated 'they used insulting language' [GW], 'said insulting things' [NCV], 'they contradicted...with violent abuse' [CBC; REB]. This verb is also translated as an adverb: 'blasphemously contradicted' [AB]. This verb means to speak against someone in such a way as to harm or injure his or her reputation, occurring in relation to persons as well as to divine beings [LN]. It means to speak in a disrespectful way that demeans, denigrates, maligns in relation to humans [BDAG].

QUESTION—What does the 'word of the Lord' refer to?

It refers to the 'word of God' [BECNT, TNTC, TRT].

13:46 And Paul and Barnabas spoke-out-boldly, saying, "It-was necessary that the word[a] of-God be-spoken first to-you. Since you-repudiate[b] it and judge[c] yourselves unworthy of-eternal life,[d] behold,[e] we-are-turning[f] to the Gentiles.

LEXICON—a. λόγος (LN 33.260) (BDAG 1.a.β. p. 599): 'word' [AB, Bar, BDAG, BECNT, CBC; all versions except CEV, NCV], 'message' [CEV, NCV], 'what is preached, gospel' [LN]. This noun denotes the content of what is preached about Christ or about the good news [LN]. It denotes a communication whereby the mind finds expression [BDAG].
   b. pres. mid. indic. of ἀπωθέω (LN 31.63) (BDAG 2. p. 126): 'to repudiate' [BDAG; NASB], 'to refuse to listen to' [LN], 'to reject' [AB, BDAG, BECNT, CBC, LN; CEV, GW, NET, NIV, NLT, NRSV, REB, TEV], 'to thrust aside' [Bar; ESV]. The phrase 'Since you repudiate it' is also translated 'seeing ye put it from you' [KJV], 'But you refuse to listen' [NCV]. This is a figurative extension of meaning of ἀπωθέομαι 'to push away' and it means to no longer pay attention to previous beliefs [LN].
   c. pres. act. indic. of κρίνω (LN 30.108) (BDAG 3. p. 568): 'to judge' [Bar, BDAG, BECNT, LN; ESV, KJV, NASB, NCV, NLT, NRSV, REB], 'to evaluate' [LN], 'to consider' [AB, BDAG; GW, NET, NIV, TEV], 'to think, to look upon' [BDAG], 'to condemn' [CBC], not explicit [CEV]. This verb means to make a judgment based upon the correctness or value of something [LN]. It means to make a judgment based on taking various factors into account [BDAG].
   d. ζωή (LN 23.88) (BDAG 2.b.α. p. 430): 'life' [AB, Bar, BDAG, BECNT, CBC, LN; all versions]. This noun refers to the life of the believer which proceeds from God and Christ [BDAG].
   e. ἰδού (LN 91.13): 'behold' [BECNT; ESV, NASB], 'look, listen, pay attention, come now, then' [LN], 'lo' [KJV], 'see' [Bar], not explicit [CBC; CEV, GW, NCV, NET, NIV, NLT, NRSV, REB, TEV]. This particle is also translated 'listen then' [AB]. This particle functions as a prompter of attention, also serving to emphasize the statement which follows [LN].
   f. pres. pass. indic. of στρέφω (LN 34.25) (BDAG 1.b.β. p. 948): 'to turn to' [AB, Bar, BECNT, CBC, LN; ESV, GW, KJV, NASB, NET, NIV, NRSV, REB], 'to go to' [CEV, NCV], 'to leave and go to' [LN; TEV], 'to shift to, to establish a relation with' [LN]. The phrase 'we are turning to the Gentiles' is also translated 'we will offer it to the Gentiles' [NLT]. This verb means to shift one's association to someone else [LN]. It means to turn around, turn toward [BDAG].

QUESTION—What is meant by 'you thrust it (the word of God) aside'? The translation has 'you repudiate it'.

It means 'you reject the word of God' [BECNT, NAC, PNTC, TH], or 'you refuse to believe the word of God,' or 'you insist the word of God is not true' [TH].

QUESTION—What is meant by 'you judge yourselves unworthy of eternal life'?

In this context, it means that due to their rejection of the word of God, they had condemned themselves and were thus not good enough to receive eternal life [TH]. The message of salvation is now equated with the hope of eternal life [BECNT].

QUESTION—What is meant by 'eternal life'?

'Eternal life' means 'real life with God which never ends, even after one's death' [TH], a broad equivalent for salvation or the kingdom of God [PNTC].

13:47 For so the Lord[a] has-commanded[b] us, saying, "'I-have-made[c] you (a)-light for (the)-Gentiles, that you may bring salvation[d] to (the)-end of-the earth'"

LEXICON—a. κύριος (LN 12.9): 'Lord' [AB, Bar, BECNT, CBC, LN; all versions], 'Ruler, One who commands' [LN]. This noun denotes a title for God and for Christ. It indicates one who exercises supernatural authority over mankind [LN].

b. perf. mid./pass. (deponent = act.) indic. of ἐντέλλομαι (LN 33.329) (BDAG p. 339): 'to command' [AB, BDAG, BECNT, LN; ESV, KJV, NASB, NET, NIV, NRSV], 'to order, to give orders' [BDAG]. This verb is also translated as a noun: 'command' [CEV, NLT], 'order' [GW], 'commandment' [TEV], 'charge' [Bar], 'instruction' [CBC; REB]. The phrase 'For so the Lord has commanded us' is also translated 'This is what the Lord told us to do' [NCV]. This verb means to give definite orders, implying authority or official sanction [LN]. It means to give or leave instructions [BDAG].

c. perf. act. indic. of τίθημι (LN 37.96) (BDAG 3.a. p. 1004): 'to make' [ESV, GW, NCV, NIV, NLT, TEV], 'to place' [CEV, NASB], 'to appoint' [Bar, BDAG, CBC, LN; NET, REB], 'to assign' [BDAG, LN], 'to designate, to give a task to' [LN]. The phrase 'I have made you a light' is also translated 'I have set you/thee to be a light' [BECNT; KJV, NRSV], 'I have set you as a light' [AB]. This verb means to assign someone to a particular task, function, or role [LN]. It means to place/appoint someone to some task or function [BDAG].

d. σωτηρία (LN 21.26) (BDAG 2. p. 986): 'salvation' [AB, Bar, BDAG, BECNT, CBC, LN; ESV, KJV, NASB, NET, NIV, NLT, NRSV, REB]. This noun is also translated 'the saving power of God' [CEV]. The phrase 'that you may bring salvation to the end of the earth' is also translated 'that you would save people all over the world' [GW], 'you will show people all over the world the way to be saved' [NCV], 'that all the world may be saved' [TEV]. This noun denotes the process of being saved [LN].

QUESTION—Where is this quote cited from?

This quote is cited from the Septuagint of Isaiah 49:6 which defines the servant's role as being a light [AB, Bar, BECNT, CBC, NAC, NICNT,

PNTC, TH, TNTC, TRT]. Here Paul says that the Lord has commanded him and Barnabas to undertake the role of being a guide to the nations concerning the way to God. This task is much like the way a light illumines a path [AB, BECNT]. God was originally talking to the Messiah in Isaiah 49:6, as Servant-Messiah, Jesus was to be 'a light to the nations.' Now the messengers of the Messiah are likewise commanded to be 'a light for the Gentiles' [Bar, BECNT, CBC, NAC, NICNT, PNTC, TNTC, TRT].

13:48 And when the Gentiles heard-(this), they began rejoicing[a] and glorifying[b] the word of-the Lord, and as-many-as were appointed[c] to eternal life believed.[d]

LEXICON—a. imperf. act. indic. of χαίρω (LN 25.125) (BDAG 1. p. 1075): 'to rejoice' [AB, Bar, BDAG, BECNT, LN; ESV, NASB, NET]. This verb is also translated as a passive verb: 'to be glad' [BDAG, LN; CEV, KJV, NIV, NLT, NRSV, TEV], 'to be pleased' [GW], 'to be happy' [NCV], 'to be overjoyed' [CBC; REB]. This verb means to enjoy a state of happiness and well-being [LN]. It means to be in a state of happiness and well-being [BDAG].
  b. imperf. act. indic. of δοξάζω (LN 33.357) (BDAG 2. p. 258): 'to glorify' [AB, Bar, BDAG, BECNT, LN; ESV, KJV, NASB], 'to praise' [LN; CEV, GW, NET, NRSV, TEV], 'to honor' [NIV], 'to give honor' [NCV], 'to acclaim' [CBC; REB], 'to thank' [NLT]. This verb means to speak of something as being unusually fine and deserving honor [LN]. It means to cause to have splendid greatness [BDAG].
  c. perf. pass. participle of τάσσω (LN 37.96) (BDAG 1.b. p. 991): 'to be appointed' [Bar, LN; ESV, NASB, NET, NIV], 'to be chosen' [CEV, NCV, NLT, TEV], 'to be prepared' [GW], 'to be ordained' [BECNT; KJV], 'to be destined' [AB; NRSV], 'to be marked out' [CBC; REB], 'to designate, to assign, to give a task to' [LN], 'to arrange, to put in place' [BDAG]. This verb means to assign someone to a particular task, function, or role [LN]. It means to bring about an order of things by arranging of a person put into a specific position [BDAG].
  d. aorist act. indic. of πιστεύω (LN 31.102) (BDAG 2.b. p. 817): 'to believe' [AB, BECNT; ESV, GW, KJV, NASB, NCV, NET, NIV], 'to believe (in), to trust' [BDAG], 'to be a believer' [LN], 'to become a believer' [Bar, CBC; NLT, NRSV, REB, TEV]. The phrase 'as many as…believed' is also translated 'Everyone…put their faith in the Lord' [CEV]. This verb means to believe in the good news about Jesus Christ and to become a follower [LN]. It means to entrust oneself to an entity in complete confidence [BDAG].

QUESTION—What is meant by 'as many as were appointed to eternal life believed'?
  The Greek word τάσσω means 'appoint/assign/designate/ordain.' Here the passive voice τεταγμένοι 'were appointed' indicates that God does the assigning [Bar, BECNT, CBC, NICNT]. This phrase refers to God's

sovereign work over salvation, where God has assigned those who come to eternal life [BECNT, CBC, PNTC, TH, TRT]. Gentiles took an active role in believing, in committing themselves to Christ; but it was in response to God's Spirit moving in them, convicting them, appointing them for life. All salvation is ultimately only by the grace of God [NAC]. Those who believed are described as those who *were ordained to eternal life*. This indicates that not all the Gentiles in the town believed the gospel. It could be taken in the sense that God had predestinated certain of them to believe. But it could also refer to those who had already put their trust in God in accordance with the Old Testament revelation of his grace and were enrolled in his people, or perhaps it means that the Gentiles believed in virtue of the fact that God's plan of salvation included them. Whatever be the precise nuance of the words, there is no suggestion that they received eternal life independent of their own act of conscious faith [TNTC].

13:49 And the word of-the Lord was-spreading[a] throughout (the)-whole region.[b]

LEXICON—a. imperf. pass. indic. of διαφέρω (LN 33.214) (BDAG 1. p. 239): 'to spread' [AB, BECNT, CBC; all versions except KJV, NASB], 'to be spread' [Bar; NASB], 'to be published' [KJV], 'to spread information about, to spread the news about' [LN], 'to carry through' [BDAG]. This verb means to spread information extensively and effectively concerning someone or something [LN]. It means to carry something through a place or structure [BDAG].

b. χώρα (LN 1.79) (BDAG 2.a. p. 1093): 'region' [AB, Bar, BDAG, BECNT, CBC, LN; all versions except NCV], 'country' [NCV], 'territory, land' [LN], 'district, place' [BDAG]. This noun denotes a region or regions of the earth, normally in relation to some ethnic group or geographical center, but not necessarily constituting a unit of governmental administration [LN]. It denotes a portion of land area [BDAG].

13:50 But[a] the Jews incited[b] the worshiping[c] women of high-standing[d] and the- leading[e] -(men) of-the-city, stirred-up[f] persecution[g] against Paul and Barnabas, and drove- them -out[h] of their district.

LEXICON—a. δέ (LN 89.124): 'but' [Bar, BECNT, CBC, LN; all versions except NLT], 'on the other hand' [LN], 'however' [AB], not explicit [NLT]. This conjunction indicates a contrast [LN].

b. aorist act. indic. of παροτρύνω (LN 39.8) (BDAG p. 780): 'to incite' [Bar, BDAG, BECNT; ESV, NASB, NET, NIV, NRSV], 'to stir up' [AB, CBC, LN; GW, KJV, NCV, NLT, REB, TEV], 'to incite to' [LN], 'to arouse' [BDAG], not explicit [CEV]. This verb means to stir up hostility against [LN]. It means to stir up strong emotion against [BDAG].

c. pres. mid. participle of σέβω (LN 53.53) (BDAG 1.b. p. 918): 'to worship' [BDAG, LN; TEV], 'to venerate' [LN], 'to be religious' [CEV]. This verb is also translated as an adjective: 'devout' [Bar, BECNT; ESV,

GW, KJV, NASB, NRSV], 'God-fearing' [AB; NET, NIV], 'religious' [NCV, NLT]. This verb is also translated as a noun: 'worshipper' [CBC; REB]. This verb means to express in attitude and ritual one's allegiance to and regard for deity [LN]. It means to express in gestures, rites, or ceremonies one's allegiance or devotion to deity [BDAG].

d. εὐσχήμων (LN 87.33) (BDAG 2. p. 414): 'of high standing' [Bar, BDAG, BECNT; ESV, NIV, NRSV], 'of high social standing' [GW, NET, TEV], 'of high rank' [AB], 'of standing' [CBC; REB], 'of prominence' [NASB], 'esteemed, honored' [LN], 'respected' [CEV], 'prominent, of high repute, noble' [BDAG], 'honorable' [KJV], 'influential' [NLT], 'important' [NCV]. This adjective pertains to having special prestige or honor [LN]. It pertains to being considered especially worthy of public admiration [BDAG].

e. πρῶτος (LN 87.45) (BDAG 2.a.β. p. 894): 'leading' [Bar, BECNT, CBC; ESV, NASB, NIV, NRSV, REB, TEV], 'important' [LN; CEV], 'prominent' [LN; NET], 'great' [LN], 'foremost' [BDAG, LN], 'first, most important, most prominent' [BDAG], 'chief' [KJV], 'of standing' [AB]. The phrase 'the leading men of the city' is also translated 'the officials of the city' [GW], 'the leaders of the city' [NCV, NLT]. This adjective pertains to being of high rank, with the implication of special prominence and status [LN]. It pertains to prominence of persons [BDAG].

f. aorist act. indic. of ἐπεγείρω (LN 68.9) (BDAG p. 360): 'to stir up' [BDAG, BECNT, LN; ESV, NET, NIV, NRSV], 'to arouse, to excite' [BDAG], 'to commence' [LN], 'to start' [NCV, TEV], 'to begin' [AB], 'to instigate' [NASB], 'to incite' [NLT], 'to raise' [Bar; KJV]. The phrase 'stirred up persecution' is also translated 'started making trouble' [CEV], 'started to persecute' [GW]. This verb is also translated as a passive verb: 'was started' [CBC; REB]. This verb means to cause to begin and to intensify an activity [LN]. It means to cause an activity to begin through provocation [BDAG].

g. διωγμός (LN 39.45) (BDAG p. 253): 'persecution' [AB, Bar, BDAG, BECNT, CBC, LN; ESV, KJV, NASB, NET, NIV, NRSV, REB, TEV], 'trouble' [CEV, NCV]. This noun is also translated as a verb: 'these people started to persecute' [GW]. The phrase 'the Jews...stirred up persecution against' is also translated 'they incited a mob against' [NLT]. This noun denotes a systematic, organized program to oppress and harass people [LN]. It denotes a program or process designed to harass and oppress someone [BDAG].

h. aorist act. indic. of ἐκβάλλω (LN 15.44) (BDAG 1. p. 299): 'to drive out/away' [AB, Bar, BDAG, LN; ESV, NASB, NRSV], 'to chase out' [CEV], 'to throw out' [GW, NET, TEV], 'to force out' [NCV], 'to run out' [NLT], 'to cast out' [BECNT], 'to send away' [LN], 'to expel' [BDAG, LN; KJV, NIV]. This verb is also translated as a passive verb: 'they were expelled' [CBC; REB]. This verb means to cause to go out or

13:51 But they shook-off[a] the dust from their feet against them and went[b] to Iconium.
LEXICON—a. aorist mid. participle of ἐκτινάσσω (LN 16.8) (BDAG 1. p. 310): 'to shake off' [Bar, BDAG, BECNT, CBC, LN; ESV, GW, KJV, NASB, NCV, NET, NRSV, REB, TEV], 'to shake' [AB, LN; CEV, NIV, NLT], 'to shake out' [LN]. This verb means to shake something out or off, in order to get rid of an object or a substance [LN]. It means to dislodge or remove something with rapid movements [BDAG].
  b. aorist act. indic. of ἔρχομαι (LN 15.81): 'to go' [AB, BECNT, CBC; all versions except KJV], 'to come' [Bar, LN; KJV]. This verb means to move toward or up to the reference point of the viewpoint character or event [LN].

13:52 And the disciples were-filled-with[a] joy[b] and with (the)-Holy Spirit.
LEXICON—a. imperf. pass. indic. of πληρόω (LN 78.46) (BDAG 1.b. p. 828): 'to be filled with' [Bar, BDAG, CBC; CEV, ESV, KJV, NCV, NET, NIV, NLT, NRSV, REB], 'to be full of' [AB, LN; GW, TEV], 'to be completely, to be entirely, to be totally' [LN]. The phrase 'were filled with joy' is also translated 'were being filled with joy' [BECNT], 'were continually filled with joy' [NASB]. This verb means to experience a complete degree of involvement in some event or state [LN]. It means to make full and refers to persons filled with powers, qualities, etc. [BDAG].
  b. χαρά (LN 25.123) (BDAG 1.a. p. 1077): 'joy' [AB, Bar, BECNT, CBC, LN; all versions except CEV], 'gladness, great happiness' [LN]. This noun is also translated as a passive verb: 'were very happy' [CEV]. This noun denotes a state of joy and gladness [LN]. It denotes the experience of gladness [BDAG].

DISCOURSE UNIT—14:1–28 [CBC, EBC, NICNT; NASB]. The topic is Jupiter and Mercury! [CBC], at Iconium, Lystra, and Derbe, and back to Antioch [EBC], acceptance and opposition [NASB], Iconium, Lystra, Derbe [NICNT].

DISCOURSE UNIT—14:1–23 [Bar]. The topic is in and around Lystra.

DISCOURSE UNIT—14:1–20 [PNTC]. The topic is the word in Iconium, Lystra, and Derbe.

DISCOURSE UNIT—14:1–7 [AB, BECNT, EBC, NAC, NICNT, PNTC, TNTC; CEV, ESV, GW, NCV, NET, NIV, NLT, NRSV, TEV]. The topic is Paul and Barnabas in Iconium [AB; CEV, GW, NCV, NLT, NRSV], in Iconium [BECNT; NIV, TEV], the ministry at Iconium [EBC], Paul and Barnabas at Iconium [ESV, NET], acceptance and rejection at Iconium [NAC], adventures in

Iconium [NICNT], converted opposition in Iconium [PNTC], conflict at Iconium [TNTC].

14:1 Now in Iconium they entered[a] together into the synagogue[b] of-the Jews and spoke in such a way that (a)-great number of both Jews and Greeks believed.[c]

LEXICON—a. aorist act. infin. of εἰσέρχομαι (LN 15.93) (BDAG 1.a.γ. p. 294): 'to enter' [Bar, BDAG, BECNT, LN; ESV, NASB], 'to go into' [AB, CBC, LN; GW, KJV, NET, NIV, NRSV, REB], 'to move into, to come into' [LN], 'to go to' [NCV, NLT, TEV], not explicit [CEV]. This verb means to move into a space, either two-dimensional or three-dimensional [LN]. It means to move into a space and here it refers to the synagogue [BDAG].

b. συναγωγή (LN 7.20): 'synagogue' [AB, Bar, BECNT, CBC, LN; all versions except CEV], 'Jewish meeting place' [CEV], 'Christian assembly place' [LN]. This noun denotes a building of assembly, associated with religious activity. Normally a building in which Jewish worship took place and in which the Law was taught [LN].

c. aorist act. infin. of πιστεύω (LN 31.102) (BDAG 2.b. p. 817): 'to believe' [AB, BECNT; ESV, GW, KJV, NASB, NCV, NET, NIV], 'to believe (in), to trust' [BDAG], 'to be a believer' [LN], 'to become a believer' [Bar, CBC; NLT, NRSV, REB, TEV]. The phrase 'a great number of both Jews and Greeks believed' is also translated 'many Jews and Gentiles put their faith in the Lord' [CEV]. This verb means to believe in the good news about Jesus Christ and to become a follower [LN]. It means to entrust oneself to an entity in complete confidence [BDAG].

QUESTION—Where was Iconium?
Iconium was 90 miles (145km.) east-southeast of Antioch, in the Province of Galatia [EBC, NAC, PNTC, TNTC]. Iconium remained largely Greek in temper and somewhat resistant to Roman influence [EBC, PNTC].

QUESTION—What is meant by spoke 'in such a way'?
Here spoke 'in such a way' refers to Barnabas and Paul's custom of initially going to the synagogue, reaching out to the Jews and then to the non-Jews like the God-fearers [AB, Bar, BECNT, CBC, EBC, NAC, NICNT, TNTC].

QUESTION—What is meant by a great number of both Jews and Greeks 'believed'?
It means that many Jews and Greeks (non-Jews) believed in Jesus, they believed in the message about Jesus that Barnabas and Paul had preached to them [Bar, EBC, NICNT, PNTC, TH, TNTC].

14:2 But[a] the Jews who disbelieved[b] stirred-up[c] the Gentiles and poisoned[d] their minds[e] against the brothers[f].

LEXICON—a. δέ (LN 89.124): 'but' [AB, Bar, BECNT, CBC, LN; all versions except NLT], 'on the other hand' [LN], 'however' [NLT]. This conjunction indicates a contrast [LN].

b. aorist act. participle of ἀπειθέω (LN 31.107) (BDAG p. 99): 'to disbelieve' [NASB], 'to refuse to believe' [LN; GW, NET, NIV], 'to refuse to be a believer, to reject the Christian message' [LN], 'to disobey, to be disobedient' [BDAG]. The phrase 'the Jews who disbelieved' is also translated 'the unbelieving Jews' [Bar, BECNT; ESV, KJV, NRSV], 'the unconverted Jews' [CBC; REB], 'the Jews who did not have faith in him' [CEV], 'the Jews who did/would not believe' [NCV, TEV], 'the Jews…spurned God's message' [NLT], 'the Jews who had not received the gospel' [AB]. This verb means to refuse to believe the Christian message [LN].
c. aorist act. indic. of ἐπεγείρω (LN 68.9) (BDAG p. 360): 'to stir up' [AB, BDAG, BECNT, CBC, LN; ESV, GW, KJV, NASB, NET, NIV, NRSV, REB, TEV], 'to incite' [Bar], 'to excite' [BDAG; NCV], 'to arouse' [BDAG], 'to commence' [LN], not explicit [NLT]. The phrase 'stirred up the Gentiles' is also translated 'made the other Gentiles angry' [CEV]. This verb means to cause to begin and to intensify an activity [LN]. It means to cause an activity to begin through provocation [BDAG].
d. aorist act. indic. of κακόω (LN 88.200) (BDAG 2. p. 502): 'to poison' [Bar, CBC; ESV, GW, NET, NIV, NLT, NRSV, REB], 'to embitter' [BDAG; NASB], 'to arouse' [AB], 'to turn someone against' [LN; CEV, NCV, TEV], 'to cause to dislike' [LN], 'to make angry' [BDAG], not explicit [BECNT]. The phrase 'poisoned their minds against' is also translated 'made their minds evil affected against' [KJV]. The idiom 'to cause a person's attitude to be bad against' means to cause someone to have hostile feelings of dislike toward someone [LN]. It means to cause someone to think badly about another [BDAG].
e. ψυχή (LN 26.4) (BDAG 2.c. p. 1099): 'mind' [Bar, CBC, LN; ESV, GW, KJV, NASB, NET, NIV, NLT, NRSV, REB], 'soul' [BDAG, BECNT], 'inner self, thoughts, feelings, being' [LN], not explicit [CEV, NCV, TEV]. The phrase 'poisoned their minds against' is also translated 'arouse bad feeling against' [AB]. This noun denotes the essence of life in terms of thinking, willing, and feeling [LN]. It denotes the seat and center of the inner human life concerning feelings and emotions [BDAG].
f. ἀδελφός (LN 11.23): 'brother' [Bar, BECNT; ESV, NET, NIV, NRSV], 'fellow believer, a Christian brother' [LN]. The phrase 'the brothers' is also translated 'the brethren' [AB; KJV, NASB], 'the believers' [GW, NCV, TEV], 'the Lord's followers' [CEV], 'the Christians' [CBC; REB], 'Paul and Barnabas' [NLT]. This noun denotes a close associate of a group of persons having a well-defined membership. In the NT ἀδελφός 'brother' refers specifically to fellow believers in Christ [LN].

QUESTION—Who were 'the brothers'?

Paul and Barnabas were not brothers in a physical sense, it means that they were fellow believers [Bar, TH]. 'Brothers' refers to both new and old converts [PNTC].

QUESTION—What is meant by 'poisoned their minds' against the brothers? This Greek idiom means to cause a person's attitude to be bad against someone [BECNT, TH].

14:3 So they-remained^a for (a)-long time, speaking-boldly for the Lord,^b who bore-witness^c to the word^d of his grace,^e granting^f signs^g and wonders^h to-be-doneⁱ by their hands^j.

LEXICON—a. aorist act. indic. of διατρίβω (LN 85.61) (BDAG p. 238): 'to remain' [AB, BECNT, LN; ESV, NRSV], 'to stay' [Bar, CBC, LN; CEV, GW, NCV, NET, NLT, REB, TEV], 'to abide' [KJV], 'to spend time' [BDAG; NASB, NIV]. This verb means to remain or stay in a place, with the implication of some type of activity [LN]. It means to remain or stay in a place [BDAG].
  b. κύριος (LN 12.9): 'Lord' [AB, Bar, BECNT, CBC, LN; all versions], 'Ruler, One who commands' [LN]. This noun denotes a title for God and for Christ. It indicates one who exercises supernatural authority over mankind [LN].
  c. pres. act. participle of μαρτυρέω (LN 33.262) (BDAG 2.a. p. 618): 'to bear witness' [Bar; ESV], 'to witness' [LN], 'to testify' [BECNT; NASB, NET, NRSV], 'to testify favorably, to speak well of, to approve' [BDAG], 'to confirm' [AB, CBC; GW, NIV, REB], 'to give testimony' [KJV]. The phrase 'the Lord, who bore witness to the word of his grace' is also translated 'he showed that their message about his great kindness/grace was true' [CEV, NCV], 'the Lord proved their message was true' [NLT], 'the Lord, who proved that their message about his grace was true' [TEV]. This verb means to provide information about a person or an event concerning which the speaker has direct knowledge [LN]. It means to affirm in a supportive manner [BDAG].
  d. λόγος (LN 33.260) (BDAG 1.a.β. p. 600): 'word' [Bar, BDAG, BECNT; ESV, KJV, NASB, NRSV], 'message' [CBC; CEV, GW, NCV, NET, NIV, NLT, REB, TEV] 'what is preached, gospel' [LN]. The phrase 'the Lord who bore witness to the word of his grace' is also translated 'the Lord confirmed the preaching of his grace' [AB]. This noun denotes the content of what is preached about Christ or about the good news [LN]. It denotes a communication whereby the mind finds expression [BDAG].
  e. χάρις (LN 88.66) (BDAG 3.b. p. 1080): 'grace' [AB, Bar, BECNT, CBC, LN; all versions except CEV, GW], 'kindness' [CEV], 'graciousness' [LN], 'good will' [GW], 'favor, gracious deed, gracious gift, benefaction' [BDAG]. This noun refers to the kindness shown to someone, with the implication of graciousness on the part of the one showing such kindness [LN]. It denotes the practical application of goodwill on the part of God and Christ [BDAG].
  f. pres. act. participle of δίδωμι (LN 90.51): 'to grant' [ESV, KJV, NASB, NET, NRSV], 'to cause' [Bar, CBC, LN], 'to bring about' [LN], 'to enable' [NIV, REB], 'to give power' [CEV, NCV, NLT, TEV], 'to allow'

[AB], 'to give' [BECNT]. The phrase 'the Lord...granting signs and wonders' is also translated 'the Lord...by having them perform miracles and do amazing things' [GW]. This verb indicates a causal relation [LN].
- g. σημεῖον (LN 33.477) (BDAG 2.a.α. p. 920): 'sign' [AB, Bar, BECNT, CBC, LN; ESV, KJV, NASB, NRSV, REB], 'miracle' [BDAG; CEV, GW, NCV, TEV], 'miraculous sign' [NET, NIV, NLT], 'portent' [BDAG]. This noun denotes an event which is regarded as having some special meaning [LN]. It denotes an event that is an indication or confirmation of intervention by transcendent powers [BDAG].
- h. τέρας (LN 33.480): 'wonder' [AB, BECNT; CEV, ESV, KJV, NASB, NET, NIV, NLT, NRSV, TEV], 'sign' [LN; NCV], 'miracle' [CBC; REB], 'portent' [Bar, LN], 'amazing thing' [GW]. This noun denotes an unusual sign, especially one in the heavens, serving to foretell impending events [LN].
- i. pres. mid./pass. (deponent = act.) of γίνομαι (LN 13.107) (BDAG 2.a. p. 197): 'to be done' [AB, Bar; ESV, KJV, NASB, NRSV], 'to be performed' [BDAG; NET], 'to be worked' [CBC], 'to happen, to occur, to come to be' [LN], 'to be made, to be created' [BDAG], 'to perform' [GW, TEV], 'to do' [NIV, NLT], 'to work' [CEV, NCV, REB], not explicit [BECNT]. This verb means to happen, with the implication that what happens is different from a previous state [LN]. It means to come into existence [BDAG].
- j. χείρ (LN 9.17) (BDAG 2.a. p. 1082): 'the hands (of)' [AB, Bar, BDAG, BECNT, CBC; ESV, KJV, NASB, NET], 'person, agent' [LN], not explicit [CEV, GW, NCV, NIV, NLT, REB, TEV]. The phrase 'to be done by their hands' is also translated 'to be done through them' [NRSV]. This is a figurative extension of meaning of χείρ 'hand' and it denotes a human as an agent in some activity [LN]. It denotes an acting agent [BDAG].

QUESTION—What is meant by the opening phrase μὲν οὖν 'so'?

These verses do not read smoothly. Verse 2 suggests that the Jews began to create trouble almost at once, whereas verse 3 speaks of Paul and Barnabas at work in Iconium for some time before 'a move was made by Gentiles and Jews together, with the connivance of the city authorities, to maltreat them' (verse 5) CBC.
1. Some think that verse 3 continues the thought in verse 1: '(Therefore) since there were so many believers in Iconium' [TRT]. This view is taken by EBC, NAC; ESV, NASB, TEV.
2. Some others think verse 3 begins a new thought: 'Paul and Barnabas stayed for a long time' [TRT]. This view is taken by AB, NICNT.
3. Some others think verse 3 shows that Paul and Barnabas' reaction to what happened in verse 2 was the opposite of what we might expect '(But) in spite of that they remained for a long time' [TRT]. This view is taken by Bar, BECNT, NAC, PNTC, TNTC.

14:4 But the people of-the city were-divided;[a] some sided with the Jews and some with the apostles.
LEXICON—a. aorist pass. indic. of σχίζω (LN 63.26) (BDAG 2.b. p. 981): 'to be divided' [AB, Bar, CBC, LN; all versions except CEV], 'to be split' [BECNT; LN], 'to become divided/disunited' [BDAG], not explicit [CEV]. This verb means to split or divide into two parts [LN]. It means to tear apart a group through conflicting aims or objectives [BDAG].
QUESTION—What does the verb ἐσχίσθη 'were divided' refer to?
The verb 'were divided' did not refer to 'divided thoughts' but to 'divided loyalties': the people of the city separated into two groups [TH]. One group sided with the Jews, the opponents; another group sided with the apostles [Bar, BECNT, CBC, EBC, NAC, NICNT, PNTC, TNTC].
QUESTION—Who were the apostles here?
Here the apostles were Barnabas and Paul. Only here and in v. 14 are Paul or Barnabas described as being an apostle [Bar, BECNT, EBC, NAC, NICNT, PNTC, TNTC]. Elsewhere 'apostle' is reserved for the twelve disciples: eleven of them named in Acts 1:13 and the new apostle Matthias named in Acts 1:26 [Bar, BECNT, NAC, PNTC, TNTC]. Here the word is used in a general sense to mean 'the missionaries sent out by the church' [BECNT, CBC, NAC, TNTC], 'the messengers of the gospel' [EBC].

14:5 When an-attempt[a] was made (by)-both the Gentiles and (the)-Jews, with their rulers, to-mistreat[b] them and to-stone[c] them,
LEXICON—a. ὁρμή (LN 30.78) (BDAG p. 724): 'an attempt' [BECNT; ESV, NASB, NET, NRSV], 'an assault' [KJV], 'an agitation' [AB], 'a plot' [NIV], 'a move' [Bar, CBC; REB], 'impulse, inclination, desire' [BDAG], not explicit [GW, NCV]. This noun is also translated as a verb: 'to decide' [LN; CEV, NLT, TEV]. This noun denotes making a decision to carry out some action, but with emphasis upon the impulse involved [LN]. It denotes a psychological state of strong tendency [BDAG].
b. aorist act. infin. of ὑβρίζω (LN 88.130) (BDAG p. 1022): 'to mistreat' [BDAG; ESV, NASB, NCV, NET, NIV, NRSV, TEV], 'to maltreat' [AB, CBC, LN; REB], 'to mistreat with insolence' [LN], 'to scoff at, to insult' [BDAG], 'to make trouble for' [CEV], 'to attack' [GW, NLT], 'to use (them) despitefully' [KJV], 'to outrage' [Bar], 'to harass' [BECNT]. This verb means to maltreat in an insolent manner [LN]. It means to treat in an insolent or spiteful manner [BDAG].
c. aorist act. infin. of λιθοβολέω (LN 20.79) (BDAG 1. p. 595): 'to stone' [AB, Bar, BECNT, CBC; ESV, KJV, NASB, NET, NIV, NLT, NRSV, REB, TEV], 'to stone to death' [LN; CEV, GW, NCV], 'to throw stones at' [BDAG]. This verb means to kill or attempt to kill by means of hurling stones, normally carried out by angry mobs [LN].
QUESTION—What is meant by the word ὁρμή 'attempt'?
The word 'attempt' suggests a determined effort [PNTC].

QUESTION—Who does 'them' refer to?
It refers to the missionaries, Barnabas and Paul [Bar, NAC, PNTC, TNTC].

14:6 **they learned-(of it)**[a] **and fled**[b] **to Lystra and Derbe, cities of-Lycaonia, and to the surrounding-country,** **14:7** **and-there they continued to preach-the-gospel**[c]**.**

LEXICON—a. aorist act. participle of συνοράω (LN 27.5) (BDAG 1. p. 974): 'to learn of' [BECNT; ESV, NLT, NRSV], 'to learn about' [LN; NCV, NET, TEV], 'to find out' [CEV, GW], 'to find out about' [LN; NIV], 'to be aware of' [KJV], 'to become aware of' [BDAG; NASB, REB], 'to perceive' [Bar, BDAG], 'to hear' [AB]. The phrase 'they learned of it' is also translated 'they got wind of it' [CBC]. This verb means to acquire information, with focus upon the event of perception [LN]. It means to receive information and make an assessment of its significance [BDAG].
   b. aorist act. indic. of καταφεύγω (LN 15.62) (BDAG 1. p. 529): 'to flee' [AB, BDAG, BECNT, LN; ESV, KJV, NASB, NET, NIV, NLT, NRSV, TEV], 'to flee for safety' [LN], 'to flee for refuge' [Bar], 'to escape' [CEV, GW], 'to run away' [NCV]. The phrase 'they…fled' is also translated 'they…made their escape' [CBC; REB]. This verb means to flee from an area [LN]. It means to get away from an area, with the implication of having a destination in mind [BDAG].
   c. pres. mid. participle of εὐαγγελίζω (LN 33.215) (BDAG 2.a.δ. p. 402): 'to preach the gospel' [AB, BECNT; ESV, KJV, NASB], 'to preach the good news' [CEV, NIV, NLT, TEV], 'to tell the good news, to announce the gospel' [LN], 'to proclaim the gospel' [BDAG], 'to proclaim the good news' [NET, NRSV], 'to spread the Good News' [CBC; GW, REB], 'to announce the Good News' [NCV]. The phrase 'they continued to preach the gospel' is also translated 'they were occupied in evangelism' [Bar]. This verb means to communicate good news concerning something and in the NT it is a particular reference to the gospel message about Jesus [LN]. It means to proclaim the divine message of salvation [BDAG].

QUESTION—Where was Lycaonia?
Lycaonia was a district in the Roman Province of Galatia [NAC, TH, TRT].

QUESTION—Where were Lystra and Derbe?
Lystra was a Roman colony about 18 miles (29 km.) southwest of the city of Iconium [Bar, BECNT, CBC, NAC, NICNT, PNTC, TH, TNTC, TRT] and about 60 miles (97 km.) west of the city of Derbe [Bar, NAC, TNTC, TRT]. Derbe was a frontier city of the province of Galatia [TH].

QUESTION—What does 'there' refer to?
'There' refers to the entire region including Lystra and Derbe [Bar, CBC, PNTC, TH].

DISCOURSE UNIT—14:8–21a [NAC]. The topic is preaching to pagans at Lystra.

DISCOURSE UNIT—14:8–20 [AB, BECNT, EBC, PNTC, TNTC; CEV, NCV, NET, NIV, NLT, NRSV, TEV]. The topic is Paul and Barnabas in Lystra [AB; CEV], in Lystra, and Derbe [BECNT; NIV, TEV], the ministry at Lystra [EBC], Paul in Lystra and Derbe [NCV], Paul and Barnabas at Lystra [NET], Paul and Barnabas in Lystra and Derbe [NLT, NRSV], encountering paganism in Lystra [PNTC], evangelism of the heathen at Lystra [TNTC].

DISCOURSE UNIT—14:8–20a [GW]. The topic is Paul and Barnabas in Lystra.

DISCOURSE UNIT—14:8–18 [ESV]. The topic is Paul and Barnabas at Lystra.

DISCOURSE UNIT—14:8–13 [NICNT]. The topic is miraculous healing at Lystra.

14:8 Now at Lystra there was- a man -sitting who could not use his feet. He was lame[a] from his mother's womb[b] and had never walked.

LEXICON—a. χωλός (LN 23.175) (BDAG p. 1093): 'lame' [Bar, CBC, LN; GW, NASB, NET, NIV, REB, TEV], 'crippled' [BDAG; CEV, ESV, NCV, NLT, NRSV]. The phrase 'He was lame from his mother's womb' is also translated 'a cripple from his mother's womb' [AB; KJV], 'a cripple from the womb' [BECNT]. This adjective pertains to a disability that involves the imperfect function of the lower limbs [LN].

b. κοιλία (LN 8.69) (BDAG p. 550): 'womb' [AB, Bar, BDAG, BECNT, LN; NASB, KJV], 'uterus' [BDAG]. The phrase 'lame from his mother's womb' is also translated 'crippled from birth' [ESV, NRSV], 'lame from birth' [CBC; NET, NIV, REB, TEV], 'he had been that way from birth' [NLT], 'born with crippled feet' [CEV], 'born lame' [GW], 'born crippled' [NCV], 'from earliest youth' [BDAG]. This noun denotes the womb [LN].

14:9 He listened[a] to Paul speaking. And Paul, looking-intently-at[b] him and seeing[c] that he-had faith to-be-made-well,[d] **14:10** said in-(a)-loud voice, "Stand[e] upright on your feet." And he-jumped-up[f] and began walking.

LEXICON—a. aorist act. indic. of ἀκούω (LN 31.56): 'to listen to' [BECNT, LN; all versions except KJV, NLT], 'to listen' [AB, CBC; NLT], 'to accept, to listen and respond, to pay attention and respond, to heed' [LN], 'to hear' [Bar; KJV]. This verb means to believe something and to respond to it on the basis of having heard [LN].

b. aorist act. participle of ἀτενίζω (LN 24.49) (BDAG p. 148): 'to look intently at' [BDAG, BECNT; ESV], 'to look at intently' [NRSV], 'to look directly at' [NIV], 'to look straight at' [LN; CEV, NCV, NLT, TEV], 'to stare intently at' [NET], 'to stare at' [BDAG, LN], 'to keep one's eyes fixed on' [LN], 'to observe' [GW], 'to gaze at' [AB]. The phrase 'Paul looking intently at him' is also translated 'Paul fixed his eyes on him' [Bar, CBC; REB], 'he had fixed his gaze on him' [NASB], 'who

stedfastly beholding him' [KJV]. This verb means to fix one's eyes on some object continually and intensely [LN].
  c. aorist act. participle of εἶδον (LN 32.11): 'to see' [Bar, BECNT, CBC, LN; all versions except KJV, NLT], 'to perceive' [AB, LN; KJV], 'to realize' [NLT], 'to understand, to recognize' [LN]. This verb means to come to understand as the result of perception [LN].
  d. aorist pass. infin. of σῴζω (LN 23.136) (BDAG 1.c. p. 982): 'to be made well' [ESV, GW, NASB], 'to be healed' [CEV, KJV, NET, NIV, NLT, NRSV, TEV], 'to be cured' [AB, CBC; REB], 'to be delivered' [BECNT], 'to be restored to health, to get well' [BDAG], 'to cure, to make well' [LN]. This verb is also translated as an active verb: 'to heal' [NCV]. This verb is also translated as a noun: 'healing' [Bar, LN]. This verb means to cause someone to become well again after having been sick [LN]. It means to preserve or rescue from natural dangers and afflictions [BDAG].
  e. aorist act. impera. of ἀνίστημι (LN 17.6): 'to stand up' [AB, BECNT, CBC, LN; all versions], 'to get up' [Bar]. This verb means to assume a standing position [LN].
  f. aorist mid. (deponent = act.) indic. of ἄλλομαι (LN 15.238) (BDAG 1. p. 46): 'to jump up' [Bar; CEV, GW, NCV, NIV, TEV], 'to leap up' [AB; NASB, NET], 'to leap' [BDAG, LN; KJV], 'to jump' [LN; NLT], 'to spring up' [BDAG, BECNT, CBC; ESV, NRSV, REB]. This verb means to leap or to jump into the air [LN]. It means to make a quick leaping movement [BDAG].

QUESTION—What is meant by 'to be made well?

Here 'to be made well' means 'to be healed physically' [AB, Bar, CBC, EBC, NAC, NICNT, PNTC, TH, TNTC, TRT], to be delivered from a crippled condition [BECNT]. The lame man's faith was made plain by his ready obedience to Paul's command to stand up. When he sprang/jumped up he then began to walk for the first time in his life [NICNT].

14:11 And when the crowds saw what Paul had-done, they raised[a] their voices, saying in Lycaonian, "The gods have-become-like[b] men and have-come-down[c] to us!"

LEXICON—a. aorist act. indic. of ἐπαίρω (LN 33.78) (BDAG 1. p. 357): 'to raise' [AB; NASB], 'to lift up' [Bar, BDAG, BECNT; ESV, KJV], 'to raise the voice, to cry out, to speak loudly' [LN]. The phrase 'they raised their voices' is also translated 'they shouted' [CBC; NCV, NET, NIV, NLT, NRSV, REB], 'they started shouting' [TEV], 'they yelled out' [CEV], 'the crowds...shouted' [GW]. The idiom 'to raise the voice' means to increase the volume with which one speaks, so as to overcome existing noise or the speech of someone else [LN]. It means to cause to move upward [BDAG].
  b. aorist pass. participle of ὁμοιόω (LN 64.4) (BDAG 1. p. 707): 'to become like' [BDAG; NASB, NCV, TEV], 'to be like, to resemble, to be similar

to' [LN]. The phrase 'The gods have become like men' is also translated 'The gods...in the likeness of men' [ESV, KJV], 'The gods...in human form' [CBC; NET, NIV, NRSV, REB], 'The gods...made like men' [Bar], 'The gods have turned into humans' [CEV], 'The gods...and they look human' [GW], 'The gods in the likeness of men' [BECNT], 'These men are gods in human form' [NLT], 'The gods have taken human form' [AB]. This verb means to be like or similar to something else [LN].

c. aorist act. indic. of καταβαίνω (LN 15.107) (BDAG 1.a.δ. p. 514): 'to come down' [AB, Bar, BDAG, BECNT, CBC; all versions except GW, NLT], 'to move down, to descend' [LN], 'to go down' [BDAG, LN], 'to come' [GW], not explicit [NLT]. This verb means to move down, irrespective of the gradient [LN]. It means to move downward [BDAG].

14:12 **Barnabas they-called**[a] **Zeus, and Paul, Hermes, because he was the chief speaker.**

LEXICON—a. imperf. act. indic. of καλέω (LN 33.129) (BDAG 1.b. p. 502): 'to call' [AB, Bar, BDAG, BECNT, CBC, LN; ESV, KJV, NASB, NCV, NET, NIV, NRSV, REB], 'to name' [BDAG, LN], 'to call by name' [BDAG], 'to address' [GW]. The phrase 'Barnabas they called Zeus' is also translated 'The people then gave Barnabas the name Zeus' [CEV], 'They gave Barnabas the name Zeus' [TEV], 'They decided that Barnabas was the Greek god Zeus' [NLT]. This verb means to speak of a person or object by means of a proper name [LN]. It means to identify by name or attribute [BDAG].

14:13 **And the priest of-Zeus, whose temple was just outside the city, brought**[a] **oxen and garlands to the gates and wanted to-offer-sacrifice**[b] **with the crowds.**

LEXICON—a. aorist act. participle of φέρω (LN 15.166) (BDAG 2.b.α. p. 1051): 'to bring' [AB, Bar, BDAG, BECNT, CBC, LN; all versions], 'to take' [LN], 'to lead' [BDAG]. This verb means to cause to move to a place, with a possible implication of assistance or firm control [LN]. It means to cause an entity to move from one position to another and here it refers to animals [BDAG].

b. pres. act. infin. of θύω (LN 53.19) (BDAG 1. p. 463): 'to offer sacrifice' [AB, Bar, BECNT, CBC; ESV, NASB, NET, NIV, NLT, NRSV, REB, TEV], 'to offer a sacrifice' [CEV, GW, NCV], 'to sacrifice' [BDAG, LN], 'to make a sacrifice' [LN], 'to do sacrifice' [KJV], 'to make a cultic offering' [BDAG]. This verb means to slaughter an animal in a ritual manner as a sacrifice to deity [LN].

14:14 **But**[a] **when the apostles Barnabas and Paul heard of it, they tore their garments and rushed-out**[b] **into the crowd, crying-out,**[c]

LEXICON—a. δέ (LN 89.124): 'but' [AB, Bar, BECNT, CBC, LN; ESV, NASB, NCV, NET, NIV, NLT, REB], 'on the other hand' [LN], not

explicit [CEV, GW, KJV, NRSV, TEV]. This conjunction indicates a contrast [LN].
b. aorist act. indic. of ἐκπηδάω (LN 15.236) (BDAG 1. p. 307): 'to rush out' [BDAG, BECNT, LN; ESV, NASB, NET, NIV, NRSV], 'to rush' [AB, CBC; GW, REB], 'to run out' [LN; NLT], 'to run' [CEV, KJV, NCV, TEV], 'to spring' [Bar]. This verb means to run or rush out quickly [LN]. It means to move forward with haste [BDAG].
c. pres. act. participle of κράζω (LN 33.83) (BDAG 2.a. p. 563): 'to cry out' [ESV, KJV, NASB], 'to shout' [AB, Bar, CBC, LN; CEV, NCV, NET, NIV, NLT, NRSV, REB, TEV], 'to scream' [LN], 'to call, to call out' [BDAG], 'to cry' [BDAG, BECNT], not explicit [GW]. This verb means to shout or cry out, with the possible implication of the unpleasant nature of the sound [LN]. It means to communicate something in a loud voice [BDAG].

14:15 "Men, why are-you-doing these-things? We also are men of-(the)-same-nature-(as) you, and we preach-the-gospel[a] to-you, that you should turn[b] from these vain-things to (the)-living God, who made the heaven[c] and the earth[d] and the sea[e] and all that is in them.

LEXICON—a. pres. mid. participle of εὐαγγελίζω (LN 33.215) (BDAG 2.a.β. p. 402): 'to preach the gospel' [NASB], 'to tell the good news, to announce the gospel' [LN], 'to proclaim the gospel' [BDAG], 'to proclaim the good news' [BECNT; NET], 'to announce the good news' [TEV], 'to spread the good news' [GW], 'to preach' [AB; KJV], not explicit [CEV]. The phrase 'we preach the good news' is also translated 'the good news we bring' [CBC; REB], 'who bring...the good news' [Bar], 'we bring...good news' [ESV, NRSV], 'we are bringing...the good news' [NCV], 'we are bringing...good news' [NIV], 'we have come to bring...the good news' [NLT]. This verb means to communicate good news concerning something and in the NT it is a particular reference to the gospel message about Jesus [LN]. It means to proclaim the divine message of salvation [BDAG].
b. pres. act. infin. of ἐπιστρέφω (LN 31.60) (BDAG 4.a. p. 382): 'to turn' [AB, Bar, BDAG, BECNT, CBC; all versions], 'to turn to, to come to believe, to come to accept' [LN], 'to return' [BDAG]. This verb means to change one's belief, with focus upon that to which one turns [LN]. It means to change one's mind or course of action, for better or worse [BDAG].
c. οὐρανός (LN 1.5, 1.11) (BDAG 1.a.α. p. 737): 'heaven' [AB, Bar, BDAG, BECNT, CBC, LN (1.11); ESV, KJV, NASB, NET, NIV, NLT, NRSV, REB, TEV], 'sky' [LN (1.5); CEV, GW, NCV]. This noun denotes the space above the earth, including the vault arching high over the earth from one horizon to another, as well as the sun, moon, and stars [LN (1.5)] or it denotes heaven, the supernatural dwelling place of God and other heavenly beings [LN (1.11)]. It denotes the portion or portions

ACTS 14:15   409

of the universe generally distinguished from planet earth forming a unity with it as the totality of creation [BDAG].
d. γῆ (LN 1.39): 'earth' [AB, Bar, BECNT, CBC, LN; all versions except GW], 'land' [GW], 'world' [LN]. This noun denotes the surface of the earth as the dwelling place of mankind, in contrast with the heavens above and the world below [LN].
e. θάλασσα (LN 1.69) (BDAG 1.a. p. 442): 'sea' [AB, Bar, BDAG, BECNT, CBC, LN; all versions]. This noun is 'a generic collective term for all bodies of water...contrasted with the sky and the land' [LN]. The combination heaven, earth, and sea denotes the whole universe [BDAG].

14:16 In the generations having-passed-by[a] he allowed[b] all the nations[c] to-go[d] their own ways[e].

LEXICON—a. perf. mid./pass. (deponent=act.) participle of παροίχομαι (LN 67.85) (BDAG p. 780): 'to be passed' [BDAG], 'to pass, to have passed' [LN]. This verb is also translated as an adjective: 'in times past' [CEV, KJV], 'past generations/ages' [AB, BECNT, CBC; ESV, NET, NRSV, REB], 'the generations gone by' [Bar; NASB]. The phrase 'In the generations having passed by' is also translated 'In the past' [GW, NCV, NIV, NLT, TEV]. This verb means to mark the passage of time, with focus upon completion [LN].
b. aorist act. indic. of ἐάω (LN 13.138) (BDAG 1. p. 269): 'to allow' [AB, BECNT, CBC, LN; ESV, GW, NET, NRSV, REB, TEV], 'to permit' [Bar, BDAG, LN; NASB, NLT], 'to let' [BDAG, LN; CEV, NCV, NIV], 'to suffer' [KJV]. This verb means to allow someone to do something [BDAG, LN].
c. ἔθνος (LN 11.55): 'nation' [AB, BECNT, CBC, LN; all versions except GW, TEV], 'people' [LN; GW, TEV], 'Gentiles' [Bar]. This noun denotes the largest unit into which the people of the world are divided on the basis of their constituting a socio-political community [LN].
d. pres. mid./pass. (deponent = act.) infin. of πορεύομαι (LN 41.11) (BDAG 2. p. 853): 'to go' [Bar, BECNT, CBC; CEV, NASB, NET, NIV, NLT, REB, TEV], 'to walk' [AB, BDAG; ESV, KJV], 'to live' [BDAG, LN; GW], 'to behave, to go about doing' [LN], 'to do' [NCV], 'to follow' [NRSV]. This verb means to live or behave in a customary manner, with possible focus upon continuity of action [LN]. It means to conduct oneself [BDAG].
e. ὁδός (LN 41.16) (BDAG 3.b. p. 691): 'way' [AB, Bar, BDAG, BECNT, CBC; all versions except GW, NCV], 'way of life' [BDAG, LN], 'way to live' [LN], 'way of acting, conduct' [BDAG]. The clause 'he allowed all the nations to go their own ways' is also translated 'God allowed all people to live as they pleased' [GW], 'God let all the nations do what they wanted' [NCV]. This noun is a figurative extension of meaning of ὁδός 'road' and denotes a customary manner of life or behavior, with probably

some implication of goal or purpose [LN]. It denotes a course of behavior [BDAG].

14:17 Yet he-did- not -leave[a] himself without-witness, for he did-good[b] by giving you rains from-heaven and fruitful seasons, satisfying[c] your hearts[d] with food and gladness.[e]"

LEXICON—a. aorist act. indic. of ἀφίημι (LN 13.140) (BDAG 5.a. p. 157): 'to leave' [Bar, BECNT, CBC; ESV, KJV, NASB, NET, NIV, NLT, NRSV, REB], 'to let, to allow' [BDAG, LN], 'to leave it to' [LN], 'to let go' [BDAG]. The clause 'Yet he did not leave himself without witness' is also translated 'But he showed that he was there' [CEV], 'Yet…he has given evidence of his existence' [GW], 'Yet he proved he is real' [NCV], 'But he has always given evidence of his existence' [TEV], 'Yet he did not remain without witness' [AB]. This verb means to leave it to someone to do something [BDAG, LN], with the implication of distancing oneself from the event [LN].

b. pres. act. participle of ἀγαθοεργέω (LN 88.3) (BDAG p. 2): 'to do good' [AB, Bar, BDAG, BECNT, LN; ESV, GW, KJV, NASB, NET, NRSV], 'to perform good deeds, good works' [LN], 'to confer benefits' [LN], 'to show kindness' [NCV, NIV], not explicit [NLT]. The phrase 'he did good' is also translated 'the good things he did/does' [CEV, TEV], 'the benefits he bestows' [REB], 'the kindness he shows' [CBC]. This verb means to engage in doing what is good [LN]. It means to do that which benefits others [BDAG].

c. pres. act. participle of ἐμπίπλημι (LN 23.17) (BDAG 2. p. 323): 'to satisfy' [BDAG; ESV, NASB, NET], 'to fill' [AB, Bar, BECNT; KJV], 'to fill with food, to satisfy with food' [LN]. The phrase 'satisfying your hearts with food and gladness' is also translated 'gives food to you and makes your hearts glad' [CEV], 'provides you with plenty of food and fills your hearts with joy' [NIV], 'gives you food and joyful hearts' [NLT], 'fills you with food and your lives with happiness' [GW], 'filling you with food and your hearts with joy' [NRSV], 'gives you food in plenty and keeps you in good heart' [REB], 'giving you food and filling your hearts with joy' [NCV], 'gives you food and fills your hearts with happiness' [TEV], 'gives you food and good cheer in plenty' [CBC]. This verb means to cause someone to be satisfied as the result of food which has been provided in sufficient quantity [LN]. It means to provide a sufficient amount [BDAG].

d. καρδία (LN 26.3) (BDAG p. 508): 'heart' [AB, Bar, BDAG, BECNT, LN; all versions except GW], 'inner self, mind' [LN]. The phrase 'satisfying your hearts with food and gladness' is also translated 'fills you with food and your lives with happiness' [GW], 'gives you food and good cheer in plenty' [CBC]. This noun is a figurative extension of meaning of καρδία 'heart,' and denotes the causative source of a person's psychological life in its various aspects, but with special emphasis upon thoughts [LN]. It denotes the heart as the center and source of physical life [BDAG].

e. εὐφροσύνη (LN 25.121) (BDAG p. 415): 'gladness' [Bar, BDAG, BECNT; ESV, KJV, NASB], 'joyfulness, rejoicing' [LN], 'joy' [AB, BDAG; NCV, NET, NIV, NRSV], 'cheerfulness' [BDAG], 'happiness' [GW, TEV]. This noun is also translated as an adjective: 'makes your hearts glad' [CEV], 'joyful hearts' [NLT]. The phrase 'satisfying your hearts with food and gladness' is also translated 'gives you food in plenty and keeps you in good heart' [REB], 'gives you food and good cheer in plenty' [CBC]. This noun denotes a state of joyful happiness [LN].

14:18 Even with saying these-words they- scarcely -restrained[a] the people from offering-sacrifice[b] to-them.

LEXICON—a. aorist act. indic. of καταπαύω (LN 68.46) (BDAG 2.b. p. 524): 'to restrain' [AB, BDAG, BECNT; ESV, KJV, NASB, NLT, NRSV], 'to cause to cease, to make stop' [LN], 'to cause to rest' [BDAG], 'to persuade' [NET], 'to prevent' [Bar, CBC; REB], 'to keep' [CEV, GW, NCV, NIV, TEV]. This verb means to cause something or someone to cease from some activity or state [LN]. It means to cause persons to be at rest by causing to give up something they have begun to do with the result that they are quiet [BDAG].

b. pres. act. infin. of θύω (LN 53.19) (BDAG 1. p. 463): 'to offer sacrifice' [BECNT, CBC; ESV, NASB, NCV, NET, NRSV, REB], 'to offer a sacrifice' [CEV, TEV], 'to sacrifice' [AB, Bar, BDAG, LN; GW, KJV, NIV, NLT], 'to make a sacrifice' [LN]. This verb means to slaughter an animal in a ritual manner as a sacrifice to deity [LN]. It means to make a cultic offering [BDAG].

14:19 But Jews came from Antioch and Iconium, and having-persuaded[a] the crowds, they stoned[b] Paul and dragged-(him)[c] out of the city, supposing that he was-dead.

LEXICON—a. aorist act. participle of πείθω (LN 33.301) (BDAG 1.c. p. 791): 'to persuade' [BECNT, LN; ESV, KJV, NCV], 'to win over' [AB, BDAG, CBC; GW, NASB, NET, NIV, NRSV, REB, TEV], 'to convince' [LN], 'to strive to please' [BDAG]. The phrase 'Jews came...and having persuaded the crowds' is also translated 'Jewish leaders...came and turned the crowds against Paul' [CEV], 'Jews arrived...and won the crowds to their side' [NLT], 'there came Jews...they got the crowds on their side' [Bar]. This verb means to convince someone to believe something and to act on the basis of what is recommended [LN]. It means to cause to come to a particular point of view or course of action [BDAG].

b. aorist act. participle of λιθάζω (LN 20.79) (BDAG p. 595): 'to stone' [AB, Bar, BDAG, BECNT, CBC; ESV, KJV, NASB, NET, NIV, NLT, NRSV, REB, TEV], 'to stone to death' [LN; GW]. The phrase 'they stoned Paul' is also translated 'they hit him with stones' [CEV], 'they

threw stones at him' [NCV]. This verb means to kill or attempt to kill by means of hurling stones, normally carried out by angry mobs [LN].
  c. imperf. act. indic. of σύρω (LN 15.212) (BDAG p. 978): 'to drag' [AB, Bar, BDAG, BECNT, CBC, LN; all versions except KJV], 'to draw' [BDAG, LN; KJV], 'to pull' [BDAG, LN], 'to drag away' [BDAG]. This verb means to pull or drag, requiring force because of the inertia of the object being dragged [LN].

14:20 But when the disciples gathered-about[a] him, he rose-up[b] and entered[c] the city, and on-the next-day he-went-out[d] with Barnabas to Derbe.
LEXICON—a. aorist act. participle of κυκλόω (LN 15.147) (BDAG 1.a. p. 574): 'to gather about' [BECNT; ESV], 'to gather around' [CEV, GW, NCV, NIV, NLT, TEV], 'to stand around' [NASB], 'to surround' [Bar, BDAG, LN; NET, NRSV], 'to be around' [LN], 'to encircle' [BDAG]. The phrase 'the disciples gathered about him' is also translated 'the disciples stood round him' [AB], 'the disciples stood round about him' [KJV], 'the converts/disciples formed a ring round him' [CBC; REB]. This verb means to move in such a way as to encircle an object [LN]. It means to move so as to encircle an object with hostile intent [BDAG].
  b. aorist act. participle of ἀνίστημι (LN 17.6): 'to rise up' [ESV, KJV], 'to stand up' [LN; CEV], 'to get up' [AB, Bar; GW, NASB, NCV, NET, NIV, NLT, NRSV, TEV], 'to arise' [BECNT]. The phrase 'he rose up' is also translated 'he got to his feet' [CBC; REB]. This verb means to assume a standing position [LN].
  c. aorist act. indic. of εἰσέρχομαι (LN 15.93) (BDAG 1.a.γ. p. 294): 'to enter' [BDAG, BECNT, LN; ESV, NASB], 'to go into' [AB, Bar, CBC, LN; CEV, GW, NCV, NET, NIV, NLT, NRSV, REB, TEV], 'to come into' [LN; KJV], 'to move into' [LN]. This verb means to move into a space, either two-dimensional or three-dimensional [LN]. It means to move into a space of structural areas and establishments [BDAG].
  d. aorist act. indic. of ἐξέρχομαι (LN 15.40): 'to go out' [BECNT], 'to go away' [NASB], 'to go' [CEV, TEV], 'to leave' [AB, Bar, CBC; GW, NCV, NET, NIV, NLT, REB], 'to depart' [KJV], 'to go out of, to depart out of, to leave from within' [LN]. The phrase 'he went out with Barnabas' is also translated 'he went on with Barnabas' [ESV, NRSV]. This verb means to move out of an enclosed or well defined two or three-dimensional area [LN].

14:21 When they had-preached-the-gospel-(to)[a] that city and had-made-many -disciples,[b] they-returned[c] to Lystra and to Iconium and to Antioch,
LEXICON—a. aorist mid. participle of εὐαγγελίζω (LN 33.215) (BDAG 2.a.γ. p. 402): 'to preach the gospel' [AB, BECNT; ESV, KJV, NASB], 'to preach the good news' [CEV, NIV, NLT, TEV], 'to tell the good news' [LN; NCV], 'to announce the gospel' [LN], 'to spread the good news' [GW], 'to proclaim the gospel' [BDAG], 'to proclaim the good news'

[NET, NRSV], 'to bring the good news' [CBC; REB]. The phrase 'when they had preached the gospel to that city' is also translated 'when they had evangelized that city' [Bar]. This verb means to communicate good news concerning something and in the NT it refers to the gospel message about Jesus [LN]. It means to proclaim the divine message of salvation [BDAG].
  b. aorist act. participle of μαθητεύω (LN 36.37) (BDAG 2. p. 609): 'to make disciples' [Bar, BECNT, LN; ESV, NASB, NET, NLT, NRSV], 'to cause people to become followers' [LN], 'to teach' [BDAG]. The phrase 'had made many disciples' is also translated 'won many disciples' [GW, TEV], 'won some people to the Lord' [CEV], 'won a large number of disciples' [NIV], 'gained/gaining many converts' [CBC; REB], 'persuaded many to become disciples' [AB], 'had taught many' [KJV], 'many became followers' [NCV]. This verb means to cause someone to become a disciple or follower of [LN]. It means to cause one to be a pupil and here it means to make a number of disciples [BDAG].
  c. aorist act. indic. of ὑποστρέφω (LN 15.88): 'to return' [AB, Bar, BECNT, CBC, LN; ESV, KJV, NASB, NCV, NET, NIV, NLT, NRSV, REB], 'to go back' [LN; CEV, GW, TEV], 'to come back' [LN]. This verb means to move back to a point from which one has previously departed [LN].

14:22 strengthening[a] the souls[b] of-the disciples, encouraging-(them)[c] to-continue[d] in-the faith,[e] and saying that through many tribulations[f] we must enter[g] the kingdom of-God.
LEXICON—a. pres. act. participle of ἐπιστηρίζω (LN 74.19) (BDAG p. 381): 'to strengthen' [AB, Bar, BDAG, BECNT, LN; ESV, GW, NASB, NET, NIV, NLT, NRSV, REB, TEV], 'to encourage' [CEV], 'to confirm' [KJV], 'to make stronger' [NCV], 'to make more firm' [LN], 'to hearten' [CBC]. This verb means to cause someone to become stronger in the sense of more firm and unchanging in attitude or belief [LN]. It means to cause someone to become stronger or more firm [BDAG].
  b. ψυχή (LN 26.4) (BDAG 2.c. p. 1099): 'soul' [Bar, BDAG, BECNT; ESV, KJV, NASB, NET, NRSV], 'heart' [AB, LN], 'inner self, mind, thoughts, feelings, being' [LN]. The phrase 'strengthening the souls of the disciples' is also translated 'encouraged the followers' [CEV], 'strengthened the disciples/believers' [GW, NLT, TEV], 'strengthening the disciples' [NIV, REB], 'making the followers of Jesus stronger' [NCV], 'heartening the converts' [CBC]. This noun denotes the essence of life in terms of thinking, willing, and feeling [LN]. It denotes the seat and center of the inner human life concerning feelings and emotions [BDAG].
  c. pres. act. participle of παρακαλέω (LN 25.150) (BDAG 2. p. 765): 'to encourage' [BDAG, CBC, LN; ESV, GW, NASB, NET, NIV, NLT, NRSV, REB, TEV], 'to exhort' [AB, Bar, BDAG, BECNT; KJV], 'to appeal to, to urge' [BDAG], 'to beg' [CEV]. The phrase 'encouraging

them to continue in the faith' is also translated 'helping them stay in the faith' [NCV]. This verb means to cause someone to be encouraged or consoled, either by verbal or non-verbal means [LN]. It means to urge strongly [BDAG].
d. pres. act. infin. of ἐμμένω (LN 68.11) (BDAG 2. p. 322): 'to continue' [LN; ESV, KJV, NASB, NET, NLT, NRSV], 'to remain' [BECNT], 'to remain firm/true/faithful' [AB; CEV, GW, NIV, TEV], 'to be true' [CBC; REB], 'to stay' [NCV], 'to remain in, to keep on' [LN], 'to persevere in, to stand by' [BDAG], 'to abide' [Bar]. This verb means to continue in an activity or state [LN]. It means to persist in a state or enterprise [BDAG].
e. πίστις (LN 31.102) (BDAG 2.d.α. p. 819): 'faith' [AB, Bar, BDAG, BECNT; all versions except CEV, GW], 'Christian faith' [LN], 'trust, confidence' [BDAG]. The phrase 'to continue in the faith' is also translated 'to remain faithful' [CEV, GW], 'to be true to their religion' [CBC]. This noun denotes the belief in the good news about Jesus Christ and becoming a follower [LN]. It denotes the state of believing on the basis of the reliability of the one trusted [BDAG].
f. θλῖψις (LN 22.2) (BDAG 1. p. 457): 'tribulation' [BDAG, BECNT; ESV, KJV, NASB], 'persecution' [LN; NET, NRSV], 'hardship' [CBC; NIV, NLT, REB], 'trouble' [TEV], 'trial' [AB], 'affliction' [Bar, BDAG], 'trouble and suffering, suffering' [LN], 'oppression' [BDAG]. The phrase 'through many tribulations we must enter the kingdom of God' is also translated 'we have to suffer a lot before we can get into God's kingdom' [CEV], 'we must suffer a lot to enter the kingdom of God' [GW], 'we must suffer many things to enter God's kingdom' [NCV]. This noun denotes trouble involving direct suffering [LN]. It denotes trouble that inflicts distress [BDAG].
g. aorist act. infin. of εἰσέρχομαι (LN 90.70): 'to enter' [AB, Bar, BECNT, CBC; all versions except CEV], 'to begin to experience, to come into an experience, to attain' [LN]. The phrase 'we must enter' is also translated 'we can get into' [CEV]. This verb means to begin to experience an event or state [LN].

14:23 And when they had-appointed[a] elders[b] for-them in-every church, having-prayed with fasting, they-committed[c] them to-the Lord[d] in whom they-had-believed.[e]
LEXICON—a. aorist act. participle of χειροτονέω (LN 37.103) (BDAG 2. p. 1083): 'to appoint' [AB, Bar, BECNT, CBC, LN; ESV, NASB, NET, NIV, NLT, NRSV, REB, TEV], 'to assign' [LN], 'to choose' [BDAG; CEV, GW, NCV], 'to ordain' [KJV]. This verb means to formally appoint or assign someone to a particular task [LN]. It means to elect or choose someone for a definite office or task [BDAG].
b. πρεσβύτερος (LN 53.77) (BDAG 2.b.α. p. 862): 'elder' [AB, Bar, BDAG, BECNT, CBC, LN; all versions except CEV, GW], 'leader' [CEV, GW], 'presbyter' [BDAG]. This noun denotes a person of

responsibility and authority in matters of socio-religious concerns, both in Jewish and Christian societies [LN]. It denotes an official among the Christians [BDAG].

c. aorist mid. indic. of παρατίθημι (LN 35.47) (BDAG 3.b. p. 772): 'to commit' [Bar, BECNT, CBC; ESV, NIV, REB], 'to commend' [AB, BDAG; KJV, NASB, TEV], 'to entrust' [BDAG; GW, NET, NRSV], 'to entrust oneself to, to commit oneself to the care of' [LN], 'to give over' [BDAG], 'to turn over' [NLT]. The phrase 'they committed them to the Lord' is also translated 'they went without eating and prayed that the Lord would take good care of these leaders' [CEV], 'Paul and Barnabas put them in the Lord's care' [NCV]. This verb means to entrust oneself to the care of someone [LN]. It means to entrust for safekeeping and here it means to entrust someone to the care or protection of someone [BDAG].

d. κύριος (LN 12.9): 'Lord' [AB, Bar, BECNT, CBC, LN; all versions], 'Ruler, One who commands' [LN]. This noun denotes a title for God and for Christ. It indicates one who exercises supernatural authority over mankind [LN].

e. pluperfect act. indic. of πιστεύω (LN 31.102) (BDAG 2.a.β. p. 817): 'to believe' [AB, BECNT, ESV, GW, KJV, NASB, NET, NRSV], 'to trust' [BDAG; NCV], 'to be a believer, to be a Christian' [LN], 'to believe in' [BDAG], not explicit [CEV]. The phrase 'in whom they had believed' is also translated 'in whom they had put their trust/faith' [Bar, CBC; NIV, NLT, REB, TEV]. This verb means to believe in the good news about Jesus Christ and to become a follower [LN]. It means to entrust oneself to an entity in complete confidence [BDAG].

14:24 Then they passed-through[a] Pisidia and came[b] to Pamphylia.

LEXICON—a. aorist act. participle of διέρχομαι (LN 15.21) (BDAG 1.b.α. p. 244): 'to pass through' [Bar, BECNT, CBC; ESV, KJV, NASB, NET, NRSV, REB], 'to go through' [BDAG; CEV, GW, NCV, NIV, TEV], 'to travel through' [AB; NLT], 'to travel around through, to journey all through' [LN]. This verb means to travel around through an area, with the implication of both extensive and thorough movement throughout an area [LN]. It means to move within or through an area [BDAG].

b. aorist act. indic. of ἔρχομαι (LN 15.81): 'to come' [AB, Bar, BECNT, CBC, LN; ESV, KJV, NASB, NCV, NET, NIV, NRSV, REB, TEV], 'to go' [GW], not explicit [CEV, NLT]. This verb means to move toward or up to the reference point of the viewpoint character or event [LN].

14:25 And when they had-spoken the word[a] in Perga, they-went-down[b] to Attalia,

LEXICON—a. λόγος (LN 33.260) (BDAG 1.a.β. p. 600): 'word' [AB, Bar, BDAG, BECNT; ESV, KJV, NASB, NET, NIV, NLT, NRSV], 'message' [CBC; GW, NCV, REB, TEV], 'what is preached, gospel' [LN], not explicit [CEV]. This noun denotes the content of what is preached about

Christ or about the good news [LN]. It denotes a communication whereby the mind finds expression [BDAG].
  b. aorist act. indic. of καταβαίνω (LN 15.107) (BDAG 1.a.β. p. 514): 'to go down' [Bar, BDAG, BECNT, CBC, LN; all versions except GW, TEV], 'to come down' [AB, BDAG, LN], 'to move down, to descend' [LN], 'to go' [GW, TEV]. This verb means to move down, irrespective of the gradient [LN]. It means to move downward [BDAG].

14:26 and-from-there they-sailed to Antioch, where they-had-been commended[a] to-the grace[b] of-God for the work[c] that they-had-fulfilled.[d]
LEXICON—a. perf. pass. participle of παραδίδωμι (LN 57.77) (BDAG 2. p. 762): 'to be commended' [AB, BDAG, BECNT, CBC; ESV, NASB, NET, NRSV, REB, TEV], 'to be committed' [Bar, BDAG; NIV], 'to be given over' [BDAG, LN], 'to be handed over' [LN], 'to be entrusted' [GW], 'to be recommended' [KJV]. This verb is also translated as an active verb: 'the believers there had entrusted them' [NLT]. The phrase 'they had been commended to the grace of God' is also translated 'they had been placed in God's care' [CEV], 'the believers had put them into God's care' [NCV]. This verb means to hand over to or to convey something to someone, particularly a right or an authority [LN]. It means to entrust for care or preservation [BDAG].
  b. χάρις (LN 88.66) (BDAG 2.a. p. 1079): 'grace' [AB, Bar, BDAG, BECNT, CBC, LN; ESV, KJV, NASB, NET, NIV, NLT, NRSV, REB, TEV], 'kindness, graciousness' [LN], 'favor, gracious care/help, goodwill' [BDAG]. The phrase 'grace of God' is also translated 'God's care' [CEV, GW, NCV]. This noun refers to the kindness shown to someone, with the implication of graciousness on the part of the one showing such kindness [LN]. It denotes a beneficent disposition toward someone [BDAG].
  c. ἔργον (LN 42.42) (BDAG 2. p. 391): 'work' [AB, Bar, BDAG, BECNT, LN; all versions except REB, TEV], 'task' [BDAG, CBC, LN; REB, TEV], 'occupation' [BDAG]. This noun denotes that which one normally does [LN]. It denotes that which one does as regular activity [BDAG].
  d. aorist act. indic. of πληρόω (LN 68.26) (BDAG 5. p. 829): 'to fulfill' [BECNT; ESV, KJV], 'to complete' [AB, Bar, BDAG, CBC, LN; CEV, NET, NIV, NLT, NRSV, REB, TEV], 'to finish' [BDAG, LN; GW, NCV], 'to accomplish' [NASB]. This verb means to finish an activity after having done everything involved [LN]. It means to bring to completion an activity in which one has been involved from its beginning [BDAG].

14:27 And when they arrived[a] and gathered- the church -together,[b] they-reported all that God had done with them, and how he-had-opened[c] (a)-door of-faith[d] to the Gentiles.
LEXICON—a. aorist mid. (deponent = act.) participle of παραγίνομαι (LN 15.86) (BDAG 1.a. p. 760): 'to arrive' [AB, Bar, BDAG, BECNT, CBC,

LN; all versions except KJV], 'to come' [BDAG, LN; KJV], 'to come to be present' [LN], 'to be present, to draw near' [BDAG]. This verb means to come to be present at a particular place [LN]. It means to be in movement so as to be present at a particular place [BDAG].
b. aorist act. participle of συνάγω (LN 15.125) (BDAG 1.b. p. 962): 'to gather together' [BECNT, LN; ESV, KJV, NASB, NCV, NET, NIV, TEV], 'to call together' [CBC, LN; CEV, GW, NLT, NRSV, REB], 'to gather in' [BDAG], 'to gather' [AB], 'to assemble' [Bar]. This verb means to cause to come together, whether of animate or inanimate objects [LN]. It means to cause to come together of persons [BDAG].
c. ἀνοίγω (LN 71.9) (BDAG 1. p. 84): 'to open' [AB, Bar, BECNT; ESV, KJV, NASB, NET, NIV, NLT, NRSV, TEV], 'to make it possible' [LN; CEV, NCV]. The phrase 'he had opened a door of faith' is also translated 'he had given...the opportunity to believe' [GW], 'he had thrown open the gates of faith' [CBC; REB]. The idiom 'to open a door' means to make possible some opportunity [LN]. It means to move something from a shut or closed position [BDAG].
d. πίστις (LN 31.102) (BDAG 2.d.α. p. 819): 'faith' [AB, Bar, BDAG, BECNT, CBC; ESV, KJV, NASB, NET, NIV, NLT, NRSV, REB], 'Christian faith' [LN], 'trust, confidence' [BDAG]. The phrase 'he had opened a door of faith' is also translated 'God/he had made it possible...to believe' [CEV, NCV], 'he had given...the opportunity to believe' [GW], 'he had opened the way...to believe' [TEV]. This noun denotes the belief in the good news about Jesus Christ and becoming a follower [LN]. It denotes a state of believing on the basis of the reliability of the one trusted [BDAG].

14:28 And they-remained[a] no little time with the disciples.
LEXICON—a. imperf. act. indic. of διατρίβω (LN 85.61) (BDAG p. 238): 'to remain' [AB, BECNT, LN; ESV], 'to stay' [Bar, CBC, LN; CEV, GW, NCV, NIV, NLT, NRSV, REB, TEV], 'to abide' [KJV], 'to spend time' [BDAG; NASB, NET]. This verb means to remain or stay in a place, with the implication of some type of activity [LN]. It means to remain or stay in a place [BDAG].

www.ingramcontent.com/pod-product-compliance
Lightning Source LLC
Chambersburg PA
CBHW071237300426
44116CB00008B/1064